MW01097272

TANGIBLE EVIDENCE:
How to Use Exhibits at Deposition and Trial

Third Edition

TANGIBLE EVIDENCE:
How to Use Exhibits at Deposition and Trial

Third Edition

Deanne C. Siemer
Attorney at Law
Washington, D.C.

National Institute for Trial Advocacy

NITA Educational Services Committee — 1996

Rudolph F. Pierce, Chair
Goulston & Storrs
Boston, Massachusetts

Joseph R. Bankoff
King & Spalding
Atlanta, Georgia

Patricia C. Bobb
Patricia C. Bobb & Associates
Chicago, Illinois

James J. Brosnahan
Morrison & Foerster
San Francisco, California

Kenneth S. Broun
University of North Carolina
Chapel Hill, North Carolina

Hon. Jim R. Carrigan, Ret.
Judicial Arbiter Group
Denver, Colorado

Joseph C. Jaudon
Long & Jaudon, P.C.
Denver, Colorado

©1996 NATIONAL INSTITUTE FOR TRIAL ADVOCACY, INC.
PRINTED IN THE UNITED STATES OF AMERICA
ALL RIGHTS RESERVED

No part of this work may be reproduced or transmitted in any form or by any means, electronic or mechanical, including photocopying and recording, or by any information storage or retrieval system without the prior written approval of the National Institute for Trial Advocacy unless such copying is expressly permitted by federal copyright law. Address inquiries to:

Reproduction Permission
National Institute for Trial Advocacy
1602 North Ironwood
South Bend, Indiana 46530
(800) 225-6482
Fax (219) 282-1263
E-mail nita.1@nd.edu

Permission is granted, however, for use of excerpts from the CD-ROM version published by the National Institute for Trial Advocacy by lawyers preparing for trial.

To my husband

SUMMARY OF CONTENTS

TABLE OF CONTENTS

CHAPTER 2
TEXT DOCUMENTS

CHAPTER 5
OBJECTS, SUBSTANCES, AND SITE VIEWS

CHAPTER 6
PHOTOS, X-RAYS, VIDEOTAPES, AND SOUND RECORDINGS

CHAPTER 7
MODELS, DEMONSTRATIONS, AND
RECONSTRUCTIONS

CHAPTER 8
COMPUTER-GENERATED DRAWINGS, SIMULATIONS, AND ANIMATIONS

CHAPTER 9
EQUIPMENT, MATERIALS, AND TECHNIQUES
FOR DISPLAYING EXHIBITS

CHAPTER 10
USING EXHIBITS AT DEPOSITIONS, OPENING STATEMENTS, AND CLOSING ARGUMENTS

ACKNOWLEDGMENTS

In preparing this third edition, I have had help from the lawyers and judges with whom I have worked. The examples in the book showing how exhibits are admitted in evidence come from transcripts including their arguments and rulings. I also have had generous assistance from lawyers and technical experts who read and commented on sections of the book.

Howard Willens, Esq., at Wilmer, Cutler & Pickering, read and edited the entire manuscript and offered his customary critique of matters small and large. Hon. Avern Cohn, United States District Judge, Eastern District of Michigan, reviewed the manuscript and pointed out areas where lawyer preparation, pretrial rulings, and the difference between evidence and testimony aids needed to be emphasized. David M. Malone, Esq., at Venable, Baetjer, Howard & Civiletti, provided material from the manuscript of his work with Peter Hoffman, of the University of Nebraska, on depositions. Lee R. Marks, Esq., at Ginsberg, Feldman & Bress, helped with electronic signatures on commercial documents.

At NITA, Shelly Goethals, Bernie Zoss, Kathy Nathan and Julie Hahnenberg worked on the manuscript. Their attention to detail and perceptive comments helped make the book much more readable. Tony Bocchino and John Maciejczyk read the manuscript and, as usual, found significant ways to improve it.

NITA Trustees Joe Jaudon, of Long & Jaudon, P.C., and Joe Bankoff, of King & Spalding, and Robert Taylor, of Howry & Simon, provided exhibits used successfully in their recent cases. Greg Mendez, on whom I have relied for help in critical matters for years, assisted in gathering illustrations.

John Martin and his colleagues at Quantum Imaging Corp. assisted with Chapter 9 and also prepared the CD-ROM version of this book and the well-designed interface that allows users easy access to the material.

Sam Solomon, the President of Doar Communications, provided excellent advice, counsel, and editorial assistance with respect to Chapter 9. Many of the techniques that Sam pioneered are described there.

Ray Hauschel, Stephanie Kelso, and Al Treibitz at Z-Axis Corporation reviewed and assisted with Chapter 8 and Chapter 9. I am also indebted to Z-Axis for excellent trial and other support over the years.

The librarians and staff at Pillsbury Madison & Sutro and Wilmer, Cutler & Pickering, where I have been a litigation partner, helped gather background materials. I also used the library collection at McDermott, Will & Emery through the auspices of colleagues Dale Church and Nathalie Gilfoyle. Other materials came from sources on the Internet too numerous to mention individually.

This third edition also reflects the contributions of those who worked on the first and second editions, who are identified in the acknowledgments to those editions. In particular, I am indebted to Ted Ciccone, the President of Litigation Communications, Inc., whose firm has provided successful creative support for trial of cases for which I was responsible as well as many others. In the end, of course, the responsibility is mine for the decisions on all materials included in the book and whatever errors have been made.

DCS

ILLUSTRATIONS

The illustrations in this book are from cases in state and federal court that were admitted in evidence in pre-trial or trial proceedings. In some cases, the exhibit labels have been changed slightly so as not to identify a particular litigant. The illustrations are referenced in the text and appear at the end of the book.

EXAMPLES

The examples of question and answer segments illustrating how to get an exhibit admitted in evidence are drawn from actual cases, but the names and details have been changed in order not to identify any living persons or actual companies.

Section	Pg. No.	Exhibit No.	Type of Exhibit	Expert or Lay	Direct/ Cross	CRIT Factors	Objections Included
1.1.1	16			Lay	Direct	C	None
1.1.1	17			Lay	Direct	C	None
1.1.1	18-20			Expert	Direct	C	Foundation
1.1.2	21-22	15	Gear	Lay	Direct	R	Relevance
1.1.3	22	15	Gear	Lay	Direct	I	See below
1.1.4	23	15	Gear	Lay	Direct	T	See below
1.1.4	24	10	Note	Lay	Direct	I, T	Condition of document
1.1.4	25	7	Gov't report	Lay	Direct	I, T	None
1.1.4	26	3	Computer printout, sales report	Lay	Direct	I, T	None
1.1.5	28	15	Gear	Lay	Direct	CRIT	Foundation
1.2.1	32-33	24, 24A, 25, 26, 27, 28, 29	Time line, enlargement	Lay	Direct	Test. aid	Foundation
1.2.1	33-34		In court sketch, blackboard	Lay	Direct	Test. aid	None
1.2.2	35-36	32	Time line, sketch pad	Lay	Direct	Test. aid	None
1.2.2	36-37		Table, blackboard	Expert	Cross	Test. aid	None
1.4.1	51	1	(Marking)	Lay	Direct		None
1.4.2	52	1	(Show to counsel)	Lay	Direct		None
1.4.3	52	1	(Hand to judge)	Lay	Direct		None

Section	Pg. No.	Exhibit No.	Type of Exhibit	Expert or Lay	Direct/ Cross	CRIT Factors	Objections Included
1.4.4	53	1	(Show witness)	Lay	Direct		None
1.4.5	54	1	(Move admission)	Lay	Direct		None
1.4.7	58-59	1	(Offer of proof)	Lay	Direct		Unfair prejudice
1.4.8	59	1	(Permission to publish)	Lay	Direct		None
1.4.9	60	1	(Publish)	Lay	Direct		None
1.4.9	60	1	(Publish)	Lay	Direct		None
1.4.9	61	1	(Publish)	Lay	Direct		None
1.7.1	69			Juror	Voir dire		
1.7.1	70-71			Juror	Voir dire		
1.7.1	72			Juror	Voir dire		
1.7.2	73-75	15	Gear	Lay	Voir dire	I, T	
1.7.2	75-76	10	Note	Lay	Voir dire		Hearsay
2.1.1	96-97	11	Assembot II, price list	Lay	Direct	CRIT	None
2.1.1	98-99	46	Certificate of completion	Lay	Direct	CRIT	Foundation
2.1.1	99-100	12	Letter	Lay	Direct	CRIT	Stipulation
2.1.1	100	4	Contract	Lay	Direct	C, I, T	None
2.1.1	101	4	Contract	Lay	Direct	C, I, T	None
2.1.1	101-02	4	Contract	Lay	Direct	C, I, T	None
2.1.1	102-03	4	Contract	Expert	Direct	C, I, T	None
2.1.2	107	44	Assembot II, brochure	Lay	Direct	C, I, T	Hearsay
2.1.2	109-10	43	Assembot II, agent letter	Lay	Direct	C, I, T	Hearsay
2.1.2	112-13	47	Production report	Lay	Direct	C, I, T	Hearsay
2.1.2	114-15	41	Personal date book	Lay	Direct	C, I, T	None
2.1.2	117-18	112	Gov't agency report	Lay	Direct	C, I, T	Hearsay Original document

Section	Pg. No.	Exhibit No.	Type of Exhibit	Expert or Lay	Direct/ Cross	CRIT Factors	Objections Included
2.2.2	124-25	35	Invoice	Lay	Direct	C, I, T	Hearsay Original document
2.2.3	127-28	30	Memo with attachments	Lay	Direct	C, I, T	Original document
2.2.4	130-31	33	Automobile title	Lay	Direct	I, T	Foundation Hearsay Original document
2.3.1	135-36	42	Assembot II, memo	Lay	Direct	I, T	Original document
2.3.2	139-40	19	E-mail message	Lay	Direct	I, T	Original document
2.3.2	141	20	Fax	Lay	Direct	I, T	Foundation
2.3.2	142-43	21	Fax	Lay	Direct	I, T	Foundation
2.3.2	143-46	22	E-mail message	Lay	Direct	C, I, T	Foundation Hearsay Original document
2.3.3	149-51	8	Workgroup document	Lay	Direct	I, T	Hearsay Original document Completeness
2.3.4	152-53	14	Library research paper	Lay	Direct	I, T	Hearsay Original document
2.3.5	155-56	13	E-mail with digital signature	Lay	Direct	I, T	Foundation Hearsay Original document Unfair prejudice
2.5.1	160	47, 48	Summary of 200 invoices	Lay	Direct	I, T	None
2.6.1	163-64	No number	Depo transcript	Lay	Cross		
2.6.1	164	33	Depo transcript	Lay	Cross		
2.6.2	165-66	9	Depo transcript	Expert	Direct	CRIT	Hearsay
2.6.2	167	36, 38	Subpoena, Depo videotape	Lay	Direct	CRIT	None

Section	Pg. No.	Exhibit No.	Type of Exhibit	Expert or Lay	Direct/ Cross	CRIT Factors	Objections Included
2.6.2	168		Depo transcript	Lay	Direct	CRIT	Rule 32(a)(2)
2.6.3	169		Depo summary	Lay	Direct	CRIT	None
2.6.4	170-71		Depo transcript	Lay	Direct		Foundation
2.6.5	175-76		Depo transcript	Lay	Direct		
3.1.1	181-82	37, 37A	Chart on 8 commodities, Enlargement	Lay	Direct	C, I, T	None
3.1.1	183	37, 37A	Chart on 8 commodities, Enlargement	Lay	Direct	Test. aid	None
3.1.1	184-85	39, 40, 41, 39A, 40A, 41A	Charts, Enlargements	Expert	Direct	I, T	None
3.1.1	185	45	Chart	Expert	Direct	T	None
3.2.1	193-94	18	Time line	Lay, expert	Direct	CRIT	See below
3.2.1	195-96	23	Time line	Expert	Direct	C, I, T	None
3.2.1	196-97	107, 108, 109	Time line	Lay	Direct	I, T	None
3.2.1	197-98	49	Table	Lay	Direct	I, T	Hearsay
3.2.2	198-99	18	Time line	Lay, expert	Direct	CRIT	Needless cumulative evidence
3.3.1	201	50	Computer printout, wages	Lay	Direct	I	None
3.3.1	205-06	50	Computer printout, wages	Lay	Direct	T	Foundation Hearsay Original document
3.3.1	208-09	51	Computer printout, power use	Lay	Direct	I, T	Foundation Original document
3.3.2	211-12	51	Computer printout, power use	Lay	Direct	I, T	Hearsay

Section	Pg. No.	Exhibit No.	Type of Exhibit	Expert or Lay	Direct/ Cross	CRIT Factors	Objections Included
3.3.2	212-14	64	Computer printout, inventory	Lay	Direct	C, I, T	None
3.3.2	216-19	17	Computer printout, testing data	Lay	Direct	I, T	Hearsay Original document
3.3.3	220-21	66, 67	Computer printout, summary	Lay	Direct	T	None
4.1.1	228	5	Plat	Lay	Direct	C, I, T	None
4.1.1	228-29	6	Map	Lay	Direct	C, I, T	None
4.1.1	230-32	52, 52A	Map Aerial photo				
4.1.1	233-34	16	Map	Expert	Direct	I, T	None
4.2.1	238-39	55	Diagram, Org. chart	Lay	Direct	C, I, T	None
4.3.1	241	34	Anatomical drawing	Expert	Direct	I, T	None
4.3.1	242-43	53	Medical illustration	Expert	Direct	C, I, T	None
4.4.1	245-46	31	Sketch in police report	Lay	Direct	C, I, T	None
5.1.1	252	2	Sprocket	Lay	Direct	C, I, T	None
5.2.1	255-57	56, 57, 58, 59, 60	Flour samples	Expert	Direct	I, T	None
5.2.1	257-58	56, 57, 58, 59, 60	Flour samples	Expert	Direct	I, T	None
6.1.1	268	61	Photo, fire scene	Expert	Direct	C, I, T	None
6.1.1	269	61	Photo, fire scene	Lay	Direct	C, I, T	None
6.1.1	269-71	70, 71, 72	Photos, assembly line	Lay	Direct	C, I, T	None
6.2.1	281-83	75, 76, 77	X-rays and labels	Expert, Lay	Direct	C, I, T	Foundation Hearsay
6.3.1	287-88	54	Videotape and label	Lay	Direct	I, T	Foundation Hearsay

Section	Pg. No.	Exhibit No.	Type of Exhibit	Expert or Lay	Direct/ Cross	CRIT Factors	Objections Included
6.3.1	289-91	62	Videotape, no audio	Expert	Direct	R, I, T	None
6.3.1	291-92	78	Videotape, no audio	Lay	Direct	C, I, T	None
6.3.1	294-97	68, 69	Summary of operator qualifications, Videotape excerpt with audio	Lay, Expert	Direct	CRIT	Foundation Hearsay Original document Unfair prejudice Confusing/ misleading
6.3.1	300	74	Videotape excerpts	Lay	Direct	I, T	None
6.3.1	301	63, 65	Transcript, Videotape of depo	Lay	Direct	CRIT	None
6.3.1	302		Transcript, Videotape of depo	Lay	Direct		
6.3.1	303-04	79, 80	Subpoena, Videotape of depo	Lay	Direct		
6.3.2	307		Edited videotape		Direct		
6.3.2	309-10	83, 84	Transcript, Videotape of depo	Lay	Direct	I, T	Unfair prejudice Leading
6.3.2	311-12	89	Videotape, edited	Lay	Direct	I, T	Completeness
6.4.1	320	62	Videotape, with audio	Expert	Direct		
6.4.1	321	62	Videotape, background sounds	Expert	Direct		
6.4.1	322-23	85	Sound recording	Lay	Direct	I, T	None
6.4.1	323-25	90	Sound recording	Expert	Direct	I, T	None
6.4.1	326-28	73	Recording of conversation	Lay	Direct	I, T	None
6.4.1	328-30	85, 86	Recording of conversation, Transcript	Expert	Direct	I, T	None

Section	Pg. No.	Exhibit No.	Type of Exhibit	Expert or Lay	Direct/ Cross	CRIT Factors	Objections Included
7.1.1	338	81	Life size model, brain	Expert	Direct	I, T	None
7.1.1	339-41	88	Scale model, boiler	Expert	Direct	I, T	None
7.1.1	341-42	93	Illustrative model, city block	Lay	Direct	C, I, T	None
7.2.1	347-48	87	Demonstration, stress on bolts	Expert	Direct	I, T	None
7.2.1	348-49	91, 91A	Demonstration, operation of machine; Video of demo	Lay	Direct	C, I, T	None
7.3.1	354-55	92, 94	Invoice, Speedometer	Expert	Direct	I, T	None
7.3.1	355-56	98	Baseball bat	Lay	Direct	I, T	None
7.3.1	356-57		Demonstration, elevator shaft incident	Lay	Direct	I, T	None
7.3.1	357-58	104, 105	Reconstruction photos	Lay	Direct	I, T	None
7.3.1	359-63	75	Reconstruction video	Lay	Direct	C, I, T	None
8.1.1	370-71	96, 96A	Engineering drawing, computer file	Lay	Direct	I, T	Original document
8.1.1	372-74	101, 101A	Engineering drawing, computer file	Lay	Direct	I, T	Original document
8.2.1	376-78	97	Financial analysis	Expert	Direct	C, I, T	None
8.2.1	378-79	97, 97A	Regression analysis, enlargement	Expert	Direct	I, T	Original document
8.2.1	379-80	97	Financial analysis, computer display	Expert	Direct	I, T	None

Section	Pg. No.	Exhibit No.	Type of Exhibit	Expert or Lay	Direct/ Cross	CRIT Factors	Objections Included
8.2.1	380-83	100, 102, 103, 106	Engineering analysis, Stress test	Expert	Direct	C, I, T	See below
8.2.2	385-86	102, 103, 106	Engineering analysis, Stress test	Expert	Direct	C, I, T	Original document
8.3.2	393-96	98	Animation, boiler operation	Expert	Direct	C, I, T	See below
8.3.2	397-98	98	Animation, boiler operation	Expert	Direct	C, I, T	Foundation
8.3.3	398-99	98	Animation, boiler operation	Expert	Direct	C, I, T	Hearsay
8.3.3	399-401	98	Animation, boiler operation	Expert	Direct	C, I, T	Original document
10.1.2	475	82	Letter	Lay	Depo		
10.1.4	478-80	99	Memo	Lay	Depo		
10.2.1	484	109	Letter	Lawyer	Opening		
10.2.2	485		Enlargement	Lawyer	Opening		
10.2.2	486	109, 55	Letter, Organization chart	Lawyer	Opening		
10.2.2	487		Icons	Lawyer	Opening		
10.3.1	489-90	43	Letter	Lawyer	Closing		
10.3.2	490-91	7, 91A	Gov't report, Video of machine operation	Lawyer	Closing		
10.3.3	491	24A	Time line, Testimony aid	Lawyer	Closing		
10.3.4	492	32	Time line	Lawyer	Closing		
10.3.5	492-93	No number, 110	Presentation aid, Letter	Lawyer	Closing		

INTRODUCTION

Tangible evidence is anything that can be presented in a courtroom other than oral testimony by a witness. It is what the fact-finder can touch, watch, read, look at, and perceive in combinations of ways—all types of documents, photographs, recordings, computer-generated displays, physical objects, substances, models, reconstructions, and demonstrations.

Almost every major point within a case can be bolstered by the sound use of tangible evidence to complement the testimony evidence given by witnesses. Most people learn and remember more readily when they can see the material being explained. Both judges and jurors find exhibits more interesting than oral testimony and, in subtle ways, more reliable. To work with tangible evidence effectively, you need to consider both legal and learning impacts: how you will meet the technical legal requirements so that the evidence is admissible and the judge or jury can consider it; and how you will meet the human learning requirements so that the judge or jury will understand and be convinced by it.

Tangible evidence is even more critical today to the outcome of the trial than it was when the first edition of this book was written in 1982. Developments in technology have provided new ways to present exhibits in the courtroom. Traps for the unwary have multiplied. Judges are more burdened by the workload and do not want time wasted on unnecessary evidence disputes.

The easiest way to master the many interlocking rules and practices that govern the admissibility of tangible evidence is to see excerpts from transcripts where an exhibit similar to yours was put into evidence cleanly and without error. This edition incorporates more question and answer segments, particularly for the newer types of evidence, such as fax transmissions and electronic mail messages, to illustrate laying foundation and meeting objections for over 100 different kinds of exhibits.

This third edition expands the step-by-step guidance on creating, presenting, and defending exhibits to include additional specialized situations and explanations about the newer technology. The book focuses on the proponent of the exhibit and shows how to lay a foundation and meet objections. The opponent of the exhibit can

1

scrutinize this suggested path to admissibility to discover where the requirements have not been met.

The discussion of qualification of exhibits and defenses against exhibits is set forth in the framework of the Federal Rules of Evidence. A copy of these rules is set out in Appendix A together with commentary on similar state rules. The guidelines presented are relevant to trials in federal courts, arbitration under the American Arbitration Association rules, or proceedings before federal administrative law judges where the federal rules may be used as nonbinding guidelines. More than half of the states have rules that parallel the federal rules in most respects, and the approaches suggested here will generally comply with the practice in these states. However, in dealing with specific evidentiary problems in state court, you will need to give careful consideration to any variation in the applicable state rules from the federal model followed here.

In this third edition, the material has been reorganized to make it easier for the practitioner to use. The guidelines for exhibits are expanded to include depositions as well as trial. Sections have been added on voir dire with respect to exhibits and jury instructions applicable to exhibits. The latest technology for creating and displaying exhibits is explained. The reorganization incorporates the helpful comments of judges and lawyers on the second edition and the questions and suggestions arising out of periodic lectures on evidence given by the author.

Chapter 1 reviews the fundamentals common to all tangible evidence so that you can lay a foundation, meet objections, and work with the exhibits in the courtroom. An understanding of these fundamentals is necessary for planning for the effective use of exhibits at deposition and trial. If you review the fundamentals carefully at the outset, your pretrial preparation will be effective and complete.

Chapter 2 is a revised treatment of exhibits that are "text documents," including the letters, memos, studies, forms, and wide variety of other documents in which most of the information is in text format. Chapter 3 covers what might be called "numbers documents," which are charts, graphs, time lines, tables, and computer data printouts. Chapter 4 deals with "picture documents" in the general categories of maps, diagrams, drawings, and sketches. All of these exhibits have characteristics common to paper documents, but there are often special considerations for getting each type admitted in evidence.

Chapter 5 discusses the actual physical things that are at issue in the case. In some instances this will be objects or substances brought into the courtroom. In other cases, it will be on-site inspections by the judge or jury of places that are at issue in the case. Chapters 6, 7, and 8 explain various alternative ways to present physical objects through photographs, x-rays, videotapes, sound recordings, models, reconstructions, demonstrations, and computer drawings, simulations, and animations. Physical objects and demonstrations of the laws of physics, chemistry, and biology that govern physical phenomena must meet evidentiary requirements different from paper documents.

Chapter 9 contains information about the equipment, materials, and techniques available for displaying equipment, including computers, exhibit frames, visualizers, laserdiscs, video players, slides, transparencies, and easels. Some federal and state courtrooms are wired for all the latest digital or electronic technology. Others may have only a single electrical outlet located inconveniently behind the judge or bailiff. Lawyers must take into account these physical limitations when planning for the use of some kinds of exhibits. This chapter also covers the use of graphic arts specialists to help design exhibits and pretrial focus groups to critique potential exhibits. A list of the manufacturers of the equipment described and some of the leading firms that supply technical assistance for creating and displaying exhibits is included in Appendix B.

Chapter 10 covers the use of exhibits at depositions, where much of the work is done to qualify exhibits for trial. Courts increasingly demand that the admission of exhibits be agreed by the parties or decided by the court in advance of trial. Exhibits qualified properly at depositions should be readily stipulated as admissible. Problems with the foundation developed at depositions can be catalogued for resolution by the court. Exhibits used at depositions are also available for settlement negotiations, and getting cases settled is always an important objective. Chapter 10 also discusses the function of exhibits in opening statements and closing arguments where the exhibits are analyzed and explained.

The materials in this book are directed to the practical problems presented by the various kinds of tangible evidence that may be available when a lawyer plans a trial. Parts of the discussion are very detailed to meet the requirements of the beginning lawyer or the lawyer with a specialized problem, and most lawyers will not need to immerse themselves in the material to this extent. For this reason, the chapters are subdivided using a standard format so that the various subject matters are easy to find. First, each chapter covers the foundation required to get the particular type of evidence admitted. If necessary elements of the foundation cannot be proved, then alternatives should be pursued. Second, there is a discussion of the objections that may be available to the other side. If one or more of these objections are likely to succeed, the trial plan should take account of that possibility. Third, each chapter contains technical information about creating, constructing, or shaping exhibits and points about various tactical considerations with respect to the use of each type of exhibit in the courtroom.

Illustrations are provided with respect to most of the types of exhibits discussed in this book. The illustrations are grouped together to make it easier to compare one style or approach with another. Of necessity, the illustrations are much smaller in this book than they would be in a courtroom, and they lose some of their effect for that reason. All of the illustrations are exhibits that were prepared for trial, and they come from cases including product liability, personal injury, commercial, construction, insurance coverage, and white collar crime.

A CD-ROM version of this book has been prepared to help in trial preparation. The CD contains the entire text and all illustrations plus search software making it easy to find the treatment of any subject or examples of particular kinds of exhibits. Permission is granted to purchasers of the CD to excerpt examples for use in notes prepared specifically for trial. This means that, without obtaining the usual copyright permission, the examples in the book may be copied from the CD to the purchaser's word processing program in order to be edited to fit the case at hand.

Citations to case law and treatises are omitted because these sources are rarely helpful for the routine tangible evidence requirements of most cases. Much more important is the very substantial discretion available to a trial judge and the peculiarities of local practice. An excellent overall guide on evidence is *A Practical Guide to Federal Evidence* (3rd Ed. 1995). Sources for further research into specific evidentiary problems related to tangible evidence and various kinds of exhibits are listed in Appendix C. Basic forms for working with exhibits are provided in Appendix D.

The problems associated with tangible evidence present some of the most critical challenges in getting a case through trial. Addressing these problems successfully will contribute significantly to the most persuasive presentation of the trial lawyer's case. When the exhibits come together to tell the story in a compelling way, the judge and jury have a well-marked and logical path to follow. The imagery of the case supports and enhances understanding of the oral testimony presented by the witnesses. The fact-finder can test alternative theories against this sturdy outline of the case and be satisfied that a decision in favor of the proponent of these exhibits is right. Solid exhibits almost always mean a solid case. The step-by-step guidelines presented here will help ensure that you get the most from your exhibits.

DCS
July 1996

CHAPTER 1

THE FUNDAMENTALS: FOUNDATION, OBJECTIONS, AND BASIC COURTROOM REQUIREMENTS

Every tangible thing used in connection with the testimony of a witness at trial must be qualified before the witness may use it or discuss it. There are two ways to qualify a tangible item for use at trial: (1) qualify it as evidence so that it may be admitted and taken to the jury room with the jury when it retires to deliberate (or may be relied on by the judge when he or she writes the opinion); or (2) qualify it as a testimony aid so that it may be displayed for the jury as the witness testifies although it is not admitted as evidence and therefore not taken to the jury room. Ordinarily, both items offered as evidence and items proposed to be used as testimony aids are called "exhibits" and given a number for ready identification in the record. The term "exhibit" is used in this book to refer to both.

The proponent of an exhibit must lay a proper foundation, the extent of which depends on the type of exhibit and the discretion of the court. In general terms, a judge will be vigilant, at his or her own initiative, to ensure that the elements of foundation are met regardless of whether a challenge is raised by opposing counsel because this is fundamental to a fair trial. This chapter covers the foundation concepts that are common to all exhibits.

Once a proper foundation is laid, the proponent of the exhibit has met the burden of going forward and is entitled to have it admitted or displayed unless a valid objection is raised. The opponent has three standard types of objections available to test whether the exhibit really meets the criteria for reliable evidence: (1) the evidence is or contains hearsay; (2) the evidence does not meet the "original document" rules; and (3) the evidence should be excluded on policy grounds. The judge usually will rely on the adversary process, and these objections will be waived unless made in a timely fashion. This chapter discusses the basic considerations in meeting each of these types of objections.

In addition to knowing the elements of foundations and objections, every advocate needs to know the nine procedural steps for handling exhibits in the courtroom. These rituals sometimes affect the pretrial preparation and handling of exhibits at depositions so each step is described here, at the outset, in order to provide a better basis for the explanations for specific types of exhibits set out in the chapters that follow.

The ethics rules impose straightforward and important requirements affecting the use of exhibits at trial, and these are explained. General tactical considerations affecting most types of exhibits are also set out in this overview.

Two more specialized topics, voir dire with respect to exhibits and jury instructions affecting exhibits, are also important in specific circumstances. The procedures are explained and samples provided so that the advocate will have a complete arsenal of tools with which to handle the exhibits offered at trial.

The fundamentals discussed in this chapter apply generally to both bench trials and jury trials. Judges may relax the evidentiary requirements in bench trials, but that is entirely discretionary. The lawyer needs to be prepared for full compliance. The term "fact-finder" is used here as a shorthand to mean either the judge in a bench trial or the jury in a jury trial.

1.1 FOUNDATION FOR EVIDENCE

The term "foundation" means the logical basis on which the court can conclude that the evidence to be presented has a proper place in the trial and should be "admitted." Evidence that is "admissible" has gotten over a hurdle designed to screen out that which is not sufficiently worthy to be the basis, partial or complete, of a finding in a trial. The concept is simple but encrusted with so many rules and procedures that lawyers must pay careful attention to the technical requirements or risk having good exhibits excluded.

The term "foundation" applies both to qualifying exhibits as evidence and to qualifying exhibits as testimony aids. Exhibits admitted in evidence can go with the jury into the jury room or can be cited by the judge in an opinion. Exhibits qualified as testimony aids can be used during the testimony of a witness to assist in the presentation or understanding of the testimony, but usually do not go to the jury room. A lawyer's first objective should be to get the exhibit qualified as evidence. If that is impossible, a fall-back position is to qualify it as a testimony aid. This section deals with qualification of exhibits as evidence. Section 1.2 covers qualification of exhibits as testimony aids.

The method for establishing foundation described in this and succeeding chapters is aimed specifically at the courtroom and, by association, at depositions. There has always been a diversity of views in the treatises about the reasons for the evidence rules, the names for various kinds of evidence, and the logic of certain requirements. Although the academic debate is interesting, lawyers need to get exhibits admitted in evidence, and judges need to decide if basic considerations of fairness and due process are being met. There is relatively little time for debate. If a lawyer does not get the foundation right on the first or second try, a perfectly acceptable exhibit may be barred from consideration. The method set out here is designed to ensure that the basic requirements are met as efficiently as possible in every case. The terminology may not match that used in every evidence treatise, but it provides an understandable and practical guide to eliciting the testimony that should result in the admission of the exhibit in evidence.

As noted by one authority in the field, "foundational requirements are essentially requirements of logic, not rules of art."[1]

The common root of the rules on the admissibility of exhibits is the burden of producing evidence sufficiently qualified to avoid an adverse ruling as a matter of law, and thus to get to the jury. The burden of producing evidence is also sometimes called the burden of going forward. It is distinguished from the burden of persuasion, which is related to the standards of preponderance of the evidence, clear and convincing evidence, and beyond a reasonable doubt. The party with the burden of producing evidence must accumulate enough evidence, before resting the case, to permit a jury to infer, after deliberating, that the fact alleged is or is not true.[2] In its deliberations, the jury may consider each exhibit admitted in evidence. Therefore, the foundation for each exhibit must demonstrate that the exhibit is of a nature that is appropriate for the jury to rely upon in reaching its decision.

In arguing the admissibility of exhibits, it is sometimes important to come back to this fundamental proposition. The issue with respect to admissibility is not whether the exhibit establishes any fact at issue, but only whether the exhibit has sufficient indicia of reliability so that it offers a fair basis for deciding whether the fact is true or not. The judge will admit the exhibit if it is something that reasonable people could use to draw a reasonable inference as to the truth of a relevant fact.

There are four factors that have to be dealt with at some point in order to complete the foundation for an exhibit to be admitted in evidence. They are:

- **C**ompetence of the witness to testify about the exhibit;
- **R**elevance of the exhibit to an issue in the case;
- **I**dentification of the exhibit distinguishing it from all other things; and
- **T**rustworthiness or authentication of the exhibit.

The acronym CRIT is useful in doing a quick mental inventory of what is needed with respect to foundation for a particular exhibit. Your trial notes should contain a brief entry for each of the CRIT factors on each exhibit, so you know you can lay the foundation.

Normally the competence of the witness to testify about the item and the relevance of the item to the case are not problems. With minimum preparation, the witness can handle the identification of the exhibit properly. The snare for the inexperienced comes in establishing the trustworthiness of the exhibit. Only certain kinds of documents and other exhibits must meet specified trustworthiness or authentication requirements under the rules. However, the court may reject any exhibit without a pending objection if the circumstances indicate that the exhibit is not trustworthy.

You have a second purpose for eliciting foundation testimony, over and above just getting past the hurdle of admission in evidence. The jury must be persuaded that the exhibit is reliable, believable, and worthy evidence. If you succeed in getting by the judge, because a technically adequate foundation is laid and the exhibit is admitted in evidence, but you fail to get by the jury, because they are not persuaded the exhibit is something on which they should base their decision, then you have not advanced the cause much. When you plan the witness's testimony, you need to include a foundation for persuasion purposes even if you have already satisfied the requirement of a foundation for evidence purposes.

For example, if the exhibit has been admitted in evidence in pretrial proceedings, you will still want to demonstrate the competence of the witness to testify about it, point out the relevance of the exhibit to an issue in the case, make sure the identification is such that it cannot be confused with anything else, and tell the jury why this is a trustworthy (or "authenticated") exhibit. So, at trial, you will go through the foundation testimony for the exhibit even though the judge has already indicated that the exhibit will be admitted in evidence. Judges know the importance of foundation testimony to a smooth trial proceeding, so many of them require you to put in the foundation even if they have indicated at a pretrial conference that they are inclined to admit the exhibit. They usually say that they want to consider the exhibit "in the context of the trial" so their ruling is tentative until the actual foundation is put in.

Another common factor in "foundation for persuasion" with respect to text documents is the evidence necessary to meet objections based on the hearsay rule and the original document rule. See discussion in Section 1.3. The fact that a record is made and kept in the ordinary course of business not only qualifies it for an exception to the hearsay rule, but also makes it more persuasive to jurors. Similarly, the fact that the exhibit is an exact duplicate of the original not only qualifies it under the original document rule, but also removes a possible question that might detract from its effectiveness with jurors. Experienced trial lawyers may include in their plan for witness testimony certain questions that normally would be asked in order to overcome objections, even though they expect no objection, just in order to be sure the jury is persuaded that the exhibit is reliable.

In this book, the elements of foundation are separated from the elements of meeting objections. In practical terms, one of the most difficult moments for lawyers who do not have much trial experience occurs when an opponent says "objection" in the middle of what was otherwise a smooth flowing chain of questions and answers. Inevitably, the first awful thought is: "I don't know what she is talking about—what basis can she have for an objection here?" If your opponent does not say any more than "objection," as is the practice of many experienced trial lawyers (trusting that the judge will also see the basis for the objection but that the opponent will not), then under the approach used in this book, you can run through the four foundation criteria—competence, relevance, identification, and trustworthiness or authentication—and demonstrate that you have met these elements. In the process, you demonstrate to the jury that you are in control of the situation. If your opponent really meant an objection on hearsay or original document grounds when he said "objection," you can quickly flush this out in an orderly fashion, establish that the foundation is adequate, and go on to address the applicable exception under the hearsay or original document rule.

Because the purpose of the examples in this book is to show how to get exhibits admitted in evidence, the examples are not focused on how to use foundation questions to persuade although most are suitable for that purpose as well. In addition, the persuasion factor is quite dependent on individual situations. The answer to the question whether to include testimony about hearsay and original document qualifications, before any objection on those grounds is made, will be different depending on circumstances. If you keep the "foundation for persuasion" factor in mind when planning the testimony of witnesses, however, you will be able to tailor the foundation questions to meet particular needs in your case.

This section discusses the elements of foundation for evidence common to all types of tangible evidence. Specific elements of foundation applicable to particular categories of exhibits, and the questions and answers necessary to lay that foundation, are set out in Chapters 2 through 8.

1.1.1 Competence

Competence is gauged by the evidence rules applicable either to lay witnesses or to expert witnesses. The latitude courts permit experts with respect to their testimony generally also extends to the exhibits they use.

Lay witnesses

Rule 601 of the Federal Rules of Evidence provides: "Every person is competent to be a witness except as otherwise provided in these rules." This is an effort to clear away all of the common law grounds for challenging the competence of a witness. The rule makes state law applicable where the substantive issue is to be decided by a federal court applying state law. This resurrects challenges based on religious beliefs, conviction of crime, connection to the litigation, spousal connection, and dead man statutes in certain situations.

Rule 602 provides the general statement of policy as to the subjects on which a witness may testify:

> A witness may not testify to a matter unless evidence is introduced sufficient to support a finding that the witness has personal knowledge of the matter. Evidence to prove personal knowledge may, but need not, consist of the witness' own testimony.

A witness has personal knowledge if he or she has personally seen, heard, felt or handled, smelled or tasted the tangible evidence or something that the tangible evidence depicts, portrays, or describes. Once some element of personal knowledge is demonstrated, the witness is competent to testify. The amount or quality of his or her knowledge goes to the weight of the evidence, not its admissibility.

Example

Q. Please state your full name.

A. Charles Walter Talbot, Jr.

Q. Where do you live?

A. In Orchard Park, New York.

Q. What do you do for a living?

A. I am a carpenter.

Q. Did you work at the house at 200 Elmhurst Drive?

A. Yes.

Q. When did you do that?

A. About three months ago.

This witness has satisfied the competence requirement, because of his first hand knowledge, with respect to anything he saw, heard, or did at this particular location.

A witness also may satisfy the competence requirement based on experience. If a company has hired a person and entrusted her with responsibilities for its business, a reasonable presumption arises that this person is competent to testify about matters within those responsibilities.

Example

Q. Ms. Jones, would you state your full name for the record?

A. Andrea Jackson Jones.

Q. Ms. Jones, what do you do for a living?

A. I am the supervisor on the first shift in the manufacturing department at the XYZ Company.

Q. What are your responsibilities in that position?

A. I assign the workers on the first shift, schedule the production, determine what is necessary in the event of a breakdown, and contact the maintenance contractor.

Q. How long have you been in that position?

A. Six years.

If the issue in the case is a broken part on equipment in the manufacturing department, this witness is competent to testify about it because she has the requisite experience with the equipment.

The competence of the witness is a fundamental requirement. Counsel should elicit testimony from each witness satisfying this requirement at the earliest possible point. Competence is usually proved with the introductory testimony on the witness's background and general knowledge of the events at issue. These matters determine the qualification of the witness to testify at trial and are necessary to support all of the exhibits the witness will sponsor.

Expert witnesses

The competence of an expert witness is established through evidence with respect to his or her qualifications, not first hand knowledge of relevant facts. Rule 702 provides:

> If scientific, technical, or other specialized knowledge will assist the trier of fact to understand the evidence or to determine a fact in issue, a witness qualified as an expert by knowledge, skill, experience, training, or education, may testify thereto in the form of an opinion or otherwise.

Note that educational qualifications are only one of the avenues by which a witness may be qualified as an expert. A person who has operated or repaired machinery for a number of years, but who has no formal education, may still be qualified as an expert based on knowledge, skill, experience, and training.

A number of equally acceptable standard ways of establishing the foundation for expert testimony may be used to qualify the witness. Getting to the point of the expert's testimony relatively quickly helps maintain the attention and interest of the jury.

Example

Q. Please state your full name and spell your last name for the record.

A. Donald Versary. V-E-R-S-A-R-Y.

Q. What is your profession?

A. I am an economist.

Q. Mr. Versary, have you come to court today prepared to give an opinion about the damages in this case?

A. Yes.

Q. Have you made a study to determine the damages suffered by Mr. Allen as a result of the injury he suffered on April 12?

A. Yes.

Q. Before we get to your study and your opinion, tell us what qualifications you have to do this work.

A. I have a B.A. degree in Economics from Penn State University, and I have a Ph.D. degree in statistics from Columbia University.

Q. Would you describe your training and experience after you got your Ph.D.?

A. Yes. I went to work for the government as an economist for the Department of Labor. I did studies of the costs involved in lost time from work due to accidents and injuries. I worked there for 10 years, and became head of the section.

Then I went into private practice in Philadelphia. In my practice, I have been employed in doing studies to determine economic losses of various kinds from work stoppages and labor disputes, injuries in accidents, construction delays, equipment malfunctions, and so on.

Q. Where do you work?

A. At Economic Analysis Group, Ltd. We have offices in New York, Philadelphia, and Washington. I work in the Philadelphia office.

Q. How long have you worked there?

A. 11 years.

Q. What knowledge and skill have you obtained as a result of your education and employment that qualifies you to testify about damages?

A. Estimating damages requires knowledge about life expectancy, earnings estimation, discounts for present value, and other tools that economists use. You have to be able to estimate how long the person who was injured would have worked, what he would have earned over that period, and what is the value in a lump sum awarded today of that income stream over a lifetime.

I have studied statistics, mathematics, and estimation techniques in undergraduate and graduate school, and I have done over 100 such estimates during my career.

Q. Have you ever qualified as an expert witness in a court proceeding?

A. Yes.

Q. How many times?

A. Four.

Q. Your Honor, we offer Mr. Versary as an expert witness on the subject of the calculation of damages.

Opposing Counsel: Objection, no foundation.

Counsel: Your Honor, the three aspects of foundation for an expert opinion have been satisfied: First, the witness will testify about "a fact in issue." This witness is offered to testify about damages. That is a contested fact. Second, the fact about which the expert will testify is something where "scientific, technical, or other specialized knowledge will assist the trier of fact to understand the evidence." The damages in this case require estimates of life expectancy, lifetime expected earnings, discounts to present value, and other matters which are not matters of common knowledge. Third, the witness is "qualified as an expert by knowledge, skills, experience, training, or education." He has a Ph.D. degree; he has training and experience through his work; and he has the necessary knowledge and skill to present an expert opinion.

Court: Objection overruled. Counsel, do you wish voir dire?

Opposing Counsel: Not at this time.

Court: Counsel, it is either now or never for voir dire of this witness. What do you say?

> Opposing Counsel: We'll reserve until cross-examination, Your
> Honor.

> Court: In that case, you may proceed with Dr. Versary's opinion.

When the court invites voir dire on an expert's credentials, the court is asking whether opposing counsel wants to test the legal sufficiency of the credentials. Counsel may elect to pass up voir dire which occurs in the midst of the direct examination and do cross-examination on the expert's credentials instead.[3] See discussion of voir dire in Section 1.7.2.

Lawyers are sometimes tempted to overdo the testimony on qualifications of expert witnesses. Asking questions about Phi Beta Kappa awards and honorary degrees may take up valuable time and cause the jury to lose interest before you finally get to the heart of the matter, which is the opinion.

Rule 104(a) assigns to the court the determination of the qualifications of a witness offered as an expert. The actual knowledge or skill of the prospective expert witness determines his or her qualification to testify, not titles or degrees. The expert need not have complete knowledge in the field, only enough to aid the jury in deciding an issue in the case.

Rule 602, requiring personal knowledge in order to qualify a witness to testify, provides: "This rule is subject to the provisions of Rule 703, relating to opinion testimony by expert witnesses." Rule 703 provides:

> The facts or data in the particular case upon which an expert bases an opinion or inference may be those perceived by or made known to the expert at or before the hearing. If of a type reasonably relied upon by experts in the particular field in forming opinions or inferences upon the subject, the facts or data need not be admissible in evidence.

Thus, Rule 703 explicitly excepts the expert from the requirement of first hand knowledge. The expert can use facts or data in forming an opinion even though he or she does not have first hand knowledge and even though such facts and data, by themselves, may not be admissible evidence.

1.1.2 Relevance

Rule 401 defines relevant evidence as:

> Evidence having any tendency to make the existence of any fact that is of consequence to the determination of the action more probable or less probable than it would be without the evidence.

One way to look at relevance is as a test of probative value. The related concept of materiality is discussed in Section 1.3.4. If anything about the evidence would help in deciding the case, then the evidence is relevant. Relevance can also be described in terms of a logical connection between the evidence offered and the determination that the trier of fact must make. If the logical connection is too remote or speculative, then the court may reject the evidence.

Generally, counsel will have little difficulty proving the relevance of tangible evidence. The relevance objection is usually more successful when directed against testimony that has strayed from the point. Nonetheless, counsel should have in mind a short defense of the relevance of each exhibit, just in case the objection is raised. The defense should state the logical connection and explain the probative value.

Example

Q. Ms. Jones, I would like you to focus now on the responsibility for maintenance on the equipment in the manufacturing department. How was that handled?

A. Mason's Maintenance Co. handled that. They sent inspectors and did periodic scheduled maintenance under a contract we had with them.

Q. What happened to parts that were replaced during routine maintenance?

A. They were delivered to me.

Q. Ms. Jones, I am handing you what has been marked as Exhibit 15. What is that?

Opposing Counsel: Objection. Relevance.

Counsel: Your Honor, may we approach the bench?

Court: You may.

(At sidebar)

Counsel: Your Honor, the objection to relevance is not well taken. It is true that this gear is not alleged to have had any part in the events at issue here, but the wear on this part shows how long the machine had been in operation without overhaul. The events at issue are alleged to have been caused by wear on other parts of the machine before overhaul. The condition of this part meets the relevance test of Rule 401 because it has at least some tendency to make the existence of a fact of consequence to this action more probable.

Opposing Counsel: That's not true, Your Honor, unless all parts wear out at the same rate. They haven't shown that, so the

      wear on this part isn't relevant to the wear on other parts of
the machine.

Court: Objection overruled. This meets the test of "any tendency."
      You may continue.

You need to have a shorthand formulation of how you get from this
exhibit to an issue in the case so that you can state the link without
hesitation. A brief reminder in your trial notes will be helpful.

An exhibit that is relevant to one issue in the case should not be
excluded because it is inadmissible as to some other issue. The
appropriate remedy in this situation is for the court to admit the exhibit
for a limited purpose. In a jury trial, the court would instruct the jury
to consider the exhibit only for a limited purpose. See discussion in
Section 1.8 with respect to jury instructions.

1.1.3 Identification

Identification is the straightforward requirement that a witness
must testify under oath as to what the thing is. Under Rule 901(b)(1),
the proponent of the exhibit offers "testimony that a matter is what it
is claimed to be." In other words, someone must have first hand
knowledge sufficient to recognize the proposed exhibit and to state what
it is in a way that distinguishes it from other similar things. The
questions to establish these facts are usually quite simple.

Example

Q. Ms. Jones, I have handed you what has been marked as
    plaintiff's Exhibit 15. Do you know what that is?

A. Yes.

Q. What is it?

A. That is the second lateral gear from the equipment in my
    department removed by Mason's Maintenance and delivered
    to me at the time of the breakdown.

Note that the witness cannot describe the substantive content or
meaning of an exhibit until it has been admitted in evidence. The
statement: "That is a letter dated June 5 from Mr. Smith to Mr. Jones"
is appropriate identification, but the statement: "That is the letter
where Mr. Smith promised to supply five widgets" is not proper as
identification.

1.1.4 Trustworthiness

Trustworthiness is a somewhat more elusive concept. Even if the
witness is competent, the information is relevant, and the witness states

the identification of the exhibit with clarity, additional testimony may be required to establish the trustworthiness or authentication of the exhibit. The court has discretion to require additional evidence of trustworthiness for any exhibit if the circumstances raise a question in that regard. The evidence rules circumscribe this discretion by providing for self-authentication under certain circumstances and giving guidance as to what will suffice to establish trustworthiness in other areas.

The trustworthiness element of foundation is different from the hearsay, original document, and policy objections although the purpose of those objections is also to ensure that the proposed exhibit is sufficiently worthy of consideration in deciding an issue. Objections are waived unless made in a timely fashion. Foundation, however, may draw the attention of the court regardless of whether there is an objection.

Basis for identification of nonunique items

One common problem as to trustworthiness is the witness's basis for identifying the exhibit. If the exhibit is not unique on its face, and possibly could be confused with another similar thing, then the witness should testify further to establish the trustworthiness of the identification.

Example

Q. Ms. Jones, how can you recognize the particular gear that has been marked as Exhibit 15?

A. There's a very distinctive pattern of wear on one side that I saw at the time it was removed from the equipment and delivered to me. I remember that pattern very clearly, so I can recognize this gear as the one that was removed at the time Mason's did the maintenance just before the breakdown.

If any question exists about the witness's basis for identifying the exhibit, counsel should elicit the facts establishing this basis.

Condition of the exhibit

Another common aspect of trustworthiness is the current condition of the exhibit. Sometimes circumstances surrounding the creation, handling, or safekeeping of the exhibit will raise reasonable grounds to question its trustworthiness. The court, in its discretion, may require evidence of trustworthiness to the extent necessary under the particular circumstances. Once again, if any question exists about whether the exhibit sought to be admitted at trial is in substantially the same condition it was at the time at issue, counsel should elicit additional testimony to complete the foundation.

Example

(After competence and relevance have been established)

Q. I am handing you what has been marked as Exhibit 10. Can you identify that?

A. Yes.

Q. What is it?

A. That is a note that I left for Mr. Lewis when I left the office on the morning of the first sexual harassment incident.

Q. How can you recognize it?

A. That is my handwriting.

Q. Your Honor, we offer Exhibit 10 in evidence.

Court: Counsel, you will have to account for the condition of the note first.

Q. Is Exhibit 10 in substantially the same condition now as it was when you left it for Mr. Lewis?

A. Yes.

Q. Can you explain the fact that the bottom part shows that some paper has been ripped off?

A. Yes. I was looking for something to write on because I was in a hurry. The sheet I wrote on had a telephone number that I had taken down shortly before, and I needed that number. So I tore off the bottom of the sheet and used the rest to write the note to Mr. Lewis.

Q. Your Honor, we offer Exhibit 10 in evidence. We have satisfied the requirements of competence, relevance, identification, and trustworthiness.

This exhibit also raises hearsay problems (see example in Section 1.7.2) and, if an objection were made, additional testimony would need to be provided to put the exhibit under one of the exceptions to the hearsay rule. The proponent might also elect to offer the exhibit for purposes of establishing notice and not for the truth of the contents.

Self-authenticating exhibits

Rule 902 provides that certain categories of documents are self-authenticating, which means that if counsel proves the document falls within one of these categories, such as newspapers, periodicals, business labels on products, and notarized documents, no further evidence of trustworthiness is required. This rule also covers domestic and foreign public documents to which a public official has attested, government publications, commercial paper and related documents, and any other documents where a statute creates presumption of authenticity.

Example

(After competence and relevance have been established)

Q. Can you identify what has been marked as Exhibit 7?

A. Yes.

Q. What is it?

A. That is a copy of the report of the Occupational Safety and Health Administration titled Job Safety in Machine Tool Manufacturing dated January 7 of last year.

Q. Your Honor, we offer Exhibit 7 in evidence. It is self-authenticating under Rule 902(5) as a publication purporting to be issued by a public authority.

Authenticated documents must still meet the requirements of the hearsay rule. These two aspects of the admissibility of an exhibit are separate. In the above example, the hearsay exception under Rule 803(8) for public records matches the self-authentication provisions of Rule 902(5) for official publications. However, that is not always the case. Some self-authenticated documents are still hearsay and have no readily available exception under the hearsay rule so, if an objection is raised in a timely fashion, they are not admissible.

Technically, when the proponent establishes competence, relevance, identification, and brings the exhibit under a provision of Rule 902 granting self-authentication, the foundation has been completed and the exhibit comes in evidence absent an objection. In this case, the proponent is not required to mention the exception to the hearsay rule under Rule 803(8) for public records and, if no objection is raised on hearsay grounds, the court typically would admit the exhibit without requiring anything more.

Standard authentication methods

Rule 901(b) approves certain methods for meeting common trustworthiness problems. Authenticating handwriting can be done under Rule 901(b)(2), (3), or (4). Public records can be authenticated by following Rule 901(b)(7); ancient documents (more than 20 years old) are covered by Rule 901(b)(8); and computer printouts are deemed trustworthy if they meet the requirements of Rule 901(b)(9). In these instances, the proponent of the exhibit has an officially sanctioned path to admissibility. All that needs to be done is to follow the exact requirements of the rule.

Example

(After establishing competence and relevance)

Q. Can you identify the document that has been marked as Exhibit 3?

A. Yes.

Q. What is it?

A. That is a computer printout of total sales in each of our stores for February of last year.

Q. Would you describe the process or system used to produce this result?

A. Yes. As each sale is made at a cash register, the cashier passes a hand scanner over the bar code on the item being sold. That bar code contains the identification of the product, the price, and the date the product was put on the shelves of the store. The information in the bar code is read by the scanner. This hand held scanner is hard-wired to the cash register, which is also a computer terminal. The information is stored in the terminal until the end of the day. After closing, all the information in all the terminals is sent electronically to our mainframe computer in Toledo. After the close of each month, the mainframe computer prints out a report in this format showing total sales in each of the stores for the month.

Q. Does this process or system produce an accurate result?

A. Yes.

Q. How long has it been in use in your business?

A. We have had a system like it for at least 10 years. The current hardware and software have been in place for more than 2 years.

Q. For what purposes do you use the monthly computer printouts in your business?

A. These are distributed to all our managers. They are used to make decisions on purchases and pricing.

Q. Your Honor, we offer Exhibit 3 in evidence.

This foundation follows Rule 901(b)(9) which provides for authenticating computer printouts through "[e]vidence describing a process or system used to produce a result and showing that the process or system produces an accurate result." The foundation under the other subparts of Rule 901 would also be structured directly from the words of the rule.

Rule 901 specifically provides for possible alternatives to the formulations set out in its subparts. The introduction in Rule 901(b) says that the succeeding 10 subparts are "by way of illustration only, and not by way of limitation." The rule also accommodates any method of authentication provided by statute or prescribed by other federal rules, such as the Federal Rules of Civil Procedure. Rule 901(b)(10).

An exhibit such as the computer printout discussed above may be challenged under the hearsay rules even if it passes muster as to foundation. In this case, the computer printout, if challenged as hearsay, qualifies under Rule 803(6) as a business record. Similarly, an exhibit that qualifies under the foundation requirements and the hearsay rules still can be challenged under the original document rules if it is not an exact duplicate of the original. In this case, Rule 1001(3) provides that the computer printout is an original. Further, an exhibit that surmounts all three hurdles—foundation, hearsay, and original document—still can be challenged successfully with a policy objection under Rule 403 on the grounds of unfair prejudice, confusion or misleading the jury, undue delay or waste of time, and needless presentation of cumulative evidence. For this reason, when preparing to offer an exhibit to which the other side refuses to stipulate, counsel must take account of several tiers of possible problems. The checklist in Appendix D or another organizational format will help with this task.

1.1.5 Challenges to the Foundation for an Evidentiary Exhibit

Objections to lack of foundation for an exhibit offered in evidence should be directed at the fundamental requirements of competence, relevance, identification, and trustworthiness. The requirements are fairly straightforward so that it will be readily apparent during trial preparation whether a given witness can provide the necessary information. With an understanding of the requirements, there should be no difficulty in formulating an appropriate response to this kind of objection. Some procedural and tactical considerations are set out in Section 1.4.6.

The response to an objection to lack of foundation should be guided by the acronym CRIT—for **c**ompetence, **r**elevance, **i**dentification, and **t**rustworthiness.

Example

Opposing Counsel: Objection, no foundation.

Counsel: Your Honor, I can run through the elements quickly. The witness is competent: she is responsible for the equipment of which the gear is a part. The condition of Exhibit 15 is relevant: the events at issue are alleged to have been caused by wear on other parts of the machine before overhaul; the condition of this part meets the relevance test of Rule 401 because it has at least some tendency to make the existence of a fact of consequence to this action more probable. The identification is satisfactory: the witness named the specific part and stated the basis upon which she recognizes it. And there is no issue of trustworthiness as to the basis for identification or the condition of the exhibit now as compared to the time it was removed from operation in the plant: the witness has years of experience with this equipment and observed the distinctive pattern of wear on the gear.

Using a checklist summarized by the acronym CRIT ensures that you have an organized approach. Going through the elements forces your opponent to identify the grounds for the objection more clearly.

Occasionally an objection phrased as "lack of foundation" means that your opponent thinks there is no proof of an exception under the hearsay or original document rules and is in the habit of phrasing this as an objection to foundation. If you respond by running through the elements represented by the acronym CRIT you will smoke out the real basis for the objection, and you will not be wondering what to do next with the witness.

The process is analogous to the law with respect to burden of proof. As explained by McCormick, "In allocating the burdens, courts consistently attempt to distinguish between the constituent elements of a premise as of a statutory command, which must be proved by the party who relies on the contract or statute, and matters of exception, which must be proved by its adversary."[4]

With respect to tangible evidence, the elements of foundation required by the rules—competence, relevance, identification, and trustworthiness—are the burden of the party offering the exhibit. When the proponent of an exhibit says: "Your Honor, we offer Exhibit 12 in evidence," this is an assertion that the four elements of foundation have been established. The judge must then rule regardless of whether the opposing party raises any challenge. If any one of these four elements is missing, the exhibit is not admitted in evidence. If all four elements are present, the exhibit is admitted, absent objection on hearsay, original document, or policy grounds. Objections are discussed in Section 1.3.

There is one other type of objection that occurs during the process of laying a foundation. If the proponent of the exhibit departs from proper procedure, for example by inquiring about the substance of the exhibit or displaying it to the jury before the court has ruled that it is admissible, the opponent may object at any point after the departure from proper procedure and before the court has ruled the exhibit admissible.

The Federal Rules of Evidence provide a good deal of help in making the admissibility of tangible evidence more certain in many situations where the older, more technical rules might have called for exclusion of the exhibit.

Rule 611(a) provides:

> The court shall exercise reasonable control over the mode . . . of . . . presenting evidence so as to (1) make the . . . presentation effective for the ascertainment of truth, [and] (2) avoid needless consumption of time . . . .

The Advisory Committee Notes point out specifically that this provision governs the use of tangible evidence. If you need exhibits to assist a witness or to make the testimony more understandable, the rule provides the necessary support.

Laying a foundation for an exhibit may take more than one witness and, if so, the exhibit normally may not be offered or used by a witness until all four requirements have been met. Under Rule 104(b) and Rule 611(a)(1), the court has the discretion to admit an exhibit subject to certain aspects of the foundation being "linked up" by testimony from a subsequent witness.

Under Rule 611(c), the questions necessary to establish a foundation may be leading, even though this is done on direct examination. This allows counsel to frame foundation questions in almost the same terms as the wording of the rule, so there can be no question that the proof meets the evidentiary requirement.

The substantive rules also provide generous latitude. For example, Rule 1006 permits summaries of voluminous documents; and Rule 406 helps solve foundation problems by permitting proof of routine habit or conduct to show what or where a particular document is.

The overall approach is summed up in Rule 102:

> These rules shall be construed to secure fairness in administration, elimination of unjustifiable expense and delay, and promotion of growth and development of the

law of evidence to the end that the truth may be
ascertained and proceedings justly determined.

This underlying philosophy of the rules provides a clear rationale for
the use of most tangible evidence.

Keep in mind the "quantum" of the burden of establishing a
foundation. The proponent of an exhibit has only the burden of
providing enough evidence so that a court can find the evidence
sufficiently worthy of consideration by a fact-finder. Many lawyers
assume the burden to be much greater and consequently spend too much
time and effort on the foundation questions. If you know what you need
and go to it directly, the foundation for most exhibits can be established
in a few minutes of testimony.

1.2 FOUNDATION FOR TESTIMONY AIDS

Testimony aids are tangible items which are not contended by
anyone to have played any part in the history of the case. They include,
for example,

- a summary made for trial showing the amount of construction
  progress at key dates;
- a list made for trial showing increases in price over time;
- a blowup of a series of related contract excerpts made for trial;
- an informal sketch on a blackboard at trial.

In each case, a witness presents relevant testimony from personal
knowledge or an expert explains an opinion. The testimony aid is
displayed during this testimony and is marked as an exhibit, but is not
offered in evidence.

The rules on testimony aids are very elastic, and the theory
governing their use requires only that the exhibit be sufficiently
explanatory or illustrative of relevant testimony to be of potential help
to the fact-finder. Courts generally accept two bases for using an exhibit
that is a testimony aid: first, that it will assist the witness in presenting
his or her testimony; and second, that it will assist the judge or jury in
understanding the testimony being presented. Usually, both
justifications are offered together. Both are drawn from the general
rules governing the conduct of a trial.

Rule 102 provides:

These rules shall be construed to secure fairness in
administration, elimination of unjustifiable expense and
delay . . . to the end that the truth may be ascertained
and proceedings justly determined.

Rule 611(a) provides:

> The court shall exercise reasonable control over the mode and order of interrogating witnesses and presenting evidence so as to (1) make the interrogation and presentation effective for the ascertainment of the truth; (2) avoid needless consumption of time; and (3) protect witnesses from harassment or undue embarrassment.

Beyond the requirements of the rules, a key practical guideline with respect to testimony aids is that each must make its point quickly and impart the necessary understanding in a single showing. Testimony aids often are exposed to the jury for just a short time. Each exhibit should deliver a specific message. It should not require any interpretation by jurors. You should test testimony aids on a group of lay people not involved in the case to see if they get the point right away. See discussion of the design for exhibits in Section 7.2 and the discussion of focus groups in Section 9.8.

1.2.1 Aid to Presenting Testimony

Sometimes a lay witness, who has no experience in testifying, will have difficulty in presenting his or her information effectively without some kind of visual presentation. If this occurs, the testimony may take more time, cause confusion, or unfairly prejudice the party who needs the testimony to support a key element of the case.

A testimony aid can be very useful with a witness who is shy, inarticulate, or intimidated by the courtroom setting. Explaining material being shown visually is much easier for these people than facing a judge or jury directly and just talking. Even some experts who are very proficient in their field, but who have never testified before, can find important support in a testimony aid that outlines important points.

Testimony aids also continuously reinforce the ideas they display or illustrate. In contrast, if a witness basically has only one important thing to say, you can have the witness testify to it only two or three times before your opponent will be on his or her feet objecting to repetitive testimony. However, a testimony aid is a continual graphic representation of the point that counsel can put before the fact-finder as a constant reminder during the testimony. No rule requires you to remove a testimony aid once the part of the witness's testimony concerning it is completed. Your opponent may request that it be taken down, but that tactic seldom works because the usual response is: "We may need to come back to this." Once the witness has left the stand, the usual, but not uniform, practice is to put away all of the exhibits used with that witness.

The rules permit the court to allow any kind of testimony aid that helps the witness present testimony fairly and effectively.

Example

Q. Mr. Jackson, what did you do in connection with the Azala project?

A. It was my job to inspect the project and to determine what progress had been made on the construction of various parts of the project since the last previous inspection.

Q. How long did you work on the project?

A. Two years.

Q. How many inspections did you make?

A. I inspected once a month—so a total of 24.

Q. How long were your inspection visits?

A. It usually took me two or three days to complete each inspection.

Q. How did you report the results of your inspections?

A. I wrote reports, and I took photographs.

Q. Over the two years, approximately how many pages of reports did you write?

A. About 2,000.

Q. Over the two years, approximately how many photographs did you take?

A. Nearly 300.

Q. Have you assisted in preparing some exhibits that would help in explaining this work that you did over a two-year period?

A. Yes.

Q. May I have these marked as Exhibits 24, 25, 26, 27, 28, and 29?

Reporter: *(Marks)*

Q. Let the record reflect that I have shown Exhibits 24 through 29 to counsel for the plaintiff.

Opposing Counsel: *(Looks)*

Q. Mr. Jackson, what is Exhibit 24?

A. That shows the dates for various phases of the project and shows the parts of the project under construction in each phase.

Q. Exhibit 24A is an enlargement of Exhibit 24. May I place this on the easel before the jury, Your Honor?

Court: Proceed.

Q. Mr. Jackson, using Exhibit 24, can you explain what principal phases the project went through while you were engaged in your inspection work?

Opposing Counsel: Objection. This exhibit has not been admitted in evidence and the witness is being asked to testify about the content of the exhibit.

Counsel: We do not plan to offer these exhibits in evidence, Your Honor. They are properly qualified as testimony aids. The witness has testified he was involved in many detailed inspections of a large project over a long period of time. We are entitled to use materials that will assist in the presentation and understanding of the testimony on this complicated matter.

Court: Objection overruled. You may answer.

A. *(Witness describes phases outlined on exhibit)*

Some courts require that lists, outlines, chronologies, and similar materials displayed for the jury as testimony aids be offered as such before they are used with the witness. The usual practice, however, is to simply mark and qualify the testimony aid, then to proceed directly with the testimony. If the exhibit is not offered in evidence, the court will assume that it is being used only for the purpose of expediting the testimony.

If the testimony aid purports to be a summary of evidence already admitted or of documents provided to the other side during discovery, Rule 1006 may provide another alternative method of establishing foundation.[5] This approach is particularly helpful with expert witnesses when you want to show how the expert draws together a number of pieces of evidence (offered by earlier witnesses) in order to formulate his or her opinion.

On occasion it can be effective for a lay witness or expert witness to provide an informal sketch on a blackboard, whiteboard, or large sketch pad as testimony goes forward in the courtroom. This practice has been common in courtrooms for decades. Because the witness is on the stand and displaying first hand knowledge with the informal sketch, the foundation is relatively simple.

Example

Q. What did you see as you came out of the door of the house?

A. There were three people standing between the fire hydrant and the elm tree.

Q. What did the three people look like?

A. There was a man in a purple sweater; a woman in a red raincoat; and a little girl in a yellow dress.

Q. Would it assist you in explaining what you saw to use the blackboard?

A. Yes.

Q. Your Honor, may the witness use the blackboard?

Court: She may.

Q. Please go to the blackboard and draw a line to show us the front of the house, then put two cross marks to show the door.

A. *(Witness draws line and indicates door)*

Q. Now please put an "X" for the fire hydrant and a circle for the elm tree to show where these were relative to your position at the door.

A. *(Witness draws "X" and "O")*

Q. Now would you put an "M" where the man in the purple sweater was standing?

A. *(Witness puts "M" next to hydrant)*

Q. Now would you put a "W" where the woman in the red raincoat was standing?

A. *(Witness puts a "W" by the tree)*

Q. Now would you put a "G" where the little girl in the yellow dress was standing?

A. *(Witness puts a "G" in front of the tree)*

Q. Does the diagram you have just made give a fair picture of the relative location of the three people?

A. Yes it does.

If the oral testimony makes the point sufficiently, you may elect to do nothing further as far as qualifying the blackboard sketch as evidence. If the sketch is needed as evidence, consider using a large sketch pad on an easel rather than the blackboard. This is a paper record that can be marked as an exhibit and preserved. The only option for preserving a blackboard sketch is to take a photograph of the blackboard after the drawing is completed and qualify the photograph.

You should not "overqualify" an informal sketch like this. It is highly unlikely that the sketch will be accurate (in the sense of scale) and therefore the question whether this is a "true and accurate" representation should be avoided. The sketch can be used so long as it is a fair representation. See Section 4.4 for additional discussion of in-court sketches.

1.2.2 Aid to Understanding Testimony

A second justification for the use of testimony aids is that they may assist the judge or jury to understand the testimony. Sometimes a witness must describe a very complicated transaction. The witness is perfectly comfortable with the material and needs no assistance in presenting the material. The fact-finder may have trouble, however, in understanding what is being presented. Most fact-finders have difficulty, for example, following multiparty transfers of money, documents, or goods. A testimony aid that uses different colored arrows and boxes to show flows of money or exchanges of documents can be effective in fostering an understanding of the transaction. Similarly, if the evidence involves a long list of dates or events, a time line or list may help the judge and jury to follow along with a fuller understanding. The same citations to Rule 102 and Rule 611(a) support this second prong of the rationale for the use of testimony aids.

This principle is important with respect to the list or sketch that the lawyer creates in the courtroom while examining or cross-examining witnesses. Anything created by the lawyer is usually not marked as an exhibit or used by the judge or jury after the examination of the witness is completed. The practice among judges varies, however, and some judges will require these materials to be marked as exhibits and will permit the jury to take this kind of material with them to the jury room.

In dealing with witnesses on direct examination, this type of visual aid can be very useful. Oral testimony, particularly testimony about financial or technical matters, passes by jurors quite quickly. If the information is unfamiliar, the jurors may not absorb or understand at all. The lawyer can slow the pace and emphasize important points by creating a visual outline as the direct testimony proceeds.

Example

Q. Mr. Morgan, let's deal first with the way this plant was supposed to work. When was the Assembot II robot ordered?

A. The order was placed on January 15.

Q. Your Honor, may I use the pad on the easel to note these steps as we go along in order to keep track of the key facts?

Court: You may.

Q. *(Writes on pad in large letters at top: January 15—order placed)* When was the robot supposed to arrive at the plant?

A. Between February 15 and March 1.

Q. *(Writes on next line on pad: Feb 15 - Mar 1—robot to arrive)* How long would it take to install?

A. We estimated 10 days for installation and testing.

Q. *(Writes on next line on pad: +10 days for installation)* When would the production line be in full operation using the Assembot II robot under the schedule you expected?

A. We expected we would be in regular operation no later than March 15.

Q. *(Writes on next line on pad: March 15—Regular operation)* What delays did you foresee?

A. None. They told us the Assembot II robot had been fully tested and that the design had been proven out.

Q. Your Honor, may I mark this page of the sketch pad as Exhibit Number 32 just so we can keep track of it for the record? I may want to refer to it again.

Court: You may.

By writing down the key points on a large sketch pad (see Section 9.3.2) in lettering large enough for the jury to see, the lawyer emphasizes key points and helps the jurors to see relationships that are important to the factual argument. With this reminder of the witness's testimony, it will be easier for the lawyer to come back to these key dates in the direct examination of other witnesses, or the cross-examination of opposing witnesses. This reminder can also be used during closing argument. See Section 10.3.3.

In dealing with witnesses on cross-examination, there may also be an extensive use of "lawyer-sponsored" visual aids. For example, a comparative table can be created during the cross-examination. (See Fig. 1.) Using this visual aid, the cross-examination would proceed as follows.

Example

Q. Mr. James, you were the accountant assigned to the XYZ Company audit, weren't you?

A. Yes.

Q. Your Honor, may I use the blackboard in the examination of this witness?

Court: You may.

Q. Now Mr. James, in the first year you worked on this account, *(Writes "First Year" on the left side of blackboard)*

> you certified that the XYZ Company had $4.5 million in short-term debt, is that right?

A. Yes.

> *(Writes "$4.5 m." in middle of blackboard)*

Q. But in fact in that year the XYZ Company had $7.9 million in short-term debt, didn't it?

A. Yes.

> *(Writes "$7.9 m. on the right side of blackboard)*

Q. And, Mr. James, in the second year you worked on this account,

> *(Writes "Second Year" under "First Year")*

> you certified $3.2 million in short-term debt,

> *(Writes "$3.2 m." under "$4.5 m." in center column)*

> when in fact there was at least $15.0 million,

> *(Writes "$15.0 m." under "$7.9 m." in right-hand column)*

> isn't that right?

A. Yes.

Q. So in the first year, when you were just getting to know this account, you were wrong by $3.4 million, isn't that right?

> *(Points to $4.5 m. and $7.9 m. previously written on blackboard and writes "$3.4 m." on same line at right side of blackboard)*

A. Well, I wasn't wrong in the sense that's what they told me.

Q. You made the certification did you not?

A. Yes.

Q. And in the second year, when you were more fully familiar with this account, your certification was wrong by $11.8 million, isn't that right?

> *(Points to $3.2 m. and $15.0 m. written on blackboard and writes "$11.8 m." on same line at right side of blackboard)*

A. Yes.

By writing out the numbers as you ask the questions and creating an informal chart, you make it easier for the fact-finder to follow the point you are making with your cross-examination.

Most courtrooms have blackboards as a standard part of the furnishings. No foundation is needed for a lawyer to write on a blackboard as the examination proceeds, if what is written is drawn from either a proper question or a proper answer. If you want to keep this kind of display to use in your final argument, write it on a large easel pad and mark it as an exhibit. What the lawyer has written is not evidence and, if done on a blackboard as in this example, can be erased when the opposing counsel gets up to examine the next witness, but it makes the presentation more effective.

Because so much discretion is given under the rules in the use of testimony aids, the lawyer can "design" a presentation to enhance the flow and not distract from the presentation by the witness. Well-planned and effective testimony aids can contribute importantly to the fact-finder's overall impression of the testimony. Chapter 9 covers the methods and materials for this kind of presentation. A graphics specialist can help plan and construct testimony aids. See Section 9.7.

1.2.3 Challenges to the Foundation for a Testimony Aid

The foundation challenges with respect to competence, relevance, and identification are the same for testimony aids as for exhibits to be admitted in evidence. If the witness has no personal knowledge of the dates on which various transactions took place, he or she cannot use a testimony aid with respect to those dates unless another witness, who does have personal knowledge, has already testified about the dates shown on the testimony aid. In that event, this witness may correlate her information with that of the earlier witness using the same testimony aid. Because a testimony aid is only a reflection of the actual testimony, there is no foundation objection to trustworthiness. If the testimony itself comes in, then the testimony aid can be used.

Any substantial "coaching" from the lawyer will probably draw a foundation objection. If the witness is making a diagram, for example, comments such as "Are you sure it should be located there?" or "Should that tree be located a little farther to the left?" are leading and objectionable on that ground. They also draw into question the competence of the witness, which is a necessary basis for the use of a testimony aid.

An experienced trial lawyer will more often use cross-examination to discredit this kind of an exhibit rather than challenging the exhibit itself. One tactic is to get the witness to make so many marks on the diagram in the course of cross-examination that the diagram is useless. This tactic can be met by covering the original testimony aid with a sheet of mylar when opposing counsel first asks the witness to mark up the testimony aid. See discussion in Section 9.3.2. That way the original testimony aid is preserved and the additional marks are only on the mylar overlay.

1.3 OBJECTIONS

If a proper foundation has been laid, your opponent can make three types of objections with respect to items of tangible evidence offered in evidence: first, that the evidence is or contains hearsay and no exemption or exception has been shown to apply; second, that the evidence does not meet the original document rules; and third, that the evidence should be excluded on policy grounds. Lawyers sometimes raise two other (what might be termed "procedural") objections, materiality and surprise, as to particular types of tangible evidence.[6] The objections with respect to testimony aids are more limited because these exhibits are not offered in evidence.

This and succeeding chapters generally deal with objections in the same order. When making and meeting objections, it helps to have a hierarchy in mind. The hearsay objection ranks first in the hierarchy because of its pervasive influence on the treatment of text documents, which are a majority of the exhibits presented. The original document objection is considered after the hearsay objection because it covers approximately the same universe of exhibits but is much narrower in effect. The policy objections are reached only after hearsay and original document are disposed of because in this area there are the fewest guidelines for the exercise of judicial discretion and thus the least predictability as to outcome.

In the courtroom, listen carefully to see if all four elements of foundation—competence, relevance, identification, and trustworthiness—are met before raising hearsay, original document, and policy objections. This order gives the lawyer responsible for objections the best possibility of success by raising the most important considerations first. Objections use up valuable trial time and therefore should be made only when a supportable basis and an important objective exist.

In preparing for depositions or for trial you should separate the testimony that establishes foundation from the additional testimony that may be needed to meet objections. An exhibit may be identified by a competent witness, relevant to an issue in the case, and trustworthy because it can be brought under one of the provisions of the rules of self-authentication, and thus the foundation is completely satisfactory. Yet the exhibit contains hearsay and cannot be brought under any of the exceptions provided in the rules. If the proponent cannot both establish foundation and meet timely objections, the exhibit will not be admitted in evidence.

Objections are the responsibility of the opponent of the exhibit. If hearsay, original document, or policy objections are to be considered by the court, the opponent of the exhibit must raise and support these objections in a timely manner. Under standard courtroom procedure, an objection is timely if made immediately after the exhibit is offered in evidence and before the court has ruled.

Once an objection is raised and supported, usually by pointing to the rule that could exclude the exhibit even if a proper foundation has been laid, the burden shifts back to the proponent of the exhibit to demonstrate either that the rule cited by the opponent does not apply or that an exception to the rule is available.

Some lawyers prefer to present the testimony necessary to meet obvious objections before offering the exhibit in evidence, thus mixing foundation testimony (competence, relevance, identification and trustworthiness) with the testimony necessary to meet the burden of going forward after an objection (hearsay, original document, or policy) is made.

It is usually easier, however, and less time consuming to think of foundation and potential objections as distinct problems. The first responsibility of the proponent of the exhibit is to lay an adequate foundation. The court may exclude the exhibit even if there is no objection if the foundation is not adequate. The proponent of the exhibit has no responsibility to do anything to meet potential objections, however, unless the objection is timely made. Your opponent may not raise an available objection either for tactical reasons or because he or she was asleep at the switch when the exhibit was offered in evidence. Most of the examples with respect to the various types of exhibits in Chapters 2 through 8 adopt the two-step approach—put in the foundation first and offer the exhibit, then put in the defense to objections only if the objection materializes.

1.3.1 Hearsay Objections

Hearsay is an objection to a statement made out of court that does not qualify for one of the three exemptions in Rule 801 or one of the 27 exceptions in Rules 803 and 804. The hearsay rules cover most "text document" exhibits, but do not affect most other types of tangible evidence. Counsel must know specifically where to look for possible problems. Once recognized, most hearsay problems with any exhibit are readily solved as the requirements of the rules are quite straightforward. Section 2.1.2 on text document exhibits contains a more detailed discussion of the exceptions to the hearsay rules.

The hearsay objection must be made in a timely fashion or it is waived. Unlike foundation requirements where the court normally will exercise a parallel responsibility to be vigilant with respect to the presence of all foundation elements before an exhibit is admitted in evidence, if no objection to hearsay is made, the court may decide it has nothing on which to rule and the opportunity to exclude the evidence will be lost. The following general guidance with respect to the hearsay rules applies in most cases.

Text documents

This type of tangible evidence is almost always within the definition of a "statement" that is the underlying basis for the hearsay rule. But many types of documents are not hearsay (under Rule 801(d)), because they are admissions by your opponent or prior statements by someone who is now a witness, or because (under the definition in Rule 801(c)) they are not offered to prove the truth of their contents. Rules 803 and 804 also establish 29 exceptions to the hearsay rule for text documents that are hearsay. See Section 2.1.2.

Charts, graphs, time lines, tables, and computer data printouts

The principal possibility of a hearsay objection in this category is focused on the input for the exhibit. If the material that went in is hearsay, then the compilation that comes out is also hearsay. You can usually overcome this, however, by using experts to qualify the information, by having available as a witness the person who generated the data, or by relying on published sources as to which a hearsay exception applies. Specialized hearsay problems exist regarding computer records generated from other documents. See Section 3.3.2.

Maps, diagrams, drawings, and sketches

You will face no hearsay problem with this category of materials providing the witness is prepared to testify to the accuracy of the facts and statements contained therein and the materials do not quote "out-of-court" statements. See Chapter 4.

Physical things at issue

Physical objects generally present no hearsay problems. Opposing counsel may object to words or symbols painted onto a physical thing, but you can overcome such an objection if the words are part of the thing and are not offered to prove the truth thereof. For the same reasons, views by the judge or jury of a place relevant to the issues in the case generally present no hearsay issues. See Chapter 5.

Materials generated by cameras and recorders

This type of tangible evidence may have some specialized hearsay problems that are usually easily overcome. Photographs, videotapes, or movies that do not have a sound track are generally not subject to a hearsay objection unless they depict nonverbal conduct intended as an "assertion" or a document that is an "out-of-court statement" and used to establish the truth of the content of the document. Sound tracks and sound recordings that include verbal statements may contain objectionable hearsay if they are offered to prove the truth of the statements. See Chapter 6.

Models, demonstrations, and reconstructions

Models, demonstrations, and reconstructions present no hearsay problem if all of the facts upon which they are based are presented by witnesses with first hand knowledge or expert qualifications. See Chapter 7.

Computer-generated drawings, simulations, and animations

Computer drawings, simulations, and animations do not face hearsay objections if all of the facts used as a basis for the exhibit are presented by witnesses with first hand knowledge or if an exception, such as business records, applies to the underlying materials and if the exhibit was built by an expert using accepted software and hardware. See Chapter 8.

Hearsay objections are very annoying to judges, particularly when the proponent of the evidence is unable to handle them even though an exception clearly applies. Rulings on hearsay objections can lead to reversal, so judges are more careful than with policy objections where a great deal of judicial discretion is recognized. It is important for you to offer at least some recognizable defense against these objections whenever they crop up. This requires that you analyze each exhibit beforehand to see whether any hearsay objection could apply. A sample form for this purpose is included in Appendix D.

1.3.2 "Original Document" Objections

The "original document" rule generally has little effect on the admissibility of tangible evidence, but there are occasional problems with certain types of exhibits. Before 1975, this objection was know as the "best evidence" objection. Beginning in 1975, the federal rules referred to this as the "original document" requirement and deliberately cut out all references to "best evidence." You will still hear "best evidence" objections from opponents, however, and their objections mean the same thing as the "original document" objection explained here.

The "original document" rule operates on two levels. First, if you want to introduce testimony to prove the content of a writing, recording, or photograph, then you must produce the writing, recording, or photograph itself before testimony about it will be admissible. Second, when you produce the writing, recording, or photograph, you must produce the original or a duplicate unless there is an acceptable excuse as to why you do not have the original, in which case you can use a "non-duplicate" copy.

Rules 1001 through 1008 of the Federal Rules of Evidence set out the "original document" concept, although they do not use the term. The federal rules are very lenient in this regard, and therefore the utility of the objection is not great. The objection applies only to three categories of things: (1) "writings," or things that have writing on them (sometimes objects have inscriptions in words); (2) photographs and videotapes; and (3) sound recordings. Moreover, the "original document" rule does not bar independent evidence of the same subject matter. For example, the existence of a photograph of a scene is no bar to witness testimony from personal knowledge about the scene even if the witness recollects fewer details (and therefore her testimony might be "weaker" evidence) than the photograph shows. The only bar is to witness testimony about the contents of the photograph before the photograph itself is admitted.

Under Rules 1001(4) and 1003, a duplicate will suffice in most cases where an original is required, and all modern methods of reproducing copies make legally acceptable duplicates. This includes photographic prints from the same negative, photocopies, printed copies, duplicate computer printouts, and sound re-recordings. Almost anything is permitted except a manual copy. Rule 1003 imposes a limitation on the use of duplicates only when a genuine question is raised as to the authenticity of the original or when it would be unfair to admit the duplicate. There is a more detailed discussion of the use of copies in Section 2.2.

Rule 406 also provides invaluable assistance in explaining where the original has gone. It permits evidence of habit or routine of a person or organization to prove that conduct on a particular occasion was in conformity with the habit or routine. Thus, for example, if it was the practice in the office to mail the original of letters and keep a photocopy or duplicate computer printout, evidence as to that practice can be presented to explain why the company does not have the original that is at issue.

Under Rule 1004(a), the explanation as to why you do not have the original (and therefore seek to use a copy) is a preliminary question and the Rules of Evidence do not apply. This means you can make the necessary showing as to the preliminary question by means of an affidavit rather than in-court testimony.

The principal problem raised under the original document rule occurs when the exhibit would qualify as a duplicate of the original but for marks or handwriting on the duplicate that do not appear on the original. Under these circumstances, the proponent of the exhibit has two choices: either provide an independent foundation for the marks or handwriting by testimony of a witness with first hand knowledge, or account for the missing original in one of the ways permitted under Rule 1004.

1.3.3 Policy Objections

Four basic policy objections are available with respect to any tangible evidence. Under Rule 403, tangible evidence may be excluded for policy reasons even if it has been properly qualified as to competence, relevance, identification, and trustworthiness, and has also survived challenges under the hearsay and original document rules. Rule 403 provides:

> Although relevant, evidence may be excluded if its probative value is substantially outweighed by the danger of unfair prejudice, confusion of the issues, or misleading the jury, or by considerations of undue delay, waste of time, or needless presentation of cumulative evidence.

The balance under Rule 403 is important. The probative value must be *substantially outweighed* by the policy reasons for exclusion. The first argument, therefore, will be about the probative value of the exhibit. If the probative value is high because the exhibit is directly connected to an important issue, then the balance will be harder to tip against admission. The second argument will be about how much is "substantially." If the probative value supporting the admission of the material in evidence and the policy reasons for excluding it from evidence are nearly in balance, then the judge should exercise his or her discretion to let the evidence in because the "substantial imbalance" test is not met.

Unfair prejudice

An objection based on unfair prejudice is generally directed at an exhibit that arouses emotion to an extent that rational thought processes may be overcome. The emotion aroused may be sympathy, resentment, revulsion, indignation, anger, or anything else that would cause a jury to deal with the fact issues in an unfair manner. An exhibit may be inflammatory, for example, if it is grisly, gruesome, or obscene. Courts have excluded photographs of corpses, body parts, traumatic injuries and facial expressions indicating great pain or agony on this ground, as well as diaries containing indecent, lewd, or obscene material. This objection is rarely raised in a trial before a judge. In theory, a judge can deal with potential emotional responses adequately and separate them from the fact-finding function.

Rules 407 through 412 in effect legislate that certain kinds of evidence are within the unfair prejudice category. These rules exclude evidence of subsequent remedial measures, settlement offers, payment of medical expenses, the existence of liability insurance, and the victim's past behavior in rape cases. Any exhibit that touches on any of these matters could be excluded by reference to the rules.

Confusion/misleading

Although Rule 403 points to "confusion of the issues" and "misleading the jury" as two separate bases for an objection to evidence that meets the fundamental requirements for admissibility, these two concepts are very close, if not identical. The court's principal concern is that the jury maintain the necessary distinction between the exhibits and the objective facts as they existed at the time of the events at issue. For example, a physical object that represents the plaintiff's theory but has some differences from the actual object at issue might be confused by the jury with the real thing. Computer simulations and animations, photographic reconstructions, and other things that "convey an impression of objective reality" also raise this concern.[7]

Another concern is that evidence may create a side issue that will distract the jury from the main issues to be decided or that the manner of presentation may affect the jury's consideration unduly. Tangible evidence may run up against this limitation if, for example, statistical evidence or data collections are presented in a way that confuses the jury. This may happen if the scales on the vertical axis or the horizontal axis of a chart are not marked off in even increments (for example, 1, 2, 3 . . .) but are uneven (such as 1, 2, 6, 8, 9, 13 . . .) causing a significant skewing of the results shown on the chart. Similarly, use of a logarithmic scale rather than an arithmetic scale on a chart risks exclusion on the ground of confusion of the jurors as most jurors are not sophisticated in mathematics. Tangible evidence that will require lengthy jury instructions as to proper and limited uses by the fact-finder may also be excluded on this ground.

Undue delay/waste of time

Rule 403 also sets out "undue delay" and "waste of time" as separate bases for an objection but the two concepts get at the same potential abuse. Evidence that may draw an extended, detailed rebuttal can be excluded on this ground if it appears likely that, after all the evidence and rebuttal is in, there will be little gain in probative value. Evidence which draws a justifiable request for a continuance in order to prepare an adequate rebuttal may also be excluded on this ground.

Needless cumulative evidence

Cumulative evidence can be entirely relevant and presented with a totally proper foundation. Indeed, the purpose of many exhibits is to pile one bit of evidence on top of another similar bit of evidence on top of another related bit of evidence until the sum is persuasive. The objection to needless cumulative evidence relates both to misleading the jury and waste of time. If the evidence on a particular point has already cumulated to the level at which the point is established, further evidence on the same point may mislead the jury as to the relative importance of the issue and waste time because the additional probative value from receiving the cumulative evidence is slight. An objection on this ground might be raised, for example, if too many documents were used with respect to a single issue.

1.3.4 Materiality Objections

Lawyers often throw in an objection to the "materiality" of the exhibit and purport to state some ground for excluding the exhibit that is separate from the "relevance" requirement discussed in Section 1.1.2. Materiality is viewed by some as the broadest test of relevance. The objection addresses a situation in which counsel asserts that the exhibit is not related at all to any issue in the case; technically, that the proposition for which the evidence is offered is not "provable" because it is not in the case. This may happen because the issue was not pleaded properly, because the issue has been removed from the case by an admission during the pleading stage, or because the substantive law is such that this evidence has no place in the required proof. For example, as the witness begins to explain the background facts, including the fact that he has worked at his present job for 48 years, opposing counsel objects stating that the allegations in the complaint about the witness's employment have been admitted, and therefore evidence about this is not "material" to the issues before the court.

The objection to relevance, by contrast, points out a situation where counsel asserts that the evidence does not make the proposition for which it is offered any more or less probable than it would be without the evidence. The proposition for which the evidence is offered is "provable"—in the sense that it is within the pleadings and therefore in the case—but the evidence with respect to it is not helpful one way or the other. For example, as the witness begins to explain the background facts, he starts to go into some detail about his previous employment. Opposing counsel objects, stating that how well the witness did or did not perform his former job is not relevant to the issues about his current job because the former employment was much different and therefore the evidence is not helpful one way or the other as to how the witness performed his job on the day in question.

The objection to materiality has been made less important, and some experts say obsolete, by Rule 15(b) of the Federal Rules of Civil Procedure that provides in relevant part:

> If evidence is objected to at the trial on the ground that it is not within the issues made by the pleadings, the court may allow the pleadings to be amended and shall do so freely when the presentation of the merits of the action will be subserved thereby and the objecting party fails to satisfy the court that the admission of such

evidence would prejudice the party in maintaining the
party's action or defense upon the merits.

Further, Rule 401 of the Federal Rules of Evidence probably absorbs
the concept of materiality into a more general approach to relevance.
The Advisory Committee Notes point out that the definition of relevance
under Rule 401 has the advantage of avoiding the loosely used and
ambiguous word "material." Moreover, under Rule 611(a) of the Federal
Rules of Evidence, the court has considerable discretion to allow
testimony to background facts that set the stage for and contribute to
the understanding of the issues although technically do not bear
directly on the issues.

1.3.5 "Surprise" Objections

With any complicated exhibit that took some time to prepare,
opposing counsel may object on the grounds of "surprise." While this is
not an objection recognized by the rules, judges can exercise their
discretion to exclude the exhibit if opposing counsel makes a convincing
argument that he or she now has no fair opportunity to respond to this
complicated exhibit in the midst of trial. This objection may also be
stated as an objection to unfair prejudice under Rule 403. An example
of this type of exhibit is a computer animation that has taken six months
to prepare and that is not delivered to the opponent until the eve of trial.
See discussion in Section 8.3.1. With respect to most types of exhibits,
counsel may avoid the "surprise" objection by disclosing the exhibit or
its existence to opposing counsel as provided in local rules at a pretrial
conference. If disclosure was not required, or if opposing counsel did not
appreciate the significance of what was disclosed, a continuance can be
requested to permit opposing counsel to work on the problem.
Complicated computer animations are an exception. Even if the
proponent of the animation has complied with a local rule that all
exhibits must be delivered at least 10 days before trial, for example, a
fair opportunity for cross-examination requires more than 10 days to
analyze the animation, and an objection on the grounds of "surprise"
should be sustained. See Section 8.3.3.

1.3.6 "Completeness" Objections

If the document, videotape, or sound recording that contains
relevant evidence is long, and parts are not needed to meet the burden
of proof, you may want to designate only a part as the exhibit. Using
portions of lengthy documents or recordings is favored by judges
because it saves trial time and is appreciated by juries who are
intimidated by the requirements of mastering lengthy exhibits. Any
time that you use only a portion of "a writing or recorded statement,"
Rule 106 gives your opponent the opportunity to object and seek to have

additional portions included in your exhibit. Rule 106 provides that the adverse party "may require the introduction at that time or any other part or any other writing or recorded statement which ought in fairness be considered contemporaneously with it. "

The Advisory Committee Note to Rule 106 explains: "The rule is an expression of the rule of completeness . . . . The rule is based on two considerations. The first is the misleading impression created by taking matters out of context. The second is the inadequacy of repair work when delayed to a point later in the trial . . . . For practical reasons, the rule is limited to writings and recorded statements and does not apply to conversations." (Citations omitted.) The reference to "conversations" means oral conversations. Recorded conversations are included in the term "recorded statement."

When a portion of something covered by Rule 106 is offered in evidence, the opposing lawyer has two choices: she can object and insist that additional portions be included in the exhibit, or she can wait until cross-examination or her own case in chief to present the additional portions. Nothing in Rule 106 limits those choices. By insisting that additional portions be included in the exhibit, the opposing lawyer has an opportunity, perhaps, to make the exhibit less effective or to disrupt the presentation of the other side's case to some extent. For these reasons, you should consider carefully your defense against such an objection whenever you have an exhibit that is covered by Rule 106. Include the necessary defense in your trial notes in case an objection is made.

The court has considerable discretion in deciding what additional portions "ought in fairness be considered contemporaneously" with the portion offered by the proponent of the exhibit. The court has additional flexibility under Rule 611(a) to extend the "completeness" doctrine to exhibits not technically within the category of "writing or recorded statement."

1.3.7 Objections to Testimony Aids

There are no hearsay objections to a testimony aid unless it is a blowup of or a quote from a document. If the testimony aid is an exact, but enlarged, representation of something to which there is a hearsay objection, then the same objection is available with respect to the testimony aid.

There are no original document objections to a testimony aid unless, as noted above, it is an enlargement of or a quotation from a document, photograph, or sound recording to which there is an original document objection. The testimony aid is not "evidence" in the sense of an item that will be offered in evidence and admitted by the court. It is only for the purpose of aiding in the presentation or understanding of the evidence.

Few reported cases discuss policy objections peculiar to testimony aids. One commentator pointed out:

> The line of demarcation falls between explanation of testimony, which is entirely proper, and the reduction of testimony to graphic form in such manner as to create the possibility of undue emphasis. Thus when the witness illustrates his testimony with a blackboard drawing, or points out on a plat the manner in which a collision occurred, his testimony is clarified but is not likely to be regarded by the trier as being anything more than oral testimony. On the other hand, when an exhibit actually presents in graphic form the testimony of a witness concerning a particular matter, it may be argued that the memorialization is likely to be given undue weight by the trier of fact and thus excludable on the grounds of misleading the jury, Rule 403. If such an exhibit nevertheless fairly and accurately depicts what it purports to represent, the exercise of discretion in favor of exclusion should be employed sparingly.[8]

The principal policy objection to the use of testimony aids as a pedagogical device in connection with witness testimony is that these exhibits will mislead the jury by unfairly emphasizing some of the evidence or will create the impression with the jury that disputed underlying facts have been established.

An opponent may object to a testimony aid if it is "argumentative" rather than sticking to the facts presented by the witness. This may be appropriate for testimony aids used with a lay witness testifying to personal observations or other first hand knowledge, but it usually would not be a valid objection to testimony aids used with an expert who is explaining (or "arguing") an opinion.

In addition, opposing counsel may challenge an informal sketch, for example, on the grounds that it may confuse the jury if it is wildly out of scale or otherwise demonstrably inaccurate. It may also be challenged as cumulative if there are other better exhibits that show the same thing. This type of problem can largely be overcome with an appropriate instruction from the judge to the jury. See Section 1.8.1. If you are going to make extensive use of testimony aids, it may be wise to propose such an instruction during a pretrial conference. Another alternative available to the court is to permit the use of the exhibit with the witness, but not to permit the exhibit to be taken with the jury to the jury room when they retire to deliberate. So long as the testimony aid contributes to the clarity of the presentation to the jury, avoids undue consumption of time, and is a reasonable method of presenting the evidence, any policy objection should be overruled.

The materiality objection does not apply to testimony aids. The "surprise" objection might apply to a complicated testimony aid that the other side has not had a fair opportunity to examine to determine whether any policy objections under Rule 403 are available.

1.4 BASIC COURTROOM PROCEDURES FOR EXHIBITS

Exhibits can create great interest in the subject matter being discussed if they are handled properly. The effect of even the best exhibit, however, can be diminished if the lawyer handling it does not follow some basic procedural steps. This section discusses the procedures applicable to most types of exhibits. Special requirements for particular types of exhibits are found in Chapters 2 through 8.

Ten simple steps apply to handling evidentiary exhibits in a jury trial. If the trial is to a judge sitting alone instead of a jury, the procedures will not include step 9 and step 10, but most judges will demand that you observe the other formalities. The general procedure and the question formats are set out below.

1.4.1 Mark the Exhibit

Every exhibit to be used in a courtroom must be marked with an identifying number whether it is going to be offered in evidence or just used as a testimony aid. Each party may mark its own exhibits; the parties may mark the exhibits together, in a pretrial conference; or the exhibits may be marked by the reporter in the courtroom during trial. Usually plaintiff has one number series and defendant has another, so that the exhibits are marked, for example, P-11 for the eleventh exhibit in the plaintiff's series, or D-3 for the third exhibit in the defendant's series. In arbitration or administrative hearings, exhibits may be numbered sequentially as they come in, regardless of which party offered them.

It may be possible to negotiate with opposing counsel an easier numbering system for the exhibits in a particular case. For example, counsel may agree that joint exhibits will have numbers 1 through 10; the plaintiff's exhibits will be numbered 100 through 300; and the defendant's exhibits will be numbered 500 through 800. This makes it much easier for the lay persons on the jury to keep track of the exhibits. The court may order that exhibits be numbered so that all those relevant to a particular issue have a similar designation, such as C-1 through C-40 for contract documents or a 200-series for damages documents so that when it comes time to decide which exhibits go to the jury room, the court will be able to deal with groups of documents without sorting through each individual exhibit.

If the marking is done at trial, it is usually done by the clerk or the court reporter, depending on the judge's practice. You do not need any permission or any foundation questions to have something marked.

Example

(Assuming the court reporter is doing the marking, carry the exhibit to the reporter and set it in front of him or her.)

Counsel: Would the reporter please mark this as plaintiff's Exhibit 1.

(It is important to stand silently while the reporter marks the exhibits because the reporter cannot mark and take down transcription at the same time.)

Some courts permit the reporter to mark exhibits before the day's session begins or at recesses in order to save trial time. If the exhibit has been marked previously, counsel need only refer to it as "what has been previously marked by the reporter as plaintiff's Exhibit 1" when it is first brought forward.

In some courts, exhibits are marked first "for identification," then if the proponent is successful in getting the exhibit in evidence, the "for identification" is stricken. As this is a time-consuming step, most courts do not require it.

Once marked, under any of the available procedures, you are under no obligation to use the exhibit or offer it in evidence. You need to keep careful track of the status of all marked exhibits, however, as offered, admitted, or refused because an objection was sustained. A checklist for this purpose is included in Appendix D.

1.4.2 Show the Exhibit to Opposing Counsel

Even if your opponent has seen the exhibit a hundred times in the course of arguments about discovery, pre-marking exhibits, or other proceedings, and even if it is an exhibit that came from his or her client's files, opposing counsel is entitled to examine everything that is used with a witness.

A silent procedure under which the exhibit is passed briefly across the desk to opposing counsel will not appear on the record, so it is necessary to say something for the record.

Example

Counsel: Your Honor, may the record reflect that I am showing to Mr. Jones, counsel for defendant, what has been marked as plaintiff's Exhibit 1.

This is the point at which opposing counsel will decide whether there is such possible prejudice that the examination of the witness to lay the foundation and get a ruling on admissibility should be done out of the presence of the jury. A request for that procedure may be directed to the court at this point.

As admissibility of evidence is a matter for the court, the jury does not have to hear the foundation testimony. If laying foundation for the exhibit is done out of the presence of the jury, you may need to repeat some of that testimony after the jury returns (if the exhibit is admitted) in order to establish the probative value of the exhibit.

1.4.3 Hand the Exhibit to the Judge

This practice varies from judge to judge but, at some point before an objection is raised, most judges want a copy of the exhibit before them. If the court has no special preference as to how this should be done, you would usually hand up the exhibit right after showing it to opposing counsel.

Example

Counsel: Your Honor, may I approach the bench with a copy of this exhibit?

Court: You may.

Counsel: *(Hands up the exhibit)*

Some judges find it more convenient to get a folder containing all the exhibits for a particular witness before the witness takes the stand. This is annoying at times for the lawyers because the judge may be perusing coming attractions in the exhibit folder rather than listening to the carefully crafted foundation testimony for the exhibit at hand. Other judges want to receive all the current day's exhibits before the jury takes their seats at the outset of the session. The court's preferences can be determined during the pretrial conference.

Local rules may require counsel to file a set of exhibits with the court. This does not necessarily mean, however, that the judge has ready access to these exhibits during the trial. Even with a complete set at hand, the judge may not want to look up the exhibit being offered and may demand the extra step of handing up an individual copy.

You must make this process flow smoothly. The jury sees every glitch in this procedure when it is done in open court, and any annoyance on the part of the judge will be readily understood by the jury as an adverse comment on the lawyer's performance and capability.

1.4.4 Lay the Foundation for the Exhibit

The foundation requirements for establishing the competence of the witness, the relevance of the exhibit to an issue in the case, the identification of the exhibit, and the trustworthiness of the exhibit are explained in Section 1.1. The foundation questions for various kinds of exhibits are set out in Chapters 2 through 8. Chapter 2 covers text documents. Chapter 3 deals with charts, graphs, time lines, tables, and computer data printouts. Chapter 4 considers maps, diagrams, drawings, and sketches. Chapter 5 considers physical objects and site visits. Chapter 6 includes photographs, x-rays, videotapes, and sound recordings. Chapter 7 covers models, demonstrations, and reconstructions. Chapter 8 deals with computer-generated drawings, simulations, and animations.

You can complete much of the foundation, including at least competence and relevance, before showing the exhibit to the witness. This helps keep the testimony flowing and avoids shifting prematurely the jury's focus from the witness to the exhibit. At an appropriate point in laying the foundation, you will need to show the exhibit to the witness. In some jurisdictions this requires certain formalities. Some courts require that you ask permission to approach witnesses. The theory is that lawyers are not allowed to intimidate witnesses by running up to them unexpectedly or "crowding" them while they are testifying. In this case, you would always put the court on notice that you are about to approach the witness.

Example

Counsel: Your Honor, may I approach the witness?

Court: You may.

In other jurisdictions, the judge will require the bailiff to hand the exhibit to the witness.

Usually you just walk up to the witness stand and record the event for posterity as follows:

Counsel: Mr. Wilson, I am handing you what has been marked as plaintiff's Exhibit 1.

Some modest pause is advisable at this point for the witness to examine the exhibit even if it is your witness and he or she has seen the exhibit dozens of times. The pause allows the fact-finder to begin to focus on the exhibit.

1.4.5 Move the Admission of the Exhibit

After you finish with the foundation questions, you must formally move for the admission of the exhibit.

Example

Counsel: Your Honor, we move the admission in evidence of the letter that has been marked as plaintiff's Exhibit 1.

It is important that you state specifically by number the exhibit for which you are requesting admission. Vague statements about moving "this" into evidence may not support an issue on appeal.

1.4.6 Meet Challenges to Foundation

When the proponent moves the admission of an exhibit, this is a declaration to the court and opposing counsel that the four basic requirements of foundation—competence, relevance, identification, and trustworthiness—have been met. At this point, opposing counsel has the opportunity to draw the court's attention to one or more respects in which the foundation is deficient. The court must then rule. Even if no challenge to foundation is raised, the court must affirmatively find that the exhibit is sufficiently worthy of consideration.

Challenge to competence

If your opponent objects to the competence of the witness—the presence of first hand knowledge—you can go back and question the witness further to establish the necessary basis. Then you can move the admission in evidence again. If the judge still is not convinced, you will have to go to another witness and wait to use the exhibit until after that witness has qualified it. Once this aspect of the foundation is established by the additional witness, the exhibit can be brought back and used with the witness who could not establish first hand knowledge.

An expert's competence is established by evidence with respect to skill, experience, training, or education. An expert is not required to have first hand knowledge of the facts or exhibits relied upon in forming an opinion.

Challenge to relevance

If your opponent objects to relevance, you should focus immediately on, and identify for the court, the fact at issue in the case to which the exhibit being offered relates. Once you have identified Fact X, you then need to explain how the exhibit has "any tendency" to make the existence of Fact X "more probable or less probable than it would be without" the exhibit.

If the court sustains the objection, you may want to proceed under Rule 104(b) which provides: "When the relevancy of evidence depends upon the fulfillment of a condition of fact, the court should admit it upon, or subject to, the introduction of evidence sufficient to support a finding of the fulfillment of the condition." In other words, the witness on the stand, who is competent to identify and discuss the exhibit, cannot provide the necessary link to an issue in the case. But another witness (who may not be qualified to provide a foundation for the exhibit itself) can provide that link. Under Rule 104(b), you ask the court for permission to proceed with the witness on the stand, and identify and discuss the exhibit, with a promise that you will call the other witness, who can provide the relevance link, at some later time.

If the court refuses, then you should fall back and move on to another point, so that you can return to this exhibit later in a better context. Arguing extensively about the relevance of an exhibit often does more damage than it is worth in terms of possibly getting the exhibit admitted.

Challenge to identification

If your opponent objects to the identification of the exhibit, he or she is usually trying to prevent the witness from testifying about the content of the document in the guise of identifying it. If the witness is identifying a document, for example, counsel is allowed to assist in getting the identification part of the foundation on the record in satisfactory fashion by saying: "Just tell us who the memo is from and the date of the memo. That will identify it."

A challenge to identification may also mean that your opponent does not think the description is sufficient to distinguish the exhibit from all other things. The description "This is a letter," without more, does not distinguish this letter from other letters. The exhibit number, of course, should do this but, because there may be misnumbering of exhibits or mislabeling plaintiff's exhibits as defendant's, the requirement for a precise identification remains.

Challenge to trustworthiness or authentication

Generally the best approach to an argument about trustworthiness is to assert at the outset that the point your opponent is making goes to the weight of the evidence, not to its admissibility. This is very often the case with the trustworthiness aspect of foundation. The task is not to ascertain at the point of foundation that the exhibit is determinative as to an issue in the case. The task is only to ascertain that the exhibit is sufficiently worthwhile that it can be considered for the purpose of ascertaining the truth of the matters at issue.

If the issue is the basis the witness has for identifying the exhibit, you should ask to approach the bench and make an offer of proof with respect to the capability of the witness in this regard. It is often difficult to separate testimony about the substance of the exhibit from testimony about the basis for identifying the exhibit. When you make a proffer in this regard, the court may allow you to proceed and admit the exhibit so that the witness can testify about its contents while, at the same time, satisfying any legitimate concern about the basis for being able to identify it.

If your opponent questions the condition of the exhibit, you might respond that any aspect of its current condition that could cause it to be untrustworthy can be explored fully on cross-examination and can be taken into account by the fact-finder in giving weight to the exhibit.

If the issue is compliance with a section of the rules that provides for self-authentication (Rule 902) or a specified method of authentication (Rule 901), get out the rule so that you can go through it with the court. Once identified, you may be able to cure the problem by asking additional questions. As an alternative, under Rule 611(a), the court may allow you to proceed with the exhibit on your representation that you will "link it up" by providing the necessary missing authentication through another witness.

If the issue is about the trustworthiness of an exhibit that is *not* one specifically covered by Rule 901 (a signature document, a handwritten notation, a public record, an ancient document, or an exhibit produced by means of a process or system), and *not* one specifically covered by Rule 902 (a document under seal, a certified or notarized document, an official or news publication, or commercial paper) you can argue that the rules contain no requirement for extrinsic evidence of trustworthiness (beyond the identification by a competent witness). You can argue that, unless the court makes a specific ruling based on some genuine question raised by opposing counsel, the exhibit should be admitted. Clarify the exact nature of the question being raised and get a ruling from the court as to the authentication necessary.

1.4.7 Meet Objections

If the challenges to foundation fail, your opponent still has an opportunity to object on any available ground. All possible objections need not be stated in the initial response to the motion to admit the exhibit in evidence. An objection on hearsay grounds, if successfully rebutted, can be followed by a separate objection on original document grounds, for example.

Your response must address the specific requirements of the rule under which the objection is raised, even if your opponent has misstated them.

Objection to hearsay

Your response to a hearsay objection should be (if factually correct) either that under Rule 801 the exhibit is not hearsay or that the exhibit is covered by one of the hearsay exceptions in Rules 803 and 804. In either case, you should cite the rule on which you are relying and show how you have complied with its requirements.

One difficult area is whether an exhibit is offered to prove the truth of its contents. Proponents of documentary exhibits will often assert that they merely wish to prove that the document exists, not the truth of what it contains. Of course, once the document comes in, even with a limiting instruction to the jury about considering this exhibit only for its existence and not for the truth of its contents, the prejudicial effect can be substantial. If the court sustains an objection on this ground, one alternative is for the parties to prepare an agreed statement to be read to the jury about the document rather than to admit the document itself. If the court admits a document for the limited purpose of proving it exists, opposing counsel likely will ask for a limiting instruction (see Section 1.8.2) and counsel offering the exhibit should have a proposed instruction at hand.

Objection on original document grounds

Your response to an original document objection should be to assert (if factually correct) that the exhibit either is an original, and therefore may be used to prove the truth of its contents under Rule 1002, or is a duplicate and may be used to the same extent as an original under Rule 1003. Occasionally you will have the defense that the exhibit is not a writing, photograph, or sound recording and therefore, under Rule 1001, is not subject to the original document requirements at all.

If the original document rules apply, and the exhibit cannot qualify as an original or a duplicate because, for example, there are handwritten markings on the copy, you will need to provide an independent foundation authenticating the additional markings. Alternatively, you will have to resort to Rule 1004 and show that: (1) the original is lost or destroyed; (2) the original cannot be obtained by discovery or subpoena; or (3) that your opponent has the original and you requested that they bring it to court, but they did not.

Objection on policy grounds

If your opponent objects to the exhibit under Rule 403 for unfair prejudice, confusion, waste of time, or unnecessary cumulative evidence, you should ask to approach the bench (in a jury trial) and argue the policy grounds. Policy objections almost always involve arguments that the jury should not hear. If you lose, you should retreat quickly and move on to another subject of questioning with the witness.

Upon further reflection at the end of the day, it may be possible to construct another route around the policy objection.

Offer of proof

If the judge rejects the exhibit, and it is important to the case, you should be prepared to make an offer of proof for the record. Note that Rule 103(a)(2) requires an offer of proof where the court's ruling excludes evidence unless the substance of the excluded evidence was apparent from the context within which questions were asked. The offer of proof simply states what the witness would have said about the exhibit.

Example

Counsel: Your Honor, we offer in evidence defendant's Exhibit 1.

Opposing Counsel: Objection. Unfair prejudice. May we approach the bench?

Court: You may.

(Both counsel and the reporter approach the bench at a position where the jury cannot hear the discussion.)

Counsel: Your Honor, under Rule 403, there must be a showing that the probative value of this exhibit is substantially outweighed by the danger of unfair prejudice.

So first, we look at the probative value. The probative value of the exhibit is high. It is a letter from the defendant to the plaintiff.

Then we look at the danger of unfair prejudice. There certainly is prejudice here. The letter establishes the defendant's intent to harm the plaintiff. But I would argue there is no unfair prejudice.

Therefore the balance between probative value on the the one hand and the danger of unfair prejudice on the other should tilt in favor of admitting this exhibit.

Opposing Counsel: Your Honor, we object to the third paragraph on page 2. This letter was sent two years before the incident in question so the probative value is low. The third paragraph is full of profanity unrelated to anything about intent, and that raises the danger of unfair prejudice. This paragraph should be excluded, although we have no objection to the rest of the exhibit.

Court: Objection sustained. Block that paragraph out and you can use the rest.

Counsel: May we make an offer of proof on that Your Honor?

Court: You may.

Counsel: The exhibit marked as plaintiff's Exhibit 1 is a letter from the defendant to the plaintiff and the third paragraph on page 2 contains a threat in which the defendant states that he would, quote get Alfie Withers, unquote. The witness would testify that the phrase, quote get Alfie Withers, unquote, was also used on other occasions when the defendant acted in a menacing manner.

An offer of proof in a jury trial must be done at sidebar or otherwise out of the hearing of the jury. While you must make a record to preserve the point for appeal, the explanation as to the importance of an exhibit that is not admitted in evidence cannot be made before a jury. Most judges have a set procedure for sidebar conferences. Some courtrooms are equipped with "white noise" devices to keep the jury from hearing what goes on at conferences at the bench.

1.4.8 Obtain Permission to Publish the Exhibit

Once admitted in evidence, an exhibit can be shown to the jury, read to the jury, passed hand-to-hand among them, or individual copies of the exhibit can be provided to each juror. The judge will want to maintain control of how the exhibit is published to the jury and therefore the better practice is to ask permission before doing it.

Example

Counsel: Your Honor, may we show (read, distribute copies of, pass) to the jury plaintiff's Exhibit 1 at this time?

Court: You may.

This tells the jurors what is coming next, and provides opposing counsel an opportunity to object to the method of publishing the exhibit.

1.4.9 Publish the Exhibit to the Jury

If you wish to pass an object among the jurors, for example an allegedly defective part, you go to the jury box and hand the exhibit to juror #1. He or she will look at it and then hand it over to the next person. When all the jurors have looked at it, the last one will hand it back to you.

If you want to distribute to the jury copies of a photograph, diagram, document, map, or similar exhibit, so that each juror has one of his or her own, just hand the copies to the first juror who will take one and then hand them on. It is generally best to have a copy for each juror when the document is relatively long and the testimony will refer to various parts of it. For example, when the witness is asked to turn to page 11, all the jurors can turn to page 11 as well.

When you distribute copies of exhibits to jurors, there are accompanying problems as to what the jurors are allowed to do with their copies. Most judges will not allow jurors to make notes on their copies or to take them from the courtroom. Usually only the official set of exhibits is permitted in the jury room.

If more than a few documentary exhibits are to be distributed to the jury, the judge may permit each juror to have a three-ring binder in which to put the documents as they are handed out. See discussion in Section 9.3.2.

If you want to read a documentary exhibit to the jury, you may do so yourself as counsel. This reading may include all or only part of the document.

Example

Counsel: *(Facing jury)* Ladies and gentlemen, plaintiff's Exhibit 1 reads as follows:

(Reads from document)

When you read from any document, even if only a few sentences, you should give the court reporter a copy to help him or her more easily transcribe the reading. If you read only a portion of the document to the jury, your opponent may object under Rule 106 and ask the court's permission to read other related and relevant portions of the document. To prevent this interruption, you should read all of the relevant portions yourself. The advantage of a reading by counsel is that you maintain control over how the jury hears the information in the document. Counsel can ensure the reading is crisp and clear with appropriate emphasis.

You may also have the witness read all or part of the document.

Example

Counsel: Mr. Jones, please read plaintiff's Exhibit 1 to the jury.

Witness: (Reads)

Having the witness read the document aloud may help to dramatize his or her involvement in the events being described. This may help the document "come alive" and can be effective on both direct and cross-examination.

Another alternative is to have the witness describe what is in the document. This summarizes the information and helps move the presentation along.

Example

Q. What does plaintiff's Exhibit 1 show about the month in which the part was manufactured?

A. This shows it was manufactured in December.

Q. What does plaintiff's Exhibit 1 show about the month in which the part was shipped to the defendant, XYZ Corporation?

A. This shows it was shipped in February.

Q. What does plaintiff's Exhibit 1 show about the condition of the part when it was received by defendant XYZ Corporation?

A. There is a box here on the third page which says "do not sign below unless the part included in this shipment is in first class condition." In the signature space there is the name Dudley Durwin.

With any of these alternatives, it may be useful to display the document so that the judge or jury can look at an enlargement of what you or the witness are describing and the important words can be pointed out. This can be done with a computer file displayed on a video monitor, by using a visualizer or visual presenter to display the document on a television monitor, by making a paper enlargement to mount on foamboard or some other stiff backing for display on an easel, by making a transparency of the relevant page and displaying it with a projector, and by other alternative. See discussion of equipment, materials, and techniques for displaying exhibits in Chapter 9.

Once an exhibit has been admitted in evidence, the exhibit may be used by any other witness without further foundation for the exhibit.

1.5 ETHICS RULES AND EXHIBITS

The ethics rules vary from state to state and this book cannot cover all of the possible impacts of these rules on the use of exhibits at trial. Certain basic requirements appear in the ABA Model Rules of Professional Conduct and the ABA opinions with respect to the current and prior versions of the rules. An outline of those rules, as applied specifically to the lawyer's tasks with trial exhibits, provides a starting point for further consideration.

1.5.1 Competence

Rule 1.1 requires that the lawyer be competent with respect to client matters. The rule requires knowledge, skill, thoroughness, and preparation. The comment points out that "Competent handling of a particular matter includes . . . use of methods and procedures meeting the standards of competent practitioners."[9] With respect to exhibits, this means that if you have never worked with a specific kind of display technique or have never appeared before the judge assigned to your current trial who has distinctive views on the admissibility of specific kinds of exhibits, you need to be sure you have done your homework.

1.5.2 Fees

Rule 1.5 requires that a lawyer charge reasonable fees to clients. Formal Opinion 93-379, issued under this rule, requires that all expenses incurred with third party vendors for exhibits be passed on to the client without any surcharge. The opinion also requires that any in-house work done on exhibits by paralegals or others be charged at cost to the law firm plus "a reasonable allocation of overhead expenses directly associated with the provision of the service."[10]

1.5.3 Confidentiality

Rule 1.6 requires that the lawyer not disclose the confidences or secrets of the lawyer's client. The lawyer is also obligated to exercise reasonable care to prevent the lawyer's employees, associates, and others whose services are utilized by the lawyer from disclosing or using confidences or secrets of a client unless the client consents. This means that when work goes outside the firm with respect to exhibits, it needs to be accompanied by an appropriate arrangement to ensure that the information transmitted is kept secure. Most vendors who work regularly in the litigation support field have established procedures for protecting materials that come to them from lawyers. The lawyer needs to inquire about these procedures and to assess whether they are adequate for the case at hand.

1.5.4 Candor Toward the Court

Rule 3.3 requires that the lawyer not make statements to the court that the lawyer knows to be false. This could apply to exhibits if the information on the displays was known by the lawyer not to be accurate. The standard is quite high—the information has to be false and the lawyer has to know that it is false.

The rule also requires that if the lawyer comes to know information is false after it has been presented to the court, the lawyer must call this to the attention of the court, unless the information is confidential in which case the lawyer must call on the client to rectify the false information.

1.5.5 Fairness to Opposing Counsel

Rule 3.4 requires the lawyer not to obstruct another party's access to evidence. This rule can apply to physical objects that may become evidence, such as broken parts, samples of products, or other physical things at issue in the case. The rule acknowledges that a lawyer may receive physical evidence from a client or from another person. If the evidence belongs to anyone other than the client, the lawyer is under an obligation to preserve and return it.

Rule 3.4 also provides that a lawyer may not "in trial, allude to any matter that the lawyer does not reasonably believe is relevant or that will not be supported by admissible evidence . . . ." This means that every exhibit mentioned in voir dire, opening statement, or during trial before being admitted in evidence must have a foundation that the lawyer reasonably believes will be sufficient.

1.6 GENERALLY APPLICABLE TACTICAL CONSIDERATIONS

Some tactical considerations apply generally to all kinds of exhibits and trials. These are summarized here. The tactical considerations in presenting specific categories of exhibits are set out in Chapters 2 through 8.

1.6.1 Preparation

Most cases settle. The potential exhibits that have been gathered for the case are never offered in evidence, and no decisions are made by the court as to whether they are admissible. For this reason, lawyers may leave questions of admissibility until immediately before trial. That is a mistake. If the assembly of foundation for each potential exhibit is a part of the litigation preparation process from the start, then there will be no unpleasant surprises if the case actually does go to trial. The admissibility of exhibits is also an important part of the settlement process. Your opponent may be assuming that you cannot qualify a particular exhibit, and the settlement offer may be adversely affected by that assumption. In addition, the foundation for some kinds of exhibits cannot be laid properly without specific pretrial preparation. If you leave it to the last minute, you may lose the exhibit.

1.6.2 Disclosure

Disclose exhibits to the other side. Most local rules require full disclosure of exhibits to be used in direct examination a certain number of days before trial. You must understand exactly what the local rule covers, and specifically whether you must disclose testimony aids that will not be offered in evidence and exhibits to be used only for cross-examination. In addition to ascertaining the scope of the local rules, it is helpful to know about the practice of the judge assigned to the case.

Photographs, videotapes, sound recordings, models, and computer-generated material should be disclosed well before any deadlines. Opposing counsel has a right to view and listen to these prior to their use at trial. Withholding this kind of exhibit until shortly before trial may cause delay and could cause substantial tactical problems if the judge's ruling on objections is adverse. See discussion in Section 1.3.5 with respect to objections based on "surprise."

There is a considerable tactical advantage to not disclosing testimony aids to the other side until they are used at trial. The foundation for these exhibits is easy to establish so you do not gain much by revealing them ahead of time unless there are unusual problems specific to the case or the predilections of the court. Testimony aids are usually prepared by or at the direction of the lawyer and therefore are not discoverable except as to expert witnesses. There is a growing disposition among judges, however, to order disclosure of all materials to be used by witnesses if the other side asks for them.

Some judges are particularly sensitive to the distinction between exhibits which are "substantive" in nature and can go with the jury to the jury room and exhibits which may reflect the testimony in summary or outline form and are used to assist a witness's presentation. These judges are concerned about allowing testimony aids to be admitted in evidence because then this form of "testimony" would go to the jury room although transcripts of the actual testimony are banned. For this reason, these judges want to see all exhibits at the pretrial conference and to understand which will be offered in evidence and which will not.

1.6.3 Stipulations and Pretrial Rulings

You should pursue vigorously pretrial stipulations with respect to all exhibits that your opponent knows you have, such as physical objects used in depositions and documents discovered from your opponent's files. At the final pretrial conference, the remaining issues (where opposing counsel has refused to stipulate) should be briefed and argued to the full extent permitted by the court. The general wisdom is that in a jury case, everything to be used with nonexpert witnesses should be stipulated or ruled on in advance in order to save time and allow for reconsideration of adverse rulings. There will probably be some exhibits as to which the court will be persuaded not to rule until seeing them in context at trial. In a nonjury case, the judge is more likely to admit exhibits that might otherwise be excluded on policy grounds on the rationale that a judge is not easily affected by unfair prejudice, confusion, or the other policy reasons for rejecting exhibits.

Judicial notice

A number of the evidence rules use terms such as "public office," "authority granted by law," "public official," "official duties," "custodian," "official record," "public authority," "authorized by law," and "provided by law." (See, for example, Rules 803, 901, 902, and 1005.) Compliance with these requirements, if challenged, can be established by judicial notice under the terms of Rule 201. Evidentiary matters are "adjudicative facts" under the rule.[11] Facts such as these examples are "not subject to reasonable dispute" as provided in Rule 201(b) because they are "either (1) generally known within the territorial jurisdiction of the trial court or (2) capable of accurate and ready determination by resort to sources whose accuracy cannot reasonably be questioned." In these examples, the sources generally are laws and regulations.

In this regard, when the law of a foreign country is to be judicially noticed, Rule 44.1 of the Federal Rules of Civil Procedure imposes an additional requirement of reasonable written notice to the other side. Judges have broad discretion as to the matters subject to judicial notice.[12] If your opponent insists on nit-picking over matters that really do not make any difference, or are obvious, a resort to judicial notice will help an impatient judge clear away the underbrush.

1.6.4 Awards of Costs and Sanctions

If your opponent refuses a reasonable request to stipulate to the admissibility of exhibits, or refuses to respond to reasonable interrogatories or requests for admissions providing the basis for a pretrial ruling that exhibits are admissible, consider requesting the court to award costs if the exhibit is offered at trial and admitted without any genuine question being raised as to its admissibility. If you have 20 or 30 exhibits to which your opponent refuses to stipulate, the trial will be extended considerably as you offer the foundation and meet objections for each exhibit. That extra cost—of lawyer time, witness time, and any associated expenses—should be borne by the opposing party if there was no reasonable basis for withholding agreement. Most exhibits are readily understood as admissible or not by even the least talented lawyer, and expending trial time on establishing technical foundations should not be encouraged. Judges have inherent power to make such awards and should be requested during pretrial proceedings to consider doing so.

1.6.5 Anticipating Objections

Lawyers have two approaches to potential objections. One view, used in the illustrations in this book, is to lay the foundation, offer the exhibit, and wait for the objection. If no objection is forthcoming, the exhibit will be admitted and you will not need to spend the time asking the questions and getting the answers to meet the potential objection. This makes the trial move along more quickly and is an approach favored by many judges and lawyers. Your opponent, who has refused to stipulate to the admissibility of the exhibit in pretrial proceedings, may lose heart at trial and not make the objection at all.

The other view, favored by perhaps an equal number of lawyers, is to elicit the testimony to meet an obvious objection along with the foundation before the exhibit is offered. That way, when the opponent hears the testimony that defeats the objection, it increases the likelihood the objection will not be made at all. Those who favor this view think that interruptions are minimized, and the jury learning process is enhanced.

A related question is what to do when an objection is made—wait for a ruling or go right back to the witness for more testimony? If the objection is a legitimate one, you can go right back to the witness, perhaps with an introductory comment such as: "I can deal with that [objection] directly, Your Honor," and not wait for a ruling. Alternatively, you can wait for a ruling. The court may not agree with your opponent and, if the objection is overruled, no additional testimony is needed. If you have adopted the first approach, and put in only the foundation testimony before making the offer, the better choice may be to go right back to the witness, provide the testimony necessary to meet the objection, and offer the exhibit again. The illustrations in this book follow this path. If you are well prepared, after a few objections your opponent may not pursue every available objection because the jury will hear the judge overrule one objection after another. If you have adopted the second approach, and have put in testimony to meet potential objections before offering the exhibit for the first time, then you may want to argue the point under the applicable rule rather than going back to the witness. Having to repeat testimony may confuse an inexperienced witness.

Jurors pay relatively little attention to the testimony that qualifies exhibits. It sounds routine and boring to them. They leave with an overall impression of how many objections were sustained and how many were overruled. This colors their view of the lawyers presenting the case and may create a feeling about whether the trial is being delayed by what is perceived as nit-picking by one side or the other as to exhibits. It is important not to be on the losing side of this impression.

Exhibit foundation checklist

With every exhibit, you must think through what the court or your opponent might do when you offer the exhibit in evidence or start to use a testimony aid. A check sheet for each exhibit can pull together a brief summary as to the testimony covering the elements of foundation and a brief potential response to each of three categories of possible objections. With that sheet in your trial notebook, if there is a challenge to foundation, you have a ready summary as to why the exhibit was offered properly and a prompt response. The check sheet can include notes on any special rules that apply and even case law if the argument is going to be over a key exhibit. A sample of this kind of check sheet is set out in Appendix D.

1.6.6 Handling and Organizing Exhibits at Trial

Once the trial begins, the lawyer's tactics and manner in handling tangible evidence can affect to a great extent the consideration of the exhibit by the fact-finder, especially a jury. Think about the impression that your exhibits make from the moment the jury is empaneled. Bring your exhibits into the courtroom in a carrying case (see Fig. 2) or wrapped so that they cannot be seen until the witness is ready to use them. They should be evident in the courtroom, so that the jury knows something interesting is coming, but not visible so as to distract from testimony on other points. Cover large exhibits; keep display equipment on wheeled carts or trays out of the way against the wall.

The handling and organization of tangible evidence is an important part of the case. The lawyer should have an organized system so that he or she can lay hands on the exhibit precisely when it is needed without any fumbling, searching, or muttering. Handle evidentiary exhibits with dignity and care. Place exhibits before the court reporter or the witness with deliberate formality and with an appropriate pause in any spoken presentation. If the exhibit has any moving or removable parts, the lawyer should be intimately familiar with how the exhibit works and practiced in working it even if it is to be handled primarily by a witness. Both witness and lawyer should practice using each exhibit in a court or court-like setting before trial starts.

Exhibit tracking list

You must keep an accurate list of all the exhibits by number, a brief identification of what they are, and a notation as to whether they were admitted. At the end of the day or at the end of the case, the judge will usually recapitulate from his or her list of exhibits which ones have been admitted in evidence. If that does not happen, you should review your list for the judge or check with the clerk, just to be sure there is no question about which exhibits were admitted in evidence. A sample exhibit list is set out in Appendix D. If you are working in a jurisdiction where it is the practice to mark exhibits first "for identification" and then to strike the "for identification" modifier when the exhibit is admitted, the exhibit itself will show whether it has been admitted.

1.6.7 Displaying Exhibits

The equipment and materials for displaying exhibits are also important. These are described in Chapter 9. To the extent possible within the budget for the case and the physical facilities in the courtroom, the exhibits should be varied in manner of presentation in order to increase impact and maintain interest. Before presenting any exhibit to the fact-finder that cannot be held in the hand or passed from juror to juror, check the lines of sight in the courtroom to be sure you have placed the exhibit where the judge, jury, and witness can all see it. A small chalk mark or piece of tape on the floor is often helpful in setting up exhibits in a predetermined position where they can be seen easily by everyone.

Once the evidence has been admitted and presented to the fact-finder, the lawyer needs to implement a plan as to what items should be kept in view throughout the trial. This helps increase the impact of the evidence and familiarity of the fact-finder with the evidence. You should take overexposure to evidence into account in this plan. For example, trial experience with particularly grisly or shocking evidence generally indicates that it should not be kept before the fact-finder continually because of the tendency to get used to it over time. When that happens, the exhibit loses its impact.

The totality of the tangible evidence for your side must be appropriate for what is at stake, and the number and type of exhibits supporting each point must be within reasonable limits. If the fact-finder believes that the amount of tangible evidence is greater than the importance of the point for which it is introduced, they will suspect that the lawyer does not know what is important in the case, or worse, that the lawyer is conducting a three-ring circus in order to fool them about something. Balance is important.

1.7 VOIR DIRE EXAMINATION ON EXHIBITS

The term voir dire covers two kinds of examination about exhibits: first, the questions put to potential jurors at the outset of the case to determine their qualification to serve; and second, the questions put to witnesses, under specialized circumstances and when permitted by the court, to determine their qualification to sponsor potential exhibits. Each is described below.

1.7.1 Voir Dire of the Jury with Respect to Capability to Understand Exhibits

The practice with respect to permissible voir dire of potential jurors varies from jurisdiction to jurisdiction. In some courts, judges give free rein to lawyers to conduct voir dire of each potential juror; in others, the judge asks a few perfunctory questions of the group as a whole and declares voir dire to be over. You need to know what the general practice is and to raise pretrial anything you would like to do that is different. This section sets out various areas where voir dire has proved highly useful. You will need to inventory the particular requirements of each case to determine what is necessary.

Color and other perception factors

If judges and jurors reflect the general population, a significant percentage, especially of the males, will be color-blind in one or more respects. It will not do you much good to have a terrific exhibit in which red and green are used to illustrate an important point if the judge or some of the jurors cannot distinguish those colors. If you have any exhibits that incorporate colors, be sure to ask about this.

As with all other voir dire of potential jurors, it is important to ask about color blindness in a neutral way.

Example

Examining counsel: The next thing I am going to ask about is color blindness. And let me explain why. In some cases, we use charts that have colors on them in order to help make certain information easier to understand. Being color-blind is not a disqualification to serve on this jury—it just means that we need to make sure we are using colors that everyone can see. For example, a lot of people cannot distinguish reds and greens. Other people have trouble with blues and browns. If we know that in advance, we just avoid those problems. So, let me ask you, is anyone color-blind in any respect?

You can use a similar approach for other eyesight problems that will affect the ability to see or read your exhibits. Ask whether potential jurors wear eyeglasses for reading or watching TV. If they do, they will have problems with documents or exhibits displayed on a video monitor unless they have their glasses on. Ask whether they have ever been treated for cataracts, glaucoma, detached retina, or other eye problems. Some of these problems do not lead to wearing eyeglasses, but they may severely disrupt a potential juror's ability to see exhibits. In a case with numerous documentary exhibits, you may want to ask the court to exercise its prerogative to excuse jurors with eyesight problems.

Jurors need to hear the explanations of exhibits. Ask about hearing aids, illnesses that cause permanent hearing impairment, temporary conditions that may adversely affect hearing, and sensitivity to loud or high-pitched sounds. Make sure that you convey your intent not to exclude anyone with a hearing aid but just to ensure any necessary adjustments are made so that everyone can hear clearly. If potential jurors think that hearing or other impairments will disqualify them, they may be reluctant to reveal that information.

Receptivity to methods for displaying exhibits

Voir dire can be used to familiarize jurors with the equipment and materials to display exhibits. If you plan to use a computer, visualizer or visual presenter, laserdisc player, whiteboard with printing capability, touch screen, or any other specialized equipment, voir dire is an opportunity to find out if jurors have any negative attitudes or have had any negative experiences that might predispose them to distrust exhibits presented with particular equipment.

One useful starting point is television viewing. If you ask whether a juror likes to watch TV, what kind of programs he or she likes best, and about how much TV watching is done per day, you will find out a good deal about the juror's attitudes and personality as well as his or her receptivity to exhibits displayed on video monitors. When you plan extensive use of video, think carefully about a potential juror who watches TV an hour or less per day. Some people who watch very little TV are generally turned off by the medium and may regard your video exhibits with suspicion.

After dealing with TV, you can move to a brief explanation of the use of the video monitor to display exhibits in somewhat the same way that TV transmissions are displayed. Jurors who are familiar with the equipment will be less distracted when you start to use it. In this context, you can also explain that if anytime there is glare on the video monitor or if any juror cannot see clearly, they should just speak up and you will make the necessary adjustments. You need to convey a concern that every juror see and hear everything presented by you as clearly as possible. You are not going to speed anything past them.

Computers

If computers have been used in any way with respect to generating any important exhibit or will be used to display your exhibits, you should find out about the level of sophistication about computers and possible negative attitudes.

Example

Examining counsel: This case involves evidence about certain computer records, and I'd like to ask about your experience with computers.

Do you have a computer in your home?

What do you use it for?

Do you use a computer in your office?

Do you have office e-mail on your computer? And what else?

Have you ever had problems with bills that were caused by
computer mistakes?

Do you think it is a good idea for young school kids to learn on
computers?

People who have never touched a computer are not necessarily
undesirable jurors in a case involving computers or computer records,
but you will need to gear the testimony to the lowest level of juror
understanding. You need to know this information at the outset. A juror
who is openly hostile toward computers may not be as good a candidate
to consider computer records carefully as some other person and may
be worth a peremptory challenge.

Photography

A committed amateur photographer may, as a juror, feel compelled
to pick apart photographic evidence. If you are using photos as
important exhibits, ask potential jurors about the cameras, video
equipment, and computer scanning equipment they may own or use.
Close friends or relatives with professional experience may also be a
significant influence.

You may want to ask about experience with or exposure to digital
cameras. Anyone who knows much about this kind of equipment (see
discussion in Section 6.1.2) also knows how easily photographs can be
manipulated to change the original while leaving no trace of alteration.
This is not necessarily a reason to exercise a peremptory challenge, but
it may affect the way you qualify or challenge certain exhibits.

Statistics

If you have key exhibits that are charts, graphs, time lines, tables,
calculations, or complicated diagrams, you may want to inquire about
experience or education with respect to statistics, mathematics, logic,
or philosophy. The latter two subjects may affect the potential juror's
attitude toward the way that your presentation attempts to persuade.

Documents

If you have important documentary exhibits, you will want to ask
about juror attitudes with respect to the particular kind of document at
issue or its close relatives. When a potential juror has had a bad
experience or has formed a relevant belief, you need to know about that.
For example, if you will be relying on a diagram of an intersection
accident in a police report and a key exhibit is an enlargement of such
a diagram, you will want to know whether any potential juror has ever
filled out such a report or had such a report made about an accident
that he or she saw or was involved in. You will also want to know

whether, drawing on that experience, the potential juror thinks such diagrams are trustworthy.

Attitudes about documents need to be pinned down to the extent possible. Some people are more willing to believe something that has been written down in a document than something asserted in oral testimony. Others believe, particularly in a commercial or corporate context, that most documents are created to protect particular interests and are unlikely to be completely truthful. You will want to know about any serious disputes or litigation in which the potential juror or close friends or relatives were involved that raised questions about the authenticity or truthfulness of documents.

Familiarity with important evidence

You may want to use certain exhibits, such as photographs of specialized equipment, maps of particular locations, or models of things at issue to inquire about jurors' familiarity with important evidence.

Example

Examining counsel: This case involves a robot called the
    Assembot II. This is an enlarged picture of the Assembot II
    robot which, you can see down here in the corner, has been
    marked as Number 64 so we can keep track of it accurately.

(Placing Exhibit 64 on the easel)

Have any of you seen one of these before?

Have you read or learned anything about this robot?

Are you familiar in any way with these kinds of robots used in
    manufacturing processes?

Exhibits that have been admitted in evidence at pretrial proceedings generally can be used for this purpose. Exhibits not yet admitted may not be used without the permission of the court. Judges will be alert to the potential for "selling" the lawyer's version of the facts if exhibits are used during voir dire, so you will want to stay strictly within the proper bounds.[13]

1.7.2   Voir Dire of Witnesses with Respect to Admissibility of Exhibits

Voir dire of a witness as to an exhibit is a limited form of cross-examination that interrupts direct examination, with the permission of the court, in order to pursue facts that bear on the admissibility of the exhibit. Voir dire should be requested before the court rules on admissibility as eliciting facts with respect to admissibility is its only legitimate purpose. Occasionally a court will allow voir dire after indicating a tentative ruling on admissibility if the opponent of the exhibit has a credible request to explore an aspect of the basis for the court's ruling.

Opposing counsel asking for voir dire may seek to challenge one of the four elements of foundation: the competence of the witness, the relevance of the exhibit, the identification of the exhibit, or the trustworthiness of the exhibit. When making the request for voir dire, counsel will be required by the court to state clearly the proposed thrust of the examination so the court can determine that it is proper.

Example

(The competence of the witness was established as described in Section 1.1.1. Relevance has been established as set out in Section 1.1.2. The witness has identified a gear part as set out in Section 1.1.3 and stated a basis for that identification as explained in Section 1.1.4. The proponent's counsel has defended the foundation as described in Section 1.1.5.)

Opposing Counsel: Your Honor, may I voir dire the witness on the foundation for Exhibit 15? It appears that the identification of this exhibit is not sufficient.

Court: You may.

Opposing Counsel: Now Ms. Jones, you haven't had continuous possession of this gear part that has been marked as Exhibit 15 from the time it was removed by Mason's Maintenance to the time it arrived in this courtroom, have you?

A. Well, our company has had it.

Opposing Counsel: But you have not personally been in possession of it, have you?

A. It was delivered to me by Mason's when they removed it, and we kept it.

Opposing Counsel: Ms. Jones, that gear part was not in your possession was it?

A. Not my personal possession, no.

Opposing Counsel: And you did not make any identifying mark on it so you could recognize it again, did you?

A. I didn't have to. It already had a distinctive pattern of wear on one side.

Opposing Counsel: But you didn't put your initials on it or anything like that, did you?

A. No.

Opposing Counsel: You are responsible for making sure the maintenance is done on all the machines in the plant, aren't you?

A. Yes.

Opposing Counsel: And there are quite a lot of those machines, aren't there?

A. About 15.

Opposing Counsel: There is maintenance going on with these machines all the time, isn't that true?

A. Yes.

Opposing Counsel: A number of these machines have second lateral gear parts just like Exhibit 15, don't they?

A. Yes.

Opposing Counsel: When these second lateral gear parts are replaced, the maintenance service delivers them to you, don't they?

A. Yes.

Opposing Counsel: So you've had many such second lateral gear parts in your possession over the past year, haven't you?

A. Well, I wouldn't say many.

Opposing Counsel: Certainly more than one, right?

A. Yes, more than one.

Opposing Counsel: All these replaced parts have wear patterns on them, don't they?

A. Yes.

Opposing Counsel: And you never saw Exhibit 15 from the time you got it from the maintenance service to the time you saw it here in court, did you?

A. I don't remember what the timing was. I know I had it when it was taken off the machine.

Opposing Counsel: Your Honor, the foundation offered by this witness just is not sufficient. The identification of Exhibit 15 is based on speculation.

Examining Counsel: Your Honor, the witness has testified that the wear pattern was distinctive and that this is the basis for her identification. This examination has not challenged that basis at all.

Court: Do you have any other identification testimony?

Examining Counsel: We have another witness who can also identify Exhibit 15 and, if necessary, we will bring in the person who actually kept Exhibit 15. We ask that we be permitted to proceed, subject to Rule 104(b), if Your Honor decides that further foundation is needed in this regard.

When challenging foundation through voir dire, you will need to make judgments about the importance of the exhibit and the amount of light to be shed on the matter by voir dire. Witnesses will be very resistant to giving you what you are seeking, and judges are almost always impatient with these interruptions unless something significant is likely to result.

Opposing counsel asking for voir dire may also seek to challenge the rebuttal to objections. Hearsay objections may be rebutted by showing that the exhibit is not hearsay under the exemptions provided in Rule 801(c) or Rule 801(d). The proponent of the exhibit may also prove facts necessary to fit under an exception in Rule 803 or Rule 804. Original document objections may be rebutted by showing that the exhibit is a duplicate or that the original is unavailable. Policy objections may be rebutted by a showing that no unfair prejudice, confusion, delay, or waste of time will result. When the proponent of the exhibit appears to have succeeded with the factual showing necessary to rebut an objection, the lawyer who made the objection is entitled to voir dire to elicit facts supporting the objection.

Example

(Exhibit 10 is offered as explained in Section 1.1.4. A hearsay objection is made on the basis that Exhibit 10 contains out of court statements and is offered to prove the truth of its contents. The proponent of the exhibit claims an exception under Rule 803(3) for a statement of the declarant's then existing state of mind and emotion.)

Opposing Counsel: May I voir dire the witness on the basis for the exception under the hearsay rule, Your Honor?

Court: You may.

Opposing Counsel: You didn't write Exhibit 10 on the morning of the first sexual harassment incident, did you?

A. I don't remember exactly when I wrote it.

Opposing Counsel: But you've already told us you were totally occupied in the lab that morning, so you certainly did not write it that morning, did you?

A. Not that morning, no.

Opposing Counsel: And you didn't write it the day before either, did you?

A. No, that day I was in New York.

Opposing Counsel: So you wrote Exhibit 10 some days before you left it for Mr. Lewis?

A. Maybe two days or so before.

Opposing Counsel: When you said in Exhibit 10: "Sexual harassment makes women feel degraded and worthless," you weren't talking about yourself, were you?

A. Well, I think it makes all women feel that way.

Opposing Counsel: But you've told us that you would not have complained but for your fear of being fired if you refused these sexual advances, isn't that right?

A. That was the reason I complained.

Opposing Counsel: You didn't feel degraded that day, did you?

A. I've always been proud of my work record.

Opposing Counsel: You didn't feel worthless that day, did you?

A. No, I am a very valuable employee.

Opposing Counsel: Your Honor, may we have this portion of Exhibit 10 stricken? This is hearsay for which there is no available exception.

Proponent's Counsel: Your Honor, that portion of Exhibit 10 is not offered for the truth of the statement, only for the fact that it was made and the company was on notice as to this problem.

Opposing Counsel: Your Honor, if this part of the note is not offered for the truth of the statement made, may we have a limiting instruction as to Exhibit 10 to explain that to the jury?

Court: You may. Do you have anything further in voir dire on Exhibit 10?

Opposing Counsel: No.

Court: Exhibit 10 is admitted. Ladies and gentlemen of the jury, this second paragraph of Exhibit 10 may be considered by you only for the limited purpose of determining the extent of the notice that the company had with respect to the matters contained in that paragraph and for no other purpose.

Often the objective of voir dire is to limit the use of the exhibit if it cannot be excluded altogether. See Section 1.8 on jury instructions with respect to exhibits. As with voir dire on foundation, voir dire on objections should be limited to instances in which it is necessary and likely to succeed.

The basic rule with respect to voir dire of witnesses about exhibits is that the examination must go only to the admissibility of the exhibit, not to its weight. If your opponent strays over the line, you are entitled to object to the voir dire on this ground. The court may order voir dire on foundation or objections to be done out of the presence of the jury. Both proponent's counsel and opposing counsel need to consider these alternatives carefully. Sometimes it is useful for an opponent to start discrediting a witness as early as possible, and interrupting the direct examination for voir dire may be a good way to achieve this objective. But jurors may sympathize with the witness if the point is not strong and they want to see the exhibit.

1.8 JURY INSTRUCTIONS ON EXHIBITS

Instructions about exhibits are important because jurors tend to rely heavily on the exhibits they believe. Lawyers need to obtain clear jury instructions that will not impede the consideration of exhibits. This is not an easy task because judges usually have standard instructions that they use in every case.

The judge usually gives jury instructions at the beginning, during, and at the end of the trial. You should try to get jury instructions resolved as early in the case as possible. Have proposed preliminary instructions ready for the first pretrial conference. Look over your opponent's proposed exhibits to see if any are likely to raise the need for limiting instructions during trial. Keep a set of proposed cautionary and limiting instructions in your trial notebook so you are prepared should the occasion arise. Put together proposed final instructions as you draft your opening and closing statements.

The court generally gives preliminary instructions orally. Final instructions are given in both oral and written form, so the jury will have a copy of the final instructions in the jury room when they deliberate. Consider requesting that the court put the jury instructions on a video monitor, either with electronic or digital technology, while the instructions are being read. Allowing the jury to read the instructions, at the same time they hear them, usually leads to better comprehension.

Each set of instructions has typical problems for some types of exhibits. This section explains the instructions that apply directly to exhibits. Other standard instructions may have implications for your exhibits in a particular case and you should examine them carefully in that regard.

1.8.1 Preliminary Instructions

The judge will give preliminary instructions at the outset of the trial just before opening statements. Many judges have a very short skeleton set of instructions that they typically give at this point in the trial. Because jurors are unfamiliar with the task ahead, instructions about evidence and exhibits are particularly useful at the outset. Consult first the pattern jury instructions issued by the court or jurisdiction in which the trial will take place. Define what you need that is not already in the pattern instructions. Then ask the judge's clerk or a court clerk for the instructions usually used by the judge in the type of case you have. Consider where these instructions depart from what you need. Gather examples from jurisdictions respected by the court. You should work hard to persuade the court that instructions about evidence and exhibits, such as those discussed in this section, are necessary for the jury's understanding of their role. The judge may have these instructions in the set typically used at the end of the case, and you may be able to persuade the court to move some of them from the final instructions to the preliminary instructions. The instructions are discussed here in the order in which they are usually given.

Evidence

The overview instruction on evidence defines what the jury can consider in deciding the case. Because jurors may have different ideas about the key terms used in trials, starting at the beginning with a short definition of terms helps get everyone on the same track.

Example

The evidence presented to you during the trial will consist of the testimony of witnesses and tangible items, including papers or documents, called exhibits.

If you will be using only papers and documents as exhibits, this basic instruction will suffice. If you have photographs, models, drawings, and other types of exhibits, you will want to try to get the court to include them in this instruction.

Example

The evidence will consist of the testimony of witnesses, documents and other things received in evidence as exhibits, and any facts on which the lawyers agree or which I may instruct you to accept.[14]

This instruction has a better formulation as to exhibits because it includes the broad category of "things." Although the last clause about stipulated facts and judicially noticed facts is common, jurors sometimes misunderstand rulings on objections to be directions with respect to their acceptance of exhibits. This clause is better left to cautionary and limiting instructions given during trial as the need arises.

Consideration of the evidence

Once the jury knows that evidence is both testimony and exhibits, they need to know how to consider the evidence. This instruction is usually given at the end of the case, but it assists the jury much more to hear it at the beginning and the end of the case.

Example

You must consider only the evidence in this case. However, you may draw such reasonable inferences from the testimony and exhibits as you feel are justified in the light of common experience. You may make deductions and reach conclusions that reason and common sense lead you to make from the testimony and the exhibits. The testimony of a single witness may be sufficient to prove any fact, even if a greater number of witnesses may have testified to the contrary, if after considering all the other evidence you believe that single witness.[15]

Researchers have done excellent work in simplifying jury instructions, and you may want to consider some of their suggestions.

Example

Your decisions should be based only on the evidence admitted in this trial and it is my duty to decide what evidence is admissible. Once evidence is admitted, only the jury can and must decide the following two things about the evidence: (1) whether it should be believed; and (2) how important it is. You should make these two decisions about each piece of evidence by using your own common sense as reasonable men and women. You should not imagine things that cannot be proven by the evidence admitted in this trial.[16]

This rewrite of a typical instruction makes it clearer and easier to understand. Judges are very cautious, however, about accepting rewrites of pattern jury instructions established in their jurisdiction. Once the appellate court has given its seal of approval to particular instructions, judges believe the safest course is to use these instructions regardless of how muddled the language appears to be.

Evidence for a limited purpose

The concept that evidence can be considered for one purpose but not for another is totally foreign to most jurors. If you expect that some of the exhibits may be so limited, you should try to have an instruction to this effect included in the preliminary instructions.

Example

Some evidence is admitted for a limited purpose only. When I instruct you that an item of evidence has been admitted for a limited purpose, you must consider it only for that limited purpose and for no other.[17]

Example

A particular item of evidence is sometimes received for a limited purpose only. That is, it can be used by you only for one particular purpose, and not for any other purpose. I shall tell you when that occurs and instruct you on the purposes for which the item can and cannot be used. You should pay particularly close attention to such an instruction, because it may not be available to you in writing later in the jury room.[18]

As noted below with respect to final instructions, the lawyer who obtains such limiting instructions should be vigilant in seeking to have the court repeat those instructions at the end of the case.

Direct and circumstantial evidence

Most jurisdictions use an instruction on direct and circumstantial evidence to explain to jurors that they may give both kinds of evidence weight according to the conclusions reached concerning the exhibits. Putting this instruction into the preliminary set assures that some juror will not spend the entire trial thinking that testimony is worth more than exhibits, only to be enlightened by the instructions at the end of the trial. By that time, most jurors have made up their minds, although instructed repeatedly by the court not to do so.

Example

Evidence may be direct or circumstantial. Direct evidence is direct proof of a fact, such as testimony by a witness about what that witness personally saw or heard or did. Circumstantial evidence is proof of one or more facts from which you could find another fact. You should consider both kinds of evidence. The law makes no distinction between the weight to be given to either direct or circumstantial evidence. It is for you to decide how much weight to give to any evidence.[19]

A "plain English" version of this instruction gives this guidance as follows:

Example

There are two general types of evidence that will be presented in this trial. One type of evidence is called direct evidence. The other type of evidence is called indirect evidence.

Direct evidence is those parts of the testimony and exhibits admitted in court which referred to what happened and were testified to by witnesses who saw or heard what happened themselves first hand.

Indirect evidence is all the testimony and exhibits which give you clues about what happened in an indirect way. It consists of all the evidence that is not direct evidence.

According to our laws, direct evidence is not necessarily better than indirect evidence. Either type of evidence can prove a fact if it is convincing enough. Thus, the important thing for you to keep in mind is whether a piece of evidence is convincing and not whether it is direct or indirect.[20]

Some jurisdictions do away with this problem altogether by just telling the jury to ignore the terms.

Example

Some of you may have heard the terms "direct evidence" and "circumstantial evidence." You are instructed that you should not be concerned with those terms, since the law makes no distinction between the weight to be given to direct and circumstantial evidence.[21]

The instruction on direct and indirect evidence will play a part in opening statements, as well as closing arguments, so you should urge the court to make it a part of the preliminary instructions.

Rulings on objections

Explaining the procedure with respect to objections helps jurors adjust to their role more quickly.

Example

There are rules of evidence which control what can be received in evidence. When a lawyer asks a question or offers an exhibit in evidence and a lawyer on the other side thinks that it is not permitted by the rules of evidence, that lawyer may object. If I overrule the objection, the question may be answered or the exhibit received. If I sustain the objection, the question cannot be answered and the exhibit cannot be received. Whenever I sustain an objection to a question, you must ignore the question and must not guess what the answer might have been. Sometimes I may order that evidence be stricken from the record and that you disregard or ignore the evidence. That means that when you are deciding the case, you must not consider the evidence which I told you to disregard.[22]

If you are counsel for the defendant, you will be doing the initial objecting, and you will want to have this instruction in the preliminary set so that the jury knows you are just doing your job.

Exhibits

Similarly, explaining the procedure with respect to exhibits is helpful to jurors who often become anxious when exhibits appear and disappear before they have had a chance to study them.

Example

Any exhibits admitted in evidence during the trial will be available to you for detailed study, if you wish, during your deliberations. So, if an exhibit is received in evidence but is not fully read or shown to you at the time, don't be concerned because you will get to see and study it later during your deliberations.[23]

This instruction contains an important caution for lawyers. Remember that unless you explain why you are using only a part or an excerpt from an exhibit, jurors will wonder what is in the rest of it. While they are wondering, they will be distracted from the task at hand. In your opening statement, try to explain why you are using excerpts or parts of the exhibits and reassure the jury by reference to this instruction.

Testimony aids

In the process of explaining the general concepts governing the trial, remember to include testimony aids that are not offered in evidence.

Example

The rules permit exhibits that are illustrations. These are a party's description or sketch or model to describe something that is involved in this trial. These illustrations are not received in evidence. If your recollection of the evidence differs from the illustration, rely on your recollection.[24]

This instruction on testimony aids is sometimes given as a cautionary or limiting instruction during trial when the first testimony aid appears. If you will be using testimony aids, you are much better off having a general description in the preliminary instructions.

Otherwise, jurors can become wary of this type of exhibit because they think they are not supposed to rely on it.

The last sentence of this instruction is sometimes worded: "If your recollection of the evidence differs from the exhibit, rely on your recollection."[25] That formulation causes jurors to think that they are not supposed to rely on exhibits. The wording is confusing, and you should try to get it changed.

Jury exhibit books

Notebook binders may be handed to each juror at the outset of the trial, and the jury instructions at the beginning of the trial may include a paragraph on the jury exhibit book and how it will be used. The explanation used by one judge is as follows:

Example

> You will be given a three-ring binder. Some of the documentary exhibits will be provided to you and can be kept in the binder. These exhibits will be handed to you, along with a tab sheet showing the number of the exhibit, by the lawyers as they go through the trial. When the lawyers or a witness refers to a particular exhibit, you may go to that tab in your binder to look at it.

Some judges prefer that the notebooks be provided to the jurors empty except for the basic plaintiff and defendant tab dividers and that the exhibits for each day be handed to the jury in a group at the outset of the day's proceedings. Others require that all exhibits admitted in pretrial proceedings be put into the juror notebooks at the outset of the trial. The instructions should be clear about how the mechanics will work.

Burden of proof

The instruction on burden of proof typically will include introductory and concluding paragraphs specific to the case telling the jury who has the burden of proof on particular issues. Embedded in that instruction, you will usually find an instruction on how to decide fact issues.

Example

> In deciding whether any fact has been proven, you may, unless otherwise instructed, consider the testimony of all the witnesses, regardless of who may have called them, and all exhibits received in evidence, regardless of who may have produced them.[26]

This instruction is important if you may be making points off exhibits offered by the other side.

1.8.2 Cautionary and Limiting Instructions

Judges give cautionary and limiting instructions as the trial goes along. When a specific circumstance calls for an instruction, the court will stop the proceedings, turn to the jury, and deliver the instruction. This is usually done at the request of counsel.

Bench conferences and recesses

When the first bench conference or recess occurs, you may want to request an instruction so that the jury knows what is going on.

Example

At times during the trial it may be necessary for me to talk with the lawyers here at the bench out of your hearing or in my chambers by calling a recess. We meet because often during a trial something comes up that doesn't involve the jury.[27]

Example

During the trial it may be necessary for me to talk with the lawyers out of your hearing, either by having a bench conference here while you are present in the courtroom or by calling a recess. Please understand that while you are waiting, we are working. The purpose of these conferences is to decide how certain evidence is to be treated under the rules of evidence and to avoid confusion and error. We will, of course, do what we can to keep the number and length of these conferences to a minimum.[28]

Jurors are always impatient with delays, and it is important to explain to them that their time is not being wasted.

Limited admissibility

Under Rule 105, anytime evidence is admitted for a limited purpose, the opponent is entitled to a jury instruction to that effect.

Example

The evidence you are about to hear (you have just heard) may be considered by you only on the issue (question) of _____. It may not be considered for any other purpose.[29]

Requests for a limiting instruction are made when a document is offered not for the truth of its content but for notice or some other purpose, when evidence is offered against one party but not against another, when prior inconsistent statements are limited to the issue of credibility, and for other similar purposes.

Deposition testimony

When the first deposition excerpt is offered in lieu of a live witness, counsel offering the deposition testimony should request an instruction explaining the procedure about to be used.

Example

Certain testimony will now be presented to you through a deposition. A deposition is the sworn, recorded answers to questions asked a witness in advance of the trial. Under some circumstances, if a witness cannot be present to testify from the witness stand, that witness's testimony may be presented, under oath, in the form of a deposition. Sometime before this trial, attorneys representing the parties in this case questioned this witness under oath. A court reporter was present and recorded the testimony. The questions and answers will be read to you today. This deposition testimony is entitled to the same consideration and is to be judged by you as to credibility and weighed and otherwise considered by you insofar as possible in the same way as if the witness had been present and had testified from the witness stand in court.[30]

If you are going to display the testimony on a monitor either as it is read in the courtroom or in substitution for a reading, you will want to modify the instruction to explain this.

Transcripts of tape-recorded conversations

Similarly, the use of sound tapes often calls for a special instruction.

Example

There is a typewritten transcript of the tape recording you are about to hear. That transcript also undertakes to identify the speakers engaged in the conversation.

You are permitted to have the transcript for the limited purpose of helping you follow the conversation as you listen to the tape recording and also to help you identify the speakers. The transcript, however, is not evidence.

You are specifically instructed that whether the transcript correctly or incorrectly reflects the conversation or the identity of the speakers is entirely for you to decide based upon what you have heard here about the preparation of the transcript and upon your own examination of the transcript in relation to what you hear on the tape recording. The tape recording itself is the primary evidence of its own contents. If you decide that the transcript is in any respect incorrect or unreliable, you should disregard it to that extent.

Differences between what you hear in the recording and read in the transcript may be caused by such things as the inflection in a speaker's voice or by inaccuracies in the transcript. You should, therefore, rely on what you hear rather than what you read when there is a difference.[31]

If you are using a television monitor or video monitor to display the transcript as the tape recording is played, this instruction should be modified to explain that.

1.8.3 Final Instructions

The court may give the final instructions before or after the final arguments by the lawyers, depending on the custom in the jurisdiction and the preferences of the court. Most lawyers prefer to have instructions fixed before the final arguments are presented but to have the court present the instructions to the jury after the final arguments are completed.

Repeat preliminary instructions

Request the court to repeat the preliminary instructions on evidence, consideration of the evidence, direct and circumstantial evidence, and burden of proof in the same form given at the outset of the trial. See Section 1.8.1.

The instructions on objections and testimony aids will need to be modified slightly to put them in a form appropriate to the end of the trial. They should, however, be repeated in nearly similar terms so as not to confuse the jurors.

Summarize limiting instructions

Most pattern jury instructions have a summary instruction reminding the jury that some exhibits were admitted for limited purposes.

Example

You will recall that during the course of this trial I instructed you that certain testimony and certain exhibits were admitted in evidence for a limited purpose and I instructed you that you may consider some documents as evidence against one party but not against another. You may consider such evidence only for the specific limited purposes for which it was admitted.[32]

This general instruction assumes, of course, that the jurors have kept perfectly in mind each limiting instruction. In fact, jurors forget most limiting instructions shortly after they are given.

If you sought and obtained limiting instructions on important exhibits, you should propose final instructions referring to those specific exhibits to remind the jury about the limitations imposed by the court. You can extract from the record each limiting instruction and propose that the court read it again. If the list is long, consider grouping exhibits together that have similar limitations.

Instructions on exhibits during deliberations

If you have excellent exhibits that you want the jury to consider carefully, you will want instructions reminding them that all the exhibits can be taken to the jury room or can be called for by the jury when they need the exhibits.

Example

When you retire to the jury room to deliberate on your verdict, you may take a copy of these instructions with you as well as exhibits which the Court has admitted in evidence.[33]

Example

There are three types of information you may ask for while discussing this case:

(1) to have repeated what a witness said during trial;

(2) to have brought to you any exhibit admitted in evidence;

(3) to have further explanation of the meaning of one of these legal instructions.

If you need any of this information, you should give a note to the officer outside your door describing what you want. The information you ask for will be given to you.[34]

You will want to use the final instructions in your closing argument to explain to the jury how they can decide in your client's favor. This exercise involves much more than the instructions with respect to exhibits but, if exhibits are an important part of your case, you will want to be sure the instructions are adequate in this regard.

ENDNOTES

1. *John W. Strong*, et al., 2 *McCormick on Evidence* § 212, at 9 (4th ed. 1992) (hereinafter *McCormick on Evidence*).

2. *McCormick on Evidence* § 337; 1 Jack B. Weinstein and Margaret A. Berger, *Weinstein's Evidence* §§ 300[01] and 301[02] (1996) (hereinafter *Weinstein's Evidence*).

3. *Steven Lubet, Modern Trial Advocacy* 196-200 (1993).

4. *McCormick on Evidence* § 337, at 430.

5. *See infra* § 2.3; *see also Weinstein's Evidence* § 1006[07].

6. The discussion in this section is not intended as an exhaustive evidence treatise on potential objections. *See generally Anthony J. Bocchino and David A. Sonenshein, A Practical Guide to Federal Evidence* (NITA Rev. 3d ed. 1996) and Appendix C of this volume for more specialized source materials. There are, in addition, objections under Rule 611(a)(1) as to testimony in the form of a free narrative rather than in answer to specific questions; objections under Rule 611(a)(3) to questions that constitute harassment of the witness or lead to undue embarrassment; objections under Rule 611(b) to questions on cross-examination that go beyond the scope of the direct examination; objections under Rule 611(c) to leading questions on direct examination; and objections under Rule 701 to opinion testimony from nonexpert witnesses.

7. *McCormick on Evidence* § 212, at 4.

8. *Michael H. Graham, Handbook on Federal Evidence* § 401.6 (3d ed. 1991).

9. *Model Rules of Professional Conduct*, Rule 1.1 (1995).

10. *A.B.A. Committee on Professional Ethics and Grievances*, Formal Op. 379 (1993).

11. *See McCormick on Evidence* § 328, at 385-87; *Weinstein's Evidence* § 200[02].

12. *See generally McCormick on Evidence* §§ 328-35.

13. *See generally Steven Lubet, Modern Trial Advocacy*, ch. 11 (1993); *James W. Jeans, Trial Advocacy*, ch. 7 (1975).

14. Ninth Circuit Jury Committee, *Manual of Modern Civil Jury Instructions for the Ninth Circuit*, No. 1.01 (modified) (hereinafter *Ninth Circuit Jury Instructions*).

15. *Pattern Jury Instructions, Civil Cases*, Fifth Circuit, No. 2.18 (modified) (hereinafter Fifth Circuit Jury Instructions).

16. *Amiram Elwork*, et al., *Making Jury Instructions Understandable*, Appendix B-1, No. 16 (1982) (hereinafter *Elwork*).

17. *Ninth Circuit Jury Instructions*, No. 1.04.

18. *Manual of Modern Civil Jury Instructions for the Eighth Circuit*, No. 1.02 (1994) (hereinafter *Eighth Circuit Jury Instructions*).

19. *Ninth Circuit Jury Instructions*, No. 1.05.

20. *Elwork*, Appendix B-1, No. 15 (modified).

21. *Eighth Circuit Jury Instructions*, No. 1.02 (part).

22. *Ninth Circuit Jury Instructions*, No. 1.06.

23. *See Edward J. Devitt & Charles B. Blackmar*, 1 *Federal Jury Practice & Instructions* § 5.08 (Aspen 1970).

24. *Fifth Circuit Jury Instructions*, No. 2.8 (modified).
25. *Id.*
26. *Id.*, No. 2.20 (part).
27. *Id.*, No. 2.7.
28. *Eighth Circuit Jury Instructions*, No. 1.03.
29. *Id.*, No. 2.08B.
30. *Fifth Circuit Jury Instructions*, No. 2.23.
31. *Ninth Circuit Jury Instructions*, No. 2.23.
32. *Fifth Circuit Jury Instructions*, No. 3.1 (part).
33. *Id.* (modified in part).
34. *Elwork*, Appendix B-1, No. 10 (modified).

CHAPTER 2

TEXT DOCUMENTS

Text documents are the normal paper records of everyday business, government, and personal life. Just to list the principal items included in this category is to demonstrate the enormous variety of documents with which the evidence rules must deal. These exhibits are: accounts, agreements, analyses, announcements, articles, bids, bills, bulletins, cards, catalogs, certificates, charges, charters, checks, compacts, contracts, credentials, daybooks, declarations, deeds, degrees, diaries, diplomas, directives, directories, dispatches, endorsements, evaluations, forms, indices, inventories, invoices, journals, leases, ledgers, legislation, letters, licenses, lists, logs, manuals, manuscripts, memoirs, memoranda, messages, notes, notices, orders, papers, passports, permits, placards, plans, proclamations, proposals, receipts, records, references, registers, releases, reports, requisitions, resolution·, reviews, rolls, rosters, schedules, scripts, settlements, signs, statements, studies, surveys, tabulations, tallies, testimonials, visas, vouchers, warrants, and other paper records consisting primarily of text information.

It is important to separate the requirements for qualifying text documents, which are normal business, government, and personal records, from other kinds of documentary materials. Charts, graphs, time lines, tables, and computer data printouts are covered in Chapter 3. Maps, diagrams, drawings, and sketches are covered in Chapter 4.

Text document exhibits are subject to the largest number of specialized evidentiary rules. These rules are simply an elaboration of the general foundation requirements that apply to all exhibits, but they are often confusing because of the ways they are applied to specific types of documents. In order to provide an easy path through the rules, the material on text documents has been divided into six categories. The basic foundation and hearsay rules that apply to all text document exhibits are set out in Section 2.1 on original documents. Section 2.2 covers copies of documents and describes the additional requirements of the "original document" rules. Section 2.3 deals with fax, e-mail, and other digital text documents. Section 2.4 explains how to use books, newspapers, and other published and multi-original documents. Section 2.5 covers summaries of documents and the special procedural requirements for qualifying these as evidence. Section 2.6 covers deposition and other transcripts which occasionally are put in evidence to present the testimony of an absent witness or for impeachment purposes.

2.1 ORIGINAL DOCUMENTS

All text document exhibits face three important sets of evidentiary requirements. First, the normal requirements of foundation—competence, relevance, identification, and trustworthiness—must be established. The use of a computer word processor to create a text document does not add any foundation requirements in cases where a hard copy (or paper copy) of the document was created and used prior to litigation. There are additional rules that apply, however, to a fax or e-mail document, a book or other published work, a summary, or a transcript. See Sections 2.3 through 2.6. Second, the hearsay requirements must be met by establishing that the document is not hearsay or that the document fits into one of the hearsay exceptions. Third, the constraints of the original document rule need to be considered. If you have the original or a duplicate of the document, this is the extent of what is required to satisfy the original document rules. If you want to offer in evidence a copy of a document that has marks on it not found on the original or differs in some other way from the original, the original document rules impose additional hurdles. See Section 2.2.

In addition, exhibits that are text documents may face a policy objection if the contents are inflammatory, grisly, obscene or otherwise unfairly prejudicial, or if the document is lengthy and only tangentially related to controlling issues and its consideration might cause undue delay and waste of time. When you use only a part of a text document, your opponent may raise a "completeness" objection and require additional material to be added to the exhibit.

2.1.1 Foundation

The foundation for a text document offered as an exhibit is the same as for other types of tangible evidence. First, a witness who is competent to testify about the document because he or she has some first hand knowledge about the document identifies it and establishes that it is relevant to an issue in the case; and second, an appropriate showing is provided that the document is what it purports to be and is sufficiently trustworthy to be considered by the fact-finder. See more detailed discussion in Section 1.1.

Competence, relevance, and identification

The basics of competence, relevance, and identification can be provided readily for most text documents.

Example

Q. Mr. Edwards, what do you do for a living?

A. I am the supervisor of the pricing unit in the manufacturing department.

Q. How long have you been in that position?

A. Four years.

Q. Does your work involve the pricing of the Assembot II that is at issue in this case?

A. Yes.

Q. Please look at what has been marked as defendant's Exhibit 11. Do you recognize it?

A. Yes, I do.

Q. What is it?

A. The price list for a robot product called Assembot II.

Q. How can you recognize it?

A. I prepared it.

This witness is competent under Rule 602 to testify about the price list because the company has entrusted him with responsibility for pricing and he has performed this responsibility, presumably adequately, for four years. The price list is relevant under Rule 401 because this is a contract dispute about price. The identification is adequate because the witness has put the document in a category (price list) and tied it to a specific item in that category (price lists for the Assembot II) so that it cannot be mistaken for anything else. This example is an instance in which no trustworthiness issue is involved. Under Rule 901(b)(1), the witness has adequate means for recognizing the list as he prepared it.

Trustworthiness: General issues as to documents

Trustworthiness issues may be raised by the means that the witness has for identifying the document. A witness who received a document may, in fact, have no basis for identifying it as coming from the person who purportedly sent it unless there has been a course of dealing in the past. A person who retrieved a document from the office files may have no basis for testifying that it is kept in the ordinary course of business if his secretarial responsibilities are limited to another area of the company altogether.

The condition of the document may also raise trustworthiness issues. If it is ripped at the bottom or if the page is shorter than standard paper sizes, for example, the condition may create a doubt that the proposed exhibit is the entire document. Some portion of the text may have been deleted thus changing the meaning of the document. If it appears that there may be a page missing, erasures made, correction fluid used, or parts of different documents taped or stapled together in a manner different from the original, the court may require extrinsic evidence of trustworthiness.

A late-appearing document that may have been generated for litigation purposes or a document located in a place where it was unlikely to have been kept for proper purposes may generate a requirement for additional foundation to confirm trustworthiness.

The proponent of the exhibit has the burden to satisfy the court that all aspects of foundation are present before the exhibit will be admitted. Because trustworthiness is a part of foundation, no objection is necessary. If the court is not satisfied with the foundation, when the proponent moves admission in evidence, the court may deny the motion. Good practice requires that the opponent rise with challenges to foundation, however, as these may be necessary to draw the court's attention to deficiencies.

Trustworthiness: Authentication of signatures and handwriting

If a document is signed, and the signature is important to establish responsibility for an action, then the authentication of the signature usually will be an essential element of the foundation for the document.

Consider first whether the document falls in the category of self-authenticating documents under Rule 902. Two kinds of signatures are self-authenticating. Rule 902(8) provides that the signatures on acknowledged documents (signed before a notary) need no further proof, and Rule 902(9) provides that commercial paper and related documents are self-authenticating, and "extrinsic evidence of authenticity as a condition precedent to admissibility is not required."

Example

Q. Ms. Andrews, what happened next?

A. I sent out a copy of our standard form certifying completion.

Q. What was the response to that?

A. I got the form back signed and dated as we require.

Q. May I approach the witness?

Court: You may.

Q. I am handing you what has been marked as Exhibit 46 and ask if you can identify that.

A. That is the signed form that I received.

Counsel: Your Honor, at this time plaintiff offers in evidence Exhibit 46.

Opposing Counsel: Objection; foundation.

Counsel: This is the certification of completion. It is an acknowledged document. The signature has been attested to by a notary public and that attestation is a part of the document itself. It is self-authenticating under Rule 902(8).

Court: Exhibit 46 is admitted.

Note that Rule 902(8) on acknowledged documents and Rule 902(9) on commercial paper make reference to other provisions of law. In the case of Rule 902(8), you must ensure: (1) that the document was executed in the manner provided by law; and (2) that the notary was authorized by law to take acknowledgments. The first requirement generally means that the person who signed the document did so personally before the notary. The notary's attestation will usually state this fact. The second requirement usually means that the notary's license had not expired when the acknowledgment was taken. In the case of Rule 902(9), you need to make sure that "general commercial law" provides a presumption of authenticity for signatures. This usually is a reference to the Uniform Commercial Code as adopted in the state where the transaction took place or where the litigation is pending.

Under Rule 201, the judge should take judicial notice of facts such as the execution of the acknowledgment "in the manner provided by law" if, in fact, it is correct. No extrinsic proof is required. The execution of the acknowledgment is an "adjudicative fact" under Rule 201, and it is one "not subject to reasonable dispute." Either the acknowledgment was taken correctly or not, which the judge can determine by reference to the requirement of the law and by inspecting the document. If necessary, the judge can rely on a presumption that "official actions by public officers . . . have been regularly and legally performed."[1] Similarly, the judge should take judicial notice that an exhibit is "commercial paper" or a document "relating to" commercial paper because those facts are readily ascertainable by reference to "general commercial law" and by inspecting the exhibit.

Consider next whether your opponent is likely to dispute the authenticity of the document. If it was produced on their letterhead, for example, it is unlikely that there will be any serious question about the genuineness of the signature. Interrogatories and requests for admissions are inexpensive ways to secure the necessary authentication for signed documents in cases where no dispute is likely.

Example

Q. Ms. Andrews, what did you do next?

A. I called the XYZ Company to get a quote on the price for the gear part.

Q. Your Honor, plaintiff offers in evidence Exhibit 12, a letter from Ms. Pepper of the XYZ Company to Ms. Andrews. This exhibit has been marked in pretrial proceedings and the admissibility of this exhibit has been conceded in the response to plaintiff's interrogatory 22. Let the record reflect that I am showing Exhibit 12 to counsel for defendant.

Court: Exhibit 12 is admitted. You may proceed.

Q. May I approach the witness?

Court: You may.

Q. Ms. Andrews, I am handing you Exhibit 12. When did you receive this?

A. I received it two days after I made the call.

When the admissibility of a document has been established through discovery, it is better not to go through the qualification again with the witness. This wastes time and also introduces a risk that the court may perceive some hypothetical problem with the document. You should, however, state the basis for admissibility of the document and get a ruling at the time it is used to avoid later possible problems with the record. Many courts will admit these kinds of documents in pretrial proceedings, so nothing by way of foundation is required at trial.

If authentication by the testimony of witnesses is required, you should get this testimony in depositions. Then, if the witness is unavailable, you will not lose the exhibit as well. A signature can be authenticated in four ways: (1) by the person who signed the document; (2) by someone who watched the person sign the document (regardless of whether he or she also signed as a witness); (3) by someone who did not see the person sign the document but can recognize his or her signature; or (4) by a handwriting expert.

Example

Q. Mr. Wells, I show you what has been marked as plaintiff's Exhibit 4 and ask if you have seen it before.

A. Yes.

Q. When was the first time you saw it?

A. On the day I met with Ms. Allen of the XYZ Company at my office at 1666 K Street, N.W., Washington, D.C.

Q. Whose signature appears at the bottom of that document?

A. This is my signature.

Q. Is the document in the same condition now as it was when you signed it?

A. Yes.

Often the person who signed the document will be the opposing party. One alternative is to depose the person who signed or call that person as a hostile witness at trial to authenticate the signature, but that may entail other risks that are unacceptable. Another alternative is to use a witness who saw the opposing party sign.

Example

Q. Ms. Walters, I show you what has been marked as plaintiff's Exhibit 4 and ask if you have seen it before.

A. Yes.

Q. When was the first time you saw it?

A. On the day I met with Mr. Wells at my office.

Q. Who prepared plaintiff's Exhibit 4?

A. I did.

Q. After preparing it, what did you do with it?

A. I gave it to Mr. Wells to sign.

Q. What did Mr. Wells do with it?

A. Mr. Wells signed it.

Q. Where were you when he signed it?

A. He was sitting right across from me in my office.

Q. After Mr. Wells signed the document, what did you do with it?

A. I gave him a copy and put the original in my files.

Q. Is plaintiff's Exhibit 4 in the same condition now as when Mr. Wells signed it?

A. Yes.

Rule 901(b)(2) makes specific provision for authentication and identification of handwriting by "nonexpert opinion as to the genuineness of handwriting, based upon familiarity not acquired for purposes of the litigation."

Example

Q. Mr. Smith, I show you what has been marked as plaintiff's Exhibit 4 and ask you to examine the signature that appears at the bottom.

A. Yes, I have looked at it.

Q. Mr. Smith, do you recognize that signature?

A. Yes.

Q. How are you able to recognize the signature?

A. I have seen this signature many times before on correspondence that I have received and on contracts that I have been involved in.

Q. Have you ever seen Mr. Wells actually sign his signature?

A. Yes, several times.

Q. Whose signature is at the bottom of plaintiff's Exhibit 4?

A. It is Mr. Wells' signature.

Qualifying a signature under Rule 901(b)(2) may be reasonable if the witness is involved in a transaction with Mr. Wells such that he has mailed documents back and forth a number of times and the document in question is one of those. If the witness routinely sends documents to Mr. Wells, they routinely come back countersigned, and the witness can recognize the signature as that of Mr. Wells, then it is likely the circumstances will give sufficient support to this method of authentication so that it will survive a challenge on voir dire. If there is a legitimate question about the signature, however, the opposing lawyer may come up with several sample signatures and ask the witness to pick out which one is Mr. Wells'. The lay witness may be unable to do so and his or her credibility will be sufficiently damaged that the foundation for the document will crumble.

Rule 901(b)(3) provides for authentication and identification of handwriting through "comparison . . . by expert witnesses with specimens which have been authenticated." There are handwriting experts available in most large metropolitan areas.[2]

Example

Q. Mr. Sanders, please describe your education.

A. I have a Bachelor of Science in Physics from the University of California at Berkeley; and I have a Master's Degree in Art in which my major field was authentication of art works.

Q. What is your occupation?

A. I am self-employed. My firm, Sanders Analysis Inc., has 5 employees. It is located at 17236 Main Street, in Berkeley, California. We have been in business, and I have been the owner of the business, for 20 years.

Q. Mr. Sanders, would you describe your experience in handwriting analysis?

A. I started out in the handwriting analysis section of the Federal Bureau of Investigation. I became chief of the handwriting analysis section and then I was hired by the CIA as the head of their handwriting analysis section. I remained in that position for three years, and then I opened my own firm.

Q. Approximately how many handwriting analyses have you performed personally?

A. At least 20,000 during the course of my career, and I have supervised people who have done hundreds of thousands of analyses during this time.

Q. Do you have a sample of the handwriting of Mr. Wells?

A. Yes, I obtained a copy of his signature from you.

Q. What was that sample?

A. I went to the clerk's office and examined the original of the answer to the complaint which contains a signature identified as that of Mr. Wells. In addition you gave me copies of that answer and several other documents purporting to be signed by Mr. Wells.

Q. Have you compared the signature of Mr. Wells on the answer to the complaint to the signature that appears at the bottom of what has been marked as plaintiff's Exhibit 4?

A. Yes, I have.

Q. Do you have an opinion as to whose signature appears at the bottom of plaintiff's Exhibit 4?

A. Yes, I have.

Q. What is that opinion?

A. It is my opinion that the signature on the bottom of plaintiff's Exhibit 4 was made by the same person who made the signature on the answer to the complaint. If Mr. Wells signed the answer, then Mr. Wells also signed Exhibit 4.

There may be several links to be connected in order to verify the exemplar before the expert can testify. The expert probably has no way of knowing whether the signature on the sample is that of Mr. Wells, so that has to be established independently. A signature on a pleading has been vouched for by filing it with the court, and it comes in without further testimony.

Rule 901(b)(3) also permits authentication and identification of handwriting by submitting both specimens that have been authenticated and the signature at issue and having the fact-finder make the comparison. This is a very risky procedure and is not recommended.

Trustworthiness: Authentication of public records

Experienced lawyers rarely dispute the authenticity of a public record because to do so unsuccessfully will raise the wrath of judges who are pressed for time. However, it may happen, and it is necessary to follow the rules carefully in these regards. The rules establish two categories of public records: those that are self-authenticating and therefore require no testimony about trustworthiness; and those that must be authenticated by the testimony of a witness.

A certified public record is self-authenticating under Rule 902(1-4). The most common is a copy rather than the original, accompanied by an appropriate certification. If you are using a copy of a public record, you will need the following: (1) a citation to a law that authorizes this document to be recorded or filed; and (2) a certification signed by a custodian or other authorized person that the document is in fact recorded or filed in the public office and that the copy is correct. The certification must bear a seal or be accompanied by a separate certification that bears a seal. The seal must either be of the agency or person who has the document or, if that person has no seal, then of a public officer in the political subdivision where the custodian is located attesting that the signer is the custodian and that the signature is genuine. Once you have the copy of the public record and the necessary certifications, the foundation is complete so long as the document is relevant.

Even if you lay a foundation properly under Rule 902(4), the exhibit will be subject to challenge under the hearsay rules. In this case, Rules 803(8) and (9) provide the necessary exception to the hearsay rule. The exception to the hearsay rule may be narrower than the self-authentication which provides the foundation. Rule 803(9) allows all reports of vital statistics, and Rule 803(8) allows all reports of the activities of an office or agency or matters observed pursuant to duty imposed by law or factual findings resulting from an investigation made pursuant to authority granted by law. If the substance of the public record does not fall within these categories, it will not be exempt from the hearsay rule. Rule 803(8) also excludes from the exception law enforcement reports used in criminal proceedings. Consequently, the hearsay rule applies to these reports even though they are public records.

Foreign public documents require two certifications to be self-authenticating. First, the document must be certified as correct by the person authorized by the laws of the foreign country to make such a certification. Second, the document must have a "final certification" by a United States diplomat in the country. The diplomat must attest to the genuineness of the signature and the official position of the foreign official who signed the initial certification. The diplomat must also attest to the genuineness of the signature and the official position of any subsequent signatures by foreign officials if some chain of certifications is required as to a particular document. Rule 902(3) provides some leeway in regard to the final certification. "If reasonable opportunity has been given to all parties to investigate the authenticity and accuracy of official documents, the court may, for good cause shown, order that they be treated as presumptively authentic without final certification or permit them to be evidenced by an attested summary with or without final certification." As the requirements for authenticating foreign documents are stringent, it is important to attend to this detail early in the litigation process in order to have the necessary certifications in time for trial. Foreign public records are also covered by the hearsay exception under Rule 803(8) for public records. As with domestic public records, the foundation requirements under Rule 902(3) and the hearsay exception under Rule 803(8) are different and each must be satisfied to make the document admissible.

Documents that are self-authenticating are not immune from challenge. The provisions of the rules for self-authentication sweep away the need for witness testimony about authentication prior to admission in evidence. After the document is admitted, however, an opponent is still free to challenge its genuineness, and the ultimate question of whether it is genuine or not is one for the jury.

If a public record is not self-authenticating, then a two-step procedure is used to satisfy the requirements of Rule 901(b)(7). First, the proponent must provide a citation to a law that authorizes the document to be recorded or filed in a public office. Under Rule 201 this aspect of the foundation is an "adjudicative fact" and is "not subject to reasonable dispute." By reference to applicable law and by inspection of the exhibit, the court can readily determine if it qualifies. No external proof is required that the office is indeed a "public office" or that the law does actually "authorize" the recording or filing of this kind of document. There is no need to request judicial notice of these facts unless there is a challenge from your opponent on these grounds.

Second, the witness must testify that the public record is in fact recorded or filed in the public office where it is authorized by law to be recorded or filed, and that the document "is from the public office where items of this nature are kept." There is no requirement that the testimony providing the foundation for a public record come from the custodian of the record. The testimony as to the facts necessary to establish that the document came from an official repository can come from any competent witness with knowledge.

When necessary, the proponent of the exhibit can rely on the presumption that "official action by public officers . . . have been regularly and legally performed."[3] The presumption shifts the burden of producing evidence so that the opponent of the exhibit must now come forward and show that the officer's conduct was, in fact, not in all ways regular and legal. Otherwise, the objection will be overruled.

With leave of court, you can also provide the necessary foundation for a public record by affidavit. Rule 104 provides that: "Preliminary questions concerning . . . the admissibility of evidence shall be determined by the court . . . . In making its determination, it is not bound by the rules of evidence except those with respect to privileges." The proponent of the public record may obtain an affidavit from a qualified official to the facts outlined above. The affidavit will substitute for witness testimony in the determination as to the admissibility of the document.

In addition, under Rule 901(b)(10), you may also authenticate public records by any method provided by federal statute or rule prescribed by the Supreme Court.

2.1.2 Hearsay Objections

Every text document is subject to a potential hearsay objection. The definition of hearsay under Rule 801(c) is "a statement, other than one made by the declarant while testifying at the trial or hearing, offered in evidence to prove the truth of the matter asserted." Rule 801(a) extends the coverage of the hearsay rule to all written as well as oral statements. You have two choices in meeting the hearsay requirements: either the document is not hearsay under Rule 801 or it qualifies for one of the exceptions under Rules 803 and 804. See general discussion in Section 1.3.1. Your checklist with respect to each text document exhibit should show how you intend to meet the hearsay requirement. See sample checklist in Appendix D. Each of these categories is discussed below.

The "not hearsay" documents

In making decisions about using text documents as exhibits and about how to deal with potential hearsay objections, look first to the three broad categories of documents that have been declared not to be hearsay at all: admissions of a party opponent, statements of a current testifying witness, and documents not offered to prove the truth of their contents. A particular document may qualify under more than one of the exemptions to the hearsay rule. These three categories of "not hearsay" documents should be considered first, as this is the easiest route through the hearsay maze. You may find it useful, in these cases, to make a note in the margin of your trial materials that this exhibit is *not* hearsay and the portion of Rule 801 on which you are relying.

Admissions of a party opponent

Under Rule 801(d)(2) admissions of a party opponent are not hearsay. Many of the documents you have discovered from your opponent should be analyzed first under this readily available standard for qualifying text documents. Although the rule speaks of admissions, it is really directed at all statements (written or oral) because it applies regardless of the circumstances in which the statement was made.

When the statement is made by the party opponent directly, then the qualification of the document is simple:

Example

Q. Ms. Owens, how did you first become informed about the Assembot II robot?

A. I attended a convention and picked up literature at a booth set up by the XYZ Corporation.

Q. I am handing you what has been marked as plaintiff's Exhibit 44 and ask if you can identify that.

A. Yes, that is one of the brochures I picked up at the XYZ Corporation booth at the convention.

Q. We offer plaintiff's Exhibit 44 in evidence.

Opposing Counsel: Objection; hearsay.

Counsel: This is a statement of a party opponent.

Court: Admitted. You may proceed.

Q. What, if anything, does Exhibit 44 say about the availability of the Assembot II robot?

A. It says that the Assembot II was fully tested and that production models were currently available.

If the party opponent is a corporation, and the statement is made by an individual on behalf of the corporation, such as in a letter or internal memorandum, a question may arise as to whether the employee is of sufficient rank within the corporation to bind the corporation as to the particular statement made. Any statement of a director, officer, management employee, or supervisor employed by a party opponent is admissible. The statements of lower level employees made about subjects that are within their specific responsibilities also usually qualify.

The rule has a broad sweep including statements by representatives of party opponents. The rule covers:

- statements by third persons that are adopted by a party opponent;
- statements by third persons that are authorized by a party opponent;
- statements by third persons who are agents (and acting within the scope of the agency) of a party opponent; and
- statements by third persons who are co-conspirators with a party opponent.

There is a corollary provision in Rule 32(a)(2) of the Federal Rules of Civil Procedure.

In making the connection to a party, you must fulfill one of the five options offered under Rule 801(d)(2). If you can connect a document to a party opponent, then the document is not hearsay and you do not need to qualify it under any exception. The methods for making the necessary connection to a party (in general order of preference) are:

- stipulation between the parties;
- discovery (interrogatory, deposition, or request for admission);
- witness testimony authenticating the signature on the document as that of a party or officer, director, or responsible agent;
- circumstantial evidence connecting the document to the opposing party.

As a first step, ask for a stipulation from your opponent that all documents on their business letterhead or that were written by one of their employees, if offered against them, are covered by Rule 801(d)(2) as statements of a party opponent. If they refuse the stipulation, you may be able to persuade a judge to extend the number of interrogatories or requests for admission available to you because your opponent refused a reasonable stipulation. Some courts will permit you to use a single question to determine the status of all of the documents of a party opponent that you want to use as exhibits, together with an attachment that lists the specific documents as to which the discovery is requested. Some judges, however, will require you to ask a separate question for each of the five subsections of Rule 801(d)(2) thus using up five of your allotted number of inquiries.

The use of witness testimony to authenticate signatures is more risky and should be used only if the stipulation and discovery routes have failed. See the discussion of signatures under Section 2.1.1.

The use of circumstantial evidence to tie a document to the opposing side is recognized in a number of common situations such as:

- reply letter (prior letter mailed to the adverse party and a reply letter subsequently received in the mail from the adverse party);
- distinct contents (material or facts known only to adverse party);
- linguistic patterns (characteristic of the adverse party).

There may also be other ways unique to the fact situation of your case to tie a document to the other side.

Example

Q. From whom did you receive information about the status of the Assembot II robot produced by the Fifer Company?

A. From Mr. Daniels.

Q. Who is Mr. Daniels?

A. Mr. Daniels is an independent sales agent who represents the Fifer Company in California.

Q. May I have this document marked as plaintiff's Exhibit 43?

Reporter: *(Marks)*

Q. Let the record reflect that I have handed the document marked as plaintiff's Exhibit 43 to counsel for defendant.

Opposing Counsel: *(Looks)*

Q. Do you recognize the document marked as plaintiff's Exhibit 43?

A. Yes.

Q. What is it?

A. It is a letter from Mr. Daniels to me.

Q. Do you recognize the signature on Exhibit 43?

A. Yes.

Q. How are you able to recognize it?

A. I've seen it many times on letters sent to us.

Q. Whose signature is it?

A. Mr. Daniels.

Q. Your Honor, we move the admission in evidence of the letter that has been marked as Exhibit 43.

Opposing Counsel: Objection; hearsay.

Counsel: It qualifies under Rule 801(d)(2)(D) as a statement by a party through an authorized agent. Fifer Company has conceded that Mr. Daniels was their agent in the response to Interrogatory #23.

Court: Objection overruled. Exhibit 43 is admitted.

Q. What information about the Assembot II robot did you receive from Mr. Daniels in this letter that he wrote to you?

A. I received information that the Assembot II was available to be installed in our plant in California within 30 days after an order was received and that it was fully tested and ready to go.

One additional concern with respect to the statements of party opponents is the admissibility problem that may arise in multiparty cases because of the requirement that the statement be offered against the party making it. This problem can be overcome through Rule 105 which provides: "When evidence which is admissible as to one party . . . but not admissible as to another party . . . is admitted, the court, upon request, shall restrict the evidence to its proper scope and instruct the jury accordingly." See discussion of jury instructions with respect to exhibits in Section 1.8.

Statements of currently testifying witnesses

Under Rule 801(d)(1) the prior statements of a witness now testifying at trial are not hearsay. Once a witness takes the stand, and is subject to cross-examination, anything he or she has previously written, testified to, told to another person, or said on videotape or audiotape is fair game if it falls into one of three limited categories. First, the statement is admissible if it is inconsistent with the current testimony and was given under oath in a prior proceeding or deposition. The most common application of this provision is to permit counsel to use prior deposition testimony on cross-examination. See Section 2.6. Second, the statement is admissible if it is consistent with the current testimony and is offered to rebut cross-examination suggesting that the witness has not been truthful in the current testimony or is subject to an "improper influence or motive." By its terms, this provision can be used only for redirect examination after cross-examination or in a rebuttal presentation. Third, the statement is admissible if it consists of an identification of a person after the witness saw that person.

If the currently testifying witness asserts a privilege, lacks recollection, or refuses to testify about a subject despite an order of the court to do so, then former testimony of this witness may be used under Rule 804(b)(1) as to the subject under examination when the assertion of privilege, lack of recollection, or refusal occurred. The limitations of Rule 801 do not apply, but Rule 804 has limitations of its own. Former testimony may be used only from proceedings in which the party against whom the former testimony is offered "had an opportunity and similar motive to develop the testimony by direct, cross, or redirect examination." Technically, Rule 804(b)(1) is an exception to the hearsay rule, but the effect is the same.

Examples of the use of a prior statement of a witness are provided in Section 2.6 on deposition testimony.

Statements not offered to prove the truth of their contents

Rule 801(c) defines hearsay as any statement "offered in evidence to prove the truth of the matter asserted." Under this definition, out-of-court statements not offered to prove the truth of their content (but just to prove the fact that they were made) are *not* hearsay.

One common application of this portion of the "not hearsay" provisions of the rules, especially when dealing with business records, is the "verbal acts" doctrine. Roughly phrased, this doctrine provides that if the document is one of the things at issue in the case, it is admitted as an "act" because the existence or effect of the document is at issue, not the truth of its content. The usual examples are contracts, notices, or price lists. When the lawsuit is about the terms of a contract, the contract document itself should be admitted, even though it is an out-of-court statement, because the issue is not the truth of what the contract says but its existence or effect. Under the definition of hearsay in Rule 801(c), this is not a document offered to prove the truth of the matter asserted in it, therefore it is not hearsay at all.[4]

Another set of documents that may fall readily under this category are those offered to show the effect on the reader or recipient rather than the truth of their contents. These effects include knowledge, notice, motive, and other state of mind effects. The value of the contents of documents offered for these purposes does not depend on the truth of the contents but rather on the fact of the contents. The fact of the contents is readily ascertainable from an examination of the document itself. Therefore it is fair to allow the exhibit to be considered by the jury in their deliberations about whether the effect on the recipient was as alleged.

Even if the document fits into one of the three "not hearsay" categories, you must establish the foundation including competence, relevance, identification, and trustworthiness (where applicable) as discussed in Section 2.1.1. In addition, although it passed muster under the hearsay rule, the document may be objectionable on original document grounds (see Section 2.2.5) or on policy grounds (see Section 1.3.3).

The hearsay exceptions

If the text document to be used as an exhibit cannot qualify as "not hearsay", then you must find an exception that fits. The most useful exceptions are those for business records, medical records, recorded recollections, statements against interest, public records, and former testimony. The different methods for approaching the hearsay problem for each of these categories are discussed below. There are also many other limited special purpose exceptions described in Rules 803 and 804. If all else fails, Rules 803(24) and 804(5) contain a general purpose exception which gives the court discretion to admit anything that is sufficiently necessary, probative, and trustworthy.

Business records

The business records exception is generally used to qualify your client's documents and the documents of third parties that are offered to prove the truth of their contents. Your opponent's business records are covered by the "not hearsay" provision of Rule 801(d)(2), and you will want to use that provision rather than the business records exception because it is easier to satisfy. Government business records are covered by a separate exception for public records discussed below.

Rule 803(6), which covers business records, is one of the most important exceptions to the hearsay rule because the definitions of "business" and "records" are very broad. Rule 803(6) specifies each element of the foundation for documents that are business records. The foundation questions are drawn directly from the rule:

Example

(After establishing relevance)

Q. Ms. Waters, please describe your job.

A. I am the administrative assistant to the General Manager of XYZ Corporation.

Q. What duties do you have with respect to the records kept by XYZ Corporation?

A. I collect, index, file, and maintain all the company's permanent records.

Q. Ms. Waters, I am handing you what has been marked as plaintiff's Exhibit 47 and ask if you recognize it.

A. Yes, that is one of our company's records. It is a production report for the month of April.

Q. Your Honor, we offer plaintiff's Exhibit 47 in evidence.

Opposing Counsel: Objection; hearsay.

Q. Ms. Waters, is Exhibit 47 a record made by a person with knowledge of, or made from information transmitted by a person with knowledge of, the acts or events appearing on it?

A. Yes.

Q. Was that record made at or near the time of the acts or events appearing on it?

A. Yes.

Q. Is it the regular practice of XYZ Corporation to make such a record?

A. Yes.

Q. Once that record was made, was that record kept in the course of a regularly conducted business activity of XYZ Corporation?

A. Yes.

Q. Your Honor, we move the admission in evidence of Exhibit 47. It qualifies as a business record of the XYZ Corporation.

Nothing further is required to qualify the exhibit under the hearsay rule.

You may use leading questions to establish this exception. Rule 611(c) provides that, although leading questions generally are not permitted on direct examination, they may be used "as may be necessary to develop the witness's testimony." This applies when the rules require that facts be elicited in a particular framework to meet an objection.

Your opponent may ask for voir dire of the witness for purposes of attacking the basis for claiming the exception, as to how the witness knows that the record was made by a person with knowledge of the acts and events appearing on it. See Section 1.7.2. For this reason you may want to have available a records custodian who is reasonably knowledgeable. The witness need not have been employed by the company during all of the time period when the records at issue were kept, although obviously someone who was there provides a stronger foundation. Someone who was not there will have to testify that, based on later-acquired knowledge, he or she knows it was the practice of the company to make such records. Your opponent may also ask for voir dire of the witness regarding the method or circumstances of preparation of the record because the rule provides for exclusion if "the source of information or the method of circumstances of preparation indicate a lack of trustworthiness." Therefore, you may want to include a few additional questions on direct examination to negate possible attacks on trustworthiness in this respect.

Medical records

Rule 803(4) provides a broad exemption for medical records that is comparable to the exemption for business records. The exception covers: "Statements made for purposes of medical diagnosis or treatment and describing medical history, or past or present symptoms, pain, or sensations, or the inception or general character of the cause or external source thereof insofar as reasonably pertinent to diagnosis or treatment."

Under Rule 803(4), the statements made by the patient to the doctor, and noted in the doctor's records, are taken out from under the hearsay rule so long as they are made for the purpose of diagnosis or treatment and reasonably pertinent to the doctor's diagnosis or treatment. Similarly, statements by a doctor, noted in the records of a hospital or of another doctor, are also covered by the exception. Using this rule, one doctor who treated the patient can testify as to all the statements he or she considered or relied on in treating the patient.

Recorded recollections

If your client is not a business or has records to which the business records or medical records exceptions do not apply, you will need to find another haven for these exhibits. Occasionally the exception for recorded recollection under Rule 803(5) may be available. If your client cannot remember the facts that he or she previously recorded in a document, the document may be used to present those facts. A document is often more persuasive than oral testimony, and this exception provides a means to get the information in those supporting documents admitted. The witness need not have totally forgotten everything about the subject matter in order to use a document under this exception. It is enough if the witness cannot testify fully. The rule imposes two foundation requirements: (1) the memorandum must have been made or adopted by the witness when the matter was fresh in the witness's memory; and (2) the memorandum must reflect the witness's knowledge correctly.

Example

Q. What were you doing during the week before your meeting with Mr. Samuels?

A. Well, I was working on the warehouse problem, I'm sure of that; but I can't remember exactly what I was doing on each day.

Q. May I have this marked as Exhibit 41?

Reporter: *(Marks)*

Q. Let the record reflect I have handed Exhibit 41 to counsel.

Opposing Counsel: *(Looks)*

Q. Please look at what has been marked as Exhibit 41 and tell us if you can identify that.

A. Yes, I can.

114

Q. What is it?

A. That is my personal date book.

Q. What information do you keep in that book?

A. I write down what I do every day.

Q. When do you write down that information?

A. Some of it is written down when I make appointments like if I have a meeting next Thursday, I will write that down in the book for Thursday. Most of it is written at the end of the day. I like to keep track of what I do.

Q. Is the information accurate at the time you write it down?

A. Yes.

Q. Does that book have entries with respect to the week before your meeting with Mr. Samuels?

A. Yes, it does.

Q. Does looking at those entries refresh your recollection about what you were doing?

A. Well, I see what is written here, but I don't remember specific things on specific days.

Q. Your Honor, we offer the contents of Exhibit 41 as to the week in question in evidence and request at this time that the witness be permitted to read those entries to the jury.

Court: You may proceed.

Note that the rule requires that the document may be read into the record by the party offering it, but the document itself may not be received in evidence as an exhibit unless it is offered by an adverse party. After the contents are admitted in evidence (because the necessary facts have been provided as to the witness's limited current recollection and the timeliness and accuracy of the recordation of information in the document), the witness can read the document to the jury.

Statements against interest

The exception to the hearsay rule for statements against interest applies only if the person who made the statement is unavailable as a witness. Rule 804(a) provides that a witness is unavailable if he or she is dead, mentally incompetent, physically ill, or beyond service of process after reasonable effort. If the witness is available, then you must call him or her to testify and use Rule 801(d)(1), discussed above under the "not hearsay" categories, to qualify the witness's prior statements.

Rule 804(b)(3) imposes fairly stringent conditions on the use of the exception for statements against interest. The exception covers only statements made under circumstances such "that a reasonable person in the declarant's position would not have made the statement unless believing it to be true." The rule provides five categories of circumstances that will meet the requirements of the rule:

- contrary to the declarant's pecuniary interest;
- contrary to the declarant's proprietary interest;
- tended to subject the declarant to civil liability;
- tended to subject the declarant to criminal liability; or
- rendered invalid a claim by declarant against another.

Rule 804(b)(3) also contains a special limitation for criminal cases that "A statement tending to expose the declarant to criminal liability and offered to exculpate the accused is not admissible unless corroborating circumstances clearly indicate the trustworthiness of the statement."

The exception for statements against interest is usually used for documents of third parties that cannot qualify as business records. Statements against interest of a party opponent would come in under Rule 801(d)(2) as "not hearsay" and that route should be preferred because it is much less restrictive than the exception for statements against interest.

Other private records

Less frequently used havens may provide an avenue for admitting private documents that do not qualify as business records. Rule 803(1) provides an exception for present sense impressions describing or explaining an event or condition while it was happening or immediately thereafter. Rule 803(2) covers excited utterances. If the person who wrote the document did it while "under the stress of excitement" caused by "a startling event or condition" and the document reports on or relates to this event or condition, the exception applies. Rule 803(3) provides an exception for a statement of the declarant's then-existing state of mind or body. Rule 804(b)(2) provides an exception, if the declarant is unavailable, for statements made under belief of impending death. This exception is available in civil actions and homicide cases. Rule 803(13) provides an exception for "[s]tatements of fact concerning personal or family history contained in family Bibles, genealogies, charts, engravings on rings, inscriptions on family portraits, engravings on urns, crypts, or tombstones, or the like. Similarly, Rule 804(b)(4) provides an exception, if the declarant is unavailable, for statements of personal or family history specified in the rule.

Public records

Rule 803 creates an exception to the hearsay rule for a wide variety of public records, including explicit exceptions for government agency reports, records of vital statistics, property records, and marriage and similar certificates. See Rules 803(8), (9), (12), and (14).

The exception for public records in Rule 803(8), and particularly the inclusion within that exception of "factual findings resulting from an investigation made pursuant to authority granted by law", covers a broad category of potentially very useful documents. The liberal construction by many courts of the term "factual findings" to include mixed findings of fact and conclusions makes this exception potentially broader than the business records exception. Under the public records exception, parties can introduce law enforcement agency reports about accidents, government agency data about the safety of products, letters from government officials about their work, scientific reports, descriptions of industry practices, production statistics, and other similar government documents.

The only significant limitation on evidence offered under Rule 803(8) is the usual caveat at the end of the rule that the court may exercise its discretion to exclude the evidence if "the sources of information or other circumstances indicate lack of trustworthiness." In applying this limitation, courts will look to how much first hand knowledge is reflected in the report as compared to how much (and what type of) hearsay; the circumstances indicating objectivity, at least with respect to the litigation at hand; the type of conclusions expressed; and the special skills of the government agency to produce the report.

The testimony required to introduce public records is usually very brief because the requirements of both the foundation and the exception to the hearsay rule are limited. As noted in Section 2.1.1, a public record requires authentication either under Rule 902(1-4) or under Rule 901(7).

Example

(After marking the exhibit and showing it to opposing counsel)

Q. Do you recognize the document that has been marked as Exhibit 112?

A. Yes.

Q. What is it?

A. It is a report issued by the Department of Transportation providing statistics gathered in their tests of automobiles.

Q. How did you get that document?

A. I called the Department of Transportation and asked for a copy of their report containing information on maximum stopping distances for all automobiles manufactured over the past five years. I learned that I could go down to their offices and pick up a copy. I did that.

Q. Where did you get the document that has been marked as Exhibit 112?

A. At the Public Information Office of the Department of Transportation on Queen Street, downtown.

Q. Is there any indication on the document that is Exhibit 112 as to who wrote it or published it?

A. Yes. It says on the cover that it is issued by the Department of Transportation.

Q. Your Honor, we offer Exhibit 112 in evidence.

Opposing Counsel: Objection; hearsay.

Counsel: Exhibit 112 is a public record which qualifies under Rule 803(8). It is a report of a public agency setting forth the activities of the agency in testing automobiles.

Court: Objection overruled.

Opposing Counsel: Objection; this is not the original document.

Counsel: Exhibit 112 qualifies as an original document under Rule 1001(3) as a published document all copies of which were intended by the publisher to be the same.

Court: Objection overruled.

If the public record is filed in the public office and came from that office, it is sufficiently authenticated. If the public record is a report of the activities of the office or agency or data collected by the agency, it comes under the exception to the hearsay rule. There is no original document problem with published documents so long as nothing has been written on or otherwise added to the published version.

Under Rule 201, the court should take judicial notice of the fact that the Department of Transportation, to which the witness has referred, is a public office or agency within the meaning of Rule 803(8) and that the matter described falls within the "activities of the office or agency." No extrinsic evidence is required on these points. These are adjudicative facts, under Rule 201, and "not subject to reasonable dispute." The judge may already be familiar with the public office, or a citation of statutory authority will suffice. If the proponent of the exhibit is correct, this can be ascertained readily from a perusal of the law and an inspection of the exhibit.

In some cases, the fact that a government agency has collected, recorded, filed, or published information will make available a presumption that its activities "have been regularly and legally performed."[5] The presumption shifts the burden of going forward so that the opponent of the exhibit must now demonstrate that the activity or report was not "authorized by law."

Rule 803(22) and Rule 803(23) govern the use of public records that are prior convictions and judgments involving family matters or property boundaries.

If a person is unavailable—that is, dead, mentally incapacitated, physically ill, or not reachable by service of process after reasonable effort—the public record of former testimony of that person may be admitted in evidence under the very limited circumstances prescribed by Rule 804(b)(1). The former testimony must have been given under oath in a court hearing or deposition. The party against whom the transcript is offered must have participated in the former proceeding and had "an opportunity and similar motive to develop the testimony by direct, cross, or redirect examination." In a civil matter, the participation of a predecessor in interest to the party against whom the transcript is offered will be sufficient.

Quasi-public records

The remaining exceptions apply to very narrow categories of quasi-public records that are used infrequently at trial. They are listed here for reference:

- Records of religious organizations (Rule 803(11));
- Documents more than 20 years old (ancient documents) (Rule 803(16));
- Statements about reputation and character (Rule 803(19, 21)); and
- Statements about property boundaries and interests (Rule 803(15, 20)).

The general purpose exceptions

If nothing else works, you can turn to the general purpose exceptions in Rule 803(24) and Rule 804(b)(5). The general purpose exceptions permit any document to be admitted that is not covered by any of the specific exceptions if it has equivalent circumstantial guarantees of trustworthiness, and the court determines that (A) the statement is offered as evidence of a material fact; (B) the statement is more probative on the point for which it is offered than any other evidence which the proponent can procure through reasonable efforts; and (C) the general purposes of the evidence rules and the interests of justice will best be served by admission of the statement in evidence.

Both Rules 803(24) and 804(b)(5) also require, to qualify for this exception, that you notify your opponent sufficiently in advance of trial to provide a fair opportunity to respond. The notice must include a copy of the document and the name and address of its author.

A note of caution with respect to the general purpose exception: some judges interpret the rule to mean that if the document *could* have been qualified under a specific exception, but the lawyer failed to do the necessary pretrial preparation, then "the general purposes of the evidence rules and the interests of justice" are *not* best served by admission of the document. For example, your client has a document from a third party that *could* be qualified as a business record of the third party by taking the deposition of an officer or custodian. You neglect to take that deposition before the discovery deadline passes. There is no other way to qualify the document, so you resort to Rule 803(24). If your opponent objects and points out your unexcused lapse, you may lose the exhibit.

2.1.3 Original Document Objections

There are no original document objections to an original of a text document, the category of exhibits considered in this Section 2.1. The application of the original document rules to duplicates and nonconforming copies is discussed in Section 2.2.2 and Section 2.2.3.

2.1.4 Policy Objections and Completeness Objections

The policy objections to unfair prejudice, confusion/misleading, undue delay/waste of time, and needless cumulative evidence are explained in Section 1.3.3. Examples of policy objections to a text document exhibit are set out in Section 1.4.8 and Section 2.3.5.

The completeness objection is available if only part of a document is used as an exhibit. This objection is explained in Section 1.3.6. Examples of completeness objections are set out in Section 2.3.3 and Section 6.3.2.

2.1.5 Production and Tactics

Handling an issue that involves a lot of documentary evidence can be a considerable problem in a jury trial. Although the significance of each document is evident to you, it probably is not at all clear to the jury. Most jurors are not accustomed to dealing with documents. They find it confusing to read bits and pieces of the story.

The first task with respect to a documentary exhibit is to ensure that the jury can read the document. They must know what the document says in order to understand why it is important. Handwritten documents almost always need to be made into special exhibits in order to convey their meaning clearly. There are basically three ways to do this. The first is to enlarge the handwriting at issue so that it is clearly legible and easily read. The enlargement is displayed next to a copy of the original. The second method is to use a side-by-side comparison of the handwritten original and a typed copy. The third method is to use a typed substitute for the original. Medical reports often fall into this category. You may need most of the information on the report, so it is necessary to reproduce it in its entirety in legible form.

The second task with respect to documentary exhibits, after ensuring that the jury can read them, is to point out what is significant about the document. You can do this by using color to highlight the significant portion. Fig. 3 is an example of this kind of exhibit. Another method is to label each of the documents and to construct an exhibit that shows how they relate to one another. See discussion in Section 9.2. If the significance of the document is its date, and you are interested in showing a chronological series of events, it is often useful to place the documents into a time line. See discussion in Section 3.2.

The third task is to promote an understanding by the jurors of the points you want to make about the document. This requires that the document have a clear and unambiguous place in your explanation of what the case is all about. You may need to use several approaches to establish and reinforce this understanding.

If the case involves a large number of documents, you may want to organize looseleaf tabbed binders for the jury so that they can each have their own set. When the witness refers to Exhibit 34, each of them can turn to Tab 34. See discussion in Section 9.3.2. If you use a notebook, it may be useful not to give the jurors copies of the exhibits in advance. When you come to an exhibit and it is qualified, then pass it out to be put in their notebooks. Otherwise, the curious jurors will always be reading ahead to see what is coming. They will miss what the witness is saying and may reach erroneous conclusions by reading the documents before they know what the documents are.

A digital (computer) system or an electronic (visualizer or visual presenter) system offers a good alternative for displaying large numbers of documents. See discussion in Section 9.6 and Section 9.5. Either can display any document on a large monitor. Either approach allows each exhibit to be labeled clearly as to what it is, zooming in on a particular sentence, highlighting a passage, or adding printed material to explain unclear passages or handwriting.

Documentary exhibits can also aid the cross-examination of experts, particularly to hammer home a single point about the expert's testimony. If the other side's expert has written a document that is useful to make a relatively simple point, it is sometimes effective to make an enlargement of the document. You then cross-examine the expert about his or her own document using the enlargement of the document to be sure the point gets across. In all dealings with the other side's expert, however, you should be extremely conservative. Experts, particularly those who have long experience in testifying, can get themselves out of difficulty with ease. Any exhibits that you use with the other side's expert should be bulletproof.

Review the basic courtroom procedures described in Section 1.4, the ethical requirements outlined in Section 1.5, and the generally applicable tactical considerations explained in Section 1.6 with respect to particular text document exhibits to ensure their effective use.

2.2 DUPLICATES AND COPIES OF TEXT DOCUMENTS

If you are not using the original document as the exhibit offered in evidence, you will need to make sure you have complied with the "original document" rule. The basic rule, set out in Rule 1002 is that "[t]o prove the content of a writing . . . the original writing . . . is required, except as otherwise provided in these rules or by Act of Congress." The original of a document is not required to prove that the document exists, or that it was signed, or that it was delivered in a certain way. None of these facts are the "content of a writing" as that term is used by Rule 1002.

For evidentiary purposes, it is necessary to distinguish between originals, duplicates of originals, and copies of originals. Duplicates are exact copies of originals. Copies have something deleted or something added in comparison to the original. Duplicates are admitted as originals. Copies require that the original be accounted for before being admitted. Therefore, duplicates are treated the same as originals and require all the aspects of foundation for original documents set out in Section 2.1.1 plus testimony that the duplicate is an exact copy of the original. Copies require all the aspects of foundation for original documents plus testimony explaining under Rule 1004 that the original is lost, destroyed, not obtainable by subpoena or discovery, in the possession of a party opponent, or limited to collateral matters.

Under the rules, there is no priority or preference among kinds of secondary evidence. If there are alternatives, for example under Rule 1005 where the contents of public records may be proved either by certified copy or by a copy that a witness has compared to the original and testifies is accurate, the proponent may select either alternative. If both duplicates and non-duplicate copies are available, the proponent may elect to provide a foundation for either one. There is no requirement to use an available duplicate instead of a copy which has markings on it that cause it to differ from the original, so long as the proponent can qualify the copy. There remains, however, the risk of an adverse inference by the fact-finder if a less desirable or less trustworthy alternative is chosen.

2.2.1 Duplicates vs. Copies of Text Documents

The first aspect of dealing with "copies" of documents is to determine what is a duplicate copy and what is some other kind of copy. Under the rules, an "original" includes several categories of documents that might otherwise be considered copies. It is useful to qualify an exhibit as an "original" or "duplicate" in order to avoid the additional evidentiary requirements applied to other copies.

Counterparts

If an original and several copies of a document are created, and all are signed by the person or persons involved, then all signed versions are "counterparts" entitled to the status of originals. Rule 1001(3) provides: "An original of a writing or recording is the writing or recording itself or any counterpart intended to have the same effect by a person executing or issuing it." Contracts are often signed with counterparts and usually recite as a part of the terms that a signed counterpart is to be treated as an original.

Computer printouts

A computer file of any type—text, graphic, image, or data—in its computer readable form as created by its author is an original. This original may be stored on any medium such as a hard disk, a floppy disk, an optical disk, a laserdisc, or a CD-ROM used by the computer with which the file was created. Any printout from a computer file is also an original, so long as the printout is an accurate version of what is in the computer file. Rule 1001(3) provides: "If data are stored in a computer or similar device, any printout or other output readable by sight, shown to reflect the data accurately, is an original."

Duplicates

Duplicate copies of originals are treated as originals. Rule 1001(4) provides: "A duplicate is a counterpart produced by the same impression as the original, or from the same matrix, or by means of photography, including enlargements and miniatures, or by mechanical or electronic re-recording, or by chemical reproduction, or by other equivalent techniques which accurately reproduces the original." Thus, a copy made on a dry paper copier of the type used in many offices is a duplicate if: (1) everything on the original is also on the copy; and (2) there are no marks, stamps, or other material on the copy that are not on the original. Copies of computer files, for example on floppy disks, CD-ROMs, or tape drives, are duplicates of the original so long as they are accurate copies. A hard copy printout from a duplicate electronic file is also a duplicate.

Under Rule 1003, "A duplicate is admissible to the same extent as an original unless (1) a genuine question is raised as to the authenticity of the original or (2) in the circumstances it would be unfair to admit the duplicate in lieu of the original." The burden is on the opponent of the exhibit to raise objections based on a genuine question or unfairness.

2.2.2 Qualifying Duplicates

The foundation for counterparts, computer printouts, and duplicate copies is straightforward. The normal foundation for an original text document is presented first. If an original document objection is made, a short additional foundation is provided to qualify the exhibit under Rule 1001 or Rule 1003.

Example

(After the exhibit is marked and has been shown to opposing counsel and the court)

Q. I am handing you what has been marked as Exhibit 35.

A. *(Looks)*

Q. Do you recognize that document?

A. Yes.

Q. What is it?

A. This is a copy of the invoice for the industrial diamonds that were shipped to Mr. Dells.

Q. How did you become familiar with that document that has been marked as Exhibit 35?

A. It is my responsibility to receive and approve all such invoices before shipment is made.

Q. Are you familiar with the original invoice from which the copy that is Exhibit 35 was made?

A. Yes. These invoices are prepared in the Administrative Department which is under my supervision.

Q. Your Honor, we offer Exhibit 35 in evidence.

Opposing Counsel: Objection, hearsay.

Q. With respect to Exhibit 35, was the original invoice a record made at or near the time by or from information transmitted by a person with knowledge of what was shown on the invoice?

A. Yes.

Q. Was it the regular practice of the business to prepare invoices such as the original of this invoice?

A. Yes.

Q. Was the copy of the invoice that is Exhibit 35 kept in the course of your company's regularly conducted business activity?

A. Yes.

Q. We offer Exhibit 35 in evidence. This is a business record.

Court: Objection overruled.

Opposing Counsel: Objection; this is not the original document.

Q. How was the copy of the document that is Exhibit 35 made?

A. This is a photocopy. It was made on our office copier.

Q. When was that photocopy made?

A. It is our practice to make a photocopy for our files after the original is prepared and before it is sent out.

Q. Is the photocopy an accurate duplicate of the original?

A. Yes.

Q. Your Honor, we move the admission in evidence of the document that has been marked as plaintiff's Exhibit 35. This is a duplicate.

No proof is required of the authenticity of the original or of the whereabouts of the original which, in this case, would have been sent along with the shipment. So long as the original would have been admissible, the duplicate copy is also admissible. The duplicate copy does not have to be made at or near the time the original was made. Copies made sometime after the original (including copies made for the purpose of litigation) are admissible if no genuine question as to authenticity is raised.

A photocopy made from a photocopy is also admissible as a duplicate of the original so long as the copy is accurate. The rule allows as a duplicate any copy made by "equivalent techniques which accurately reproduces the original." The purpose is to ensure that whatever is being used as the exhibit is an exact duplicate of the original. If you are dealing with this situation, sometimes it is useful to change the formulation from: "Is the photocopy an accurate duplicate of the original?" to the following:

Q. Is there anything ON that copy that DID NOT appear on the original?

A. No.

Q. Is there anything NOT ON that copy that DID appear on the original?

A. No.

Then counsel may offer the copy as a "duplicate" of the original.

Although Rule 1001(3) requires that, in qualifying a computer printout as an "original," the proponent must establish that the printout "reflect[s] the data accurately," this is rarely applied to the printouts of text documents that are reduced to hard copy in the ordinary course and not produced specially for litigation. Those are treated as normal documents, and the computer printout made at the time is the original. If more than one printout was made at the time, all the printouts are originals. If a set of documents is retrieved from computer files for litigation purposes, and printouts are made at that time, but were not made in the ordinary course of business, then the extra step of qualifying these text documents as accurately reflecting the data in the computer should be taken.

2.2.3 Qualifying Copies That Are Not Exact Duplicates

Copies may not be exact duplicates of the original because they have additional marks, stamps, or handwriting on them. These additions take the copy out of Rule 1003, which allows duplicates to be admitted to the same extent as originals, and requires the proponent to proceed under Rule 1004 if an original document objection is made.

The options under Rule 1004 are to establish that:

(1) The original is lost or destroyed, and that did not happen by any bad faith of the proponent; or

(2) The original is in the hands of a third party and cannot be reached by subpoena or discovery; or

(3) The original is in the hands of a party opponent who has not turned it over; or

(4) The document goes to a collateral issue, and therefore the copy should be allowed as an efficient means of proceeding.

One alternative to proceeding under Rule 1004 is to seek a stipulation from your opponent that the document is a duplicate because the marks on it are inconsequential for purposes of the case.

Another alternative is to have the marks or handwriting on the document identified by the person who made them and qualified independently of the underlying document, which returns the underlying document to its "duplicate" status.

Using either the options under Rule 1004 or these alternatives requires some pretrial preparation. When you locate a document that would be useful at trial and that has marks or handwriting on it apparently made after the original was created, try to get the original or a duplicate copy (without the marks or handwriting) through discovery. If you are using an imaging system, it is easy to search through the entire document collection to see if there is a "clean" copy somewhere among the documents already turned over. If none is located, a special document request may have to be made. If the marks or handwriting were made by a party opponent or a third party, the deposition of that person can establish either the whereabouts of the original or an independent foundation for the subsequently added material. If the marks or handwriting were made by your client, cross-examination at a deposition of your client or your client's testimony at trial can clear up this problem.

Example

Q. Can you identify the document that has been marked as Exhibit 30?

A. Yes.

Q. What is it?

A. That is a memorandum from me to Mr. Atkins, who is the president of Atkins Financial Co., which I sent just before the merger.

Q. What is attached to the memorandum?

A. The first attachment is an assessment of the merger by Atkins Financial. The second attachment is an analysis of the French market.

Q. Your Honor, we offer Exhibit 30 in evidence.

Opposing Counsel: Objection. This is not the original document.

Q. Your Honor, I will qualify the documents. *(To the witness)* Is Exhibit 30 an original?

A. No, it is a photocopy.

Q. Directing your attention first to the memorandum itself. Is there anything on the memorandum that was not on the original?

A. Yes.

Q. What is that?

A. The notation "Merger file" and the check marks along the right margin.

Q. Who made those notations?

A. I did. The first is an instruction to my secretary as to where the document is to be filed, and the second is a set of marks I made indicating significant points. Those check marks were made as I read the document.

Q. Other than the notations you have identified, is the memorandum an exact duplicate of the original?

A. Yes, it is.

Q. Directing your attention to Attachment A, the financial analysis, is that an exact duplicate of the original?

A. No. It has some underlining on two of the pages, and there is a date stamp on the first page.

Q. Who put those marks on Attachment A?

A. I don't know.

Q. Where is the original of Attachment A, the financial analysis?

A. We lost it. We had it at the time, but we can't find it now. We had the original and a number of copies. One of the copies must have substituted for the original. It is hard to see the difference because Mr. Atkins' signature is in black ink and that is difficult to distinguish from a copy.

Q. Directing your attention to Attachment B, the analysis of the French market. Is that an exact copy of the original?

A. I don't know. I never saw the original.

Q. Where is the original of Attachment B, the analysis of the French market?

A. That was done by a consultant in France. We never had the original of that document.

Q. Your Honor, we offer Exhibit 30 in evidence. The memorandum is a duplicate, except for the markings for which an independent foundation has been provided. Attachment A is a copy and we have accounted for the original, which was lost. Attachment B is a copy, and we have accounted for the original which is beyond the process of this court.

Court: Objection overruled.

If you have a document that has several parts, one may qualify as a duplicate while others may not. An independent foundation will be needed for any attachments to a document that are not, themselves, exact duplicates.

There might have been a hearsay objection to the documents in the example. The memorandum would likely be qualified as a business record. The first attachment is not hearsay if it is a statement of a party opponent and the second attachment may be offered for the purpose of showing what information was available at the time and not as proof of the truth of its contents.

2.2.4 Qualifying Copies of Public Records

Public records have a special status under the original document rules. If they are self-authenticating under Rule 902 because they bear the required certification of a public official, then under Rule 1005 they are also qualified under the original document rule.

Several aspects of the technical requirements to meet an objection under the original document rules with respect to an exhibit that is a public record will be resolved by judicial notice under Rule 201 and no testimony from a competent witness is required. Rule 1005 refers to an "official record" and "a document authorized to be recorded or filed." The status of a document as an official record is provided by law or practice in the relevant jurisdiction. Judges may take judicial notice of the laws of their own jurisdiction or a sister state.[6] You may need a citation to the applicable law if the judge is not familiar with the public office involved, but once cited, no further proof is required. These are "adjudicative facts" under Rule 201 and thus subject to judicial notice. However, if the citation is to the law of a foreign country, Rule 44.1 of the Federal Rules of Civil Procedure requires reasonable written notice to the other side before the court may "determine" foreign law. It is not clear that a citation in connection with Rule 1005 is such a determination, but it may be prudent to provide written notice before offering the exhibit.

Rule 1005 permits the court to admit any copy "certified as correct in accordance with rule 902." Rule 902(1) refers to the political subdivisions, departments, offices, and agencies of the government of the United States, the 50 states, and U.S. territories. The status of these entities is subject to judicial notice. Rule 902(2) refers to a public officer who has official duties under the district or political subdivision. The status of the officer and the existence of official duties that qualify under this rule are also subject to judicial notice.

In addition, the court may rely on a presumption that "official activities by public officers . . . have been regularly and legally performed."[7] If the court invokes the presumption, which is discretionary, then the burden shifts to the opponent of the exhibit to demonstrate that there is some defect in the status of this exhibit.

Example

Q. Would you state your full name, please?

A. Janice Owens Edmonn.

Q. Ms. Edmonn, are you the owner of the property located at 112 Oak Street?

A. Yes.

Q. When was the white Chevrolet shown in the photograph left on your property?

A. Sometime last summer.

Q. Your Honor, at this time we offer in evidence Exhibit 33, which is a certified copy of the title to the white Chevrolet.

Opposing Counsel: Objection, lack of foundation.

Counsel: Your Honor, Exhibit 33 is a copy of an official record, the title to an automobile. Under Section 4-113 of the state statutes, this record is authorized to be filed with the Bureau of Motor Vehicles. This copy is certified as having been actually recorded in that public office and as being correct. The certificate is made by the Records Clerk of the Bureau of Motor Vehicles, who is authorized to make the certificates. All of this appears on the face of the document. This is self-authenticating under Rule 902(4). No testimony of a witness is required.

Court: Objection overruled.

Opposing Counsel: Objection, hearsay.

Counsel: Your Honor, Exhibit 33 is a public record that falls under the exception to the hearsay rule in Rule 803(8). It is a record of a public agency setting forth the activities of the agency, in this case the Bureau of Motor Vehicles, which include the issuance of titles to automobiles. It is also covered by Rule 803(14) as a record of a document affecting an interest in property. It is a record of a public office and a statute, in this case Section 4-113, authorizes the recording of automobile titles in the Bureau of Motor Vehicles.

Court: Objection overruled.

Opposing Counsel: Objection, original document. This is a copy, not an original.

Counsel: Your Honor, under Rule 1005, the contents of an official record can be proved by copy, certified as correct in accordance with Rule 702.

Court: Objection overruled.

Rule 1005 also allows copies of public records to be admitted based on the testimony of any competent witness who has compared the copy with the original and says that it is correct. Moreover, if a party exercises due diligence and still cannot get a certified copy or a copy verified by a witness, then "other evidence of the contents may be given."

Even with a public record, you will need to be prepared to establish foundation (that the document is what it purports to be), to overcome the hearsay objection (that the document is an out-of-court statement), and to overcome the original document objection (that the document is not an original). The intent of the rules is to collapse all of these requirements into one showing that the particular record is authorized by statute and is certified by a person authorized to do so. Not many experienced lawyers will require you to go through these steps because the outcome is quite certain, and the court's tolerance for lawyers who make these objections will be very limited. All public documents, if relevant, should be stipulated as admissible in pretrial proceedings. Refusal to do so should result in an assessment of costs. See discussion in Section 1.6.4.

2.2.5 Original Document Objections

Duplicates and non-duplicate copies of documents are subject to the hearsay objections described in Section 2.1.2 and the policy objections described in Section 2.1.4. In addition, the proponent of the exhibit must take account of the requirements of the original document rules. The very liberal approach of Rules 1001 through 1008 sweeps away most of the technical obstacles to the use of photocopies, computer printouts, photographic prints, and other common duplicates of originals. Meeting original document objections is usually a matter of eliciting only very summary statements from the witness and, for this reason, the objection is not often raised.

Status as a duplicate

When an original document objection is made, the proponent of the exhibit should first ensure that the exhibit qualifies as a duplicate, if possible.

Rule 1001 requires testimony supporting computer printouts to the effect that the printout accurately reflects the data in the computer. If a computer printout of text documents has been made specially for litigation purposes, then the witness must have a basis for knowing that the printout is accurate.

Rule 1001 also requires testimony supporting photocopies and other reproductions to the effect that the means used to make the copy accurately reproduces the original. If the witness testifies that the copy accurately reflects the original, the requirements of the rule have been met even if the witness does not identify the process by which the copy was made. There may be an objection, however, if the witness has no basis for the assertion that the copy accurately reflects the original. The rule provides such a basis to the witness who knows what process was used to make a copy.

If the duplicate has become illegible in part, the court may require that the original be produced. If the duplicate is not complete or the duplication process left gaps, the original may be required. If the illegible or missing portions of the duplicate are not relevant to issues in the case, then the duplicate may be allowed.

Genuine question

Rule 1003 creates an exception to the general rule on the admissibility of qualified duplicates if a genuine question is raised as to the authenticity of the original. Two common questions as to authenticity or trustworthiness of the original, often found to be "genuine" in the sense intended under Rule 1003, are (1) the basis that the witness has for identifying the exhibit and (2) the condition of the exhibit. See discussion in Section 1.1.4 on trustworthiness. In ruling on foundation, of which trustworthiness or authenticity is one element, a court needs to consider only whether reasonable jurors could find the exhibit to be genuine. The ultimate question of genuineness of the exhibit does not have to be reached at this point. When an original document objection is made, because a duplicate is being offered rather than the original, and the genuineness of the original is questioned, the court needs to consider whether, under the circumstances, reasonable jurors could rely on the duplicate as a stand-in for the original.

If the original is readily available to one of the parties, the court will normally resolve the problem by ordering the original produced so that the jury can consider it, rather than the duplicate. If the original has been lost or destroyed, the court may consider whether the proponent of the duplicate was responsible for the loss or destruction of the original in bad faith. If neither of these options resolves the problem, the court may allow or refuse the exhibit conditionally and await further evidence. The court may issue a cautionary instruction to the jury with respect to the exhibit. See Section 1.8.2. The basic question for the court is whether the duplicate is something on which a reasonable juror could base a decision on the issue.

Unfairness

Rule 1003 also creates an exception to the use of duplicates if it would be unfair to admit the duplicate in lieu of the original. This may arise if one party offers a copy of a document and the opposing party suggests that the original of the document was changed after the copy was made, so that the copy no longer reflects accurately the content of the original or that the original was never signed so that it does not qualify as a statement of a party. If the dispute is centered on fraud with respect to the original and one party is questioning the genuineness of the original or the signature on the original, an objection may be raised to use of the copy because that may prevent the challenger from doing the kind of scientific analysis necessary to determine genuineness.

Additions/deletions

Rule 1004 makes available objections to documents that are not exact copies. If the proponent of the exhibit claims that the original was lost or destroyed, the opponent may make a showing that the original was lost or destroyed in bad faith by the proponent. If the proponent claims that the original is not obtainable by judicial process or discovery, the opponent may demand evidence that any effort to subpoena the original or obtain it through discovery was made. If the proponent of the exhibit claims that the original is in the hands of the opponent, the opponent may demand proof of notice that the original was required at trial. If the proponent of the exhibit asserts that the copy should be admitted, although the original cannot be accounted for, because the document goes to a collateral issue, the opponent may address the discretion of the court as to the relationship of the exhibit to a controlling issue.

Rule 406 is helpful in establishing the whereabouts of the original in some cases. For example, you can put in proof under Rule 406 of the routine practice in the office of mailing the original to the person to whom it was addressed. In this case, the original was addressed to your opponent, the proof of routine practice is sufficient to establish that the original is in the hands of your opponent. Once that is established, Rule 1004(3) can be applied and the copy can be admitted.

2.3 FAX, E-MAIL, AND OTHER DIGITAL TEXT DOCUMENTS

Documents produced through facsimile and computer equipment are treated for evidence purposes as duplicates of original documents. The "original" may be a paper document that has been scanned into digital form, or it may be a computer file for which there is no paper document at all.

The definitions for digital documents merge at various points because any computer-readable file can be transmitted and printed out by various means given the necessary equipment. It is useful to distinguish among several basic types of digital documents, such as word processing documents, fax documents, e-mail documents, workgroup documents, and scanned documents, for purposes of tracing the evidentiary requirements. Illustrations in each category are set out below.

The proponent of a digital text document must first establish the competence of the witness, the relevance of the subject matter, and the identification of the document. See Section 1.1. In addition, Rule 901(9) provides a standard method of establishing trustworthiness or authenticity.

Under Rule 901(9), a text document that is the result of a process or system can be authenticated by "[e]vidence describing a process or system used to produce a result and showing that the process or system produces an accurate result." With most computer, fax, and e-mail systems used in commercial businesses, the description of the system as a commercially available system using standard equipment and software provided by established suppliers should be sufficient. Similarly, for home or personal systems using standard equipment from recognized suppliers, a basic description of the equipment should be sufficient. A problem may arise if the equipment was specially built or assembled from nonstandard parts. In this case, it may be more difficult to qualify the system as one that produces an accurate result.

Every digital text document is subject to a hearsay objection unless it is "not hearsay" under Rule 801 or falls under an exception provided by Rule 803 or Rule 804.

When anticipating original document objections to digital text documents, it is useful to focus on the qualification for a duplicate copy as described in Section 2.2.1. Rule 1001(1) defines a "writing" to include "letters, words, or numbers, or their equivalent, set down by . . . magnetic impulse, mechanical or electronic recording . . . ." Rule 1001(4) defines the term "duplicate" to include copies made by "mechanical or electronic re-recording . . . or by other equivalent techniques which accurately reproduces the original." Copies are qualified as duplicates regardless of when they were made and regardless of whether they were part of the same transaction as the original. Copies must have no additions to or deletions from the original in order to qualify as a "duplicate." Otherwise, the nonconforming copy must be qualified under Rule 1004 by accounting for the nonavailability of the original.

The policy objections often focus on considerations of undue delay and waste of time. See Section 1.3.3. Opposing counsel may argue that, although relevant, digital text documents require an undue amount of time to inquire into the particulars of the system that produced them. This may focus on the time and date stamp when offered to prove when a particular communication occurred. Every system can be reprogrammed to change the date and time from the correct indication to something else, and opposing counsel may argue this will require extensive cross-examination. If the proponent has established an adequate foundation, however, this objection should be overruled.

2.3.1 Word Processing Documents

A word processing document was created on a computer using word processing software. Once created, it usually exists as a digital file in a computer storage medium such as a hard disk, an optical disk, a floppy disk, a CD-ROM, or a tape. It may also exist in paper or "hard copy" form. When a word processing document is transferred into hard copy format, the digital file generally is transmitted through cabling from a computer to a printer and the printer causes the characters corresponding to the digital file to be transferred to paper. There are a variety of types of computers, word processing software, and printers, but these are irrelevant for evidentiary purposes.

The hard copy of a document created with word processing software in the ordinary course of events and not for litigation purposes is treated, for evidentiary purposes, like any other text document. If the document was circulated and used in a business or personal context in its hard copy form, and is being offered in evidence in that hard copy form found in the files or among the papers of one of the parties, there is no reason to apply additional requirements of trustworthiness just because it was created using a computer word processing program rather than a typewriter.

The availability and searchable nature of computer files, however, means that the document offered in evidence may have come from files kept in a digital format rather than in a hard copy format. In this case, the foundation needs to take account of the ease with which computer files can be changed.

Example

(After competence and relevance are established; assuming XYZ Co., is a party opponent)

Q. Can you identify what has been marked as Exhibit 42?

A. Yes.

Q. What is that?

A. That is a memo from Mr. John Delaney, the product manager for the XYZ Company, sent to Mr. Talmadge, their agent, just before the Assembot II robot was shipped.

Q. We offer Exhibit 42 in evidence.

Opposing Counsel: Objection. This is not the original document.

135

Q. Your Honor, we can qualify that as a duplicate. *(To the witness)* Can you identify what has been marked as Exhibit 42A?

A. Yes.

Q. What is that?

A. That is one of the disks containing copies of computer files that was delivered to us in discovery. It came from the XYZ Company.

Q. How do you know that?

A. Each disk that was delivered in discovery was logged in and labeled. This is disk #31. It was produced in response to our request for the relevant documents in Mr. Delaney's files.

Q. Was Exhibit 42 one of the documents on the disk that is Exhibit 42A?

A. Yes.

Q. Is Exhibit 42 a true and accurate printout of the corresponding digital file that is contained on the disk that is Exhibit 42A?

A. Yes, it is.

Q. How do you know that?

A. When we received the disk that is Exhibit 42A, we searched it for documents generated by Mr. Delaney about the Assembot II robot that were created prior to the ship date. Exhibit 42 is one of the documents that was identified in that search. After the documents were identified, they were printed out. After I examined this document, I compared the contents of the digital file as displayed on the screen to the hard copy that had been printed out, and they were the same.

Q. Your Honor, we offer Exhibit 42 in evidence. It is a duplicate under Rule 1001(4) because the printout is an accurate reflection of the computer file.

Note that there would be no hearsay objection in this example. The document was generated by a party opponent and delivered by them in discovery. The document is covered by the exemption from the hearsay rule in Rule 801(d)(2) for the statements of a party opponent.

This is a belt-and-suspenders example for purposes of illustration. It is not necessary to have in court the disk produced in discovery or to mark it as an exhibit, but this practice ensures that there will be no successful objection. It is also not necessary to have the person testify who actually first printed out the copy used as an exhibit. An affidavit to this effect will suffice if there is any contest about the exhibit. Normally an exhibit printed out from digital files delivered during discovery will be submitted for authentication through the process of requesting pretrial stipulations or responses to requests for admissions. Some documents, particularly those to be used for cross-examination purposes, however, may be kept as "surprise" exhibits and a foundation would be laid at trial.

In addition, questions may arise about the completeness of the copies. For example, if your opponent produced the digital computer files and you created the hard copy, you may need an affidavit from the appropriate person stating that the materials on the disk produced by your opponent were printed out in a standard computer operation with no additions or deletions. It is a common practice to add a header to documents that were produced from computer files indicating their origin. If anything has been added to the document, you will need a stipulation from the other side or testimony indicating what was added. If you obtained direct access to your opponent's computer system through a discovery order, and you created both the computer files and the hard copy, you may need qualifying testimony as to each step in the process. It is best to use a neutral expert for this purpose and to prepare an affidavit immediately upon completion of the work.

2.3.2 Fax and E-mail Documents

A fax document is one that was transmitted in a digital format by a fax machine or a computer via the telephone system to a telephone number. The transmission goes directly from sender to receiver like a telephone call. When a document is sent over the telephone lines to a telephone number, a machine hooked up to that telephone number by a modem will "answer" and receive the transmission. The receiving machine can be either a fax machine or a computer, and it will translate the digital signals into a printed copy or a display on a computer monitor. Both the sending and receiving machines generally attach a time and date stamp, page numbers, and an identifier for the machine.

An e-mail document is one that was transmitted in a digital format by a computer to a computer address from which it can be retrieved by another computer. These transmissions are also generally accomplished through the telephone system, but there is an intermediary between the sender and receiver, somewhat analogous to the post office. When the message is transmitted, the receiving computer at the "address" may operate as a storage facility, holding the message in a "mailbox" until the owner of the mailbox comes onto the system to collect his or her mail. E-mail may be sent through computer systems within an organization that are linked by a computer network, through a commercial on-line system that provides e-mail services, or through the Internet, which is a link among computer networks. An e-mail message is transmitted with header information indicating the e-mail address of the sender, the e-mail address of the recipient, the date and time of transmission, and the path along which the document was transmitted if it is coming from an outside source.

Fax and e-mail documents are one step removed from normal word processing documents. In the facsimile process, the "original," so to speak, may be a word processing document, which has been printed out and the resulting hard copy has been put in a freestanding fax machine, which converted a picture of the document to digital form, and sent it to a fax machine or a computer on the other end. Alternatively, the "original" computer file may have been used to send the text to a fax machine or a computer on the other end, and there may be no intervening hard copy on the sending end at all. If a fax is sent by a computer and the telephone on the other end is answered by a computer, there may be no hard copy on either end.

If the proponent of the exhibit received the document, the copy that was received may be the only one available. The original document may not have been preserved on the system that sent it, or it may be unavailable through normal process. If the system is reliable in transmitting and receiving exact duplicates, however, the computer file or the printout at the proponent's end is sufficient. No "original" is required. If the fax is coming from a party opponent or its agent, then it is not hearsay. If the fax is coming from a third party, then it will have to be qualified as a business record of the third party (by a showing that they both made and kept the document in the ordinary course of business), or some other exception to the hearsay rule will have to be found.

If the proponent of the exhibit generated the document and it was kept in electronic form until the time of the use for litigation, then the trustworthiness of the exhibit must be established by negating the possibility of tampering with or changing the files, and the exhibit must be qualified as a business record or as coming within some other exception in order to survive a challenge under the hearsay rules. If the document was kept in hard copy form from the time it was generated, then there is usually no litigation-related motive that would require additional foundation to establish trustworthiness.

Example

(After competence and relevance have been established, the exhibit has been marked and shown to opposing counsel and the court; assuming that XYZ Co. is a party opponent.)

Q. After you sent out your inquiry about the delay in the delivery of the gear part, what happened?

A. Nothing much.

Q. Can you identify the document that has been marked as Exhibit 19?

A. Yes.

Q. What is it?

A. It is an e-mail message sent to our company in early September last year.

Q. From whom did you receive it?

A. From the XYZ Co.

Q. Was Exhibit 19 a response?

A. Yes, this is what the XYZ Company sent to us responding to our inquiry about the delay in delivery of the gear part.

Q. How was the e-mail message received?

A. It was received at our company's e-mail address on the Internet.

Q. What is the process or system by which e-mail messages are received at your company?

A. We have an internal computer network. It consists of servers and personal computers. E-mail going to places outside the company or coming from places outside the company is routed from or to our network via an established commercial Internet provider.

Q. What experience have you had indicating that the process or system that your company uses to transmit and receive e-mail messages produces an accurate result?

A. We have been using this system for commercial purposes in our business for several years and we have had no problem with it.

Q. We offer Exhibit 19 in evidence.

Opposing Counsel: Objection, this is a copy and it is not the original document.

Q. How are e-mail messages stored at your company?

A. They are stored on our network server for a month; then the computer files are transferred to our archive system. The files are kept on tape drives in our archive system for three years.

Q. How was the printout that is Exhibit 19 made?

A. We located the computer file in a search of our computer records for all documents relevant to our transaction with the XYZ Company. Once we located the file, we downloaded it from the archive file, and printed it out.

Q. Is there anything on the paper copy that was not a part of the original e-mail message and its routing information?

A. No.

Q. Is the content of the e-mail message exactly the same on the paper copy as what was received on your computer system?

A. Yes.

Q. Your Honor, we offer Exhibit 19 in evidence. This is a qualified duplicate.

Court: Objection overruled. Exhibit 19 is admitted.

In this example, no hearsay objection would be made because the e-mail message is exempt from the hearsay rule as a statement of a party opponent.

In this example, the proponent of the exhibit has established trustworthiness in a traditional way, by showing that the e-mail came in as a response to something that was sent out. Under Rule 901(b)(4), a text document can be authenticated by ". . . contents, substance, internal pattern, or other distinctive characteristics." It has long been the rule under the common law that if one person sends out a letter to a specific addressee about a particular subject, and the letter offered in evidence purports to be written by that addressee in response, the fact that the incoming letter either refers to the outgoing letter or is responsive to its terms will authenticate it.[8] This principle is useful in authenticating faxes, e-mail messages, and other incoming digital texts as well.

The amount of evidence about the outgoing message needed to authenticate the incoming message depends on the circumstances. In the example above, the witness testified that an inquiry went out, and presumably the duplicate or copy of that outgoing message could be qualified as an exhibit if necessary to explain the facts. Then the witness is asked about the incoming message and authenticates it with testimony that the incoming message is a response. In most situations, that is all that is needed. If time is a critical factor, it will be necessary for the foundation to include the date of the transmission of the outgoing message and that the incoming response was received without unusual delay.

An incoming message may also be authenticated by the header line printed by the fax machine that sent it.

Example

Q. Can you identify the document that has been marked as Exhibit 20?

A. Yes.

Q. What is it?

A. A fax that we received from the XYZ Company.

Q. How can you tell that it came from the XYZ Company?

A. The header line at the very top of the page identifies the sender as the XYZ Company and gives the fax number from which it was sent.

Q. Whose telephone number is that?

A. The XYZ Company's fax number.

Q. How do you know that?

A. We have sent faxes to them at that number that were received and acknowledged by them.

Q. Have you received faxes from the XYZ Company before you received the one that is Exhibit 20?

A. Yes.

Q. What header was on those faxes?

A. The same header—it has their name and fax number, just like this one.

Q. Your Honor, we offer Exhibit 20 in evidence.

Opposing Counsel: Objection, lack of foundation.

Counsel: Your Honor, the elements of foundation have been established. The witness is competent; Exhibit 20 is relevant to the issue of the state of knowledge on the part of the XYZ Company; the witness has identified the exhibit properly; and the exhibit has been authenticated under Rule 901(b)(4) by the appearance of the fax header line taken in conjunction with circumstances.

Court: Objection overruled. Exhibit 20 is admitted.

Outgoing faxes, e-mail messages, and other electronic transmissions can be authenticated by analogy to Rule 901(b)(6) under which telephone conversations can be authenticated "by evidence that a call was made to the number assigned at the time by the telephone company to a particular person or business, if (A) in the case of a person, circumstances, including self-identification, show the person answering to be the one called, or (B) in the case of a business, the call was made to a place of business and the conversation related to business reasonably transacted over the telephone."

Example

Q. Can you identify Exhibit 21?

A. Yes.

Q. What is that?

A. This is a fax that we sent to an alternate supplier right after we got the response from the XYZ Company.

Q. To what telephone number was that fax sent?

A. Area Code 202, number 296-7600.

Q. Whose fax number is that?

A. That is the fax number of Access Alternatives, Inc.

Q. Is that a business fax number?

A. Yes.

Q. How do you know that?

A. That is the fax number on their letterhead, and that's where we sent it.

Q. Was the fax received?

A. Yes.

Q. How do you know that?

A. The indicator on our fax machine showed a connection and the report generated by our fax machine showed that this transmission was completed.

Q. Your Honor, we offer Exhibit 21 in evidence.

Opposing Counsel: Objection, lack of foundation.

Counsel: Your Honor, we have provided a proper foundation. Competence, relevance, and identification are obvious. We have met the trustworthiness requirement by analogy to Rule 901(b)(6) for telephone calls. A fax is a transmission by telephone links. We showed that the call was made to a business number, it was answered in the ordinary course by the fax machine on the other end, and the sending machine reported that it completed the transmission. Rule 901(b) says that its specific examples are by way of illustration only and not by way of limitation, so using an analogy is appropriate.

Court: Objection overruled. Exhibit 21 is admitted.

The same underlying assumptions that have provided the bases authenticating telephone calls should be applicable to fax calls. Many fax machines have a display that indicates the number of the fax machine that has responded (or "answered") the call plus a report capability that will print out the status of the transmission as either received, no answer, or busy.

A fax sent to a business may arrive at a fax machine used by numerous people associated with the business. The question whether the fax was delivered from the machine to the specific addressee should not keep the fax from being admitted (if hearsay and original document objections are met adequately). That is a question as to the weight to be given the fax message after it is admitted.

There are two reasons why a fax machine that "answers" a call may not, in fact, receive the message: the receiving machine may be out of paper or the receiving machine may be out of memory because it has received numerous other messages and has not been able to print them out. In either case, the receiving machine will connect and the sending machine will record that fact. The proponent of the exhibit that is a fax document should not have to negate these possibilities. The document should be admitted on the foundation shown above and then the opponent may argue that the fact-finder should give it no weight because of evidence that the message itself was not received.

Outgoing e-mail may be analogized to the U.S. mail. Systems have been set up to ensure that messages properly addressed are received. The public exchange through the Internet system should be entitled to the same presumption as applies to the mail: "A letter properly addressed, stamped, and mailed is presumed to have been duly delivered to the addressee."[9]

Example

Q. What is Exhibit 22?

A. That is a printout of an e-mail message that I sent to Elisa Willoughby right after the tree fell on the house.

Q. How did you send it?

A. I sent it through the regular commercial on-line service that I use.

Q. Does the on-line service offer e-mail services through the Internet?

A. Yes, they do.

Q. Are those e-mail services a part of their commercial offerings to the public?

A. Yes, they are.

Q. How did you address the message?

A. I addressed it to Ewill, which is Elisa Willoughby's e-mail name, at, using the "at sign," the lower case letter "a" in a circle, aol.com. The last part, aol.com, stands for America OnLine, a regular commercial on-line service.

Q. Where did you get that address?

A. From Ms. Willoughby's business card.

Q. Was your subscription to the on-line service fully paid up and in effect at the time you used the on-line service to send the message?

A. Yes.

Q. Have you used this e-mail service before sending Exhibit 22?

A. Yes.

Q. With what result?

A. I have never had any trouble with it.

Q. What information do you have about whether the message was received?

A. The on-line service provides an e-mail interface that includes the message "Your e-mail has been delivered" when the communication has been sent through to the addressee's e-mail box. That message was displayed with respect to Exhibit 22.

Q. Your Honor, we offer Exhibit 22 in evidence.

Opposing Counsel: Objection, lack of foundation.

Counsel: Your Honor, we have established all four aspects of foundation. The witness is competent. She sent Exhibit 22 and has first hand knowledge. Exhibit 22 is relevant to the issue of knowledge about the condition of the house. The witness has identified the exhibit sufficiently to distinguish it from all other things. And the exhibit is trustworthy. It was properly addressed, and mailed through an established commercial on-line service provider, using a subscription that was fully paid up. This is entitled to the same presumption as a letter properly addressed, stamped and mailed. Such a letter is presumed to have been delivered to the addressee.

The commercial service has every incentive to ensure that
e-mail messages are delivered properly, and has the
demonstrated capability to do so. Therefore there is a very
strong probability that the e-mail was, in fact, delivered.

Opposing Counsel: Even if that is so, they have only proved the
e-mail was delivered to a commercial provider's mailbox for
Ms. Willoughby. They have not proved Ms. Willoughby got on
her computer, dialed up her service provider, and actually
retrieved this e-mail.

Counsel: In the case of a letter put in the U.S. mail, we do not
have the burden of proving Ms. Willoughby actually opened
her letterbox and took out the mail. It is enough to show the
letter was properly addressed, stamped, and mailed through a
system that by and large gets the mail through. We have done
that. There is no challenge to the address, or the fact that the
witness's commercial provider is fully capable of delivering
the mail and has a commercial incentive to do so accurately.

Opposing Counsel: But anyone could have gotten on a computer
and retrieved this message. There is nothing to connect Ms.
Willoughby to the particular message.

Counsel: Again, the analogy to the U.S. mail is instructive. The
mail is usually delivered to a letterbox or mail slot. There isn't
any guarantee that Ms. Willoughby is the only person with
access to that mail. The presumption merely shifts the burden
of going forward. Here, only a person with the password to get
into Ms. Willoughby's mailbox with her commercial provider
has access to that message. One can argue that it is far more
likely the e-mail message actually came into Ms. Willoughby's
hands than a letter mailed to her address.

Opposing Counsel: It would not be fair to allow them to establish
that Ms. Willoughby had this knowledge on the flimsy basis of
an e-mail that she may or may not have received.

Counsel: Admitting Exhibit 22 in evidence is not the same as
establishing the contested fact. Exhibit 22 is evidence that
can be considered by the jury in its deliberations about
whether the contested fact has been established. All we have
to show by way of foundation is that the exhibit is something
a reasonable person could rationally use to arrive at a
decision on this issue. We submit that an e-mail, duly
addressed, and transmitted through an established
commercial provider that has an incentive to deliver, meets
the fundamental test of something on which a reasonable

juror could base a decision. It is open to Ms. Willoughby to deny she got the message, and the jurors can also consider that.

Court: Objection overruled.

Opposing Counsel: Objection, hearsay.

Counsel: Exhibit 22 falls under Rule 803(1). It is a present sense impression. The witness testified that she sent it right after the tree fell on the house. As Your Honor can see from the text of the message, this meets the requirement of a "statement describing or explaining an event or condition while the declarant was perceiving the event or immediately thereafter."

Court: Objection overruled.

Opposing Counsel: Objection, original document. This is a copy.

Counsel: I can go back to question the witness and establish that this is an accurate reflection of what is stored in the computer. Under Rule 1001(3), the printout, if it is accurate, is an original, and the original document rule does not apply.

Court: Is there any issue as to whether there is something in the printout that was not on the computer version of this?

Opposing Counsel: We don't know.

Court: Objection overruled. Exhibit 22 is admitted.

There is a question, under the literal terms of the business records exception, whether a fax or e-mail message coming from outside the company can qualify as a business record. If it is the regular practice of the business to put incoming e-mail or fax messages into a computer or hard copy file, it might be said, in computer terms, that it is the "regular practice of that business activity to make the memorandum, report, record, or data compilation," that is, the incoming e-mail or fax is "made" at the receiving end in the sense that it is printed out there and reduced to hard copy. By analogy to written correspondence, however, that is not the intention of the rule. The sender of the fax or e-mail message is the "maker" of the memorandum, report, record, or data compilation contained in the message.

There may also be a variety of policy objections raised with respect to e-mail messages, sometimes based on the misconceptions of opposing counsel as to how the Internet, a commercial provider's e-mail system, or a business establishment's internal network e-mail system works. It is useful to flush out these potential objections in pretrial discovery and deposition. See Section 10.1.

The objection to additions or deletions discussed in Section 2.2 will be available as to an e-mail message if the "header" information is not also printed out on the copy. A computer file containing the e-mail message itself should also contain header lines indicating the computer address from which the message was sent, the date and time it was sent, and the data path through which the message was transmitted. This information is technically a part of the original because it was generated with the original. If this information is missing on the copy, the exhibit may be subject to challenge as being incomplete and therefore not a "duplicate" of the original that can qualify under Rule 1003.

There is some debate about whether the computer file received by the fax or e-mail process is an original or a duplicate because the same file is kept at the sending end. Rule 1001(4) provides a definition of "duplicate" that includes any "electronic re-recording" of the original "which accurately reproduces the original." If it is an "original," then no objection is available under Rule 1003 based on a "genuine question as to the authenticity" of the message on the originating end or an argument that "it would be unfair to admit the duplicate in lieu" of the message on the originating end. Because of the ease with which computer files can be altered without leaving any trace of the alteration, the better practice may be to treat the message on the receiving end as a "duplicate" and the message on the sending end as the "original" and to focus on what kind of showing will be necessary by the opponent of the exhibit to raise a genuine question or sufficient unfairness to exclude the exhibit.

Once the fax or e-mail message is received, any paper copy of the message has equal status with the computer version. If the computer version is an original, then the paper copy is an original. If the computer version is a duplicate, then the paper copy is also a duplicate. This is the intent of Rule 1001(3), which provides: "If data are stored in a computer or similar device, any printout or other output readable by sight, shown to reflect the data accurately, is an original."

If the paper copy printout from the computer file is not an exact duplicate of the computer file from which it was taken, then, under Rule 1004, the original (or duplicate received when the original was sent) will have to be accounted for before the non-duplicate copy can be used. This may happen when notes are affixed to the incoming fax or e-mail while it is on the computer system or after the hard copy is made.

Note that the original document rule covers photographs, videotape, and sound recordings. To the extent that multimedia files are a part of an exhibit, these components must be separately qualified if they are not "originals." See Section 6.1.3 (photographs), Section 6.3.2 (videotapes) and Section 6.4.2 (sound recordings).

2.3.3 Workgroup Documents

A workgroup document is one that was generated using workgroup, workflow, or other shared access software. Typically, one person generates a first draft that is passed along via some form of e-mail to the next person, who adds comments or additional text, and that combined draft is either passed back to the first person or on to yet another person. All of the people contributing to the document may be in the same location on a local computer network or they may be on different continents. Those working with the document may be individuals or groups. The materials they add to the document may be text, sound, short "post-it" notes, graphics, or data.

Documents generated with workgroup or workflow software create an additional level of complexity for evidentiary purposes. These documents have the characteristics of word processing documents because they are created on a computer with word processing software; they are like fax or e-mail documents because they are sent from one place to another through a computer network; and they have additional features because anyone on the network who has access to the document or the project can add text, sound, image, or graphics files. The people with access may be independent contractors, agents, consultants, representatives, or employees of the company for whom the document (or project) is being created. In addition, some of these workgroup or workflow software packages have replicating database features so that the underlying information can be updated everywhere on the network that it exists as new information becomes available or is added.

Some documents generated with workgroup software are simple forms: one person fills out part of the form and sends it to someone in another department who fills out the rest. This process is very similar to what would happen with a hard copy of the form if it were filled out manually. Other documents are much more complex. The sound files added to the document may be the verbal comments of one of the members of the team attached at key points in the document so that the principal author can take account of these comments in producing the next draft. Sound files may also be attached from outside sources, however, such as a speech made by a stock analyst or expert in the field. Similarly, someone in the group that is working on the project may add graphics files, such as a scanned photo, or image files, perhaps a reference document, that complicate the problem of establishing the trustworthiness and hearsay exceptions.

The foundation for a workgroup document must take account of all of the input to the document and thus will be highly particularized to the exhibit.

Example

(After establishing competence and relevance)

Q. Can you identify Exhibit 8?

A. Yes.

Q. What is it?

A. That is a printout of the analysis of the competition based on which our company decided to go into the business of selling an on-line matchmaking service.

Q. Your Honor, we offer Exhibit 8 in evidence.

Opposing Counsel: Objection, hearsay.

Counsel: Your Honor, we can qualify Exhibit 8 as a business record.

Court: You may proceed.

Q. Is Exhibit 8 a memorandum, report, record, or data compilation of acts, events, conditions, opinions, or diagnoses that was made at or near the time of the analysis recorded?

A. Yes.

Q. Was Exhibit 8 made by or from information transmitted by persons with knowledge?

A. Yes.

Q. Was it the regular practice of your company's business activity to make Exhibit 8?

A. Yes.

Q. Was Exhibit 8 kept in the course of a regularly conducted business activity?

A. Yes.

Q. Your Honor, we move the admission in evidence of Exhibit 8. It is a qualified business record.

Opposing Counsel: Objection. This is not the original document.

Counsel: Your Honor, we can qualify Exhibit 8 as an original under Rule 1001(3). It is a printout that reflects accurately the data stored in the computer.

Court: You may proceed.

Q. From what source was this printout made?

A. That was made from the computer file for this project on our network.

Q. Is Exhibit 8 an accurate reflection of the text and graphics included in that computer file?

A. Yes.

Q. How do you know that Exhibit 8 is an accurate reflection of the text and graphics files for the competitive analysis stored in the computer?

A. I compared Exhibit 8 to the computer files and determined that the printout was accurate.

Q. Is there anything in the computer file that is not also included in Exhibit 8?

A. Yes.

Q. What is that?

A. The sound files are not included and the notes and e-mail files are not included.

Q. Can you identify what has been marked as Exhibit 8A?

A. Yes. That is the computer disk that contains all of the files on this competitive analysis—including the sound files and the notes and messaging files.

Q. Why have certain of the files not been included?

A. The sound files are not included because they are suggestions for musical backgrounds intended to be played on a multimedia computer system. There is no way to "play" them in a hard copy. They are available, however, in Exhibit 8A. The notes files appear on the screen as yellow "post-it" notes indicating a comment on a particular paragraph or graphic. In a computer context, these can be moved around the screen so that you can read what is underneath. There is no practical way to print these out in hard copy without obscuring some of the text. The messaging files indicate when a particular draft is being delivered from one personal computer to another one. They are not a part of the text of the document itself. All of these files are on Exhibit 8A.

Q. We offer Exhibit 8 in evidence. It accurately reflects the text and graphics files that are a part of the original data stored on the computer.

Court: Objection overruled.

Opposing Counsel: Objection, this exhibit is only part of the original.

Counsel: Your Honor, under Rule 106, any additional parts may be introduced if a proper showing can be made that these missing parts "ought in fairness to be considered contemporaneously with" the exhibit. No such showing has been made.

Court: Objection overruled. Exhibit 8 is admitted.

If a computer file contains some information, such as sound components, that cannot be printed out, that is not a reason to exclude the printout of the text and graphic files. The sound files can be treated as a separate part of the document subject to Rule 106 or the exhibit with the sound files can be displayed on a computer monitor and the sound files can be played by the computer's audio system at the places where they are affixed to the text.

The foundation questions about a computer printout should refer to it as a "printout" rather than a "copy" to avoid confusion under the rules.

It is not necessary to identify all of the authors who contributed to a group process, nor is it necessary, as a part of foundation, to attribute particular work to specific authors. In some kinds of group work software, the database is replicated wherever it is located when it is updated by one of the authorized members of the group. There may be multiple versions of the database saved as distinct computer files. None of the other versions need be introduced or identified in order to qualify one of the versions, perhaps the one that was extant on a particular date. Earlier versions produced in a workgroup context may be required by the opponent of the exhibit under Rule 106.

2.3.4 Scanned and Downloaded Documents

Scanned and downloaded documents are usually computer-readable copies of documents from some outside source. A scanned document started out as a hard copy. It was processed by a scanner to turn it into a computer-readable file. This file may produce an image of the document, such as a photo, drawing, or computer-generated graphic, or it may produce a text document. The text document will be either a text file, in which case it can be edited and changed in the same ways as any word processing document, or it will be an image file, in which case it can only be printed in its original form unless it is processed with optical character recognition software to turn it into editable text. A downloaded document is a file that was located on one computer system and transferred ("downloaded") to another computer. Files obtained through the Internet, for example, are typically "downloaded" from some other computer on the net.

The foundation for a scanned or downloaded document arises from the source of that document. Records or reports downloaded from computers maintained by government agencies are covered by Rule

901(b)(7) and Rule 902(5). Newspapers and periodicals are covered by Rule 902(6). Other scanned or downloaded documents are established as trustworthy by the testimony of a witness that the document "is what it is claimed to be" or testimony that a process or system produced an accurate result. See Section 1.1.

Example

(After establishing competence and relevance)

Q. What is Exhibit 14?

A. That is a copy of one of the research resources I used in preparing my article on the problems with water pollution coming from the XYZ Company's plant on the Thick Water River.

Q. Where did you get it?

A. I got it from the University of Arawan's library of graduate research papers.

Q. How did you get it?

A. I went onto the Internet and searched for the subjects "water pollution" and "river." I found the university's home page, which listed the papers available. I downloaded the files covering both water pollution and rivers that were available. Exhibit 14 was one of those papers.

Q. What is the process or system that you used to retrieve material from the Internet?

A. I subscribe to a commercial Internet service that provides a browser to locate specific information and downloading capability to get the information that has been located. My personal computer is connected to the commercial Internet service.

Q. What can you tell us about whether this process or system produces an accurate result?

A. I have used it many times, and the copies of the files that I retrieved were accurate.

Q. Is the content of Exhibit 14 exactly the same as the content of the file you retrieved from the University?

A. Yes, it is.

Q. Your Honor, we move the admission of Exhibit 14 in evidence. Its trustworthiness is established under Rule 901(b)(9) by the process or system by which it was produced.

Opposing Counsel: Objection, hearsay.

Counsel: This document is not hearsay. Under Rule 801(c), it is not offered to prove the truth of its contents, only to prove that reasonable research was done.

Court: Objection overruled.

Opposing Counsel: Objection. Original document.

Counsel: It is a qualified duplicate. The original is in the library at the university. An electronic duplicate has been made for access via the university's Internet home page. This duplicate was re-recorded when it was downloaded, producing another exact duplicate. Each duplicate is treated as an original under Rule 1001.

Court: Objection overruled. Exhibit 14 is admitted.

In this example, the offer of a document on the basis that it is not offered to prove the truth of the content should trigger a request for an instruction to that effect. See Section 1.8 on jury instructions.

There is no provision of Rule 901 or Rule 902 that specifically contemplates materials retrieved electronically from the Internet. Under Rule 902(5), materials retrieved from government sites on the Internet can be qualified as having been "issued by public authority." Material available on the Internet has been "issued" by the site from which it is retrieved. Rule 902(6), however, covers newspapers and periodicals in their "printed" form. It seems logical that materials used in printed form and also available in computer-readable form from the Internet should not be disqualified as evidence just because the particular printed version offered in evidence came via a computer.

The broadest rule applicable to Internet materials is Rule 901(b)(9) which allows authentication through description of a process or system that produces an accurate result. This allows the proponent to establish that the exhibit is what it purports to be.

Scanned and downloaded documents are hearsay, unless exempted under Rule 801, and must be brought within an exception to the hearsay rule. In addition to being hearsay themselves, these documents may also contain other hearsay, in which case, under Rule 805, the proponent will need to qualify each part of the hearsay within hearsay under an exception.

Scanned and downloaded documents are also subject to the original document rule. Downloaded documents are duplicates under Rule 1001(4). Downloading is an "electronic re-recording" which accurately reproduces the original. On occasion, however, there may be some electrical or software interference that disrupts the download and causes a gap in the downloaded document. Normally the burden of raising this challenge should be on the opponent. Scanned documents should also qualify as duplicates under Rule 1001(4). The scanning process qualifies as one of the "techniques which accurately reproduces the original."

The scanning process makes an exact duplicate in a way analogous to the normal office copier. Confusion is sometimes caused by the processing of scanned documents by optical character reader software into computer readable text. The scanned document is like a photograph. It is an exact copy but cannot be "read" by the computer. Once the optical character reader software has processed the scanned image, every letter has been identified. This software may make occasional mistakes. Blurred, faded, or poorly printed originals may increase the error rate. Normally your exhibit will be the scanned document (the "photo" of the original) and not the text version that has been converted to computer-readable format. In this case, the mistakes in the text version are irrelevant. If for some reason you are using a printout from the text file rather than the image file as your exhibit, the burden should be on the opponent of the exhibit to demonstrate that under the circumstances in which the optical character reader software processing was done, it would be unfair to admit the duplicate in lieu of the original.

2.3.5   Digital Signatures

The signature on an e-mail, fax, workgroup, or other computer-generated text document may have been scanned from an exemplar and affixed as a graphic insert. The process is as follows: (1) a person signs a blank piece of paper; (2) that paper is put through a scanner and made into a digital file—like a picture or other non-text material; (3) the digital file containing the signature is stored in a computer until it is needed on a document; (4) when a document is completed that requires a signature, the digital file is called up and a copy is "pasted" into the appropriate place. When the document is printed out or transmitted electronically, an exact copy of the signature will appear on it. In this case, the document itself was never physically "signed." The digital signature is the equivalent of a rubber stamp.

Fraud is considerably easier to accomplish in this context than with actual handwritten signatures. A person's signature can be scanned from any document that he or she in fact signed. The non-signature remainder of the document can be discarded by the software, leaving only the signature which can then be affixed to any other document. The signature is an exact duplicate of the real thing and, as such, is indistinguishable by handwriting analysis. So, to the extent that the signature is digital, the underlying rationale for the evidence rules on signatures—ensuring that they are genuine and preventing fraud—might support a more rigorous foundation. Within the business context, it is useful to provide at least some testimony from a competent witness as to prior practice with digital signatures.

Example

(Assuming relevance; and the document is offered against a party)

Q. Can you identify Exhibit 13?

A. Yes.

Q. What is it?

A. That is a letter from Mr. Bailey agreeing to purchase 5 tons of palm oil for delivery next year.

Q. Whose signature appears on the document?

A. Donald Bailey.

Q. How are you able to recognize the signature?

A. I have seen this signature many times on correspondence I have received.

Q. How did you receive this document?

A. By e-mail.

Q. Have you on prior occasions received a document by e-mail signed by Mr. Bailey?

A. Yes.

Q. How does the form of those prior documents compare to this one?

A. The same. There is an order form and a signature in the box at the bottom.

Q. Have you acted on previous occasions on the basis of this kind of signature from Mr. Bailey?

A. Yes.

Q. Were those transactions completed satisfactorily?

A. Yes.

Q. Your Honor, we offer Exhibit 13 in evidence.

Opposing Counsel: Objection, lack of foundation. This is a computer copy of a signature; it could have been put there by anyone.

Counsel: We have provided an adequate foundation. The witness is competent; she has been involved in prior transactions with Mr. Bailey and has personal knowledge. The exhibit is relevant. This is part of the contested course of dealing. The witness has identified the exhibit properly. And the trustworthiness of the exhibit has been established under Rule 901(b)(4). The appearance and contents are similar to other uncontested transactions and, taken in conjunction with circumstances, this evidence is sufficient to support a finding that Exhibit 13 is what it is claimed to be, namely, a document signed by Donald Bailey. If Mr. Bailey's counsel wishes to put in evidence contesting the signature, that would be considered by the jury in weighing the evidence, but Exhibit 13 should be admissible on the present foundation.

Court: Objection overruled.

Opposing Counsel: Objection, hearsay.

Counsel: This is not hearsay. Mr. Bailey is a party. This is a statement by Mr. Bailey offered against him. Under Rule 801(d)(2), this statement is not hearsay.

Court: Objection overruled.

Opposing Counsel: Objection, original document. This is a copy.

Counsel: This is not a copy, it is an original. There is nothing on this printout that was not exactly the same as the message received on the computer system. Under Rule 1001(3), any printout that reflects accurately data stored on a computer is an original. I can put these questions to the witness if the court would prefer.

Court: That will not be necessary. Objection overruled.

Opposing Counsel: Objection, unfair prejudice, confusion and misleading the jury, and delay and waste of time. This signature will be mistaken by the jury for a real signature and it will require a substantial amount of additional trial time and witness testimony to make this point.

Counsel: Exhibit 13 may be excluded on these grounds under Rule 403 only if its probative value is substantially outweighed by the danger of unfair prejudice and so on. The burden is on opposing counsel to make the case that there is a substantial outweighing, and this has not been done.

Court: Objection overruled. You may proceed.

As pointed out in Chapter 1, just because you succeed in laying a proper foundation does not necessarily mean you can succeed in overcoming hearsay, original document, and policy objections. You should consider each separately.

There is a separate jurisprudence on the admissibility of fax documents that have been signed in person. In this case, there is an original that was signed in person. The original was then sent by fax, and the recipient has the fax copy. So long as the fax is a duplicate, it is as sufficient as the original.[10]

If the court treats the header information (the imprint added by the sending and receiving fax machines indicating time, date, page number, and machine identifier) as separate information, then the fax is not a duplicate, and either a separate foundation must be provided for these marks, or under Rule 1004 the original must be accounted for. The better practice is to treat the fax header lines as if they were the cancellation of a stamp by the post office and not requiring any separate foundation unless a genuine question is raised as provided by Rule 1003(1) on the admissibility of duplicates.

2.4 PUBLISHED AND MULTI-ORIGINAL DOCUMENTS

Occasionally an excerpt from a book, pamphlet, or other document which was created as one of many "originals" will be needed in evidence.

2.4.1 Foundation

The requirements of competence, relevance, identification, and trustworthiness must be established for any published work. See Section 1.1. The sponsoring witness must have used or relied on the published material in some way that is relevant to the issues in the case. Pay particular attention to the definition of relevance under Rule 401. It is often the case that published works cannot be demonstrated to "make the existence of any fact that is of consequence to the determination of the action more probable or less probable than it would be without the evidence."

Most published works do not require extrinsic evidence of trustworthiness. Two categories of published documents are self-authenticating. Under Rule 902(5), "Books, pamphlets, or other publications purporting to be issued by a public authority" are self-authenticating. Similarly, under Rule 902(6), "Printed materials purporting to be newspapers or periodicals" need no extrinsic evidence of authenticity as a condition of admissibility.

Published works that are written by nongovernmental authors and that are not newspapers or periodicals could be authenticated using the general provision of Rule 901(a), by presenting testimony "sufficient to support a finding that the matter in question is what its proponent claims."

Excerpts from published works are used by experts to bolster their testimony. Published works are readily authenticated in this context by an expert who regularly uses the book in his or her professional work.

2.4.2 Objections

All published materials are out-of-court statements, so it is necessary to identify an exemption or exception to the hearsay rule in order to have portions admitted in evidence. See Section 1.3.1.

Under some circumstances, a passage in a published work may be used to explain why a person took a particular action—that the person relied on published authority, for example. In this case, under Rule 801(c) the published work is not hearsay because it is not offered to prove the truth of its contents. If the book or pamphlet was published by a party opponent, it is "not hearsay" under Rule 801(d)(2). The same may be true if the book is used by the party opponent in its business or is otherwise endorsed by it—that is, the use or endorsement is what is sought to be proved, not the truth of the contents. If the witness who is testifying wrote the book or published material, it may be used to support the witness's testimony as a prior statement under Rule 801(d)(1), but only on rebuttal after an attack on the witness for recent fabrication or improper influence or motive.

In using a book or published work to cross-examine a witness about inconsistent statements, you must distinguish between the lay witness and the expert witness. A book written by a lay witness that contains statements inconsistent with the current testimony cannot be admitted in evidence, under Rule 801(d)(1), because it is not a statement that was "given under oath subject to the penalty of perjury at a trial, hearing, or other proceeding, or in a deposition." However, a book written by or acknowledged as authoritative by an expert falls under a special exception in Rule 803(18). That rule allows statements from published works to be read in evidence, although the book or excerpts may not be received as exhibits.

A published work may fall under three other hearsay exceptions. The work may qualify as recorded recollection under Rule 803(5), as a public record or report under Rule 803(8), or a stock market report or commercial publication under Rule 803(17).

Published works do not raise original document objections. Rule 1001(3) provides that an original is "any counterpart intended to have the same effect by a person . . . issuing it." All identical books produced in a single printing or press run, for example, are intended by the publisher to have the same effect, and all qualify as originals.

Published works generally raise policy objections of unfair prejudice, undue delay, and wasting time. Needless presentation of cumulative evidence is also an occasional ground for objecting. See Section 1.3.3. Most courts will not allow you to offer an entire published book in evidence unless the book itself is at issue, as might be the case in a copyright or libel action. Jurors are intimidated by the prospect that they must read the entire book and, as an ancillary issue, may defer entirely to the one or two jurors who do so. Some experienced judges recount instances where an entire published work went to the jury room and an industrious juror who read it came up with a novel theory not considered by any of the lawyers based on passages not at issue in the case. To avoid this kind of unfair prejudice, most courts limit the proponent of the exhibit to excerpts.

2.4.3 Production and Tactics

If you need something from a published work, be sure to have the entire work available in the courtroom and show it to the jury. Otherwise, the more skeptical jurors will think you are keeping something from them.

When you are making a point to the jury and you pick up a book that contains material important to your case, handle it with respect. Convey by your action that this is a worthy source. If you are using excerpts, you will probably want to have the witness explain generally what is in the book and why the excerpt has been singled out for particular attention.

A visualizer or a visual presenter is a good way to show excerpts from a book because the entire book can be placed on the surface below the transmitting camera, making it clear to the jury that you are not tampering with what is in the published book. See Section 9.5.1. An opaque projector has the same advantage and is a lower cost display option. See Section 9.4.1.

2.5 SUMMARIES OF DOCUMENTS

The rules make available a valuable aid in dealing with large quantities of documents or information. Under Rule 1006, a summary may be admitted in evidence in place of the underlying documents.

2.5.1 Foundation

A summary of data or documents can be brought in under Rule 1006 without any detailed foundation. There are three simple requirements: First, the material being summarized must be voluminous to an extent that it cannot be examined conveniently in court. This can mean anywhere from 10 to 10,000 pages of materials depending on the importance of the document and its susceptibility to summarization. Second, the underlying material must itself be admissible. Third, the voluminous materials underlying the summary must have been made available to the other side at some point. This does not mean that they have to have been presented in a group. As long as they were turned over sometime during discovery and have been identified, that will suffice.

Example

Q. Ms. Wilson, I show you what has been marked as Exhibit 47 and ask you if you can identify that.

A. Yes, that has all of the invoices that involve shipments of parts to the XYZ Company.

Q. Ms. Wilson, how many pages of documents are included in Exhibit 47?

A. About 200.

Q. I show you what has been marked as Exhibit 48, and ask if you can identify that?

A. Yes, that is a summary I prepared of the documents in Exhibit 47.

Q. Ms. Wilson, does Exhibit 48 fairly and accurately summarize the documents in Exhibit 47?

A. Yes.

Q. Your Honor, the documents included in Exhibit 47 were delivered to Ms. Clark, counsel for plaintiff, in response to plaintiff's first request for documents. We move the admission in evidence of Exhibit 48.

In this case, Exhibit 47, which is the collection of documents underlying the summary, need never be moved in evidence because the witness will use only the summary.

There are two kinds of challenges to foundation you could face here: (1) the underlying documents are inadmissible; and (2) the summary contains something that is not to be found in the underlying documents. The latter objection may be made when opposing counsel believes that the summary is an inaccurate reflection of the underlying documents or that the witness has injected his or her own opinion into the exhibit as well as information from the voluminous documents. Rule 1008(c) suggests that the accuracy of a summary is a jury question, but the judge will usually require opinion not reflected in the underlying documents to be removed.

There is no requirement that a summary, in order to be accurate, must include your opponent's version of the facts as well as your own.

2.5.2 Objections

No hearsay objection applies to a summary on the ground that the person who prepared the summary is not the one testifying about it.

The commentators agree that the underlying documents, which are available to the other side, adequately substitute for the person who prepared the summary.[11] Generally it is better practice not to lift quotes out of the underlying documents for use in the summary, but to make an "independent" summary so that your opponent cannot argue that you are using the summary as a backdoor device to admit hearsay statements from the documents.

The original document objection does not apply to a summary. Rule 1006 on summaries is, itself, an exception to the original document rule.

The titles used on a summary chart may draw a policy objection if they can be characterized by your opponent as unfair or as having independent meaning or if they are conclusory or argumentative as to an issue in the case. For example, if the documents are bank records and the issue is whether payments were made, a title or heading of "Payments Made" may draw a successful objection. See Section 1.3.3.

2.5.3 Production and Tactics

Summary exhibits are very useful for a witness who has to go through a long series of documents where the main point is that the documents exist, or that the contract provisions have certain requirements, or that there are certain similarities and differences. This lets the fact-finder follow along without difficulty and keeps the witness from having to refer to extensive documents or notes.

In order to qualify the summary, you must represent to the court that the underlying documents have been disclosed before trial. There is no precise time limit; the rule requires only a "reasonable time." Reasonableness requires sufficient time to allow opposing counsel to prepare for cross-examination and to prepare his or her own summary if necessary. It is important to keep a log showing all the documents used in the summary and the date on which they were delivered to your opponent.

Normally you will want to produce the summary in two ways: an 8½ x 11" size and a blowup to be displayed for the jury. It is useful to have an 8½ x 11" copy for your exhibit book and to hand up to the court.

The tactical question arises whether to disclose the proposed summary to the other side before trial in order to seek a stipulation on admissibility or a pretrial ruling. As the underlying documents must be submitted before trial and as the court will usually allow time for your opponent to examine a summary for the purpose of making objections, it is usually a good idea to disclose summaries to the other side at the pretrial stage. Sometimes it is possible to use a summary in depositions during discovery of the other side's witness and to remove the bases for any objection in that manner.

Another tactical consideration is whether to have the witness who will use the summary participate in its preparation. This is not required under the rules in order to have the summary admitted, but it is very useful in fending off cross-examination about the accuracy of the summary.

The final tactical consideration is whether to offer the underlying documents in evidence once the summary is admitted. Some lawyers like to do this for the sake of completeness of the record, although the underlying documents may add nothing but volume. You should consider the risk. An enterprising judge or juror may examine the underlying documents and decide that the summary is inadequate in some respect. This conclusion may be wrong, but if it is reached after the case is submitted, you will never have the opportunity to correct it.

2.6 DEPOSITION AND OTHER TRANSCRIPTS

There are two principal uses to be made of deposition and other transcripts at trial: (1) to cross-examine an adverse witness by impeaching him or her with prior inconsistent statements made under oath at a prior deposition, and (2) to substitute entirely for the personal appearance of a witness.[12] Occasionally it will also be useful to offer a summary of the deposition or other testimony of a witness who is not central to the case. The use of deposition transcripts should be planned carefully before trial so that the technical requirements of the rules can be met and the transcripts themselves can be handled with ease in the courtroom.

Because all deposition transcripts contain out-of-court statements, they are governed by the hearsay rules. Special exceptions have been created, however, for deposition transcripts. Some of these are in the Federal Rules of Civil Procedure and others are in the Federal Rules of Evidence.[13]

The rules have a number of technical requirements that are important to master. These technical requirements rest on three factors:

- whose deposition: some rules distinguish between the deposition of a party to the action (including various kinds of employees and agents) and the deposition of a witness who is not a party;

- whose use of the deposition: some rules permit the use of a deposition by any party; others permit use only by an adverse party; and

- what use of the deposition: some rules permit use for any purpose once the requirements as to the deponent and the party using the deposition are met; others permit use only for a specified purpose.

Each of these technical requirements is discussed below with respect to specific examples. The examples, however, do not cover all uses of depositions at trial.

2.6.1 Foundation for Cross-Examination

The most common use of deposition transcripts is in cross-examination. During direct examination the witness says something directly contrary to a statement he or she made at deposition some months earlier. Rule 801(d)(1)(4) applies here:

> A statement is *not* hearsay if . . . [t]he declarant testifies at the trial or hearing and is subject to cross-examination concerning the statement, and the statement is . . . *inconsistent* with the declarant's testimony, and was given under oath, subject to the penalty of perjury . . . in a deposition. (Emphasis added.)

The deposition transcript can be used for impeachment as soon as a foundation can be laid that this witness was the one who appeared at the deposition from which the transcript you are using was produced.

Example

Q. Ms. Woods, weren't you heavily in debt at the time you executed the document that has been marked as plaintiff's Exhibit 6?

A. No.

Q. Ms. Woods, on October 5, 1988 you appeared for your deposition in my office at 1700 Pennsylvania Avenue, N.W. in Washington, D.C., right?

A. Yes.

Q. At that time you were put under oath and you swore to tell the truth, did you not?

A. Yes.

Q. At that time I asked you the following question, which appears on page 47, beginning at line 12, of the transcript of that deposition *(reading from the transcript):*

"Weren't you heavily in debt at the time you signed the letter to Mrs. Vulture?"
and you said in response to that question:
"Yes."

You remember that, don't you?

A. Yes, I said that.

Q. And that was the truth, wasn't it?

A. Yes.

When the witness admits that she said something different at deposition and does not argue about what it was, it is not necessary (or proper) to put the deposition transcript in evidence as an exhibit.

Rule 613(a) does away with any requirement that the witness be shown his or her prior statement before being examined on it. The rule does require, however, that the prior statement be shown to counsel on request. This can be done by referring during questioning to the page and line number of the deposition transcript where the witness's statement appears, assuming that opposing counsel has his or her own copy of the transcript.

Sometimes a witness will be reluctant to say he or she remembers saying something different. In that case the deposition transcript is used.

Example

(Same circumstances as above)

Q. You remember that, don't you?

A. I don't remember that.

Q. Your Honor, I request that this excerpt from the deposition transcript, duly attested by the court reporter, be marked as plaintiff's Exhibit 33 and admitted in evidence.

Court: Admitted.

Counsel: Your Honor, may I read what has been marked as plaintiff's Exhibit 33 to the jury?

Court: You may.

Counsel: *(Reads excerpt again)*

Any use of an excerpt from a deposition transcript, like any other document, is subject to Rule 1006 which provides: "When a . . . recorded statement or part thereof is introduced by a party, an adverse party may require the introduction at that time of any other part or any other writing or recorded statement which ought in fairness to be considered contemporaneously with it." Therefore, when you quote a part of a transcript, opposing counsel may insist on having more of the surrounding pages read into the record at the same time.

2.6.2 Foundation for Substitution for a Live Witness

A number of situations may arise where deposition transcripts would be helpful at trial because the witness is not going to appear at all. This occurs when: (1) the witness is busy and would prefer not to appear as a matter of convenience; (2) the witness refuses to appear; (3) the witness cannot appear because he or she is dead, ill, or incapacitated; (4) the witness is adverse and you would prefer that he or she not appear as a part of your case because you don't want to take that risk. In each of these cases, helpful portions of the deposition transcript can be used at trial. In planning for such situations, if the deposition transcript is likely to be used at trial, you should consider videotaping the deposition. See discussion of videotaped depositions in Section 6.3. Without a very interesting person in the witness chair reading the transcript, it is difficult to conduct a reading from a transcript for more than 10 minutes and sustain the attention of any but the most avid juror.

If your witness is busy and would prefer not to appear at trial, you are entitled as a matter of right to use his or her deposition if the witness is located more than 100 miles from the place of the trial or out of the United States (so long as you didn't temporarily send him or her there). Fed.R.Civ.P. 32(a)(3)(B). If the witness is closer than 100 miles, you must request the court's permission to use the deposition in place of live testimony. Fed.R.Civ.P. 32(a)(3)(E). This method is often used for expert testimony from medical doctors or other specialists who are needed to meet emergencies or other important commitments that would be interrupted if they were called to testify.

The format is quite simple:

Example

Court: Call your next witness.

Counsel: Our next witness is Dr. Helen Siegfried. Dr. Siegfried is the botanist who examined the plant growth at plaintiff's sheep ranch after defendant's nuclear generating plant came on line.

We ask the court's leave under Rule 32(a)(3)(E) to present Dr. Siegfried's testimony by videotape of her deposition which was taken three months ago.

The notice required by the rule was given to defendant in our notice of her deposition. I have a copy of that notice here and am handing it up to the Court.

Dr. Siegfried has extensive teaching commitments and would have to cancel large classes of over 200 students at the university if she were to schedule an appearance in this trial.

We have an affidavit from Dr. Siegfried to this effect and we
have served a copy on defendant *(hands up the affidavit to the
Court)*.

Court: Any objection?

Opposing Counsel: We object on the ground that teaching
commitments are not the sort of "exceptional circumstances"
contemplated by Rule 32(a)(3)(E).

Court: Are you injured in any way by using the videotape instead
of Dr. Siegfried's live testimony?

Opposing Counsel: Yes, there are several new lines of inquiry we
would like to pursue with Dr. Siegfried on cross-examination
that were not explored at her deposition.

Court: Did you have notice that they might seek to use the
videotaped deposition?

Opposing Counsel: Yes.

Court: Objection overruled. You may proceed with the videotape.

Counsel: May I have this videocassette marked as Exhibit 9?

Reporter: *(Marks)*

Counsel: Let the record reflect that I am handing the
videocassette that has been marked as Exhibit 9 to counsel for
defendant. This is the same videotape as the copy we supplied
to the defendants after the deposition.

Opposing Counsel: *(Looks)*

Counsel: At this time we offer the tape that has been marked as
Exhibit 9 in evidence.

Opposing Counsel: Objection; hearsay.

Counsel: The videotape of the deposition is admissible under Rule
803(24) which is the general exception for the hearsay rule.
This covers situations in which the Federal Rules of Civil
Procedure allow the use of a deposition transcript at trial. We
have met the requirements of the civil procedure rules in this
instance.

Court: Overruled.

Counsel: Your Honor, may we play Exhibit 9 at this time?

Court: You may.

Under Rule 104(a), the availability of the witness is a preliminary
question and the rules of evidence do not apply. An affidavit is, therefore,
appropriate.

This example deals with a third party witness. If the witness is a party opponent or the employee or agent of a party opponent, then Rule 801(d)(2) takes the deposition transcript out of the hearsay rule.

If the witness refuses to appear, you must proceed under Rule 32(a)(3)(D) and Rule 804(b)(5), both of which permit the use of a deposition if the witness has failed to appear after a subpoena has been issued.

Example

Court: Call your next witness.

Counsel: Our next witness is Thomas Tully. Pursuant to Rule 32(a)(3)(D), we intend to present Mr. Tully's testimony through the transcript of his deposition. We have subpoenaed Mr. Tully to appear, but he has failed to do so. Mr. Tully has on previous occasions explained that he cannot appear because if he takes time off from work he will be fired.

May I have this subpoena marked as Exhibit 36?

Reporter: *(Marks)*

Counsel: Let the record show that I am handing what has been marked as Exhibit 36 to counsel for plaintiffs. Exhibit 38 is the transcript of Mr. Tully's deposition signed by Robert Redmond, certified shorthand reporter.

At this time we offer Exhibit 38 in evidence.

Court: Any objection? Admitted.

Counsel: May we read portions of the deposition into the record?

Court: Proceed.

(Single or dual reading by lawyers; see subsection 2.6.5)

If the witness is physically unable to appear, you will need to proceed under Rule 32(a)(3)(A) or (C) and Rule 804(a)(4) and (b)(1), both of which permit the use of a deposition if the witness is dead, ill, infirm, or incarcerated. The form is the same as the preceding example except that the foundation exhibit is usually an affidavit instead of the subpoena. An affidavit is appropriate because, under Rule 104(a), the availability of the witness is a preliminary question and the rules of evidence do not apply.

If the witness is adverse and you do not want to call him or her during your direct case, but you need some specific facts in order to make out the elements of your cause of action, you can turn to Rule 32(a)(2) if the witness is a party or if you can make a showing that the witness is an officer, director, or managing agent of a party.[14] Generally these aspects of foundation are established during discovery. Any statement provided during discovery is admissible.

Example

Counsel: Your Honor, at this point I wish to turn to the deposition of Elvin Emwell, taken under oath before Les Martin, a certified shorthand reporter. I intend to offer pages 20-25, 31-52, and 67. May I approach the bench?

Court: You may.

Counsel: I am handing up a copy of the deposition transcript of Mr. Emwell. May I proceed?

Court: You may.

Counsel: By way of foundation, I refer to the Defendant's Response to Plaintiff's Requests for Admissions as follows:

Response to Request #47: the employment of Elvin Emwell with Daniel Welding Co. as the manager of the bookkeeping department was admitted.

Response to Request #48: the fact that indexing and filing invoices was within Elvin Emwell's scope of employment was admitted.

The excerpts from Elvin Emwell's deposition that are offered in evidence have to do with actions taken by Mr. Emwell with respect to certain invoices.

Court: *(to opposing counsel)* Any objections?

Opposing Counsel: We object on the ground that Mr. Emwell is not a managing agent and therefore the deposition may not be used under Rule 32(a)(2).

Counsel: Mr. Emwell's title is a manager. When the business itself calls an employee a manager, that is sufficient.

Court: Objection overruled.

If the point is narrow and can be made effectively with a ten-minute excerpt from a deposition, this procedure is usually much more efficient than calling a live witness. When a deposition transcript is used, it is not necessary to show the transcript to opposing counsel before using it. Counsel are assumed to have copies of transcripts, and a reference to the page numbers is sufficient. It is necessary, however, to be sure that the judge has a copy on the bench.

2.6.3 Foundation for Summaries of Transcripts

If it is necessary to put in evidence long portions of a deposition transcript because of an absent witness, an alternative technique is to prepare a deposition summary under Rule 1006. See discussion of summaries at Section 2.5. The summary reads like a narrative and shortens the presentation while preserving the necessary details.

Example

> Elvin Emwell has been employed at the XYZ Co. for five years. His duties were to index and file all invoices for industrial grade diamonds. Mr. Emwell received an invoice for six industrial grade diamonds of one-half carat each from the ABC Co. Mr. Emwell filed the invoice in the normal course of the company's business and the files where he stored the invoice were subsequently destroyed through no fault of the XYZ Co.

This narrative could summarize 80 to 100 pages of deposition transcript. Because the summary, once read into the record, becomes a part of the transcript, generally it does not have an exhibit number.

In deciding whether to use a summary of a deposition, consider carefully that, without a very engaging "reader" on the witness stand, ten minutes is about the longest "reading" of a deposition segment that is effective for juror comprehension. Effective reading of depositions at trial, especially using someone to read the witness responses, requires a lively, interesting, effective reader. The deposition summary is often a useful alternative. Normally the narrative is submitted to opposing counsel during the pretrial proceedings for additions or corrections. Any disputes that cannot be resolved by the parties are decided by the judge at pretrial conference.

2.6.4 Objections

It is rare that all of any deposition or any substantial portion of a deposition will be admissible. Usually the pretrial conference includes designation of portions of the deposition to be admitted as evidence at trial. Under this procedure, the opponent submits objections and counter-designations and the court rules on all disputes before trial. Some judges, however, require all objections to be made in open court.

There are essentially only four objections when a party seeks to use a portion of a deposition transcript at trial: compliance with the rules on use of deposition transcripts, relevance, objections preserved for trial, and truncated selection.

Compliance with the rules

If the deposition transcript is being used in substitution for a witness, an objection may be raised if the technical requirements of the rules are not met.

- If the witness is more than 100 miles from the place of trial, Fed.R.Civ.P. 32(a)(3)(B) applies. If the deposition transcript itself does not establish the witness's location as one that can be judicially noticed as more than 100 miles from the courthouse, you will need an affidavit to that effect.
- If the witness is closer than 100 miles and "available" but has other commitments, Fed.R.Civ.P. 32(a)(3)(E) applies and you must make a motion for permission to use the deposition.
- If the witness is closer than 100 miles and refuses to appear, Fed.R.Civ.P. 32(a)(3)(D) and Fed.R.Evid. 804(b)(1) apply and you must have served a subpoena and produce it in court.
- If the witness is closer than 100 miles but is dead, ill, infirm, or incarcerated, Fed.R.Civ.P. 32(a)(3)(A) or (C) and Fed.R.Evid. 804(a)(4) and (b)(1) apply and you will need an affidavit as to the facts with respect to the witness's unavailability.
- If the witness is adverse, Fed.R.Civ.P. 32(a)(2) applies and you must make a showing that the witness is an officer, director, or managing agent of a party.

In most cases, deposition transcript selections are stipulated by the parties. It is useful to seek stipulations or to narrow the issues by negotiation wherever possible.

Relevance

The latitude provided in discovery depositions is very broad and by the time the matter reaches trial, the issues may have been narrowed by stipulation, responses to request for admission, or rulings by the court. If the section of the deposition to be read includes any material that cannot meet the test of relevance under Rule 401, the nonrelevant material can be excluded on objection.

Example

(After the portion of the deposition transcript has been offered)

Court: Any objection?

Opposing Counsel: Yes. There is not an adequate foundation for this testimony, Your Honor. It is not relevant. May we approach the bench, Your Honor?

Court: You may.

(At sidebar out of hearing of jury)

Opposing Counsel: Part of this transcript describes the actions of
 Elvin Emwell in trying to open one of the invoice files. The file
 had been rigged with a bomb and Mr. Emwell's hand was
 blown off. The police never found the bomber and the bomb
 incident is not relevant here. This case has to do only with
 payment on an invoice for 100 industrial grade diamonds. The
 invoice for the diamonds was in the file cabinet that was
 blown up, but we object to pages 31-52 where the bomb blast
 is described.

Court: *(to proponent)* Why do you need the description of the
 bomb?

Counsel: Mr. Emwell has first hand knowledge and is therefore
 competent. Mr. Emwell's actions in dealing with the records
 for the industrial diamonds that are at issue here are
 relevant. The act of opening the files is a part of what
 happened. There is no challenge to the accuracy of Mr.
 Emwell's description. We have satisfied all foundation
 requirements.

Opposing Counsel: The receipt and filing of the invoice are
 relevant. The bomb blast is not at issue in the case and is not
 relevant.

Court: Pages 31-52 are excluded; you may proceed with the rest.

The testimony about the bomb blast might also have been
challenged as unfairly prejudicial under Rule 403. The challenge to
relevance comes first, however, because Rule 403 permits the court to
exclude evidence that, although relevant, has probative value that is
substantially outweighed by the danger of unfair prejudice. If you want
to have two opportunities to exclude this evidence, you could start with
relevance and get to unfair prejudice only if the court found relevance.
Under Rule 32(d)(3)(A) of the Federal Rules of Civil Procedure,
objections to relevance are preserved even if not made at the deposition.
The rule contains an exception for objections that the examining lawyer
might have cured at the deposition, but the exception almost never
applies to relevance objections made at trial.

Objections preserved for trial

Rule 32(b) of the Federal Rules of Civil Procedure states the general
rule with respect to the admissibility of deposition transcripts:

> [O]bjection may be made at the trial . . . to receiving in
> evidence any deposition or part thereof for any reason
> which would require the exclusion of the evidence if the
> witness were then present and testifying.

This general rule is subject to two exceptions. The first is a narrow
exception under Rule 28(b) that covers foreign deposition. The second
is Rule 32(d)(3) that provides, under certain circumstances, for a waiver
of objections not made at the deposition.

Rule 32(d)(3)(A) provides:

> Objections to the competency of a witness or to the
> competency, relevancy, or materiality of testimony are
> not waived by failure to make them before or during the
> taking of the deposition, unless the ground of the
> objection is one which might have been obviated or
> removed if presented at that time.

The rule says that objections *are not waived* unless the condition is met.
Therefore, the lawyer who did the examination at deposition must make
the showing that he or she could have avoided the objection at the
deposition. Under Rule 104(a), this showing can be accomplished by
affidavit. No personal appearance by the witness is required.

Rule 32(d)(3)(B) provides:

> Errors and irregularities occurring at the oral
> examination . . . in the form of the questions or answers
> . . . and errors of any kind which might be obviated,
> removed, or cured if promptly presented are waived
> unless seasonable objection thereto is made at the
> deposition.

This rule is phrased differently. Objections *are waived* unless made at
the deposition. Therefore the lawyer who defended the deposition is
bound by the objections made at the deposition and must make the
showing that the objection made at trial is to something that could not
have been obviated, removed, or cured if the objection had been made
at the deposition.

The practical question, under both rules, is what can be termed
"curable" at the deposition and therefore the objection must be made or
waived. With respect to exhibits, the following is a list of the most
common areas where judges find that something was curable under
either Rule 32(d)(3)(A) or Rule 32(d)(3)(B) and therefore objections *not
made* at depositions *are waived*.

Foundation

The identification and trustworthiness elements of foundation may be curable if the questioner uses the opportunity at the deposition to ask the necessary questions. Identification is almost always curable unless a nonunique object or substance is at issue. Trustworthiness may be curable if the questioner could have brought the exhibit under one of the provisions of Rule 901 on methods of authentication or Rule 902 on self-authentication.

Hearsay objection

Hearsay is curable if the statement can be put under one of the exemptions in Rule 801 or one of the exceptions in Rule 803 or Rule 804. If the objection had been made at the deposition and the questioner could have asked the necessary questions to invoke an exemption or exception, the objection is waived for trial. Hearsay that cannot be put under an exception is not curable, and in these cases, the objection would not be waived if not made at the deposition.

Original document objection

Original document problems are generally curable. The questioner at a deposition can establish the location of the original or a duplicate, can establish a foundation for marks or writings on the document that make it a non-duplicate copy, or can bring the exhibit under one of the provisions of Rule 1004 for the use of copies when the original is not available.

Some aspects of the foundation and objections with respect to exhibits generally are found by judges *not* to be curable at a deposition, and these objections even if *not made* at the deposition are *not waived* for trial.

Competence of the witness

State law may determine whether a witness is competent to testify as to a particular matter, and generally these matters are not curable at deposition. Rule 32(d)(3)(A) gives competence of the witness as an example of an objection not waived.

Relevance of the exhibit

See discussion above. Relevance is always fair game.

Policy objections

Unfair prejudice is determined using a balancing test set out in Rule 403. That balancing cannot be done at a deposition, and the unfair prejudice objection is not waived. Confusion of the issues, misleading the jury, undue delay, waste of time, and needless presentation of cumulative evidence can be determined only in the trial context, and therefore these objections are not waived.

Materiality objections

The materiality objection goes to whether the issue as to which the exhibit is relevant is still in the case. See Section 1.3.4. That can be determined only in the context of trial. Rule 32(d)(3)(A) specifically mentions the materiality objection as one that is not waived.

Theoretically any type of objection is curable under a conceivable set of circumstances, but generally judges will not stretch to find something in these categories to be curable unless it is fairly plain on the face of the deposition transcript that the opponent knew the objection was curable and refrained from making it.[15]

Completeness

When a party offers a selection from a deposition transcript, opposing counsel may object and ask that more of the deposition transcript be put in evidence in order to provide a "fair" presentation. See Section 1.3.6. Judges follow different practices in this regard. Rule 106 provides a general opportunity to supplement a writing or recorded statement when only a part is offered by one party. Rule 32(a)(4) provides opposing counsel an opportunity to designate additional portions of a deposition transcript if parts are offered in evidence by the other side. This rule was intended to cover situations where the witness does not appear at all, rather than situations where the witness is being cross-examined. If the excerpt offered during cross-examination is part of an answer or an answer that the witness immediately clarified in subsequent statements during the deposition, most judges will entertain requests by opposing counsel to supplement the exhibit offered. If the exchange with the witness is oral and no exhibit is offered, most judges will not permit an objection that seeks to supplement parts of the deposition testimony, but will require opposing counsel to wait and try to bring out the point on redirect examination.

The completeness objection is of some tactical advantage to your opponent because he or she will thereafter refer to these additions as your exhibit. If you use an excerpt in your part of the case, your opponent, in his or her part of the case, may also introduce without further foundation (although subject to the usual objections) any other part of the deposition transcript that was not put in as a part of your exhibit.

2.6.5 Production and Tactics

The method to be used at trial for presenting the information in a deposition transcript varies substantially depending on the circumstances. Some alternatives are described below.

Display by exhibit

If the relevant passages of the deposition are short, a special exhibit can be prepared such as an enlargement shown on an electronic or digital display system that can move from one passage to another very efficiently and that can zoom in on particular words or highlight passages in color. See discussion in Section 9.5 (electronic display) and Section 9.6 (digital displays). A static display on a foamboard backing or a transparency is a lower cost alternative allowing counsel to focus the fact-finder's attention on the precise words to be emphasized. Such an exhibit is usually an enlargement of part of a page of the deposition transcript. See Section 9.3.2 (foamboard) and Section 9.4.2 (transparencies). Any accurate copy, however, will be permitted if the original of the transcript, prepared by the reporter, is available for comparison.

Reading by lawyer

The lawyer can simply pick up the deposition transcript after it has been admitted in evidence and, after the usual amenities, begin to read to the jury. This is more difficult than it sounds. The lawyer's voice must somehow maintain the jury's interest in what they are hearing. Pacing, inflection, tone and projection are all important. If a long portion is being read, a copy may be displayed on a monitor or given to the jury so they can follow along. It may be wise to read the deposition in portions between the testimony of witnesses, if that will not break up the flow and dilute the meaning.

In reading a deposition excerpt, the lawyer's presentation must be fair. The lawyer may not use a mocking tone of voice when reading the witness's answers or engage in histrionics when reading the important stuff. Being fair usually means being dull. For this reason, unless the passage is very short and the point is very easy to understand, most lawyers prefer either an exhibit, such as a series of excerpts on an electronic or digital display system, or a responsive reading.

Responsive reading

If part or all of a deposition transcript is to be used under this exception, it can be done as a responsive reading by having someone play the role of the witness and actually take the witness stand. This can be done even if the real witness (for example, the opposing party) is sitting in the courtroom.

Example

Q. Your Honor, at this point I wish to turn to the deposition of Daniel Deford, taken under oath before Les Martin, certified shorthand reporter. I intend to offer pages 43 through 52, and pages 56 and 57.

May I have this transcript marked as plaintiff's Exhibit 10?

Reporter: *(Marks)*

Q. May I approach the bench?

Court: Yes.

Q. I am handing up a copy of the transcript.

Court: *(to opposing counsel)* Any objection?

Opposing Counsel: *(makes any objections to the transcript on grounds reserved under Rule 32(d)(3) of the Federal Rules of Civil Procedure)*

Court: *(Rules on objections)*

Q. Your Honor, I would like to request permission to have my colleague Larry Lawrence, who is a lawyer in our firm, take the stand and read the portions of the transcript that record the answers of Daniel Deford to my questions on pages 43 through 52 and pages 56 and 57.

Court: Proceed.

Hand the court reporter a copy of what is about to be read so he or she can follow along and use the written version to check the accuracy of his or her transcript later. Your colleague then takes his place in the witness chair; you read the questions from the transcript (playing the part of the lawyer); and he reads the answers (playing the part of the witness).

This role playing works particularly well if the person reading the answers is the same age and sex as the person whose testimony was taken and if the reader tries to make this testimony come alive. The person doing the reading from the witness stand need not be a lawyer. Many secretaries, administrative assistants, and paralegals are much better at making the part come alive than lawyers are.

One caution: If there is material in the deposition transcript that you would rather not have the jury read, then you should offer an excerpt (even if you have to prepare it and offer it later in the day or the following day) rather than offering the whole transcript.

ENDNOTES

1. *See, e.g.*, 2 *McCormick on Evidence* § 343, at 455.

2. *Henry M. Philo, Lawyer's Desk Reference: Technical Sources for Conducting a Personal Injury Action* (8th ed. Supp. 1995) (§ 1.17 contains a list of handwriting experts).

3. *See, e.g.*, 2 *McCormick on Evidence* § 343, at 455.

4. *See Weinstein's Evidence* § 801(c)[01], 2 *McCormick on Evidence* § 246.

5. *See, e.g.*, 2 *McCormick on Evidence* § 343, at 455.

6. 2 *McCormick on Evidence* § 335, at 415-17.

7. *See, e.g.*, 2 *McCormick on Evidence* § 343, at 455.

8. 2 *McCormick on Evidence* § 225, at 49-51; 5 *Weinstein's Evidence* § 901(b)(4)[01].

9. 2 *McCormick on Evidence* § 343, at 455.

10. *L. Marks & C. Marrion, The Facts on Fax, NAPN Insights* (May 1993).

11. *See, e.g.*, 5 *Weinstein's Evidence* 1006[06].

12. *See David M. Malone & Peter T. Hoffman, The Effective Deposition: Techniques and Strategies That Work*, ch. 16 (NITA, 2d ed. 1996) (thoroughly describing deposition transcripts) (hereinafter *The Effective Deposition*).

13. The two sets of rules are easily distinguishable through their numbering system. The Federal Rules of Civil Procedure are numbered 1 through 86. The Federal Rules of Evidence are numbered 101 through 1103.

14. *See* Rule 804(a)(5) (defining "unavailable witness"). *See also* Rule 801(d)(2) (more broadly defining "party" and allowing your own witness to testify, if the witness has first hand knowledge, as to what an adverse witness said; such testimony is not hearsay under 801(d)(2)).

15. *See The Effective Deposition* §§ 9.4 and 14.5 for a more extensive discussion of curable and non-curable objections.

CHAPTER 3

CHARTS, GRAPHS, TIME LINES, TABLES, AND COMPUTER DATA PRINTOUTS

Documents that display primarily numbers rather than text are qualified readily as exhibits so long as the accuracy of the numbers can be vouched for by a qualified witness. Charts, graphs, time lines, tables, and computer data printouts fall within this "non-text" category of documentary exhibits. These exhibits face a narrower range of objections than the text documents described in Chapter 1 and Chapter 2, but may also face greater skepticism from jurors unless presented carefully. Section 3.1 covers basic charts and graphs. Section 3.2 deals with time lines and tables. Section 3.3 sets out special considerations with respect to computer data printouts.

3.1 CHARTS AND GRAPHS

A chart, as the term is used here, is a simplified, organized display of numerical information using shapes of various kinds. This category includes bar charts and pie charts which are the most common forms used in litigation exhibits. A graph, as the term is used here, is a representation of numerical data by positioning a line or lines. These devices are usually used to help a witness explain the effect or relationship of data and to help the judge or jury understand what the data mean. The chart or graph may have existed in the files of someone connected to the issues in the case or it may have been prepared specially for litigation purposes.

3.1.1 Foundation

This kind of exhibit can be qualified either as evidence or as a testimony aid. See Section 1.1 and Section 1.2. Generally you will want to offer charts and graphs in evidence because the way of organizing the data can qualify as "substantive evidence" and it is valuable to have the organized data before the jury during its deliberations. A chart or graph may be qualified by either a lay witness or by an expert witness.

Lay witness

If the witness is not an expert, the qualification questions for a chart to be admitted in evidence need to demonstrate the competence of the witness by showing first hand knowledge, the relevance of the data shown on the chart, an identification of the chart, and evidence of the trustworthiness of the chart, generally consisting of testimony about the source and accuracy of the information on the chart.

Example

Q. Mr. Wallet, do you know about the amounts of commodities shipped on the S.S. Queenship on its fall voyage?

A. Yes.

Q. How did you come to know about that?

A. I personally handled all of the transactions with respect to those shipments.

Q. How many commodities were involved?

A. There were eight different kinds of things aboard.

Q. What happened to the value of these commodities when the S.S. Queenship was detained in Sri Lanka?

A. Well, the value of the commodities decreased, but the different commodities were affected differently.

Q. I show you what has been marked as Exhibit 37 and if you can identify that?

A. This is a chart that I assisted in preparing with respect to these commodities.

Q. Is the information on that chart accurate?

A. Yes.

Q. Your Honor, we offer Exhibit 37 in evidence.

Court: Admitted.

Q. Your Honor, we have an enlargement of Exhibit 37 so that the jury can see the chart Mr. Wallet is using. May we mark it as Exhibit 37A and display it?

Court: You may.

Q. *(After putting the blowup of the chart on the easel where the jury can see it)* Mr. Wallet, would you tell us what happened to the first commodity when the ship was detained in Sri Lanka?

A. *(Witness explains.)*

This is a chart that was prepared for litigation. It did not exist in the files of the company prior to the time Mr. Wallet began preparing his testimony. Nonetheless, the foundation format is the same. What is important, from a foundation viewpoint, is that the chart is accurate, not when it was prepared.

At the point that this chart was offered in evidence, it is difficult for the opposing counsel to figure out whether it contains hearsay. If the witness has first hand knowledge of the information on the chart, then there is no hearsay objection. If the chart is merely a summary of documents, however, there may be a hearsay objection. For this reason, opposing counsel may ask for voir dire with respect to the exhibit before it is admitted. See discussion in Section 1.7.2.

Alternatively, to qualify the chart as a testimony aid, which will not be admitted in evidence or go to the jury room when the jury deliberates, you need show only that it will aid the witness in the presentation of the testimony or aid the finder of fact in understanding the testimony.

Example

Q. What happened to the value of these commodities when the S.S. Queenship was detained in Sri Lanka?

A. Well, the value of the commodities decreased, but the different commodities were affected differently.

Q. Would it assist you in presenting your testimony about the eight different commodities to use a chart?

A. Yes, it would.

Q. Can you identify the chart that has been marked as Exhibit 37?

A. Yes.

Q. What is it?

A. That is a chart showing the data about the eight commodities on the ship and the effect of the delay in Sri Lanka.

Q. Your Honor, may I display an enlargement of Exhibit 37 on the easel? We have marked the enlargement as Exhibit 37A. This chart is not being offered in evidence. It is merely to assist in the presentation of testimony so that we can move along efficiently.

Court: You may.

Q. Using Exhibit 37A, would you explain what happened to the first commodity?

A. *(Witness explains.)*

In this instance the chart is being used as a testimony aid, and there is no offer in evidence. But before you display the chart to the jury, be sure that the court is in agreement that it is an appropriate testimony aid. A hearsay objection can be made with respect to a testimony aid as well as to an exhibit and, if sustained, will keep the testimony aid from being displayed to the jury. The witness may, of course, continue to use the chart as a part of his personal notes at the witness stand.

It is important, once the exhibit is qualified as a testimony aid, to refrain from leading questions while eliciting the testimony for which the witness is using the chart. The presence of a chart tends to encourage counsel to slip into leading questions, which may draw a disruptive objection.

Expert witness

Rule 703 provides that an expert may use any fact or data in forming his or her opinion whether it was received before, during, or after the occurrence at issue so long as it is "of a type reasonably relied upon by experts in the particular field in forming opinions or inferences upon the subject." The data or the facts that the expert uses need not be admissible in evidence. Therefore the hearsay objection typically is not available. The foundation questions are drawn from the rule.

Example

(After qualification of the witness as an expert and establishing relevance)

Q. Ms. Essex, did you bring with you any charts that would assist in your explanation?

A. Yes. I brought three charts.

Q. May I have these charts marked as plaintiff's Exhibits 39, 40, and 41?

Reporter: *(Marks)*

Q. Let the record reflect that I am showing counsel for defendant what has been marked as Exhibits 39, 40, and 41.

Opposing Counsel: *(Looks)*

Q. Your Honor, may I hand these exhibits up to the bench?

Court: You may.

Q. Ms. Essex, is the information shown on the charts that have been marked as plaintiff's Exhibits 39, 40, and 41 included among the data or facts upon which you base your testimony?

A. Yes.

Q. Is the information shown in the charts of a type reasonably relied upon by experts in your field?

A. Yes, it is.

Q. Is the information in these charts that have been marked as plaintiff's Exhibits 39, 40, and 41 accurate?

A. Yes.

Q. Your Honor, we offer in evidence plaintiff's Exhibits 39, 40, and 41.

Court: Admitted.

Q. Have you produced larger versions of these charts as well?

A. Yes, we have 30 x 40 inch versions.

Q. Are they the same as what has been marked as Exhibits 39, 40, and 41?

A. Yes, exactly the same, just enlarged.

Q. May I have these enlargements marked as plaintiff's Exhibits 39A, 40A, and 41A?

Reporter: *(Marks larger 30 x 40" versions of charts)*

Q. Your Honor, may we display the blowups on the easels for the jury at this time?

Court: You may.

The question with respect to the accuracy of the information on the charts is not necessary in situations in which the chart merely sets forth the factual information on which the expert bases his or her testimony. Because the expert often has no first hand knowledge of these facts, he or she cannot testify whether the information is accurate.

If there is anything unusual about the scale or the way the scale is presented on charts, the foundation should include information about the scale.

Example

(After other foundation questions and before the chart is offered in evidence)

Q. What scale is used on the horizontal axis of the chart that has been marked as Exhibit 45?

A. The horizontal axis shows the dates on which the defendant's trucks delivered rolls of paper to the plaintiff's plant.

Q. Is that a continuous scale?

A. No. The horizontal axis simply shows the exact dates on which the deliveries were made. It is used for the purpose of showing the variation in the amounts of those deliveries.

Q. What scale is used on the vertical axis of this chart?

A. That scale is thousands of two-pound rolls. In other words, the number 5 indicates 5,000 two-pound rolls; the number 10 indicates 10,000 two-pound rolls, and so on.

Q. Is that a continuous scale?

A. Yes. Each marked increment on the vertical axis from 0 at the base to 30 at the top represents one unit of 1,000 two-pound rolls.

(Offer the chart)

If the chart purports to be a summary of evidence already admitted, Rule 1006 may provide yet another alternative for establishing a foundation.[1] See discussion of summaries at Section 2.5.

The foundation for a chart or graph is very straightforward, and there is rarely an objection to the fundamentals. There is no objection based on a failure to produce the person who prepared the chart. It is immaterial who prepared the chart so long as it is presented by a witness as a representation of his or her knowledge or by an expert who used the data in reaching an opinion.

3.1.2   Objections

The hearsay objection may be available when a lay witness does not have first hand knowledge of the information contained in the chart. See Section 1.3.1. Generally no hearsay objection is available when a chart is offered in evidence based on the testimony of an expert. Usually no hearsay problem arises with charts as testimony aids. See Section 1.3.7. A chart, though made out of court, is nevertheless subject to cross-examination through the witness who verifies and uses it. Charts should present information, not quote out-of-court statements. Most charts that deal with numbers and quotes will not be a problem. For example, if someone said that the stock of a new company would sell at 43, the quote or a paraphrase of that statement would be hearsay. There is no hearsay problem, however, if the price "43" is put on a chart along with other data points and the witness explains what the financial consequences would be of a stock price at several of these points, including 43.

Although the original document rules apply, there should be no original document problem with a chart or graph made for litigation purposes. See Section 1.3.2. The "original" is the exhibit itself when the witness using the exhibit testifies that it is accurate. If the witness is using a duplicate made from the original computer printout, for example, that is qualified under Rule 1001(4). An opponent may demand earlier versions of the chart in discovery to show that an expert's opinion changed as his investigation proceeded. But the chart as presented in court summarizes the underlying numbers and, if it is accurate, there is no requirement to produce the "first" original. There is no original document problem with an enlargement. The enlargement is a "duplicate" under Rule 1001(4) and, under Rule 1003, is admissible in evidence to the same extent as the original.

The policy objections under Rule 403 are the most important obstacle to this category of exhibits. These are discussed at Section 1.3.3. The grounds for these objections are highly specific to the exhibit. Generally, as long as the underlying testimony is proper, the charts that assist in the presentation of the testimony will survive challenge. If you use a form of chart for a purpose for which it is not suited, however, you will likely be faced with an objection. As explained below, bar charts, pie charts, and line graphs each have suitable uses. If a bar chart were offered for some unsuitable or inappropriate use, a misleading/confusion objection should be sustained.

If a chart or an enlargement shows only a part of the document the opponent may demand under Rule 106 that any other part of the document be introduced at the same time.

3.1.3 Production

The decisions that go into the production of a chart or graph for use at trial are the most important factors in assuring the success of this type of exhibit.[2] Foundation is rarely a problem and most objections are easily overcome, but the effectiveness of a chart is not achieved just by getting it before the fact-finder. A mass of numbers does not reveal its significance easily. Some observations with respect to specific kinds of charts and their appropriate uses are set out below, preceded by a description of some general factors that affect all charts.

General factors

Design and labeling can make any chart more easily understood and therefore more persuasive. To a large extent, the design and labeling used in a successful chart are independent of the method of presentation of the chart. However, the method of presentation should also be considered carefully at the design stage. An 8½ x 11" version of a chart can be displayed on a video monitor using a digital computer display (see Section 9.6). The same chart can be displayed by a visualizer or a visual presenter using a television monitor (see Section 9.5). Charts can be enlarged and mounted on illustration board or foamboard and displayed on an easel or exhibit frame (see Section 9.3). They can be displayed using slides or transparencies (see Section 9.4). The choice may depend on the expert witness's preference or the budget for the case (see Section 9.1). Anything that is large enough, colorful, and readable will make an impact.

Charts have three important types of labels—the title, the labels for the axes, and the labels for the items shown on the chart. The title should have the largest size lettering and should appear at the top of the chart. It should be very short. A subtitle is preferable to a long main title. The labels for the axes should be concise and should tell exactly what units of measurement are being used. The label for the vertical axis should appear at the top of that axis and the label for the horizontal axis should appear just below the middle of that axis. The labels for pie charts should be set out around the circle. Arrows connecting labels to parts of the chart are ineffective. The labels for items shown on the chart should be as simple as possible. Labels for lines on multiple line charts should be just above or below each line. A legend key for double column or double bar charts should be placed in an appropriate open space. See Section 9.2.2.

The size of the exhibit and its distance rating are critical to the impact that the exhibit will have. Charts and graphs are often perceived by jurors to be difficult to understand and, if they are too small, this problem will be compounded. See Section 9.2.1 on size factors. The use of typefaces and color are covered in Section 9.2.2. These factors are very important in making charts readable and understandable.

Bar charts

There are two kinds of bar charts—vertical and horizontal. A vertical bar chart is one in which the information is conveyed by the relative size of vertical columns or bars. See Fig. 4. The horizontal axis is usually a time factor or the titles of categories being compared and the vertical axis is the measurement factor. A single bar can be subdivided to show effectively the relationship among several factors of different size. See Fig. 5. A time scale on the horizontal axis does not have to be continuous. Specific dates can be picked to illustrate relationships as of the precise dates at issue in the case.

Vertical bar charts are best suited to comparing amounts or emphasizing differences over time. However, they are not very good for showing a trend over time. The line graphs discussed in this section are better for that purpose. Overlays (discussed in Section 9.3.2) are also effective with vertical bar charts to show before and after effects. See Fig. 6 as an example.

Double vertical bar charts are useful in comparing two sets of data over time. See Fig. 7. The bars may be placed side by side, or front and rear. Subdivided double bars can be used if the chart is kept relatively simple. See Fig. 8. Triple bar charts should be used only rarely, because multiple bars are too confusing in a courtroom setting.

Some of the more complicated vertical bar charts used in economic treatises or other publications are not effective in a courtroom. These include floating vertical bars, subdivided double vertical bars and 100-percent vertical bars. The spatial relationships are hard to digest simply by looking at the chart from a distance and the interrelationships often appear to be more complicated than they are.

Positive/negative vertical bar charts are particularly useful for emphasizing profits and losses. The information conveyed by this kind of chart is immediately apparent, and it can be made more effective by using black for the columns indicating profit and red for the columns indicating loss. See Fig. 9. Or, if the positive/negative chart is for the purpose of emphasizing the positive, a pleasant color can be used for the positive and a barely-there pastel for the negative.

Horizontal bar charts have bars that go sideways instead of up and down. A horizontal bar chart typically has the units of measure on the horizontal axis and an identification of the entity being measured on the vertical axis. See Fig. 10. These are best used to compare the size of a number of different items at one specified time. Put the longest bar at the bottom and work up from there if this is compatible with the point being made.

Double horizontal bar charts are useful in comparing items for two time periods. Any more than two bars used for time comparisons, however, can be too confusing for use in the courtroom. Other types of horizontal bar charts, for example subdivided bars, paired bars, and 100 percent bars sometimes used to illustrate scientific or other written materials, are usually too complicated for effective courtroom use. Several sets of simplified bar charts will work better than trying to crowd too much information on one chart.

The principal design factor for a chart is defining the vertical and horizontal axes—deciding what measurements should be shown where. The next design factor is the unit of measurement to be used—hundreds, thousands, or millions. The measurement scale should always start at zero and should be set out in equal units to avoid an objection that the chart is misleading. The broken scale should be avoided if possible as it too invites an objection. With a few exceptions such as a Fahrenheit/Centigrade scale, avoid double scales. Even when used with good color coding these are usually confusing and will very likely draw objections that will be sustained. Comprehension is often enhanced by placing identical vertical scales on both left and right sides.

You also need to consider whether the chart will have a grid background, a line background, or a plain background. The less detail you include in the background, the better the chart will look. A plain background is usually preferable if the material can be understood without reference to lines or grids. Sometimes a one-line reference point will suffice. When the chart is assembled, the background lines or grids should be the lightest, thinnest lines. The vertical axis and horizontal axis should be heavier lines, and the lines for the columns or bars should be the heaviest and most emphatic. You can also use representative shapes in place of plain bars if that helps convey the meaning.

Pie charts

Pie charts are quite familiar to most laymen and are useful for relating the size of the component parts to the size of the whole. See Fig. 11. Pie charts can be very effective if there are not too many parts and if the parts are of substantially different sizes. However, they do not work well for relatively small differences in size. For example, if the parts to be compared are 5 percent, 10 percent, 15 percent, and 70 percent of the whole, it is easy to get a visual picture of their relationship from a pie chart. If the parts to be compared are 12 percent, 14 percent, 15 percent, 18 percent, 19 percent, and 22 percent, and the point to be made arises out of the differences in these percentages, the point will be difficult to convey using a pie chart. A table or vertical bar chart will better illustrate these smaller differences.

Pie charts may require an additional element for the foundation with respect to the scale used. If a section of a pie chart represents 12 percent of the whole, then that section should measure 12 percent of the 360 degree whole or 43.2 degrees. Graphs and charts made with the aid of computer graphics will present no problem in this regard as the computer will automatically make the necessary computations and measurements to an accuracy of two or three decimal places.

Pie charts should be assembled according to the size of the parts (from largest to smallest) proceeding clockwise from the top. It is usually wise to limit pie charts to five or fewer parts. Color is very important here to help distinguish the parts.

Line graphs

A line graph is generally used to show change over time. The time factor—hours, days, months, years—is plotted on the horizontal axis and the size of the item being displayed is plotted on the vertical axis. The time factor shown on the horizontal axis usually must be equally divided (each increment represents "X" number of days, months, years) in order to avoid an objection with respect to confusion. Fig. 12 shows a simple line graph. Each axis must be labeled clearly.

Line graphs are useful to summarize a long series of data or to compare several series of data. They are best for showing movements or trends, and are not particularly suited to showing amount of change. Bar charts such as those shown in this section are better for this purpose.

When values for two subjects are shown on the same line graph, the lines should contrast sufficiently to avoid confusion. One solid line and one broken line or two different colors are standard methods for accomplishing this objective. See Fig. 13. When two lines are used, clear labeling is important. In addition, if the two lines intersect it may be useful to cut one of the lines so that at the point of intersection one line appears to go underneath the other and the relationship between the two lines is clear. Generally use no more than two lines on any one chart. If more comparisons are necessary, additional charts can be used.

Silhouette line charts show the line graph with the area beneath it filled in. In some cases, these silhouettes make the line graph easier to understand. Fig. 14 shows a simple silhouette line chart. Fig. 15 shows a more sophisticated exhibit using color. Fig. 16 shows a double line graph that has been made into a silhouette chart to emphasize a growing shortfall in funds.

Some alternative illustrative methods for line charts used in publications, such as multiple bands, do not work particularly well in the courtroom. These are visually distracting when the viewer is sitting some distance away. Fig. 17 shows this kind of chart. Line charts in which the points have not been connected with a line are often too difficult to read for effective courtroom use.

The comments with respect to the measurement scales and background for bar charts also apply to line graphs. Always prefer simplicity in constructing charts because most people have some level of resistance to mathematical concepts that will make them think the chart is "hard" to understand. The chart should not be "busy" or look confusing on first glance. Ideally, its message should be immediately apparent.

3.1.4 Tactics

The witness who will be using the chart in the courtroom should do the preparation for his or her testimony using the actual exhibit. The witness must be fully familiar with the chart and able to use it effectively to illustrate points in the testimony. If possible, let the witness practice working with the chart in the courtroom where the testimony will be given.

The most common way of using a chart or graph exhibit in the courtroom is to enlarge it to a 30 x 40" size or to a 40 x 60" size and to mount it on foamboard or other stiff backing so that it can be placed on an easel or exhibit frame. See Section 9.3.1 with respect to the use of easels and exhibit frames in the courtroom. When you use this method of presentation, have smaller 8½ x 11" versions available to hand up to the court, the clerk, and your opponent. Generally the enlargements can be marked with the same exhibit number and the letter A to identify them in a way that is connected to the smaller charts that may be the ones to go to the jury room. If you prepare a three-ring binder of documentary exhibits for the jury, the 8½ x 11" versions of the larger exhibits can be incorporated.

When using a chart in a courtroom, always place it where the fact-finder can see it easily. See the discussion of distance rating in Section 9.2.1. The witness need not use the chart from the witness stand; he or she can come down off the stand and testify standing next to the chart if necessary. You will want to try out the exhibits in the courtroom where they will be used at some time when court is not in session, and perhaps put a small chalk mark or piece of tape on the floor to mark the proper spot for the exhibit. If you cannot place the large exhibit where both the judge and jurors have a good view, make sure the jurors have a direct view and give the judge a small version to refer to from the bench.

In testifying with the aid of a chart, it is important to have the witness keep the record as clear as possible. The witness should not use terms like "here" or "there" when pointing to places on a chart because the reference point will be unclear on the written record. The lawyer should observe this same caution in framing questions about a chart. Reference points should be described plainly (as "the first column or the line labeled 'B') and the chart should always be referred to by its exhibit number.

3.2 TIME LINES AND TABLES

Time lines and tables use layout and format to convey data. Generally time lines are related to other documentary exhibits, and tables are related to charts and graphs.

A time line is usually a single axis display pinpointing events over time. The units of time are measured on a horizontal line, and labels, pictures, or documents are affixed to the exhibit to indicate the occurrence of a relevant event. Use a time line when it is important to make an evidentiary point about the relationship of events over time.

A table is a systematic arrangement of data into rows and columns so that numbers representing two factors can be read by locating each of the factors on the horizontal and vertical axes of the table and reading the number at the point where the row and column meet. Use a table when the exact numbers are required instead of a graph or chart.

3.2.1 Foundation

Both time lines and tables have evidentiary value over and above the factual information they present. The layout of the information also conveys important conclusions or interpretations that aid the fact-finder in ascertaining the truth. Thus, your foundation must pay attention to both the factual information and the layout. See Section 1.1.

Time lines

The foundation for a time line to be used with a lay witness must be laid with a witness who has first hand knowledge of the dates that appear on the time line. That may be the testifying witness or some previous witness. This type of exhibit can be qualified at the outset as a finished product or can be "built" in the courtroom as the witness testifies about each significant event.

Example

Q. Ms. Evans, where were you when Mr. Bellville was injured?

A. At my house on Whistler Drive, at number 200.

Q. Where is your house located in relation to the site where Mr. Bellville was working?

A. It is right across the street. I liked to sit in my front yard and watch the construction during the morning when the sun was out.

Q. What was the first thing you observed on the morning that Mr. Bellville was injured?

A. Well, I saw everybody come to work as usual around 7:30 a.m.

Q. *(Approaching a large sketch pad on an easel near counsel table where the judge and jury can see it)*

Your Honor, if I may, I'd like to make a time line here as Ms. Evans tells us what she saw.

(Writes 7:30 a.m.—workers arrive)

What did you see next?

A. I saw Mr. Bellville and two other men go up to the roof at around 9:00 a.m.

Q. *(Writes 9:00 a.m.—Bellville on roof)*

What did you see next?

A. Then three people on the ground began using a high lift to put materials up on the roof where Mr. Bellville was working. One of them was driving the high lift and two others were loading it.

Q. When was that?

A. About 30 minutes after they got up on the roof.

Q. *(Writes 9:30 a.m.—high lift operating)*

What happened after the high lift began operating?

A. On the first lift, Mr. Bellville was knocked off and fell to the ground.

Q. When did that happen?

A. About three minutes later.

Q. *(Writes 9:33 a.m.—Bellville knocked off roof)*

What did you see immediately after Mr. Bellville fell?

A. Well, I rushed over to see if I could help. They said they
    needed a blanket, so I ran home to get one. And then I ran
    back. As I ran back, I saw someone on the telephone in the
    truck. I thought they were calling the emergency line. I took
    the blanket to the man who was tending to Mr. Bellville and
    he put it over him. That was about four minutes later.

Q. *(Writes: 9:37 a.m.—Ms. Evans brings blanket)*

    Ms. Evans, did the emergency truck come?

A. Yes, they did.

Q. When did they get there?

A. It was about five minutes after 10.

Q. *(Writes: 10:05 a.m.—Ms. Evans sees emergency truck arrive)*

    Your Honor, I am finished with this part of the time line for
    now. May I mark this for identification as plaintiff's Exhibit
    18?

Court: You may.

Q. *(After marking the sketch pad page)*

    How did Mr. Bellville look to you as he lay on the ground?

A. *(Witness explains pain and suffering.)*

                              * * *

Q. Dr. Moriarty, when did you first see Mr. Bellville?

A. I was in the emergency room at 10:25 when the emergency
    truck brought him in.

Q. Your Honor, may I go back to Exhibit 18 which is our time
    line and add Dr. Moriarty's items?

Court: You may.

Q. *(Writes 10:25—Dr. Moriarty first sees Bellville)*

    What did you do?

A. I determined the extent of his injuries, started an intravenous
    line, and sent him to surgery.

Q. What time did you send him to surgery?

A. At 10:32, according to my notes.

Q. *(Writes 10:32—Bellville sent to surgery)*

    What was Mr. Bellville's condition when you sent him to
    surgery?

A. *(Witness explains.)*

This kind of time line helps focus the jury on the chronology of the events and puts them at ease with respect to the burden of remembering all the details of the testimony. See also example in Section 1.2.2.

A time line presented by an expert witness normally will have been prepared in advance. The foundation will draw on the witness's status as an expert and her task of sifting the available information to decide what is important.

Example

Q. What did you do next, Dr. Tenzer?

A. I examined all the records and made a time line so that I could analyze the intervals between important events.

Q. Directing your attention to what has previously been marked as Exhibit 23, can you identify that?

A. Yes, that is the time line I prepared.

Q. Does the time line accurately portray the data you found in the records with respect to the events that you determined were important?

A. Yes.

Q. Your Honor, we offer Exhibit 23 in evidence.

Opposing Counsel: Objection; hearsay and original document rule.

Q. Are the facts and the data reflected in this time line of a type reasonably relied upon by experts in your field in forming opinions or inferences upon the subject you were asked to examine?

A. Yes.

Q. Are the facts displayed on this exhibit drawn from the contents of voluminous documents which cannot be conveniently examined here in court?

A. Yes, they are.

Q. Your Honor, we offer Exhibit 23 in evidence.

Court: Admitted.

Q. Dr. Tenzer, what is shown on the horizontal axis?

A. Those are the units of time, in this case days, weeks, and months. The months are the large lines and are labeled with the name of the month. The weeks are the lighter lines and are labeled with the numbers 1, 2, 3, and 4 for each month. The days are the lightest lines and they are not labeled, but there are 7 spaces within each week.

Q. What is on the rest of the time line?

A. Those are labels identifying each significant event.

(Witness goes on to testify about what the time line shows.)

The response in this example to the hearsay objection draws from Rule 703 with respect to the data that may be used by experts and the response to the original document objection draws on Rule 1006 with respect to summaries of voluminous data.

A time line may also be constructed using the juxtaposed documents technique. See discussion in Section 9.3.2.

Example

(After the results have been admitted in evidence)

Q. Mr. Welsh, what did the XYZ Company representative tell you about their test results?

A. They said the test results were uniformly favorable.

Q. Was that true?

A. No.

Q. Let's look at their test reports. First, would you refer to Exhibit 107. *(Clips a copy of Exhibit 107 to the top left side of the blank backing material and writes "Exhibit 107" in large letters immediately below it)* What was the date of the test reported in that report?

A. June 12.

Q. *(Writes "June 12" below the exhibit number)* And what was the result of that test?

A. 4 units passed and 0 units failed.

Q. *(Writes "4 passed—0 failed" below the date)* Now would you refer to Exhibit 108. *(Clips a copy of Exhibit 108 to the top of the backing material to the right of Exhibit 107, already there, and writes "Exhibit 108" immediately below it)* What was the date of the test reported in that report?

A. August 30.

Q. *(Writes "Aug. 30" below the exhibit number)* And what was the result of that test?

A. 2 units passed and 2 units failed.

Q. *(Writes "2 passed—2 failed" below the date)* Now would you refer to Exhibit 109. *(Clips a copy of Exhibit 109 to the top of the backing material to the right of Exhibit 107 and Exhibit 108, already there, and writes "Exhibit 109" immediately below it)* What was the date of the test reported in that report?

A. September 6.

Q. *(Writes "September 6" below the exhibit number)* And what was the result of that test?

A. 1 unit passed and 3 units failed.

Q. *(Writes "1 passed—3 failed" below the date)* What is a fair characterization of these test results? *(Pointing to the three successive sets of results written below the exhibits)*

A. The test results were initially favorable but then were unfavorable. Taken together, the overall test results are 7 units passed and 5 units failed. Those are unfavorable test results.

The written reiteration of the testimony as it is given helps the jurors see the relationship between the dates and the outcomes.

Tables

The foundation for a table is similar to the time line. The witness, usually an expert, testifies to the numbers on each axis and how the other numbers on the table were derived. If the witness has first hand knowledge of the numbers used on the axes of the tables, no hearsay problem arises. If the table uses market quotations or is a published tabulation "generally used and relied upon by the public or by persons in particular occupations," it falls under the hearsay exemption in Rule 803(17).

Example

(After establishing the competence of the witness and relevance of the information)

Q. Mr. Arnold, can you identify the document that has been marked as Exhibit 49?

A. Yes.

Q. What is it?

A. That is the table of home mortgage interest amounts that was used in calculating the amount due under this loan.

Q. What can you tell us about the use of Exhibit 49 in your business?

A. This is the standard table that we use with loans like this one.

Q. Your Honor, we offer Exhibit 49 in evidence.

Opposing Counsel: Objection; hearsay.

Q. By whom is the table published?

A. By the National Board of Realtors.

Q. Is it generally used and relied upon by the public or by persons in your particular occupation?

A. Yes.

Q. Your Honor, we offer Exhibit 49 in evidence. It is a published tabulation, not prepared for trial, and it qualifies under the exception to the hearsay rule in Rule 803(17).

Court: Objection overruled. Exhibit 49 is admitted.

Life and work expectancy tables and present value tables are normally used by expert witnesses and fall under the exception in Rule 703 for facts or data used by experts.

Most time lines and tables can be qualified either as evidence or as testimony aids. The challenges to foundation are similar to those for charts and graphs, as explained above. If the foundation is not sufficient to support admission in evidence, the court may still allow you to use the exhibit as a testimony aid if the witness asserts that it would assist in the presentation of the testimony.

3.2.2 Objections

The response to particular hearsay objections is illustrated with the examples above. In the first example, with respect to Mr. Bellville's injuries, no hearsay problem arises because this time line summarizes testimony given in court and subject to cross-examination. In the second example, with respect to the time line prepared by an expert, Rule 703 provides that the facts or data used by an expert need not be admissible in evidence. See Section 1.3.1.

There is no original document problem with this category of exhibits, as explained in Section 3.1.2 above.

The policy objections—unfair prejudice, confusion/misleading, undue delay/waste of time, or needless presentation of cumulative evidence—may arise in a number of difference contexts.

Example

(After the last entry is made on Exhibit 18 in the example in Section 3.2.1 with respect to Mr. Bellville's injuries)

Counsel: Your Honor, plaintiff offers Exhibit 18 in evidence. It is a time line showing the key events with respect to Mr. Bellville's injury and treatment. The time line was made as the witnesses testified, and it is an accurate reflection of that testimony.

Opposing Counsel: Objection, this is needless cumulative evidence. Why isn't the testimony about the events sufficient?

Counsel: Both the testimony about the times involved and the intervals between these times are relevant to the issues in this case about why Mr. Bellville's injuries had the effect that they did. The testimony is about the times. This exhibit shows the intervals. Under Rule 611(a), the court should allow us to present the evidence in this way because it makes the presentation effective for the ascertainment of truth.

Court: Admitted.

Your opponent may make policy objections to the manner of labeling, if the time line or table emphasizes some events unfairly, or uses argumentative statements in labeling. See Section 1.3.3.

3.2.3 Production and Tactics

The time line is a very functional exhibit in any case where the progression of events lends force to the arguments as to the facts or the law. See Fig. 18. One of the principal design considerations is whether to present the time line all at once, as a completed exhibit, or to "build" it in the courtroom as the testimony proceeds. If the process by which a conclusion is reached is important, and the trial is to a jury, then you may want to take the jury through the building of the time line step by step. If the conclusion is fairly obvious and the process of building the time line is unimportant, then you may want to use a static exhibit to present the time line all at once.

Some time lines are a simple list made on a sketch pad mounted on an easel with the lawyer writing the date and event as the witness testifies. Others are magnetic boards or Velcro exhibits with the units of time (days, months, years) printed on the board so that labels identifying individual events can be affixed as the testimony unfolds. See discussion of equipment in Section 9.3.1 and materials in Section 9.3.2. Time lines can also be displayed using projector screen displays (Section 9.4), electronic displays (Section 9.5), and digital displays (Section 9.6).

In designing a table, you should not to put too much information on it. Several "clean" looking tables are preferable to one table containing a maze of information. Less than ten lines of information is ideal; no more than 20 lines should be attempted. If possible, tables should be introduced only after a more general chart or graph has given the fact-finder an overview. Fig. 19 is a table showing damages claims.

Size and presentation features are important for both time lines and tables. See discussion in Section 9.2 with respect to typeface, color, white borders, and various formats that might be used.

3.3 COMPUTER DATA PRINTOUTS

The computer is becoming a prime generator of evidence. In many industries, computers create more business records, financial analyses, engineering reports, blueprints, and statistical work than humans do, and the computer's share of many kinds of tasks is growing. The computer is also becoming less expensive to use, making its analytical and visual display capabilities more affordable for many kinds of litigation.

This chapter discusses data output produced by computers that is itself substantive evidence and sets out a summary of the foundation requirements for various types of computer-generated data printouts. This computer-generated evidence is usually the product of a spreadsheet or other statistical analysis program or a database program. Text documents generated using word processing software on a computer are handled in the same way as other text documents, as explained in Chapter 2. Chapter 8 discusses computer drawings, simulations, and animations that are accomplished using sophisticated graphics software. Chapter 9 covers the use of computers to assist in the display of exhibits.

There is also an important dichotomy between computer-generated evidence that will be presented through the testimony of a lay witness and that which will be presented by an expert. Lay witnesses can get ensnared in hearsay rules; experts have an exemption available to them that clears away most problems with the hearsay rules.

Section 3.3.1 covers the fundamentals with respect to qualifying any computer-generated exhibit involving data compilations. It is important to be able to convey to the judge exactly what the computer has done and how the requisites of competence, relevance, identification, and trustworthiness will be met during the foundation. Section 3.3.2 covers the avenues available to get past hearsay objections.

3.3.1 Foundation

When qualifying computer-generated data as evidence, it is necessary to satisfy the requirements of competence of the witness, relevance of the information, identification of the exhibit, and trustworthiness of the exhibit. See Section 1.1. The trustworthiness requirement is important in this context. It requires that the lawyer be able to explain to the judge exactly how the proposed exhibit was generated, and it is necessary to think through what errors theoretically could have been made during the computer processes so that you can include in the foundation sufficient evidence on trustworthiness.

Competence and relevance

The witness who testifies with respect to the information in the computer data printout may not have much knowledge about how the printout was generated. If the exhibit is something other than a routine business record, it may be necessary to plan for two witnesses to sponsor the exhibit—one for the technical computer requirements and another for the substance of the information.

Computer printouts that are voluminous may be met with a relevance objection because they contain information not relevant to the issues as well as that which is relevant. The amount of nonrelevant information that will be permitted is left to the discretion of the court.

Identification

The witness must state specifically (and usually from personal knowledge) what the printout is with sufficient particularity that it can be distinguished from all other things. This requirement is generally very simple to meet:

Example

Q. I hand you what has been marked for identification as defendant's Exhibit 50 and ask you to examine it.

A. *(Witness looks over Exhibit 50.)*

Q. What is it?

A. That is a computer printout of wages and salaries for the XYZ Corporation for last year.

Q. How are you able to identify it?

A. As a part of my duties as the manager of data processing services for the XYZ Corporation, I routinely prepare printouts of annual wages and salaries. This is the printout for last year, and I prepared it. My initials are in the upper right-hand corner in the code line identifying this particular report.

Trustworthiness

The computer printout must be an accurate report of the data it contains. Establishing this aspect of the foundation is normally no problem if you follow the requirements of Rule 901(b)(9) which provides that an exhibit can be authenticated by "evidence describing a process or system used to produce a result and showing that the process or system produces an accurate result." The data, input, hardware, software, and security are elements in the "process or system" of computer-generated data printouts. If you expect a challenge to foundation, each element must be described, and a showing must be made that, taken together, the system will produce an accurate result.

Even the simplest computer input is acted on in some way by the computer (e.g., stored, retrieved, sent to a printer), and thus the output is potentially subject to a claim of unreliability or inaccuracy. Information is typically put into a computer by a person using either a keyboard and monitor, a CD-ROM disk, a scanner, a computer disk, a magnetic tape, or a computer-to-computer transfer using telephone lines or other hard wired connections. The person who enters the information may have first hand knowledge of the input or may be working from receipts or other documents generated by someone else. The steps of assembling the information, entering it into the computer, storing it, retrieving it, performing calculations on it, and printing it out or displaying it on screen provide many theoretical opportunities for the introduction of inaccuracy into the system. These need to be taken into account in deciding how much foundation is required for a particular computer-generated exhibit.

Data

Examine the data first. Where did the data come from; how good are the data; who can verify the data? If the data being used for the computer-generated printout are insufficient in some critical way, then nothing that the computer hardware or software can do will make up for this deficiency. In order to provide an adequate foundation, you will need to know all of the relevant facts with respect to the source of data being used.

Input

Next, examine the method used to get the data into the computer so that it can be used or processed to create the necessary exhibit. There are basically three methods of data input: (1) human input; (2) intermediary data transfers; and (3) direct computer-to-computer transfers.

Human input involves the most potential for error. If the person entering the data is the same person who is engaged in the transaction that he or she is recording (such as a sale of goods in a department store), there may be a mistake concerning the details of the transaction. If the person entering the data is working from a receipt or other document, the data may be misread, creating a mistake in the input. And the creator of the document from which the input is done may have made an error in recording the original transaction. Assuming that the underlying document is accurate and the person entering the data has perceived the underlying transaction or document accurately, he or she may make a mistake in inputting the information into the computer by striking the wrong key on the keyboard. The person entering the data may enter the correct information into the wrong file or may fail to take steps to ensure that the information, once entered, is stored properly by the computer. The lawyer needs to consider these possibilities and the effect they may have on the foundation for the exhibit.

Intermediary data transfers usually involve tapes, disks, or scanners. The data may be transferred from a computer to a tape or disk and then subsequently loaded onto the computer that will generate the exhibit. In so doing, there may be transfers from one format to another. One common transfer is from the format being used by one computer to ASCII (American Standard Computer Information Interchange) which is a format that can be used by many types of computers. Data transfers from tapes or disks can be checked by electronic comparisons and generally present the fewest problems.

Data transfers by scanners convert printed or typed material into digital form. You need to distinguish between the scanning process, which produces an "image" or photo of the document, and the optical character reader software that processes the image into a computer-readable format. The image will be very accurate, probably better than a typical office copier could produce. The conversion of the information in the image (letters and numbers) to computer-readable format may contain errors. The software may identify a "7" as a "1," for example. Normally, you will be using the "image" as the exhibit and not the "text file." If, for some reason, you are using the text file, be aware that even if the optical character software has a very low error rate, and can produce 99 percent accuracy, there will be errors on nearly every page of material that is translated into computer-readable form. You will need to involve some human or computer error-checking methods to get 100 percent accuracy if that is needed.

Computer-to-computer transfers usually occur over the telephone lines or dedicated data transfer lines. Occasionally they occur through direct "hard-wired" connections. Most data transmission programs have error-checking methods that, once understood by the lawyer, are sufficient to qualify the product as trustworthy enough to meet evidentiary standards.

Hardware

You may need to be able to identify the computer hardware used in generating the exhibit. Hardware is usually identified by manufacturer, model name, and model number. You also need to know how widely this hardware is used for non-litigation purposes and what safeguards are available against equipment malfunctions. Even if there is no error in data input, there may be a malfunction in the computer that causes information to be stored incorrectly or destroyed. The circuitry or computer chips may be faulty. A surge of electricity or other environmental problem may cause a malfunction. Most of these malfunctions can be prevented by common office practices such as the use of surge protectors between the electrical outlet and the computer. Hardware malfunction is rarely a problem in practice, but the evidentiary foundation will need some basis for asserting that the hardware operated properly.

Software

You may need to be able to identify the software that the computer is using in the operations that generated the exhibit sought to be admitted. Software is generally identified by the name and version of the product. You will also need to know the name and address of the publisher and the year in which the version used to generate the exhibit was released.

You need to be prepared to explain the safeguards with respect to proper operation of the software. The program that drives the computer may have "bugs" or design errors in it. As a result, the computer may not store, retrieve, perform calculations on, display, or print the information properly. Most commercially available software has been used in thousands of installations and has been "debugged" sufficiently to meet evidentiary standards. If you are using proprietary or special purpose software written for the specific litigation, you will need to have sufficient evidence that it has been "debugged" satisfactorily. If there is any choice, it is always better, for litigation purposes, to use commercially available software that is used for business purposes other than litigation. It is far easier to qualify exhibits generated with this kind of software.

Security

Even if the data are correct when received, the input operations are flawless, and the hardware and software operate properly, unauthorized persons may gain access to the computer and may alter the information stored on it. Unlike forgeries or alterations of paper documents, alterations to data stored in a computer might be difficult to detect because there is no document reflecting the alteration. You will need to be familiar with the security precautions that are taken such as passwords and identification requirements for internal computer operations and dial-in protections for computers that are linked in any way to the outside world.

It is a matter of judgment as to how much material on these subjects to put into the foundation. If the printout is routine, a very simple foundation will suffice. If the printout is the result of a unique program, application, or event, more should be added to the foundation as to accuracy. The opposing side may elect to voir dire on any of these subjects of competence, relevance, identification, and trustworthiness prior to the ruling on admissibility. See Section 1.7.2. After hearing the voir dire, which may be done out of the presence of the jury, the judge will rule on admissibility. Usually if the judge believes the proponent has not met the trustworthiness requirement, further direct examination of the witness will be permitted to supply the missing information.

Example

(After establishing competence, relevance, and identification)

Q. Is the information stored in the computer accurate?

A. Yes.

Q. How do you know that?

A. These printouts on wages and salaries are prepared from data input into the computer by experienced personnel. I have a regular testing method to detect input errors. The data comes from reports filled out by XYZ Corporation supervisors and I regularly cross-check to make sure those records are accurate.

Q. How are these printouts used in the company?

A. These are the regular reports that we use for accounting and tax purposes.

Q. Your Honor, we offer defendant's Exhibit 50 in evidence.

Opposing Counsel: Objection; lack of foundation.

Counsel: Your Honor, this exhibit has been qualified under Rule 901(b)(9). It is the result of a process or system that has been shown to produce an accurate result.

Court: Objection overruled.

Opposing Counsel: Objection; hearsay.

Q. Going back to Exhibit 50, for a moment, is it a report or record of events or conditions made at or near the time of the events or conditions it contains?

A. Yes.

Q. Was Exhibit 50 made by, or from information transmitted by, a person with knowledge?

A. Yes.

Q. Was the regular practice of your business to make this kind of record or report?

A. Yes.

Q. Was Exhibit 50 kept in the course of your regularly conducted business activity?

A. Yes.

Q. Your Honor, we offer Exhibit 50 in evidence. It qualifies under the exception to the hearsay rule for business records.

Court: Objection overruled.

Opposing Counsel: Objection; this is not the original document.

Q. Is the printout an accurate reflection of the data stored in the computer?

A. Yes.

Q. Your Honor, we offer Exhibit 50 in evidence. Under Rule 1001(3), it is an original. There is no original document problem.

Court: Objection overruled. The exhibit is admitted.

The foundation for a computer printout qualifies the accuracy of the data stored in the computer which is necessary to establish the trustworthiness of the exhibit. The accuracy of the printout as a reflection of the data stored in the computer is necessary to qualify the printout as an "original" for purposes of the original document rule.

With more complicated printouts representing more sophisticated computer functions, the foundation witness or witnesses should testify that:

(1) the computer used to generate the printout is standard equipment and is reliable;

(2) the software program used to enter, store, and retrieve the information is standard and reliable;

(3) the data entry process is checked regularly for accuracy and the data stored in the computer are accurate;

(4) the data are stored in a manner secure from loss or alteration; and

(5) the printout is an accurate representation of the data stored in the computer.

Even with relatively simple exhibits, the witness should be prepared on each of these matters in case any problem arises.

The simplest kind of computer data exhibit is that which replicates or mirrors the information that was previously entered and stored in the computer memory and sorted but not otherwise processed or changed in any way by the computer. The most common example of such evidence is a printout of a business's records of its transactions. Formerly maintained in manual ledgers or typewritten reports, such reports may now routinely be entered into a computer and printed out as needed in the ordinary course of business. Examples include customer accounts at a business such as the telephone company or a bank and records of transactions such as the purchase of an airplane ticket or the rental of a car.

In the case of simple computer records maintained on standard computer equipment using standard programs, your opponent may be willing to stipulate to the admissibility of the document. If no stipulation is forthcoming, the witness can supply the necessary foundation if he or she has personal knowledge of the accuracy of the data stored in the computer. This may be established by experience over a substantial period of time with the equipment and software or by personal knowledge of checks for accuracy.

When faced with challenges to the trustworthiness of records created by a computer, the courts have adapted three standard criteria used with other types of evidence: the use of routine procedures designed to assure accuracy; the presence of a motive to assure accuracy; and the absence of anticipated litigation when the data were generated.

Routine procedure designed to assure accuracy

The custodian or supervisor of the relevant department can testify concerning the procedures that resulted in creation of the computer file. For example, Witness A, the custodian of business records for a Company A, testifies that employees of the company transfer to backup tape information contained on claim forms submitted by the various claimants. Witness A further testifies that two employees then check the accuracy of the transfer of information before supplying the tape to Company B. Witness B, the director of claims processing for Company B, then testifies that the information is transferred from the tape into Company B's computer and used as the basis for generating the information on claims contained in the computer-generated evidence. Under Rule 104, all of this evidence as to admissibility can be provided by affidavit rather than testimony in court.

Motive to assure accuracy

If the foundation witness testifies that the business relies on the computer records in conducting its regular business, the trustworthiness of the records will be enhanced. The reliance may be in any part of the business—inventory, purchasing, paying—so long as some business function could be affected adversely if the records were inaccurate.

Data not prepared in anticipation of litigation

The opponent of an exhibit which is a computer printout might object that the printout was created solely for use in the litigation and thus is suspect. The operative fact, however, is not when the printout was generated, but when the data that are contained in the printout or used in producing the printout were first entered into the computer and the circumstances under which they were entered.

For example, suppose the proposed exhibit is a computer printout of the electricity used by a particular plant during one month. The issue is whether the plant was operated efficiently, thus entitling the owners to a bonus that was set out in a performance-oriented contract. A foundation could be provided by the plant manager as follows:

Example

Q. I show you what has been marked for identification as defendant's Exhibit 51 and ask you to examine it.

A. *(Witness looks over exhibit.)*

Q. What is it?

A. This is a computer printout showing the amounts of electricity used during each 24-hour period during the month of September at the River Run plant.

Q. How do you know that?

A. As plant manager, I get daily, weekly, and monthly performance reports on many aspects of the River Run plant operations. I have been receiving this report on electricity usage for the past three years. This one has headings and markings on it that I recognize as our usual monthly report. It is identified as the report for September by the date in the lower left hand corner of each page.

Q. How was it prepared?

A. There are meters on the electricity lines coming into the plant. These meters are read daily at 6 a.m. by a person in the Utilities Management Section. That person enters the data from the meters into a computer terminal and the computer stores the information. When we need information about how much electricity has been used in a particular day, month, year, or other time period, we have the computer sort the data that have been entered and print out the requested information.

Q. What kind of computer equipment is used for this purpose?

A. We use equipment manufactured by Hewlett Packard.

Q. Is the computer hardware reliable?

A. Yes it is. We have had it installed for over a year and it has worked fine.

Q. What kind of software is used for this purpose?

A. We use standard database software.

Q. Is the software reliable?

A. Yes it is. We have also used it for over a year with no problems.

Q. Does this computer process or system produce an accurate result?

A. Yes, it does.

Q. How do you know that?

A. We have cross-checks built into the system and we manually inspect a sample of the data on a regular basis to ensure accuracy.

Q. What security precautions are taken with the computer system?

A. Only operators with a current password can get into the system. There is no dial-in capability, so no one from outside the company can access the computer. The passwords are changed every week.

Q. How is the information on the amount of electricity used during each 24-hour period at the River Run plant used in the operation of the company's business?

A. This is very important operational information that we use to make decisions about production runs and expected expenses. We also use it to make maintenance decisions.

Q. How long has the company been collecting this data?

A. For almost five years.

Q. Your Honor, we offer Exhibit 51 in evidence.

Opposing Counsel: Objection; lack of foundation.

Counsel: Your Honor, the printout has been qualified under Rule 901(b)(9) as trustworthy because it is the result of a process or system shown to produce an accurate result.

Court: Objection overruled.

Opposing Counsel: Objection; this is not the original document.

Q. Is the printout that is Exhibit 51 an accurate reflection of the data stored in the computer?

A. Yes, it is.

Q. Your Honor, we offer defendant's Exhibit 51 in evidence. The printout is an original under Rule 1001(3).

Court: Objection overruled. Exhibit 51 is admitted.

If the computer printout is a summary, then the additional requirements of Rule 1006 must be met.

3.3.2 Objections

Computer data printouts are subject to the usual range of objections. See Section 1.3. Although the foundation for computer data printouts is different from that for computer text documents, the objections available are nearly the same.

Hearsay objections

Some printouts will not present a hearsay problem. If the printout was made by a party or its agent and is offered in evidence against that party, it is admissible as a nonhearsay admission of a party opponent under Rule 801(d)(2). Some printouts may be admissible because they are not offered to prove the truth of what they assert. For example, the manufacturer of a mechanical part may offer a computer analysis or design of the part not to prove that the part was in fact safe but simply to show that the manufacturer took every reasonable precaution, including computer-aided design techniques, to make it safe.

When computer data printouts face a hearsay objection, several exceptions to the hearsay rule are available.

Business records exception

The hearsay exception most often applicable to computer printouts is the business records exception set out in Rule 803(6). The federal courts have routinely held that printouts of information recorded and stored in the regular course of business are admissible as business records if a proper foundation is laid. The requirements of Rule 803(6) are straightforward. They are summarized here.

First, the witness need not have personal knowledge. The data compilation may be made "by, or from information transmitted by, a person with knowledge" of the transaction being recorded. Thus, Employee A may fill out manually a form reflecting a transaction and transmit the form to Employee B, who enters the data from the form into the computer. As long as the data entry occurs "at or near the time" of the transaction, the resulting printout is admissible. Moreover, the witness called to lay the foundation for the printout need not be either Employee A or Employee B, but can be their supervisor, the records custodian, or another qualified witness. Rule 803(6) provides that "all" of its requirements can be shown by the testimony of "the custodian or other qualified witness." The Advisory Committee Note points out that the rule is derived from prior state and federal statutes designed to

> relax the requirement of producing as witnesses, or
> accounting for the non-production of, all participants in
> the process of gathering, transmitting, and recording

information which the common law had evolved as a burdensome and crippling aspect of using records of this type.

Under this rule, any witness who has familiarity with the computer processing procedure used by a particular company or office, for example, can be used to qualify any printout that came from that company or office.

Second, the definition of business is very broad. As set forth in the text of the rule, the requirement that the information be regularly kept in the course of a regularly conducted business activity includes any "business, institution, association, profession, occupation, and calling of every kind, whether or not conducted for profit." The intention is to segregate purely personal records from the records made for some kind of public venture.

Third, the burden of persuading the court on the question of trustworthiness is on party objecting. A printout or other business record is admissible under Rule 803(6) "unless the source of information or the method or circumstances of preparation indicate lack of trustworthiness." This language gives the trial court wide discretion in allowing or disallowing a printout. The possible sources of inaccuracy outlined in Section 3.1.1 give the opponent considerable opportunity to conduct a voir dire of the foundation witness in order to show that the proffered printout is unreliable and therefore inadmissible. See Section 1.6 on voir dire.

Example

(After testimony on competence, relevance, identification, and trustworthiness and an offer based on that foundation)

Opposing Counsel: Objection, hearsay.

Q. We can deal with that objection under the business records exception, Your Honor, if I may proceed.

Court: You may.

Q. Was Exhibit 51 made by a person with knowledge of, or made from information transmitted by a person with knowledge of, the acts or events appearing on it?

A. Yes, it was. The entries into the computer are made by experienced personnel. They use records created by supervisors who have knowledge of the amounts paid to employees.

Q. Was each of the records on Exhibit 51 made at or near the time of the acts or events appearing on it?

A. Yes, the entries are made weekly at the time our employees are paid. The printout contains a collection of all of those entries for the previous year.

Q. Is it the regular practice of the XYZ Corporation to make such a record?

A. Yes, we make entries every week and we make a printout summarizing the whole year every year.

Q. Once that record was made, was that record kept in the course of a regularly conducted business activity of XYZ Corporation?

A. Yes. Once the records are entered into the computer, they are kept as a regular part of the accounting activity of the XYZ Corporation.

Q. Your Honor, we move the admission in evidence of Exhibit 51. It qualifies as a business record of the XYZ Corporation.

Court: Objection overruled. Exhibit 51 is admitted.

All of the questions on this part of the foundation are taken directly from (and phrased exactly the same as) Rule 803(6). All of the questions are leading, but that is permitted in establishing compliance with one of the hearsay exceptions. See Rule 104(a) and Rule 611(c).

The questions used to establish the business record exception may be asked all at once, as in the example above, or interspersed in the questions on trustworthiness if the lawyer elects to anticipate the objection by eliciting the necessary testimony to meet it before offering the exhibit. If you know there is a determined objection to a particular exhibit, you may want to use this approach.

Example

Q. Mr. Adams, please describe your job.

A. I am the Director of Information Systems for the XYZ Company.

Q. What duties do you have with respect to the records of the XYZ Company?

A. I am in charge of all data processing systems. This includes all the computer processes by which XYZ Corporation generates computer databases for various purposes and produces records from those databases.

Q. How long have you held this position?

A. For about six years.

Q. Mr. Adams, I show you what has been marked as plaintiff's Exhibit 64 and ask if you can identify that document.

A. Yes. That is a computer-generated report on potential irregularities in our inventory of radioactive materials.

Q. What computer equipment is used by XYZ Computer to generate reports such as plaintiff's Exhibit 64?

A. We use our mainframe equipment which is manufactured by IBM.

Q. How long has the XYZ Company used this equipment for the purpose of generating reports such as plaintiff's Exhibit 64?

A. For about five years.

Q. Is the use of the computer for this purpose a systematic and routine procedure?

A. Yes.

Q. What input is used to generate this report?

A. Each storage facility that keeps radioactive materials makes a daily, weekly, and monthly report of its inventory. These reports are made by different people and serve as a cross-check. Each delivery unit that transfers materials makes a daily report on transfers. Each production unit that generated radioactive material makes an hourly report on production. All of these reports are made at computer terminals located on the various sites where the radioactive material is handled. The computer collects and compares all of this information. If there are any discrepancies, a report such as this Exhibit is generated.

Q. Was the input for plaintiff's Exhibit 64 made by a person with knowledge of, or made from information transmitted by a person with knowledge of, the acts or events appearing in it?

A. Yes.

Q. Was the input for plaintiff's Exhibit 64 made at or near the time of the acts or events appearing on it?

A. Yes.

Q. What precautions, if any, are taken to detect or avoid errors in the data?

A. We have programmed a double cross-check system under which every number entered into the system is confirmed for accuracy.

Q. What precautions, if any, are taken to detect or avoid unauthorized tampering with the data?

A. We have a security system programmed into the database so that no unauthorized person can add data or take data out.

Q. In what form is the report produced?

A. Just as you see it in this Exhibit. The computer activates a printer which prints the information in that format.

Q. What precautions, if any, are taken to detect or avoid malfunctions in the system?

A. We have programmed three different safeguards to protect against equipment failures.

Q. Is the printout that is Exhibit 64 an accurate reflection of the data stored in the computer?

A. Yes.

Q. Is it the regular practice of XYZ Company to make a computer record such as plaintiff's Exhibit 64?

A. Yes.

Q. Was plaintiff's Exhibit 64 a record that was kept in the course of a regularly conducted business activity of XYZ Company?

A. Yes.

Q. Your Honor, we offer plaintiff's Exhibit 64 in evidence. The foundation has been established. In addition, it is a business record under Rule 803(6) and it is an original under Rule 1001(3).

It is useful to keep the foundation questions as precisely aimed at meeting the requirements as possible. Once the exhibit is admitted, you may want to go back over some of this ground in more detail if any of this is important to an issue in the case. If the exhibit has been admitted at pretrial proceedings, it is often a good idea to give the jury some background on how the exhibit was created.

Public records

Computer printouts that are public records can be qualified under Rule 803(8) and Rule 803(9). They include any "records, reports, statements, or data compilations" from any public agency and also "records or data compilations, in any form, of births, fetal deaths, deaths, or marriages, if the report thereof was made to a public office pursuant to requirements of law."

Nonoccurrence of event

Computer data printouts may be used to prove that something *did not* occur. Bank records, for example, may be admitted as proof that a person or company did not make a deposit during a certain month. The foundation requirements under Rule 803(7) (absence of a business record) and Rule 803(10) (absence of a public record) follow the same general path as the rule governing proof from these records that something *did* occur. However, counsel is well advised to pay added attention to the procedures used to collect and input the data. If those procedures were sloppy, with the result that the records may not reflect an event that did occur, the opponent may be able to argue that the circumstances under which the records were created are untrustworthy and therefore that the records should be excluded.

Market quotations and commercial lists and directories

Rule 803(17) permits admission of computer printouts that are: "Market quotations, tabulations, lists, directories, or other published compilations, generally used and relied upon by the public or by persons in particular occupations." If the compilation is prepared or printed by computer, that should be no bar to admissibility provided that the requirements of general use and reliance are established.

Other specific exceptions

Most computer data printouts can be fit under one of the specific exceptions. Some personal records, which is the largest group of data printouts other than business and public records, can be fit under the exceptions for statements as to present sense impression, excited utterance, or then existing mental, emotional, or physical condition. See Rules 803(1), (2), (3), and (4). For example, a person who kept track of weight loss, pulse rate, and body temperature on a personal computer probably could qualify that record under one of these exceptions.

Some personal data records can be qualified as recorded recollections under Rule 803(5). Examples might be records kept on a personal computer of cash payments to a relative or friend. Records of household expenses, inventories of household goods and their value, and similar personal data may qualify under this rule.

If the computer data printouts are from a third party who is now unavailable to testify, you may be able to qualify them under Rule 804 which covers former testimony, statements against interest, statements under belief of impending death, and statements of personal or family history.

General purpose exception

Rule 803(24) permits admission of

> A statement not specifically covered by any of the foregoing
> exceptions but having equivalent circumstantial
> guarantees of trustworthiness, if the court determines that
> (A) the statement is offered as evidence of a material fact;
> (B) the statement is more probative on the point for which
> it is offered than any other evidence which the proponent
> can procure through reasonable efforts; and (C) the
> general purposes of these rules and the interests of
> justice will best be served by admission of the statement
> in evidence. However, a statement may not be admitted
> under this exception unless the proponent of it makes
> known to the adverse party sufficiently in advance of the
> trial or hearing to provide the adverse party with a fair
> opportunity to prepare to meet it, the proponent's
> intention to offer the statement and the particulars of it,
> including the name and address of the declarant.

Rule 804(5), which covers statements of a declarant who is not
available, is phrased in the same terms as Rule 803(24).

When you qualify a computer printout, or any other exhibit, under
the general purpose exception, you should expect a more determined
objection from your opponent and more careful scrutiny from the court.
You will need to pay particular attention to the requirements of Rule
803(24) and have a well thought out explanation of the balancing of
interests that is required.

The most likely circumstance to resort to the general purpose
exception for a computer data printout will occur when you have failed
to lay the necessary foundation during discovery. If the necessary
witness is beyond the subpoena power of the court or otherwise
unavailable, you may not be able to get the necessary testimony to
qualify the printout as a business record or to take advantage of one of
the other available exceptions. You then must fall back on the general
purpose exception.

Example

(After establishing competence and relevance)

Q. Mr. Akbar, I am handing you a document that has been
    marked as Exhibit 17. Can you identify that?

A. Yes. That is a computer printout of the performance testing
    data on plastic molded cases to protect instruments.

Q. Where did you get it?

A. From Performance Plastics, a Canadian company.

Q. What do you know about the business of Performance Plastics?

Opposing Counsel: Objection, hearsay. The witness has no first hand knowledge of Performance Plastics.

Counsel: Your Honor, if I may proceed, we have a Dun & Bradstreet report and a Standard & Poor's listing with respect to this company. Both are commercial publications generally used and relied upon by the public or by persons in Mr. Akbar's particular occupation. Under Rule 803(17), there is an exception to the hearsay rule for these publications.

Opposing Counsel: Objection, original document. If they want to prove the content of a writing, they have to use an original of the writing.

Counsel: If necessary, Your Honor, we are prepared to mark these as exhibits. But Mr. Akbar learned facts about Performance Plastics from these publications. He is now testifying about what he learned. That is not covered by the original document rule. Counsel can cross-examine on this point.

Court: You may proceed.

Q. Mr. Akbar back to the question. What do you know about the business of Performance Plastics?

A. They make and sell plastic molded cases to protect instruments. They have substantial sales in Canada, where they are located, and in the U.S.

Q. How did you get Exhibit 17?

A. I learned of the company from a search that we did. I wrote to them and asked for data on their plastic molded cases to protect instruments. Exhibit 17 is what they sent me.

Q. What efforts did you make to obtain testimony from Performance Plastics?

A. We asked them, but they didn't want to get involved in any lawsuit.

Q. Why didn't you pursue discovery against them?

A. They are in Canada, and it would have been too expensive for us. We are a very small company, and we just don't have the resources.

Q. When did you provide Exhibit 17 to the defendant?

A. A few days after I got it. I sent it to them.

Q. To whom did you send it?

A. To Ms. Stilton. She is my counterpart, with whom I had been dealing in this matter.

Q. Do you know whether she received it?

A. Yes, she did. We talked about it.

Q. Your Honor, we offer Exhibit 17 in evidence. It is relevant because it shows there was an alternative source for the kind of plastic needed to protect the instruments at issue in the case. Mr. Akbar is competent to testify on this subject, as shown by the testimony. He has identified the exhibit, and we have shown that it is trustworthy as it was received in the ordinary course from the company that published it.

Opposing Counsel: Objection, hearsay. This is an out-of-court statement offered to prove the truth of its contents. It did not come from us, therefore it is not an admission under Rule 801(d)(2). It cannot be qualified as a business record of Performance Plastics because Rule 803(6) requires a custodian or other qualified witness to testify to the creation of the document. It is not a public record. Plaintiff has not established that Performance Plastics is unavailable under Rule 804, and even if they did, Exhibit 17 is not a statement against interest. There is no way they can qualify Exhibit 17.

Counsel: We concede that Exhibit 17 is hearsay. We rely on the general purpose exception under Rule 803(24). First, Exhibit 17 is offered as evidence of a material fact. In this case, the availability of a better protective shield for the instrumentation is such a material fact because the defendant is claiming they used the best available technology. Second, Exhibit 17 is more probative on the point for which it is offered than any other evidence which we can procure through reasonable efforts. This is a computer printout of performance data in response to a specific request. It was put out in a business context. There is nothing suspect about it. Third, the purposes of the evidence rules and the interests of justice will be served by admission of Exhibit 17. This is a business record. But we cannot qualify it in the traditional way because we do not have sufficient financial resources to go all the way to Canada and pursue discovery there against a reluctant, if not hostile, witness. Performance Plastics is a potential supplier to the defendant. They don't want to cooperate in any lawsuit against the defendant. Fourth, we turned this document over as soon as we got it. We listed it on our exhibit list, and we gave defendant the name and address of the person we got it from. If they think there is something untrustworthy about it, they can cross-examine. I have a short memorandum on this point, Your Honor.

Court: I am going to allow Mr. Akbar's testimony on this point. I would like a responding memorandum on the admissibility of Exhibit 17 by tomorrow morning, and I will rule then.

Because of the balancing of interests required under the general purpose exception, courts will often require a short memo on the qualification of the exhibit under the rules. Disputes under this exception are often extensions of discovery wrangles, and courts are reluctant to admit hearsay unless discovery has been done in a reasonable fashion.

Original document objections

The original document rules apply to computer data printouts. They fall within the category of "[w]ritings and recordings consist [ing] of letters, words, or numbers, or their equivalent" as provided in Rule 1001(1). A computer file of any type—text, graphic, image, or data—in its computer-readable form as created by its author is an original. This original may be stored on any medium such as a hard disk, a floppy disk, a CD-ROM, an optical disk, or tape used by the computer with which the file was created.

Any printout from a computer file is also an original, so long as the printout is an accurate version of what is in the computer file. Rule 1001(3) provides: "If data are stored in a computer or similar device, any printout or other output readable by sight, shown to reflect the data accurately, is an original." If the witness testifies that the printout accurately reflects the data stored in the computer and has some reasonable basis for that testimony, then there is no original document objection to the printout.

Policy objections

The policy objections used most often against computer data printouts are undue delay, waste of time, and needless presentation of cumulative evidence. See Section 1.3.3. An opponent may argue that substantial time will be required to voir dire the witness about the foundation or bases for objections or to cross-examine the witness about the printout. This can support an objection under Rule 403 for undue delay or waste of time if the probative value of the exhibit is not strong. An opponent may also argue that one or more witnesses has already testified to the facts shown on the printout and that the printout is needlessly cumulative for that reason.

To meet the undue delay/waste of time objection, it is important that the exhibit have been identified in the pretrial process when there was an opportunity to have objections heard in a setting where a jury is not waiting while evidentiary matters are thrashed out. To meet the needlessly cumulative evidence objection, introduce the printout early in the chain of evidence about the point. Oral testimony that follows an exhibit is much less likely to be excluded than an exhibit that follows extensive oral testimony.

Occasionally a printout contains information that is the target of an objection with respect to unfair prejudice or confusion of the issues. These objections generally are directed at extraneous information included with relevant information or the labeling and format of the printout. If there is extraneous information in a normal business report that you plan to present in its customary form, you may want to have with you a special printout that excludes this information, just in case the objection is sustained. Any labels or departures from the usual wording of a business printout may raise a need for the same kind of backup exhibit.

3.3.3   Summaries of Computer Printouts

A computer can rapidly prepare a summary of information that has been gathered and input during the regular course of business. The summary can take the form of a table, graph, pie chart, or bar chart. The use of such printouts raises additional considerations with respect to foundation.

A summary prepared in the regular course of business is admissible as a business record if it meets the requirements of Rule 803(6). However, if prepared specifically for use in litigation, printouts that are special summaries or charts may not qualify for admission under the business records exception, and some other basis for admission must be proffered. A summary or graph prepared for litigation, whether by computer or otherwise, must meet the requirements of Rule 1006. Under that rule, the underlying data from which the summary is prepared must be made available to the opponent for examination or copying or both. The person who prepared the summary or caused it to be prepared can lay the foundation. As long as the underlying printouts are admissible as business records and are made available to the opponent, the computer summary can be admitted without the underlying printouts being admitted.

Example

(You want to prove the amount of wage payments made by the company in each quarter of the year. The company regularly creates a weekly printout of the wage payments made that week but does not regularly create a printout of the wages paid each quarter. For purposes of the litigation, the company prepares a new printout,

based on the same data as the weekly printouts, summing the wage payments for each quarter. After Exhibit 66 has been identified and qualified as a business record)

Q. How many pages long is Exhibit 66?

A. About 200. The company has a lot of employees, and every wage payment is recorded there. It is quite voluminous.

Q. I now hand you what has been marked for identification as Exhibit 67 and ask if you can identify that.

A. Yes, that is a summary, prepared by the computer, of the contents of Exhibit 66. For each quarter of last year, it shows the sum of the weekly wage payments made in each quarter.

Q. How was it prepared?

A. Our computer is programmed, using commercially available, off-the-shelf software, to produce summaries of some of our regularly produced reports on command. This particular program simply took the same data that is contained in Exhibit 66, divided the data into quarters, and then calculated the sum of the payments in each quarter.

Q. Does Exhibit 67 represent an accurate calculation of the sum of the quarterly wage payments contained in Exhibit 66?

A. Yes.

Q. Your Honor, the printout that has been marked as Exhibit 66 was delivered to Ms. Jones, counsel for defendant, in response to a discovery request. We move the admission in evidence of Exhibit 67.

Under Rule 1006, the court may order that Exhibit 66, the underlying data, be produced in court, so it is important to have a copy at hand. The court may wish to examine the underlying voluminous document if there is any question as to the accuracy of the summary.

3.3.4 Production and Tactics

There are three basic ways to present the results of computer work at trial. Although these methods have common elements, they present different evidentiary problems. The method chosen depends on a number of factors in the trial setting. See discussion in Chapter 9.

Oral testimony about the results of computer work

A lay witness or an expert may testify concerning the results of computer work. A lay witness must rely on one of the hearsay exemptions (business records, opposing party's records, public records, and so on) to qualify the data. The resulting exhibit may be a summary generated in court (see example in Section 1.2.2 and Section 3.2.1) or a prepared testimony aid (see Section 1.2).

An expert witness may testify about computer work performed by the expert witness or someone else without the constraints of the hearsay rule. Although the underlying computer work must be made available to the opponent for purposes of cross-examination, it is not invariably offered in evidence for independent consideration by the trier of fact. This use of computer output is governed by Rules 702 through 705, and its foundation generally is the same as for other aspects of expert opinion delivered orally.

Printouts of computer work

The different types of computer printouts can be illustrated by considering possible presentations of data concerning a company's wage payments to employees. A printout may contain: (1) a simple representation of data stored in computer memory, such as the thousands of individual wage transactions (e.g., date and amount of each wage payment to each employee); (2) a selected segment of data retrieved from the computer's memory (e.g., wage payments to a particular employee; wage payments by a particular branch office; wage payments over a particular period); (3) the results of computations routinely performed by the computer on the stored data (e.g., amount of FICA and social security tax withheld from wages); (4) a summary of stored data (e.g., a calculation of the total dollar amount of wage payments during a specific period); (5) a graphic summary of the data (e.g., a graph showing monthly total wage payments over a five-year period); or (6) projections or analyses based on the data (e.g., projected wages based on past payments and assumed inflation, bargaining results, employment levels, and the like). The level of detail selected for the exhibit will depend on particular trial objectives. Generally, simpler is better.

The computer printout may be in exactly the same format as used for commercial purposes, or the format may be altered to make the information easier to present to jurors. If you alter the format, be sure to acknowledge that in the foundation testimony for the exhibit.

Screen displays of computer work

Computer-generated evidence can be presented as screen displays rather than as hard copy printouts. The screen display can come directly from the computer (or from the computer file displayed by another computer, such as a portable, used in the courtroom) and displayed on a video monitor. See Section 9.6. Alternatively, a printout can be displayed by an electronic system on a television monitor (see Section 9.5) or by a projector screen system on a large reflective screen (see Section 9.4).

The witness can also use a computer in court to perform calculations or other functions in response to questions from the examiner, with the results displayed on the video display monitor normally used in conjunction with the computer. This is a much riskier method and opens some unusual opportunities on cross-examination.

ENDNOTES

1. 5 *Weinstein's Evidence* 1006[07].
2. *See Scott McGregor, Graphics Simplified* (1979). This illustrated text provides an excellent source of helpful pointers relevant to the use of charts as trial exhibits.

CHAPTER 4

MAPS, DIAGRAMS, DRAWINGS, AND SKETCHES

Representations of objects or places at issue that are produced by artists or technicians fall in the general category of "documents," and thus share some of the characteristics of the "text documents" described in Chapter 1 and Chapter 2 and the "numbers documents" described in Chapter 3. The key to admissibility of representational or "picture documents" such as maps, diagrams, drawings, and sketches is the degree of fairness and accuracy with which they represent the "real" thing—that is, the place, organization, object, or other thing being illustrated. Section 4.1 covers maps; Section 4.2 deals with diagrams; Section 4.3 explains drawings done by qualified artists or technicians; and Section 4.4 distinguishes sketches done by witnesses or officials on duty.

4.1 MAPS

A map, as the term is used here, is a drawing made to scale showing the location of certain physical features. Maps can assist in developing an overview or a perspective of the events at issue. Maps are also important when distances or the operation of physical principles based on distances are at issue.

Not every geographic fact requires an exhibit. The court will take judicial notice of many aspects of geography including the boundaries of political subdivisions, the intersection of roads, the location of particular well-known sites as north, south, east, or west of others, and similar matters that, under Rule 201, are either: "(1) generally known within the territorial jurisdiction of the trial court or (2) capable of accurate and ready determination by resort to sources whose accuracy cannot be reasonably questioned." The sources for geographic facts referred to by this rule generally are official or published maps.

4.1.1 Foundation

There are three types of maps: a standard map published by the government or reputable private publisher; an aerial photo that has been made into a map by a reputable mapmaker or surveyor; and a map made from measurements by a surveyor or mapmaker on the ground. The foundation requirements are as follows.

Foundation for standard map

The proponent of the map must first establish the competence of the witness to testify about the map and the relevance of the map to an issue in the case. The witness must identify the map and then provide the element of trustworthiness. See Section 1.1. If the map has been produced by a federal, state, or local government, Rule 902(5) provides the authentication as a publication "purporting to be issued by public authority."

Example

Q. Mr. Martin, where are you employed?

A. At AAA Realty Co., 925 Main Street, Centerville.

Q. Are you acquainted with the property at the intersection of Oak Road and First Street that is involved in this case?

A. Yes.

Q. How did you come to know about that property?

A. I have lived in the community for 25 years and I have visited that property many times. More recently, I did an appraisal of that property. For that purpose I made a detailed inspection.

Q. May I have this marked as Exhibit 5?

Reporter: *(Marks)*

Q. Let the record reflect that I have shown what has been marked as defendant's Exhibit 5 to counsel for plaintiff.

Opposing Counsel: *(Looks)*

Q. Mr. Martin, are you familiar with what has been marked as Exhibit 5?

A. Yes.

Q. What is it?

A. This is a plat of the area including the property at the intersection of Oak and First.

Q. By whom was that plat made?

A. This plat is published by the Lavelle County government.

Q. Where did you get it?

A. I got it from the County Recorder's Office.

Q. Your Honor, we move the admission in evidence of what has been marked as plaintiff's Exhibit 5.

In this case, the map is made by a county government, so it qualifies under Rule 902(5) and is self-authenticating.

If a well-known company in the field published the map and it was not made for any purpose connected with the litigation, a similar foundation is available.

Example

Q. Ms. Gerardi, do you know about the overseas operations of XYZ Co.?

A. Yes.

Q. How did you come to know about that?

A. As a officer of the company, I traveled periodically to each overseas installation.

Q. May I have this marked as plaintiff's Exhibit 6?

Reporter: *(Marks)*

Q. Let the record reflect I have shown what has been marked as plaintiff's Exhibit 6 to counsel for defendant.

Opposing Counsel: *(Looks)*

Q. Ms. Gerardi, are you familiar with what has been marked as Exhibit 6?

A. Yes.

Q. What is it?

A. It is a map of the world.

Q. Who made the map?

A. It is a standard Mercator projection map published by the National Geographic Society.

Q. Is this map available for sale to the public?

A. Yes.

Q. Was the map made for any purpose connected with this litigation?

A. No. It is a standard map sold by the National Geographic Society.

Q. Have any additions been made to the map?

A. Yes. There are red dots at each of the locations of the company's engineering offices; white dots at each of the company's manufacturing plants; and blue dots at each of the company's construction projects.

Q. Who put those marks on the map?

A. I did.

Q. Are the locations indicated by the red, white, and blue dots accurate?

A. Yes.

Q. Have any other additions or changes been made to the standard published map?

A. No.

Q. Your Honor, we move the admission in evidence of plaintiff's Exhibit 6.

This is not a map published by a public authority, so it is not self-authenticating. However, there should be little controversy about any map from a source not connected in any way with the litigation. Under Rule 901(b)(1) the testimony of a witness who describes the map should establish the necessary identification and trustworthiness.

Standard maps are often used as background for testimony aids showing how something was transported from point A to point B. Lawyers rarely challenge the map portions of these exhibits, and no foundation as to the map itself may be necessary if the exhibit has been presented to the other side and there has been no objection directed at the map. You can lay the foundation for the testimony aid incorporating a map the same way as described in Section 1.2.

Foundation for aerial photo map

A map made from an aerial photo traces relevant detail on the photo (or blocks out nonrelevant detail) and preserves on the resulting map the same scale and relationships as shown on the photo. The map can then be made larger or smaller than the photo through standard copying processes. The foundation for this kind of map qualifies the aerial photo first and then qualifies the changes to make it into a map.

Example

(A two-witness procedure to qualify one map)

The photographer:

Q. Ms. Kershner, would you give us your full name?

A. Jacqueline Avery Kershner.

Q. Where are you employed?

A. At National Air Survey, Inc.

Q. What do you do there?

A. I am a camera operator for an aerial photography team.

Q. How long have you been employed in that position?

A. I was an apprentice for one year and I have been an operator for three years.

Q. Would you describe for us the procedure by which aerial photographs are taken?

A. *(Witness describes how the pilot determines position, how camera is mounted in place.)*

Q. May I have this marked as defendant's Exhibit 52A?

Reporter: *(Marks)*

Q. Let the record reflect that I have shown counsel for plaintiff what has been marked as Exhibit 52A.

Opposing Counsel: *(Looks)*

Q. Ms. Kershner, what is Exhibit 52A?

A. That is an aerial photograph that I took.

Q. When was it taken?

A. In October of last year.

Q. What equipment did you use?

A. *(Witness describes type of camera, lens, shutter speed, and other relevant technical details)*

Q. What film did you use?

A. *(Witness describes)*

Q. From what location was this photograph taken?

A. *(Witness describes altitude, latitude, and longitude)*

Q. Does Exhibit 52A fairly and accurately represent the ground features in the area covered by the photograph?

A. Yes, it does.

Q. Were any alterations or deletions made to the photograph?

A. No.

The map maker:

Q. Mr. Nelson, would you give us your full name?

A. Wendell Axel Nelson.

Q. Where are you employed?

A. At Map Resources, Inc.

Q. What do you do there?

A. I am a mapmaker.

Q. How long have you been employed in that position?

A. For five years.

Q. Would you describe your qualifications as a mapmaker?

A. *(Witness describes training and experience)*

Q. Have you had occasion to make maps from aerial photographs?

A. Yes, we often do that.

Q. How often have you done that?

A. I have probably made about 60 maps from various kinds of aerial photographs.

Q. Would you describe for us the procedure by which maps are made from aerial photographs?

A. *(Witness describes equipment and procedures used)*

Q. May I have this marked as Exhibit 52?

Reporter: *(Marks)*

Q. Let the record reflect that I have shown to counsel for plaintiff what has been marked as Exhibit 52.

Opposing Counsel: *(Looks)*

Q. Mr. Nelson, what is Exhibit 52?

A. This is a map that I made.

Q. Are you familiar with what has been marked as Exhibit 52A?

A. Yes.

Q. How did you become familiar with that?

A. Exhibit 52A is the photograph that I used to make the map that is Exhibit 52.

Q. When was Exhibit 52 made?

A. I completed my work toward the end of October last year.

Q. Would you describe what you did with Exhibit 52A to make Exhibit 52?

A. *(Witness describes)*

Q. Is Exhibit 52 a fair and accurate representation of the area bounded by Woods Road, Welcome Road, Trevor Road, and State Highway #1?

A. Yes it is.

Q. Your Honor, we offer Exhibit 52 in evidence.

Court: Admitted.

These two witnesses with personal knowledge establish the identification and trustworthiness of this exhibit. No special authentication requirements need be met for this category of exhibit.

Often, a description of the process by which a map is made from an aerial photograph makes it more convincing as an exhibit. If the map is particularly critical, you may want to have the qualifying witness provide more details. The underlying materials may be marked as exhibits but not offered in evidence if there is a concern that the fact-finder might become confused.

A valid challenge to foundation arises if the qualifications of the mapmaker are not sufficient. However, this is rarely used because the court will usually rule that this is relevant to the weight to be given to the exhibit, but not to its admissibility.

Foundation for litigation map

If a map is made specially for litigation, and it is to be qualified as accurate, you must qualify it by a surveyor, professional mapmaker, or someone else who made all the necessary measurements.

Example

(After establishing qualifications and relevance)

Q. May I have this marked as Exhibit 16?

Reporter: *(Marks)*

Q. Let the record reflect that I have shown what has been marked as Exhibit 16 to counsel for plaintiff.

Opposing Counsel: *(Looks)*

Q. Mr. Jensen, can you identify what has been marked as Exhibit 16?

A. Yes.

Q. What is it?

A. It is a map of the school and grounds of the East Brentwood High School located at 47th and East Roads.

Q. Who made Exhibit 16?

A. That is a map that I made.

Q. When did you make the map?

A. About six months ago.

Q. How did you make the map?

A. I went to the school and grounds with two of my assistants and measured all significant distances to establish the relationships between objects shown on the map. I recorded all the measurements in my notes and made a preliminary sketch. Then I went back to my office and prepared the map from my notes and my sketch.

Q. Does the map include all objects at the school and grounds?

A. No, only significant objects.

Q. What scale is used on the map?

A. The map was prepared using a scale of one inch equals 10 feet. That scale is indicated in the lower right-hand corner.

Q. What, if anything, did you do to check the accuracy of the map?

A. After I completed the map, I returned to the school and grounds and made a visual inspection to check the accuracy of the map.

Q. What did you determine?

A. I determined that the map was accurate.

Q. Your Honor, we move the admission in evidence of the map that has been marked as defendant's Exhibit 16.

Court: So ordered.

Q. Your Honor, may we distribute copies of Exhibit 16 to the jury at this time?

Court: You may proceed.

(Hand copies to juror #1 who passes them along to other jurors.)

Q. Mr. Jensen, what symbols are used on the map?

A. The symbols are described in the legend in the lower left-hand corner. The double solid lines indicate brick exterior walls. The single solid lines indicate interior walls. The wavy lines indicate temporary movable interior walls.

Q. What do the colors mean?

A. The colors are also described in the legend in the lower left-hand corner. The blue area is the part where water damage occurred; the brown area is the part where blast damage occurred.

Q. What labels are used on the map?

A. I placed seven labels on the map. The label "sidewalk" indicates a normal concrete sidewalk. The label "driveway" indicates a macadam road two lanes wide. The label "parking lot" indicates a paved area with horizontal lines marking parking spaces for cars. The label "main entrance" indicates the doorway facing East Road. The label "side entrance" indicates the doorway facing 47th Street. The label "back entrance" indicates the doorway facing the parking lot. The label "tree" indicates several large maple trees.

It is important to note that generally the testimony about what is on the map can come in only after the map has been admitted in evidence. After the map has been qualified as evidence, the person who made it can testify about what it shows, and other witnesses can use it to describe their knowledge of relevant events.

It is theoretically possible to put in a foundation for map through someone who watched the measurements being made, but that is quite risky if the exhibit is important.

4.1.2 Objections

Maps generally do not fall under the category of a "written assertion" and therefore are not "statements" within this coverage of the hearsay rules.[1] Judges differ in their approach, however, and if there are extra words and labels on the map placed there after the map was published by someone not testifying, the exhibit may be met with a hearsay objection. No hearsay objection should be sustained to a map drawn by the witness who is on the stand. That witness is subject to cross-examination about his or her work. See Section 1.3.1. If a hearsay objection is made, and the court thinks the map qualifies as a "statement" under Rule 801(a)(1), you can meet that objection by the exception under Rule 803(8) for maps published by public authorities and by the exception under Rule 803(17) for maps published by private publishers. Some maps will qualify as records of documents affecting an interest in property under Rule 803(14). The general purpose exception under Rule 803(24) is also available.

Maps may be subject to the original document rule because they include "letters, words, or numbers, or their equivalent" although they are not "writings" as that term is usually used under Rule 1001.[2] Judges may entertain an original document objection, however, so you should be prepared. See generally Section 1.3.2. Under Rule 1001(3), when thousands of maps are published in one printing or issue, each individual map is a "counterpart intended to have the same effect by a person . . . issuing it" and is qualified as an original. There is no original document objection to exact duplicates of maps of which only a single original was made. To qualify a duplicate, under Rule 1001(4), a witness will need to testify that the exhibit "accurately reproduces the original." Once qualified in this fashion, under Rule 1003 the duplicate is admissible to the same extent as the original unless the opponent of the exhibit shows some genuine question as to the authenticity of the original or unfairness in admitting the duplicate. These factors are usually not relevant to maps. There is no original document objection to an enlargement of a map. An enlargement that is an exact copy is a duplicate. If marks have been made on the map that cause it to be different from the original, either the marks must have an independent foundation (see example in Section 2.2.3) or the proponent of the exhibit must account for the missing original as specified in Rule 1004.

A map is subject to the policy objections under Rule 403 of unfair prejudice or confusion/misleading if there is any significant distortion, over- or under-inclusion of details, or use of details beyond the expert capability of the mapmaker. Opponents may also object to argumentative labels and inappropriate colors on the same basis. Occasionally an objection to confusion/misleading arises when the underlying map is accurate, but a lay witness has sketched in additions to the map with no consideration for relative size. See Section 1.3.3.

If a portion of a map or enlargement of a portion of a map is offered in evidence, under Rule 106 your opponent may demand that additional parts of the map be offered at the same time. The application of Rule 106 to a map depends on whether the court considers it a "writing." Courts go both ways on this question as many maps originate from aerial and satellite photos which are not writings.

4.1.3 Production and Tactics

There is an enormous library of maps produced by government agencies and reliable private agencies like the National Geographic Society. Nearly every federal agency produces maps of areas within its jurisdiction, and many state and local agencies have excellent maps available for a very modest price.

A mapmaker can draw a map of an area only a few hundred feet square, as in the mapping of skid marks on a pavement, or an area hundreds of miles square, as in an environmental case. In small-area mapping situations, the mapmaker usually works from direct measurements. The mapmaker will accompany the lawyer to the site and get instructions on what is to be done. Then measurements are made in a careful systematic manner; the measurements are recorded; and the map is produced from the record. For larger maps, a surveyor may be used and the map will be made from the surveyor's notes.

Maps are made from actual measurements and are intended to be produced to scale. Diagrams, by contrast, are not made from exact measurements and need not be drawn exactly to scale. See discussion in Section 4.2. The scale for a map can be any one chosen by the lawyer as most efficient for use in the courtroom. A professional mapmaker can produce a map to any scale from a given set of measurements.

It is important to decide at the outset and to discuss with the mapmaker how much detail should be put into the map. As with photographs, it is important not to include too much extraneous detail or an objection will be forthcoming. Maps are most effective with jurors when they show all the essential features but are not cluttered with (even relevant) detail. If you require a large number of details, consider using several versions of the same map.

Once you have settled on an appropriate approach to the problem and level of detail, then you must address how the map will be used in the courtroom. The factors such as size, weight, color, typeface, and other design considerations with respect to a map as an exhibit are discussed in Chapter 9. An example of a map using color keys is shown in Fig. 20.

Some lawyers advise that in order to make the map into a more integral part of the witness's testimony, the witness should add something to it in the courtroom. This could be a mark noting where the witness stood or a line showing a route taken. Unless the witness is an expert or a seasoned courtroom veteran, it is probably more prudent to limit the witness to very simple tasks with respect to a map and to practice the markings numerous times before the actual testimony is undertaken.

At trial, you can use overlays with maps in the same way you do with photographs, charts, and boards. See discussion in Section 9.2.3. The marks to be made on the map by one witness can be made on an overlay; then the next witness can mark on the map using a separate overlay. This minimizes confusion by keeping the map itself clean and simple.

Maps often must be very large exhibits to be effective—larger than the standard chart or board that rests comfortably on the standard easel. You may need special frames for these very large exhibits. This type of map can be mounted on a very large piece of foamboard (up to 4 x 8'); it can be divided and mounted onto panels of foamboard for larger freestanding displays; it can be put up on a convenient wall if the courtroom configuration is suitable; or it can be mounted on an exhibit frame. The exhibit frame is discussed in Section 9.3.1.

Alternatively, depending on the configuration of the courtroom, you may try taping large map exhibits to a wall. Often the wall to one side of the jury box is available. If there is a door, the door can be blocked off temporarily from the other side and the exhibit can be mounted on the wall stretching across the door.

4.2 DIAGRAMS

Diagrams are line drawings that can be used to simplify the description of technical processes, manufacturing production lines, or the construction of a building or product. Diagrams can also be schematics or flow charts that summarize how certain actions were taken, sources of financing or supply, or the relationship between parts of an organization. Diagrams may be used to substitute for simple maps showing an intersection or the location of a building on a lot.

4.2.1 Foundation

In framing a foundation for a diagram that is to be offered in evidence, do not ask it to do too much. Diagrams are simplified representations of complicated information. One often hears lawyers ask if diagrams are a "fair and accurate" representation of something. A better approach is to establish that the diagram itself is a "fair"

representation and that the information it contains is accurate. A
diagram cannot be an *accurate* representation of a totality of
information about a subject (such as "the organization" of a company)
because it omits many details. You can, however, characterize it as a
fair representation of the "general plan of organization" of the company.

Example

Q. Ms. Monsen, by whom are you employed?

A. By the XYZ Company.

Q. What is your position with XYZ Company?

A. I am the Senior Vice President for Manufacturing.

Q. Do you know about the current organization of the XYZ
Company?

A. Yes.

Q. How did you come learn about that?

A. I have been with the company for 10 years.

Q. May I have this marked as Exhibit 55?

Reporter: *(Marks)*

Q. Let the record reflect that I have shown Exhibit 55 to counsel
for plaintiff.

Opposing Counsel: *(Looks)*

Q. Ms. Monsen, are you familiar with Exhibit 55?

A. Yes.

Q. What is it?

A. It is a diagram showing the organization of the XYZ Company.

Q. Who made Exhibit 55?

A. That was made by Janet Jones who works for the Graphic
Arts Design Co.

Q. What information did Ms. Jones use in preparing this
diagram?

A. She used our company organization manual, and I also
explained the company organization to her.

Q. Does the diagram fairly represent the general organization of
the XYZ Company?

A. Yes, it does.

Q. Is the information portrayed by the diagram accurate?

A. Yes, it is.

Q. Your Honor, we move the admission in evidence of the diagram that has been marked as Exhibit 55.

Court: So ordered.

Q. Ms. Monsen, directing your attention to the diagram, what do the squares indicate?

A. Those are major manufacturing components.

Q. What do the circles indicate?

A. Those are consulting or engineering components.

Q. What do the triangles indicate?

A. Those are subsidiary companies.

Q. What do the solid lines indicate?

A. Those are direct lines of authority within the company. Any lower unit connected to a higher unit by a solid line is under the authority of the higher unit and reports to the head of the higher unit.

Q. What do the dotted lines indicate?

A. Those are coordinating lines within the company. Any unit connected to another unit by a dotted line is supposed to keep that unit informed of its activities, although there is no direct line of authority.

Q. Using this diagram that is Exhibit 55, would you explain to the jury how decisions are made at the XYZ Company with respect to manufacturing changes?

A. *(Explains)*

In this example the foundation includes relatively little about the qualifications of the person who made the diagram and the reliability and accuracy of the information on which the diagram is based. That is usually the case with the diagrams because they are relatively simple representations as compared to maps, drawings, or models. But a complicated diagram on a difficult point might require a fuller explanation before you establish a foundation. See the foundation requirements for a litigation map in Section 4.1.1.

Foundation challenges to diagrams rarely arise because the diagram usually represents something about which the witness has personal knowledge. No special formulations exist under the evidence rules with respect to identification or trustworthiness beyond the requirement that the diagram be a fair representation. See Section 1.1.

Diagrams can also be qualified as testimony aids if they assist in the presentation or understanding of the testimony. See Section 1.2.

4.2.2 Objections

There are no hearsay objections to a diagram. Titles are not subject to a hearsay objection because the witness can testify from first hand knowledge as to the meaning conveyed by the title. This is also usually the case with any labels on the diagram.

There are no original document objections to a diagram because it is not a "writing" within the meaning of Rule 1001(1). The fact that it is drawn from other information is not sufficient to invoke the original document rule. Duplicates or enlargements of it are entitled to be used to the same extent as the original diagram.

Your opponent may raise valid policy objections. Courts will sustain objections to a diagram if it is poorly executed and therefore may confuse the jury. Other potentially valid objections arise if the labels on the diagram are inaccurate, unfair, argumentative, or suggestive; or if the diagram is needless cumulative evidence because of photographs or other material with a subject matter common to the diagram. See Section 1.3.3.

4.2.3 Production and Tactics

Diagrams should use simple shapes or outlines in bold black lines. You should be able to comprehend the overall pattern or message of the diagram quickly. E.g., Fig. 21 (technical process). Every significant item on the diagram should have a clear, simple label in type large enough to be read at a distance of 10 to 15 feet or wherever the fact-finder will be located. E.g., Fig. 22 and Fig. 23. You should usually avoid complicated designs like zebra stripes or cross-hatching as tools for distinguishing one part of the diagram from another. These present a visually confusing message and make the diagram *look* as if it is going to be hard to understand.

The tactics with respect to the use of a diagram with witness testimony are generally the same as those described in Chapter 3 with respect to charts and graphs. Suggestions for displaying diagrams are included in Chapter 9.

4.3 DRAWINGS

On occasion, a drawing will permit the most effective presentation of a point because it can illustrate internal workings or a perspective not visible through a photograph or videotape. Medical illustrations, anatomical drawings, and cutaway drawings of machinery are examples that fall in this category.

4.3.1 Foundation

A drawing is an artist's rendition of reality and is, perhaps, more susceptible to subjective presentation than a photograph or videotape. For this reason, a standard drawing published by a reputable publisher and used for purposes other than litigation may be the best alternative, if available. Establishing competence, relevance, and adequate identification is done through the witness who will use the drawing. Establishing trustworthiness is done through a witness with first hand or expert knowledge vouching for the drawing and the credentials of the publisher or artist. See Section 1.1.

Sometimes it is adequate simply to use a standard medical illustration for purposes of assisting an expert's testimony. A standard illustration from a reputable source that does not purport to be a representation of anything special about the case can be used to describe what happened.

Example

Q. May I have this marked as plaintiff's Exhibit 34?

Reporter: *(Marks)*

Q. Let the record reflect I am handing what has been marked as plaintiff's Exhibit 34 to counsel for defendant.

Opposing Counsel: *(Looks)*

Q. Doctor, can you identify what has been marked as plaintiff's Exhibit 34?

A. Yes.

Q. What is it?

A. It is a standard anatomical drawing of the leg.

Q. Who made the drawing?

A. The drawing is published by XYZ Company for use in medical schools, teaching hospitals, and other similar institutions. We use it for teaching purposes at the Mount Everest Hospital.

Q. When was it published?

A. This one was copyrighted two years ago.

Q. Is the drawing a fair and accurate representation of the muscle and ligament tissues of the leg?

A. Yes.

Q. Your Honor, we move the admission in evidence of plaintiff's Exhibit 34.

A drawing need not be done to scale. Any questions as to scale go to the weight given to the exhibit, not its admissibility.

In special cases, where the injuries to be described are fairly unique and standard anatomical drawings do not permit the expert to make the point, it may be necessary to prepare a special drawing for litigation purposes. This will require a more extensive foundation.

Example

(After qualifying the doctor as an expert)

Q. When did you first examine Ms. Miller?

A. It was eight months ago.

Q. What did you do on your first examination?

A. Ms. Miller was brought into the emergency room on a stretcher. She was unconscious and there was no one who could tell us anything about her injuries. Nothing was known about her from our records, so I first quickly checked all the vital signs and, finding them stable, proceeded to a detailed examination of Ms. Miller to determine the extent of her injuries.

Q. Did you determine the extent of Ms. Miller's injuries?

A. Yes, I did.

Q. May I have this drawing marked as plaintiff's Exhibit 53?

Reporter: *(Marks)*

Q. Let the record reflect that I am handing what has been marked as Exhibit 53 to counsel for defendant.

Opposing Counsel: *(Looks)*

Q. Doctor, can you identify what has been marked as plaintiff's Exhibit 53?

A. Yes. That is a medical illustration showing a cross section of the chest and abdominal area.

Q. Who made this drawing?

A. It was made by Alvin Adelaide, a medical illustrator on the staff of Mount Everest Hospital.

Q. Are you familiar with Mr. Adelaide's qualifications?

A. Yes, I am. He has worked as a medical illustrator for the hospital for seven years. He produces illustrations for the hospital's teaching functions and has worked with several hospital staff and faculty to produce medical illustrations for published texts.

Q. Do you have an opinion as to the quality of Mr. Adelaide's work?

A. Yes I do.

Q. What is that opinion?

A. It is excellent.

Q. Who directed Mr. Adelaide's work with respect to Exhibit 53?

A. I did.

Q. What reference materials, if any, did you use in directing Mr. Adelaide's work?

A. I used the hospital records with respect to Ms. Miller and the x-rays that were taken of Ms. Miller, plus my own observations of Ms. Miller.

Q. Is the medical illustration that has been marked as Exhibit 53 a fair portrayal of Ms. Miller's injuries?

A. Yes, it is.

A. Your Honor, we move the admission in evidence of plaintiff's Exhibit 53.

Normally the hospital records and x-rays will have been admitted in evidence and the drawing can be qualified by reference to prior exhibits. However, the witness is an expert and, under Rule 703, she can use material not admitted in evidence on which to base her opinion. Her opinion, in this case, is the nature of Ms. Miller's injuries.

It makes no difference whether the artist had any first hand knowledge through observation of Ms. Miller as long as the witness, who does have first hand knowledge affirms the accuracy of what the artist did.

Objections to foundation matters, such as the qualifications of the artist, generally go to the weight to be accorded the exhibit rather than its admissibility.

4.3.2 Objections

Because drawings are not statements under Rule 801(a), no hearsay objections arise as to them.[3]

The original document rule does not apply to drawings because they are not writings or recordings under Rule 1001(1).[4] A drawing may have been made using writings, photographs, or x-rays as reference materials but it has an independent status.

However, your opponent may assert valid policy objections under Rule 403. These objections usually arise when a drawing is incomplete, places undue emphasis on a particular aspect or relation to the whole, or is not accurate in some important detail. This objection may be phrased as "unfair prejudice" because the drawing is unduly suggestive or is "confusing or misleading" the jury. See Section 1.3.3.

4.3.3 Production and Tactics

A number of medical publishing companies produce standard anatomical drawings used by medical schools and teaching hospitals.[5] These companies usually have lists of their products and can supply the information on the qualifications of the person or persons who made the illustration. Most medical research institutions have medical illustrators available on a consulting basis. These people often take private consulting assignments and have a good rapport with the medical personnel so that they can get enough of their time to get an accurate description of what should be portrayed. Examples of various kinds of medical drawings are shown in Fig. 24, Fig. 25, Fig. 26, and Fig. 27.

Cutaway drawings are particularly useful in helping the fact-finder envision the internal workings of machinery or other equipment. It is important to have clear, concise, easily-read labels on cutaway drawings because the whole point of the exhibit can be lost if the fact-finder cannot identify what is being presented. Standard cutaway drawings are available for many kinds of equipment and can be enlarged or modified to suit particular litigation purposes. Engineering draftsmen and illustrators are often available through engineering schools, professional associations, or firms specializing in the preparation of exhibits.

Drawings can also be useful in dealing with very complicated photographs. Using photo editing software, the photograph can be turned into an illustration that eliminates nonessential details and emphasizes important ones by the addition of color, contrasting, or outlining. Some of the complexity may be alleviated by using drawings with overlays. Drawings done exactly to scale are also very useful to depict witness accounts or investigator reports.

Any drawing used in a courtroom should be large enough so that the jurors in the back row can see it and should be colored in a way that assists the witness's explanation. See discussion in Chapter 9 of methods for presenting drawings.

The tactical considerations for the use of drawings with witness testimony in the courtroom are generally the same as those described in Chapter 3 with respect to charts and graphs.

4.4 SKETCHES

Sketches are informal drawings, usually by lay witnesses, made to illustrate a point or the relationship between or among objects observed by the witness. They are different from maps, diagrams, and drawings which are usually done by professionals with special credentials. Sketches generally fall into three categories: those done at the time of a particular occurrence; those included in reports or depositions; and those done in court. The approach to foundation and objections is uncomplicated. See Section 1.1.

4.4.1 Sketches Done at the Time of a Particular Event

The documentary record of an event may include a sketch by a witness who was at the scene. Sometimes persons involved in or witness to a traffic accident will make a contemporaneous drawing of what they saw. A police officer may make a sketch as the basis for a later report. An insurance investigator may make measurements and include a sketch in order to make clear how the measurements were made. If the person who made the sketch does not testify, anyone who was present at the event, and who has first hand knowledge of the making of the sketch, can qualify it by providing the necessary testimony as to identification and trustworthiness.

Example

(After establishing competence and relevance)

Q. Mr. Dougherty, can you identify what has been marked as Exhibit 31?

A. Yes.

Q. What is it?

A. That is a sketch made shortly after the accident by Officer Wells when she arrived at the scene.

Q. Where were you at the time?

A. I was standing right next to Officer Wells, and I described what happened.

Q. Is Exhibit 31 a fair representation of the intersection where the collision happened?

A. Yes.

Q. Is Exhibit 31 a fair representation of how the cars collided?

A. Yes.

Q. Is Exhibit 31 a fair representation of where the cars were after the collision?

A. Yes.

Q. Your Honor, we offer Exhibit 31 in evidence.

If there is no problem in identifying the sketch, then the witness needs only to have first hand knowledge of what the sketch portrays to be able to qualify it as a fair representation of the events at issue.

4.4.2 Sketches Made in Reports and Depositions

Investigative reports, police reports, witness statements, and depositions may contain sketches in which the relative position of persons or objects is illustrated.

The first choice for a witness to provide the foundation for a sketch included in a report is the person who made the sketch. That person, while testifying in court, can authenticate the sketch as a fair representation of what he or she saw.

It is unclear whether a sketch is a "statement" as defined by Rule 801(a) and therefore included in the definition of hearsay under Rule 801(c). A statement is defined as "an oral or written assertion . . . if it is intended by the person as an assertion." No definition of "written" is included in Rule 801, although in Rule 1001, the definition of "writings and recordings" is something that "consist[s] of letters, words, or numbers, or their equivalent, set down by handwriting, typewriting, printing , photostating, photography, magnetic impulse, mechanical or electronic recording, or other forms of data compilation." Judges rule both ways on the question whether a sketch included in a report is a "statement" and therefore subject to this hearsay rule so, unless there is a definitive opinion controlling in your state, the better practice is to be prepared for the objection.

Some sketches made in reports will qualify for the exception under Rule 803(1) as a present sense impression. Rule 803(1) allows "a statement describing or explaining an event or condition made while the declarant was perceiving the event or condition or immediately thereafter." If the sketch was not made close enough to the event at issue to fulfill the "immediately thereafter" requirement, you will need to go to the general purpose exception under Rule 803(24) and use the fact that the witness who made the drawing is on the stand and available for cross-examination. Rule 801(d)(1) usually does not apply because that requires the statement to be inconsistent with the declarant's testimony before it can be used on direct examination. Note also that Rule 803(5) on recorded recollection is not useful in this context because it does not permit the admission of the statement itself as an exhibit.

As in the example in Section 4.4.1, if the person who made the sketch is not available, any person who has first hand knowledge of the making of the sketch can identify it and anyone with first hand knowledge of the events depicted can testify that the sketch is a fair representation.

Sketches made by police officers or other personnel employed by public offices or agencies can be brought under an exception to the hearsay rule for public records and reports, but only in civil cases. Rule 803(8) covers reports of public officers or agencies setting forth:

> (B) matters observed pursuant to duty imposed by law as to which matters there was a duty to report, excluding, however, in criminal cases matters observed by police officers and other law enforcement personnel, or (C) in civil actions and proceedings and against the Government in criminal cases, factual findings resulting from an investigation made pursuant to authority granted by law, unless the sources of information or other circumstances indicate lack of trustworthiness.

The foundation for sketches done during depositions should be completed during the deposition, as the deponent may not show up to testify at trial. These sketches are covered in Section 10.1.5.

4.4.3 Sketches Made in Court During Trial

Occasionally you will need to ask a witness to make a sketch on a blackboard, whiteboard, or sketch pad to illustrate some part of the testimony. An example is set out Section 1.2.1. This should be done only when there is no time to have the sketch done ahead of time and when the witness has sufficient experience or presence of mind to be able to deliver a credible sketch.

In-court sketches are, in general, very risky. Witnesses, both expert and lay, are under considerable pressure in the courtroom. This often makes them too nervous to draw accurately or to get relationships fixed accurately on a blank blackboard. Many people just have no artistic ability and, even if they were not under pressure, their drawings would be hard to follow. Only rarely should you allow a witness (other than an expert who is accustomed, for example, to using sketches in classroom lectures) an extemporaneous exercise at a blackboard, whiteboard, or sketch pad. Too often the resulting exhibit simply convinces the fact-finder that the witness is hopelessly muddled. Testimony aids prepared ahead of time and checked for accuracy are much safer and more effective.

Your opponent may try to get the witness to make additional marks on the sketch. If this happens, it is useful to preserve a copy of the sketch as it was when the witness finished with it. Have the witness mark up a piece of transparent plastic mylar that has been put over the sketch, or mark up the sketch on the blackboard only after a photograph of it has been made to preserve the original. See discussion of overlays in Section 9.3.2.

ENDNOTES

1. 2 *McCormick on Evidence* §§ 213, 246.

2. *Id.* §§ 230-36.

3. *Id.* § 246.

4. *Id.* at 97-99.

5. *See, e.g., Henry M. Philo, Lawyer's Desk Reference: Technical Sources for Conducting a Personal Injury Action,* §§ 2.58, 2.59 (8th ed. Supp. 1995). Two other sources for medical illustrations: Guild of National Science Illustrators, Inc., P.O. Box 652, Ben Franklin Station, Washington D.C.; Association Medical Illustrators, Route 5, Box 31 IF, Midlothian, Virginia.

CHAPTER 5

OBJECTS, SUBSTANCES, AND SITE VIEWS

The exhibits discussed in this chapter are the "real" thing. They are the physical things that are the issues in the case, such as defective parts and physical injuries. This chapter also includes "views" by the judge or jury when they go to the site to examine something too large to bring into the courtroom.

For purposes of laying a foundation, physical objects and substances fall into two categories: those that are unique and can be recognized on sight and those that cannot be identified reliably just by looking at them and for which a chain of custody or possession must be established. In dealing with this category of tangible evidence, the key issue as to admissibility is whether the object really is what it purports to be. In addition, the foundation testimony must establish that the exhibit is in substantially the same condition now as it was at the time in issue. This kind of evidence has the most interest for the fact-finder and therefore should be handled carefully in order to obtain the maximum benefit. Concomitantly, losing an exhibit in this category because an objection is sustained can appear to jurors to have an importance far beyond the actual legal significance. The inference drawn is usually adverse to the proponent of the exhibit, so caution and full preparation are necessary.

A "view" by a judge or jury of places or things at issue in a case is not a matter covered by the Federal Rules of Evidence. Under the common law, the court has an inherent power to order a view by the jury or by the court itself. This power extends to personal property as well as real property. Most jurisdictions also have statutes covering this practice.[1] The view is important because it is another aspect of the lawyer's option to have the fact-finder look at the actual thing at issue instead of a photograph, diagram, or other representation.

5.1 UNIQUE OBJECTS

The rules and practices with respect to this kind of evidence are quite straightforward and easy to master.

5.1.1 Foundation

If something relevant to the case can be recognized because the witness saw it previously, the witness can lay the foundation by testifying that he or she recognizes the object, can identify it, and it now is in substantially the same condition as it was when the witness saw it at the relevant time. This may be a part that can be identified because it has a particular serial number, an object that can be identified because it has recognizable characteristics such as scratches in the paint, or something that is just so unique that there could not be any other.

Example

Q. Please describe the part that is attached to the end of the shaft on the milling machine installed at plaintiff's plant.

A. It is a small round sprocket with a serial number stamped on it.

Q. May I have this metal part marked as plaintiff's Exhibit 2?

Reporter: *(Marks)*

Q. May the record reflect that I have passed plaintiff's Exhibit 2 to Mr. Smith, counsel for defendant.

Opposing Counsel: *(Looks)*

Q. Mr. Gordon, I show you what has been marked as plaintiff's Exhibit 2 and ask if you have seen it before.

A. Yes.

Q. When was the first time you saw plaintiff's Exhibit 2?

A. I inspected the milling machine at plaintiff's plant on the day it broke down.

Q. How are you able to recognize plaintiff's Exhibit 2?

A. I remember that two of the teeth were broken off the sprocket. *(Points to place where teeth are missing.)* I recorded the serial number in my report. Also, I scratched my initials on the part so that I could identify it easily in the future. Those initials are still there.

Q. Is plaintiff's Exhibit 2 in substantially the same condition today as when you inspected the machine at plaintiff's plant?

A. Yes.

Q. Your Honor, we move the admission in evidence of plaintiff's Exhibit 2.

The witness may have one or more means of recognizing the item so long as the means are reasonably likely to produce an accurate identification. If the object has an inscription, sign, tag, or label "affixed in the course of business and indicating ownership, control, or origin," the object is self-authenticating under Rule 902(7) and does not require the testimony of a witness beyond establishing relevance.

The principal challenge to foundation is the means that the witness has for identifying the object. Sometimes this goes to the competence of the witness because the necessary first hand knowledge is not present. The rules are generous, however, with respect to the admissibility of relevant physical objects. Under Rule 901(b)(1), if the proponent offers testimony that "a matter is what it is claimed to be" and the witness has sufficient knowledge to support that testimony, then the requirements with respect to identification and trustworthiness have been met and the item is admissible.

5.1.2 Objections

Physical objects rarely draw hearsay objections.[2] Generally, the label or other words that are a part of an object are not a written "assertion" such that the label comes within the definition of a "statement" under Rule 801(a)(1). For that reason, the label is not within the reach of the hearsay rule. If the label bears a slogan, such as "The Best In The World", then the proponent may offer the object with the label as a part of the object and not to prove the truth of the statement on the label, which under Rule 801(c) would mean that it is not hearsay. Alternatively, the slogan may be one put there (and therefore adopted) by a party opponent, and thus is not hearsay under Rule 801(d)(2).

There is no original document objection to physical objects. The requirement of an original applies only to "a writing, recording, or photograph" and thus testimony about physical objects may be received without having the object itself before the court and jury. See Rule 1002. This means that the witness can testify about the physical object, after competence and relevance are established, and the object itself can be introduced later.

The most frequent objection to a physical object is one of the policy objections. If the object is gory or grisly, the judge may exclude it on unfair prejudice grounds. Pickled bodily parts have long fallen into this category. Exhibits of scars, injuries, or other bodily marks may also draw an objection on unfair prejudice grounds. Opponents of this type of evidence may also object on "confusion/misleading" grounds. One example is a witness who wanted to exhibit an 11" scar extending from the pubic bone to the sternum. The court sustained an objection to the proposed display on the ground that it could mislead the jury because the knife wound at issue was only one inch long; the remainder of the scar was a surgical incision to repair the damage done by the knife wound. Moreover, a surgeon was available to testify as to the location and nature of the scar.

Objections may be raised to exhibits that cause disruption in the courtroom. If the exhibit has some danger attached to it, such as acidic chemicals, gasoline engines, or high-pressure or high-temperature equipment, the judge may exclude it. Similar problems exist if the exhibit is very large or would affect the dignity of the proceedings. The judge may require photographs, models, drawings, or diagrams to be substituted. If the exhibit will take time to move into the courtroom and set up, there may be an objection on grounds of undue delay and waste of time.

5.1.3 Production and Tactics

Relatively few production problems arise with physical objects in creating the exhibit or using it effectively in the courtroom.

Large or bulky items

You will want to consider mounting very large, heavy pieces of equipment or other bulky items on a four-wheel dolly so that it can be brought before the jury with a minimum of effort and can easily be turned around if the witness wants to point to something on the back or the sides.

Very small items

An exhibit may be a very small gear, microchip, or other item that is difficult to handle because of its small size. Sometimes such exhibits can be mounted in clear blocks of plastic to make an exhibit of a size that can be handled readily and in which all sides can be examined.

Parts of the human body

Plaintiffs or defendants may want to exhibit some body part to show an injury, a scar, an identifying mark (such as a distinctive tattoo), or for some other purpose. Make sure that the witness is wearing clothes that permit the display without undue undressing or delay. If the witness is asked to show limitations in motion or aches that cause pain, technically that is regarded as a demonstration and could be subject to additional foundation requirements. See discussion in Section 7.2.

Personal injury lawyers often advocate having victims display their scars, burned tissue, amputated stumps, and the like in open court. Some even ask permission to have the jury touch something like burn tissue to feel how hardened it has become or a dent in the scalp to feel how serious the injury was. For the afficionados of terminology, having the jury touch a body part or other object in order to ascertain its condition for themselves is sometimes called "autoptic evidence" or "autoptic proference." An alternative is to videotape a medical or psychiatric examination to get an overview of the injuries that can be edited if objections are sustained.

Fish, insects, and other preserved things

Small fish or insects that may be important in an environmental case, for example, may cause jurors to feel squeamish if passed from hand to hand in their natural state. The exhibit may work better mounted in a block of clear plastic. See Fig. 28.

Other problems

Perishable, greasy, living, or dangerous things all have peculiar problems that can be resolved by careful thought and perhaps a conference with the judge. If an exhibit will be helpful in explaining your case, it should not be rejected because of handling problems until all possibilities have been explored. Sometimes a knowledgeable court clerk can offer suggestions or precedent from previous cases. Frequently the fact-finder has great interest in these physical objects. Therefore, you want to make the inspection as easy as possible to avoid any sense of frustration by the fact-finder.

The primary tactical consideration with respect to use of physical objects is the impression the object will have on the fact-finder. If the object is very small, the fact-finder (whether judge or jury) may think that such a small thing could not have caused so much trouble. Enlarged photographs may be a useful addition or substitution for making the point.

Generally if the actual item at issue is available it should be produced and made an exhibit. Otherwise jurors will speculate as to what happened to it or why it was not produced, often to the detriment of the proponent.

5.2 NONUNIQUE OBJECTS AND SUBSTANCES

If the object or material cannot be identified readily just by looking at it, then the foundation must include the chain of custody in order to establish that it really is what it purports to be. Things like samples of fluids, powders, food substances, common parts or items of equipment that have no serial numbers or other identifying marks, and chips of paint or other small pieces of things are examples of this type of evidence.

5.2.1 Foundation

The chain of custody necessary to the foundation for these nonunique objects can be established in two ways: (1) the object has been in the custody of one or more persons during the entire time and these persons so testify; or (2) the object was sealed in a tamper-proof container and marked at the time, the still-sealed container is produced in the courtroom, and the person who did the sealing testifies.

Example

Q. When did you go to the warehouse for the inspection?

A. About a week after they called me about the problem with the flour shipment.

Q. What did you do when you went to the warehouse?

A. I took samples of the flour from one bag in each lot.

Q. What did you do with the samples after you removed them from the bags?

A. I put each one in a separate special envelope that we use for storing samples. I marked each envelope showing the lot from which it had come.

Q. What did you do with the envelopes?

A. I took them back to my lab, tested them, and stored them in my sample cabinet.

Q. Did anyone else handle the samples?

A. No.

Q. What does your sample cabinet consist of?

A. It is a steel cabinet about 6 feet high by 4 feet wide with 10 shelves and a lock on the door.

Q. Who has access to your sample cabinet?

A. Only me.

Q. After placing the samples in your sample cabinet, what did you do?

A. I locked it.

Q. From the time you placed the samples in your cabinet until today, did you ever remove the samples from your cabinet?

A. No.

Q. Did you ever allow anyone else to open your sample cabinet?

A. No.

Q. What did you do with the samples today?

A. I opened my sample cabinet this morning, took out the samples, and brought them with me to court.

Q. Have the samples been in your possession since you removed them from the sample cabinet this morning?

A. Yes.

Q. May I have the samples?

A. *(Hands them over)*

Q. May I have these marked as plaintiff's Exhibits 56, 57, 58, 59, and 60?

Court reporter: *(Marks)*

A. Let the record reflect that I am showing what has been marked as plaintiff's Exhibits 56, 57, 58, 59, and 60 to counsel for the defendant.

Opposing Counsel: *(Looks)*

Q. Ms. Burns, I hand you what has been marked as plaintiff's Exhibits 56, 57, 58, 59, and 60. Are these samples in substantially the same condition now as when you collected them at the warehouse?

A. Yes.

Q. Your Honor, we move the admission in evidence of plaintiff's Exhibits 56, 57, 58, 59, and 60.

The exhibits may have been removed from the locked case on one or more occasions so long as the witness (or other witnesses) can account for the complete chain of custody. Any break in the chain could lead to an objection being sustained.

Alternatively, the nonunique objects or substances can be put in sealed containers that can be demonstrated not to have been opened or altered after the sealing and that can be identified with certainty.

Example

Q. When did you go to the warehouse for the inspection?

A. About a week after they called me about the problem with the flour shipment.

Q. What did you do when you went to the warehouse?

A. I took samples of the flour from one bag in each lot.

Q. What did you do with the samples after you removed them from the bags?

A. I tested each sample with my field kit and then placed each sample in a separate plastic bag. Then I labeled each bag and sealed it.

Q. How did you label it?

A. I put the date, the place, the lot number, the time, and my name on the label pasted to the inside of the bag.

Q. How did you seal it?

A. I have a special device that seals plastic bags by heating the open end so that the two sides melt and stick together. The sealed strip is about half an inch wide and is colored pink.

Q. What did you do with the bag after you sealed it?

A. I took it back to the lab and gave it to the lab technician who is in charge of the files.

Q. What was the condition of the bags at the time you turned them over to the lab technician?

A. They were sealed.

Q. May l have these marked as plaintiff's Exhibits 56, 57, 58, 59, and 60?

Court reporter: *(Marks)*

Q. Let the record reflect that I am showing what has been marked as plaintiffs' Exhibits 56, 57, 58, 59, and 60 to counsel for the defendant.

Opposing Counsel: *(Looks)*

Q. Ms. Burns, I show you what has been marked as plaintiffs' Exhibits 56, 57, 58, 59, and 60. Do you recognize these?

A. Yes.

Q. What are they?

A. Those are the bags that I sealed and labeled on January 20, 1988.

Q. How can you recognize these bags?

A. The labels pasted to the inside of the bag have the date, the place, the lot number, the time, and my name and signature on them.

Q. Is the seal on these bags in the same condition today as when you sealed the bags at the time, of your inspection?

A. Yes.

Q. Are the contents of Exhibits 56, 57, 58, 59, and 60 in substantially the same condition now as they were when you sealed the bags?

A. Yes. The flour samples look the same now as they did when I took the samples at the warehouse.

Q. Your Honor, we move the admission in evidence of plaintiffs' Exhibits 56, 57, 58, 59, and 60.

If more than one person has been involved in either of these processes, then each one will have to testify or provide an affidavit before the exhibit can be admitted. For example, if the lab technician performed some tests on the samples, then this witness can take the chain of custody up to the point when the lab technician gets the samples. The lab technician will then have to testify about custody from there. This means that each person in the chain has to have a means of identifying the materials and, under the chain of custody method, must have a separate seal.

In most cases where the proponent has no difficulty in establishing all links in the chain of custody, it is prudent to do so through stipulation of the parties, a procedure which is cheaper and more expeditious than parading before the fact-finder a host of custody witnesses offering predictable testimony and perhaps irritating the court. Alternatively, if the opponent refuses to stipulate, the proponent of the exhibits can ask the court for a separate hearing, either pretrial or when the jury is not sitting, when the witnesses who provide the foundation can be called. Under Rule 104(a), foundation evidence is for the court, not the jury, and need not to be a part of the trial itself.

The foundation challenges with respect to nonunique objects generally go to the adequacy of the showing of complete chain of custody. The foundation must either account for the exhibit at all times from the point at issue to the time it was produced in court or provide an acceptable way of identifying the object or substance.

5.2.2 Objections

The factors governing the hearsay objection, the original document objection, and the policy objections are the same as explained in Section 5.1.2 with respect to unique objects.

5.2.3 Production and Tactics

The factors affecting the packaging or presentation of nonunique objects are generally the same as those discussed in Section 5.1.3 with respect to unique objects.

When a labeling procedure is used, it is helpful to have printed labels if they are available, so that the identifying witness has just filled in the blanks on the label and signed his or her name or initials. When the exhibit is a powder, paint chips, or similar material, it is useful to display it in glassine or clear plastic envelopes with the label attached so that the fact-finder can easily see the nature of the material. See Fig. 29.

You must keep the exhibits straight. It is important not to hold up Exhibit 3 when your witness is talking about Exhibit 2. Confusion by the lawyers may add to the propensity of a jury to distrust this kind of exhibit.

5.3 SITE VIEWS BY THE FACT-FINDER

The judge or jury can leave the courthouse to view the site or building or whatever is at issue. If you have a large facility or a special location that must be seen to be appreciated, then you need to press to have the fact-finder go see it. The inaccuracies inherent in verbal communication are enormous. Words mean different things to different people. The picture that builds in a judge's or juror's mind as oral testimony proceeds may be based on a faulty preconception that is totally unknown to the lawyer. By assuring that you and the fact-finder have seen the same scene, you will have some assurance that you are on the same wavelength and therefore that the oral testimony is building on the same base.

5.3.1 Governing Law

The request for a view is raised by motion and is addressed to the court's discretion.[3] The factors affecting whether the judge will exercise discretion to order a view include:

> (1) the importance (to the issue) of the information to be gathered by the view;
>
> (2) the extent to which this information can be secured from photographs, maps, or diagrams;
>
> (3) the extent to which the place or thing to be viewed has changed since the controversy arose; and
>
> (4) the inconvenience or disruption to the trial caused by the view.

The motion must set out clearly the balance to be struck in considering these factors. Get a ruling on such a request at an early stage in the pretrial proceedings because the availability or nonavailability of a view may affect the approach you take to other potential tangible evidence.

5.3.2 Timing

The view can be made at any point in the trial. Because first impressions are lasting ones, you should think about the best time to have the view. If the thing speaks eloquently for itself, the general wisdom is that the view is best at the outset of the case. If the fact-finder is likely to be surprised at the condition of the site or thing until there has been some explanation of why it is in its current condition, then you may want to wait until after one or more witnesses have testified.

Also, nothing limits the fact-finder to only one view. Therefore, it may be useful to schedule a series of views throughout the trial, particularly if it is a trial to a judge sitting alone.

5.3.3 Procedure and Tactics

Generally the judge tries to get the parties to agree on a procedure for conducting the view. Procedural matters are more difficult with a jury view than if the judge alone is making the tour. For a jury, the judge needs to appoint officials to take the tour with the jury and to point out relevant matters. This may be the bailiff or clerk of the court. The judge may also appoint other persons familiar with the site if the view is complicated. These must be neutral third parties who have no stake in the outcome, unless the parties agree otherwise.

The moving party usually prepares a list of items that the jury is to look at once they are at the site. This list is served on opposing counsel who can add items to the list or object and ask that items be stricken from the list. The court-appointed official generally reads this agreed-on list to the jury verbatim at the site. Counsel for both sides attend to make sure no hearsay evidence is put before the jury. The owner of the facility being "viewed" may have a decided advantage because he or she can post signs or other visual aids that become part of the place that is being "viewed," and hearsay evidence can be communicated in this manner. If counsel is alert, some ground rules are usually negotiated in advance to get at this problem. The presence of the judge is not required but usually is a good idea to prevent procedural disputes and to ensure that the judge has the same information as the jury. For a view by a judge alone, the parties may agree on their own representatives to act as guides and counsel may decide not to accompany the party.

No testimony should be received during a view and no experiments or demonstrations should be done unless the judge has expressly ruled on these beforehand. The status of a view is unclear—whether it is evidence in itself or just a means of assisting the fact-finder in evaluating the evidence. Because of that legal issue, taking testimony or doing experiments outside the courtroom during a view just invites an appeal with respect to whether that evidence was properly before the fact-finder.

The expenses of the view usually include fees for the guides and transportation costs associated with getting the fact-finder to the site. The party demanding the view generally bears these expenses, although occasionally they may be taxed as costs at the end of the trial.

If the court refuses to order a view or if a view is impractical under the circumstances, consider the use of a videotape, introduced and qualified by a witness, as a substitute for the view. See discussion in Section 6.3. The videotape should be noncontroversial in substance and should provide the fact-finder with a neutral overview of the site. The video can be made with a sound track or the witness can offer a live narration from the stand.

Another alternative to a traditional "view" is to have a witness on the stand next to a television or video monitor. An assistant can be stationed at the plant or facility to be viewed. If the assistant has a video camera, the witness can direct the assistant via a cellular telephone or two-way radio to various spots at the plant while the witness testifies. These live video images can be brought back to the courtroom via standard computer communications technology. This is very effective in creating an interesting "live" presentation. "And now Fred, would you just move the camera to your left a little. Point and zoom in on those rusted bolts. Now here we see . . . ." Because the jurors are seeing what the camera sees, they generally trust the presentation more than a "prepared" exhibit. The images sent by the camera can also be stored and marked as an exhibit. See discussion of digital cameras in Section 6.1.2.

ENDNOTES

1. 4 *Wigmore* § 1163, n. 8 (Chadbourne rev. 1972).

2. *See, e.g.*, David W. Christensen & J. Douglas Peters, *A Guide to the Use of Demonstrative Evidence*, 61 *Mich Bar J.* 818 (1982) (defining common objections to the use of demonstrative evidence and describing ways to properly enter demonstrative evidence at trial).

3. *See generally* 1 *McCormick on Evidence* § 216; 1 *Weinstein's Evidence* 403[05], at 403-81.

CHAPTER 6

PHOTOS, X-RAYS, VIDEOTAPES, AND SOUND RECORDINGS

In evidentiary terms, the next best thing to the object or the scene itself is a reproduction or representation of the object or scene made by a highly accurate camera or recorder. Photographs, x-rays, videotapes, and sound recordings fall into this category. Under Rule 1001(2), all of these forms except sound recordings are treated as "photographs." This kind of evidence has been used in courts for a long time. The first question of the admissibility of a daguerreotype reached the Supreme Court in 1859.[1] The Ohio Court of Appeals admitted a photographic exhibit in 1916.[2] Videotape evidence has been considered since 1969.[3] Because it has a long history, the foundation has become routine, and judges admit evidence in this category with relatively little supporting testimony.

Technology advances have, however, made these exhibits much easier to manipulate. All of the types of exhibits in this category can be changed to digital files and manipulated by computers in large and small ways. For example, small objects shown in photographs can be eliminated; objects can be added to the photograph, or parts of the image can be moved from one place to another on the photograph. No trace of the manipulation remains in the finished product and, for that reason, there is a substantial opportunity for untrustworthy exhibits to survive the initial foundation hurdle.

6.1 PHOTOGRAPHS

Photographs are very common as trial exhibits and much has been written about this category of tangible evidence.[4] The foundation is quite straightforward and the potential objections, although many, are not usually successful. The production factors and tactics for using photographs, however, are somewhat more difficult. Because it is a very common medium, lawyers tend to give less thought to how to maximize the impact of photographs on the fact-finder although photographs are sometimes quite difficult for the lay juror to interpret.

6.1.1 Foundation

The foundation for a photograph must include the basis on which the witness is competent to testify about the photo. The photo must be relevant to an issue in the case. The identification of the photo need be only a general statement as to what the photo shows. The trustworthiness aspect of foundation for still photographs has become quite abbreviated in the more than a century that they have been used as exhibits. In most instances, a witness need only testify that he or she saw the object or the scene at the time in issue and that the photograph is a fair and accurate representation of what he or she saw. See Section 1.1.

You have two choices when laying a foundation for a photograph. You can use the person who took the photograph; or you can use a person who was present at or about the relevant time and who can testify that the photograph is an accurate representation, regardless of who took it.

If you elect to use the photographer to qualify the photo, it is not necessary to present testimony about the qualifications of the photographer in order to lay the foundation for admissibility for the photograph. Nor is it necessary to establish a chain of custody for photographs.

Example

Q.　Where were you on the evening of the fire?

A.　I was at the Smith Building on Main Street.

Q.　Why were you there?

A.　I was called by the owner, Mr. Smith, to come and take pictures of his building, which was burning down.

Q.　What time did you arrive at the Smith Building?

A.　At 8:02 p.m.

Q.　What did you do after you arrived?

A.　I took photographs on three rolls of film.

Q.　May I have this photograph marked as plaintiff's Exhibit 61?

Reporter: *(Marks)*

Q.　Let the record reflect that I have handed the photograph marked as plaintiff's Exhibit 61 to Mr. Jones, counsel for defendant.

Opposing Counsel: *(Looks)*

Q.　I show you what has been marked as plaintiff's Exhibit 61 and ask you if you can identify that.

A.　Yes, that is a photograph that I took from the Main Street side of the Smith Building.

Q.　Does plaintiff's Exhibit 61 fairly and accurately represent the scene as it appeared on the evening of the fire?

A.　Yes.

Q.　Your Honor, we move the admission in evidence of plaintiff's Exhibit 61.

An important note here: when you seek to get a photograph in evidence, you cannot ask the witness to describe the details of what it shows (for example, the smoke coming from the second story window if that is a key item) until you complete the foundation and the court admits the exhibit in evidence.

If you elect to use a witness with first hand knowledge of the event or object recorded on the photograph, you need establish only a reasonable basis for the ability of the witness to conclude that the photo is a fair and accurate representation of what the witness saw.

Example

Q. Where were you on the evening of the fire?

A. I was in my office at the Smith Building on Main Street until the fire started, and then I was outside on Main Street watching the fire until it was all over.

Q. How long have you worked in the Smith Building?

A. For 4 years.

(Marks exhibit and shows to opposing counsel)

Q. I show you what has been marked as plaintiff's Exhibit 61 and ask if you can identify it.

A. Yes, that is a photograph of the Smith Building from the Main Street side while it was on fire.

Q. Does that photograph fairly and accurately portray the scene as it appeared on the evening of the fire?

A. Yes, it does.

Q. Your Honor, we move the admission in evidence of plaintiff's Exhibit 61.

Even if the photograph was taken substantially after the fact, it can qualify for admission in evidence if the witness can testify that the photograph fairly and accurately represents the scene as of the time the events in issue took place. Your opponent may try to demonstrate, by voir dire or cross-examination of the witness or by argument to the court, that despite the witness's testimony, the photograph really is not a fair and accurate representation and therefore should be excluded. See Section 1.7.2 on voir dire examination. If the photograph was taken well after the event, you may want to put in a more detailed foundation to show that the witness has the necessary information to support the conclusion that the photograph is indeed fair and accurate.

Example

Q. Where do you work?

A. At the XYZ Company plant located at 1200 Twin Locks Road.

Q. How long have you worked there?

A. I have worked there as a production supervisor for 12 years.

Q. Does your work involve the robot assembly line within the plant?

A. Yes.

Q. What do you do in that part of the plant?

A. It is part of my responsibility to visit that part of the plant every day to be sure there are no production problems.

Q. Did you have occasion to visit the robot assembly line on the date that the robot in question in this case was manufactured?

A. Yes.

Q. May I have these photographs marked as defendant's Exhibits 70, 71, and 72?

Court reporter: *(Marks)*

Q. Let the record reflect that I have handed the photographs marked as defendant's Exhibits 70, 71, and 72 to counsel for plaintiff.

Opposing Counsel: *(Looks)*

Q. I hand you what has been marked as defendant's Exhibits 70, 71, and 72 and ask you to examine those carefully.

A. *(Witness looks)*

Q. Can you identify those exhibits?

A. Yes. They are photos of the robot assembly line in the plant.

Q. Is there anything shown in those photographs that is different from the conditions present on the date the robot at issue in this case was manufactured?

A. The equipment used to manufacture the robots is all the same. We have not made any changes in that. But we did change the position of the receiving clerk's desk, which you can see at the edge of the photograph. We moved it to the other side of the door. So the photograph shows it in its new position. And we were using a new type of bin to store parts at that time. That is shown in photograph 72. Otherwise, the production line is the same in these photographs as it was on the date the robot was manufactured.

Q. What effect does the position of the receiving clerk's desk have on the operation of any of the manufacturing equipment on the production line?

A. None. It is just a place where a clerk checks the invoices of things that are delivered. It has nothing to do with the operation of the production line equipment.

Q. What effect does the type of storage bin used for parts have on the operation of any of the manufacturing equipment on the production line?

A. None. We changed from a square bin to a rectangular bin when our suppliers changed their packaging. The parts are removed from their packaging and delivered from the storage bin to the production line by conveyors. The shape of the storage bin does not affect the operation of the production line equipment.

Q. Do the photographs that have been marked as defendant's Exhibits 70, 71, and 72 fairly and accurately portray the robot assembly line as it appeared on the date when the robot at issue in this case was manufactured?

A. Yes, they do.

Q. Your Honor, we move the admission in evidence of defendant's Exhibits 70, 71, and 72.

Changes in the objects portrayed in a photograph are not objectionable unless the changes affect objects that are relevant to a determination of the issues in the case. Even changes in the objects at issue may go to the weight to be given the photograph rather than its admissibility.

Alternatively, if there are substantial differences between the photograph, taken before or after the fact, and the scene as it appeared when the events at issue actually occurred, the photograph may be qualified as a testimony aid. See discussion in Section 1.2. This allows the witness to use the photograph in explaining what happened, although the exhibit will not go to the jury room when the jury deliberates.

There are a number of ways in which the trustworthiness—that is, the fairness and accuracy—of a photograph may be attacked even if a witness vouches for the it.

Lens distortion

Photographs taken with a wide-angle or telephoto lens contain inherent distortions that may cause the photograph to differ substantially from the actual scene depicted. Telephoto lenses tend to shorten apparent distances and couple intermediate range objects together unrealistically. Wide-angle lenses give a false sense of greater-than-actual space and distance.

Color distortion

Color film and printing can fail to reproduce certain colors with sufficient fidelity under some lighting conditions. If the color of something is actually at issue in the case, a photograph showing this color may be challenged successfully unless a standard color bar is included in the image area of the photograph. The color bar which was used in making the photograph can be produced in court as a means of comparing the color fidelity of the print or slide. More often, the color shown on a photograph, such as a scar or a bruise, goes to the weight of the evidence, not its admissibility. If the color reproduction on a photograph of a bruise is not exact, the photograph may still have significant evidentiary value with respect to the size of the bruise.

Printing distortion

Occasionally a negative will be printed backwards which causes the left and right sides to be reversed in the print. You can bring this out by comparing the original negative and the print to be used in evidence.

Optical illusions

Certain optical illusions can cause the photograph not to be a fair representation even though it is accurate. Bright objects will appear to be larger than dark objects of the same size; vertical lines will appear longer than horizontal lines of the same length; and a space containing objects or details will appear larger than an empty space. Photographs are usually offered for the purpose of showing physical details as to which these optical illusions are not significant and therefore the objections on this ground are quite specialized.

The fundamental question before the court, with respect to almost any challenge to the foundation for a photograph, will be whether the questions raised about the photograph offered in evidence should go to the weight of the evidence rather than the admissibility.

The foundation for photographs that are specially staged to recreate a scene or events at issue is discussed in Section 7.3.

6.1.2 Digital Cameras and Image Manipulation

The evidence rules and case law with respect to photographs were developed from more than 100 years' experience with cameras that use light to create an image on film. Once developed, that film negative can be used to make a positive print on photographic paper or can be used directly as a slide. Each step in this process can be monitored. The negative can be checked for alteration, and the print can be compared to the negative to determine if it has been altered.

Digital cameras change all that. A digital camera creates no negative. Instead, it creates a digital file that can be read by a computer to produce an image. That image can be printed on any printer hooked up to the computer. In between, the image can be altered in many ways, none of which are detectable. But the images from digital cameras qualify as evidence under the same rules as photographs from traditional cameras. For that reason, the trial lawyer faced with a photograph as an exhibit needs to know whether a digital camera was used and must be aware of the possibility that the photo has been altered during processing.

A digital camera has similarities to a traditional camera. Both have a lens, shutter, and diaphragm. The difference is in the back end where the image is saved. A traditional camera stores its images on light sensitive film. That film is later developed, using a series of chemicals, and the image is permanently fixed on the film. A digital camera saves its images in the camera's memory, which is like the storage on a computer. When called up from this memory, the image can be transferred to a computer and stored in the computer's memory. From there, the image can be displayed on the computer's monitor or printed out like any other computer file.

The digital camera achieves this capability through the use of a charge-coupled device, or CCD, which is a postage-stamp sized semi-conductor chip. The lens focuses the image on CCDs. Each CCD contains a very large number of resistors. When the shutter opens, the light striking the CCD creates electricity. The more light, the more electricity. These electrical states in each of the resisters are then translated into zeros and ones by an analog-to-digital converter (ADC) chip. The resulting digital data are compressed and saved to the camera's memory.

Another kind of digital camera operates like a camcorder and is usually called a "still video" camera. It captures an image as described above but does not immediately convert the analog information to digital data. Instead, it saves the data in analog form on miniature floppy disks. Later, the disk is put into an external ADC drive and the data are converted into digital format.

The images from a digital camera are uploaded to a personal computer by attaching a serial cable from the camera or converter to the computer. Special software resident on the computer is opened, and a button appears that enables the command to send and save the images to the computer's hard disk. One click on the button is all that it takes, and the image is now on the computer.

Once this digital file is in place, every pixel (picture element) can be moved alone or in groups to alter the image. Objects can be made larger, smaller, fatter, thinner, nearer, and farther away. Colors can be changed, figures can be removed entirely, and the orientation of the image can be rotated in any direction.

Similar results can be achieved without a digital camera. A photograph from a traditional camera (either negative or positive) can be fed through an optical scanner to produce a digital file. The scanner's file can be transferred to a personal computer where the same kind of editing can take place. Off-the-shelf photo-editing software is available with very sophisticated capability. A photograph of three people standing in front of a house, one of whom is wearing a blue shirt, can be changed so that two of these people are standing in front of a tree (the house is now gone) and both are wearing blue shirts. No trace of this alteration remains.

For this reason, it is helpful to ascertain in discovery whether your opponent's photographs came from a digital camera or a traditional camera and to inquire whether they have been altered in any way. In making these inquiries, remember that opposing counsel may not know how the photos were made, so some questions about the genesis of the exhibit may be in order.

6.1.3 Objections

Objections to photographs rarely succeed, even when they should. If you have a serious objection to a photograph, you will need to be well-prepared. See general discussion of objections in Section 1.3.

Hearsay objections

Hearsay objections to a photograph do not arise unless it depicts a written statement. A photograph of objects, scenes, or people is not a "statement" within the definition contained in Rule 801(a)(1) which covers "an oral or written assertion." Because it is not a statement, the hearsay rule does not apply. If the photo depicts a written statement, such as a warning sign on a building or a label on an object, one defense against a hearsay objection is that the photo is not offered to prove the truth of the statement and therefore, under Rule 801(c), the photo is not hearsay. If the sign or label was provided by a party opponent then, under Rule 801(d)(2), the photo is not hearsay.

One caveat exists to the general proposition set out above. Under Rule 801(a)(2), "nonverbal conduct of a person, if it is intended by the person as an assertion" is hearsay. Thus a photograph of a person doing something might be objectionable as hearsay if the action depicted was "intended to say that something is so" which is a common definition of "assertion" in the evidence context.[5] The objecting party bears the burden of showing the requisite intent so as to invoke the hearsay rule.

Original document objections

Rule 1001(2) makes the original document rule applicable to photographs. The negative of any photograph is an original. Under Rule 1001(3), all of the prints made from a photographic negative are also "originals." This means that there may be many "originals" from a single photographic negative. The prints that qualify as originals may be made all at the same time or at any subsequent time. In order to qualify a photograph, it is technically necessary to have the negative available in order to demonstrate that the photograph was made from a negative and not from some other process. Lawyers have rarely invoked this requirement in the past, but with the advent of computer processes to alter photographs, it has once again become important.

The challenge to trustworthiness is directed at the proposition that the photograph is a fair and accurate representation of the real thing. This is different from the policy objection on the basis of confusing or misleading the jury. A photograph can be an accurate representation and still be excluded on the grounds that it will confuse or mislead the jurors.

Marks

An objection may be based on retouching done in the production process or on marks made on the photograph on the ground that the photo, as retouched or marked, is not a fair and accurate representation of what the witness saw. There should be no labels, numbers, or writing on the print or back of a photograph except the exhibit number and those markings for which the witness is prepared to lay a foundation by means of first hand knowledge. Any other marks may cause the court to reject the exhibit.

Computer manipulation

If the photograph has been changed by computer manipulation, it no longer qualifies as an original. If the photograph is offered to prove its content, as almost all photographs are, Rules 1002 and 1003 require that the proponent use the original or a duplicate. A photograph that has been manipulated by computer processes may still qualify as a testimony aid (see discussion in Section 1.2) because it can assist the witness in presenting testimony or assist the judge or jury in understanding testimony. If offered as a testimony aid, however, an altered photograph would face policy objections because jurors might be confused or misled. Photographs that have been changed in order to reconstruct events as the witness remembers them can be qualified as reconstructions. See Section 7.3. The original document rule does not preclude the use of these photos.

Policy objections

Both prejudice and confusion/misleading objections are available with respect to photographs. The most common are outlined below.

Unfair prejudice

Photographs that show grisly, gory, or indecent material may be excluded on grounds of unfair prejudice even if the foundation is proper.

Photographs of corpses, traumatic injuries, bodily parts, and similar items are subject to attack on this ground, although many are admitted. Photographs showing pained facial expressions or grimaces may also be excluded as prejudicial if the expressions would inflame the average person. If only a part of the photograph contains prejudicial material, there may be a request to "crop" the photo to cut out the offending parts while permitting the use of the rest.

Confusion/misleading

There are additional objections based on confusion or misleading the jury even if the foundation is established adequately.

First, there may be over-inclusive subject matter. A photograph may show much more than is relevant to the case at issue and the additional material may be confusing or misleading.

Second, there may be omissions. A photograph may include only a small part of a scene which, standing by itself, could be confusing or misleading as to the rest of the scene. For this reason, when using close-ups it is advisable to have a distance shot that puts the close-up in perspective.

Third, the photograph may have a single viewpoint. If only a single photograph is available, there may be an objection based on confusion or misleading because the aspect shown by the photograph may seem more real than other aspects which must be described by testimony and which have no supporting photographs. There may be a similar objection when a photograph represents only one instant in time and the events at issue occurred over a substantial period of time. The jury may believe that the photograph also depicts what went before and what followed the time when it was taken.

Fourth, enlargements may be unfair. Where enlargements increase the size of the object being photographed beyond its normal size, the foundation should include a justification for this to avoid an objection. The jury may remember the size of the object they saw in the photo and fail to understand testimony about the actual size of the object. The usual explanation is that the enlargement is needed for clarity or in order to see important details.

Fifth, a time lapse may have occurred. Objections to changes in circumstances are directed to the lapse of time between the event at issue in the case and the time the photograph was taken. The objection may be based on differences in:

- season of the year (snow vs. full foliage on trees causes substantial changes in the appearance of the scene);

- time of day (sun position varies, producing different shadows and visibility conditions);
- weather conditions (clouds vs. full sunlight produce different shadows or visibility); or
- physical changes at the scene (things have been added or deleted over time, thus changing the appearance of the scene).

The viability of this objection depends on the purpose and level of detail for which the photograph is offered. A photograph offered to show the angle at which one street joins another will not be excluded on an objection that the cloud cover conditions were different on the day of the accident and the day the photograph was taken.

Despite the range of objections available, most photographs can be qualified as evidence without difficulty.

6.1.4 Production

When photographs are needed to enhance the understanding of the judge or jury with respect to the facts, the use of a professional photographer is probably justified. Most professionals will work for an hourly rate plus a per-print charge.

You should explain clearly to the photographer what you are trying to accomplish. He or she may have useful ideas about composition, lighting, or emphasis in order to convey the information that is important to the case. If the photograph is for the purpose of showing what a witness saw or could see, it should be taken from the position the witness describes as his or her vantage point, and the camera should be at the witness's eye level. If the photograph is for the purpose of showing the relative positions of the objects, buildings, trees, and shrubs, or other things, the camera angle should not exclude important details.

You should go along with the photographer to the site when the photographs are made. On-site assistance is necessary to ensure that, from an evidentiary point of view, there are no problems with the resulting work. It may be necessary, for example, to use a measurement indicator to display dimensions or distances. A photograph of a pothole in a road could be made more effective by placing a yardstick next to the pothole to show width or vertically in the pothole to show depth. This will help prevent an objection to confusing or misleading the jury.

Photographs of buildings, sites, highways, and similar areas are normally done with a 35 mm camera because it is light, portable, and provides good definition. A 35 mm camera's regular lens will produce images in which relative distances or sizes are very close to what is seen with the unaided eye. When possible, you should have photographic work done with available light rather than with the flash. Sometimes, the photographer can use more sensitive film to make up for the lower level of available light and avoid using a flash. It is difficult to get a good reproduction of what the unaided eye would see when a flash is used because the light is most intense nearest the flash and is much less intense farther away. This means that nearby objects are lighted more than they would appear to the unaided eye and objects farther away are surrounded by more darkness.

As a precaution, the background information on every photograph to be used in evidence should include the name of the photographer; the time and date when the photograph was taken; an identification of the camera, lens, and film used; the shutter speed and lens aperture used; a description of the artificial lighting if any; and the distances from the camera to various points of importance in the photo. The information may not be necessary to lay a foundation, but it should be available in case of questions from the judge or challenges from opposing counsel.

Although the foundation for a photograph does not require the production of the negative, it is a good idea to avoid disputes about foundation by making negatives available. You should store negatives and photographs separately in order to avoid accidental loss before trial. Negatives should be kept in a cool dry place in envelopes or plastic folders to prevent damage.

6.1.5 Tactics

To maximize the effectiveness of the witness testimony about the photograph, the fact-finder should be looking at the photograph at the same time the witness is testifying about it. Any of the four display technologies described in Chapter 9—digital, electronic, projector screen, or paper graphics—can be used with photographs. See discussion of alternatives for displaying photographs set out in Section 9.1.1. Whenever possible, keep all the jurors focused on the same photograph at the same time. If the jurors have their own sets of photographs, they may be looking through those while other important testimony is being presented.

Enlargements are routinely permitted usually after a smaller version of the photograph has been marked and admitted. In one case plaintiff's counsel had admitted in evidence a six-foot high, full color enlarged photograph of a plaintiff who had been badly burned over much of his body. The plaintiff was clad, for the occasion, only in a loincloth. The photograph remained before the jury during all of the plaintiff's case until the defendant finally settled. Note that others advise that particularly shocking evidence not be kept before the fact-finder for a long time because jurors become accustomed to it, and familiarity depreciates its effect. Fig. 30 shows an imaginative use of a life-size photo of a medical device and Fig. 31 shows how parts can be added to or taken off the underlying photo to illustrate the use of the device. If an enlargement is used, and the enlargement makes the subject matter larger than real life, this should be made clear in the foundation testimony to prevent an objection.

Occasionally a photograph to be used for evidentiary purposes is too complicated to get the point across effectively. It may show too many details or, as with enlargement of medical photographs, may be difficult to interpret. In these cases it is useful to have an illustrator make a simplified drawing from the photograph and to have the witness use both in presenting his or her testimony. See discussion of drawings in Section 4.3.

If color is critical to an issue in the case, there may be a question whether photographic slides are better than prints. See discussion of slides at Section 9.4.2. Color is impossible to reproduce accurately using photographic methods, whether the medium is slides or prints, because the pigments used to render color are not the same as those of the subject photographed. Slides render their colors by subtracting from four color layers which exist in the unprocessed film. Characteristics of these dyes vary with film type and manufacturer. Exposure time can have an effect on how they produce color. Processing procedures, because of temperature variations and chemical replenishment variations, can taint the image, yielding false color. Even the projector lamp color can affect perceived color because the whites actually are clear on the slide and therefore can be untrue. The printing process allows the professional color printer to correct some kinds of problems. But the color may be better with a projection from a slide.

Often situations arise where you would like to have witnesses mark on photographs. If more than one or two marks are to be made by the witness, it may be better to use more than one copy of the photograph as an exhibit. Too many marks on one photo can be confusing when the jury takes the photo into their deliberations. Several copies of the same photograph can be marked as subparts of the same exhibit; for example, the photograph itself is Exhibit 17; the marks of the first witness to use the photograph are on a copy marked as Exhibit 17A; the marks of the next witness are on a copy marked as Exhibit 17B; and so on. If more than one witness is to mark the same photograph, you should have different witnesses use different color markers and put their names or initials on what they have marked so their marks are readily distinguishable from those of other witnesses.

Clear plastic overlays are preferable when there are a number of photographs to be marked by witnesses or a single photograph is to be used for more than one purpose. See discussion of overlays in Section 9.3.2. The photo can be discussed in testimony by itself; it can be used with the overlay created by one witness; or it can be used with the overlays created by several witnesses in any combination. When you use overlays, you should mark each overlay as a separate exhibit, usually with the same number as the underlying photograph plus a letter designation, for example, Exhibit 17 is the photograph; then Exhibits 17A, 17B, and 17C are the overlays to that photograph. It is also useful to have the witness initial the overlay when he or she has completed the marks on it. If more than one witness works with a single overlay, have each witness use a different color marker and initial the overlay using that color.

6.2 X-RAYS, CAT SCANS, MAGNETIC RESONANCE IMAGES, AND SONOGRAMS

X-rays are very common exhibits in personal injury cases. Computer assisted tomography (CAT) scans, magnetic resonance images (MRI), endoscopy images, nuclear medicine scans, and sonograms, while based on different and more complicated technology, are used for the same kinds of diagnostic purposes and present the same basic evidentiary problem. Because they depict something that cannot be seen unless surgery has been done, no witness has seen "the real thing" and can testify that the image is a fair and accurate representation of the real object at issue.

6.2.1 Foundation

An expert medical witness is generally used to meet the requirements of competence, relevance, and appropriate identification for this category of exhibits. See Section 1.1. The trustworthiness of the exhibit must be established under Rule 901(b)(9) which applies to processes or systems. The output from this medical equipment can be qualified by testimony that the process or system produces an accurate result. This is useful because the doctor who testifies seldom has any first hand knowledge of the taking of the x-ray of the patient. The doctor, however, can testify about the process or system used by the hospital to take and identify x-rays and can qualify the x-ray as an exhibit in that way.

Sometimes the treating physician is not closely connected with the hospital or other place where the x-rays were taken and cannot testify as to their procedures. In that case, two witnesses must lay the foundation if the exhibit is contested.

Example

(After qualifying the treating physician as an expert)

Q. Doctor, when did you first treat Mr. Peters?

A. I first saw him last August.

Q. At that time, what was your diagnosis of Mr. Peters' condition?

A. Mr. Peters appeared to have a broken rib.

Q. Doctor, did you order any x-rays made of Mr. Peters to assist you in your treatment of him?

A. Yes, I did.

Q. Are you familiar with the x-ray process?

A. Yes, I am.

Q. How does that process work?

A. *(Witness describes process)*

Q. Does the x-ray process produce an accurate result?

A. Yes, it does.

Q. Were x-rays of Mr. Peters taken?

A. Yes, they were.

Q. Where were those x-rays taken?

A. At Mount Everest Hospital in the Radiology Department.

Q. Did you review those x-rays?

A. Yes, I did.

Q. May I have these marked as Exhibits 75, 76, and 77?

Reporter: *(Marks)*

Q. Let the record reflect that I have handed to counsel for defendant what has been marked as Exhibits 75, 76, and 77.

Opposing Counsel: *(Looks)*

Q. Doctor, I hand you what has been marked as Exhibits 75, 76, and 77. Can you identify those?

A. Yes.

Q. What are they?

A. They are x-rays of Mr. Peters' rib cage.

Q. How do you know that?

A. Because they depict the condition for which I treated Mr. Peters and because they are so labeled by Mount Everest Hospital.

Q. Your Honor, we offer Exhibits 75, 76, and 77 in evidence.

Opposing Counsel: Objection, foundation.

Counsel: There is sufficient foundation, Your Honor. The witness is the treating physician. She is competent to testify about the x-rays of the patient she treated. The x-rays are relevant. They show Mr. Peters' injury. The identification is sufficient; the doctor recognizes them. The x-rays are trustworthy because the doctor can relate them to the condition for which she treated Mr. Peters.

Court: Objection overruled.

Opposing Counsel: Objection, hearsay. The witness relied on the labels and those are out-of-court statements offered to prove the truth of their contents—that these really are Mr. Peters' x-rays.

Counsel: I can qualify those as business records, if that is required.

Court: Please do so.

(After qualifying the custodian of hospital records from Mount Everest Hospital)

Q. Would you describe the process for labeling and filing x-rays at the Mount Everest Hospital?

A. *(Witness describes process)*

Q. I hand you what has been marked as Exhibits 75, 76, and 77. Are those records of the Mount Everest Hospital?

A. Yes. These are x-rays taken at the hospital and kept by us.

Q. How do you know that?

A. They have our standard labels on them and our log numbers.

Q. Directing your attention to the label on what has been marked as Exhibit 75, was that label made in the ordinary course of the hospital's business?

A. Yes, that is one of our standard labels.

Q. Was that label affixed to the x-ray at the time it was taken?

A. Yes.

Q. Was that label made by a person with knowledge or made from information transmitted by a person with knowledge of what appears on that label?

A. Yes. The label is made out by the technician who is with the patient.

Q. Was it the regular practice of the hospital's business to make that label?

A. Yes, that is standard practice.

Q. Once this label is made and affixed to the x-ray, is the x-ray kept on file in the course of the hospital's regularly conducted business activity?

A. Yes.

Q. Would your testimony be the same with respect to the labels on Exhibits 76 and 77?

A. Yes.

Q. Your Honor, we offer Exhibits 75, 76, and 77 in evidence at this time.

Court: Objection overruled. Admitted.

(Call the treating physician back to the stand and proceed with questions about what the x-rays show)

The most common foundation challenge is that the x-rays have not been sufficiently identified to link them definitively with the person whose injuries they allegedly portray. Meeting this objection requires careful planning of the expert's testimony.

In this example, you might want to use the affidavit or deposition of the hospital records administrator to avoid inconvenience. You must get through the foundation for x-rays smoothly and get into the substantive part of the testimony as quickly as possible. Most of the foundation information is of little interest to jurors. They just want to see the x-rays. Another approach, if your opponent refuses to stipulate to the foundation for the x-rays, is to request the court to allow affidavit or deposition testimony to substitute for live testimony as to the foundation, and for the court to review the foundation materials and make a ruling in advance of trial.

6.2.2 Objections

An x-ray is not a "written assertion" under Rule 801(a)(1) and, for that reason, there are no hearsay objections to x-rays or similar exhibits. However, there may be an objection to the contents of the labels because those usually are offered to prove the truth of their contents—that is, that the x-ray is of the person whose name appears on the label. The business records exception under Rule 803(6) is available to meet this objection. See general discussion in Section 1.3.1 and example in Section 6.2.1.

CAT scans, magnetic resonance images, and sonograms are labeled by typing the identification of the patient into the computer terminal that is used to process the images. You may assert that qualification under Rule 406 is sufficient. The theory is that the name is a code, just like an identification number, and the fact that x-rays are those of a specific patient can be proved by evidence that it is the routine practice of the hospital to label x-rays after having ascertained the name of the patient.

Rule 1001(2) makes the original document requirement applicable to x-rays by including x-rays in the definition of photographs. Under Rule 1001(3), "An original of a photograph includes the negative or any print therefrom." Positive or "negative" prints of x-rays can be made from the original and also qualified as originals. The rules do not address the status of CAT scans, magnetic resonance images, and sonograms but, because these processes are all controlled by computer, their output can be qualified as "originals" under Rule 1001(3) which provides: "If data are stored in a computer or similar device, any printout or other output readable by sight, shown to reflect the data accurately, is an original." See Section 1.3.2.

A policy objection, sometimes successful, is that the x-ray does not assist in presenting or understanding the witness's testimony because the details sought to be explained are so small or insignificant that only a trained eye can perceive them on the x-ray. See Section 1.3.3. Similar objections might be raised with respect to sonograms, CAT scans, and magnetic resonance images. Sonograms, in particular, sometimes produce very fuzzy images that, to the untrained eye, are difficult to understand. This objection goes to prejudice (the exhibit is being used to bolster the expert's testimony, not for what is shown on it) or to misleading/confusion of the fact-finder (what is being testified about is not shown on the x-ray). An appropriate instruction can cure both of these possible problems. See Section 1.8 on jury instructions with respect to exhibits.

6.2.3 Production

Few production problems exist with x-rays, CAT scans, magnetic resonance images, or sonograms. You will have to take them as they are. Any hospital radiology department can duplicate the films themselves for a nominal cost. Some engineering photo houses can accommodate full size x-rays as negatives.

An effective alternative with x-rays is to convert from a "negative" into a "positive"—black images on a white background—which can be handled, marked, and shown to the fact-finder like any other photograph. Another alternative is to create a colored medical illustration from the x-ray to delineate soft tissue and other relationships that do not show up clearly on x-rays. See discussion of drawings in Section 4.3.

Most CAT scan, MRI, and sonogram equipment can also create color printouts which can be used like photographs. You can enlarge all of these images for easier understanding. By adding color and labels for the specific features to be discussed in the testimony you can make more effective exhibits. See discussion in Chapter 9.

6.2.4 Tactics

If your opponent refuses to stipulate to the admissibility of x-rays as to which there is no real issue, consider asking for costs for testimony to prove the foundation and any facts required to meet meritless objections. Judges have discretion to make such awards when one side insists on making technical objections that have no apparent purpose but to waste time.

The traditional method for displaying x-rays is to use a backlighted display. X-rays are generally difficult to see even on a good display cabinet, so the display may have to be set up very close to the fact-finder. The witness can come down from the stand and point to the critical places on the x-ray as he or she explains.

You can also use electronic systems (see Section 9.5) and digital systems (see Section 9.6) to display x-rays. An x-ray can be videotaped by putting the negative on the backlighted display cabinet and then using a high quality video camera to videotape the image. This technique allows the camera operator to zoom in on specific parts of the x-ray or CAT scan which will appear as enlarged images when the videotape is played. You can also display x-rays and CAT scans on an electronic system using a visualizer or visual presenter (see Section 9.5.1). Magnetic resonance imagery systems and sonogram systems create digital files which are displayed on a monitor when used for medical purposes. A special disk can be made so that these images can be projected in the courtroom using a digital display system if it is necessary to rotate the images on the screen.

6.3 VIDEOTAPES AND MOVIES

Television is an important factor in nearly every fact-finder's life. The television screen is a familiar, comfortable source from which to obtain news and information, as well as entertainment. Videotape equipment is also versatile and reliable. For these reasons, videotape evidence presentations are an important part of the tangible evidence media. Movies are rarely used as trial exhibits except where the movie itself is an issue in the case.

6.3.1 Foundation

Videotapes are basically photographs that involve motion, and the foundation follows the same principles. A witness must establish competence and provide a suitable identification. The material on the tape must be relevant to an issue in the case. And the witness must testify that the tape fairly and accurately represents what is portrayed on it. The trustworthiness of the exhibit is established by testimony adequate to support the accuracy of the representation. See Section 1.1.

Before high quality and easily portable videotaping equipment became available, movies were sometimes used as trial exhibits. Movies did not include a method for embedding the date and time in the exhibit, and typically were made in a number of segments. For this reason, the foundation for movies, although basically the same as for videotapes, needed an additional assurance that the filming had not been manipulated by starts and stops in unobservable ways that would make it unreliable as evidence. Because of the expense involved, it would be very unusual for a trial lawyer to choose to use a movie rather than videotape as an exhibit. Instances may arise, however, where a segment of a movie is itself relevant to an issue in the case. In that case, the movie would qualify either as a physical object (see discussion in Section 5.1) or as a photograph (see discussion in Section 6.1). In other respects, the foundation for a movie would proceed in the same manner as that for videotapes as described in this section.

Your opponent is entitled to demand a viewing of any videotape before it is admitted in evidence. This is similar to the requirement that you hand your opponent a document or physical object for his or her inspection during the process of qualifying it as an exhibit. You are not required to stop in the midst of your qualification of the videotape, however, to complete this step. If your opponent asserts this right, when you have finished qualifying the tape, the judge will declare a recess and excuse the jury. Under most circumstances, these videotapes will have been exchanged in discovery long before trial, making this interruption unnecessary.

Foundation problems vary with the kind of videotape used. Five are discussed here: first, videotapes taken at times or places at issue; second, videotapes of places or events at issue made for litigation purposes; third, day-in-the-life videos to illustrate injuries; fourth, videotapes used to help explain the work done by experts or other witnesses; and fifth, videotapes of deposition testimony. In addition, videotape summaries or excerpts may be put together in a special presentation. The foundation for each is described below.

Videotapes taken at the time or place at issue

There are a number of possible sources for videotapes made at the time or place at issue. All or part of an event may have been recorded. The trustworthiness of this kind of tape could be qualified under the "process or system" described in Rule 901(b)(9).

Example

(After establishing competence and relevance)

Q. Can you identify what has been marked as Exhibit 54?

A. Yes. That is the videotape from the video monitoring system in our warehouse.

Q. When was it made?

A. On the date of the accident.

Q. How do you know that?

A. We have a standard label for these tapes that is filled out when each tape is taken out of the video recorder. It gives the dates and hours covered.

Q. Your Honor, we offer Exhibit 54 in evidence.

Opposing Counsel: Objection, no foundation.

Court: Sustained.

Q. Ms. Keller, let's go back a moment to the video observation system in the warehouse. Would you describe the system?

A. Yes. A video camera is mounted in the upper northwest corner of the warehouse near where the wall meets the ceiling. The focus and direction of the camera are fixed. The recording equipment is located in a locked cabinet at floor level below the camera. The images from the camera are recorded on tapes. At the beginning of each 8-hour shift, the tape is changed.

Q. Does the video observation system produce an accurate result?

A. Yes.

Q. Your Honor, we offer Exhibit 54 again. The competence of the witness, the relevance of the subject matter of the tape, and the duplication of this tape are not challenged. The trustworthiness of the tape has been shown under Rule 901(b)(9) as the accurate result of a process or system.

Opposing Counsel: Objection; hearsay.

Counsel: There is no basis for a hearsay objection. This is essentially a photograph.

Opposing Counsel: The objection is to the contents of the label.

Q. Ms. Keller, let's focus now on the label. Is that a record of the acts or events with respect to the video observation system, made at or near the time, by a person with knowledge, or from information transmitted by a person with knowledge?

A. Yes, it is.

Q. Is it the regular practice of the business activity to make the record?

A. Yes.

Q. Was this videotape with the label on it, as we see it now, which is Exhibit 54, kept in the course of a regularly conducted business activity?

A. Yes. We have a regular practice with respect to filling out the labels, putting them on the tape cassettes, and filing the cassettes.

Q. Your Honor, we offer Exhibit 54 in evidence. The label qualifies as a business record.

Court: Admitted.

A videotape made at the time or place at issue might also be made by a bystander, a news photographer, or a government investigator. In this case, either the photographer or a witness who saw the place or event at the time at issue and who can testify that the videotape is an accurate representation of what was seen at the time can qualify the tape. This foundation is the same as for a photograph. See examples in Section 6.1.1.

Videotapes of places or events made for litigation purposes

If you use a videotape created specifically for litigation purposes to support a contention regarding the places or events at issue, and the use of the tape is contested by your opponent, you need to establish trustworthiness as completely as practicable under the circumstances. The ideal is a five-step approach as follows:

> (1) the video camera was tested before it was used to create the tape and it was in normal operating condition and transmitted images accurately;
>
> (2) the video recording machine had the capability to record accurately;
>
> (3) the witness saw and heard what was being recorded;
>
> (4) after the recording was finished, the tape was replayed and the witness saw that the tape was an accurate recording; and
>
> (5) the recording machine that is in court is in normal operating condition and can accurately reproduce the images on the tape.

If there is a sound track, additional foundation is required. This foundation is discussed at Section 6.4.1.

Some courts have required foundation evidence as to both the qualification of the equipment and the operator. This is unnecessarily burdensome in a civil case. The qualifications of the operator should go to the weight of the evidence, not its admissibility. The witness should be familiar with the qualifications of the operator so he or she can respond effectively on voir dire or cross-examination.

If a specific challenge to the technical capability of the equipment arises, a witness (not necessarily the same one) may need to qualify the video equipment as capable and reliable in producing accurate representations. Unless a specific challenge is asserted, however, this should not be necessary. The fairness and accuracy of what appears on the tape is the heart of the trustworthiness of the exhibit, not the technical aspects of the equipment that made the tape. If you think the judge may require you to qualify the video camera operator and the video equipment, consider getting an affidavit from the operator at the time the video is made. This evidence is part of the foundation and, under Rule 104(a), may be provided by affidavit.

Example

(After establishing qualifications as an expert)

Q. Ms. Ellis, why are sea grasses important to the ecology of the beach area at Radnor Island?

A. Without the sea grasses, the effect of the tides and waves in the beach area would cause much greater erosion. To understand this effect, you have to look at the overall topography of the area.

Q. Have you made a videotape of the overall topography at Radnor Island?

A. Yes, I have a videotape of the whole area.

Q. May I have this videotape cassette marked as plaintiff's Exhibit 62?

Reporter: *(Marks)*

Q. Let the record reflect that this videotape was delivered to Ms. Smith, counsel for defendant, before the discovery cut-off date and that I am handing the cassette to Ms. Smith for her examination.

Opposing Counsel: *(Looks)*

Q. Who made the videotape that has been marked as Exhibit 62?

A. It was made by Videotape Productions, Inc. Their offices are located at 221 Franklin Street, Miami, Florida.

Q. When was the tape made?

A. It was made last summer, in July.

Q. Were you present when the tape that has been marked as Exhibit 62 was made?

A. Yes. I directed the technicians with respect to making the tape.

Q. Was the video equipment tested before the tape was made?

A. Yes. The technicians took three test segments of Radnor Island.

Q. What was the result of the testing?

A. The equipment was in normal operating condition and the video output was accurate and of high quality.

Q. Did you see what was recorded?

A. Yes.

Q. Was any sound recording made?

A. No. This tape contains only video. There is no audio portion.

Q. What did you do after the recording was finished?

A. We rewound the cassette and played the tape.

Q. What did you see when you played the tape?

A. I saw the recording of the scene at Radnor Island.

Q. Is the videotape that has been marked as Exhibit 62 the one you observed being made and that you checked after it was made?

A. Yes.

Q. Is Exhibit 62 a fair and accurate representation of the topography at Radnor Island?

A. Yes, it is.

Q. What did you do with the tape after it was made?

A. I labeled the cassette with my name, the date, and the place.

Q. Has the tape been edited?

A. No.

Q. How do you know that?

A. We used a date/time generator in making the tape. That shows the date and time with a minute and second clock in the lower margin of the tape. The minute and second clock shows that all of the original tape is there.

Q. Do you have a video playback machine with you today?

A. Yes, I do.

Q. Have you tested this equipment?

A. Yes, I tested it this morning. It is in good operating condition and plays the tape accurately.

Q. Your Honor, we move the admission in evidence of plaintiff's Exhibit 62 and request permission for the witness to play it as her testimony proceeds.

Some courts have gone further than qualifying the video equipment and required the foundation to include evidence that the tape was sealed or otherwise protected to guard against tampering. This appears to be a requirement that had its genesis in criminal cases and is not necessary in civil proceedings.

If the videotape depicts a scene that represents to the fact-finder the way things were when the issues in the case arose, then you must qualify the videotape in the same way as a photograph that is used for this purpose. See discussion in Section 6.1.1. The foundation must include proof that the places depicted are the same as or sufficiently similar to the places at issue.

Example

Q. When did the XYZ Corporation vacate the facility at 120 Center Road?

A. Last summer, in July.

Q. Why did they vacate?

A. There was terrible flooding in the basement and covering some part of the first floor.

Q. Where were you when that flood occurred?

A. I was at the facility at 120 Center Road all day. I directed the evacuation.

Q. Did you personally observe the condition of the facility?

A. Yes, I was in and out of the building all day.

Q. May I have this videotape cassette marked as plaintiff's Exhibit 78?

Reporter: *(Marks)*

Q. Let the record reflect that I have handed Exhibit 78 to Mr. Smith, counsel for defendant.

Opposing Counsel: *(Looks)*

Q. I show you what has been marked as Exhibit 78 and ask you if you can identify that.

A. Yes, that is a videotape of the facility at 120 Center Road.

Q. When was that videotape made?

A. It was made three days after the day of the flood.

Q. Have you seen that videotape played?

A. Yes, I have.

Q. How can you tell that Exhibit 78 is the videotape you saw?

A. I put my initials on the yellow marker on the front of the cassette *(points to marker)*.

Q. How does the depiction of the facility at 120 Center Road, shown on this videotape that has been marked as plaintiff's Exhibit 78, compare with what you saw at the facility on the day of the flood?

A. It looks the same.

Q. Are there any differences at all?

A. The flooding in the basement and on parts of the first floor is the same. Some pumping equipment had been moved into place on the second day after the flood and that is shown on the videotape. That was not present at the beginning of the flood. By the time the tape was made, they were just about to start pumping out the water so that repairs could be made.

Q. Mr. Schilde, is the videotape that is Exhibit 78 a fair and accurate representation of the condition of the facility as you saw it on the day of the flood?

A. Yes, it is.

Q. Your Honor, we move the admission in evidence of the videotape that has been marked as plaintiff's Exhibit 78.

The principal challenge to the foundation for nondeposition videotapes goes to the trustworthiness of the representation of the subject matter. The objection may be to lens distortion, color distortion, or time lapse. These are the same objections as described at Section 6.1.3 with respect to photographs.

This example deals with a lapse of time over a period of several days. The lapse of time can be several weeks or months, so long as there is no substantial change in what is depicted from the time at issue that would confuse or mislead the jury. Foundation problems can also exist if the videotape is taken at a different time of day in cases where the issues arise out of an event that happened at a particular time of day and the time is relevant to the issues in the case. Sometimes issues will be raised as to the time of year when the videotape was taken if foliage, angle of sunlight, or other details affected by the season are relevant to the case. See discussion in Section 6.1.3 with respect to photographs. When changes are an issue, any resulting confusion can be eliminated by a proper jury instruction. See Section 1.7.2.

The proponent of a videotape must understand and be able to explain to the judge that standard videotape equipment records only in real time. And except with special equipment, the playback of videotapes cannot be speeded up or slowed down like movies, therefore there is no distortion of the representation by showing the recorded events at a speed faster or slower than they occurred.

Similarly, videotape does not require developing like film. Both the image and the sound are recorded directly onto the tape. Therefore the potential problems with still camera film or movies, such as the quality of processing or possible image reversal, do not exist with videotape.

Occasionally the inherent limitations of the video camera may draw an objection to the fairness of the representation. A videotape that shows the approximate view the plaintiff or defendant had just prior to an accident is limited by the video camera lens. A wide-angle lens shows a field of vision of approximately 46 degrees. The human eye, however, with normal peripheral vision has a field of vision of more than 70 degrees. In this instance the videotape may not be a fair representation. Using a computer-generated animation may overcome this limitation. See discussion in Section 8.3.

Musical background to an evidentiary videotape offers a possible objection on relevance grounds and usually should be avoided.

Day-in-the-life tapes

In personal injury cases, the plaintiff may seek to define the extent of his or her injuries, the painful and extensive therapy required, and the losses in quality of life by preparing a videotape showing a daily routine. The foundation for this type of videotape may be offered by the plaintiff, a close relative who supervises the care of the plaintiff, a nurse or other medical specialist familiar with the care of the plaintiff, or an expert who observed or tested the plaintiff. You should carefully plan videotaping to avoid extraneous persons and irrelevant material. One example would be showing preexisting and unrelated disabilities as a part of a day-in-the-life tape. Both of these problems give your opponent an opportunity for an objection on grounds of relevance and perhaps also on the grounds of "confusion" and might cause unhelpful editing of the tape by the court before permitting the tape to be used at trial.

Medical or psychiatric examinations may be videotaped to document injuries or defend against overstated claims. The foundation for this type of videotape could be provided by the examining physician.

Environmental and property cases also may benefit from this kind of videotape evidence so that jurors can see unfamiliar scenes in context.

Example

(After establishing competence and relevance)

Q. Mr. Wilkens, when did the United States Army start to use the land next to your home?

A. Just about two years ago.

Q. What effect, if any, did that have on your farming operation?

A. A large part of my income is derived from raising mink. The mink get very upset when they hear a loud noise. When they get upset they get very agitated, and often they just die.

Q. What exactly are the effects of loud noises on the mink?

A. Well, there are a lot of different effects which can be seen in their behavior.

Q. Do you have any pictures of this behavior?

A. Yes. I have a videotape that shows what happens to the mink when these artillery blasts go off.

Q. May I have this cassette marked as plaintiff's Exhibit 2?

Reporter: *(Marks)*

Q. Let the record reflect that I am showing the cassette to Mr. Smith, counsel for the United States, and that Mr. Smith received a copy of this videotape during discovery.

Opposing Counsel: *(Looks)*

Q. Who made the videotape that is marked as plaintiff's Exhibit 2?

A. I hired Sarah Jones, who is a professional photographer, to make the film.

Q. Did you investigate Ms. Jones' qualifications to make this film?

A. Yes I did. Ms. Jones had made 30 to 40 such films, mostly for industrial firms. She owns her own equipment and has two people who work for her on these films. Ms. Jones has been in business at the same location for 10 years.

Q. Your Honor, Ms. Jones' deposition was taken in this case and sworn testimony from that deposition is available with respect to Ms. Jones' qualifications if more is required. We have prepared a summary of Ms. Jones' testimony with respect to the type of camera used, the sensitivity of the film, the type of lens used, the camera and lens settings used, the speed at which the film was taken, and the sound process used. May I have this summary marked as plaintiff's Exhibit 3?

Reporter: *(Marks)*

Q. Let the record reflect that I have shown Mr. Smith, counsel for the United States, a copy of this summary. This summary was submitted to Mr. Smith for stipulation and was the subject of a ruling by Your Honor at a pretrial conference that the summary is admissible in evidence.

Court: You may proceed.

Q. *(Distributes copies)* Your Honor, may we now read the summary?

Court: You may.

Q. *(Reads)*

Q. Mr. Wilkens, when was the videotape that is plaintiff's Exhibit 2 made?

A. Videotaping was done every day for a week, during the first week of September last year.

Q. Were you present when the videotaping was done?

A. Yes, I was.

Q. Who else was present?

A. The photographer, Ms. Jones; one of her assistants; and Butler Welborn, who knows a lot about mink.

Q. Was any special lighting used?

A. No. We used the air vent panels on the mink pens to let in natural light. These panels can be closed with special covers during bad weather.

Q. How was the videotaping done?

A. Ms. Jones set up her camera in front of one of my three mink pens. The camera was on a tripod, but it could be swung from side to side. Every day we would start filming about 11:00 a.m. Then about noon, the Army would start doing their shelling and making these loud blast sounds. We would keep on filming to record what happened to the mink during the blasts and afterward. It went that way pretty much every day.

Q. Is there any sound track on this film?

A. Yes.

Q. Is there anyone heard speaking on the sound track?

A. Yes.

Q. Who is that?

A. I speak sometimes and Mr. Welborn speaks sometimes.

Q. Are the statements made by you on the sound track true and accurate?

A. Yes.

Q. Is the videotape that has been marked as Exhibit 2 a fair and accurate depiction of the activities of your mink during times when the Army conducted this shelling and blasting activity?

A. Yes.

Q. Are the activities of your mink during the week when this videotape was made a fair and representative sample of their activities during all of the weeks since the Army has conducted this shelling and blasting activity?

A. Yes. It has been pretty much the same all along.

Q. Does the videotape that is Exhibit 2 include all of the taping that was done at your farm?

A. No.

Q. How much was left out?

A. At the end of the week, we had about 20 hours of tape. Exhibit 2 includes only part of one day. It is a single excerpt that is about 35 minutes long.

Q. Why did you select this part and leave out the rest?

A. A lot of the tape shows the mink doing the same kinds of things. We selected one part of the tape showing this behavior, instead of showing every incident.

Q. Was the selection a fair representation of the behavior of the mink that is included in the whole taping?

A. Yes.

Q. Where are the tapes from the whole 20 hours?

A. We saved them all. I brought them with me.

Q. Your Honor, Mr. Welborn will be offered by plaintiff as an expert in the raising of mink. We represent that he will testify that the statements made on the film sound track are true and accurate and he so testified under oath at his deposition. Subject to that linking up, we offer Exhibit 2 in evidence and

we request permission to show the videotape now. Mr.
Welborn's testimony will be quite lengthy and it would be
disruptive to have to produce him now for this limited purpose.

Opposing Counsel: Objection; foundation. There is no showing
that the selection of one excerpt from the videotape hasn't
distorted the activities it portrays. The excerpt is not
trustworthy.

Counsel: The only requirement that must be met is that the
videotape is what it is claimed to be. Mr. Wilkens' testimony
is sufficient in that regard. He was there and has first hand
knowledge.

Court: Objection overruled.

Opposing Counsel: Objection; the sound track is hearsay.

Counsel: The statements on the sound track are hearsay, but they
are admissible under Rule 803(24). The statements are
offered as evidence of material facts; the statements, which
describe and explain the behavior of the mink are more
probative on the point than other evidence; and the general
purposes of the rules are served because both persons who
spoke on the sound track will be present in the courtroom and
can be cross-examined. These are the three requirements of
Rule 803(24).

Court: Objection overruled.

Opposing Counsel: Objection; the single portion of the videotape
is not the original document that shows the behavior of the
animals.

Counsel: I can clear that up, your Honor.

Q. Is Exhibit 2 an exact duplicate of the corresponding portion of
the whole unedited tapes?

A. Yes.

Q. Your Honor, we offer Exhibit 2. The portion on Exhibit 2 is a
duplicate of the corresponding portion of the original that has
been re-recorded. As such, this segment is admissible to the
same extent as the corresponding portion of the original.

Court: Objection overruled.

Opposing Counsel: Objection, unfair prejudice and confusing and
misleading. The single sequence doesn't provide the time
intervals that would be present in real life.

Court: We'll have a recess and the court will view some of the
originals and the excerpts that have been offered.

Judges, like jurors, are wary of selected portions of videotapes made for litigation purposes. If the selection is fair, however, and saves time, no policy objection should be sustained.

Videotapes of demonstrations and reconstructions by experts

If you want an expert to demonstrate something, it may be better to have him or her do it on videotape than to try to do it live in the courtroom. This gives you the obvious advantage of organizing a smooth presentation and trying again if the method of presentation is not sufficiently clear the first time. If the expert is working in his or her lab or in another controlled environment and he or she is the main subject of the videotape, the foundation requirements are more relaxed. Generally, courts require no evidence with respect to the equipment. The expert is qualified to opine as to the fairness and accuracy of the videotape representation of his or her work. This kind of foundation is described in Section 7.2.1 and Section 7.3.1.

The special foundation required for a videotape that depicts a reconstruction of scenes or events at issue is discussed in Section 7.3.1.

Videotapes of depositions

Videotaped depositions permit the use in court of a "live" presentation by the witness rather than a reading from a transcript record. Although there are techniques for putting some life into a reading from the deposition transcript, if the reading takes more than 10 to 15 minutes, it will be very hard to maintain the jury's attention. A videotape of the witness testifying is much better in this regard. It gives the fact-finder a person to whom to attach the testimony, and it makes the testimony more interesting.

The foundation for videotaped depositions is governed by the Federal Rules of Civil Procedure.[6] The Uniform Audio-Visual Deposition Act[7] is a good source for states which do not follow the federal rule and have no state rule. The foundation must show that the requirements of the rules have been met. The following elements are necessary for a proper foundation:

Stipulation or order

Under Rule 30(b)(2) of the Federal Rules of Civil Procedure, a deposition may be videotaped as the sole means of recording the deposition (with no written stenographic transcript). For convenience, however, it is common to have a stenographic transcript made at the same time that the deposition is videotaped.

Deposition officer

Under Rule 28 of the Federal Rules of Civil Procedure, a deposition must be taken before an officer qualified to administer the oath and the record must be prepared by that official or under his or her direction. The operator of video equipment usually does not have that qualification. Under Rule 28(c), the deposition officer cannot be "a person who is a relative or employee or attorney or counsel of any of the parties." This precludes the use of in-house video equipment operators as deposition officers. All of these problems are obviated, however, if a stenographic transcript is taken at the same time. Under those circumstances, the court reporter is the deposition officer and swears the witness. The video equipment operator can be anyone designated by the lawyer.

Testimony under oath

The testimony must be taken under oath. In order to take testimony under oath, as noted above an officer qualified to administer the oath must be present at the deposition and must administer the oath in proper form.

Proper use at trial

Rule 32(a) of the Federal Rules of Civil Procedure sets out the uses that may be made of deposition transcripts at trial. Rule 32 is consistent with Rules 801, 803, and 804 of the Federal Rules of Evidence. While the two sets of rules are worded differently, they are intended to exclude the same categories of uses.

The videotaped deposition of a *party* can be used at trial by an *adverse party* for any purpose. This means that you can use the videotaped deposition of your opponent or their officers, directors, and managing agents, but you *cannot* use the videotaped deposition of your own client or his officers, directors, or managing agents because of the adverse party requirement.

The videotaped deposition of a *witness* may be used by *any party* at trial in lieu of live testimony in court if the witness is:

- dead;
- more than 100 miles from the place of the trial;
- unable to attend because of age, illness, or imprisonment;
- not available pursuant to subpoena; or
- if other circumstances indicate that use of the deposition would be in the interests of justice and the court so orders.

Under Rule 104(a), all of these matters as to witness availability are preliminary questions and the rules of evidence do not apply. Therefore, you may establish the pertinent facts by affidavit.

If you want to use the videotape of the deposition of a witness, perhaps a medical expert who is in a distant city and not conveniently available, you must proceed under Rule 32(a)(3)(B) of the Federal Rules of Civil Procedure or get a ruling from the court under Rule 32(a)(3)(E).

Example

Counsel: Your Honor, we would now like to turn to the testimony of Dr. Christine Chemmer. Plaintiff offers the testimony of Dr. Chemmer through a videotape of her deposition which was taken last year at her offices at 12 Mulberry Lane, Honolulu, Hawaii. Dr. Chemmer's deposition is offered under Rule 32(a)(3)(B) of the Federal Rules of Civil Procedure. Dr. Chemmer is located more than 100 miles from this courtroom. Testimony with respect to that fact is included in the deposition. May I have this videotape cassette marked as plaintiff's Exhibit 63?

Reporter: *(Marks)*

Counsel: May I have the transcript marked as plaintiff's Exhibit 65?

Reporter: *(Marks)*

Counsel: Let the record reflect that I have handed Exhibits 63 and 65 to Ms. James, counsel for defendant.

(Also hands copy of transcript to judge.)

Counsel: Your Honor, Exhibit 65 is a transcript prepared by Les Martin, certified court reporter. Mr. Martin's certification is on page 2 of Exhibit 65. We move the admission in evidence of plaintiff's Exhibits 63 and 65.

Court: So ordered.

Counsel: Your Honor, at this time may we play plaintiff's Exhibit 63 for the jury?

Court: You may proceed.

Because this witness is not an officer, director, or manager of either of the parties, Rule 32(a)(3) of the Federal Rules of Civil Procedure applies. This permits the use of deposition testimony of any witness by any party for any purpose if the witness is more than 100 miles away or if he or she is within the 100 mile radius of the courthouse but exceptional circumstances exist that make it desirable to allow the deposition to be used.

Rule 32(a) permits the use of a deposition "so far as admissible under the rules of evidence *applied as though the witness were present and testifying*." (Emphasis added.) The Advisory Committee Note makes clear that this provision of Rule 32(a) was to "eliminate the possibility of certain technical hearsay objections which are based, not on the content of the deponent's testimony, but on his absence from court."

This testimony does not fall under Rule 801(d)(1) because it is not offered to impeach the witness or for any other purpose listed there. This testimony does not fall under Rule 804 because the witness is not "unavailable" as defined by that rule.

One alternative used on occasion is to publish both the transcript and the tape for the jury.

Example

Counsel: Ladies and gentlemen, I am handing you copies of the official transcript of the deposition of Robert Russian. Mr. Russian's testimony was taken under oath, just as it would have been if he were appearing here in the courtroom today. I will put the videotape of Mr. Russian's testimony on the machine in a moment and you will hear him present the testimony under oath that appears in the transcript you now have before you. Mr. Russian speaks English with a heavy accent so you may find it useful to read along in the transcript as the videotape is played.

(Play videotape.)

You should do this, however, only in special situations where the voices on the tape are garbled. Jurors are distracted by trying to watch the tape and turn the pages of the transcript at the same time.

Another option is to display each line of the transcript on a large video or television monitor as the tape is played, so that the jurors can both see and hear the words at the same time. The methods for displaying segments of transcripts on a monitor in the courtroom are described in Chapter 9.

Usually the grounds under Rule 32(a)(3) for using a videotaped deposition in lieu of live testimony will appear as a part of the deposition transcript and therefore you need not establish the foundation by independent means. If that is not the case, you should be ready to establish compliance with the rule by affidavit or other testimony.

When a witness simply refuses to appear, a different foundation is required.

Example

Counsel: Your Honor, we would like to turn to the testimony of Thomas Teclo. Plaintiff offers the testimony of Mr. Teclo through the videotape of his deposition which was taken last year at our offices at 12 Main Street in this city.

Mr. Teclo's testimony is offered under Rule 32(a)(3)(D). A subpoena has been issued to obtain Mr. Teclo's testimony here this morning and Mr. Teclo has refused to appear. May I have this marked as plaintiff's Exhibit 79?

Reporter: *(Marks)*

Counsel: Exhibit 79 is a copy of the subpoena to Mr. Teclo and the return of service. Mr. Teclo has refused to appear today because he is afraid that if he misses work he will be fired from his job. May I have this marked as plaintiff's Exhibit 80?

Reporter: *(Marks)*

Counsel: Exhibit 80 is the videocassette containing the videotape of Mr. Teclo's deposition.

Let the record reflect that I am handing Exhibits 79 and 80 to counsel for the defendant for his examination.

Opposing Counsel: *(Looks)*

Counsel: We move the admission in evidence of plaintiff's Exhibit 80.

Court: So ordered.

Counsel: At this time, Your Honor, may we play plaintiff's Exhibit 80 for the jury?

Court: You may proceed.

When a witness is unavailable to appear and you want to establish illness, infirmity, incarceration, or one of the other elements of Rule 32(a)(3) of the Federal Rules of Civil Procedure or one of the subsections of Rule 804(a) of the Federal Rules of Evidence, usually you should produce an affidavit which states the reason for unavailability. Most courts, particularly in your home jurisdiction, will accept an oral representation. An affidavit provides additional security if your opponent challenges the basis for using a deposition videotape.

The use of deposition testimony for purposes of cross-examining a party or a witness at trial is explained at Section 2.6.1. This use is generally on a question-by-question basis, and segments of either a written transcript or a videotape may be used. Videotape segments may be selected during pretrial preparation and put on an electronic system (see Section 9.5) or a digital system (see Section 9.6). See discussion of tactics in Section 6.3.4.

Videotape summaries and multiple excerpts

In the mink farm example above, the videotape used at trial might have been a composite of several excerpts rather than a single segment of the original tapes. If a large number of videotapes contain relevant material, you can prepare a summary tape under the provisions of Rule 1006. Composite tapes can condense the relevant material, put it in chronological or other order to make it easier to understand, and provide a more efficient presentation.

In order to qualify a summary tape under Rule 1006 the proponent must show that: (1) the underlying tapes are voluminous; (2) the underlying tapes fairly and accurately depict the subject matter (and therefore could, themselves, be admissible); (3) the summary tape fairly depicts the underlying tapes; and (4) opposing counsel has had a fair opportunity to inspect the summary before its use at trial. See discussion of Rule 1006 in the context of documents at Section 2.5.1.

Example

Q. Ms. Stakowski, I show you what has been marked as Exhibit 74 and ask if you can identify that.

A. Yes. That is a videotape cassette containing excerpts from the videotapes generated by the cameras installed around the boiler equipment in the Detroit plant of the Jones Company.

Q. How long is the videotape that has been marked as Exhibit 74?

A. About 35 minutes.

Q. Directing your attention to the videotapes from which Exhibit 74 was prepared, how many of those videotapes are there?

A. There are 76 videotapes, one for each day during the months of January, February, and March when the boiler equipment was in operation.

Q. How long are the 76 videotapes?

A. They would require about 1500 hours to play.

Q. How were the 76 videotapes made?

A. They are made automatically by cameras trained to focus on a particular area. Each day, the maintenance supervisor takes out the tape from the previous day and inserts a new tape.

Q. Who made the summary videotape that has been marked as Exhibit 74?

A. I did, with technical assistance from Legal Video Services, Inc., an Oakland, California firm.

Q. When was the tape made?

A. It was made in August, last year.

Q. How was the tape made?

A. I reviewed all 76 tapes and made note of the places where the tapes showed instrumentation readings that indicated stress on the boilers. Then I had the 76 tapes edited to collect these excerpts on one tape and to label them.

Q. What did you do after the tape that has been marked as Exhibit 74 was completed?

A. I looked at the tape and compared it to my notes to be sure that it included the segments I had designated.

Q. What did you see when you played the tape?

A. I saw that the covered segments had been included and that they were in the proper time-sequence order.

Q. Is the videotape that has been marked as Exhibit 74 a fair and accurate summary of the underlying 76 videotapes?

A. Yes, it is.

Q. Your Honor, the underlying 76 videotapes that Ms. Stakowski has described were delivered to Ms. Appleby, counsel for defendant, during discovery. The summary tape that has been marked as Exhibit 74 was delivered to counsel at the pretrial conference. We move the admission in evidence of Exhibit 74.

Whenever you are using more than one excerpt from a videotape, you will need to have a reasonable basis for the selection of segments to be shown, and you should give careful consideration to the production considerations set out in Section 6.3.3.

6.3.2 Objections

Videotapes are generally very effective exhibits and will tend to draw objections on every available ground. The objections are somewhat different as to videotapes of depositions and videotapes made for other purposes because of the special rules that apply to videotaped depositions. See general discussion of objections in Section 1.3.

Objections to videotapes other than depositions

Most objections to videotapes are based on hearsay or on policy grounds. Each of these objections is examined below.

Hearsay objections

The hearsay objections to sound tracks on videotapes are easily overcome by putting the person who spoke the words heard on the sound track on the witness stand to testify (and be cross-examined with respect to the assertion) that the sound track's narrative is accurate. If the person who made the sound track is not available, the videotape can be played with the audio turned off, and a different witness can narrate from the witness stand. A somewhat more difficult situation would be created if a professional narrator were used. In that case, it should be possible to qualify the person who wrote the script to testify in the courtroom that the narrative is accurate.

A separate hearsay objection is sometimes raised to videotapes that show the conduct of a person on the ground that it is a nonverbal assertion and therefore should be treated like oral testimony. This objection is most often raised with respect to day-in-the-life videos. Rule 801(c) defines hearsay as "a statement, other than one made by the declarant while testifying at the trial or hearing, offered in evidence to prove the truth of the matter asserted." Rule 801 (a)(2) defines the term "statement" to include "non-verbal conduct of a person, if it is intended by the person as an assertion." The opponent of a day-in-the-life video may argue that the scenes of the plaintiff trying to walk with artificial legs, for example, are statements of the plaintiff about his condition offered to prove the truth of his condition and not subject to cross-examination. Several courts have upheld this objection, finding that the videotape was a "statement" rather than "tangible evidence" like a photograph of an inanimate object. Faced with the objection, the exception under Rule 803(3) for statements about mental, emotional, or physical conditions, or the catchall provision of Rule 803(24) may be helpful.

Original document objections

Rule 1001(2) includes videotapes in the definition of "photograph" and makes videotapes subject to the original document requirements. Rule 1001(3) provides that: "An original of a photograph includes the negative or any print therefrom." Thus, when you play a videotape directly on a video player connected to a monitor, this is a display of an original.

If the videotape has been copied onto a computer storage medium for display (see discussion in Section 9.6.2), the computer version is a "duplicate" under Rule 1001(4) which is admissible under Rule 1003 to the same extent as an original.

If you use excerpts from a videotape as an exhibit, the excerpts qualify as "electronic re-recording . . . which accurately reproduces the original" under Rule 1001(4). The requirement of an accurate reproduction applies to the frames of the videotape that have been re-recorded and does not mean that the whole videotape must be re-recorded in order for the exhibit to qualify as a "duplicate."

The sound track to a videotape may also be subject to an original document objection if the sound has been brought from another source and was not recorded at the same time as the videotape. See Section 6.4.2 with respect to objections to sound recordings.

Policy objections

Objections to unfair prejudice are generally the same as are available with respect to photographs. See Section 6.1.3. Videotapes may arouse emotions because of the physical injuries or devastation that is depicted. If the tape zooms in for close-ups of agonized facial expressions or tears, an objection on undue prejudice grounds likely will succeed. Sound tracks that include groans or cries of pain probably will be excluded on grounds of unfair prejudice. Any mention on the tape of the case or the cause of the injury will also draw an objection, and it is better to avoid these potential traps.

A videotape is not inadmissible on prejudice grounds, however, unless the prejudice is unfair so that rational thought processes on the part of the fact-finder might be overcome. See Section 1.3.3. One alternative is the bifurcation of the trial of liability and damages, so that the inflammatory videotape is used only after liability has been established.

Videotapes may also draw an objection on grounds of confusion/ misleading of the jury. See discussion in Section 1.3.3. One rationale often used in this area is that the videotape is "confusing" because it is not identical to the physical objects or events at issue. However the foundation requirement is only that the videotape is "fair" and "accurate," not that it is identical.

Another aspect of the "confusion/misleading" objection is the assertion that the tape shows more than can be justified by the purpose for which it is being offered. A videotape that is offered as a "view" of the scene may in fact contain action that makes it a demonstration or a reconstruction. This may be inherently misleading and, faced with an objection on policy grounds, the court may require that the videotape be qualified as a demonstration or reconstruction. See discussion in Section 7.2 and Section 7.3.

Editing of videotapes often produces objections although editing is proper so long as it is not misleading or unfair. In order to provide a basis for arguing against this type of objection, it is often useful to have the witness describe during direct testimony the editing that was done and explain why it was done.

Example

Q. Has the tape been edited?

A. Yes.

Q. How was it edited?

A. I reviewed the tape and noted segments that were repetitive or not directly relevant to what I am testifying about today. Then I gave my notes and instructions to Thomas Teller, and he edited the tape.

Q. Did you review the tape after it was edited?

A. Yes.

Q. How had Mr. Teller done in complying with your instructions?

A. He did exactly as I had instructed. Nothing was edited except the segments I designated.

Q. What happened to the segments that were edited out?

A. They were preserved on the master tape.

The last question is not necessary, but it serves to assure jurors that nothing is missing that the other side might have wanted to use.

Sometimes videotapes draw an objection on the ground that they are cumulative. See general discussion of this objection in Section 1.3.3. A videotape is not cumulative merely because some testimony or other photographic evidence on the same point has preceded it. But if it adds nothing new or incorporates a great deal of prior photographic evidence, the objection may succeed. To avoid this potential objection, the videotape can be offered early in the trial before a substantial quantity of other evidence about its subject matter has been received.

Completeness objections

Under Rule 106, when you select portions of a videotape, your opponent may ask that additional segments be selected and played together with your segments. These requests are sometimes made for tactical reasons, to make your videotape presentation too long for sustained juror interest.

Rule 106 provides: "When a writing or recorded statement or part thereof is introduced by a party, an adverse party may require the introduction at that time of any other part or any other writing or recorded statement which ought in fairness to be considered contemporaneously with it." Technically, Rule 106 applies only to recorded "statements" which does not cover all types of evidentiary videotapes. Courts also use Rule 611(a), however, to order that segments of "non-statement" videotapes designated by an opponent be played together with segments designated by the proponent. See discussion in Section 1.3.6.

If your exhibit is limited to one point, the court generally will not allow your opponent to add material on other unrelated points. That material would be reserved to your opponent's case. The proponent of the tape may ask the court to allow playing the segments of the videotape relevant to the proponent's case first, followed by the segments relevant to different points that are a part of the opponent's case.[7] The court will often order the segments played in the order they occur on the tape, however. This offers the opportunity for your opponent to obscure important points by surrounding them with lengthy, boring testimony about other things. All of this becomes a part of the proponent's exhibit. The opposing party may use any of the remaining material on the videotape (not relevant to the subject matter of the edited tape) as a part of his or her case without further foundation.

Objections to videotapes of depositions

Objections with respect to videotaped depositions are somewhat broader in scope because they include evidentiary objections to the testimony shown on the tape. See discussion of objections to videotape transcripts in Section 2.6.4. Under Rule 32(b) of the Federal Rules of Civil Procedure, opposing counsel may make any objection to the testimony shown on the tape that could have been made if the testimony were presented "live" in the courtroom. Rule 32(d)(3)(A) and (B) impose limitations on raising certain objections at trial if the ground of the objection is one which might have been cured had it been raised during the deposition. This type of objection generally requires a pretrial motion in limine challenging specific portions of the videotape so that the judge can rule on each objection. If an objection is sustained, you can edit the tape to remove the material that was the subject of the objection. This kind of objection can also be raised at trial but, because it requires the judge to excuse the jury, hear the objection, and then have the tape edited, considerable time is wasted. An alternative to editing is to have the tape played for the jury up to the point where the objectionable material begins and then the recorder can be set on fast forward to move the tape beyond that point without the jury seeing the objectionable material. Because of the possibility of technical mistakes with the latter technique resulting in the jury seeing some of the objectionable material, the editing alternative is recommended.

Your opponent may object to production matters such as camera angle, the use of close-ups, and other camera techniques. Depending on the circumstances and the location of the deposition, the camera operator may focus only on the witness, or on the questioner and the witness together, or on the questioner, the witness, and the opposing counsel together. The camera operator may also shift focus from one to another of the participants and change the length of focus, for example, from a medium length focus on both the questioner and the witness to a closer focus just on the witness. Extreme close-ups should be avoided because the court may hold them to be prejudicial. Generally you should use just one camera angle for the entire deposition, focused just on the witness. Have the witness at the deposition view herself on the monitor screen at the outset of the deposition before any questioning and, on the record, declare herself satisfied with the camera angle, lighting, and other production details.

Example

Counsel: Your Honor, plaintiff's next witness is Eldon Erdly. Mr. Erdly's testimony is quite short and he is now working in San Francisco; therefore we will use a videotape of his deposition, taken under oath, three months ago at 1666 K Street, N.W. in Washington, D.C. The deposition was taken before Michele Trahan, certified shorthand reporter, and a written transcript of the testimony has been certified by Ms. Trahan. May I have this videotape marked as plaintiff's Exhibit 83?

Reporter: *(Marks)*

Counsel: May I have this transcript marked as plaintiff's Exhibit 84?

Reporter: *(Marks)*

Counsel: The videotape marked as Exhibit 83 was played for Mr. Smith, counsel for the defendant, immediately after the pretrial conference at my offices, and, at his request a copy of the tape was furnished to him at that time. The videotape that has been marked as plaintiff's Exhibit 83 is exactly the same as the videotape provided to Mr. Smith.

Opposing Counsel: We would still like an opportunity to examine this videotape.

Court: You may do so. We will have a short recess.

Opposing Counsel: Your Honor, there are also two objections that we wish to press at this time.

Court: The jury is excused. *(After jury leaves)* Please proceed with your objections.

Opposing Counsel: Your Honor, if you will turn to page 45 of the transcript, beginning at line 12, counsel asks a question about what Mr. Erdly saw when he arrived at Mr. Dveny's offices. The camera at that point moves substantially closer to Mr. Erdly and this close-up emphasizes unfairly Mr. Erdly's evident disgust with the dead chickens found in Mr. Dveny's offices. This change in camera angle is unfair. A jury would view Mr. Erdly from a constant perspective. This move was engineered knowing the videotape would be used instead of testimony.

Counsel: The camera angle is not unfair; it does not distort Mr. Erdly's response at all. Let me show you the disputed sequence. The camera operator was moving in to get a better view of the invoice to which Mr. Erdly was pointing. *(Plays sequence)*

Court: Overruled.

Opposing Counsel: Your Honor, if you will turn to page 47 of the transcript, beginning at line 18, counsel asks a question that is grossly leading and improper on direct examination.

Counsel: Leading in that situation was proper under Rule 611(c) because it was necessary to elicit the testimony.

Court: That provision applies to foundation questions for exhibits, not to descriptions of dead chickens. Strike that question and the answer.

Counsel: With your permission, Your Honor, we will edit that question and answer out of the tape. We will proceed with the next witness and will have the tape ready after the noon recess.

Court: Granted. Please make sure that Mr. Smith has had an opportunity to review the edited tape. Subject to any objections to the editing, the tape will be admitted after editing.

Though not required by the rules, providing a copy of the tape to opposing counsel helps speed the in-court presentation.

Some courts require the tape, as edited after objections are resolved, to be given a new number or to have a letter designation. In this case, the videotape submitted by plaintiff is Exhibit 83 and the edited videotape would be Exhibit 83A.

Editing deposition videotapes is almost always necessary because much of what happens at the typical deposition is not needed at trial. There is usually disagreement, however, about whether the editing, which shows the points useful to one side, can be used without also including testimony designated by the other side.

Example

Counsel: Your Honor, plaintiff's next witness is Sam Tilden, whose testimony we will present by videotape. Mr. Tilden died last summer. The videotape records Mr. Tilden's deposition which was taken before Michele Trahan, a certified shorthand reporter, and a written transcript of the testimony has been certified by the reporter. May I have this videotape marked as plaintiff's Exhibit 89?

Court Reporter: *(Marks)*

Counsel: Let the record reflect I have handed to counsel for defendant what has been marked as plaintiff's Exhibit 89. Let the record also reflect that this videotape has been edited to remove statements by lawyers and the segments of Mr. Tilden's deposition that are not necessary at this time. We have attempted to shorten the testimony where possible so that we can complete the trial expeditiously.

Opposing Counsel: I object, Your Honor, all of Mr. Tilden's testimony should be played; not just selected parts.

Counsel: May we approach the bench, Your Honor?

Court: Yes.

(At sidebar)

Counsel: The portions of Mr. Tilden's testimony that have been deleted are not necessary to establish plaintiff's case, Your Honor.

Court: *(To opposing counsel)* What have they left out?

Opposing Counsel: They left out the part where Mr. Tilden describes his grandfather's bootlegging business, and they left out all of my cross-examination of the witness.

Counsel: The testimony about Mr. Tilden's grandfather's bootlegging business is not proper character or reputation evidence with respect to Mr. Tilden and does not come within Rule 608. The cross-examination is not required to be introduced at this time under Rule 32(a)(4) of the Federal Rules of Civil Procedure because the cross-examination was on different topics than the excerpt plaintiff is offering. If Mr. Smith wants to introduce any portion of Mr. Tilden's testimony on these other subjects, he is supposed to do that during the presentation of his own case and not during plaintiff's evidence.

Court: The testimony about the bootlegging business is stricken. I will review the cross-examination as to substance. I think that the spirit of Rule 32(a)(4) requires that the opposing party be able to require the introduction of supplementary relevant testimony from the deposition transcript at the conclusion of the reading of the deposition rather than having to wait until the defendant's case is presented.

It is important to make clear to the jurors that the tape has been edited. Most jurors will spot the places where the tape has been edited and, unless there is an explanation, may draw adverse inferences.

The hearsay, original document, and policy objections to videotape depositions are the same as described in this section with respect to other videotapes. Rule 32(a)(4) which applies to deposition transcripts uses almost the same wording with respect to "completeness" objections as Rule 106 which applies to other types of exhibits as well as deposition transcripts.

6.3.3 Production

Videotaping is often more difficult than it appears, particularly where you need a polished "television quality" product. Two questions should be addressed at the outset of the case. First, how likely is it that the videotape will be used at trial. (A key consideration here is whether the case is likely to go to trial.) Second, if the videotape is used at trial, how important is it likely to be to the outcome of the case. For any videotape likely to be used at trial, and certainly with respect to anything important to the outcome of the case, the use of a professional videotape consultant is probably justified. See references to qualified consultants in Appendix B.

When producing videotape exhibits remember that the average judge or juror has been conditioned by television as to the quality and length of videotape presentations. Television tapes are of very high quality with excellent focus and organization of material. If your material looks careless or "homemade," the fact-finder will give it less credibility. Jury studies and interviews support the conclusion that virtually all jurors expect the quality of the video they see in the courtroom to be as well-paced and well-produced as what they may see on their television set at home.

Date/time generator

Most video cameras have a built-in date/time generator which is very useful for videotaping depositions or trial exhibits. This equipment generates and transmits a signal indicating the date on which the taping is being done and the time of day. The time of day is generated by the hour, minute, and second. The signal from the date/time generator is displayed in the upper or lower margin of the picture. This display shows the time clock running continuously during the taping.

In a situation where the objective is to demonstrate that there has been no editing at all, reference to the date/time display establishes this fact. In a situation where only part of the tape will be played at trial, the date/time generator functions as an efficient "locator." Do not rely on the "digital counter" on the videotape player. This records only the number of revolutions the videotape reel has made, not the number of feet or inches of tape that have passed by. It also varies from one player to another. Therefore the digital counter is difficult to use for locating a particular segment to play back at trial. The counter is also subject to operator error because it must be set at zero every time a cassette is used. In contrast, the date/time generator provides a precise indicator that is a permanent part of the tape and that can be used in the videotape logs or to locate a specific portion to play back.

Another alternative is to put the video in digital format in which each frame of the videotape has a separate identifier number. Using controls for a computer-driven system (see Section 9.6.3), any individual frame can be located and displayed. The video can be advanced or moved backward frame by frame.

Logs

In order to facilitate handling the videotape in the courtroom, you should prepare a log which contains a written description, item by item, of the things or scenes depicted on the tape together with notations from the date/time generator or digital frame numbers indicating where on the tape they are located. If the final tape is edited, the material taken out should also be noted on this log.

Length

Most videotaped evidence should be in fairly short segments. Three- to five-minute tapes are common. Most jurors are conditioned by the ten to twelve-minute segments on television between commercial breaks, and they have difficulty concentrating on longer segments.

Even with respect to day-in-the-life videotapes, which could tend to be quite long compared to other types of videotape evidence, most experienced personal injury lawyers aim for an edited copy not exceeding twenty minutes in length. Problems with length can be solved by creating separate videotape segments or by having a different witness testify as to different parts of the tape.

Copies

Videotapes are easily damaged by magnetic fields such as those produced by copy machines, computers, audio speakers, beepers, magnetic paper clip holders, and other common office equipment. Videotapes also can be damaged by heat or moisture. Several copies should be made of each evidentiary videotape for protection of the tape and for responding to discovery.

Editing

Videotapes can be edited electronically or digitally with much the same result as is achieved in editing film but with the additional advantage that the original material is preserved intact. At least two machines are used and the videotape is actually re-recorded on the second tape. The process is more difficult than film editing and is best done by a professional. Audio dubbing can also be done during editing. The original audio can be replaced, audio can be added to a tape that was video only, or new audio can be added to the original audio.

You should always consider editing any videotape, both to shorten the exhibit and to concentrate on the key points.

Deposition videotapes

A conservative approach should be taken to adding "special effects" to deposition videotapes. Straight cuts, which put nothing between the edited segments, are the simplest form of editing. However, this may make the viewers uncomfortable with the jumps from one segment to the next. This technique also sometimes causes jurors to think there is something wrong or to become momentarily distracted and lose the flow of the material.

"Video black" can be inserted at cuts between edited segments. The black period can be anywhere from a few frames (there are 30 frames of video per second) to as many as five seconds. Cuts to black can be used as an editing convention to signal to the viewer that a new segment is coming or to give emphasis to particular pieces of testimony. Fades to and from black give an additional effect.

Switcher effects, such as wipes and dissolves, are very effective in creating a smooth flow and assisting in making the editing less jarring. Digital effects, however, should be used only very occasionally in deposition videos. These effects emphasize the presence of editing and may cause objections.

Nondeposition videotapes

A full range of digital effects may be added to editing videotape exhibits. Flips, spins, page turns, floats, infinite expansions and shrinks when used appropriately can add to the effectiveness of the exhibit. Switcher effects, such as wipes and dissolves, create a smooth flow and assist in making the video easy to understand. A combination of switcher and digital effects is very useful in creating side-by-side and overlay comparisons.

Editing should proceed in stages. Start with a "paper edit." Using a written transcript from your deposition or a copy (dub) of your videotape taken in the field, note time codes for the beginning and end of each of the segments you think will work in the product that you want to use at trial. Then go to an "off-line edit" in which you edit a copy of the tape to produce a video draft of what you are going to use at trial. This version will not contain the transition effects that you will add during the last stage, an "on-line edit." The final "on-line edit" is done from the original tapes. Never use the original tapes until ready for final editing in order to avoid the risk of damage to the master tapes.

Editing may include producing a narration for the tape. You should avoid any narration while recording in the field because all of that material will be discoverable. Often there is little advantage to narrating on-the-spot what the camera is seeing. You can write the necessary narration later and add it to the final videotape.

Combined with other media

Videotapes can be combined effectively with other media. They can incorporate photographs or computer animations. The videotape of a conveyor belt in operation could, for example, include a 20-second segment on a "still" photograph of the part that broke and a computer animation depicting, by means of a cutaway, how the internal braking system of the conveyor belt works.

If the videotape contains particularly effective images, consider using blowups of the images on the tape as static exhibits displayed on an easel so that the witness can point to specific areas more easily or can actually mark on the exhibit. See discussion of overlays in Section 9.3.2.

One cautionary note: if the videotape is a day-in-the-life presentation, combining home video segments or still photographs of the plaintiff with the videotape images of the plaintiff's current condition to create a before-and-after story will lead to vigorous objection and likely will support a ruling that the tape is inadmissible unless the "before" material is edited out.

6.3.4 Tactics

The courtroom use of videotape has several advantages over using other media. First, for many people, including judges and jurors, videotape is a more "believable" medium. It gives the flavor of "on-the-spot" reporting and may not carry the assumption of "staging" associated with still photos. Most people are accustomed to receiving news from a television screen and most news broadcasts use videotape for reports from remote locations. Second, videotapes do not require a darkened room. A television monitor will produce adequate contrast and color under normal room lighting. Third, placement of the playback unit does not have to disadvantage anyone in the courtroom. Multiple monitors can be used—in front of the judge, jury, and opposing counsel—and operated from a single playback unit. Everyone in the courtroom will have a good vantage point from which to see the evidence. Fourth, the videotape can be locked temporarily onto one image while a point is being explained by the witness. Then, when the witness is finished with the point, the playback can continue. The witness thus can establish a comfortable pace and control the medium for presenting the tangible evidence.

Situations in which to consider videotapes

One potential use for videotape is as a substitute for a "view" by the judge or jury as described in Section 5.3. If an actual tour is impossible because of the distance (as in a foreign country) or logistics, then videotape can bring the tour to the courtroom. In this kind of taping, the video camera goes from place to place in the facility or at the site showing carefully all the surroundings in which the events at issue took place. This kind of a tape is also very useful during testimony about the surroundings because you can stop the video player at particular points to "freeze" an image on the screen while the witness in the courtroom describes the significance of the things at which the fact-finder is looking.

Videotape can also help to describe facilities involved in small, but important, parts of the case where the judge might not want to take the time for a full-scale tour. For example, if the issue is the care with which certain work was done, a part of the proof may deal with the training of the people who did the work. A short videotape showing the training facilities may help make this testimony more meaningful. You can use "split screen" videotape to show two separate sets of actions that occurred simultaneously and how they were interrelated.

If you have a long, complicated story involving a number of people, you may want to tape short depositions from the "minor" characters so they can be played with dispatch as the trial proceeds. This avoids the scheduling problems and expense if all these people were to appear in person. Fact-finders usually succumb to boredom most quickly when written material is being read to them. On the other hand, people are accustomed to watching television for hours at a time and are well able to relate to what they see on the screen. For this reason, videotapes of depositions generally make a better presentation than using a written transcript or an oral reading of the transcript. An important consideration here is the demeanor of the witness, which will be evident on the videotape but probably not through the reading of a stenographic transcript. If demeanor is a negative factor for your case, you may want to stay with the transcript.

Videotape allows the expert to testify using a full range of exhibits and testimony aids because the camera can capture all of the props as well as the testimony of the witness. If you have an expert with a very busy schedule, a videotape of his or her deposition will permit you to use the testimony "live" even if the trial is delayed and the expert is unavailable when you finally reach his or her part of the case.

Videotapes of your opponent's witnesses are helpful in four situations. First, if your opponent is unlikely to bring the witness to trial, you might want to preserve your option to use some of that testimony by making a videotape. Second, if the witness is arrogant or difficult, videotapes generally will keep witness demeanor within acceptable bounds during the deposition. Third, and in the same vein, if the opposing lawyer is given to excessively aggressive deposition tactics, a videotape to play at a sanctions hearing can be helpful. Fourth, if the witness will use a scale model or other demonstration in his testimony, and your expert cannot be present, you may need to record the demonstration or reconstruction.

Videotapes may also present an opportunity to present the testimony of a child without the trauma associated with a courtroom appearance.

The flexibility of videotape permits the evidence to be collected as it happens. This is particularly important in personal injury cases where the effects of the injury and pain and suffering may be much less apparent several years after the accident when the case goes to trial.

Another interesting use for videotapes is to make comparisons. If you want to dramatize how big an improvement Invention A is over Standard Method B, make a videotape of the use of Invention A to perform a particular task with a date/time generator recording the minutes and seconds as a part of the picture. Then make a videotape of the use of Standard Method B to perform the same task, also using the date/time generator to record elapsed time. This may show clearly for the fact-finder the benefits such as efficiency, cleanliness, safety, amount of space needed, and other claims with respect to Invention A.

Precautions while making videotapes

If the videotape is an important part of your evidence, you should have the client, rather than the lawyer, hire the photographer and put in writing the instructions to those who are making the tape. Those involved in the taping should be instructed to ensure that the tape will be fair and accurate.

Nothing requires you to notify your opponent when videotaping exhibits or to permit representatives of the other side to attend. You cannot, however, keep the resulting videotape a secret until trial if you intend to use it as an exhibit. Attempts to protect videotapes during discovery by claiming that they are work product or trial-preparation materials are ill-advised. You will eventually meet an objection based on "surprise", see Section 1.3.5, along with motions for discovery sanctions. Your opponent is entitled to a fair opportunity to inspect any exhibit, and most judges will require disclosure and delivery of the tape at least by the time of the final pretrial conference.

As a tactical matter, you might want to consider inviting your opponent to the final taping. This allows you to have the benefit of appearing to be open and concerned only with an efficient presentation at trial. If your opponent attends, he or she will be faced with an argument that objections not voiced at the taping have been waived. If your opponent does not attend, the court may be less patient with speculative assertions as to what might have been done to affect the fairness of the taping.

Useful production guidance has been published by the Federal Judicial Center.[8]

Editing videotapes

Two types of edits to evidentiary videotapes should be distinguished carefully: first, "practice" tapes in which the entire tape is re-recorded when the "final" tape is made; and second, edits to remove segments from the "final" tape. There is no restriction, other than the obvious opportunities for cross-examination, on redoing the tape. You should carefully consider in advance whether to make "practice" tapes, and if made, whether you will keep them. The final tape may be produced by using the same tape as was used for previous work because the video recorder erases just before it records. Nothing in the rules requires you to keep "practice" tapes, and the damage that might be done by cross-examination about any "practice" taping differs greatly from case to case.

If the final tape is edited, however, you should keep the original containing the material edited out. Your opponent generally is entitled to discovery of the material edited out of the final tape if you intend to use the tape in evidence. Moreover, sometimes an objection to editing can be overcome if the judge can be shown that the outtakes were just repetitive material or hearsay comments. Conversely, if the material edited out of the final tape is not available, the tape may be held inadmissible.

Editing of videotapes should always be acknowledged during the direct examination. When you edit a videotape, formulate a plan for ensuring its admissibility. The plan should include keeping the "outtakes" on a master tape and offering a plausible reason for the editing, such as saving time, deleting irrelevant material, or avoiding needless presentation of cumulative evidence. Similarly, if you plan to have a sound track on a videotape, then you will need an appropriate witness in order to have the sound track admitted.

Playback in the courtroom

The equipment for displaying videotapes in the courtroom is described in Section 9.5 (electronic systems) and Section 9.6 (digital systems). A smooth presentation without time-wasting pauses to find the right segment is very important to the effectiveness of videotape exhibits. Having someone assigned to this task who is familiar with the equipment and can handle minor technical glitches provides insurance in this regard.

6.4 SOUND RECORDINGS

Sound recordings and sound tracks for videotapes can be very effective evidentiary presentations. Because sound recordings are often statements or conversations, they raise special hearsay problems.

6.4.1 Foundation

Evidentiary sound recordings are generally of three kinds: sound tracks for videotapes, recordings offered for the quality of particular sounds, and recordings of conversations. The foundation fundamentals for sound recordings are the same as for visual recordings made with video cameras. First, a witness must establish competence by testimony that he or she heard or made the actual sounds relevant to the issues in the case. Second, the sound recording must be relevant to some issue in the case. Third, the witness must be prepared to identify the sound recording. And fourth, testimony must be offered as to the trustworthiness of the sound recording. See Section 1.1. The testimony on trustworthiness generally establishes that the sounds on the tape are a fair and accurate reproduction of the sounds of which the witness has first hand knowledge.

Some commentators find necessary the additional qualifications that the sound recording equipment and operator be capable and reliable in making accurate reproductions. This is basically a carry-over from criminal cases that is unnecessary in civil cases. Some courts have required the proponent of the tape to demonstrate that it has been preserved intact and unaltered from the time of making to the time of playing at trial. Again, this requirement arises from criminal cases and should not be applicable in civil cases. If the witness is competent to testify that the recording as played in court is a fair and accurate reproduction of the sounds he or she made or heard, that is sufficient for foundation purposes.

Sound tracks for videotapes

A video recorder is capable of recording sound at the same time as it records video images. The tape passes over a video head which records the video image and then over an audio head, which records the sounds. The audio head operates in the same manner as an audio tape recorder, placing the sounds directly onto the videotape. A control mechanism synchronizes the sound with the video images.

The sound tracks on most videotapes used as tangible evidence are the verbal statements of someone who is explaining something portrayed on the video portion of the tape. This is an out-of-court statement, because it was made wherever the videotape was made, and thus is hearsay. It may also be an "off-camera" statement by someone who cannot be seen and identified, and a proper foundation requires that the voice be identified.

The most common way to deal with the hearsay problem and the trustworthiness problem at the same time is to produce, in court, the person who made the statements recorded on the tape and have him or her testify that the statements are true and accurate. This qualifies the out-of-court statements with in-court statements and should be sufficient for an exception under Rule 803(24) to overcome any hearsay objection because the declarant is in court and available for cross-examination. It also authenticates the voice on the tape and provides the necessary foundation in that respect.

Example

(After other qualifying questions about the video portion of the tape)

Q. Is there anyone heard speaking on this videotape?

A. Yes.

Q. Who is that?

A. Me.

Q. Are you the only speaker heard on the tape?

A. Yes.

Q. Is all the information you provided as the speaker on the tape true and accurate?

A. Yes.

This approach is not foolproof. Some judges will require the witness to replicate the narrative from the stand. This is generally not difficult with a knowledgeable witness.

Often the audio portion of the videotape is made later when the tape is edited and dubbed in to fit the edited tape. This eliminates distracting background noises and permits a carefully crafted narration that will not be open to objection on grounds related to the substance of what is said. The foundation remains the same. On direct examination, you need not go into how the sound track was made, but you should prepare the witness for these questions on cross.

If the sound track on a videotape consists only of nonverbal sounds, the foundation is the same as that for any other nonverbal sound recording. It must be a fair representation of the sounds as they actually existed at the time that is relevant in the case.

Example

Q. Are there any sounds in the audio portion of the tape other than the spoken voice?

A. Yes, the videotape was taken at the beach area of Radnor Island and there are background sounds from waves and birds and the like.

Q. What equipment was used to record those sounds?

A. We used the built-in sound recording capability in the video recorder that I described earlier. We used a high-impedance shotgun microphone with an independent power supply.

Q. Are there any sounds on the audio portion of the tape that were not recorded at the time and place the videotape was made?

A. No. Nothing was added. We used the sound track exactly as we recorded it, without change.

Q. Did you listen to the sounds at the beach area when the videotape was made?

A. Yes, I did.

Q. Have you listened to the sounds on the videotape?

A. Yes, I have.

Q. Are the sounds on the videotape a fair and accurate reproduction of the sounds you heard at the beach area?

A. Yes.

If a precise understanding of the words on the tape is important and the sound track is somewhat garbled, a transcript can be prepared and handed out to the judge or jury so they can follow along while the tape is being run. Or the words on the sound track can be displayed on a computer monitor as the tape is played. You must qualify the transcript separately before it can be used. The witness does not have to be an expert and is required only to testify that he or she listened carefully to the tape; that the transcription was made carefully; and that the transcription was cross-checked against the tape.

Recordings of sounds

Sound recordings are sometimes used as proof of a physical fact: there is a warning bell on a bridge; certain noise is so loud as to constitute a violation of noise pollution regulations; or the sound unit supplied with particular equipment does not meet specifications because there are frequent gaps in the transmission. If the sound recording is offered only to give the fact-finder information about the type of sound and the technical attributes of the sound are not at issue, a simple foundation will suffice.

Example

Q. Mr. Hotchkiss, what do you do for a living?

A. I am the operator of the drawbridge at 58th Street.

Q. Mr. Hotchkiss, in your job, do you hear the sound of the warning bell on the 58th Street Bridge?

A. Yes.

Q. How often do you hear that sound?

A. As the operator of the drawbridge, I am on duty eight hours a day at the bridge and I hear the warning bell every time it goes off.

Q. How often does it go off?

A. About six times a day.

Q. How long does it ring when it goes off?

A. Exactly 30 seconds.

Q. May I have this marked as defendant's Exhibit 85?

Reporter: *(Marks)*

Q. Let the record reflect I have shown to Mr. Smith, counsel for plaintiff the tape cassette which has been marked as defendant's Exhibit 85.

Opposing Counsel: *(Looks)*

Q. Mr. Hotchkiss, I show you what has been marked as Exhibit 85.

A. *(Looks)*

Q. Mr. Hotchkiss, have you listened to the tape recording that is Exhibit 85?

A. Yes.

Q. How do you know that?

A. I put my initials on the white sticker on the side of this cassette after I listened to it.

Q. Were you able to identify the sounds on the tape?

A. Yes.

Q. What were they?

A. This is a recording of the warning bell on the 58th Street Bridge when it is ringing.

Q. Is the sound on the tape a fair and accurate reproduction of the type of sound made by the warning bell?

A. Yes, it is.

Q. Is the sound on the tape a fair and accurate reproduction of the length of time the warning bell rings when it goes off?

A. Yes.

Q. Your Honor, we move the admission in evidence of defendant's Exhibit 85.

Court: So ordered.

Q. Your Honor, may we play the tape that has been admitted in evidence as Exhibit 85?

Court: You may.

If you offer the sound recording with respect to specific attributes of the sound, generally you must qualify the exhibit with an expert who is an audio engineer.

Example

(After the engineer's qualifications are established)

Q. Mr. Engle, did you make any measurement of the noise level at the facility located at 320 Hill Street?

A. Yes.

Q. At what time of day did you make those measurements?

A. At noon.

Q. How did you make the measurements?

A. I placed an audiometer five feet off the floor at a point 10 feet inside the front door and at a point 10 feet inside the rear door.

Q. Was your audiometer in good working order on the day you used it at the facility at 320 Hill Street?

A. Yes. I have it calibrated every week. I had it calibrated just the day before.

Q. What reading did you observe on the audiometer at the facility at 320 Hill Street?

A. The highest reading was 100 decibels; the lowest reading was 87 decibels.

Q. What else did you do?

A. I placed a tape recorder next to each audiometer and made a recording of the noise.

Q. Was the tape recorder capable of making an accurate recording of the sounds?

A. Yes. The tape recorder I use is very accurate and I have used it frequently in my work.

Q. May I have this tape marked as plaintiff's Exhibit 90?

Court reporter: *(Marks)*

Q. Let the record reflect that Mr. Smith, counsel for defendant, received the tape that has been marked as Exhibit 90 during discovery. I have handed Exhibit 90 to Mr. Smith for his examination.

Opposing Counsel: *(Looks)*

Q. Mr. Engle, I am handing you what has been marked as Exhibit 90.

A. *(Looks)*

Q. What is Exhibit 90?

A. That is the tape made at the 320 Hill Street location.

Q. How do you know that?

A. It has my standard label on it showing the date and place where it was made.

Q. Who made that tape?

A. Thomas Teller made this tape under my supervision.

Q. Is the tape that has been marked as plaintiff's Exhibit 90 a true and accurate recording?

A. Yes.

Q. How do you know that?

A. After the tape was made, I rewound it and played it. The tape was an accurate recording of what I personally had heard.

Q. Have there been any additions, deletions, or other changes to the tape since you made it?

A. No.

Q. Do you have an audiometer with you today?

A. Yes, I do.

Q. Is it in good working order today?

A. Yes. I had it calibrated yesterday.

Q. Using your audiometer to check the decibel level, can you play the sound recording tape that has been marked as Exhibit 90 at the levels that you observed at noon at the facility at 320 Hill Street?

A. Yes. I can.

Q. Your Honor, we move the admission in evidence of plaintiff's Exhibit 90.

Court: Admitted.

Q. Your Honor, may the witness play for the jury plaintiff's Exhibit 90?

Court: You may.

The details with respect to what equipment was used and who operated the equipment used by the expert are not essential to the foundation. Some lawyers include these facts as a part of the foundation in order to help the witness appear to be in command of the situation. Similarly, details about where the tape was stored after it was made and what safekeeping procedures were used to make sure it was not altered are not a part of the basic foundation. If you know your opponent has some points that can be made in this area, you may want to bring these factors out on direct, rather than waiting for them to be raised on voir dire. See Section 1.7.2 on voir dire.

Recordings of conversations

Sound recordings of conversations present some different problems. One is the requirement that the voice on the tape be identified properly. Rule 901(b)(5) provides for:

> Identification of a voice, whether heard firsthand or through mechanical or electronic transmission or recording, by opinion based upon hearing the voice at any time under circumstances connecting it with the alleged speaker.

If the witness has heard the speaker before, he or she can testify as to the identification of the speaker. This is an opinion that falls under Rule 701 and may properly be offered by a nonexpert witness. Voices may also be identified without first hand knowledge or exposure to the speaker through self-identification coupled with circumstantial evidence. If the speaker says, "I am George Whimple" in a telephone conversation in which the person on the other end dialed a number listed in the phone book for George Whimple and the telephone which the speaker is using is located at an address where George Whimple lives, this self-identification coupled with circumstantial evidence should be sufficient.

A second possible problem, although not technically a part of the foundation, is the legal requirement for consent or statutory authorization. If the conversation was taped with the consent of one or more of the parties, the qualifying testimony should include facts to establish consent. Although taping with the consent of one of the parties satisfies the Fourth Amendment,[9] and the federal wiretap law,[10] there may be additional requirements under the laws of the state where the recording is to be made. If neither party consented to the taping, but it was done by an authorized law enforcement officer in a manner consistent with the constitutional requirement for a judicial warrant and the procedural safeguards of federal law,[11] the qualifying testimony should include facts to establish the legality of the taping. If the taping was done without consent and without statutory authorization, it may still be admissible in a civil case in some jurisdictions, but the person who did the taping may be subject to prosecution.[12]

Third, because this is a recording of an out of court statement, it must qualify under the hearsay rules. Rule 801(d)(2) establishes a hearsay exception for recording of conversations of a party, a party's agent or representative, or a party's co-conspirator. The requirements are explained at Section 2.1.2 in connection with documentary exhibits. This exception is the primary vehicle for use of sound records of conversations although there are other specialized circumstances in which such recordings are also admissible. For example, Rule 801(d)(1) and Rule 803(l), (2), and (3), also discussed in Section 2.1.2, may cover some conversations.

There are two types of foundation witnesses for a tape recording of a conversation: (1) a person who heard the actual conversation can testify that the tape recording is a fair and accurate representation of the conversation he or she heard; and (2) the person or persons who placed the recording device (if the two are separate as in a transmitter/receiver situation) can establish a chain of custody for the tape.

Example

Q. Mr. Marshall, where were you on the evening of January 10?

A. I was at home.

Q. What happened on that evening?

A. I called Daniel Deford at about 8:20 p.m. to discuss pricing of self-locking bottle caps. It was about time for another price increase, and I was going to check with Mr. Deford about that.

Q. Did you make any recording of that call?

A. Yes.

Q. How did you make the recording?

A. The FBI came and put a voice-activated recording device on my telephone. That recording device automatically records all conversations.

Q. Did you consent to this recording?

A. Oh yes. I was the one who called the FBI and suggested they do it.

A. May I have this tape cassette marked as plaintiff's Exhibit 73?

Court reporter: *(Marks)*

Q. Let the record reflect that Ms. James, counsel for defendant, received a copy of this tape during discovery.

Court: *(Waits for James to ask for another opportunity to examine what has been marked)*

Q. Have you listened to the tape that has been marked as Exhibit 73?

A. Yes. Those are my initials and the date on the white label on the reverse side.

Q. What is recorded on that tape?

A. The conversation I had with Daniel Deford on the evening of January 10.

Q. How many voices are recorded on that tape?

A. Just two.

Q. Whose voices are they?

A. Daniel Deford's and mine.

Q. How are you able to identify Mr. Deford's voice?

A. I have talked to him on several previous occasions, and I recognize his voice. Also, I dialed the phone number listed under his name in the book and asked for Daniel Deford. He said: "This is Daniel Deford," when he answered.

Q. Do you recall that conversation on the evening of January 10?

A. Yes.

Q. Is the recording on the tape a fair and accurate representation of that conversation?

A. Yes, it is.

Q. Your Honor, we move the admission in evidence of plaintiff's
Exhibit 73.

You need not have the witness label the tape cassette but it helps avoid
any confusion.

Your opponent may ask to see a copy of a transcript of what is on
the tape. You need to produce such a transcript, however, only if you are
going to use one to allow the fact-finder to follow the tape more easily.
Otherwise, your opponent is entitled only to the same opportunity to
examine (in this case listen to) the tape which is the exhibit as he or she
is accorded with every other kind of exhibit.

Example

Q. Mr. Itman, where were you on the evening of January 10?

A. I met with Irma Wilson at her home at 240 Peachtree Lane
about 8:30 p.m.

Q. Why were you there?

A. Ms. Wilson had arranged a meeting that evening with Daniel
Deford to discuss the pricing of self-locking bottle caps.

Q. What did you do there?

A. I put a concealed transmitter on Ms. Wilson and adjusted the
equipment to be sure it was in proper operating order. It was
working fine.

Q. Did Ms. Wilson consent to carrying this transmitter?

A. Yes. As a matter of fact it was her suggestion.

Q. What experience, if any, have you had in working with this
equipment?

A. I have used this transmitter and receiver equipment for the
last two years. Before that, I used similar equipment for the
past ten years. There are new developments in the field
constantly, and I upgrade the equipment from time to time.

Q. Is the transmitter equipment you used with Ms. Wilson
capable of recording accurately and clearly the conversations
Ms. Wilson had with others?

A. Yes. This transmitter picks up conversations within a 25 foot
radius and transmits up to half a mile.

Q. To what are these conversations transmitted?

A. To a receiver, usually in a nearby car or building.

Q. What did you do after you put the concealed transmitter on
Ms. Wilson?

A. I went out to my car where the receiving equipment was installed and checked to be sure it was in proper operating order. It was working fine.

Q. Then what did you do?

A. I drove to the intersection of 17th and K Streets, N.W. and parked my car. Ms. Wilson had arranged a meeting with Daniel Deford for 10 p.m. in Farragut Square Park. I waited until the meeting took place, recorded the conversation, and then took the tape back to my office.

Q. What did you do with the tape?

A. I played the tape and created a transcript by typing the words that I heard on the tape. Then I made a copy of the tape.

Q. Are you able to recognize the voices on the tape?

A. Yes.

Q. How are you able to recognize those voices?

A. One voice I recognize because I have heard it many times before, and I have also heard it on test recordings on the equipment. The other voice identified himself on this tape, and thereafter I was able to recognize that voice and distinguish it from the other.

Q. Whose voices are on the tape?

A. One voice I recognize as that of Irma Wilson. The other voice was a male who identified himself as Daniel Deford.

Q. Have any changes, deletions, or additions been made to the tape?

A. No.

Q. Did you bring the tape with you this morning?

A. Yes. *(Hands it over)*

Q. May I have the tape cassette marked as plaintiff's Exhibit 85 and this transcript marked as plaintiff's Exhibit 86?

Court reporter: *(Marks)*

Q. Let the record reflect that I have handed plaintiff's Exhibits 85 and 86 to counsel for the defendant.

Opposing Counsel: *(Looks)*

Q. Mr. Itman, I show you the tape cassette that has been marked plaintiff's Exhibit 85 and ask if you can identify it.

A. Yes.

Q. What is it?

A. That is the tape I made from the transmitter carried by Irma Wilson.

Q. Mr. Itman, I show you the transcript that has been marked as plaintiff's Exhibit 86 and ask if you can identify that.

A. Yes.

Q. What is it?

A. That is the transcript I prepared from the tape that is Exhibit 85.

Q. Is that transcript an accurate representation of what is on the tape that has been marked as plaintiff's Exhibit 85?

A. Yes, it is.

Q. Your Honor, we move the admission in evidence of plaintiff's Exhibits 85 and 86.

Some lawyers add questions about the details of safekeeping of the tape during the foundation testimony because they help illustrate the professionalism of the investigator and the trustworthiness of the tape. These questions are not, however, a part of the basic foundation. If any editing has been done to the tape, the foundation should include questions to demonstrate that nothing has been done that would affect the fairness or accuracy of the exhibit.

If you use a transcript of the tape at trial to help the fact-finder understand the material on the tape, you can satisfy the original document rule by introducing the tape (which is the "original") first, then the transcripts. You must lay a foundation that the transcript is accurate. You can do this by having a witness testify that the transcript is an accurate representation of the conversation the witness heard. Alternatively, anyone can testify that he or she listened to the tape and prepared the transcript accurately.

6.4.2 Objections

The use of sound tracks and other sound recordings must be planned carefully because a wide variety of objections are available. See Section 1.3.

Hearsay objections

Some haven must be found under the exceptions to the hearsay rule for all statements on sound recordings. Rule 801(d)(2) provides an exception for statements by a party or the party's employees and agents. Rule 803(1), (2), and (3) covers statements made while events at issue were going on. Rule 804(b)(1), (2), and (3) provides exceptions for former testimony, deathbed statements, and statements against interest applicable only to unavailable witnesses. Finally, the general purpose exceptions permit the judge discretion to admit recordings under Rule 803(24) for available witnesses and Rule 804(b)(5) for unavailable witnesses.

Original document objections

Sound recordings are covered by the original document rules. Rule 1002 provides: "To prove the content of a . . . recording, . . . the original . . . recording . . . is required except as otherwise provided in these rules or by Act of Congress." If you have a tape on which sound recordings have been copied, you will need to qualify the tape as a "duplicate" if possible. Under Rule 1001(4), "A duplicate is a counterpart produced . . . by mechanical or electronic re-recording . . . or by other equivalent techniques which accurately reproduces the original." Once qualified by testimony from a competent witness that the tape offered in evidence was produced by means that accurately reproduced the original recording, the duplicate is admissible, under Rule 1003, to the same extent as the original. The original document rule also applies to sound tracks dubbed onto other media such as videotapes or computer files. If the copy is not a duplicate, then it must be qualified by accounting for the original under Rule 1004.

Policy objections

A sound recording can be stricken for prejudice for the same reasons that apply to photographs. See discussion in Section 6.1.3. For example, a sound track for a videotape that includes a plaintiff moaning in pain during rehabilitation therapy might be stricken as prejudicial.

The objection to confusion/misleading of the jury may also apply under certain circumstances. See Section 1.3.3.

Audibility

Portions of the tape may be inaudible because of background noise. If the inaudible portions are substantial enough, they may make the recording untrustworthy as a whole.

Irrelevant portions

Portions of the conversations may be irrelevant to the issue in the case and at the same time prejudicial. Sometimes this can be cured by producing an edited version of the tape.

Quality of transcript

Your opponent is entitled to a voir dire on the accuracy of transcript. See Section 1.7.2. Your opponent is entitled to ask how many people listened to the tape for the purpose of preparing the transcript, how many drafts were prepared, and how many changes were made. This can bring out the interpretations and choices made where the tape itself may be unclear or ambiguous. Your opponent is also entitled to have his or her own audio expert listen to the tape, make a transcript, and then testify that transcript you offered is mistaken in important respects.

Some judges will exclude your transcript if they believe it contains mistakes. The better practice is to treat the accuracy of the transcripts offered in evidence as an issue of fact. The jury can use both transcripts and decide for itself which one is correct.

Completeness objections

If excerpts from a sound tape or sound track are offered as an exhibit, under Rule 106 the opponent of the exhibit may demand that additional portions be introduced and played at the same time if considerations of fairness warrant. See Section 1.3.6.

Constitutional and statutory objections

When conversations are recorded without consent, even in a civil case you may need to comply with constitutional and statutory procedures. Objections based on these procedures involve specialized case law not summarized here.

6.4.3 Production

The quality of an audio recording will vary dramatically with the quality of the microphone and recording equipment used. The consultants who do videotaping work will have their own sound equipment and can adapt it to the circumstances of the taping or filming. With respect to sound recordings for anything but the most standard recording of an interview, you should seek professional assistance from knowledgeable firms or consultants.

If any enhancements are done to improve the quality of the tape, for example filtering out background noise, be sure to get an affidavit from the audio expert who did the work and to keep copies of the original as well as the enhanced tape.

When evidence is to be put in through tape recordings not associated with videotapes, it is almost always necessary to prepare and qualify a transcript as evidence. Reading a transcript while listening to a tape greatly improves the fact-finder's comprehension of the tape. Particularly significant passages of transcript may be enlarged into exhibits to be used with witness testimony, opening statements, or closing arguments. Color can help highlight which person is speaking. Transcripts must be prepared with meticulous attention to detail. Having transcripts prepared by two people independently helps to identify places where reasonable people could differ.

If the transcript was prepared by someone familiar with the speaker, that familiarity may have affected the interpretation of garbled phrases. The person preparing the transcript is not supposed to add his or her own knowledge to the material on the tape. A technician or paralegal who does not know anything about the speaker may make mistakes about places or names. These mistakes can be corrected by someone who recognizes the name from the tape, but new information should not be added. The transcript should indicate unintelligible or doubtful portions in the tape. If reasonable people could disagree about a particular portion of a tape, your transcript may be regarded as less than forthcoming if it does not say so.

6.4.4 Tactics

When working with audiotapes, it is important for safekeeping of the exhibit (and probably also for discovery) to have several high-quality copies made of the original.

You should try to negotiate a stipulated version of the transcript with the other side. Sometimes it will be possible to agree on a single interpretation of a garbled phrase. In any case, the judge will appreciate the effort.

If there are several related transcripts—such as National Transportation Safety Board transcripts of dispatchers, block operators, and others made available after major railroad accidents—it may be useful to prepare transcripts in side-by-side columns indicating what each transcript contains for a given point in time. This is an easy way of displaying the interrelationships among the transcripts.

Audiotapes played in a courtroom, particularly those of conversations, usually require a set of earphones for each juror, the judge, and each counsel. This equipment should be set up and tended by a professional. Although the equipment itself is not technically complex, the wiring and connections can be confusing.

ENDNOTES

1. *Luco v. United States*, 64 U.S. (23 How.) 515 (1859).

2. *Duncan v. Kiger*, 6 Ohio App. 57 (1916).

3. *Paramore v. State*, 229 So.2d 855 (Fla. 1969), *modified in part* 408 U.S. 935 (1971).

4. *See generally Charles C. Scott, Photographic Evidence* (2d ed. 1969). This three-volume work covers both the presentation and preparation of photographic evidence including movies and slides. It discusses a number of more esoteric subjects not covered here such as photomicrography, radiography, ultraviolet photography, infrared photography, stereoscopic photography, and photogrammetry.

5. *See, e.g., 2 McCormick on Evidence* § 246, at 97-98.

6. *See The Effective Deposition*, ch. 18 (providing an excellent discussion of videotaped depositions).

7. *Unif. Audio-Visual Deposition Act*, 12 U.L.A. 8 (1978).

8. *See 4A James Wm. Moore et al., Moore's Federal Practice* § 32.06 (2d ed., 1988).

9. *Guidelines for Pre-Recording Testimony on Videotape Prior to Trial* (Federal Judiciary Center Pub. No. 76-3, 1976); *see also Audio/Video Technology and the Courts for Court Managers* (National Center for State Courts Pub. No. R0034, 1977).

10. *Katz v. United States*, 389 U.S. 347 (1967).

11. 18 U.S.C. § 2511(2) (1996).

12. 18 U.S.C. §§ 2510-22 (1996).

CHAPTER 7

MODELS, DEMONSTRATIONS, AND RECONSTRUCTIONS

Models, demonstrations, and reconstructions can be used in the courtroom to help the judge or jury picture what happened. Models are three-dimensional scale constructions to re-create the object at issue or the area where the events at issue took place. Demonstrations show how scientific principles or types of equipment operate as a part of providing background information on what happened. Reconstructions are reenactments of events at issue, usually recorded in photographs or on videotape. This category of exhibit is different from computer animations covered in Chapter 8 where a computer calculates or estimates what happened.

7.1 MODELS

A model brings three-dimensional assistance to the problem of explaining complicated fact situations. Models may be either standard teaching tools used in a profession or specially built projects relevant only to the case being tried.

7.1.1 Foundation

For purposes of laying a foundation, there are four principal kinds of models: (1) exact life-size replicas; (2) models made to scale—either larger or smaller than life-size; (3) cutaway models that show the interior of structures or equipment; and (4) other models that are not exactly to scale but are generally fair representations. Each has the same requirements with respect to competence, relevance, and identification but somewhat different requirements with respect to the trustworthiness aspect of foundation. See discussion of foundation in Section 1.1.

The competence of the witness to testify using a model can be established by background information about the first hand knowledge or expert status of the witness. A lay witness may use a model to explain what he or she saw or how something happened. An expert witness uses a model to explain conclusions and opinions.

Relevance is shown by linking the model to an issue in the case. The proponent can argue that using a model to help support the reasoning process in arriving at a conclusion meets the test under Rule 401 of having "any tendency" to make the existence of the fact at the end of the reasoning process more or less probable than it would be without the model.

The witness identifies the model by describing briefly its scope or coverage. The identification should state whether the model is life-size, made to scale, cutaway, or illustrative. The witness should also describe what the model shows: "This is a scale model of the fuel storage yard at the XYZ Company plant located at Naylor Road."

Trustworthiness is established by showing that the model is a fair representation of the real thing as explained below.

Life-size model

Some models are exactly life-size, such as a skeleton or skeletal parts of the body, a model of a heart or a brain, or a green plant. These present the fewest difficulties. If the model is made by a reputable firm, an expert can qualify it with relatively few questions. The format is the same as is used for drawings or illustrations. See Section 4.3.1.

Example

Q. Dr. White, the model that has been marked as Exhibit 81 is on the table in front of you. Could you identify that for us?

A. That is a model of the human brain.

Q. Is it actual life-size?

A. Yes. Human brain sizes differ slightly from person to person, but this is an average size.

Q. Who made it?

A. This was made by Medical Education Devices, Inc. of Scranton, PA. Their label is at the bottom.

Q. What are the differences between this model and the real thing?

A. Well, the model is made of hard plastic pieces. The brain is soft tissue. The model has colors and labels on its various parts; the actual brain does not have these. And the model's parts come apart, so we can see how they fit together. The actual brain is tightly connected and none of its parts can be removed without very substantial damage.

Q. What do you use this model for in your practice?

A. This is a model that we use for teaching purposes at the university, and we also use it to explain various operations of the brain to patients.

Q. Is it a fair representation of the human brain?

A. Yes, it is.

Q. Your Honor, we offer Exhibit 81 in evidence.

It is helpful if the model has an "accepted use" such as teaching or training. Carefully explain colors, if those are not exactly what appear in the "live" version, and any other departures from the real thing.

A model of this type can also be qualified as a testimony aid. See Section 1.2.

Scale model

A model built exactly to scale is usually used for the purpose of recreating an event or occurrence and proving, with the assistance of the model, how the events at issue actually occurred. The proponent must prove that all the necessary measurements were taken and that all aspects were reduced accurately to scale. Because exact scale models are relatively expensive, consider other alternatives unless the model is required to reconstruct the event because no witness with first hand knowledge is available or the witness accounts of the events at issue are fragmentary and the evidence is mainly circumstantial.

For more complicated scale models, the foundation requirements increase. Building a model to scale may require land surveys to get exact measurements, photographs to record the scene, or other studies to provide the information for building the model. You must qualify the witness who presents a model built exactly to scale to testify as to the accuracy of the exhibit—that it is identical with the original except as to size, which may be smaller or larger, and irrelevant details, which may be omitted. Usually this witness must be an engineer or someone with similar formal training. When you lay the foundation for this type of model, all of the maps, photographs, documents, and measurements used to construct the model must be admitted in evidence first. Then, after all of the information on which the model is based has been admitted, you can offer the model. You should consider photographing the construction of the model and using the photographs in laying the foundation for the care with which the model was built.

Cutaway model

Sometimes it is necessary to show the internal aspects of a structure or piece of equipment. A cutaway model may be life-size or built to scale. It is not a full replica of the real thing, however, because half has been cut away to expose the internal workings. The foundation is the same as for a life-size or scale model, but explains what is missing.

Example

Q. Mr. Allen, what do you do for a living?

A. I am the Vice President for Engineering at the Imperial Energy Corp.

Q. What do you do in that job?

A. I am responsible for the design, installation, and operation of our electrical generating plants.

Q. How long have you had that job?

A. Five years.

Q. What experience have you had with fluidized bed boilers?

A. Our company has built and operated fluidized bed boilers at three installations. I was responsible for the engineering of two of those three installations, and I have worked extensively with the third during its operation.

Q. What responsibility did you have for the installation at the Western Valley site?

A. I was responsible for the engineering decisions on that installation.

Q. What type of boiler was installed?

A. A fluidized bed boiler.

Q. Mr. Allen, before we get to the explanation of how a fluidized bed boiler works, do you have a model that shows such a boiler?

A. Yes. The company built a model that it uses to explain the fluidized bed boiler at scientific conferences and with other engineers and businessmen.

Q. Have you brought that model with you?

A. Yes.

Q. May we have this marked as Exhibit 88?

Reporter: (Marks)

Q. Mr. Allen, can you identify what has been marked as Exhibit 88?

A. That is a cutaway scale model of a fluidized bed boiler so that you can see how the internal parts of the boiler work.

Q. What is the scale that was used?

A. 1 to 20. One inch on the model equals 20 inches on the real thing. Or 1 foot on the model equals 20 feet on the real thing.

Q. What action does the model show?

A. It shows how air is forced up through the sand bed to support combustion and how the sand circulates within the boiler during combustion.

Q. How does the model differ from the real thing?

A. The model has been sliced in half lengthwise, so half is not shown. The actual boiler has pumps and a power plant that are simulated in model by a small electric engine. The internal parts of the actual boiler are a dark color as the result of the combustion that occurs in the boiler. The internal parts in the model have been painted different colors to illustrate where the fuel enters and where the combustion occurs. The model shows the action of the fluidized bed. It does not show the fuel entering the boiler or actual combustion taking place.

Q. Is the model that has been marked as Exhibit 88 a fair representation of the aspects of the fluidized bed boiler that it shows?

A. Yes, it is.

Q. Your Honor, we offer Exhibit 88 in evidence and request permission for Mr. Allen to use the model in his explanation of how a fluidized bed boiler works.

This model has the advantage of having been constructed for purposes other than litigation. If a model actually used in the business is available, it is usually more convincing to jurors than one built specially for litigation. Colors that are not on the original should not disqualify the model if they have a legitimate purpose in assisting to explain how the real thing works. Any question about such colors should go to the weight of the evidence, not its admissibility.

Illustrative model

If you intend to use a model to show the relative position of objects or relative distances, and the exact dimensions are not important facts, then the model need not be built to scale. Even if not built to scale, however, the model must meet the requirement that it is a fair representation. In fact, this type of model is usually built reasonably nearly to scale to avoid any objection under Rule 403 that it is confusing or misleading. The foundation, however, need not go into any matters of scale. As with any other model, irrelevant detail (present in the original) may be left out. You should carefully explain in the foundation any differences between the model and the actual item or scene.

Example

(After establishing competence and relevance)

Q. What is the address of the building you own?

A. 1772 K Street.

Q. Is that in the 1700 block of K Street?

A. Yes.

Q. How often do you go there?

A. I have visited the building I own very often over the past five years. Also, the buildings owned by Mr. Franklin are located there, and I have also visited them.

Q. Do you have a model that would assist you in explaining where your building is located relative to the buildings owned by Mr. Franklin?

A. Yes.

Q. May I have this model marked as plaintiff's Exhibit 93?

Reporter: *(Marks)*

Q. Let the record reflect that Mr. Jones, counsel for defendant, has had several prior opportunities to inspect this model at pretrial conferences.

Court: Proceed.

Q. What is plaintiff's Exhibit 93 a model of?

A. This is a model of the 1700 block of K Street Northwest, in Washington, D.C. It shows the buildings on the north side of the street.

Q. Who made the model?

A. It was made by Janet Jones of Graphic Arts Inc. of Washington, D.C.

Q. What information was used to make the model?

A. She used photographs of the site plus visits to the site. She also made measurements at the site.

Q. Does the model show every structure on the north side of the street?

A. No. The model does not include trees, streetlights, mailboxes, and other small structures because they are not necessary to the explanation about Mr. Franklin's building.

Q. Is the model that is plaintiff's Exhibit 93 built exactly to scale?

A. No. It is generally accurate as to the relative size of the buildings but it is not exactly to scale.

Q. Is the model that is Exhibit 93 a fair representation of the north side of the 1700 block of K Street?

A. Yes.

Q. Your Honor, we move the admission in evidence of plaintiff's Exhibit 93.

You may also offer illustrative models as testimony aids and not introduce them in evidence. See discussion of the foundation for testimony aids in Section 1.2. The witness would use the model in the courtroom to help explain what happened, but the model would not go to the jury room when the jury deliberates. This may be a problem if jurors need the model to defend their viewpoint about the evidence. Therefore, you should qualify the model as evidence if possible.

7.1.2 Objections

There are no hearsay or original document objections to a model. There may be an objection that rather than use a model, the judge and jury should go to the site and view the real thing.

The policy objections to a model include distortion in the making of the model such as parts which are relatively larger or smaller than they would be in an exact scale model, colors that do not appear on the originals, and argumentative or inaccurate labels. Policy objections will also arise if some parts of a scale model are made to one scale, and other parts use a different scale. A magnetic board model of an intersection made to one scale is objectionable if the objects (cars, trucks, stop signs) are not made to the same scale. See Section 1.3.1.

7.1.3 Production

Life-size medical models are available from a number of supply houses. Also, some laboratories build special medical models to illustrate particular injuries. Businesses often have models used for sales presentations that are also adaptable to courtroom use.

A persuasive life-size cutaway model of a product can be made by purchasing a new or used product of the same make or model involved in the case. The representative item can then be sectioned longitudinally or horizontally to expose the aspect of the design or construction at issue in the case. Labels and color will make the model easier to understand. See Fig. 32.

Casting is another method for creating a life-size model. This permits the reproduction of a part such as a pipe connection that cannot be moved. A very simple casting method is to rub the object with clear grease, such as Vaseline, then press clay around it. After the impression is made in the clay, plaster of Paris is poured into the clay impression and allowed to set. When the plaster is hard, the clay can be removed. The plaster may then be painted to replicate the original.

If a model is to be built exactly to scale, the work necessary to support the foundation usually will have to begin very soon after the events at issue while the physical evidence still exists and before changes occur to the site or structures. Fig. 33 and Fig. 34 show a model of a bridge built exactly to scale.

The simplest three-dimensional scale model is a magnetized map upon which magnetic cars, trucks, fences, and the like can be placed. See Fig. 35. This offers an alternative to the two-dimensional diagram that fact-finders often find hard to follow. This kind of model can be made by gluing an accurate map made to scale on a thin magnetized metal sheet. You qualify the model in three steps. First qualify the map. See discussion in Section 4.1.1. Then qualify the objects to be placed on the magnetic board as being reasonable with respect to the scale used on the map. Then a witness or witnesses with first hand knowledge of the events or expert qualifications can place the objects on the map. Other types of scale models can also be effective using magnetized figures or parts.

Two general types of scales are used to build models. An architectural scale is used for buildings or parts of buildings. This ranges from 1/32 of an inch = 1 foot or 1/16 of an inch = 1 foot for large buildings; ¼ of an inch = 1 foot for residential buildings; and ½ inch or 1 inch = 1 foot for details of parts of rooms. An engineering scale is used for roads, bridges, and other large works. This ranges from 1 inch = 20 feet through 1 inch = 100 feet, depending on what is appropriate. A model may be accurate to horizontal scale and inaccurate as to vertical scale if only the horizontal scale is relevant. The vertical scale may also be different from the horizontal scale if the horizontal scale is the one of primary relevance.

The materials used to make the model can also contribute to its overall effectiveness. If the plaintiff fell down a set of stairs and the model is for the plaintiff's case, the model might be made of hard-looking chip board that helps reproduce the hard, dangerous character of the stairs. The model must have a neat appearance in order to promote its acceptance as accurate.

7.1.4 Tactics

Unlike charts, photographs, maps, and other tangible evidence, it is difficult to tailor a model for your particular view of the case and still get it admitted in evidence. For that reason, some trial lawyers advise that the first tactical consideration is whether the model may be of more use to your opponent's case than to your own case. A model can help your opponent's witnesses illustrate their points more effectively than they might be able to do without it. A model may also make your opponent's theory seem less speculative because it can be played out more realistically using the model. Computer animations may be a good alternative. They are usually less expensive and more flexible than physical models. See discussion in Section 8.3.

Models of geographic or topographic features can be very effective because they can be viewed from a number of vantage points. The fact-finder gets a good overview of the area at issue and the relationship of key components. Small models of very large equipment or structures and large models of very small parts, molecular formations, or organisms can enhance the explanation of technical points. These kinds of models, however, carry the inherent danger that the fact-finder will comprehend only the dimensions of the model and not those of the object it represents. Very large things can become too small in the fact-finder's mind and very small things can become too large. You can cure this, of course, by combining the use of the model with a "view" of the actual thing by the fact-finder. See discussion of "views" in Section 5.3. Another response to the problem of scale is to attach to the model (or display in close proximity to the model) a legend that will remind the fact-finder of the true scale. The legend may also be in picture form, and can contrast, for example, the object that the model depicts with another object (such as a human being or a car) more familiar to the fact-finder.

The model itself should be large enough to be viewed easily, and detachable parts or components of the model should also be large enough to be understood readily. In cases where this is difficult, use a separate model of the smaller part or component.

Ease of handling is very important, particularly if you intend to have your witnesses work with the model. You should practice before the witness testifies. A fumbling witness looks bad and diverts the fact-finder's attention from the points you want to make.

Models and their component parts should be made of resilient material that is not easily broken. When you are trying to convey to the fact-finder how carefully your client has built or fabricated the machinery or structure in question, it doesn't help to have your model fall apart.

Operational models with moving parts can be useful in illustrating how machinery works. These models, however, bring the additional risk of some malfunction in the courtroom. There is also the possibility that one of the other side's witnesses may use the model to demonstrate a variety of other ways in which it could operate. This may confuse the jury about the very point that the model was intended to illustrate. A related problem is that jurors may construct their own speculative theories with the assistance of a model, which may subvert the intended purpose of the model.

If you use a model to reconstruct what happened or to demonstrate the exact dimensions of objects within the model, you should have a special ruler with the scale dimensions on it so that the witness can demonstrate measurements without having to make conversion calculations in the courtroom. If the scale of the model is one inch to 10 feet, the ruler would be marked off in tenths of inches, each representing one foot. When the witness approaches the model to testify about the distance from the high-tide mark to the proposed pilings for the high-rise development, he or she can use the special ruler to make the measurement on the spot.

You should also have photographs of the completed model to use both at trial and on appeal. After the model is admitted, the photograph can be used in place of the model when a witness has only one or two points to make and most of his or her testimony is about something else. Use photographs to record the testimony of witnesses when they work with the model. A witness may point to a spot, arrange the model cars and trucks as he or she saw them, or make measurements. Photographs of the witness as these acts are performed help keep the record clear.

Consider storage of the model when it is not being used. If a model is simply sitting in the middle of the courtroom, the fact-finder may spontaneously ask a witness to make a point with the model, and thereby distract the witness and possibly counsel. Large scale models present some difficulty in logistics within the courtroom. If possible, it is wise to construct the model so that it can be taken out of the courtroom or stored on its side against the wall of the courtroom when not needed.

7.2 DEMONSTRATIONS

A demonstration, as the term is used here, is a showing of the operation of scientific principles or the physical possibility that events occurred in a particular way so as to support a legal theory. Demonstrations assist a witness in explaining some technical part of the testimony. Demonstrations of physical injuries to a person can also involve having the injured person perform motions or actions to show pain or impairments. Demonstrations can be done "live" in the courtroom or can be captured in photographs or on videotapes. An in-court "live" demonstration is a risky way to put in evidence. If the demonstration does not work, the impression left with the fact-finder may be irremediable. Photographs or videotapes of demonstrations are much safer.

7.2.1 Foundation

Demonstrations will be relevant only if you use objects or materials that are substantially the same as those involved in the case. Demonstrations may require that the objects used in the demonstration be in substantially the same condition as the objects at issue in the case or as the objects were when the issue arose.

A demonstration usually exhibits the operation of scientific principles or the operating capabilities of equipment. For example, a demonstration may be a videotape showing the operation of a conveyor belt, or perhaps the operation of safety equipment—when you place both hands and both feet on the stops, you cannot get your limbs caught in the cutting machine. This does not reenact or reconstruct events that did happen, but demonstrates that something does or would happen in a particular way. See discussion of reconstructions in Section 7.3. Demonstrations can also be tests or experiments conducted in a laboratory or even at the scene of the events at issue to highlight facts that are relevant to a claim. You may use these tests or experiments to help an expert testify in lay terms.

Example

(After establishing the expert's credentials and relevance)

Q. Ms. Wallace, what happens to a bar of copper that has been bolted to steel under these circumstances?

A. The copper expands at a different rate than the steel, putting a great deal of stress on the bolts.

Q. Have you done a demonstration of this effect?

A. Yes.

Q. Where did you conduct that demonstration?

A. In my laboratory at 12 Oak Street, Philadelphia, Pennsylvania.

Q. How did you record the results?

A. In two ways: I made notes from which I produced a written report, and I made a videotape while the test was being conducted.

Q. May I have this videotape cassette marked as plaintiff's Exhibit 87?

Reporter: *(puts sticker label on casing of the tape cassette)*

Q. Let the record reflect that I am handing to Mr. Smith, counsel for defendant, the cassette that has been marked as Exhibit 87. A copy of this tape was delivered to Mr. Smith at the last pretrial conference.

Counsel: We wish to examine the contents, Your Honor.

Court: We will have a 10-minute recess. The jury is excused.

(Videotape is played and court hears any objections. Proceeding begins again after jury returns.)

Q. Is there any sound track to this videotape?

A. No.

Q. Is the videotape recording that has been marked as Exhibit 87 a fair and accurate depiction of the testing work you did?

A. Yes.

Q. Your Honor, we move the admission in evidence of what has been marked as plaintiff's Exhibit 87.

Court: So ordered.

Q. Your Honor, at this time I request permission to have Ms.
   Wallace play Exhibit 87.

Court: You may proceed.

(Move video monitor in front of jury or judge if necessary)

Q. Ms. Wallace, will you step down from the witness stand and
   start the tape, please.

If the expert is working in the field or doing a survey outside his or
her lab, however, you should use the fuller foundation, including
qualification of the equipment.

Example

(After establishing competence and relevance)

Q. Mr. Kling, what safety devices, if any, are incorporated into
   the PRD Model 3 cutting machine?

A. There are two hand stops and two foot stops.

Q. What are hand stops?

A. Hand stops are devices that the operator's hands must be
   resting on in order for the machine to operate. They ensure
   that the operator's hands cannot get into the cutting machine
   when it is in operation.

Q. What are foot stops?

A. Foot stops are devices that the operator's feet must be resting
   on in order for the machine to operate. They ensure that the
   operator's feet cannot get into the cutting machine when it is
   operating.

Q. Are you able to demonstrate how the hand stops and foot
   stops operate?

A. Yes.

Q. What experience have you had with this safety equipment?

A. I have been in charge of safety for the fabricating department
   where the cutting machines are located for about six years.
   Part of my responsibility is to check the hand stops and foot
   stops on the machines when they are installed or returned
   from overhaul to be sure the stops are operating.

Q. Do you have a PRD Model 3 cutting machine on which you
   could demonstrate the operation of this safety equipment?

A. Yes. We have a machine mounted on a dolly so that we can
   use it in the courtroom.

Q. *(Wheels the dolly into position)* May I have this machine marked as defendant's Exhibit 91?

Reporter: *(Puts label on machine)*

Q. Mr. Kling, what is Exhibit 91?

A. That is a PRD Model 3 cutting machine.

Q. Is that the cutting machine on which Mr. Peters, the plaintiff was injured?

A. No.

Q. How is Exhibit 91 similar to the cutting machine on which Mr. Peters was injured?

A. It is the same make and model. It is approximately six years old, so it is the same age. It has been used in our fabrication department for six years, so it has been subjected to approximately the same use.

Q. How is Exhibit 91 different from the cutting machine on which Mr. Peters was injured?

A. It was serviced on a different schedule although the service cycle was the same. It was located in a different place in the assembly line; and it was operated by different people.

Q. What changes, if any, have been made in the hand stops and foot stops on Exhibit 91?

A. None. It is exactly the same as it was manufactured and used in our fabricating shop.

Q. Your Honor, we will not offer Exhibit 91 in evidence because it is very bulky, but we request permission to have Mr. Kling demonstrate the operation of the hand stops and foot stops using Exhibit 91.

Court: You may proceed.

Q. Your Honor, we request permission to make a videotape of this demonstration in order to preserve it for the record. We will mark the videotape for identification as Exhibit 91A.

Court: *(To opposing counsel)* Any objection? Proceed.

Q. Mr. Kling, will you step down from the witness stand and demonstrate the use of the hand stops and foot stops on this machine?

Witness: *(Demonstrates)*

Counsel: Your Honor, we offer Exhibit 91A, the videotape of this demonstration, in evidence.

Court: Admitted.

This example is one where a videotape of the demonstration made out of court probably would have been better. The demonstration in court may raise a problem in getting a high capacity electrical connection with which to operate the machine and the danger that the machine might malfunction during the demonstration in court. With a videotape, the ability to "freeze" frames and stop the action which the witness explains would permit an effective explanation. A videotape presentation would take less time to set up and, if the fact-finder had taken a trip to the factory for a "view" of the setting, there would be no loss of clarity in the explanation. The foundation for a videotape of a demonstration by an expert is discussed in Section 7.3.1.

Challenges to the foundation for demonstrations are primarily to relevance—that the conditions under which the demonstration is done are not sufficiently similar to the events at issue to make the demonstration relevant. Often counsel will argue about the demonstration's trustworthiness and whether both the instrumentalities and the circumstances are sufficiently the same as the events at issue. Only the instrumentalities (the things used to do the demonstration) need to be substantially similar to those at issue. The similarity of the circumstances goes to the weight of the evidence, not its admissibility.

7.2.2 Objections

If a demonstration has been videotaped or photographed, then a hearsay objection may arise. Statements on a videotape sound track are hearsay. You may overcome this objection by presenting the maker of the statements as a witness. See discussion of videotapes at Section 6.3. In addition, under Rule 801(a)(2) a videotape of the actions of a person may fall within the hearsay rule if the actions shown are "nonverbal conduct of a person, if it is intended by the person as an assertion." See discussion of photographs at Section 6.1.3 and of videotapes at Section 6.3.2. An objection based on the nonverbal conduct rule usually must be met by resort to the general purpose exception in Rule 803(24).

Because the original document rule covers only writings, photographs, and recordings (see Rule 1002 and Section 1.3.2), no original document objections apply to demonstrations.

Occasionally a demonstration raises a policy objection because the actions proposed are inappropriate for a courtroom, pose a possible danger to those in the courtroom or those doing the demonstration, or would take up too much time for the benefit to be gained. See Section 1.3.3. The reported cases include a witness who offered to swallow a teaspoon of ground glass;[1] a medical doctor who offered to swallow certain drugs and demonstrate that he did not become drowsy as a result;[2] burning a piece of carpet;[3] igniting and burning nail polish;[4] bringing gasoline into contact with a hot surface;[5] and firing a gun.[6]

How the trial court exercises its discretion will be affected by the relevance of the circumstances in the proposed demonstration and whether there are reasonable alternatives, such as an out-of-court videotaping, that might be better.[7]

7.2.3 Production

The first consideration with respect to a demonstration is whether to do it in-court as a "live" demonstration or whether to use photographs, videotapes, models, or computer-generated animations. The best photograph or videotape is not as effective as having the physical object itself in the courtroom. Having the actual product in the courtroom is an advantage because jurors can examine it themselves and can become familiar with it over time as the case proceeds. In-court demonstrations that involve very complicated action are, however, very risky. A videotape is usually a better alternative.

One type of in-court demonstration that can be effective is to show how certain instruments looked when the operator should have known something was wrong. For example, if you allege that operator error caused a large industrial boiler to explode, you may want to dramatize the magnitude of the error by showing how the instruments gave their warnings. Verbal explanations of the movement of a needle from 350 to 450 pounds per square inch may lack impact. No videotape of the needle moving from 350 to 450 is possible because the boiler can not be operated that way to permit making the tape. Bringing examples of the instruments into court would show the needle and the scale, but no movement. However, an expert could stage an in-court demonstration by mounting the instrument on the front of a box containing the necessary batteries and switches to make the needle move as it would when the boiler pressure went up. After foundation testimony by the expert who assembled it, you could offer the box in evidence and then "play" it for the jury.

If you decide to risk an in-court "live" demonstration, one insurance policy is to have the witness practice the demonstration several times before the trial right in the courtroom where it will be presented. You will probably need to do this after the day's court proceedings are finished, but the clerk will usually grant permission. So far as possible, use the exact equipment, electric connections, lighting conditions and acoustics that will be present at trial. Remember, of course, to prepare the witness for cross-examination on this "practice" session.

A demonstration of physical principles may be made more effective by using a different medium from the material at issue. For example, a rubber rod can demonstrate certain physical effects on a steel rod. The rubber rod is marked clearly at equal increments. Then forces of compression, tension, or torque are applied and the markings on the rod

351

spread, converge, or spiral demonstrating what cannot be seen on a steel rod.[8]

When making a videotape of a demonstration by an expert, you must insure that any narration on the audio portion of the tape is free of argument or comment that goes beyond technical statements, as this kind of audio provokes an objection on the ground of unfair prejudice even after the hearsay objection is overcome. When using a videotape, you can have the expert describe what is going on using an audio portion of the tape itself (see discussion of sound tracks at Section 6.4) or you can play the tape silently and have the expert testify as the tape proceeds. You may play a portion of the tape, then have the expert explain the next point, then play another portion of the tape. Or you may elect to play the whole tape at one time. You may also "freeze" a frame of the videotape on the screen so that the expert can present a detailed explanation of what is shown, then start up the player and proceed to the next point where a "freeze" is required. In planning this kind of presentation, you should keep in mind that the attention span of most jurors is very short. If they are required to concentrate on a videotape for more than 10 to 15 minutes at a time, they will begin to lose the capability to retain details. The attention span of many judges is not a great deal longer. Switching back and forth from live testimony to taped materials helps insure better retention of the information communicated.

Demonstrations effectively establish probable future results. For example, if it is the plaintiff's theory that the transportation of nuclear waste on a particular two-lane road is dangerous and should be prohibited because the trucks could go into dangerous skids, a video could effectively illustrate this point. The video would use a truck of approximately the same size and configuration as the trucks to be used to transport the nuclear waste and would show, with the aid of an expert driver, how the wheels could catch on the edge of a dangerous curve throwing the truck into a skid or spin.

When videotaping demonstrations, you should run the demonstration several times to satisfy yourself that what will be videotaped will be effective. Videotaping a failed demonstration creates discovery disputes when your opponent asks for copies of all relevant videotapes. Experienced lawyers advise avoiding hurried, last-minute videotaping to rebut an unexpected theory presented by the other side.

7.2.4   Tactics

Demonstrations may be useful when the issue of liability is difficult. A demonstration of what could happen under certain circumstances will help persuade the fact-finder that such an accident or event can in fact occur. The witness testimony about the accident or event will be more credible after removing the question whether such an occurrence could happen at all.

When you do an in-court demonstration, you must be careful to create an adequate record. The witness's actions will not show up on the record, so you may need to narrate while the witness works.

Example

Counsel: Let the record reflect that Mr. Scientist has just inserted the metal bar into the drill press.

This insures that there is at least a sketchy record in the transcript of what was done.

When you present demonstrations by means of a videotape, the tactical considerations with respect to equipment, editing, and placement in the courtroom are generally the same as for any other use of a videotape. See discussion in Section 6.3. Also, you can display a videotaped demonstration in the courtroom using either electronic systems (see Section 9.5) or digital systems (see Section 9.6).

One other relevant consideration with respect to demonstrations is that a court may take judicial notice of scientific principles.

> [T]he principle involved need not be commonly known in order to be judicially noticed; it suffices if the principle is accepted as a valid one in the appropriate scientific community. In determining the intellectual viability of the proposition, of course, the judge is free to consult any sources that he thinks are reliable, but the extent to which judges are willing to take the initiative in looking up the authoritative sources will usually be limited. By and large, therefore, it is the task of counsel to find and to present in argument and briefs such references, excerpts, and explanations as will convince the judge that the fact is certain and demonstrable.[9]

Judicial notice is a powerful tool and should be sought whenever a credible argument supporting it is available.

7.3 RECONSTRUCTIONS

A reconstruction attempts to show that certain things or events at issue actually did or did not happen by recreating the situation. Reconstructions are useful for any case in which the fact-finder must consider movements in three dimensions in order to reach a decision. Combinations of factors such as speed, time, distance, height, direction changes, or rates of ascent or descent are difficult for the fact-finder to put together from oral descriptions alone. This difficulty is complicated when the context is not a familiar one, like cars crashing at an intersection, but involves structures or substances that the fact-finder has never seen before, such as the force of an explosion or the pressure that caused a part to fail. Simple reconstructions can be done "live" in the courtroom; more complicated events are usually recorded in photographs or on videotape.

7.3.1 Foundation

The foundation for a reconstruction depends on the method used to present the reconstruction. See general discussion of foundation in Section 1.1. Some of the possibilities are set out below. When a reconstruction is done, you must establish a foundation showing that the instrumentalities (the factors involved in the events at issue) and the circumstances under which they are used are the same as or substantially similar to those at issue.

Reconstructions involving people in the courtroom

One kind of reconstruction is a staged event in the courtroom where the witness shows the fact-finder how the events unfolded, perhaps by use of several other people playing the roles of various individuals involved in the events at issue or by the use of specially constructed models.

The simplest kind of in-court reconstruction is to have the witness come down off the witness stand and re-create something before the jury:

- how the defendant swung at him with a baseball bat;
- how far away the defendant was standing when he observed the defendant burn the records.

You should use objects that are the same type or model as the objects at issue in the case to help explain the witness's testimony. The foundation for admissibility can be either that the object is exactly the same as the object at issue and therefore is a visual substitute, or that the object is generally the same as the object at issue and will assist in explaining the testimony. The instrumentalities need to be qualified before the reconstruction can proceed.

Example

(The speedometer of an automobile is alleged to have been installed improperly, to have come loose, and caused injury.)

Q. What kind of speedometer was installed in the car that the defendant was driving?

A. The car came equipped with a Himmlich 482 speedometer.

Q. How do you know that?

A. It was listed on Exhibit 92 which is the invoice for the car.

Q. Do you have the Himmlich 482 speedometer that was installed in the car that the defendant was driving?

A. No. The car was totally wrecked in the crash and the speedometer was demolished.

Q. May I have this marked as plaintiff's Exhibit 94?

Court reporter: *(Marks)*

Q. May the record reflect that I am showing what has been marked as plaintiff's Exhibit 94 to counsel for the defendant.

Opposing Counsel: *(Looks)*

Q. Ms. Adams, I show you what has been marked as plaintiff's Exhibit 94 and ask if you can identify it.

A. Yes. That is a Himmlich 482 speedometer.

Q. How does Exhibit 94 compare to the speedometer that was installed in defendant's car?

A. Exhibit 94 is the same model and type of speedometer as was installed in defendant's car.

Q. Your Honor, we move the admission in evidence of what has been marked as plaintiff's Exhibit 94.

Dealing with comparisons of complicated objects may require expert testimony because the court may hold that the comparison is an opinion and may hold further that such an opinion is not proper from a nonexpert witness.

If the representational object is not a duplicate of the object at issue in the case, the foundation will have to establish sufficient similarity so that use of the object will assist the jury.

Example

Q. Where were you on the evening that Mr. Wilson and Mr. Atkins got into a fight?

A. At Joe's Tavern.

Q. What happened that evening?

A. I was coming out of the bar when Danny Wilson got out of his car with a baseball bat in his hand. Jerry Atkins was standing next to his own car. Danny switched the bat from one hand to the other and laughed kind of funny. Then all of a sudden he hit Jerry.

Q. What kind of a baseball bat was it?

A. A softball bat, pretty standard size. I didn't see the label or anything. It had a wrapped handle though.

Q. Do you know where the softball bat is now?

A. No. I never saw it again after Jerry was taken away to the hospital.

Q. Please mark this as plaintiff's Exhibit 98.

Court reporter: *(Marks)*

Q. May the record reflect that I am showing what has been marked as plaintiff's Exhibit 98 to counsel for defendant.

Opposing Counsel: *(Looks)*

Q. I show you what has been marked as plaintiff's Exhibit 98 and ask you to compare that to the softball bat you saw in Mr. Wilson's hands outside Joe's Tavern.

A. That is just like the one he had.

Q. Are you able to step down here before the jury and show them exactly what you saw Mr. Wilson do with the baseball bat?

A. Yes, I certainly am able to do that.

Q. Would it assist you in your explanation to be able to use what has been marked as plaintiff's Exhibit 98?

A. Yes, it would.

Q. Please step right down here in front of the jury, take this bat that has been marked as plaintiff's Exhibit 98, and show us what you saw.

A. *(Witness reenacts what happened)*

In this case the bat probably could not be offered in evidence. The qualification is, however, necessary before the witness can use the bat in his reconstruction.

Similarly, you can ask a witness to step to the floor of the courtroom and reconstruct how he or she reacted to events. The foundation for this type of in-court reconstruction is not complicated.

Example

Q. Ms. Nellis, what did you do after you saw that you were about to step into an empty elevator shaft?

A. I reached around behind with my left arm and with my right arm I held onto the edge of the doorway.

Q. Can you show the court exactly what you did?

A. Yes, I can.

Q. Would you step down off the stand and come over here to the center of the floor so everyone can see you. Then would you show the court exactly what you did after you saw that there was no elevator in the elevator shaft?

Witness: *(Proceeds to reenact)*

Q. Let the record reflect that Ms. Nellis showed what she did by moving her arms and upper torso.

Another type of reconstruction performed by a witness in a courtroom is done with the assistance of a scale model. The foundation for and use of such models is explained in Section 7.1. Similarly, the court may permit the witness to mark on the courtroom floor with chalk to show the relative position of things or people when the events at issue took place.

Photographs that reconstruct the scene

Another relatively simple reconstruction is a photograph showing the scene as it has been reconstructed to conform to the testimony of a witness. The foundation for such a photograph must show a substantial similarity to the scene as it was at the time relevant to the issues in the case.

Example

Q. Where were you standing when you saw the explosion?

A. I was standing about three feet outside the main entrance door to the south wing of the building.

Q. Which way were you facing?

A. I was facing directly down the sidewalk that leads from the doorway.

Q. What were you doing?

A. I had just opened the door and walked through. The door was closing behind me. I was walking normally.

Q. What time of day was it?

A. 12:05 p.m.

Q. May I have these photographs marked as plaintiff's Exhibits 104 and 105?

Reporter: *(Marks)*

Q. Let the record reflect that I have handed what have been marked as Exhibits 104 and 105 to counsel for defendant.

Opposing Counsel: *(Looks)*

Q. Ms. Dell, I hand you what has been marked as Exhibits 104 and 105 and ask if you can identify those exhibits.

A. Yes. Exhibit 104 is a photograph showing me about three feet outside the main entrance door to the south wing of the building. Exhibit 105 is a photograph facing directly down the sidewalk that leads from the doorway.

Q. From what point was Exhibit 105 taken?

A. That was taken from a point three feet outside the main entrance door at my eye level.

Q. Is Exhibit 104 a fair and accurate representation of where you were when you saw the explosion?

A. Yes.

Q. Is Exhibit 105 a fair and accurate representation of your field of view when you saw the explosion?

A. Yes.

Q. Your Honor, we move the admission in evidence of plaintiff's Exhibits 104 and 105.

The relevance in this example is field of view, not the object seen. If you want to reconstruct the object seen, as it was viewed by the witness, you may need expert testimony from a photographer as to the lens setting that would reproduce the size of the image seen by the witness's eye.

Videotape reconstructions

One effective means of reconstruction is to take the witness who was involved in the events at issue back to the scene to recreate what happened. The reconstruction is recorded on a videotape to be played in the courtroom as the witness testifies.

The foundation requires that the instrumentalities and circumstances depicted in the reconstruction be the same as or substantially similar to those in the events at issue that the reconstruction attempts to depict. You must carefully catalog all of the instrumentalities (people and things) to be used in the reconstruction along with a detailed comparison of them to the originals. Similarly, you should carefully examine the circumstances—weather, lighting conditions, temperature, location—to ensure the close match required to establish a foundation for a reconstruction.

Example

(The control panel of a large oil refinery is alleged to have been defective, causing a serious explosion. A defendant, the supplier of one critical section of the control panel, is reconstructing how it was assembled.)

Q. What is your job?

A. I supervise our controls unit. The people who design, construct, and install controls work for me.

Q. Did your job involve the control panel that was installed at the Brego Refinery Unit #1?

A. Yes.

Q. How?

A. I designed the flow sensing unit and supervised its construction. I also supervised the installation of that unit in the completed control panel.

Q. When did you do that?

A. That was about three years ago.

Q. Are you able to describe the assembly of the control panel?

A. Yes, I am.

Q. Have you participated in a reconstruction of that process?

A. Yes, I have.

Q. Was that reconstruction recorded?

A. Yes, it was.

Q. How was it recorded?

A. We videotaped it.

Q. When was the videotape made?

A. It was made about a year ago.

Q. How long was that after the explosion at Brego?

A. About one month.

(For the rest of the foundation for the videotape, see Section 6.3.1; and for the foundation for the sound track, see Section 6.4.1.)

Q. Who were the people who participated in the reconstruction?

A. There were three. The first one is the stockman who selects the parts from the supply area and delivers them to the technician's workbench. The second one is the technician who puts the parts together to construct the unit that the customer has ordered. The third one is the inspector who checks out the completed unit.

Q. Can you identify them?

A. Yes. The stockman was James Allway. The technician was Roy Meade. The inspector was Stella Manley.

Q. Are they the same people who participated in the assembly of the flow sensing unit delivered to Brego?

A. Yes, they are.

Q. How do you know that?

A. Each person at our company who has anything to do with the construction of a unit signs a log with respect to that unit. We keep the log in our files. It is numbered with the identification number of the unit. Each of these people signed the log with respect to the unit delivered to Brego.

Q. Are they the people who are shown on the videotape of the reconstruction?

A. Yes, they are.

Q. How often do you see these people?

A. I usually see them every day.

Q. Did you see them every day during the period when the unit delivered to Brego was built?

A. Yes I did, just about every day.

Q. Had any of the three people you have identified changed in any significant way, from the time when they participated in assembly of the unit delivered to Brego to the time when you made the videotape?

A. No.

Q. Where was the videotape made?

A. It was made at our plant on Queen Street.

Q. Where in the plant was the videotape made?

A. At three places: the supply room where the parts were obtained, at the technician's workbench where the unit was assembled, and at the inspector's workbench where the unit was inspected.

Q. Was there any difference in the appearance of the three places—the supply room, the technician's bench, and the inspector's bench—between the time when the actual unit was made and the time when the videotape was made?

A. No.

Q. How do you know that?

A. I am in those areas of the plant every day and I did not see any changes. Also, I checked our maintenance records and they do not show any changes. Everything was the same.

Q. What time of day was it when the actual unit that was delivered to the Brego plant was assembled by your company?

A. It was made from 1 p.m. to 4:30 p.m. in the afternoon.

Q. How do you know that?

A. From the time records that each of our technicians and inspectors kept. Each technician and inspector records when they start and when they stop work on each unit. They keep track by the identification number assigned to each unit.

Q. At what time of day was the videotape made?

A. From 1 p.m. to 4:30 p.m.

Q. Can you tell us how the materials used in the reconstruction compared to the materials used in the actual unit?

A. Yes, I can. The board and microcircuitry chips were drawn from the same supply lots. The flow dial numbers 21, 22, and 23 were drawn from the same supply lots. The flow dial number 24 was drawn from a different supply lot—the next one that was delivered to us, but the supplier was the same and the specifications were the same. The wiring was the standard supply that we always use.

Q. How do you know that?

A. I checked the supply numbers on the internal supply form that was made out for the Brego units, and I checked the supply numbers on the parts that were used for the reconstruction.

Q. Thank you. You may step down for a moment.

(Stockman is sworn in)

Q. Did you participate in the assembly of the unit that was delivered to Brego?

A. Yes, I did.

Q. How do you know that?

A. My signature is on the supply form for that unit.

Q. Did you participate in the reconstruction that was videotaped at the plant?

A. Yes, I did.

Q. Can you compare your actions with respect to the unit that was delivered to the Brego plant and the unit that was a part of the reconstruction?

A. Yes. They were the same. I always do the same thing. It is part of my routine.

Q. Thank you. You may step down.

(Technician is sworn in)

Q. Did you participate in the assembly of the unit that was delivered to the Brego plant?

A. Yes, I did.

Q. How do you know that?

A. My initials are on the internal supply form.

Q. Did you participate in the reconstruction that was videotaped at the plant?

A. Yes, I did.

Q. Can you compare your actions with respect to the unit that was delivered to the Brego plant and the unit that was a part of the reconstruction?

A. To the best of my knowledge, they were the same. I assembled one of those units every week or so, and I always follow the same procedure. The procedure is set out step-by-step in the engineering instructions for that unit.

Q. Thank you. You may step down.

(Inspector is sworn in)

Q. Did you participate in the construction of the unit that was delivered to the Brego plant?

A. Yes, I did.

Q. How do you know that?

A. My signature is on the inspection form for that unit.

Q. Did you participate in the reconstruction that was videotaped at the plant?

A. Yes.

Q. Can you compare your actions with respect to the unit that was delivered to the Brego plant and the unit that was a part of the reconstruction?

A. Yes. I did the same thing. I followed the inspection procedure in both cases. The inspection procedure for those units is set

out on a sheet that hangs on the wall in front of my
workbench. I follow each step on the sheet whenever I get one
of those units to inspect.

Q. Thank you. You may step down.

Q. Your Honor, we move the admission in evidence of the
videotape that has been marked as Exhibit 95. We have
established that the instrumentalities and circumstances with
respect to the reconstruction portrayed on the tape are the
same as the instrumentalities and circumstances with respect
to the unit at issue.

Court: Admitted.

Q. Your Honor, may we play the videotape for the jury at this
time?

Court: You may.

(Bring back whichever witness will testify with the videotape)

Some lawyers prefer to have each witness (the stockman, the
technician, and the inspector) describe what they actually did before
the videotape is played. In most cases, however, you should get the
reconstruction before the jury as quickly as possible so they can see the
process for themselves and then recall the witnesses to describe in
testimony what they did if that is necessary.

The challenges to the foundation for a reconstruction are likely to
be so varied and scattershot that it is wise to prepare a short
memorandum for the court summarizing the testimony that will be
offered as foundation and the reasons why that foundation is adequate.
If a reconstruction is an important part of your evidence, consider
making a motion in limine before trial to get a ruling that the
reconstruction will be allowed.

Other challenges to the foundation for a reconstruction generally
will be directed to the degree to which both the instrumentalities used
in the reconstruction and the circumstances under which the
reconstruction was done are the same as those in the events at issue.
Because no rule directly applies, judges have considerable discretion
under Rule 611 to permit reconstructions. You will need a careful
point-by-point explanation as to each of the instrumentalities and
circumstances to support the reconstruction.

A court may exclude a reconstruction if the proponent fails to show
that all the factors that may have been relevant to the events at issue
have been included in the reconstruction. There may simply not be
enough evidence to support a visual reconstruction of the entire series
of events at issue. In that case, the expert may reconstruct only one

critical portion of the events at issue or may turn to a demonstration rather than a reconstruction.

7.3.2 Objections

Hearsay objections to a reconstruction are focused on any spoken or written words and the nonverbal acts. These objections are met as described in Sections 1.3.1, 1.4.8, 6.1.3, and 6.3.2.

There are no original document objections to a reconstruction unless a photograph, videotape, or sound recording used for the reconstruction is subject to those objections. See Section 6.1.3 (photographs), Section 6.3.2 (videotapes), and Section 6.4.2 (sound recordings).

One policy objection often raised with respect to photos or videotapes of reconstructions is that they emphasize certain testimony unduly. Another is that the reconstruction will so confuse the jury that it will be substituted for the objective facts in the jurors' minds. In other words, the realistic nature of the depiction may lead jurors to think it is the real thing. This argument is generally raised when one party has a reconstruction exhibit and the other does not. With the exhibit, the proponent's version of contested facts may seem more "real" to the jury. However, this argument should not prevail unless there are important deficiencies in the foundation for the reconstruction.

If the witness uses facial expressions or verbal utterances of pain, fear, disgust, or other factors, this could cause an objection to unfair prejudice. See discussion of this type of objection at Sections 1.3.3, 6.1.3, and 6.3.2.

In states not following Rule 704 of the Federal Rules of Evidence or a similar rule, testimony is inadmissible if it is an opinion on the ultimate issue for jury determination. Under this kind of rule, a photo or videotape of a reconstruction may be viewed as evidence on the "ultimate issue" and may be excluded on those grounds.

7.3.3 Production and Tactics

To produce photographic or videotaped reconstructions, you must have the assistance of professionals. Because testimony with respect to these exhibits must be clear and persuasive, consider personal appearance and courtroom experience in choosing an expert. The production considerations with respect to each of the media are discussed in Chapter 6 (photographs and videotapes).

You can produce convincing reconstructions through photographs taken with digital cameras and then altered through computer processes to conform to what the witness remembers. See discussion of digital cameras in Section 6.1.2. The scene may have changed since the events at issue but the digital image may be changed in the same ways so as to render an accurate reconstruction.

You may also want to consider the use of a professional stuntman to do reconstructions in personal injury cases. The plaintiff or other witness describes what happened to the car, truck, motorcycle, boat, or other vehicle, and the stuntman recreates the scene. This may be a dramatic crash, rollover, fall, or slide. The stuntman's work is videotaped and used as an exhibit. The stuntman testifies as the qualifying witness.

In-court "live" reconstructions are usually available only where the events do not involve many people or props. Most full-scale "live" reconstructions are impossible because of the limitations inherent in the courtroom setting and the reluctance of judges to allow large-scale construction projects in their courtrooms. A videotape of the reconstruction at the scene is usually better.

The same general tactical considerations apply to videotaped reconstructions of events outside the courtroom as apply to other types of videotapes. See discussion in Section 6.3.4. If the reconstruction is not successful, the tape can be protected as work product and cannot be discovered.

ENDNOTES

1. *Coca-Cola Bottling Co. v. Langston*, 127 S.W.2d 263 (Ark. 1939) (demonstration allowed).

2. *Otte v. Taylor*, 146 N.W.2d 78 (Neb. 1966) (demonstration allowed).

3. *Metropolitan Property & Liability Ins. Co. v. Shepherd,* 304 S.E.2d 74 (Ga. Ct. App. 1983) (demonstration allowed).

4. *Whitehurst v. Revlon*, 307 F. Supp. 918 (E.D. Va. 1969) (demonstration not allowed).

5. *Beasley v. Ford Motor Co.*, 117 S.E.2d 863 (S.C. 1961) (demonstration not allowed).

6. *Schleunes v. American Casualty Co.*, 528 F.2d 634 (5th Cir. 1976) (not allowing demonstration was an abuse of discretion).

7. *See generally 2 McCormick on Evidence* §§ 214-15.

8. *See Max Schwartz & Neil F. Schwartz, Engineering Evidence* § 8.06 (1987).

9. 2 *McCormick on Evidence* § 330, at 395; 4 *Weinstein's Evidence* 801(c)[01].

CHAPTER 8

COMPUTER-GENERATED DRAWINGS, SIMULATIONS, AND ANIMATIONS

Computer work done with graphics, simulation, and animation software creates highly persuasive courtroom exhibits. This chapter covers the three general categories: computer-generated drawings, simulations, and animations. Like television and video, computers have become a part of the lives of many jurors. Those who do not have first hand experience usually have friends or relatives who work with computers at the office or use them for home entertainment or communication. In the past, jurors viewed computers with some suspicion, focusing for example on the mistakes computers made in their utility bills. However, now jurors generally accept computers as an ordinary tool.

Computer drawings are two or three dimensional engineering drawings usually produced by an off-the-shelf engineering software or graphics program. These computer assisted design (CAD) programs are used for many purposes other than litigation, and their output usually can be qualified without difficulty. The advantage of a computer-generated engineering drawing is that, once completed, the display of the drawing can be rotated to any viewing point. The object can be turned around, looked at from the top or bottom, and taken apart, all without doing any new drawing.

Computer simulations are usually built with financial or engineering software that projects what will happen in the future under a given set of circumstances. Financial experts can project the effect of their assumptions by building forecasts, for example, as to cost, price, profit and loss, sales, or other business or economic performance. Engineers can use computers to test structural designs by making calculations about stress or other performance factors.

Computer animations recreate an object, event, or series of events in a visual format using the computer to display data in the form of images linked together to produce motion over time. Animations are produced with specialized software that can combine many forms of data with color and perspective to create a very lifelike reconstruction.

Because these kinds of computer-generated exhibits are difficult to cross-examine fairly without the help of an expert, they should be disclosed early in the discovery process and copies of all the computer files required to generate the exhibit should be turned over well before trial.

8.1 COMPUTER-GENERATED DRAWINGS

Many corporations and engineering firms use standard off-the-shelf software such as ProEngineer for most of their computer design work. They store their designs in computer files and rarely make hard copies for in-house purposes. When litigation issues arise with respect to products or structures made using these computer-generated drawings, it may be necessary to use the drawings as exhibits.

8.1.1 Foundation

The foundation requirement that a witness have the necessary competence to testify about the exhibit is generally met by qualifying an expert. Computer-generated exhibits are almost always used with a professional engineer or other expert witness. The broad latitude provided for experts under Rule 703 is useful in providing a foundation for the computer-generated exhibit. Once the exhibit is qualified by an expert, other witnesses may refer to the computer-generated drawing during their testimony.

As with any type of drawing you must establish the exhibit's relevance by linking it to an issue in the case. See discussion of drawings by artists in Section 4.3.1.

The identification of the drawing should include the facts that the drawing was generated by a computer and shows a particular part or structure.

Use Rule 901(b)(9) to establish the trustworthiness of the drawing with "[e]vidence describing a process or system used to produce a result and showing that the process or system produces an accurate result." If the engineering drawing that is the exhibit is also used in the regular course of the company's engineering functions, or is used by professional engineers elsewhere for nonlitigation purposes, the foundation is straightforward. See general discussion of foundation in Section 1.1.

Example

(After establishing the witness's engineering qualifications and the relevance of the drawing)

Q. Directing your attention to Exhibit 96, can you identify that?

A. Yes.

Q. What is it?

A. That is a printout of an engineering drawing of the retrieval arm on the Assembot II robot.

Q. What is the process or system that produced this design?

A. It was generated on the computer system used in our engineering department. We use ProEngineer software, which allows us to do engineering design work at a computer workstation. The software is on our server, and each engineer can access it through a desktop workstation. The server and desktop units are standard Hewlett Packard models. The designs are also stored on the server and can be called up and printed out if a hard copy is needed. We use a special printer, designed for engineering work also from Hewlett Packard, to make the hard copies.

Q. How long have you been using this process and system?

A. We have had the current version of the software for about 18 months and we upgraded to the current hardware about a year ago. We installed the printer about six months ago.

Q. What did you do to produce Exhibit 96?

A. I entered the identification number for the retrieval arm design using a workstation unit and entered the print command. The computer located the design and sent the data to the printer which created the printout.

Q. What can you tell us about whether your system produces an accurate result?

A. It produces very accurate drawings.

Q. Directing your attention to Exhibit 96A, can you identify that?

A. Yes. That is a diskette which has a copy of the computer file containing the design for the retrieval arm. It is what was used to print Exhibit 96.

Q. Is Exhibit 96A an exact duplicate of the computer file?

A. Yes.

Q. Your Honor, we offer Exhibit 96 in evidence.

Opposing Counsel: Objection, this is not the original document.

Q. We can qualify the printout, Your Honor. (*To the witness*) Is Exhibit 96 an accurate representation of the data stored in the computer system with respect to the design used to build the retrieval arm?

A. Yes.

Q. Your Honor, we offer Exhibit 96 in evidence. Under Rule 1001(3), the printout is an original because it has been shown to reflect accurately data stored in a computer.

Court: Objection overruled.

Counsel: In addition to Exhibit 96 itself, which is the printout, we would like to use the computer monitor to display the digital version of the design. We will use Exhibit 96A for that purpose. We do not intend to offer Exhibit 96A in evidence.

You may not need to mark a duplicate of the computer file as an exhibit in order to display on a computer monitor an exhibit that has been admitted in evidence as a computer printout. Judges follow different practices. Some will accept a representation from counsel that what is on the computer screen is the same as what is in the printout exhibit. You should have a duplicate of the computer file ready, however, in case your opponent is alert enough to demand it. An engineer would normally want to work with a computer display in a courtroom rather than a printout because the computer version can be rotated to different points of view in order to explain particular points and can be displayed in a lifelike three-dimensional representation. The witness can show a section or cutaway view. Or the witness can use a window to show two or more representations simultaneously. This capability may be useful in defending against cross-examination when the witness is challenged by an assertion in a leading question and wants to show on the screen why the assertion is not correct.

Another common evidentiary situation involving computer-generated drawings is the hard copy design that is put into computer-readable form for litigation purposes. Regular engineering drawings are difficult to handle as exhibits in a courtroom. When they are put into a computer, it is easier to use color, rotation to a convenient angle, labels, and zoom-in features to explain the design.

Example

(After establishing competence and relevance)

Q. Directing your attention to Exhibit 101, can you identify that?

A. Yes.

Q. What is it?

A. That is the engineering drawing for the seat latch that holds the back of the seat up while the driver is sitting in the seat.

Q. By whom was the drawing made?

A. By Jackson Controls, one of our suppliers for seats.

Q. Do you have a computer-readable copy of this drawing?

A. Yes.

Q. Directing your attention to Exhibit 101A, can you identify that?

A. Yes.

Q. What is it?

A. That is a diskette containing the computer file that is the computer-readable version of Exhibit 101.

Q. How do you know that?

A. I checked the diskette myself, and compared the computer file to the hard copy design

Q. Who prepared the computer-readable version of the design?

A. Our engineering department.

Q. What hardware and software did they use to do that?

A. The same hardware and software we use to do our designs for our products. We simply feed all the measurements and design elements from the hard copy design into the computer using standard techniques.

Q. How does the design in Exhibit 101, from your supplier, compare to the design in Exhibit 101A, the computer-readable version?

A. It is exactly the same.

Q. How do you know that?

A. I checked it. And we also have software that does a checking process, so we used that as well.

Q. Why did you make Exhibit 101A, the computer-readable version?

A. This allows us to display the design on the computer monitor, to turn it around to look at it from different angles, to zoom in to particular features, and to add colors and labels to help explain the design.

Q. Your Honor, we offer Exhibit 101A in evidence.

Opposing Counsel: Objection. Exhibit 101A is not an original.

Counsel: Your Honor, the original document rule does not apply to drawings. It applies to writings and recordings. This is an engineering drawing, it is not letters, words, or numbers as set out in the definition to Rule 1001(1). In any case, we have the original. It is Exhibit 101. And Exhibit 101A qualifies as a duplicate.

Opposing Counsel: Your Honor, they have added colors and labels, and they intend to rotate the design to an angle different from the original.

Counsel: Your Honor, under Rule 611(a) the court can allow labels, colors, and rotation of an image if it will make the presentation effective for the ascertainment of the truth or to avoid needless consumption of time. We are required to present engineering drawings to lay jurors, and we should be permitted to use these standard techniques for these purposes.

Court: Objection overruled. You may proceed. I will rule on
   specific objections to labels, colors, or rotation as they come up.

When using the "process or system" method for establishing
trustworthiness, the lawyer needs to think through all the parts of the
system that were used to get to the result that is the exhibit. In the
examples above, the witness has qualified the software and hardware
as standard items. With off-the-shelf items sold to many businesses and
not used only for litigation purposes, you need not qualify the publisher
of the software or the producer of the hardware. In addition, when the
design of a part is at issue in the case, there is no need to qualify the
data, the input process, the security, or the procedures to assure
accuracy in order to get the exhibit admitted in evidence. All of those
factors might affect the quality of the design, and therefore be relevant
to liability, but the exhibit showing the design is admissible regardless
of the inherent quality of the design so long as the exhibit is an accurate
representation of the design.

8.1.2 Objections

There are no hearsay objections to a computer-generated drawing
itself. The labels on the drawing indicating the date on which it was
initially prepared and last updated and the person who did the work
can be qualified as business records if they are challenged. See the
example in Section 6.2.

There are no original document objections to an accurate printout
from a computer file. Rule 1001(3) provides that "If data are stored in
a computer or similar device, any printout or other output readable by
sight, shown to reflect the data accurately, is an original."

The policy objections to a computer drawing may be directed at
argumentative or inaccurate labels, newly affixed colors not in the
original data file, the angle or viewpoint from which it is displayed, and
the size of the display compared to the size of the actual object.

8.1.3 Production and Tactics

Computer-generated drawings may be displayed by printouts and
enlargements (see discussion in Section 9.3), by electronic systems (see
Section 9.5), and by digital systems (see Section 9.6). Choose a view of
the design that adequately displays the features at issue and reduce
this to hard copy so that there is at least one exhibit in the set of paper
copies the jury takes to the jury room. The computer file and portable
computer to run it can be kept at hand in the courtroom in case the
expert needs to rotate the viewing angle to explain a particular feature
or to meet some argument on cross-examination. Explain in your closing

argument that the jury can request a replay of any display of the computer-generated drawing that they saw in the courtroom.

Opposing counsel may demand a copy of the computer software used to generate an exhibit. One advantage to using standard, off-the-shelf software is that the court will rarely order you to turn it over. Your opponent will have adequate access to the software through consultants and other commercially available services.

It is important, in this regard, to distinguish the software from the underlying data. Your opponent is entitled to the data in a usable format. If the data can reasonably be used only in computer-readable format, then the court likely will order you to turn over a disk (rather than reams of paper) if your opponent demands it.

8.2 COMPUTER-GENERATED SIMULATIONS

A computer simulation is generally used to predict what will happen in the future or what will happen under certain combinations of circumstances. It is a mathematical model that may be summarized in a chart or graph but generally is not a picture of the thing at issue. An animation, by contrast, is based on mathematical data but is displayed as a picture or series of pictures. See Section 8.3.

In cases where lost profits or lost earnings are an issue, experts can use statistical software to project different returns depending on past earnings and different assumptions concerning future market conditions and the like. They can easily display to the trier of fact the results of the projection for each year, as well as a calculation of the present value of the projected amount.

Engineering simulations are useful in product liability litigation and breach of contract or warranty litigation, where the question often is how a part of a machine failed and whether the failure was the result of a defect in design or manufacture. With the aid of computer software, stress tests or failure analyses can be conducted with respect to the design to predict how it would perform under specified conditions. Some of the computer software used for this work is well-recognized in the engineering profession and used by manufacturers to predict how designs will operate in practice.

8.2.1 Foundation

The foundation for a simulation requires, after establishing the competence of the witness, the relevance of the information, and the identification of the exhibit, a reliable basis for the trustworthiness of the exhibit. See Section 1.1. In this respect, the foundation is more complicated than for a computer-generated drawing as explained in Section 8.1.1. The foundation for this type of exhibit is highly particular to individual exhibits. Two examples are set out below to illustrate some common approaches.

Example

(Assume that the plaintiff company has gone out of business and is claiming as damages its lost profits because of being forced out of business. The plaintiff wants to put in damage proof calculated through the use of a computer simulation or model. A proper foundation has been laid for the introduction of lost profits with the type of contract involved and the circumstances of the breach.)

Q. Would you state your full name, please?

A. My name is Al Hoft.

Q. Where do you live?

A. I live on Long Island, in New York.

Q. What do you do for a living?

A. I am a certified public accountant.

Q. For what company do you work?

A. Price & Co. I am a partner in the firm, and I work in our worldwide litigation consulting practice.

Q. Are you prepared to give an opinion as to the amount of money that the XYZ Company lost as a result of its dealings with the ABC Company?

A. I am.

Q. What are your qualifications to give that opinion?

A. *(Witness reviews education and work experience)*

Q. How did you determine the amount of lost profits to the XYZ Company?

A. I followed our standard methodology that we have used many times.

Q. What does that involve?

A. The first step in general terms is to gain an understanding of the facts, the causes of relevant events, and the historical information to the extent that it is available from the affected company. We take that data and historical information and make sure it is correct. Then we create a database from which we can work with the computer.

Q. How did you do that?

A. We did an audit of the XYZ Company's historical financial results and its operating results until the year it shut down operations. We also audited sales transactions.

Q. What have you done to ensure against errors in the data?

A. We use very strict quality control procedures on our assignments. We test the data, confirm it by alternative means, and we recheck the calculations against the calculations made by the computer.

Q. What equipment did you use?

A. We use a network system. The server and desktop workstations are manufactured by Compaq.

Q. What software did you use?

A. We use commercially available statistical analysis software. This software is also used by investment bankers, industry analysts, and others who need to project results from current data using a variety of assumptions.

Q. What do you do to protect against errors in entering the data?

A. We cross-reference the data that comes out of the analysis back into the historical financial statements of the company. This will highlight any errors in input.

Q. On the basis of your knowledge and experience, were the underlying data that you used in your computer analysis reliable and sufficient for the purpose?

A. Yes, the data are reliable.

Q. What does the analysis do?

A. It projects the net income during and after the XYZ Company failure by using balanced statistical measures called a historical regression analysis. This is a procedure for taking past financial results and projecting what the future would be if it had been consistent with the past. Then it compares the projected income with actual income to calculate the amount of lost profits.

Q. Does the hardware and software system that you used produce an accurate result?

A. Yes.

Q. How do you know that?

A. I have used this system on a number of assignments. In my experience, using this hardware and software system does produce a result that reflects the amount of damages sustained in this kind of situation.

Q. In developing this analysis, what assumptions did you make?

A. The most significant assumption was that the XYZ Company would have had no other disruptive events affecting its future income. This assumption was based on the testimony of its officers. The next assumption was what the XYZ Company's price-earnings ratio would have been if it had not been for the problems with the ABC Company.

Q. Based on your study and work in this matter and based on the damages analysis that you used on your computer, do you have an opinion based upon a reasonable degree of certainty as to the total amount of damages suffered by the plaintiff XYZ Company as a result of its experience with ABC Company?

A. Yes, I do.

Q. What is that opinion?

A. In my opinion, the amount of lost profits is $15,372,000. That amount is stated in accordance with the accounting principles normally applied in this area for this purpose.

At this point, the evidence about the computer work supports the conclusion reached by the expert, but there is no exhibit representing that work. If you decide to use an exhibit, there are a number of options. One is a static display of the principal calculations.

Example

Q. Directing your attention to the document that has been marked as Exhibit 97, can you identify that?

A. Yes.

Q. What is it?

A. That is an exhibit that shows a graphical picture of the regression analysis that the computer performed.

Q. Does the process or system you used produce an accurate regression analysis?

A. Yes it does.

Q. How do you know that?

A. We checked a sample of the calculations by hand. Also, we have used this software extensively and it produces an accurate result.

Q. Your Honor, we offer Exhibit 97 in evidence.

Opposing Counsel: Objection, this isn't the original document.

Q. We can qualify it, Your Honor. *(To the witness)* Is Exhibit 97 an accurate reflection of the data stored on the computer?

A. Yes.

Q. How do you know that?

A. I used the report module of the software to print this out after the calculations had been made and checked.

Q. Your Honor, we offer Exhibit 97 in evidence. Exhibit 97, the printout, is an original under Rule 1001(3) because it accurately reflects the data stored in a computer. There is no original document problem here.

Court: Objection overruled.

Counsel: Exhibit 97A is an enlargement of Exhibit 97. We offer that as well.

Court: Exhibit 97 is admitted. Exhibit 97A is admitted. You may proceed.

At this point, one aspect of the computer analysis has been reduced to a printout and is in evidence. This will permit the expert witness to explain what a regression analysis is and why it is a reliable method for estimating what would happen in the future under specific assumptions.

In some situations, the lawyer may want the expert to demonstrate the changes in the result that come from making different assumptions. This may be a situation where large changes in some assumptions make relatively little difference in the outcome. The proponent of the exhibit may expect cross-examination along this line and, in order to present this testimony in the most favorable light, may want to include this in the direct.

Example

Q. Are you able to demonstrate the use of your analysis to reach this opinion?

A. Yes.

Q. What equipment do you have with you for that purpose?

A. I have a portable computer that I use regularly in my work.

Q. Is the equipment in proper working order?

A. It is. I tested it this morning.

Q. How will the output of your computer work be displayed?

A. There is a monitor there in front of the jury box, another monitor on the judge's desk, and a third monitor on trial counsel's table over there. All three will have the display from the computer output simultaneously.

Q. Using this equipment, are you able to vary the assumptions that were made in reaching your estimate with respect to the amount of lost profits?

A. Yes.

Q. Your Honor, may the witness to use his computer to demonstrate how changing some of the assumption would affect the result?

Assuming that the court consents, the expert would then explain the variations in several key assumptions, make the appropriate keyboard entries to make the computations, and display them in chart or graph form on the monitors as the explanation proceeds. Using a "live" demonstration is risky except with the most experienced experts. Charts or other static exhibits illustrating the computer analysis and its results are a safer alternative.

Another common type of exhibit involving computer simulation is stress testing of component parts to demonstrate that a design was reasonable or unreasonable under the circumstances.

Example

(An engineering company was hired to determine whether a part would break under certain kinds of stress. A representative of the engineering company is called as a witness to establish a foundation for the computer work that will be used by other witnesses and experts.)

Q. Ms. Jackson, will you state your name and address for the record?

A. Jane Jackson, 223 Primrose Path, Elkville, Michigan.

Q. Ms. Jackson, where are you employed?

A. I am an engineer with Addison Engineers Inc.

Q. What do you do there?

A. I am a design engineer.

Q. What kinds of things do you design?

A. Mainly I work on automobile parts.

Q. Ms. Jackson, are you familiar with the axle that has been admitted in evidence as Exhibit 100?

A. Yes, I am.

Q. How did you become familiar with that?

A. Our company was asked to test the design of that axle.

Q. What testing did your company do?

A. We did the stress testing.

Q. What is that?

A. That is testing to determine how the axle will perform under various loads.

Q. Who performed the tests?

A. I supervised this work.

Q. What are your qualifications to do that?

A. *(Witness explains)*

Q. How is that testing done?

A. We put all of the parameters of the axle design into a computer and used a computer program to make the calculations of the stresses on the axle that will result from various kinds of loads put on the design. We then analyze how those stresses will cause the axle to perform under those loads.

Q. I show you what has been marked for identification as Exhibit 102 and ask you to examine it.

A. *(Witness looks)*

Q. What is that?

A. That is a printout of a computer file containing the design of the axle.

Q. What is in the computer file containing the design of the axle?

A. That contains the actual engineering dimensions and material specifications that make up the design of the axle.

Q. How do you know that?

A. I looked at the contents of the file after it was loaded onto our network. I am familiar with this kind of file, and this one was complete.

Q. I show you what has been marked as Exhibit 103.

A. *(Witness looks at exhibit)*

Q. What is that?

A. That is a computer printout showing the calculations made in the stress testing of the axle.

Q. How do you know that?

A. I did the computer work that this printout reflects. I recognize the title and the headings, and my initials are in the upper right hand corner along with the date and the project number.

Q. When was it prepared?

A. On the day we did the work. The date is entered automatically by the computer.

Q. How was it prepared?

A. First, one of our technicians entered into our computer system the contents of the computer file containing the design of the axle. Then I entered the various loads for which I wanted the calculations done. Then I examined the results of those calculations and had the computer display the results of the stress on the axle.

Q. What is the process or system that was used in your work?

A. I used the hardware in our computer network, which consists of a server and workstations. This is all commercially available equipment used in many engineering offices. I used analytical software published by a recognized firm and used for stress testing in the automotive industry.

Q. What can you tell us about whether this hardware and software system that you used produces an accurate result?

A. I have used it many times, and it is very accurate.

Q. How was the stress test conducted?

A. I broke the axle design down into separate elements, each of which represents a different segment of the axle. Each element is square or nearly square in shape, and all of the elements together form a mesh of the entire axle. Each element in turn contained four corners or "nodes." The stress analysis involved determining the different loads that could be expected to be exerted on each node of the axle in actual operation, and then calculating the effect that each load or combination of loads would have on the axle. The predicted effect of any load could be calculated by standard formulas of mechanics and dynamics, based on mass, friction, velocity, torque, and the design and composition of the axle.

Q. I show you what has been marked for identification as Exhibit 106 and ask you to examine it.

A. *(Witness looks at exhibit)*

Q. What is that?

A. That is a graph produced by the computer. It shows the places where the stress was put on the axle and the results of the stress that was applied.

Q. How was Exhibit 106 produced?

A. That is a printout from the software we used for the stress analysis. It was produced on the printer in our office.

Q. How did you check the accuracy of the data put into the computer?

A. After the stress analysis was performed, two other employees of our company checked the results of the calculations by doing a manual spot check of some of the calculations and by performing physical tests of a prototype physical axle in the laboratory and on the test track.

Q. How do you know that the data are secure from alteration by some unauthorized person?

A. We have a security system programmed into the database so that no unauthorized person can add data or take data out. In order to get access to the database for this computer analysis of the axle, or any other file on our system, you need to know a ten-character password. I created the password for this particular assignment. I am the only person who knows the password, and I have not given it out to anybody.

Q. How do you know that the data are secure from any computer malfunction?

A. The network has two different safeguards to protect against failures and to detect them if they occur. No failures occurred on this project.

Q. How do you know that the data are secure from any software malfunction?

A. In addition to the procedures I described earlier, we have programmed a double cross-check system under which every calculation performed by the computer is confirmed for accuracy. In addition, the commercially available programs we used have been tested for accuracy and certified as accurate by a nationally recognized testing organization.

Q. Your Honor, we offer what has been marked as Exhibit 103 and Exhibit 106 in evidence.

In this case, the trustworthiness aspect of the foundation includes evidence with respect to the quality of the data input and also the three principal security concerns: that an unauthorized person tampered with the file, that the hardware malfunctioned, and that the software malfunctioned. It is an option to leave these factors to be developed on cross-examination. The foundation is complete when the requirements of Rule 901(b)(9) are satisfied by evidence identifying the process or system used to get the result and evidence that it produces an accurate result.

One common challenge to the foundation for a computer simulation points out that the witness has not explained how the computer reaches an accurate result. This objection goes beyond the requirement of Rule 901(b)(9) and should not be sustained. The rule requires "evidence describing a process or system." This is met by an identification of the hardware and software used together with the information that these components have commercial uses outside the litigation arena. The rule also requires a "showing that the process or system produces an accurate result." This showing can be made through testimony that the witness has had prior experience with the system and that it has produced accurate results. Exploring the possible deficiencies of the system is the burden of the cross-examiner.

8.2.2 Objections

Because computer simulations are exhibits sponsored by experts, the objections available to the opponent, once an adequate foundation is laid, are limited.

Hearsay objections

A hearsay objection is sometimes raised on the grounds that the data input to the computer is a "statement" made out of court and therefore subject to the hearsay rule. See Section 1.3.1. The usual response to a hearsay objection to the data used by an expert is the exception in Rule 703 which provides:

> The facts or data in the particular case upon which an expert bases an opinion or inference may be those perceived by or made known to the expert at or before the hearing. If of a type reasonably relied upon by experts in the particular field in forming opinions or inferences on the subject, the facts or data need not be admissible in evidence.

The computer printout is usually the work product of the expert, and admissible on that ground independent of the underlying data. Other exceptions to the hearsay rule, such as business records and public records, may also be available. Or, if the data were obtained from a party opponent, they may come under the exemption for admissions.

Original document objections

A computer simulation generally involves a number of computer files, and an original document objection may succeed if the proponent does not have available the information necessary to meet this challenge. See Section 1.3.2.

Example

(Using the example set out above with the engineering exhibits)

Opposing Counsel: Objection, this printout is not the original document under the applicable rules.

Q. Your Honor, there is no problem here. It is just a matter of identifying the computer files as originals and the printouts as exact duplicates. *(To the witness)* Ms. Jackson, let's go back to the computer files that were used here. First, where did you get the computer files that contained all of the parameters of the axle design?

A. I obtained them from the mainframe computer containing the design files.

Q. Is the mainframe computer file the original design itself?

A. Yes, it is.

Q. Was the computer file you used made by an electronic re-recording of the mainframe computer file?

A. Yes, it was.

Q. Is Exhibit 102, the printout of the computer file containing the design of the axle, an accurate reflection of the data stored in the computer?

A. Yes, it is.

Q. Is the computer data file containing the calculations with respect to the stress test an original in the sense that it is the file that was created when the calculations were done?

A. Yes.

Q. Is Exhibit 103, the printout of those files, an accurate reflection of the data stored in the computer?

A. Yes.

Q. Is the computer file containing the image an original in the sense that it was created when the image was created?

A. Yes.

Q. How do you know that Exhibit 103, the printout of the calculations, is an accurate representation of the data that are stored in the computer?

A. The computer's printing device is programmed to print out the results of the calculations. It is programmed to detect printing errors. In addition, I checked the printout for accuracy against calculations that were displayed on the computer screen.

Q. Is Exhibit 106, the printout of the image, an accurate reflection of the computer file?

A. Yes.

Q. How do you know that Exhibit 106, the graph showing the testing results, is an accurate representation of the data that are stored in the computer?

A. The reason is the same.

Q. Were any other computer data files used by you in doing your work that is shown in Exhibits 103 and 106?

A. No.

Q. Your Honor, we offer Exhibits 103 and 106 in evidence. The computer data file used by Ms. Jackson to transfer the data with respect to the axle design is a duplicate under Rule 1001(4). The computer data file containing the calculations of the stress test is an original under Rule 1001(3). The computer file containing the image is an original under Rule 1001(3). The printouts that are Exhibit 103 and Exhibit 106 are also originals under Rule 1001(3) because they are printouts that have been shown to accurately reflect the data stored in the computer. That is all that is required under the original document rules.

An original document objection can be raised here because the printout being offered in evidence originates from computer files from another system. The design for the axle appearing on the printout came from the "original" file in the mainframe via the "duplicate" on the computer on which the expert was working. This is different from the situation where an expert uses data drawn from a number of computer files to create a new computer file and the printout offered is from the new computer file. In that case, the source files need not be qualified as originals. It is enough that they are data properly relied on by the expert under Rule 703. See example in Section 8.3.2.

Policy objections

Computer simulations generally do not raise policy objections. They do not arouse emotions in the way that supports an objection of unfair prejudice. They do not usually cause undue delay or a waste of time because they are a summary of what otherwise would take quite a long time to present. And computer simulations usually do not fall under the category of needless cumulative evidence. Occasionally an objection will be made on the grounds of confusing the jury by the method with which a computer simulation is presented if the screen displays and hard copy exhibits do not fit together well. See Section 1.3.3.

The most common objection is "surprise," which is not technically a policy objection under Rule 403 but which is allowed in every court. See Section 1.3.5. If the underlying data have not been produced in a fair manner during discovery, this objection may be sustained. The "surprise" objection may also be based on the failure to produce the simulation exhibit itself during pretrial proceedings. The discovery requirements under Rule 26(a)(2) of the Federal Rules of Civil Procedure with respect to expert testimony are intended to result in the pretrial disclosure of all such expert work product.

8.2.3   Production and Tactics

When using the results of a simulation as an exhibit, it is helpful to turn over in discovery the underlying data, even if your opponent has not made a demand with sufficient particularity. This avoids delay at trial and a possible "unfair prejudice" or "surprise" objection. If the simulation was done using commercially available, off-the-shelf software, generally you will not be required to turn over the software. Your opponent should have reasonable access to the software through consultants who use it every day in their business.

Disputes will often arise in discovery when data are turned over in hard copy format but can be used only in computer-readable format. As the cost of turning the hard copy into computer-readable format can be considerable, particularly if manual error-checking is necessary, and if your client has the data in computer-readable format, it is likely you will be ordered by the court to turn it over in computer-readable format.

8.3 COMPUTER-GENERATED ANIMATIONS

A computer animation is produced by linking a series of images, each of which is technically accurate, to show motion over time. Courts have admitted computer animations in evidence to show how automobile or airplane accidents occurred, how fire spread through a building, how construction was completed, how personal injury accidents occurred, how manufacturing operations progressed, how machinery or equipment failed, and many other types of events.

Computer animations give the judge or jurors the sense of making their own judgments and discovering their own conclusions from the computer work being shown. This is much more satisfying than listening to oral testimony about the judgments and conclusions of lay or expert witnesses. For this reason, this form of exhibit is unusually powerful.

There are three kinds of animations—models, demonstrations, and reconstructions—paralleling in the computer context what has been done for many years using other media. See Chapter 7 on models, demonstrations, and reconstructions using techniques other than computer animation. A computer animation that is a model simply shows, through a visualization of the data used to construct the real thing, how an object looks. This may be an object that was destroyed when the events at issue took place, an object that is too large to bring into the courtroom, or an object that is too small to be seen with the naked eye. The model may have a cutaway feature so that the inside workings of the object can be displayed. A computer animation that is a demonstration shows how some physical principle works. For example, an expert may need to explain the optics in a camera. The animation shows the lines of sight, how light strikes the object, and how the images are formed. This does not show a part of the expert's actual opinion in the case. It is a tutorial about background information so that the jury can understand the opinion. A computer animation that is a reconstruction shows how the events at issue occurred. This is the most complicated and controversial type of animation. It usually depicts the expert's theory of what happened in the case, such as an aircraft crash or an automobile accident.

8.3.1 Pretrial Disclosure

In order to use a computer-generated animation at trial, you must disclose during discovery the identity of the expert who is available to testify about the production of the animation, the identity of the hardware and software used to construct the animation, the documents and other sources of the data included in the animation, and the computer data files that make up the completed animation. Computer animations take a good deal of time to create, usually more than a month. Sufficient pretrial disclosure is required for the opponent of the animation to have a fair chance to understand the animation and cross-examine the expert.

You should make the necessary disclosure regardless of whether an outstanding discovery request covers this information. If no disclosure is made, your opponent may make an objection based on "surprise" when you seek to introduce the animation. See discussion in Section 1.3.5. Under Rule 611(a) the court has the discretion to exclude the animation if the opponent has not had a fair opportunity to prepare for cross-examination. A well-prepared computer animation is a very powerful exhibit, usually overshadowing everything else at trial in the minds of jurors. In the case of a complicated reconstruction, a fair opportunity to cross-examine requires at least 90 days. The opponent has to engage an expert, examine the preparation and construction of the animation closely, and prepare either a counteranimation or cross-examination segments. See discussion in Section 8.3.5.

The trial lawyer may elect to present as a witness only an expert whose conclusions are supported or illustrated by the computer animation, not the expert who produced the animation. The opponent is entitled, however, to depose the person responsible for making the animation as well as the expert who will use it. There should be no delays or excuses in this regard. The name, address, and resume of the producer of the animation should be turned over well within the discovery deadline for depositions. In some cases, lawyers have chosen not to disclose the existence of an animation until very close to trial, arguing that the animation is work product until a decision is made to use it at trial. That rationale should be rejected. No sophisticated animation can be cross-examined successfully at trial without a deposition of the producer of the animation and sufficient time both to prepare for that deposition and to use the results of the deposition in preparing for cross-examination.

Most experts who make animations for litigation purposes use standard hardware and software. Otherwise the potential objections and discovery complications increase exponentially. The proponent of the animation should provide the name and address of the computer manufacturer, the model number of the computer and its basic specifications, and the identification of any peripherals used. The proponent should also provide the name and address of the software publisher, the name of the software program and the version used, and any modifications or ancillary programs used in preparing the animation.

All of the data used in constructing the animation must be turned over in discovery. The animation is a summary under Rule 1006, which provides: "The contents of voluminous writings, recordings, or photographs which cannot conveniently be examined in court may be presented in the form of a chart, summary, or calculation. The originals, or duplicates, shall be made available for examination or copying, or both, by other parties at reasonable time and place. The court may order that they be produced in court."

In addition, if the animation depicts the events at issue in the case, you also should be prepared to deliver the actual computer files making up the animation on a computer disk so that the other side's expert can examine not only the final product but the underlying computer files from which the animation was constructed. Sometimes an animation is changed a number of times before trial, and some lawyers will use the excuse that the "final" animation is not ready for delivery to the other side until shortly before trial. Courts should not permit this kind of delay, particularly with a complicated reconstruction. At least 90 days are required to have an expert examine the computer files used in a reconstruction, analyze the data, and decide whether there are flaws that need to be exposed during cross-examination. If no final animation is ready, the court should order the proponent to deliver what is available 90 days before trial and should not tolerate substantial changes at the last minute.

A computer animation may be presented via computer or videotape, and you should deliver a copy of this presentation to the other side well before trial. It is for this reason that vendors generally make a videotape copy of the animation even if a digital system will be used to display the animation in court. A videotape is easier to mark as an exhibit and to deliver a copy to the other side.

Sometimes an issue is raised as to whether the actual software used to make the animation must be produced. (This is different from the computer data files making up the animation. Those show what data have been used in the animation and how the data have been arranged and shaped. The software is what has been used to create those data files.) If commercial animation software has been used, and it is readily available to experts in the field, then normally a court will not order the proponent to produce a copy of the software. Because of licensing restrictions, it costs both parties an equal amount to acquire this extra copy. Moreover, a qualified expert in the field likely already has the software or has access to it. If proprietary software has been used, then the court should either order that the proponent of the animation provide access to that software for the opponent's expert or produce a copy. See Fed.R.Civ.P. 26(b)(4)(C).

Another situation involves publicly available software that has been modified to some extent. The modifications could be extensive, involving reprogramming or changing the fundamental nature of the way the program operates. Conversely, the modifications might be slight, such as creation of field names or use of macro instructions to make the program operate more efficiently. If the modifications do not change the essential way the data is manipulated by the software and could be easily explored in detail with the expert during a deposition or even at trial, providing a copy of the actual software should not be ordered. If the modification changes the software or the way it functions, the adversary would be in a stronger position to ask for production.

If a court orders production of proprietary software you should apply for a protective order to limit disclosure pursuant to Fed.R.Civ.P. 26(c)(7).[1]

8.3.2 Foundation

The foundation for any computer animation is highly specific to the exhibit. The foundation for an animation that is a "model" could be supplied by a lay person intimately familiar with the real thing. The foundation for an animation that is a "demonstration" will be supplied by the expert who can testify that it is an accurate rendition of the operation of the relevant laws of physics, chemistry, or biology that the jury needs to understand. The foundation for an animation that is a "reconstruction" may need both the substantive expert and the producer of the animation to lay a proper foundation.

The seven-step procedure set out below can be adapted to qualify any animation produced by a capable firm using commercially available hardware and software. An example of the foundation for a reconstruction drawn from an actual case follows the discussion of the general guidelines.

Qualify the expert

Step 1: Computer animations must be qualified by an expert who can supply the requirements under Rule 901(b)(9). The person in charge of the production of the animation must be prepared to testify that the process or system employed to make the animation produces an accurate result. The producer of the animation may supervise a number of people including animators, paint artists, designers, and video editors. The selection of an expert is critical to the success of this kind of exhibit. The expert must have sufficient qualifications to support the reasonableness of the uses of the data, the data input operations, the computer hardware and software used, and the accuracy of all of the results reached.

Qualify the computer hardware

Step 2: This qualification is similar to that discussed in Section 3.3.1, Section 8.1.1, and Section 8.2.1. The expert should emphasize the nonlitigation uses of the hardware in commercial applications.

Qualify the computer software

Step 3: This qualification is similar to that discussed in Section 3.3.1, Section 8.1.1, and Section 8.2.1. Again, it is very important to have the expert emphasize the commercial applications of the software to design commercial products or to analyze failures in a nonlitigation setting and to do other analytical work.

Qualify the data

Step 4: You must identify all of the data used to construct the animation and have hard copy form available to be produced in court. The source must be specified and someone must vouch for its accuracy.

The data used for computer animations or reconstructions come from five principal sources:

- physical measurements;
- design drawings, blueprints, and other technical specification documents;
- data recorders such as the black boxes on planes and trains, geological survey tapes, readings from test instruments, and satellite photographs and data collections;
- expert witness calculations, mathematical models, opinions; and
- lay witness testimony (usually eyewitness accounts).

In an automobile accident reconstruction, for example, some of the data may come from physical measurements at the scene as to the width of the road, the friction of the surface, the shoulders and road markings, and the configuration of the intersection. Some data may come from the specifications of the vehicles involved. Still other data may come from expert calculations concerning the likely speed involved, the force on impact, and the results of that force on the vehicles. Finally, an eyewitness on the scene who observed the vehicles in a particular position may supply that data.

Qualify the quality checking operations

Step 5: A witness should describe in detail the method used to input the data into the computer and the accuracy checks. Your expert can provide the necessary qualifications for the processing operations; usually these involve hand calculations in which a small part of the computer's operations are checked to ensure that they are accurate. Your expert may be able to use benchmark tests to demonstrate that the software has processed the data properly. And some software programs have certifications that can be used in this regard.

Identify and prepare to defend the assumptions used by the expert

Step 6: Nearly every computer animation involves assumptions made by the expert about what happened and how it happened. It is important to be able to identify each assumption and defend it. Normally the assumptions are not made a part of the foundation questioning, but a careful voir dire will attack assumptions and the proponent must be prepared to put in testimony identifying and qualifying the assumptions if the court requires this as a part of establishing the trustworthiness of the exhibit. Assumptions, if reasonably made by a qualified expert, normally go to the weight to be given the animation as an exhibit, not to its admissibility.

Qualify the presentation media

Step 7: Most computer-generated animations are presented on a computer or videotape display. You will need to present testimony that what appears on the display medium accurately represents the computer's output. Normally this can be done by describing the methods by which the computer output was transferred to the display medium. This is technically a part of meeting an original document objection and normally would not be a part of the foundation. See Section 1.6.5. With an animation, however, in order to minimize confusion, it is useful to put this explanation into the testimony given before the exhibit is offered in evidence.

Example

(Steps 1 through 7 for a reconstruction animation after relevance is established)

Q. Please state your name and spell your last name for the record.

A. David Jannsen. J-A-N-N-S-E-N.

Q. Mr. Jannsen, have you produced an exhibit that shows the operation of the stoker boiler at the Straw Valley plant?

A. Yes, I have.

Q. What kind of exhibit is it?

A. It is a computer animation that shows how each element of the plant operates.

Q. How can we see this animation?

A. I can display it on the monitors that have been set up at the jury box, at counsel table, and on the judge's bench.

Q. What are your qualifications to produce this animation?

A. I have a Bachelor's Degree in Mechanical Engineering from the University of Michigan. I have a Master's Degree in Mechanical Engineering from the University of Pennsylvania. I worked for 10 years as an engineer for the Ford Motor Company. During that experience, I used computer hardware and software to design and test automotive components. After I left Ford, I joined Z-Axis Inc. which specializes in making computer animations for the analysis and correction of problems, the settlement of disputes, and for litigation. I have been at Z-Axis for eight years. During that time, I have produced over 50 computer animations such as the exhibit for this case.

Q. What hardware did you use in your work on this animation?

A. I used computer workstations produced by Silicon Graphics. They specialize in making workstations for computer animations and other engineering work. These workstations are commercially available and are used by most of the firms in my field.

Q. What software did you use in your work on this animation?

A. I used the most recent version of WaveFront software. This is commercially available software published for uses in computer animation and engineering design. This software is used by many other firms in my field.

Q. What data did you use in your work on this animation?

A. I used five kinds of data: First, I gathered all the designs for the plant. Some of these were in hard copy and some were done on computers. That gave me all the information from which the plant was built. I put all of this information into the computer. Second, I went to the plant and made physical measurements and observations of the key components. This allowed me to test whether the plant was actually built according to the plans. Third, I obtained the production data from the plant. This included records on how much fuel was put into the plant and how much electricity came out the other end. Fourth, I gathered as many photographs of the plant as I could locate, including an aerial photograph that was made of the plant for purposes of litigation. And fifth, I consulted with Percy Nelson, a boiler expert with 35 years of experience.

Q. How do you know that the data you used were accurate?

A. The plans and designs for the plant were confirmed by the owners of the plant. I relied on my expert capability as an engineer in making the measurements and observations. I was careful in my work. The production data were produced by the operators of the plant. The photographs were verified in discovery. And Mr. Nelson's credentials as a boiler expert are beyond question.

Q. How do you know that the input of the data to your computer was done accurately?

A. For data that are entered manually, we have a system of manual checks of samples of the data to ensure that the input was done correctly. Much of the data is already in computer-readable form, and those data are transferred directly. We have an error checking protocol in our data transfer procedures.

Q. What assumptions did you make?

A. I made three assumptions. First, I made physical measurements of the key components at the plant. Those showed that the design drawings were accurate in these respects. I assumed that the drawings were also accurate in all other respects relevant to the animation. Second, because there are no flow meters in the plant that would tell us how fuel actually flowed along the conveyors, I assumed the average rate specified by the design. Third, I assumed that the plant production records were correct, and I did not independently verify those.

Q. Why are those assumptions reasonable?

A. I was satisfied that I tested enough of the physical measurements to have an accurate animation, and I also used photographs as a cross-check. The assumption about average flow rates is standard engineering practice in the absence of specific data. And the plant production records were produced in discovery by the other side and those are the records they used in their case.

Q. Does the process or system that you used to make the animation produce an accurate result?

A. Yes, it does.

Q. How do you know that?

A. As I said, I have made over 50 animations and I have extensive experience with this system. It is the best in the industry.

Q. Does the display accurately show the results of your work?

A. Yes it does.

Q. How is the display prepared?

A. Once the animation is completed, we make a videotape of it and also transfer it to a computer storage medium. In this case we used a digital video disk.

Q. Is there any sound track with the animation?

A. No.

Q. How is the display put up on the monitors we have here in the courtroom?

A. The computer is hooked to the digital video disk player and to the video monitors. The computer generates the necessary commands to the digital video disk player which retrieves and displays the animation on the video monitors in the same general way that a videotape player would display material on a videotape on television monitors.

Q. Is this equipment in operating order?

A. Yes, it is. I tested it this morning.

Q. Directing your attention to what has been marked as Exhibit 98. Can you identify that?

A. Yes.

Q. What is it?

A. That is the videotape cassette containing the videotape of the computer animation of the stoker boiler at the Straw Valley plant.

Q. Is the animation in Exhibit 98 a fair and accurate representation of the stoker boiler at the Straw Valley plant?

A. Yes, it is.

Q. Would you identifiy what has been marked as Exhibit 98A?

A. Yes. That is the digital video disk containing the digitial version of the computer animation.

Q. Your Honor, we offer Exhibit 98 in evidence. The videotape is a convenient way to make the animation a part of the record. The animation is qualified under Rule 901(b)(9) on the authentication of the results of processes or systems. We will use Exhibit 98A to present the animation on the monitors we have set up in the courtroom, but we are not offering the disk in evidence.

Note that the expert who produced the animation is not an expert with respect to boiler design. His experience is in the automotive field. For that reason, a boiler expert has been retained to validate any assumptions that are necessary in bridging gaps in the data. No foundation has been laid with respect to these assumptions in this example. If assumptions have been exposed and attacked during discovery, you may want to include testimony in the foundation defending the reasonableness of these assumptions.

The easiest way to deal with a computer animation as an exhibit is to mark and offer the videotape version. Normally a computer animation will be displayed using a laserdisc or digital video disk that has been made from the original animation computer files. You may not want to mark the disk itself as an exhibit because you may have documents and other testimony aids on the disk, as well as the animation. The animation is a compilation of computer files, which were either played on a high resolution monitor in order to make the videotape or transferred directly from the computer on which the animation was made to the computer storage medium from which the animation will be displayed. The court may require that the underlying data disks be produced in court and marked as a composite exhibit, but normally you need not offer the data in evidence.

Foundation challenges to computer animations are often very broad and unspecific because your opponent does not know enough about the process to be precise. A computer animation is likely to be central to an expert's testimony, so your opponent will want to preserve the broadest possible range of options on appeal. To combat these generalized objections, it is important to focus the judge's attention on the dividing line between what is required to qualify the animation so that it may be considered by the jury and what is required to persuade the jury of the point of view advanced by the animation.

The response to a foundation objection should refer to the rule and attempt to pinpoint the technical bases for the objection.

Example

Opposing Counsel: Objection. The foundation for this exhibit is not sufficient.

Counsel: Your Honor, we have qualified the computer animation under Rule 901(b)(9) which is a permitted way of authenticating or establishing the trustworthiness of this exhibit. We have qualified the expert, the computer hardware and software, the data, the quality checking operations, the reasonableness of the assumptions, and the presentation media. Nothing further is required for purposes of determining the admissibility of the exhibit. Anything else would go to the weight to be given the exhibit.

Further, Your Honor, if opposing counsel believes there is any technical basis on which to attack the foundation for this exhibit, he should voir dire the witness.

Court *(to opposing counsel)*: Do you wish an opportunity for voir dire?

Opposing Counsel: We don't have the burden of establishing a foundation, Your Honor. This foundation is not sufficient.

Counsel: Your Honor, they need either to voir dire the witness or to specify the respects in which they contend the foundation is inadequate. Under Rule 901(b)(9), our burden is to describe the process or system used to produce the animation and to present adequate testimony showing that the process or system produces an accurate result. We have done that.

Court: Objection overruled.

If your opponent takes the opportunity for voir dire, it is important to contain this examination to the narrow purpose of exploring the technical bases for the foundation. See discussion in Section 1.7.2.

8.3.3 Objections

You should expect the full range of objections to an animation and prepare accordingly. Getting a resolution of objections at a pretrial conference is a good idea as it may be necessary to brief the issues.

Hearsay objections

Because computer animations are produced by experts and are, in essence, the expert's "opinion" about facts at issue in the case, the rules make available a special exception to the hearsay rule. Rule 703 provides:

> The facts or data in the particular case upon which an expert bases an opinion or inference may be those perceived by or made known to the expert at or before the hearing. If of a type reasonably relied upon by experts in a particular field in forming opinions or inferences upon the subject, the facts or data need not be admissible in evidence.

This is an important and very broad exception to the hearsay rules.

Example

Opposing Counsel: Objection. Hearsay.

Counsel: Your Honor, we can qualify the data used with respect to the animation. *(To the witness)* Mr. Jannsen, are the data you used in constructing the computer animation that is Exhibit 98 of a type reasonably relied upon by experts in your particular field in forming opinions or inferences on the subjects included in the animation?

A. Yes.

Q. Does Exhibit 98 reflect your expert opinion about the operation of the stoker boiler at the Straw Valley plant?

A. Yes, it does.

Q. Your Honor, we offer Exhibit 98 in evidence. Under Rule 703, data that are of a type reasonably relied upon by experts need not be admissible in evidence.

Opposing Counsel: The computer animation that is Exhibit 98 is an exhibit, not an opinion. Therefore Rule 703 does not apply.

Counsel: Nothing in Rule 703 requires an opinion to be rendered in words as opposed to images. Rule 703 covers images that are expert opinions such as Exhibit 98, and specifically provides that the data used by an expert in formulating an opinion need not be admissible in evidence.

Court: Objection overruled.

There are, of course, other methods of qualifying data either as "non-hearsay" or under an exception to the hearsay rules. See discussion in Section 1.3.1 and Section 2.1.2.

Original document objections

If an original document objection is raised in this example where the expert has drawn on data from various computer files to create a "new" computer file, the objection is readily met.

Example

Opposing Counsel: Objection, the videotape that is the exhibit is not the original document as required under the rules.

Counsel: We can qualify the exhibit under the original document rules, Your Honor. Exhibit 98 is a videotape of the computer animation. For purposes of displaying the animation in court this morning, we will use Exhibit 98A, a duplicate version of the animation which has been put on a computer storage system. I can qualify both. (*To the witness*) Mr. Jannsen, was the data that you collected from various sources combined into one data file?

A. It was initially combined into three files: the first controls the relative size and shape of the objects; the second controls the texture and color of the objects; the third controls the positioning of the objects. Then, when the animation was completed, the contents of the three files were merged into one file.

Q. Does the final merged file constitute the animation itself?

A. Yes.

Q. How is the animation transferred from the final merged computer file to the videotape?

A. The computer files are encoded to a television video format and recorded onto videotape.

Q. Is the videotape an accurate re-recording of the animation?

A. Yes.

Q. Does the output from the videotape to a television monitor reflect the data accurately?

A. Yes.

Q. How is the animation transferred to the computer storage medium from which it is displayed on the monitors we have in this courtroom?

A. We transfer an exact duplicate of the computer file from the hard disk on the computer with which the animation was created to a digital disk.

Q. Is the process of transferring the file a re-recording?

A. Yes.

Q. Does this re-recording accurately reproduce the original?

A. Yes.

Q. Does the output from the digital video disk to the video monitor reflect the data accurately?

A. Yes.

Q. Is the animation that is Exhibit 98 a summary of the contents of voluminous writings, recordings, and photographs?

A. Yes.

Q. Are the data you used available to be produced in this courtroom?

A. Yes, they are.

Q. Have these data been made available to Mr. Owens, counsel for the defendant?

A. Yes, they have. We produced all the data for them more than three months ago.

Q. Your Honor, we offer Exhibit 98 in evidence. This exhibit qualifies as a duplicate under Rule 1001(4). The videotape is a duplicate because it is a re-recording by a technique that accurately reproduces the original. The computer files on the digital video disk used to display the animation are also a duplicate of the original animation files.

The exhibit also qualifies under Rule 1006. It is a summary of the contents of voluminous documents, all of these documents were turned over to counsel, and the documents are available in court.

Under either Rule 1001 or Rule 1006, the original document objection is overcome.

Court *(to opposing counsel)*: Are you prepared to make a showing of a genuine question as to the authenticity of the original?

Opposing Counsel: No, we concede that the original is what it has been represented to be by the expert. But we contend that it is unfair under the circumstances to admit the duplicate, which is the videotape in lieu of the original. They are not actually using the videotape to display the animation in court. We think that we need the original computer files.

Counsel: We have delivered copies of the original computer files to opposing counsel in discovery. We are not under any requirement to mark the computer disks containing these duplicates as an exhibit during our case. If opposing counsel wants them marked, they should do so in their case. We have marked the videotape as a convenient way to put the animation into the record of this case.

Court: What is it about the display from the computer they have here as compared to the display from the original computer that is unfair? The originals are available.

Opposing Counsel: The videotape gives the impression that this animation is a tangible object. It is just a bunch of computer files. The jury should know that from the outset.

Court: You can bring that out on cross-examination. Overruled.

Policy objections

Serious challenges to a computer animation may be available under Rule 403 which sets out the policy objections.

An objection to unfair prejudice is available if the completed animation, the underlying computer files, and the data used in construction of the animation are not turned over in discovery sufficiently in advance of trial. See discussion in Section 8.3.1 on pretrial disclosure. It is not fair to provide an opponent a complicated computer-generated exhibit in a time frame too short to allow effective cross-examination. This objection may also be phrased as "surprise."

An objection to confusion or misleading the jury is available if the labels on the animation are argumentative or substantially incorrect, the assumptions used in making the animation result in a representation that could lead the jury to misunderstand "the real thing," the colors displayed on the animation are confusing when compared to the colors on the thing at issue, or any other aspect of the animation is suggestive of something that is demonstrably not so. The judge has a great deal of discretion as to an objection on these grounds, so it is better to flush these out in pretrial proceedings, if possible, when sufficient time remains to change the animation or persuade the court.

An objection to undue delay and waste of time is sometimes raised when there is the prospect of lengthy proceedings at trial to resolve objections. This should not succeed, however, as the foundation for a computer animation is no more complex than for expert testimony of other types.

An objection to needless presentation of cumulative evidence can be a problem if there already has been quite a lot of testimony about the subject matter of the animation at the time the animation is offered in evidence. To guard against this, the trial plan should call for a relatively early appearance for the animation.

8.3.4 Production

The computer animation has great versatility as a litigation tool. It offers the lawyer flexibility in displaying the theory of the case. As new data appear in the case or the assumptions change, the animation can show quickly the effect on the outcome. Animations are also a very useful tool in settlement. They help the other side literally see the points that you would make at trial.

The cost of computer animations, once quite high, has been decreasing dramatically as new hardware and software make the engineering job of constructing the animation easier. A good expert can provide an animation that will fit the litigation budget. It may be a spare, low cost, wire frame with none of the fancy colors, shadings, or details of a more expensive animation. If the initial version produces the necessary assistance for the case, it can be used "as is" or a decision can be made to expand the budget to incorporate a few more features that would make it even stronger. Most experts who are experienced in producing animations can show you a variety of options from their collection of past work. See Section 9.7 on working with specialists to create trial exhibits.

Once the animation is constructed, you can "play" it from any angle, observing the impact, for example, from above, behind, to one side, to see if all angles comport with your theory. The computer does this by using mathematical calculations to rearrange the image on the screen as it would appear if viewed from different angles. In the process of making decisions on how best to display the animation, you will need to consider which angle of view is best for the case.

Like a static exhibit, labels at critical points in the animation can help to focus the jury's attention on important points. The computer's color palette can color any part of the model for emphasis. The computer can combine the animation with photographs of the real thing (see

Section 6.1), static diagrams (see Section 4.2), or excerpts from documents (see Section 2.1) to explain the issues. If the scene of the accident has changed, the animation can reproduce the scene as it is now (shown in photographs) and can then rearrange things to show how it was at the time of the events in issue.

The easiest way to display an animation in the courtroom is to have the animation put on videotape. The computer file containing the animation is output to a standard video encoding device and is recorded by a professional video recording machine. A videotape player is relatively inexpensive, stable, and easy to operate. It has limitations, however, because it is difficult to move to particular segments accurately, and to "freeze" a particular image in a stable fashion so that the expert can explain a point without rushing. See Section 6.3 and Section 9.5.

Alternatively, a digital system can "play" the computer file directly. See Section 9.6. Computer controls use random access to find any segment of the animation almost instantly and can isolate any frame for the required period of time with no degradation in image quality. Animation files are very large and require substantial computer storage. If they contain motion, they require high performance video capability. A digital video disk with its large capacity and very high speed can display computer animations very effectively. Hard disk or optical disk storage has the required speed, but one gigabyte will accommodate only five to six minutes of animation. A laserdisc player has the required speed and one laserdisc will accommodate about 20 minutes of animation, so it was the storage medium of choice for longer animations until digital disk became available. A CD-ROM player, except very high end equipment, does not have the required speed and will produce a jerky motion. A CD-ROM disk also has more limited storage capacity.

8.3.5 Tactics

A computer animation is an extraordinarily powerful tool as evidence. Although it is constructed by an expert with the specific purpose of influencing a jury toward a particular conclusion, most jurors feel more comfortable with a computer animation showing a conclusion than with expert testimony orally describing a conclusion. With an animation, jurors feel that they are making up their own minds. With expert testimony, jurors feel that they are being told what to think.

Given the very significant impact of a computer animation, you should anticipate that your opponent will exercise the full range of objections. To avoid long delays at trial and possible surprises as to what the court will require by way of foundation, consider getting a ruling on admissibility in pretrial proceedings. This can be sought by a pretrial motion in limine to admit the computer animation and a hearing at which the expert's affidavit or live testimony is considered.

On occasion, there may be two alternative theories about the event at issue, such as the cause of a fire. An animation can show how both theories would have led to the same or similar results. An animation can also contrast proper procedure with faulty procedure. If there are varying accounts of what happened, sometimes you can display why your opponent's theory is wrong by putting their assumptions into the animation and showing the resulting images.

You should also anticipate that your opponent will hire an expert to work with the computer files you have provided with respect to the animation and to change them in some way to assist in cross-examination. Although it takes a great deal of work to create an animation, it takes much less time and effort to modify an existing animation. You will need to ensure that any modifications to the animation to be used in cross-examination are not a surprise to your expert. There may be gross errors in your opponent's manipulation of your animation, but your expert may not be able to defend against them adequately without adequate time to examine the computer files carefully.

Handling a computer animation in a courtroom setting requires an easy familiarity with the display equipment and an ability to get quickly from one point to another without difficulty. Either the lawyer or the expert witness can be in charge of the display, but a good deal of practice is helpful to a smooth presentation. See Section 9.5 (electronic equipment) and Section 9.6 (computer equipment) for details on presenting animation exhibits.

ENDNOTE

1. *Manual for Complex Litigation* §21.446 (Federal Judicial Center 2d ed., 1995).

CHAPTER 9

EQUIPMENT, MATERIALS, AND TECHNIQUES FOR DISPLAYING EXHIBITS

The trial lawyer must create an interesting and well-paced presentation that is easy to understand. To do this, the lawyer needs to understand some fundamentals of design and the basic technology alternatives. The trial lawyer's involvement in the actual production of exhibits or operation of technical equipment in the courtroom varies depending on individual preferences and technical proficiency. However, anyone who has responsibility for a trial must make the critical decisions and direct the overall effort.

The traditional way to display exhibits to the jury is to hand the exhibit to the first juror and have that person pass it hand to hand down the row until all the jurors have had a chance to see it. That method can be effective with some kinds of physical objects or photographs. See discussion in Section 1.4.9. There are important drawbacks to this technique, however. Jurors each have only a very short time to examine the exhibit before passing it to the next person. They cannot listen effectively to a witness while passing exhibits from hand to hand. The lawyer either has to stop while the jury examines the exhibit or take the risk that jurors will miss part of the witness's presentation. Most important, you cannot control the jurors' attention by focusing them on the part of the exhibit about which your witness or expert is testifying. Without this focus, people tend to give their attention to the area of an exhibit most familiar and comfortable to them. This area may be totally beside the point of your presentation. This chapter catalogs the alternative methods available for the display of important exhibits.[1]

Alternatives for displaying exhibits to the jury have accumulated gradually over the years driven by the need to save time and by the more complicated concepts about which jurors are asked to make decisions. Section 9.1 discusses the four general options for displaying exhibits at trial and the factors that affect the choice of the "backbone system" with which most exhibits will be displayed. The trial lawyer, who bears responsibility for presenting the client's case in the most persuasive manner permitted under the rules, must decide which of the available alternatives to use in a particular courtroom. Section 9.2 discusses factors that affect the display of all types of exhibits. Section 9.3, Section 9.4, Section 9.5, and Section 9.6 give guidance with respect to each of the four options. Unfortunately, lawyers are often not good judges of the effectiveness of exhibits. Graphic arts specialists can be of great assistance in this regard because they focus on the exhibit's message, not the fine points of the case. Suggestions on how to use these firms effectively are set out in Section 9.7. The ultimate test, however, is with a focus group of lay people from the general population from which the jury will be drawn. Section 9.8 discusses the use of focus groups for evaluating exhibits.

9.1 DECIDING ON THE BACKBONE SYSTEM FOR DISPLAYING EXHIBITS

Early in the trial planning, you will need to decide on the backbone system for displaying exhibits in the courtroom. To some extent, the physical layout of the courtroom and the personal preferences of the judge will limit your options. Your opponent may seek competitive advantage by trying to force agreement on a common system for displaying exhibits. You will also have to take into account the budget for the case and any time limits imposed by the court. The needs of the case must predominate, however, and increasingly those needs will demand more technology for better and more effective exhibit displays.

9.1.1 An Overview of the Four Options

Your backbone system for displaying exhibits is the medium through which you will display most of the exhibits to the judge and jury. You may use two or three of the four options during the course of the trial, but the backbone system does most of the work. The backbone system also has the most influence on your cost, flexibility, trial time, and impact.

Digital system

A digital display system is run by a computer that transmits images to a video monitor for display. A computer can deal only with materials in digital form, which means that the information has been processed so that it is represented by digits or numbers. When you select a computer (or digital) display system as the backbone for courtroom presentations, all of your exhibits must be converted to digital form. Exhibits in paper or hard copy form, such as documents, maps, drawings, diagrams, photographs, and x-rays, are converted to digital form using a scanner. Exhibits in electronic (or analog) form such as videotapes or sound recordings are converted to digital form using a specialized analog to digital converter. Some exhibits, such as computer-generated documents, drawings, simulations, and animations already exist in digital form and do not need to be converted. The digital images are stored on a hard disk, an optical disk, a laserdisc, a CD-ROM, a digital video disk, or other storage medium that can be accessed by the computer.

Electronic system

An electronic system is run by a videotape player, a laserdisc player, or a visual presenter (also called a visualizer or document camera), all of which transmit images to a television monitor for display. A television monitor can deal only with materials in analog form. A videotape player, a visual presenter, or a television camera operate with analog signals and can transmit directly to a television monitor. Anything that can be put within range of a television camera, such as documents, maps, drawings, diagrams, photographs, and x-rays, can be displayed in an analog system. An audiotape player also transmits information in analog form and sound tapes can be played with the speakers on the television monitor or with separate high fidelity speakers. A computer's digital output must be converted to analog form, usually by a digital scan converter, before it can be displayed on a television monitor. Converting digital signals to analog format usually degrades the image quality, which may be a more significant issue for document exhibits than for graphics. Digital exhibits are generally better displayed on digital video monitors.

Projector screen system

A projector screen system is run by some type of optical projector that enlarges an image and projects it onto a fabric screen, wall surface, or other available surface. Optical projectors can deal only with materials in film or paper format. They use lenses, light sources, and reflective surfaces to transmit the enlarged image to the screen or other viewing surface. Projector screen systems usually operate with manual controls and sometimes require the room lights to be dimmed.

Paper graphics system

A paper graphics system uses paper copies displayed directly by passing them to the jury or in enlarged format on an easel or exhibit frame. It also includes sketches and notes made on a large sketch pad hung on an easel or made on a blackboard or whiteboard in the courtroom. This is the traditional method for displaying exhibits in the courtroom, and all courtrooms accommodate this method. The equipment includes copier machines, poster enlargement equipment, photographic enlargement processes, and various equipment used by graphic arts firms to create static exhibits.

9.1.2 Factors to Consider

In deciding on your backbone system, you will need to think about the principal factors that determine the availability and effectiveness of exhibit displays. If you can assess these factors and make this decision early in the case, you will have a competitive advantage over your opponent. You will also have the best opportunity to lower your client's costs, maximize the impact of your exhibits, and adapt your personal style to the extent necessary.

The court's discretion

Judges have almost total discretion about how exhibits are presented in their courtroom. Some judges will embrace electronic and digital technology because it saves time. Others will reject it because they fear a glitch will happen that will mean the trial must stop until the equipment is repaired. In some jurisdictions, courtroom demonstration projects will have paved the way for high tech equipment. If a judge has formed an impression that trial lawyers gain an unfair advantage through technology, he or she may want a single system open to both sides. You cannot assume that a particular display system will be available just because you decide it is right for the case. Even relatively low tech equipment, such as an exhibit frame, may be totally new to a judge and require careful consideration before he or she grants permission for its use.

In some jurisdictions, judges worry about the state of the record if an electronic or digital system incorporates drawing and marking capability. They want to have a record of everything the jury sees on the monitor, even though they would not hesitate for a second in allowing a lawyer to erase a sketch from a blackboard without making a photo of it. When these concerns are raised, you will need to know if the system you propose has recording capability. Most electronic or digital systems have an output line that facilitates videotaping, printing, or storing any marks or other additions by the lawyer made during the presentation to the jury.

You need to treat a judge's decision about the backbone system you plan to use with the same seriousness you would treat a dispositive motion. Find out what the judge has experienced in previous trials; research the kinds of equipment that have been used in other courtrooms in the same building; inquire about demonstration projects or judge education efforts going on in the jurisdiction. Raise the question about options with respect to exhibit display systems at an early conference with the court. Make sure you know the benefits of using new systems from the court's point of view. Prepare a short memorandum if necessary.

Some lawyers hesitate to discuss electronic systems or digital systems with the court at an early point in the pretrial proceedings for fear of giving up a competitive advantage to their opponent. Others are reluctant to commit to a particular system early in the case preparation process because they think the case will settle. The benefits from delay in either competitive advantage or cost saving are very small. Most trial lawyers have read about all four options even if they have never tried the higher end systems. You will not be giving away any state secrets by letting the judge know you might use a particular backbone system and inquiring whether the court has any reservations. Settlement prospects increase with better control over exhibits; and the agility with which you can go to trial if settlement does not materialize increases exponentially if you have included the exhibit display system in your case planning.

The physical layout of the courtroom

Visit the courtroom where the case will be tried to assess the physical layout and the limitations that may be imposed on your choice of a backbone system for displaying exhibits. Nothing replaces your first hand view. Sit in each position in the courtroom—jury, judge, and counsel—to determine how a system will "play" in that particular location.

Estimate the distances between the bench, counsel table, and the jury box. Figure out how much working space you will have for easels, exhibit frames, special tables for projectors, computers, and other equipment. In some courtrooms, for example, it may be possible to place the jury monitor on the floor, tilted upward to the jurors' view. This depends on the amount of space in the well and the height of the jury rail. Use the various categories of exhibits in this book as a checklist. Make a tentative assessment about where the equipment would be placed. Ask the clerk whether lawyers have used this kind of equipment in this courtroom before. Check on storage space and whether it is locked, so you know if you have to cart exhibits and equipment back and forth to the courthouse every day.

You should look at lighting, both natural lighting from windows and artificial lighting from ceiling or other fixtures. If the windows are behind the jury box, there will be a glare on any monitors placed in front of the jury box. Overhead lights directly above a monitor will produce the same effect. If the windows do not have shades, dimming the lights for a projector screen system is probably not an option.

Check all the electrical outlets. Do not assume that all outlets work. Courthouse maintenance rarely meets expectations. Think about how the cabling, wiring, and electrical cords would be put down so as to minimize disruption to the operation of the courtroom. If the courtroom has only one outlet, find out from the maintenance department whether there is another nearby outlet from which an extension could be run. It is very difficult to deal with a digital or electronic backbone system when you have only one outlet.

The logistics of supporting a trial in a particular courtroom may be complex, depending on the length of the trial and the number of exhibits. Give consideration to using a courtroom media professional who can develop a courtroom presentation strategy, advise on appropriate technology, and provide a catalog of the necessary infrastructure support for the system you choose. See Appendix B, Part II. There are many hidden costs in the support work for a complicated trial. Your client will benefit if these costs are known from the outset. The assessment of an expert is insurance against exhibits that do not work in a specific courtroom.

The number and type of exhibits

If yours is a one-day case about a one-page contract, a paper graphics system serves well. You can use blowups of the relevant provisions of the contract and testimony aids made into poster-sized exhibits to help explain damages. An easel will display everything you need, and an exhibit frame might be helpful if you want to take apart the contract language to show the meaning that you are urging the jury to accept.

If you know that you will present videotapes of depositions because one or more witnesses are not available to testify at trial, then you will need either a television or video monitor. If a monitor is installed for one purpose, it may make sense to use it for many other purposes. This might lead you to an electronic or digital backbone system.

When you estimate that the trial will involve hundreds of documentary exhibits, you may want to use a digital system for speed and convenience, combined with some paper graphics exhibits for emphasis. The digital system enables you to move from one document to another with a minimum of disruption. It decreases trial time from 20 percent to 40 percent and helps ensure that the jurors focus on the specific language being drawn to their attention. Having all your exhibits on a digital system also gives you the maximum flexibility for opening statements and closing arguments. Paper graphics exhibits are often combined with a digital backbone system to provide the "big picture." Overview charts on an easel keep jurors grounded in the context of what they are seeing on the monitors.

An expert witness may prefer a particular exhibit display system. The electronic system using a visual presenter or visualizer provides the flexibility to shift control of the system from the witness to the lawyer so that the expert can control his or her own testimony aids but the lawyer can control the testimony aids for lay witnesses. Some experts are most comfortable with slide presentations because they use them in their classrooms. Others like overhead projectors. Technical experts may be supported by computer animations, in which case they will want to use an electronic or digital system. If the expert's testimony is a significant part of the case, you may want to adopt that display system for the rest of the case.

Your opponent's demands

If you use any of the four options for displaying exhibits, the court may require that a single system be available to both sides. This avoids cluttering the courtroom with competing equipment, and some judges believe it gives each side fair access to the technology. If you propose the use of particular equipment, you should be prepared to accede promptly, on fair terms, to any request by the other side for access to the equipment. Making the first proposal puts you in an advantageous position with respect to the type of equipment and the ground rules for its use. In fact, access to equipment never gives the other side any significant advantage unless they are thoroughly prepared to use it as an integral part of presenting their case.

When you are using a paper graphics system, you may have an easel, exhibit frame, or whiteboard in the courtroom. This equipment is discussed in Section 9.3. The only ground rules you need to establish for an exhibit frame are that the materials put on it be of an appropriate weight. Heavy exhibits may fall off the Velcro backing and may cause the Velcro backing itself to detach from the frame. A whiteboard usually requires dry ink markers; permanent markers will damage its surface and make it unusable. You need to extract a promise to use only the correct markers and to replace the unit if the wrong markers are used. If you are renting the equipment, the court will usually require your opponent to shoulder half the cost. If you own the equipment, however, the court sometimes regards it as a professional courtesy to allow the other side to use the equipment without reimbursement.

If you are using a projector screen system, the only ground rule relates to the carousels for the slide projector. In order to keep the slide exhibits for each side in order, you should request your opponent to supply his or her own carousel. See Section 9.4. If you have rented the equipment, you may ask for reimbursement of half the rental and the cost of any technician employed to set up or operate the equipment.

An electronic system is more complicated to install, and the court may wish to exercise more control. If there are monitors for the judge and counsel, you may want to suggest that they be connected to a switcher so that an exhibit can be displayed only on these monitors and not on the jury's monitor while objections are being considered. A debate usually arises about control of the switch. Some judges leave this to examining counsel. Other judges want the switch at the bench or in the hands of the bailiff. A videotape player, with its associated cabling and TV monitor, is standard equipment that should raise no special issues. If your opponent is supplying the equipment, however, you will need to be attentive to quality. Some of the less expensive player units have poor freeze-frame capability, and the controls are not very well marked. See Section 9.5. The TV monitor for the jury may be too small and have poor resolution. You should specify that the wiring and key monitors have S-video capability in order to have high video quality. Because a visual presenter is so easy to learn to operate and offers such a quantum increase in capability, defendants often wait to install the equipment until the plaintiff rests. If you are sharing a visual presenter with your opponent, make sure it has the capability you need. Not all visualizers can control video, provide projection adequate for x-rays, and support split screen capability. Some dealers do not offer on-site service, which can be disastrous when the equipment breaks down in the midst of trial. Specialists who are in the business of supplying equipment for trials provide better service. See listing in Appendix B.

A digital system raises the most difficult protocol issues. The simplest system uses one computer, equipped with a hard disk and a CD-ROM player, connected to the required number of high resolution video monitors. All of the exhibits for both sides may be put onto one CD or each side may supply their own CD containing their exhibits. If the court permits only one system, the equipment is neutral territory, sometimes operated by the bailiff or a neutral contractor not an employee of either party. A much better alternative is a common set of monitors and cabling connected to individual computers that each side supplies for itself. Lawyers may have different preferences as to the storage system. See Section 9.6.2. The CD player is the slowest alternative for displaying exhibits in a digital system. An optical disk will be several times faster than the CD, and the computer's hard disk will be faster than the optical disk. The storage speed is not so important with documents, but becomes crucial with digitized video that one side may use and the other side may not. Moreover, computer systems can be optimized in numerous ways that provide advantages in displaying exhibits. Lawyers may also have different preferences as to the control system. See Section 9.6.3. Having a common set of monitors but individual computers allows each side to optimize the computer in its own particular way, to use its own software, and to mark the controls in the way best suited to its purposes. When plaintiff's counsel is examining a witness, plaintiff's computer system is switched into the monitor system and the display is controlled from that computer. When defendant's counsel cross-examines, defendant's computer system is switched into the monitor system and its operator controls the display of exhibits.

Control of the computer equipment is a high priority item if you plan to use a digital backbone system for any kind of complicated display. You should be prepared to argue to the court why having common monitors but individual computer systems is a fair method. Some judges have had experience with a relatively low tech digital trial in which both sides showed up with individual CD-ROM disks containing their exhibits, and both CDs could be played on a common system. If that is the court's view of a "digital trial," you will be called upon to explain why you need something else. In fact, a computer system used at trial must be "idiot proof" and totally redundant. The interface between the trial lawyer and the computer system must be very simple so that there are no computer commands, mouse clicks, or anything else that distracts from the trial lawyer's focus on the witness testimony. Because you will lose control of all your exhibits if the computer system crashes during trial, you need to have a totally redundant backup system available in the courtroom at all times. No courtroom common system will provide this level of support.

Your client's budget

Lawyers often assume that the selection of a backbone exhibit display system will be dominated by cost considerations. That is usually not the case. The lower end systems involve less equipment and lower cost units, but they are not necessarily cheaper overall because the cost per exhibit can be quite high. The higher end systems involve more equipment and higher cost units, but this equipment can be rented rather than purchased and has a low cost per exhibit.

Costs for exhibits can vary enormously from place to place depending on the availability of experienced suppliers with up-to-date equipment and on local price structures. In addition, some lawyers plan efficiently and get the exhibit right the first time; others require several tries until they get what they want, making the cost of the finished exhibit considerably higher. However, once you have decided what types of exhibits might be effective for a particular trial, the information provided in this book should make it possible to get a quick, accurate price quote and this, in turn, will enable you to make realistic decisions about priorities and possible tradeoffs among the types of exhibits that might be used. The list in Appendix B sets out some of the firms specializing in creating exhibits for lawyers. They will provide examples of their work and summaries of their credentials to do the specific type of work necessary for a particular case. Choosing a firm or a person to do work on evidentiary exhibits should be done carefully with an eye toward both cost and capability. See Section 9.7.

In dealing with the costs for exhibit display systems, try to account for all costs including competitive advantage and time. Lawyers sometimes fail to consider the costs involved in having paralegals or clerks sorting through documents to find and copy exhibits, the costs inherent in a longer trial, and the very high costs of an increased risk of an adverse result.

For example, a construction case may involve 50 photographs that will be exhibits of the progress at the construction site.

- The lowest cost alternative is to make one set of 4 x 5" prints of these photographs to pass among the jury as the testimony proceeds. That results in a low unit cost for 50 exhibits, but a higher risk that the jurors will not see or understand the construction defects about which the expert is testifying. Jurors cannot all look at a particular photograph at once, and they may miss the point if they do not both see and hear the information at the same time.

- An alternative is to obtain 10 x 12" or 11 x 14" enlargements and pass those enlarged prints to the jury. This entails a higher unit cost, and somewhat better juror comprehension, but still presents a significant risk that the information will not be communicated very well.

- Another alternative is to make poster-sized enlargements that are 30 x 40" or 40 x 60" mounted on foamboard or some other backing material that can be set on an easel or used with an exhibit frame so the expert can point to the specific defect, and the jurors can all see it at the same time. Making 50 enlargements of this size is a very substantial increase in cost, but produces a much better learning experience for the jurors. Handling and storing 50 large exhibits in the courtroom, however, is time consuming and may result in mixups.

- The 50 photographs can be enlarged to 6 x 8' or 8 x 12' by using a projector screen system, with a slide projector, an overhead projector, or an opaque projector. Each 4 x 5" color photograph is put, in turn, on the viewing surface of the projector or 50 slides are prepared and installed in a carousel for a slide projector. The rental of the projector and screen should be much less than the cost of poster-sized enlargements. The larger image on the screen gives the expert an opportunity to point to the specific aspects he or she is talking about, but these projection systems cause shadows when pointers are used, blocking out some of the photo. Once the projection system is installed, it becomes available for other standard sized documentary exhibits, thus spreading the cost.

- The 50 photographs can be displayed electronically, using a visual presenter (also called a visualizer or document camera). The small 4 x 5" color photos are put on the visual presenter's viewing surface, under the TV camera, and an enlargement appears on a large TV monitor. The visual presenter allows the expert to zoom in and enlarge a portion of the photo to see particular details. The expert can now also draw or mark with a light pen similar to those used by sports commentators to make x's and o's appear on the TV screen. The rental of the visual presenter and monitor should be about the same as the cost of the 50 poster enlargements. But with the visual presenter, the expert has much more capability to explain the exhibit. And the visual presenter can be used to present other types of exhibits as well, including documents, videotapes, x-rays, and computer-generated materials converted from digital format, thus lowering the per unit cost.

- Another alternative is to scan the 50 photographs into digital form using a high resolution color scanner. The digital files, controlled by a computer, can be displayed in enlarged format on a large video monitor. The rental of the computer system will cost considerably more than the 50 poster enlargements. But the computer system allows you to store as well as present all forms of exhibits except physical objects and substances. When you factor in the cost savings from the storage as well as the presentation, the per unit cost of this display system usually competes favorably with the other options.

You will want to look carefully at each of the four options as soon as you have some overall estimate of the number and type of exhibits required for the case. Work up a basic cost estimate for the various options you are considering. You may want to do a risk analysis to help quantify the risk associated with failure to win particular issues.

9.1.3 Your Personal Courtroom Style

Your own personal comfort level with each of the four options also plays an important role in your assessment of the display system best suited for the case. Your personality and style of trial management may also affect your choice. A detailed treatment of this subject is beyond the scope of this book because it involves so many of the factors that affect the personal effectiveness of individual lawyers before judges and juries.[2] A few of the key considerations are suggested below.

Energy level and pace

Your personal style may be high energy and very warm or lower energy and calm or anything in between. The paper graphics display system accommodates the personal style of the high energy, very warm personality. The paper displays do not compete with the lawyer for the jurors' attention. They are there when called upon, but they usually do not intrude. The digital display system is best adapted to the lower energy, calm personality. A digital trial is full of images flashing on the screen. It feels to jurors like a high-speed chase movie compared to one about Walden Pond.

Of course, any personal style can be turned up or down to some extent to accommodate the needs of the case. You simply need to be aware that if you are a "hot" personality and you adopt a "hot" medium, like television, to display your exhibits, the resulting atmosphere in the courtroom may turn some jurors off. Similarly, if you talk fast, and you adopt a "slow" medium, like paper graphics, jurors may find your presentation more comprehensible. The suspicious ones will be less likely to think you are rushing something past them.

Establishing credibility

Lawyers have different styles for establishing their own credibility with a jury and different intuitions about the pace at which this can best be done in the courtroom. The more technology you use, the earlier you will have to establish credibility with the jury. The jury will need to understand who you are and what you stand for—face to face—before they will pay close attention to and accept exhibits flashed at them from a monitor. If the jury accepts you as credible and real, then anything you show them will be viewed within the context of this personal credibility you have established.

Tolerance for complexity

The more technology you use, the more you will need the balance of low tech exhibits to help establish an overview and to make sure the jury has a context into which to fit what they are shown on the monitor. This makes your job in the courtroom more complex. You need to be sure you can change the pace of the presentation at regular intervals to enhance the jury's attention and learning. You need to shift from the exhibits flashed on the monitor to a list you do on your sketch pad mounted on an easel and then go back to more exhibits on the monitor. This keeps your presentation from becoming monotonous and mind numbing. You need to master not only the digital or electronic system, but the requirements of good presentation with a paper graphics system as well. You do not get rid of the easel, foamboard enlargements, sketch pad, and other basic tools by going to a high end digital system. You get an overall system that is more persuasive, faster, and more powerful, but more complex as well. Your trial management system needs to be stronger; your trial team needs to be better trained and more experienced; and you need to have the necessary patience and command presence to get by the glitches that inevitably will occur.

Technophobia

Your attitude toward technology shows in a courtroom. If you hate computers, it will be difficult for you to project respect, warmth, and confidence in your exhibits that reside in a computer system. You might want to use an electronic system instead as you will probably have an easier time feeling comfortable with a visual presenter. If, every time you touch a piece of display equipment, you act as if you expect it to cause a disaster, the jurors will receive a negative message. If you cannot get comfortable with the technology, you probably should elect to stick with a paper graphics system.

Relying on others

The higher you get up the technology chain, the more control you must cede to others. Ceding control sounds easy, but for some lawyers it affects their courtroom style in uncomfortable ways.

At the lowest rung on the technology chain, the principal trial lawyer is in control of everything that happens in the courtroom. He or she puts the exhibits on the easel for examining the witness, physically points to the relevant portion of the exhibit displayed, and takes the exhibit back to its assigned place when it is no longer needed. The equipment, such as an easel or exhibit frame, is typically owned by the lawyer or law firm and used in many trials. Exhibits are made by processes that can be understood thoroughly by the least technologically proficient lawyer so that the reasonableness of lead time and cost is readily assessed.

At mid-level, with a projector screen system or an electronic system, the equipment can also be used directly by the lead trial lawyer, although it is usually advisable to have someone else assigned to help with the equipment. The equipment for these systems may be owned by the law firm or rented for a particular trial. The overhead projector, slide projector, and opaque projector have only two controls: the on-off switch and the focus. Once those are fixed, the lead trial lawyer can put exhibits on or take them off the projector without much disruption in concentration. Similarly, a visual presenter has only three controls: the on-off switch, the focus, and the zoom-in control. Training time is minimal. A hands-on lawyer should have no difficulty with this technology. A videotape player and laserdisc player require additional controls to get to the right spot on the tape or disk to display what the lawyer is looking for. A bar code system for running a laserdisc player is easy for the trial lawyer to operate. It involves simple point-and-shoot operations with the bar code reader. A videotape player has controls with which the trial lawyer may have considerable comfort from home or office use.

At the top rung, with a digital system, it is unlikely that you will want to own the equipment. Lawyers and law firms are not in the technology business, and it is very difficult for them to keep up with the latest equipment. You will probably rent a system for a particular trial. In this way, you will be able to avoid the capital cost and also assign the entire cost of using the system where it belongs, with the client for whose benefit it is being operated. But, in so doing, you will be relying heavily on the skill and ability of your supplier. Similarly, it is very difficult for the principal trial lawyer to handle a computer-driven display system, although some do. If you go to a digital system, you will almost always want to have a dedicated operator for the system. That operator may be supplied by the firm from whom you rented the equipment or it may be one of your paralegals who has been trained by your supplier. If that person does not operate the system correctly, Exhibit 64 will not appear when you ask for it. You may not be comfortable with putting this control over your exhibits in the hands of a technician.

Tolerance for risk

The higher you get up the technology chain, the more risk you must assume and the greater the protective measures you must take. You may decide that you have enough to worry about in the courtroom without concerns about the redundancy of the system or the calamitous effects of a computer crash.

With a paper graphics system, you have no risk that the exhibits cannot be displayed. If you have gotten them done in time, they are with you in the courtroom and you can pull them out at any time. Of course, you may not be able to find them very conveniently, if you have a large number of exhibits, but you will have the comfort of knowing they are there somewhere. The principal risk in a paper graphics system is the time that it takes to make and modify exhibits. Enlargements and poster mounting may require that the exhibits be done at the shop of your graphic arts specialist. If you need to change an exhibit at the last minute, for your opening statement or closing argument, you may not be able to get the exhibit done in time.

With a projector screen system, the only technical risk is that the projector will blow a light bulb, so you will need to have a spare and know how to install it. The remaining parts of the projectors and screens are sturdy mechanical and electrical systems that rarely fail to perform. If there is an outlet in the courtroom and you know how to plug in the projector, you can be assured that your exhibits will be displayed. Your backup is a rental firm that can deliver substitute equipment within a few hours.

With an electronic system, you have increased the technical risk considerably. The cables from the source equipment (videotape player or visualizer) may not operate properly. The monitor may produce a fuzzy image or be subject to interference. And the videotape player or the camera in the visualizer equipment may break down. This equipment is all quite common and reliable, however, so if you have a good supplier you can get a replacement for almost anything in an hour. Be sure you have those arrangements in place because, although you will have control over the physical exhibits (the documents, things, and tapes), you will be unable to display them as you had planned until replacements arrive.

With a digital system, you have the most technical risk. If the system does not operate properly, you cannot locate or display any of your exhibits. You will lose all control over your exhibits. And, particularly if the hard disk crashes, you will have no readily available alternative that can be set up in a few hours. The only acceptable way to meet this risk is to have a totally redundant computer system. That means two of everything with all of the computer files on both systems. A totally redundant system requires extensive testing every day to be sure everything in both the main system and the backup system is operating properly. Increased time and attention must be devoted to making sure that files are updated as necessary and that everything winds up on both systems. This may be more hassle than you want to accommodate.

Favored juror types

Every trial lawyer believes that there exists a certain juror type who is naturally attuned to the lawyer's every nuance. If only a sufficient number of these ideal persons could be found in the venire, every trial would be won. In selecting juries, you need to understand the vast differences in the generations and the sexes with respect to learning styles. For example, the baby boomers tend to be people oriented. They learned from teachers, read books and newspapers, and talk to their friends on the phone. The Generation X folks tend to be isolationists in some respects. They learned from audio and video, they watch a lot of television, and they communicate with their friends via the Internet. If you like to pick baby boomers as your jurors, you need to be more cautious in using extensive digital displays. These jurors need to be warmed up to this medium because they may think this is an excess like those they have heard or read about in other trials. If you like Generation X types on your juries, they will expect a multimedia presentation at trial because that is the way it was done in all the big-time trials they watched for hours on television. Women tend to be more concerned than men when images flash by on the screen. They are more anxious about their ability to retain and use what is presented at trial and become more worried when they think that information is appearing and disappearing faster than they can assimilate or examine it. The over-50 contingent may have a harder time reading screen displays than their younger colleagues, although they will be grateful if you use large type and make things easy to see from their seats. Factors like this are numerous, pervasive, and important to the success of your backbone display system. Most of these factors, however, can be overcome by careful presentation in your opening statement and attention to detail during the trial. The more technology you use, the more careful you must be not to leave anyone on the jury behind.

9.2 TECHNIQUES APPLICABLE TO ALL EXHIBITS

Certain techniques apply to nearly all exhibits, regardless of the system with which they are displayed. For planning purposes, consider the method by which the exhibit is created separately from the method by which it is displayed. Materials made by hand, for example artists' renditions, can be displayed by any of the four backbone systems. Materials generated by a digital system, for example by using computer graphics software to generate a pie chart, can also be displayed by any of the four backbone systems. This section deals with making rather than displaying exhibits. The factors discussed here will cause the exhibit to have more impact regardless of the system used to display it. You will need to make decisions on size that incorporate distance ratings and viewing angles; presentation factors such as titles, white space, typeface, and color; and design features like add-ons, take-aparts, and pop-outs. These are the factors that help make exhibits legible, understandable, and good vehicles for teaching the facts of the case. The factors for making successful exhibits specifically for one of the four backbone systems are described in Sections 9.3 through 9.6.

9.2.1   Size Factors and Enlargements

When working with exhibits to be displayed before the jury (rather than given to them as copies in their notebook or passed from hand to hand), you need something that is large enough to be seen easily by the judge and jury. It also needs to be of a size that will make an impact. Small things get lost in a large courtroom.

Distance rating

The design for each display exhibit should include a distance rating—the number of feet from the most distant reader with whom the exhibit may be used effectively. The typeface and type size must be readable from the back row of the jury box. Pick the approximate place in the courtroom where the exhibit will be displayed. Then calculate the distance from the juror who is farthest from that point. Write that distance on the back of the preliminary version of the exhibit so that you can test the final design for the enlarged version to determine that the written portion can be read and the graphics portion can be seen clearly from that distance. If you will not know until shortly before trial which courtroom will be used, pick a distance rating of at least 20 feet for your enlarged exhibits. It is better to have the print size a little large than too small.

Viewing angle

A sketch of the courtroom showing the distances from the jury box to the witness stand, the counsel table, and the judge's bench will allow you to plan where exhibits might be placed, should the court allow. The placement of exhibits must be at an angle close enough to 90 degrees (head on) to allow for easy viewing. The maximum and minimum angles will depend on lighting conditions in the courtroom and the equipment and materials used for displaying the exhibit. Someone should sit in the seats in the jury box that are farthest away from the exhibit to determine at what angle the exhibit becomes too difficult to see clearly. The placement of exhibits in the courtroom needs to be kept within a range of angles that permit each juror to read or view them without leaning out of normal position in his or her chair.

9.2.2 Presentation Factors

Every display exhibit should make use of standard advertising presentation features, the most important of which are amount of information, white space, titles and labels, typeface and type size, and color. Some guidelines which apply to most kinds of exhibits are set out below.

Amount of information

Limit each exhibit to a single image or point. The text material on the exhibit should be able to be comprehended in 30 seconds or less although you will normally leave it displayed much longer during your presentation. If the exhibit is a testimony aid that contains text, about 10 lines of printed text per exhibit is the maximum and the lines should be relatively short—about 30 to 35 letters per line. The presentation should have a consistent format for developing each point. Shifting layout and pattern too often will distract the fact-finder.

White space

The layout or design for the exhibit should include ample white space around the edges and between major parts of the message on the exhibit. This will help make the exhibit easier to read and understand.

Titles and labels

Each exhibit should have a short heading or title to identify it. The information identifying the exhibit should be presented in a spare style. Avoid adjectives and adverbs where possible. Edit the proposed text a number of times to reduce to the bare minimum the number of words used to express each idea. The heading needs sufficient white space around it to set it off properly.

Labels are needed if the exhibit has several aspects on which the jury is supposed to focus. For example, charts and graphs need labels on each axis and on the lines, bars, or pie slices that provide relevant information. The labels on other types of exhibits might identify the exhibit number, show relevant dates, describe the exhibit (as the insurance company's fire report, for example), or point out possible vulnerabilities of the document. The labels are usually displayed above the exhibit or below the exhibit. You may want to adopt a consistent style for all your exhibits. When you use electronic or digital systems, the label can stay with the image as long as it is displayed, or the label can be made to disappear after 30 seconds. Labels should be in a smaller type size than titles.

Typeface

Pick a typeface for titles, labels, or anything else you generate for an exhibit that has clean lines and will enlarge well. A typeface that is condensed or one that has very thin or fat letters will not be sufficiently legible. The space between letters and words is also important. There should be a standard space between words and between the end and beginning of sentences. If the exhibit will have several sizes of letters on it, they should all come from the same type family. Mixing styles presents a confusing image.

Color

Use color on exhibits to differentiate one point from another, to emphasize particular points, or to catch the fact-finder's attention with respect to the exhibit as a whole. Contrasts in color are important. Generally, do not use light colors together, or dark colors. White letters should not be put on light backgrounds or black letters on dark backgrounds. One expert advises[3] that the most legible color combinations are:

Lettering	Background
Black	Yellow
Black	White
Dark Green	White
Dark Blue	White
White	Dark Blue

The choice of a color combination, of course, varies with the actual shades of color used. Black letters on a deep yellow are less legible than dark blue on white. Black on white is actually the same as dark blue on white from a distance.

You can use color effectively in borders, dividing lines, blocks surrounding key words, and item markers. Use the most important color for the most important item in the graphic.

> Important colours [sic] are those with high intensities and are at the light end of the value scale. The pure hues—green yellow, yellow, yellow orange, orange, and orange red, all warm colours are considered more attention getting, especially when used in moderation

and when placed against a darker colour of low chroma [intensity or brightness]. Warm colours seem to advance while cool colours—red violet, violet, blue and blue green recede and should be reserved for backgrounds.[4]

Color is often important in linking exhibits together or helping to emphasize the logic of the presentation. For example, if a witness has a very long presentation to make, you can use a "summary exhibit" followed by "detail exhibits" and tied together by colors. The summary exhibit describes the overall subject broken down into component parts. Each component part has a heading or a border in a different color. One separate detail exhibit then deals with each of the components shown on the summary exhibit. The detail exhibit has the same color heading or border used for that subject on the summary exhibit. If the lawyer leaves the summary exhibit in place during his or her examination about each of the detail exhibits, the judge or jury will know at all times by quick reference to the color the part of the outline with which the witness is dealing.

For paper graphic systems and projector screen systems, color can be added to a black and white exhibit in the photographic process by using color printing techniques, by adhering transparent color films to the exhibit, or by using paint or colored markers. Color photographic processes are the most expensive. Transparent films require accurate hand work, but can be done relatively quickly by experienced graphic artists. One system that works well and is relatively inexpensive utilizes Pantone color films. These are translucent colored sheets with an adhesive backing. A piece is cut to fit the area to be colored and is pressed onto the surface. The printed copy underneath it shows through the color film. This system produces a neat, clean product and has relatively little glare. It is easily repaired in an emergency and colors can be matched to exhibits made at another place or time. Each Pantone color has a code number which allows exhibits produced in different areas of the country to have matching colors.

For electronic systems, color can be added with markers as the exhibit is examined on the visualizer. For example, text emphasized by the witness can be underlined in yellow. For digital systems, the computer system makes a full palette of colors available for highlighting any exhibit.

9.2.3 Design Features

At times, a design feature will help make a static exhibit more interesting and demonstrative of the point to be made. These design features are zoom-in, add-on, take-apart, and similar ways to make the exhibit say something by the way it is designed. These features can be implemented in a number of different ways depending upon the display system selected.

Zoom-in

If a portion of an exhibit has particular importance, a zoom-in can focus the jury on this portion as it relates to the whole. The zoom-in feature enlarges one area of the exhibit, usually with a border around it separating this area from the rest of the exhibit. The zoom-in can be active with an electronic or digital system where the equipment shows the process of enlarging a particular area, or it can be static with a paper graphic or projector screen display where the enlarged area is simply pasted onto one corner of the exhibit.

Add-on

You may want to emphasize how things relate to one another by adding to an exhibit or by taking the exhibit apart visually.

One method for add-on exhibits is to have a time line constructed by adding labels as the witness testifies. Or a photograph can be displayed and key words can be placed alongside as the witness makes points about the photo. Add-ons to enlarged photographs can help make key points. See Fig. 30 and Fig. 31.

Add-on exhibits are often useful in the cross-examination of an expert. You can take the expert's key table, for example, enlarge it, cover up one column or part of a column of the expert's numbers, and replace it with your own. During cross-examination, you can now force the expert to re-examine his own exhibit without keeping his exhibit before the judge and jury the whole time. You can alter his exhibit in a number of different ways and question him about a number of different variations or alternatives using only the materials sponsored by the lawyer. As the questioning proceeds, you can ask the expert to assume or (if already in evidence) to substitute the facts shown on each of the place-overs. Later, your own expert will testify to the accuracy or appropriateness of the facts on the place-over strips and, if successful, you can use the exhibit once again in final argument to demonstrate the flaws in the other side's theory.

Exhibits of this type may be marked for identification but need not have any foundation or any other evidentiary formalities. They are the lawyer's props to assist in the cross-examination and require no permission for their use. Opposing counsel may object to the use of exhibits like these as misleading, but if there is a legitimate objective in cross-examination, this should be easily overcome.

In paper graphic systems, add-on exhibits can be constructed using Velcro strips pasted unobtrusively on a foamboard exhibit. See Fig. 36. Later, small sections can be added to make a particular point. Each small section has a matching Velcro strip on its back side that will attach to the strip on the main board. The add-on exhibit can be displayed on an easel or an exhibit frame. Using Velcro makes the board reusable and presents a neat and orderly look.

In opaque projector screen systems, strips can be placed over the exhibit while it is being projected. In overhead projector systems, the lawyer marks the "add-on" information to the transparency using standard markers.

In electronic and digital systems, the lawyer can use a "light pen" to mark up the exhibit on the screen or can use the computer to change the appearance of the exhibit.

Take apart

Take-apart exhibits show the entire exhibit at the outset and then disassemble it to make a point. If you need to contrast one thing to another, you may want to have a part of the exhibit visually pop out showing, for example, what would have been, could have been, or should have been had your client been treated properly.

In paper graphic systems, Velcro strips can be used to create take-apart boards. Two pieces of foamboard are used for this kind of construction. The information is placed on the top board, which is cut into sections and fastened to the bottom board with Velcro strips. As the various sections are explained in testimony or oral argument, they can be lifted from the board, physically taken apart, and set out for display on a separate "holding" board nearby. See Fig. 37. As the testimony or argument proceeds, the pieces can be reassembled. You can also use this kind of take-apart board effectively with an exhibit frame. See Section 9.3.1. The main board is displayed on the exhibit frame by means of small pieces of Velcro attached to its backing, and the take-apart pieces are then set next to it by means of the small Velcro patches that are also attached to them. The exhibit frame is an easier method for dealing with this type of exhibit because all of its parts are kept in one area. See discussion of exhibit frames in Section 9.3.1.

Similar effects can be achieved with electronic and digital systems, using the computer's capability to cut and paste to achieve the necessary effect.

Write-as-you-go exhibits

In eliciting expert opinion about a variety of factors all of which led the expert to a particular conclusion, it may be useful to have a write-as-you-go exhibit. This kind of exhibit is set up so that as the expert gives "Yes" or "No" answers in response to questions about the interaction of various factors, those answers can be written in the appropriate place on the exhibit. The exhibit should be designed so that the pattern of "Yes" or "No" answers written on the exhibit helps make the point.

For example, four different chemicals were shipped to a warehouse and, because of faulty drums, some of the chemicals leaked, causing an explosion. Plaintiff wants to show that the fault had to be with XYZ Corporation that manufactures one of the chemicals. To negate other possibilities, plaintiff's board lists each of the four chemicals and the name of the manufacturer across the top of the exhibit and lists the various combinations (air, water, heat, cold, other chemicals) of things that could have happened down the left side of the exhibit. As the expert testifies that chemical #1, manufactured by ABC, could not explode when combined with air, the lawyer writes "No" in the appropriate block, and so on through this portion of the testimony creating a visual record of the testimony. After exploring each item and completing the chart, the expert gives his or her overall opinion.

Another example of write-as-you-go exhibits is the "report card." A chart is created with the key elements that were required to be accomplished or the key results that were to be attained. As you review each element, your expert is asked to rate or "grade" the other side's results. If designed correctly, a series of "D's" and "F's" will fill the report card and send a clear message of failure. This exhibit can be used in closing as a powerful visual summary of your expert's opinion.

With paper graphic systems, this kind of exhibit would be on a posterboard or sketch pad and the lawyer would mark on the exhibit with a marker pen. With projector screen systems, the lawyer would write on the film transparency on an overhead projector using special markers. With electronic or digital systems, the lawyer would use a light pen to create the effect of "writing" on the television or video monitor.

Flip charts

A series of related testimony aids can be presented as flip charts so that the lawyer turns the pages as new topics in the outline are reached.

In a paper graphics system, this can be done by putting each sheet on a piece of flexible paper and attaching all the sheets to a stiff backing. The stiff backing piece is mounted on a square frame easel. As the testimony proceeds, the sheets are "flipped" or turned over the top of the backing to expose the next sheet. A special easel is required so that the pages can be easily turned, and it is nevertheless still difficult to go backward and forward in the presentation.

In a projector screen system, this can be done by a series of slides or vuegraphs. In an electronic or digital system, the computer graphics capability can be used to simulate the turning of pages as each testimony aid comes up on the screen.

Juxtaposed documents

Jurors often have difficulty following the points lawyers and witnesses are making about the relationship between documentary exhibits. You can alleviate this problem by using a juxtaposed display.

In a paper graphics display system, put a large blank piece of stiff backing material, preferably 40 x 60", on an easel. Clip a copy of the first exhibit to the top left-hand side of the backing material. Write its exhibit number right below so the jury sees what you are talking about. List the points about the exhibit by writing them below the exhibit as the witness explains. Then clip the next exhibit to the top of the backing material some distance to the right. Write its exhibit number clearly below it, and then list the points made about this exhibit as the witness testifies. If you have a third document in this series, for example, continue the process. See example in Section 3.2.1.

In an electronic or digital system, use the split screen capability to display more than one document at once. Using this process, the jurors have a visual reference for each point that is being made and can follow the testimony more easily. Usually the jurors will have copies of the exhibits in their juror notebooks, and they can see more readily how you are using the exhibits as the testimony proceeds. If the court has allowed them to take notes, the more industrious of them will copy down what you have written, thus reinforcing it again.

9.3 PAPER GRAPHICS DISPLAYS

The paper graphics display system for exhibits is the traditional method that has been used in courtrooms for decades. It relies on simple equipment and inexpensive materials available from most office supply outlets.

9.3.1 Equipment

Lawyers use six types of equipment in paper graphics displays: easels, exhibit frames, poster generators, magnetic boards, whiteboards, and blackboards. Each has been used so many times that you are unlikely to face any limits imposed by courts.

Easels

Many courtrooms provide easels that are less than ideal for working with exhibits. Do not accept an easel just because it is the one that is on hand. A good easel can make the display of exhibits much smoother. The best type of easel is a simple lightweight model that can be folded up for easy carrying and storage when not in use.

Easels come in three-legged and four-legged models. See Fig. 38. The three-legged models are generally lighter and less obtrusive than the four-legged models. However, four legs provide more stability.

Easels also come in wooden or metal versions. Some lawyers prefer wooden easels because they are easier to handle and make less noise when moved around in a courtroom. Wooden easels may also be less expensive than their metal counterparts. However, metal easels usually have more flexibility in adjusting the height at which the exhibit is displayed.

The midsection of the easel should have a tray or cross-member or small pegs on which exhibits can be supported. If you have different sized exhibits, all of which are to be displayed on a single easel, you should use an easel which has a tray or supports for the exhibit that you can adjust in height to accommodate the size of the exhibit. In any case, the base of the exhibit must not be down so far that the jurors cannot see it over the bar in front of the jury box.

The top of the easel may include a clamp device or prongs so that a sketch pad can be hung from it. This is very useful as an alternative to using a blackboard or whiteboard.

You will need to test the easel in the courtroom to be sure that it supports exhibits in a way that allows the jury to see them fully. You should practice with the easel and the exhibits. Set it up in the courtroom several weeks before trial when the courtroom is empty at a bench recess or at the end of the day. Look at sample exhibits from the jury box. Also look at them from the judge's position on the bench. Your first priority is the jury. The exhibit should be easy to read from anywhere in the jury box. The judge should be included in the line of sight if possible. If the angle is bad, the judge may be satisfied with a small 8½ x 11" copy of the exhibit. You do not need to accommodate opposing counsel. If a reasonable position from the jury's point of view excludes opposing counsel from the line of sight, he or she can either rely on your smaller 8½ x 11" copy or get up from counsel table and move to a better position.

Exhibit frames

An exhibit frame is a large but very light tubular frame which supports large Velcro mats. Exhibits are displayed on the exhibit frame by placing small Velcro patches on the four corners of the back of the exhibit. When the back of the exhibit touches the Velcro mats on the exhibit frame, the Velcro attaches, and fastens the exhibit to the frame. To remove the exhibit, the lawyer simply supplies some pressure to the exhibit and the Velcro parts. This operation is similar to the Velcro closing on jackets, shoes, and other articles of clothing.

The exhibit frame fits into a compact case. The frame and case together weigh only 32 lbs. See Fig. 39. The frame sets up in about one minute. It has no parts to be fit together manually, but simply expands and locks into place. See Fig. 40 and Fig. 41. Setting up an exhibit frame always creates interest and excitement in the courtroom because few jurors have ever seen one. The frame comes in 6' and 8' heights and 6', 8', and 10' lengths. Use one that fits your height. If you can reach eight feet into the air, use the larger size. If you can't, stay with the six foot height. The backing is available in dozens of colors. Black, dark blue, and dark green are the colors most often used in the courtroom, but some lawyers prefer zestier colors.

The exhibit frame allows you to mount several 30 x 40" charts or boards side by side. It is particularly effective with take-apart boards and other exhibits that have "moving" parts because everything can be placed on the frame when you are working with it. See Fig. 42. If a sequence of exhibits is important for making a particular point, each exhibit can be displayed on an exhibit frame (or clipped to a 40 x 60" foamboard backing supported on two easels). The significance of the relationship among the exhibits can be noted as the witnesses testify. This allows the jury to grasp the point while the evidence is coming in, instead of having to put it together for the first time while listening to closing argument. Exhibit frames are available from a number of companies that make displays for conventions and meetings. See Appendix B.

Poster generators

Poster generators are small, versatile devices that create very inexpensive enlargements of document and photographic exhibits. See Fig. 43. They are used to create enlarged exhibits on-the-spot in the courtroom when an unexpected document becomes important and an enlargement is needed to use with the jury. They are also used to prototype exhibits before sending them out for professional enlarging and mounting in order to avoid unnecessary expense incurred for poorly conceived exhibits.

The poster generator has a built-in scanner and a two-foot wide roll of paper, usually 100 feet in length. The system uses a thermal, not ink, process and, for that reason, has essentially no maintenance. The half-tone printer in the poster generator does a respectable job of enlarging black and white photographs. The entire system is about 30 inches wide, 12 inches deep, and 6 inches high. It weighs under 30 pounds. A shipping case is available for the unit.

The document to be enlarged is placed in the scanner and 60 seconds later the poster generator produces a 2 x 3' enlargement. The poster generator has settings for creating larger exhibits. A 3 x 4' exhibit can be produced in two sections that are easily spliced together. A 4 x 5' exhibit is produced in the same manner. The poster generator produces banners for time lines by using a long original.

Charts can be produced in black on white, blue on white, and black on yellow. The color is changed by switching to a new roll of paper. A second color for a title or label can be added with a companion labeling system. Labels are generated in different colors, on a clear backing, up to 4 inches in height.

The poster-sized exhibits that are produced by the poster generator can be mounted in standard Velcro frames with borders. A transparent cover places the enlargement on a lightweight plastic backing. Velcro adheres the transparent cover to the backing. These frames may be used repeatedly with different enlargements, thus reducing the cost of each exhibit very substantially.

A computer interface is also available. You can generate graphics on a computer and transmit them to the poster generator for instant enlargement and printing. The poster generator acts as a printer for the computer. You can also transmit graphics from another location, such as your graphics firm or your law firm's graphics department, directly to the poster generator in the planning room for the case or in the courtroom.

Magnetic boards

Thin magnetized surfaces can be mounted on foamboard or other stiff backing material. The magnetized surface may have a diagram of a traffic intersection, for example, marked or pasted on its surface. This will allow small metal objects, such as tags, labels, colored shapes, and similar items to be placed on the exhibit as a witness testifies, creating an overall explanation of the facts in issue.

Magnetized boards can also be used to create good time lines or events charts. The board has the days, months, and years relevant to the case on its surface. The magnetic figures attached to it are in the shape of boxes with pointers that, when attached to the board, will point to a specific date. You can write the names or descriptions of events that are relevant to the case in the boxes and affix them to the magnetized board one by one as the witnesses testify to particular dates and events. This kind of exhibit works well in conjunction with an electronic or digital system. As materials are put on the monitor screen, the point of reference is the magnetized board which contains the overview for the case.

Whiteboards

Some courtrooms are equipped with whiteboards on which colored markers can be used. The whiteboards produce a better image and allow the use of more colors than blackboards. You should check the supply of markers. As court budgets often omit this kind of supplies, you may have to bring your own. Whiteboards require special dry markers. Marks from regular markers cannot be erased. Be sure you have the right kind on hand. If the courtroom where your trial will be located does not have a whiteboard, consider bringing one in and putting it just in front of the traditional blackboard. You will need a small camera to record anything significant put on the board that needs to be preserved.

A more versatile form of whiteboard has a printing capability. This equipment has a large white surface about the size of the standard whiteboard, mounted in a narrow frame, and the white surface can be marked with ordinary markers and erased in the same way as a fixed whiteboard. The image on the white surface is transmitted to a copier by a variety of means, depending on the manufacturer, and the copier creates a duplicate image that is printed on 8½ x 11" paper and deposited in the bin at the bottom of the board. A number of manufacturers produce this kind of equipment and they can be obtained from school and office supply companies. A computerized version of the whiteboard transmits anything written on it to a computer file in storage or printing. See Section 9.6.

Blackboards

Many courtrooms have blackboards that use the traditional chalk and eraser. Although blackboards have been used by lawyers and witnesses for years, this is not a particularly effective mechanism for displaying information. Typically the witness sketches a diagram on the blackboard to illustrate his or her testimony. The blackboard may not be very clean and therefore the contrast between the chalk and the board may be diminished. Chalk lines are often not very precise, and effective labeling is difficult. After the witness is finished, the blackboard may be erased.

If any use of a blackboard is likely, either by you or by your opponent, it is useful to have colored chalk available so that different points or contrasts can be indicated. It is also useful to have a small camera available to make a permanent record of what was put on the board. The photograph of the blackboard can be marked as an exhibit, thus preserving the actual markings rather than relying on a verbal description in the record.

9.3.2 Materials

The paper and plastic materials used to create paper graphics exhibits are available at office supply stores. Many exhibits to be displayed in paper graphic format are generated on computers using graphic arts software for shapes, colors, and lettering.

Jury exhibit books

Some judges like to use juror notebooks. Under this basic format for presenting documentary exhibits, counsel mark each exhibit during pretrial proceedings and put together a notebook for each juror containing important documentary exhibits that have been either stipulated to be admissible or that have been ruled on by the court in pretrial proceedings. The notebook is tabbed for plaintiff and defendant exhibits and for the number of each exhibit within those dividers. Separate notebooks for plaintiff and defendant exhibits do not work well as there is too much clutter in the jury box and a good deal of confusion as jurors try to find the right book.

The juror notebooks should not be larger than a 2" binder and 1½" is a preferable size. Only the key documentary exhibits, to which the jury will refer several times, should be put in the notebooks. Bulky documentary exhibits usually are not included. Documentary exhibits admitted in evidence and not in the notebooks will be available to the jury when they retire to deliberate.

If your case involves more than 10 key documentary exhibits, consider using a juror notebook and inquire at a pretrial conference as to the preferences of the court in this regard. Counsel can usually work out a stipulation as to what will be put in the juror notebooks once the court decides they may be used.

The mechanics of putting exhibits into the juror notebooks are important and should proceed smoothly once the trial is underway. After opening statements, and before the first witness is called, the bailiff should hand out the jury notebooks. The court bailiff will usually collect the juror notebooks at the end of each trial day and hand them out again in the morning. For this reason, it is useful to have a sticker on the lower right corner of the cover where each juror can put his or her name. Be sure to check with the bailiff as to his or her procedures with respect to juror notebooks. Find out from the court whether the notebooks are to be provided to the jurors empty except for the basic plaintiff and witness dividers.

The judge may order that the exhibits be put into juror notebooks all at once at the beginning of each party's case, or in a group for the expected witnesses during an entire day, or in a group at the outset of each witness's testimony, or individually as they are admitted in evidence. This will depend upon the extent of pretrial ruling on admissibility. You need to know how the procedure will work and have exhibits ready to hand out.

Make the copies for the juror notebooks on three-hole punched paper. That way, the exhibits will fit into the notebooks readily and the pages will turn easily. When you punch holes in individual exhibits with a manual punch, inevitably some are crooked, some are long and others are short, and some have no holes at all. Jurors are easily frustrated if the pages of their notebooks do not turn easily because the holes in the paper are not aligned with the rings in the notebook.

Work out a method for delivering the exhibits to the jurors that does not waste time. In some courts the bailiff can do this very quickly for you. The bailiff has more latitude to talk to jurors so if someone is having trouble getting something into the notebook or is missing an exhibit they may feel more comfortable in speaking up.

Some judges allow jurors to take notes during the trial. If jurors will be able to take notes, you should redouble your efforts to persuade the judge to allow jury exhibit books. When you make points with respect to document exhibits, the jurors can write their notes directly on the exhibit. You may want to incorporate this approach into your opening statement. To minimize the clutter in the jury box, counsel may supply blank pages at the front of the notebook for notetaking purposes.

If juror notebooks are to be used, include a proposed instruction explaining these books in your set of preliminary instructions. See Section 1.8.1.

Large sketch pad

A large sketch pad mounted on an easel is a basic part of the courtroom system for displaying information. This approach has been used in courtrooms very effectively for decades. Some lawyers outline dates on the sketch pad—every time a witness mentions a date, the lawyer writes it on an informal time line. Other lawyers outline the points made on cross-examination as the testimony comes in so that the jury understands what is going on. This kind of outline can be used effectively in closing argument because the jury saw it being made. Witnesses make sketches or diagrams on the sketch pad, each page of which can be marked as an exhibit and preserved. If the witness makes a mistake, he or she can go to the next page on the pad and start over again.

These pads are usually 30 x 40" in size and come with a plain surface or with a grid surface. The grid is often helpful with diagrams involving distances. If the witness thinks that the tree was 10 feet from the fire hydrant, he or she can just count off 10 blocks on the grid and get the two objects in the right distance relationship to each other. If the witness makes light pencil markings on the pad to guide the sketch made during the testimony, be sure to disclose that fact on direct and be prepared for cross.

The sketch pad needs to have a good backing so that it can be hung from the easel and be written on without fumbling. Some easels have a cross piece at the top with two prongs from which a sketch pad can be hung. A four-legged easel that has a square top is easier to use with a sketch pad (than a three-legged easel with a pointed top) because the pages of the sketch pad can be folded back over the top of the easel more readily.

You will need a broad tipped marker in order to make your writing legible at a distance. Black, blue, red, and dark green markers all work well. Lighter colors are not legible.

When you use a sketch pad in a courtroom, you will need to practice in order to produce a useful means of conveying information. First, you need to make sure the letters and numbers written on the sketch pad are large enough to be read easily by the jury from where they are sitting. See Section 9.2.1 on size factors. Second, it is not easy to write in a straight line on a sketch pad hanging on an easel. Most people will tilt to one side or another, which makes the resulting product hard to read. Third, your normal handwriting or printing may not be very legible. You will have to slow down and concentrate in order to do well.

Penmanship is very important. Poor handwriting on a chart may actually be less persuasive than oral testimony alone because it may cause a perception of lack of preparation or professionalism. If your handwriting is sloppy or difficult to read, use some alternative other than a sketch pad.

Foamboard

Light foamboard, which is a sandwich material made of stiff styrofoam in the middle and finished paper glued to both sides, is the best material for large paper graphics exhibits. Foamboard is light, stiff, and durable, making it easy to handle. The enlargement or printed exhibit is usually glued to the foamboard in the same manner as posters are made. Foamboard is also manufactured as displayboard, which has only one finished side. The back is raw cardboard. Presentation board is a form of foamboard that has two finished sides and a fold-out construction so that the main board, usually 30 x 40" or 36 x 48", is flanked by two fold-out panels each of which is half the size of the main board. Together the fold-out panels completely cover the main board when it is closed.

Poster board

Poster board (sometimes called illustration board or tagboard) can be purchased in any art supply store. This can be clipped to an easel or mounted on an exhibit frame when displayed to the jury. It is light and holds its shape reasonably well. If bent, however, it is difficult to straighten out. Poster board comes in many sizes and colors.

PVC sheets

PVC (polyvinyl chloride) sheets are a flexible durable plastic material that can be rolled up for storage. The material has a "memory" that allows it to return to a totally flat position after being installed. Exhibit material can be printed directly on these sheets.

Mylar overlays

Mylar is a form of lightweight, flexible, clear plastic that comes in sheets or rolls. It can be cut to any size with ordinary scissors and has a surface that allows marking with the same type of colored markers used with sketch pads.

Clear mylar sheets can be used as overlays for exhibits so that cumulative pieces of information can be displayed seriatim. A single mylar overlay can be taped to the top of the board and turned over the back of the exhibit. Multiple overlays can be affixed by hanging them on small prongs drilled through the top of the board. Another method is to attach the prong or register pin to the front surface of the board with filament tape which can then be camouflaged with white or black tape. See Fig. 44.

This type of material has a very substantial advantage when you want to build a picture for the fact-finder that has a number of sequentially related elements. If the whole picture were presented all at once, the effect might cause confusion. By building the picture step-by-step with overlays, the relationships become logical and confusion is avoided.

The disadvantages of overlays are: (1) they reflect light and, under certain lighting conditions, create a glare that makes the exhibit hard to see; (2) the mylar sheets are somewhat hard to handle because they make a distracting noise if not put in place smoothly; and (3) once attached to the prongs, the mylar sheets can be unruly and refuse to lie flat against the surface of the board, thus producing a wavy image.

You can also use mylar overlays in "lawyer-sponsored" visual aids for cross-examining the other side's expert. Exhibits prepared by the other side's expert can sometimes be used effectively to demonstrate—by altering some features, covering up particular parts, or adding small items—that the exhibit is misleading. Because you cannot mark on the other side's exhibits, you will need a clear overlay or an enlargement of your own that reproduces the offending exhibit and includes the means to demonstrate its inadequacies. If you are using an overlay, grease pencils or colored markers will allow you to highlight weaknesses.

Standard sizes

Graphic artists and demonstrative evidence specialists who make display exhibits for lawyers work with standard sized materials. They can cut materials to any size, but exhibits are less expensive if they use standard sizes. If you are using charts or exhibits with written material that you expect the fact-finder to read, 30 x 40" is often a good size, although you should not hesitate to use a 40 x 60" size if needed to get the point across effectively. It is unlikely that anything smaller than 30 x 40" will be effective before a jury.

There are several other factors to be considered in deciding on the appropriate size for exhibits. The 30 x 40" exhibits will rest comfortably on a very inexpensive unobtrusive easel and can be put on an exhibit frame. Larger exhibits will require a heavier, steadier easel and usually are too heavy for an exhibit frame. Another ancillary consideration is transportation of exhibits back and forth from the courtroom. The large-size artist carrying case, see Fig. 2, will accommodate about ten 30 x 40" foamboard exhibits, but larger exhibits will have to be specially wrapped or otherwise protected while bringing them to court. Ease of handling in the courtroom is also affected by the size of the exhibit, and you may need someone with you in the courtroom to assist in handling larger exhibits.

9.4 PROJECTOR SCREEN DISPLAYS

A projector and screen system is low-key, reliable, and easy to use. The rental or purchase cost is low, there are few moving parts to replace so you can expect long equipment life, and good suppliers exist in nearly every city. The principal problems with using this display technology in a courtroom are the need to dim the lights to get a crisp image on the screen, and the need for adequate space between the projector and the screen to get the enlargement you want. These projectors do not zoom in on a part of the material they are projecting.

9.4.1 Equipment

The three types of projectors most often used in trials are the overhead projector for transparencies, the slide projector, and the opaque projector for paper documents. The overhead projector is somewhat more versatile because it allows the lawyer to mark on the transparencies as they are being used. The slide projector provides the best color images. An opaque projector is sometimes used for sections of books or treatises. Projectors are also available for the images produced on computers. Those are discussed in Section 9.6.6.

Overhead projector for transparencies

Transparencies are projected onto a screen or blank wall space using an overhead projector. See Section 9.4.2 with respect to transparencies. The transparency is put on the glass plate of the projector, which projects a strong beam of light up through the transparency to a mirror and lens arrangement and thence out onto the screen or wall. The positive transparency can be magnified to many times its size and projected at various angles and distances using this method.

Overhead projectors require only a standard electrical plug outlet and perhaps an extension cord. They can be placed on a wheeled cart for easy use in the courtroom. Portable models fold up for easy transport and storage. Look for a unit that has no fan and therefore operates quietly. You will want a model that is small, has a low profile, is lightweight, and folds into a hard shell carry case. See Fig. 45. A built-in tray for markers is useful. Some models come with an automatic transparency feeder which allows the lawyer push button convenience. You will want to have a spare bulb in case of failure, but usually nothing else can go wrong with the unit.

One disadvantage of using an overhead projector is the "trapezoid shape" that results on the screen. It is very difficult to get a good angle with an overhead projector given the space limitations in most courtrooms. This means that the top of the image on the screen will be larger than the bottom. This is acceptable with text material, but may draw an objection with graphics or other pictorial material.

Slide projector

Photographic slides can be used with a portable projector, dual projectors, or a rear projection unit as described below. See Section 9.4.2 with respect to slides.

Portable projector

You can find a standard portable slide projector at any camera store. Look for one that has good brightness, excellent optics, and a long power cord. The slides to be used as exhibits can be inserted into a standard circular carousel that has numbered slots. The carousel is mounted on the projector and the slides are shown on a screen, blank wall, or other suitable surface. Most projectors are very flexible, providing adequate focus at distances ranging from three feet to 30 feet. There is usually a remote control available by which the witness or lawyer can advance the slides without having to stand next to the projector.

Dual projectors

For a wide-screen effect or for comparing one thing to another side-by-side, it may be useful to set up two projectors and have two sets of slides. The paired slides can be projected simultaneously or at intervals during the testimony.

Rear-screen projector

A viewing unit, much like a large TV set, which uses a standard slide projector inside the unit (instead of in front of it as with standard projectors) is useful in situations where a high degree of clarity is needed or where there is a great deal of natural light in the room that cannot be blocked out during the slide presentation. See Fig. 46. These projectors are limited in size and do not have any flexibility in the size of the image produced. The largest standard rear-screen projection unit is about 30 x 40", although for special cases (and quite high daily rental fees) larger units can be found. The rear-screen projection unit allows your witness to point to objects on the screen without creating blocking shadows as would be the case with a standard projector. A disadvantage to this type of display, however, is that viewers must be directly in front of the screen. If viewers are too far to the left or right, the image fades and disappears. This may mean the unit will have to be placed farther away from the jury than you would like.

An alternative to slides displayed with a projector on a screen is a computer using presentation graphics software. See Section 9.6.5. The computer can produce the same visual effects as photographic slides with greater flexibility and in considerably less time. Computer-generated slides can be displayed on a video monitor or a large screen via a digital projector system.

Opaque projector for books and paper documents

An opaque projector does not require a special medium for projection like transparencies or slides. It will project whatever you put on its surface: pages of open books, documents, photographs, and objects. See Fig. 47. These projectors are light, portable, and easy to use. They have good focus control, although the enlargement capability is not as great as the overhead projector. If you decide to use this option, you will need an opaque projector adequate for courtroom use. These projectors were originally designed for grammar school teaching and artist sketching. The ordinary commercial opaque projectors do not have sufficient brightness or image size for use in trials.

Screen

A basic screen for use with any of these projectors is available in 6 x 6', 6 x 8', and 8 x 10' sizes, either on rental from an audiovisual supply firm or sale from an office supply store. Some courtrooms are equipped with pull-down screens that can be used for this purpose. Another alternative is to cover the courtroom blackboard or whiteboard temporarily with screen fabric.

Look for a screen that has a good "gain" factor so that you will not have to dim the lights much in order to get a sharp image on the screen. Most portable screens roll up into a compact tube for easy transport and storage. Be sure to try the screen out with your projector in the courtroom before trial. Many smaller courtrooms just do not have enough space to position a projector and screen in a way the jury can see well.

9.4.2 Materials

The materials used with projector screen display systems are inexpensive, flexible, and widely available.

Transparencies

Transparencies are 8 x 10" sheets of clear plastic. Printed or graphic information on these sheets is projected onto a screen or wall using an overhead projector. They are also called vuegraphs, foils, vuegraph transparencies, and overhead projection transparencies. Transparencies are made using a copying process that is the same as the process used to produce paper copies. Special sheets of clear plastic film that can be purchased at any art or office supply store are put in the paper tray of a standard dry paper office copy machine, and the exhibit is copied. The process causes toner to be deposited on the clear plastic film in the same fashion as it would have been put on copying paper had that been in the paper tray. Computers can also be used to generate black and white or color transparencies by using the plastic sheets instead of paper in the paper tray of the printer that is connected to the computer.

Color copiers and color printers can produce color transparencies. Your selection of colors will depend in part on how much light there will be in the courtroom when the transparencies are shown. Color can also be added to black and white transparencies through the use of Pantone color sheets, which are translucent colored acetate with adhesive backing. See Section 9.2.2.

The completed transparency is usually put into a light cardboard frame to make it easier to handle. These are also available at office supply stores.

Transparencies can be somewhat difficult to handle for the uninitiated because they are placed by hand, face up, on a lighted glass plate. If they are placed incorrectly, the image comes out upside down, backward, or crooked. On most machines there is no clip or other device to hold them in place, so bumping the table or the machine may cause the transparency to slide off the machine. One remedy for this is to tape a strip across the top of the projector's glass plate that has two prongs to hold transparencies in place. Each of the transparency frames can then be punched with holes to fit precisely over the prongs and marked with a colored dot to show the right side up. If the transparency is placed on the prongs with the dot side up you know the image will come out right side up on the screen.

Because they must be handled individually, transparencies can also easily get out of order. Good labeling is a requirement. Another aid to ease of handling is to punch the transparency frames with holes so they will fit in a regular three-ring notebook. That way you can return each transparency to its place behind a number tab in the notebook, and easily locate it if you need it again.

Transparencies can also be presented as overlays, in the same general manner as the mylar overlays discussed in Sections 9.3.2. Transparencies are better than paper charts or slides for some situations where the witness will make marks on the material. You can mark on them with a grease pencil or colored marker and then "erase," if necessary, by wiping the marks off with a clean cloth. An alternative technique is to put a piece of clear plastic over the transparency and to make marks on it. Both the transparency material and marks will show up on the projected image. This is particularly useful if you want to have your witness mark up your opponent's transparency to illustrate conceptual or factual mistakes. If your opponent uses transparencies and the lawyer or witness marks on them, you may want to preserve the marks. Paper copies can be made of transparencies by putting the transparency directly on a photocopier and copying it like any other document.

Transparencies have a relatively quick production time, low cost, good durability, and ready adaptation to color. You can use the projector in a room with normal daytime lighting without lowering or turning off the lights which is an advantage over slides. But most transparencies show up better with some decrease in normal lighting. Transparencies also can look more "down home" than slides. They can present a less polished, less-expensive image, which may be useful, particularly in cases where a large number of exhibits will be used. Computer-generated transparencies, of course, will look just as sophisticated as other media, perhaps more so.

Transparencies are a useful complement to a paper graphics system that uses exhibits enlarged and mounted on foamboard. This medium is close to the paper graphics method, but creates interest and breaks monotony when a long string of exhibits need to be displayed.

Slides

Slides are photographic film that has been processed and mounted in individual cardboard frames for use with a slide projector. Slides can be either photographic exhibits presented to prove what something is or looks like, or they can be testimony aids, presented to assist the witness or the fact-finder with the testimony. Slides have several advantages: a large volume of material can be presented without bulky exhibits; the medium is very flexible and exhibits are quickly produced or repaired; the cost is relatively low; and the medium is easy to handle in a courtroom. Slides are also a good way to break up a long series of exhibits displayed on an easel or exhibit frame. In a long trial, you should use different media to help maintain the jury's interest and attention. Slides are often particularly useful with expert witness presentations of complicated testimony.

You should place slides in a carousel for easy handling. The carousel should have a lock ring on top to keep slides in place in case the carousel falls or is dropped. Qualify the carousel as one exhibit number and each slide as A, B, C, and so on within that exhibit number. You can also lay the foundation for the whole group of slides at once. An index to the carousel identifying each slide by number or letter and a short description can be included as an ancillary exhibit.

Slides can be produced by regular photographic processes or with computer-assisted equipment. Many graphic arts firms can produce colored slides overnight with either a photographic process or a computer set-up. When a photographic process is used, the underlying material is camera-ready "mechanical art" which displays the necessary printed material and illustrative material. When slides are made, this material is photographed and the color negatives are mounted as slides. Computer software is useful in producing the underlying material for slides to be used as testimony aids. If the material is text, the words are typed into a form that appears on the computer screen along with the instructions about typeface, color background, size, and spacing. If the material is a chart—bar chart, column chart, line graph, or pie chart—the instructions as to horizontal and vertical axes and the points on the chart are put onto the computer screen. The software composes the chart. If the material is artwork more complicated than charts, an artist can actually draw the image with a mouse or stylus. A transparency generator can be used to expose the film pixel by pixel. This method yields very high quality images.

Slide screens offer a relatively large area for big, bright, colorful projections. Slide presentations can be tailored in various ways by changing the order of the slides in the carousel or by making new slides to further explain a particularly difficult point. This versatility has a counterbalancing problem, however, in that the room generally must be darkened somewhat to use slides effectively. This causes disruption and may cause the fact-finder's attention to wander. Another problem occurs when slides get mixed up and are out of order when it comes time to present them in court. One way to deal with this problem is to use small colored stick-on numbering circles in different colors so that you can tell instantly if a slide is upside down, backwards or out of order.

Several companies make a flashlight pointer that is useful when working with slides. The pointer projects the image of a small arrow on the slide screen. By using the arrow to point to various parts of the image on the screen, the witness avoids the necessity of using an arm or pointer which will interfere with the beam of light from the projector and darken part of the screen.

When using slides, you may want to make printed copies of the slides as exhibits. It may also be helpful, when a slide is needed for use with another witness or in a closing argument, to enlarge the slide. You can enlarge a color slide through a standard copying process to a maximum size of 11 x 17". To get larger exhibits, you will need to use different processes. A visualizer (see Section 9.5.2) can be used to zoom in on prints from slides to produce an enlargement. As with any photograph, slides can be digitized and displayed through a computer system. See Section 9.6.

A slide presentation may include some topics, other than those shown on the slides, about which the witness will testify at length. For example, the expert shows slide #1, talks about that; shows slide #2, talks about that and, then before coming to slide #3, explains in detail his or her evidence-gathering process or something else that is not illustrated with slide. Do not leave a slide about topic #2 up on the screen while the expert is talking about the introductory material to slide #3. However, turning the projector off and on is sometimes quite distracting. A practical alternative is to use a blank slide in the set at this point to block out the screen and have someone man the light switches or dimmers to raise and lower the lights.

9.5 ELECTRONIC DISPLAYS

An electronic display system for a courtroom uses analog signals (which are frequency based) to produce images on a television monitor. The digital equipment described in Section 9.6 can also be used with an electronic display system through the use of a converter to put digital signals into analog form.

9.5.1 Videotape Player

Videotape exhibits can be displayed for a judge or jury either with videotape player equipment discussed here, or with computer equipment discussed in Section 9.6. The choice between the two display technologies is a trade-off between cost and quality. A videotape played on a videotape player is a lower cost exhibit that has a lower quality. Putting a videotape on a computer system so that it can be played on a video monitor results in a higher cost exhibit of higher quality. The start and stop controls and the "freeze frame" capability on a videotape player are not as high as provided by a computer.

Videotape players are small and compact and can be used easily in a courtroom. They are readily portable, quite sturdy, and not ordinarily subject to glitches in operation. The playback equipment used for particular videotapes depends upon the type of equipment used in making or editing the videotape. Make sure that the video player to be used in the courtroom will play the type of tape that you have.

The player needs a good "freeze-frame" feature so that the witness can stop the tape at critical points and explain to the fact-finder the image that appears on the screen. The image must not wobble or degrade significantly when the tape is stopped. Many less expensive players do not provide a "freeze-frame" image satisfactory for courtroom use. Good videotape equipment can be purchased or rented from most audiovisual suppliers.

The player needs a counter that is readily visible so that the lawyer or operator can find specific locations on the tape. The operator should have a small monitor and a switcher that can maintain a blank screen on the monitors for the judge, jury, and opposing counsel while the operator is looking for the beginning of a particular segment. Video player counters are not very accurate and often the same reading on the counter will result in slightly different places on the tape with each replay.

It is often useful to paint the key controls red (for the stop button), yellow (for pause or freeze frame) and green (for the play button) so that, under the demanding conditions in a courtroom, the player is easy to use.

A case for transporting the player and its associated cabling will help ensure that everything arrives at and leaves the courtroom in good working order.

9.5.2 Laserdisc Player

A laserdisc player retrieves data from a laserdisc and displays it on a standard television monitor. The equipment has relatively high capacity to display quality full motion video, such as computer animations, and also can display documents, photographs, graphics, and other static exhibits. The discussion about the laserdisc player is set out in Section 9.6.2 to facilitate comparison with digital systems using hard disks, optical disks, CD-ROM, and digital video disks. The laserdisc technology has been available since the late 1970s and is very reliable for courtroom use. The digital video disk, which displays its output on a video monitor (not a television monitor) is the technological successor to the laserdisc system insofar as trial exhibit display systems are concerned.

9.5.3 Visual Presenter or Visualizer

A visual presenter, also called a visualizer or document camera, is the simplest and most versatile of the input devices for an electronic display system. A visual presenter is a miniature television camera mounted over a surface that has a sufficient light source to get good images from the camera. When the camera is on, it transmits to the television monitor an image of anything within its field of focus. See Fig. 48.

A visual presenter can be used to display text documents, charts, graphs, computer data printouts, maps, drawings, diagrams, objects, photographs, and x-rays. The exhibit to be displayed is placed on the display surface beneath the camera. The image appears immediately on the monitor. See Fig. 49.

The camera can be raised or lowered to zoom in on a portion of the document or photo, thus instantly enlarging it to the full size of the monitor. The lawyer or witness can mark on the exhibit, adding a highlight color, for instance, to important words, as the exhibit is discussed in testimony.

A light pen can be used with a visual presenter for drawing or pointing capability on the television screen. See Fig. 50. Anywhere the light pen is placed on its table, a corresponding mark will appear on the monitor. The lawyer or witness can circle objects, draw lines, or mark over anything being displayed on the screen. When the light pen is switched to the pointer, anywhere the lawyer or witness touches the pen to its tablet, an arrow will appear on the screen. Videotaping and printer capability can be added so that a permanent record can be made of any markings shown to the jury.

Some visual presenter systems have been designed specifically for trial work. They include built-in monitors, wireless video transmission between the visual presenter and television monitor, integration of the display of computer graphics on the same television monitor, and carrying cases. Suppliers who specialize in trial work can supply instructional videos and on-call support.

If you need to compare exhibits, you should use a visual presenter that has a split screen capability. With two windows open on the television monitor, you will be able to put a photograph and document together side-by-side. You will also be able to play the videotape deposition of a key segment of testimony in one window while the written transcript appears in the other window.

A visual presenter can also use a system to record video images on a disk for instant and random-order recall. Images are retrieved either with a remote control or bar code scanner. Images may be recorded or moved to different locations instantly. Various lists of images for different witnesses may be maintained on the same disk. This is different from a digital recording system because in this case the recording and displaying of the video images is done on a regular television set. The input "scanner" is the visual presenter itself.

The visual presenter is low-cost, flexible, portable, and highly effective. A visual presenter can also be integrated into a digital system. A computer switch can "scan double" video images so that they can be displayed on digital monitors. Reliable suppliers are listed in Appendix B.

9.5.4 Television Monitor

A television monitor for displaying the output of a videotape player or visualizer is usually just a television set tuned to the channel for video input. The key factors in the successful use of television monitors are size and location. No dimming of lights is necessary to read the material on the monitor and a distance factor of 15 to 20' can be accommodated

The basic setup in a courtroom is a monitor for the jury, a monitor for the judge, a monitor for opposing counsel, a monitor for the witness, and a monitor for the visualizer or videotape operator. If the lawyer doing the direct or cross-examination is required under local court rules to stand at a particular spot, and none of the monitors can be seen from that position, an additional monitor for the questioner will be necessary.

The monitors for everyone except the jury can be small—13 to 20" television sets will do. The judge, opposing counsel, and the operator are very close to their screens and a small image is sufficient. These monitors sit on desktops and need no special mounting. An unobtrusive table for the operator, if there is one, may be useful.

The best size single screen for a 12-person jury is 35", and larger standard monitors should be available from a rental firm. With a six-person jury a smaller 27" monitor may be sufficient, depending on the layout of the courtroom. Very large screen capability with a 60" monitor is available from specialized audiovisual suppliers but more often if you need anything beyond 35", you will want to use a digital projection system. See Section 9.6.6.

The jury monitor should be put on stand that has a swivel base, making it easy to adjust the viewing angle, and the stand should be put on a wheeled cart so that the monitor can be brought out and removed without a lot of effort. Depending on the geometry of the jury box and the lighting in the courtroom, it may be advisable to have two or more monitors for the jury. This will ensure that each juror has a comfortable view. It is often impossible to avoid glare on a monitor screen and get a clear line of sight from every juror viewpoint with a single monitor. It is necessary to check out the glare from the proposed location for the jury monitor or monitors in both morning and afternoon. If the monitor will be wheeled in and out several times, a small piece of tape can be used to mark the spot on the floor where the glare is minimized and all jurors have a clear line of sight to the monitor. Sometimes tilting the monitor downward slightly will reduce glare significantly.

No dimming of lights in the courtroom is necessary with a good television monitor. This is a significant advantage (over slide and transparency projectors) in moving the trial along with efficiency.

It will be necessary to wire all of the monitors to the visual presenter or videotape player. Usually a distribution amplifier will be necessary to get the signal to more than two monitors at the same time. Any wires that go across a floor space will need to be taped down so that people don't trip over them. If the jury monitor is to be moved in and out of place as the need arises, it is easiest to unhook the monitor and leave the cabling taped in place rather than taking up all the cabling each time the monitor is moved. Wireless transmission offers more flexibility. Typically in a wireless setup, the television set for the jury is still cabled but all the other monitors in the courtroom do not need to be wired. This reduces the amount of work for setup and teardown (after trial) of the television system.

Cabling should be checked out thoroughly in exactly the place in the courtroom where it will be used. Special plugs and long extension cords may be required. Glitches can develop with the best of equipment when it is moved from place to place. The person who will operate the equipment in the courtroom should make several practice runs "on location."

9.6 DIGITAL DISPLAYS

A digital display system for a courtroom uses digital signals generated by a computer to produce images on a video monitor. The electronic equipment described in Section 9.5 can sometimes be used with a digital system through the use of a converter to put analog signals into digital form. This section describes the hardware, presentation software, and associated projectors and whiteboard that can be used with a digital system.

9.6.1 Computer Equipment

A digital system requires a high-end personal computer to locate and retrieve exhibits and a computer switch to control the link between the computer and the various monitors in the courtroom

Personal computer

A powerful personal computer is the most capable and flexible equipment for courtroom use. The computer can display all types of tangible evidence—documents, photographs, videotapes, maps, drawings, deposition transcripts, charts, and computer animations—on a high resolution monitor. Because the computer has a high capacity and produces excellent quality images, it is a very useful tool in a courtroom. It can store hundreds of thousands of potential exhibits and retrieve any of them with total accuracy in milliseconds. Its display on a video monitor has resolution much higher than any projection screen or television monitor. The computer transmits images to a video monitor with very precise start and stop controls. It allows the witness to use many documents, and to zoom in on the relevant words in documents, with a full display to the jury and without the necessity of shuffling papers every time a new exhibit comes up. It saves a very significant amount of time with the testimony of witnesses who use many exhibits—more than one-third in most cases—and it keeps the jury's interest alive by varying the images and making the images interesting. The built-in graphics capability can produce zoom-in, color, labeling, and all the special effects available in any other system, usually with better quality and faster turn-around time. A good computer system will display exhibits that impress even the most skeptical juror and will make the trial faster and more efficient.

Higher risk comes with the computer's greater capability. Computer equipment is complex. Any of its parts may stop working at any time causing all the rest of its parts to become nonfunctional as well. It is subject to quirks in the court building's electrical system and given to crashes at inopportune times. You will need an experienced supplier or system integrator, an excellent operator, and a totally redundant system in order to prevent disaster.

The safest way to use a computer system in a courtroom setting is a rental for the duration of the preparation and trial from a well-established firm that has supported trials successfully in the past.

Rental is more practical than purchase for most law firms. You will need a relatively new model computer with high-end capability that is well integrated as far as storage and controls are concerned. Law firms are not well equipped to make these investments frequently and wisely.

Computer switch

A computer switch controls the link between the computer and the monitors used in the courtroom. A good switch will accept at least two inputs (from plaintiff's computer and from defendant's computer) and direct the signals to at least six monitors other than the monitors on the two input computers. The switch allows the jury's monitor to be turned off while sidebar conferences are held by the court with counsel. The monitors for opposing counsel, the judge, and jury can be turned off when the lawyer is finished with one exhibit and no other exhibits will follow. The better switches also have the capability to "scan double" video signals so that they can be displayed on digital monitors. This means that a visual presenter or videotape player can be connected to a digital system. Having a visual presenter available in a digital trial is a substantial advantage because it helps with the necessary balance of low tech exhibits (see Section 9.1.3), provides an on-the-spot capability to present exhibits immediately that may not exist on the digital system, and operates as a backup to the digital system.

9.6.2   Storage Options

The storage system used with a courtroom computer system determines the amount of material that can be managed and the speed with which it can be retrieved and displayed. Some types of exhibits, such as documents, are not very sensitive to the speed of the system. Others, like computer animations, can only be used on a system that is fast enough to accommodate the exhibit's full motion video.

Hard disk and optical disk

The computer's hard disk is the fastest storage option. Removable hard disks provide more storage capability if exhibits can be stored on one disk and discovery documents, for example, on another. The optical disk is usually a larger but somewhat slower storage option than the hard disk. Hard disk and optical disk storage is generally measured in gigabytes (or thousand megabytes). One gigabyte of storage can accommodate about 28,000 pages of documents or 100 minutes of ordinary deposition videotape. This storage option can handle photographs and any other type of graphics exhibit.

This storage is read-write, which means that files can be erased and replaced with something else. The read-write capability makes this medium more flexible, so that you can add exhibits and other documents as you go along, but it is also more prone to error and catastrophe. When you use either of these options, you need a systematic backup procedure to ensure that you do not lose your data.

CD-ROM

CD-ROM means compact disk, read-only memory. You cannot add anything to the CD once it has been made, but you do not risk losing any data either. The principal attraction of the CD-ROM technology, which was introduced in 1984, is the approximately 650 megabytes of memory that fit on a thin, light, polycarbonate disk. A CD-ROM disk is about 4½" in diameter and the player is a small unit that can fit in the computer case or, alternatively, can be plugged in as an external unit. The disks are nearly indestructible and are estimated to last for at least 10 years. Once something has been stored correctly on a CD-ROM disk, it is free from error and will always be there in exactly the same form you stored it. A CD-ROM disk offers random access, which means you do not have to play through the whole disk to find something stored near the end—each item has an address to which you can go directly.

Suppliers charge a fee for making the master disk and provide copies at less than $10 apiece. When CD-ROM disks are made, the data are etched onto the surface of the disk. Pits or indentations distinguish data from lands or flat areas. When a laser hits a land, the laser reflects. When it hits a pit, the laser light scatters. Other systems use a translucent dye and burn tiny spots in the dye to reduce the laser reflectivity at that spot.

One CD will hold about 10,000 pages of documents, depending on the compression technology that is used when the files are put on the disk. Some vendors can load 25,000 pages of documents. Video can also be put on CD-ROM but the quality and retrieval time is generally not good enough for courtroom application. Photographs are also generally not used with CD-ROM for trial work.

CD-ROM disk players have slower random access times and slower transfer times than hard disks or optical disks. This means that after you send the command to retrieve an exhibit, you wait longer for it to appear on the screen. You can improve the access time by structuring the data put on the disk into directories and files. Multiple CD-ROM disks can be accessed by a single computer system using a jukebox which first locates the correct disk and then locates the correct file on the disk. CD-ROM is an excellent medium for archiving case materials when the trial is over.

Laserdisc

The laserdisc technology was introduced in the late 1970s and is a bridge between a digital system (that uses digital signals) and an electronic system (that uses analog signals). A laserdisc stores pictures and sound in analog, but stores the table of contents in digital format. Because the locating information is in digital format, the laserdisc player can find any point on the disk by random access and with exact precision. A laserdisc player can be controlled by a standard remote control (which operates similarly to the remote on your television or VCR), by a bar code reader, or by computer controls. See Section 9.6.3.

The disk itself is about 11½" in diameter, and the player is about the size of a standard videotape player. The disk can hold 54,000 documents or about 20 minutes of very high quality video, such as a computer animation. A laserdisc system works well with photographs and all other types of graphic exhibits. Like a CD-ROM, it is relatively sturdy and not subject to damage by fingerprints, magnetic fields, or moderate heat and cold. Like a CD-ROM, this is a read-only medium. Once you have put your exhibits on the disk, nothing else can be added. The laserdisc player generally provides better quality video, and is a more expensive option, than a CD-ROM player. For this reason, it has long been used to present computer animations and deposition videotape excerpts in courtrooms. The laserdisc does not provide as high quality video, and is a less expensive option, compared to a digital video disk. DVD provides 480 lines of horizontal resolution; a laserdisc provides 425 lines. The laserdisc player displays material on a standard television monitor and, for that reason, is more properly within the electronic system. The information on the laserdisc is presented here to facilitate comparison.

Digital video disk

A digital video disk (DVD) stores all information digitally. Unlike many consumer formats, DVD stores images using component signals. The component format stores pictures in three forms: black and white (luminance) and two channels of color (chrominance). All three signals are retained at significantly higher bandwidth than laserdiscs, so performance (details and colors) is better. DVD stores pictures at 720 by 480 lines of digital resolution and produces excellent images on video monitors. DVD also handles documents, photographs, graphics, and all other types of static displays.

A DVD disk is the same size as a CD-ROM disk or an audio CD disk, but is designed specifically to achieve the speed and capacity needed to play long full motion videos, such as movies. The DVD technology is an extension of the CD-ROM format and the DVD player will also play CD-ROM disks or audio CD disks. The player is plugged into and controlled by a computer. A DVD disk has a storage capacity of about 4.7 gigabytes, or about seven times that of a CD-ROM disk. The player has much faster access times than a CD-ROM system and accommodates full motion computer animations with very high fidelity. DVD-ROM equipment and disks are significantly more expensive than high-end CD-ROM systems or laserdisc systems.

Digital video disks solve the problem of displaying video from a digital source that is both "full screen" and "full motion." Older computer systems did not have enough power to play video that would fill the screen (like television) and provide for smooth motion of the video. However, with the development and standardization of compression techniques, video clips can be stored efficiently and displayed in a full screen with full motion. A special graphics card is required in the computer to play the video and a sound card is needed to play the audio. If the system has high wattage speakers, the sound will be of excellent quality. With this system, you can play a segment of a deposition videotape while the key documents being discussed at the deposition are displayed on the screen at the same time. Documents can be changed, zoomed in, and annotated while the video plays. Digital video can be edited easily, and bar codes can be used for easy access.

The DVD format will not work well with ordinary television monitors. There is a long technical explanation for this, but the basic problem is that DVD is a component format and American (but not European) television uses only a composite format. Therefore, a DVD player must downgrade its high quality signals into a video signal that television monitors can accept. Even then, the television must have an S-video input to receive composite signals from this source without distortion. In the courtroom, you will want to use a DVD player only with a digital system and not with an electronic system unless your supplier has an advanced television monitor.

9.6.3 Control Options

There are four types of controls available for a computer system used for litigation displays and each has different advantages and disadvantages in the courtroom setting.

Standard keyboard or mouse control

The standard keyboard unit that comes with the computer allows you to give the command to search for the image, and "still" or "play" commands that tell the computer what to do with the image when it is located. The advantage of this kind of control is that it is flexible and inexpensive. Most computer systems include the keyboard in the price of the equipment. The disadvantage is the need to punch in a five-digit number accurately every time you want to change the exhibit on the screen. Under pressure in the courtroom, this can be too difficult.

You can also create special screen displays to make finding exhibits easier. You can for example, create an exhibit list for plaintiff and defendant that will call up a particular exhibit when you click a mouse on the number, or a "script list" can be created of exhibits to be used by the expert witness. Subject matter word lists may be used to help locate documents by a word description of the document. The advantage of this system is its total flexibility and tailoring of the system to the particular needs of the trial. The disadvantages (compared to other controls) are primarily additional complexity of the operations required in the courtroom. Normally a computer-operated system requires a paralegal or other technician dedicated to operating the system. The keyboard and mouse system is an interface for a trained operator, not for a trial lawyer.

Bar code reader

The necessary commands for the computer can be put into standard bar codes with English subtitles. The bar codes are a series of vertical lines that provide the five-digit locator number, the "search" command, and the "play" or "still" commands. These are like the bar codes you see on products in the supermarket that are scanned at the checkout counter. See Fig. 51. Bar codes can be produced on small stickers or labels that are easily attached to the lawyer's notes or the witness outline. The lawyer uses a hand-held scanner to read the bar code and transmit the necessary information to the computer. The scanner is a very small unit which scans the information from the bar codes and, with one click of the control button, displays the image on the video monitor. See Fig. 52. Hand-held scanners may be either hard wired to the laserdisc player or battery operated portable units that beam information to the computer.

The advantage of using this system of control is that its operation in the courtroom is very simple. The lawyer or the witness simply holds the hand-held scanner over the bar code. (Units that require a pen to be passed from one side of the bar code to the other have a higher risk of error.) The operator then presses one button on the scanner that sends the scanned information to the computer. One disadvantage is that bar codes must be prepared in advance. Preparing the bar codes does not take very long; 10 or more code stickers can be prepared in an hour. And, you can also use the standard keyboard input unit for anything you decide you want to retrieve for which you do not yet have a bar code prepared. Another disadvantage (relative to the standard keyboard control unit) is cost. The scanner unit is an additional cost, and the bar codes must be prepared by someone with the necessary equipment, usually on an hourly-charge basis. However, these costs are very modest compared to the capability that the bar coding brings to the courtroom. One cautionary note: a hand-held scanner operates on batteries, so it is necessary to have on hand a supply of spare batteries.

Light pen

A light pen attached to the computer acts just like a mouse, except that the light pen is used directly on the video monitor screen in front of the lawyer. With the light pen, the lawyer can zoom in on documents, annotate and highlight passages in documents, and compare sections of different documents on the screen. The actions commanded by the lawyer using the light pen on the lawyer's monitor are shown on all the other monitors on the system. The tip of the light pen acts like the click of the mouse, so you just press to execute the command. The light pen also has a draw and point capability. When you "write" with it on the screen, every motion of the pen is reflected on top of the image on the screen like the systems used by the television sports commentators to draw x's and o's on the screen during football games. When the point feature is used, any place where the light pen touches the screen produces a directional arrow pointing to a particular part of the underlying image on the screen.

Touch screen controls

A touch screen unit can be used to control the computer. The touch screen is like the bank ATM machine. See Fig. 53. The screen shows a series of buttons labeled "Exhibit 5" or "Jones letter" or any other short descriptive title. When you press on the screen with your finger, the necessary information to retrieve and play the exhibit is transmitted to the computer. The touch screen has the advantage of being easier for a lawyer to operate than the keyboard or the bar code reader. Its disadvantages are that it is more expensive to prepare touch screen programming than bar codes and the touch screen unit is much larger than a bar code reader.

A touch screen also has drawing and pointing capability. If you want to emphasize something on the screen, you can touch the screen with your finger or a matchstick and trace a circle around the object, perhaps a particular part of a photograph being displayed on the video monitor. A circle will appear on the video monitor exactly where you put it on the touch screen control. You can underline a word, draw a line from one element to another, or do any other kind of hand-drawn graphics. This capability is like the x's and o's used on the television screen by sportscasters. When you switch to the pointing feature, a small arrow appears wherever you touch the screen. If you want to point out the swelling at a particular point, you simply touch the point with your finger and an arrow appears at that spot pointed in the correct direction. The arrow stays on the screen until you touch the screen at some other point. You can switch back and forth between the drawing and pointing capability at any time. The control system should have an output line to allow your marks to be recorded on videotape or a printer for the record, if necessary.

9.6.4 Digital Monitor

A digital monitor performs the same type of function as a television monitor, but it processes digital signals rather than analog signals. The resolution on a video monitor is much higher than on a television monitor. But the size is smaller and the cost is higher. The largest TV monitor for courtroom use is 60". The largest video monitor is 41". The courtroom setup for digital monitors is the same as for television monitors. See discussion in Section 9.5.4.

Flat panel displays are thin, portable video monitors with high resolution. Prices are decreasing and sizes are increasing so that these units are becoming more practical for courtroom use.

Developments in the electronics industry are bringing electronic systems and digital systems closer together. HDTV, high definition television, uses a digital television monitor rather than the standard analog television monitor currently in standard television systems. Digital signal processor (DSP) capability allows digital output to be displayed on analog systems.

The quality of the display on a video monitor is measured by three factors: a "dot pitch" rating (the number of dots per inch (dpi)), maximum resolution numbers, and the refresh rate. All three factors work together to affect the sharpness of the image and the absence of flickers. A smaller dot pitch number means a sharper image. The dot pitch for courtroom work should be .28 dpi or less. A larger maximum resolution number means a larger amount of information will be displayed within a given area on the screen. The maximum resolution should be 1024 x 768 or higher. The resolution may be interlaced or non-interlaced. Non-interlaced is better. The refresh rate has to do with the speed at which images can be displayed. A refresh rate of 60Hz or higher means the presentation will look professional when images are changed on the monitor. Maximum resolution and refresh rate are often provided together, as in "1280 x 1024 @ 60Hz." The quality of the display is also affected by the architecture of the screen. A vertically flat screen works best in the courtroom setting because it has the least glare and distortion. Some monitors have a special anti-glare coating on the screen which is also helpful.

A good monitor cannot produce excellent images on the screen without a good video card in the computer. The amount of random access memory (RAM) devoted to video has the biggest impact on speed. RAM comes in DRAM, VRAM, and WRAM. DRAM was once the memory type of choice for good video images, but VRAM and WRAM offer considerably better performance in terms of high resolution, high color, and high refresh rates.

9.6.5 Presentation Software

A "slide show" of the kind presented by photographic slides can be done using presentation graphics software on a laptop computer in the courtroom. Sometimes presentation graphics are prepared by experts and controlled from the witness stand. If the expert has documents to show, testimony aids to present, or photographs to analyze, the presentation graphics software has the capability to provide titles, labels, color emphasis, and zoom-in views. This approach has the advantage of allowing immediate changes, on site in the courtroom, if circumstances require additional material or editing to existing material.

The computer output can be shown on a video monitor, if that is the system being used for other exhibits, or through a digital projector to a large screen of the type used in projector screen systems. The image will also show on the laptop screen so the witness will be able to see what the jury is seeing.

Once the slide show has been prepared, the expert can go from one "slide" to the next by pressing a single key on the computer. The presentation can go backwards or forwards and can skip from one "slide" to any other. A strong advantage of this alternative is the control that the expert witness has over his or her own material. The expert need not use unfamiliar equipment in the courtroom and can practice the presentation wherever the laptop computer is kept.

Presentation software also allows the trial lawyer to prepare an advanced form of trial notes that show how exhibits and testimony aids will be laid out and displayed. For example, if you intend to use exhibits when Mr. Smith testifies, you can put together a set of trial notes (some call it a "script") for Mr. Smith's testimony that include the photograph, the zoom-in that you intend to use to highlight the defective part shown in the photograph, the video clip of the defective part in action, the document that is the page of specifications for the defective part, the yellow highlighted portion of the specification showing exactly where the specification was not met, the order form on which the part was described, and so on. Your trial notes, in software format, contain all the exhibits and the ways in which the exhibits will be displayed. To move from one exhibit to the next as Mr. Smith testifies, you just click on the bar code reader or the keyboard. This allows you to organize your presentation completely before you enter the courtroom. Good presentation software allows you to switch between the prepared format of your trial notes and a random access format so that you can retrieve any exhibit at any time.

9.6.6 Digital Projectors

If you want an image that is larger than the 35" video monitor can provide, an LCD panel for an overhead projector or a digital projector can put the computer output on a large screen of the type discussed in Section 9.4.1.

An LCD panel is a projection aid that is placed on top of a standard overhead projector described in Section 9.4.1. The panel is cabled to a computer and displays the computer output. The overhead projector shows what is displayed on the panel as if it were a paper exhibit. Fig. 54. An overhead projector using an LCD panel usually requires the courtroom lights to be dimmed and does not achieve very high resolution on the screen. For testimony aids that are primarily text and other kinds of exhibits that do not need very fine colors or details, this kind of projector is an inexpensive alternative and fits in well with a projector screen backbone system.

A digital projector takes output directly from the computer and projects it to the screen with high color resolution approaching what would be achieved with a video monitor. It produces good images in ambient light conditions. The digital projector is a freestanding unit (see Fig. 55) cabled to the computer that is larger than an overhead projector and will require a special cart or table in the courtroom. This is a higher cost alternative used when good resolution for a larger number of exhibits is required.

9.6.7 SoftBoards

A SoftBoard is a computerized version of the blackboard. A large white drawing surface, usually 4 x 6', mounted on a frame is connected to a computer. See Fig. 56. The lawyer or witness writes, draws, or marks on the SoftBoard with special markers, somewhat like the dry markers used with whiteboards. See Section 9.3.1. Anything drawn on the SoftBoard is transmitted to a computer file and becomes an digital image (like a photograph) that can be printed out in the same fashion as any other computer file.

The SoftBoard is actually an infrared laser system that uses components similar to those found in laser printers and compact disc players. The infrared laser continuously scans the entire area of the whiteboard, about a quarter inch above the surface. The dry-erase markers used with the SoftBoard are equipped with reflective bar coded sleeves. When a lawyer or witness writes on the board with these markers, the laser system locates, identifies, and tracks the color and position of the markers in real time. The data stream is sent to a digital signal processor, which in turn sends the processed data to the computer which then presents the corresponding graphic image on the computer monitor. The file is saved and can be transferred or printed out like any other file. A special eraser functions the same way as the special markers so that information erased from the board with the encoded eraser is also removed from the computer file in case the lawyer or witness makes a mistake and wants to write or draw something over again. When the lawyer or witness is finished, the SoftBoard is erased, like a blackboard, with a regular eraser and is ready for the next use.

If colored markers are used to make particular points, the colors can also be saved in the computer file and later copies can be printed out in color. This means that anything put before the jury can be automatically recorded without the need for a photograph of the board. What has been constructed on the SoftBoard can be recalled readily for use with another witness or for final argument. When the file is retrieved from the computer, it can be displayed on any computer medium that is being used in the courtroom—a video monitor, a digital projection system, or an electronic system (through digital signal conversion). Two such files can be retrieved and displayed by the computer side by side on the monitor or screen. The SoftBoard is an excellent tool for courtroom use and is available on a rental basis from some litigation support vendors. See Appendix B.

9.7 USING SPECIALIZED VENDORS TO CREATE EXHIBITS

The principles and techniques for producing successful exhibits and testimony aids are drawn from psychology, advertising, and graphic arts. Qualified specialists can apply these methods to produce exhibits that jurors will trust and remember.

If you have a choice, it is better to use a specialist than for a lawyer to try to design exhibits. Few lawyers have sufficient art skills or familiarity with the necessary computer software to make cost-efficient use of their time in this manner. If possible, choose a specialist who has considerable experience with litigation exhibits over one who does advertising or other design work. Some techniques that work well in other contexts do not work at all in a courtroom. When cost is a consideration, it is important to have someone who can get it done correctly the first time.

If you don't have someone to whom you turn regularly for litigation graphics, the list of evidence specialists in Appendix B will provide a place to start. These firms will provide you with samples of their work in trial matters and references from lawyers for whom they have worked.

Budget is the most important factor. Tell the vendor how much you can spend in order to provide a context within which they can make suggestions and proposals. The price quotes for enlargements, foamboard exhibits, and electronic and digital systems are fairly standard within a particular market, so it is not hard to work out a budget that fits the needs of the case.

A clear theory of the case is a second key factor. Explain to the specialist your client's position with respect to the key issues. This will help the specialist to suggest a knowledgeable and critical approach for using exhibits to enhance your presentation. One good place to start is to give the specialist a copy of your rough draft of a closing argument. Ask for ideas about how the key points could be illustrated. Another useful method is to invite the vendor to listen while you do the preparation of key witnesses. The investment in these hours will be returned in better exhibits.

Time is the third key factor. The specialist must have enough time to do a good job. The trial lawyer will also need enough time, after seeing the proposed work product, to make necessary changes. Exhibits must be an integral part of the case planning, not something tacked on at the last moment. You will usually want to retain a vendor firm when you are about halfway through discovery in a commercial or personal injury case, for example. By this time, you will have a reasonably good idea who the witnesses will be and what the conceptually difficult issues are. By this point you can spot the areas in which prepared exhibits may be most helpful.

Consultants who provide digital trial support should be brought in well before trial. A great deal of planning and expertise goes into a digital trial. The consultants will need to go over all your documents, graphics, videos, and photographs to offer advice on the best ways to display them. The consultants will need to provide power backup for the computers and printers, on-the-spot scanning capability for new exhibits that show up at the last moment, software to correct scanning mistakes when new images are made, software to crop photographs, and a plan for total redundancy of the system. In order to make the most of the extraordinary power that a digital system offers at trial, you will need to have the system plan in place as you prepare witnesses and exhibits so that the whole effort fits together seamlessly.

9.8 USING FOCUS GROUPS TO CRITIQUE EXHIBITS

As the trial preparation goes forward, give some attention to the total picture presented by the exhibits to be offered in evidence and the testimony aids to be used with key witnesses. Most jurors find trial procedures, such as objections, conferences at the bench, interruptions for motions, and extended exchanges between the court and counsel to be irrelevant to the reason they are in the courtroom—to decide the case. Jury interviews confirm that jurors find long stretches in trials to be boring and incomprehensible. They welcome polished exhibits that fit well together and help tell the story. They love to be entertained.

A focus group is made up of 8 to 10 people whose backgrounds reflect the general pool from which jurors are drawn. They may be hired from temp agencies, recruited from senior citizen centers, located through church groups or other community organizations, or even pressed into service from among friends and relatives of employees of the lawyer.

A focus group usually works from 3 to 6 hours on a single day and is paid a modest hourly stipend plus a meal. It may be important to have them meet at a location other than the lawyer's offices, depending on the nature of the case, so that no more information about the actual case is disclosed than is necessary to a good critique of potential exhibits.

In most cases, the focus group is told that materials have been prepared to explain the facts in a matter that is the subject of a dispute, and that it is important to have these facts explained clearly and fairly. Their job is to look at certain of these materials and to give their views on whether the materials are clear and fair.

You will want to emphasize fairness because the best exhibits are those that do not give an impression of covering up or hiding anything. Jurors are always alert to the possibility that they are being misled, and you will want to ferret out any such impression so that the offending exhibits can be fixed before trial.

Two people work with the focus group: a lawyer who explains the facts and displays the potential exhibits and a moderator who asks the group questions about the exhibit during and after the presentation. The moderator may be a lawyer, but a professional who has experience in conducting focus groups is usually better. The graphic artists or vendors who prepared the exhibits and the witnesses who will use the exhibits may also be present. Some lawyers prefer to videotape the proceedings and have the graphics personnel and witnesses see the tapes at a later time.

The consulting firms that do focus group work for jury selection also usually offer services geared to critique of exhibits. Some are listed in Appendix B.

You will want to take into consideration the state of the law with respect to attorney work product in your state before exposing witnesses to focus group exercises. In some states, this work is considered an integral part of the lawyer's preparation, but in others this work may be subject to discovery if anyone not employed by the lawyer has any contact with the process.

Arrange the focus group members in a row to represent the second row of the jury box. During the presentation, the lawyer and the exhibits should be at the same distance from the focus group as they would be from the jurors in the back row of the jury box.

The lawyer making the presentation to the focus group should just tell the story: this is what happened and how it happened. Try to avoid referring to a "case"; call it a dispute. Stay away from legal terms like "evidence," "alleged," "plaintiff," "defendant," and so on. (This is also good practice for the opening statement). As the narrative comes to a key point to be illustrated by an important exhibit, that exhibit is displayed as it would be in the courtroom. If you are planning to use a computer system, visualizer, transparency, or sketch pad, now is the time to try it out. If you plan to hand out copies of documents, try that out too. The narrator talks about the exhibit as he or she would if the presentation were being made in a nonlegal context: this chart shows the number of units sold; this diagram shows the intersection where the accident happened; and so on.

Every 20 or 30 minutes, at natural break points in the story about what happened, the narrator stops and the moderator asks questions about the exhibits to find out if they are easily understood, effective for making the point, and subject to any unintended impressions. At the end of the lawyer's presentation, the group is asked to discuss the exhibits to decide which one is the most important, which is the best display, and which should be done over. Typically this discussion is held out of the presence of the moderator and lawyer, but is videotaped. The focus group is given a sheet of specific questions and asked to spend up to an hour giving collective answers.

This process, if done in an atmosphere conducive to comment and discussion by the focus group members, will highlight any problems with exhibits. Documentary exhibits in which language is clear to lawyers may have ambiguous meanings to lay persons. It is useful to search for these. Charts and graphs may appear too hard to understand. You will get suggestions about how to make them more friendly. Time lines may have gaps that raise questions; computer printouts may lead to suspicions of manipulation; drawings may use colors that are misinterpreted; and models or demonstrations may give rise to unintended speculation. If you hear about these problems in the context of a constructive discussion, they can usually be remedied so that the presentation at trial will be effective.

ENDNOTES

1. The techniques and technologies described in this chapter apply to any form of presentation to include: deposition, mediation, arbitration, bench trials, summary jury trials, and client presentations. Visual presentations will significantly improve consensus, advocacy, retention, and learning any time that you need to communicate facts or persuade someone to adopt your position.

2. *See Sonya Hamlin, What Makes Juries Listen* (1984).

3. *See Scott MacGregor, Graphics Simplified* 38 (1979).

4. *Id.*

CHAPTER 10

USING EXHIBITS AT DEPOSITIONS, OPENING STATEMENTS, AND CLOSING ARGUMENTS

The use of exhibits at pretrial depositions, during the opening statements, and in closing arguments relates closely to the admission of exhibits in evidence at trial. In order to get the most out of the available exhibits, the lawyer must use them effectively in each of these settings. Section 10.1 covers depositions. Section 10.2 deals with opening statements. Section 10.3 explains closing arguments.

10.1 DEPOSITIONS

The work done with exhibits at depositions can determine how the court will treat the exhibit at trial. Important elements of foundation may be available during depositions and at no other time. If the examining lawyer does not establish the foundation correctly at deposition, the exhibit may not be admitted in evidence at trial. Even if the case will most likely settle, when the examining lawyer does a skillful job at a deposition to tie up all the loose ends with respect to the admissibility of an exhibit, this effort reduces the uncertainty about the case's value.

To deal successfully with exhibits at depositions, the lawyer must understand how the court treats exhibits at trial. With the ability to look ahead and picture the nature of the contests about exhibits at trial, a lawyer taking a deposition is well armed. The use of deposition transcripts at trial is covered in Section 2.6. The use of deposition videotapes at trial is explained in Section 6.3. This chapter deals with procedures and tactics at depositions to ensure that the necessary groundwork is done for a successful outcome at trial.

The objective is to ensure that each necessary exhibit is admissible at trial. If you have adequate foundation in the deposition transcript, you should be able to obtain a pretrial ruling on a written submission if your opponent refuses to stipulate to admissibility. Some judges prefer to rule on exhibits only at trial in the context of witness testimony. This causes the trial to be substantially longer than it would be if the court made most of the evidence rulings in pretrial proceedings and introduces considerable uncertainty (causing extra time to be spent) in preparing the case. If you have solid support in the sworn deposition testimony, however, and if the court can make evidence rulings on written submissions so that a time-consuming hearing is unnecessary, even the most recalcitrant judge may issue pretrial evidentiary rulings.

At trial, a witness who is competent to testify because of first hand knowledge or expert qualifications must establish that the exhibit is relevant to an issue in the case, identify the exhibit, and provide any necessary assurances of trustworthiness required by the rules or the circumstances of the case. In addition, a witness must have the knowledge necessary to overcome hearsay and other available objections. The general requirements with respect to foundation and objections are discussed in Chapter 1. The additional requirements for laying a foundation and meeting objections for specific kinds of exhibits are set out in Chapters 2 through 8. Much of this work should be done at depositions. If you are going to incur the expense of a deposition anyway, it might as well be a productive one.[1]

10.1.1 Preliminary Steps

You can increase the useful outcome of the deposition considerably, in terms of what will happen at trial, if you do some additional preparation with respect to the exhibits.

Find and number potential document exhibits

Lawyers typically prepare for the depositions in a case by locating potential document exhibits. This includes, in the first instance, copying whatever documents their opponent has produced voluntarily, if disclosure rules apply, and serving interrogatories and document discovery requests to obtain materials relevant to the case.

Discovery from third parties and research in public databases through the Internet and established database suppliers is also important. The latter will yield all significant news coverage, government agency reporting, and other published material relevant to the deponent or the specialized subject matter associated with the deponent. The methods for discovery under federal and state rules or through public computer resources are beyond the scope of this text but are not difficult and need not be costly.

Once you have received the documents, you should code them to show the source from which and the date on which the document arrived in your possession. Bar coding, bates stamping, and automatic numbering in an imaging system are all established methods for accomplishing this step. Information about the sources of documents often leads to useful lines of inquiry at a deposition.

If your case involves more than 100 pages of documents, put the results of the discovery into a computer database, preferably a good imaging system.

Assemble working sets of potential document exhibits

For each deponent, make a database query to locate all the interrogatory answers and documents that mention the deponent or the special subject matters with which the deponent is associated. This book cannot cover the methods for assembling and querying a computer database system, but the system should be able to identify all documents that include the deponent's name, initials, and title; the name, initials, and titles of persons reporting to the deponent; and the relevant subject matters for which the deponent is responsible.

The querying of the computer database for names and titles is the first but not the only step in finding potential document exhibits. Remember to include in your deposition outline for each exhibit questions about the types of documents that other people generated or received so that you gain an understanding of the paper flows relevant to the issues in the case. The writings of third parties or materials to be found in public sources may also be a fruitful area for questioning. An imaging system also provides the capability for constructing pattern analyses, chronologies, subject correlations, and other advanced discovery research techniques that are beyond the scope of this book.

Next, you should assemble a set of the documents that relate to the deponent because he or she wrote or received them, engaged in or supervised activities described in them, or knows something about the subject matter. If you are using an imaging system, these sets of documents will be stored in a computer system. Otherwise, assemble a file of hard copies.

Third, identify and study documents that are copies. Pull from the deposition set identical copies from the same source. Documents are not identical copies if one has on it any meaningful handwritten notes and the other does not. Also pull copies that are identical but for insignificant handwritten notes. Keep these non-duplicate copies in a separate file for later double-checking (after depositions have developed the issues in the case) to ensure that what you initially thought was insignificant remains so. You should also pull identical copies from different sources from the set if the source is not relevant to the issues in the case. Again, keep these in a separate file in case the source later becomes an issue. Set aside copies that are identical but for attachments for further consideration as deposition preparation proceeds. Different attachments may have significance such as a different level of disclosure, different time frames, and different file keeping practices.

Fourth, cull out the documents that you need not cover in the deposition because they are: (1) not relevant to any issue in the case, (2) relevant to an issue that other evidence can establish conclusively in your favor, (3) better pursued with another deponent, (4) routine documents the significance of which you understand fully and for which you do not need a foundation, or (5) covered by an adequate stipulation establishing admissibility. Do not waste time at a deposition on documents where the payoff for trial purposes is likely to be extremely low. If you have sufficient time and budget, code the culled documents to record the reason they were rejected for inclusion in the deposition. Assign each reason a unique code that does not overlap with the deposition preparation coding discussed below. For example, in one such system NO means not relevant, AR means a fact has already been established conclusively, RO means a routine document, and ST means an adequate stipulation covers the document. This coding is not vital to a successful deposition but it saves a considerable amount of time in the long run (as does any measure to record work done or judgments made so future efforts are not repetitive). Keep the culled documents in a separate hard copy file on the deponent, or marked in the imaging system, so that you can review them again if need be as the trial preparation proceeds.

Fifth, pull out materials that fall in the categories covered in Chapter 3 (charts, graphs, tables, and computer printouts), Chapter 4 (maps, diagrams, and drawings), Chapter 6 (photographs), and Chapter 8 (printouts of computer drawings and simulations). Each of these requires foundation that is somewhat different from text documents covered in Chapter 2. Place these materials in a special folder for the deposition marked Additional Foundation, or something similar.

Sixth, make the necessary copies. You will need to produce three sets of documents to use at the deposition: one set for the questioner with appropriate notes and codes; a clean set for opposing counsel; and a second clean set to be marked individually with exhibit numbers by the reporter. If you are working with a good computer imaging system, this step can be accomplished quickly because your notes and coding can be done on the system that can always print out "clean" copies. If you are working with hard copies, make sure you maintain a "clean" copy with no extraneous marks on it to use as the actual exhibit.

Each of the sections below with respect to particular types of deponents focuses on the most important factors that you need to consider in the overall context of foundation and objections. See Section 1.1 and Section 1.3.

10.1.2 Depositions of a Party Opponent

The depositions of the opposing party or parties include the officers, directors, employees, representatives, and agents of those parties. The limits of employment, representation, and agency relationships are established by state law in your jurisdiction, so you need to have a usable working definition drawn from the relevant cases to be sure you qualify exhibits properly in this regard.

Discovery should include, in the case of a party opponent that is a corporation, requests for the organization charts for the years relevant to issues in the case, job descriptions for persons who have functions relevant to issues in the case, and descriptions of the terms of agency or consulting arrangements for people who have knowledge of issues in the case. This information will assist in providing the foundation for documents that are "not hearsay" because they are statements of the party opponent. You should also send a request for stipulation or admission that covers the signatures on useful documents generated by your opponent. This will avoid time spent at deposition authenticating routine signatures about which there should be no controversy.

Locate and qualify the "not hearsay" text documents

The most important aspect of the depositions of party opponents, as far as exhibits are concerned, is usually establishing the "not hearsay" status of documents generated by the party opponent. All of the documents that appear relevant to the deponents should be reviewed carefully to decide which text documents potentially qualify as admissions of a party opponent.

Someone should code these documents under Rule 801(d)(2) so that the person taking the deposition knows how each document might fit under the definition of admissions by a party opponent and thus qualify as "not hearsay" for purposes of the evidence rules. An easy way to do this is to use the five categories set out in the rule and mark the copy of each document used by the lawyer taking the deposition accordingly:

> 2A—the party's own statement in either an individual or a representative capacity. If the party opponent is an individual, this category includes any document written by him or her. If the party opponent is a partnership, corporation, or other entity, this category includes any document written by employees who are of sufficient rank to bind the company with respect to the particular subject matter. Anyone whose job appears on a company organization chart will usually suffice in this regard.

> 2B—a statement which the party has adopted or manifested a belief in its truth. Attachments (written by someone else) to documents written by the deponent often fall into this category.

> 2C—a statement by a person authorized by the party to make a statement concerning the subject matter. This category includes documents prepared by consultants, outside lawyers or accountants, and public relations or advertising firms.

> 2D—a statement made by the party's agent or servant concerning a matter within the scope of the agency or employment. This covers sales and other agents, and lower level corporate employees if they are writing about something that is within their responsibilities.

> 2E—a statement by a co-conspirator of a party during the course and in furtherance of the conspiracy. This is a very specialized category that covers antitrust violations,

various frauds, and other crimes where conspiracy is an aspect of the charges.

00—a document that does not come within one of the five categories for admissions of party opponents and therefore an exception under the hearsay rule must be found.

There are two other categories of "not hearsay" documents: (1) those under Rule 801(c) that are not offered "to prove the truth of the matter asserted," and (2) those under Rule 801(d)(1) that are prior statements of the witness who is on the stand and testifying. Neither of those rules is particularly helpful in preparing for a deposition. The exemption for documents not offered to prove the truth of the matter asserted is useful primarily for documents like contracts and invoices for which stipulations are readily available. You will use this category as a fallback position when other strategies fail, so it rarely plays a role in deposition planning. Similarly, the exception for prior statements of witnesses usually is not relevant at deposition because it applies only if the deponent testifies. With a deposition witness, you will not be sure whether he or she will show up at trial to testify.

Most of the documents that qualify as "not hearsay" because they are statements of your opponent are also business records under Rule 803(6) because they were both made and kept in the ordinary course of the business. You can more easily qualify a document as "not hearsay," however, than as a business record, particularly with a hostile witness. Most deposition examiners will choose the former.

Decide what to do about the hearsay text documents

All of the documents coded 00 are probably hearsay documents. You need to study the documents coded 00, that do not fit in the category of admissions of a party opponent, to decide whether anything can be done in the deposition to bring them under one of the exceptions to the hearsay rule. Although Rule 803 has 24 exceptions and Rule 804 has five, most cannot be established in the deposition of a party opponent.

Most of the documents turned over by your opponent that were *not* generated by them (and therefore do *not* fall under Rule 801(d)(2) as admissions of a party opponent) were received by them from third parties and maintained in their files. Rule 803(6) requires a business record to have been both made and kept in the ordinary course of business. Therefore, these documents are usually business records of the third parties who generated them, but they are not the business records of the party opponent just because they received and kept them in their files.

There are only a few other hearsay exceptions available for documents held by a party opponent.

- Medical records held by the party opponent should qualify for an exception under Rule 803(4).

- Recorded recollections (such as date books, calendars, and personal memos) are covered by Rule 803(5). This kind of personal record may not qualify under the business records exception if it is not a practice of the business itself (rather than the individual) to make the record.

- Public records held by the party opponent should qualify for an exception under Rule 803(8).

- Documents that are 20 years old or more are covered by Rule 803(16).

- Stock market reports and commercial tabulations, lists, or directories held by the party opponent are exempt under Rule 803(17).

You should code these documents with an appropriate notation showing that they will come in under a particular exception. A simple system like 00-3-16 showing that Rule 803(16) applies will usually suffice.

Every hearsay exception requires that you establish a few simple facts. You can draw the questions directly from the wording of the rule. You will find examples in the chapters covering particular kinds of exhibits. Remember, under Rule 611(c) you can use leading questions to establish foundational matters. Also, under Rule 104(a) the court is not bound by the rules of evidence when considering the admissibility of an exhibit.

Plan the foundation for the non-text documents

After you have organized the text documents, you should next plan the foundation for the non-text documents. The foundation requirements are set out in the chapters dealing with these types of documents, including charts, graphs, tables, computer data printouts (see Chapter 3); and maps, diagrams, drawings, sketches (see Chapter 4). In addition to the standard requirements of the competence of the witness, relevance of the exhibit, and an adequate identification, most of these types of exhibits need some special foundation to establish trustworthiness. You should decide what portion of the required foundation you can obtain from the particular deponent and what you must obtain from other sources.

(1) Competence: Include factors affecting the competence of the witness to testify to foundational matters for particular exhibits or groups of exhibits in the standard

set of questions about the witness's background and experience.

(2) Relevance: If there are fact matters that affect the relevance of particular exhibits, these should be listed and included in the examination of the witness.

(3) Identification: Require the witness to identify each exhibit that is discussed during the deposition and always make a record that includes both the exhibit number and its identifying features.

(4) Trustworthiness: The requirements for establishing the condition of the exhibit, the source or publisher of maps, drawings, or diagrams, and results produced by processes or systems such as computer-generated graphs or tables materials are specified in Rule 901 and Rule 902.

You must keep track of the foundation requirements for non-text documents as depositions in the case are completed. It would be an unhappy result to reach the discovery cutoff date with several key aspects of the foundation for important exhibits still not completed. If you are using an imaging system, you can keep notes with documents as to what parts of the foundation are still needed. Some lawyers use an exhibit log for this purpose.

Non-text documents such as charts, graphs, and tables, may show up at trial as enlargements, juxtaposed comparisons, color highlighted versions, and other specially prepared items. Remember to ask each deponent if he or she has seen or heard about non-text exhibits in these formats. Opposing counsel may raise an objection to the "heard about" question because these conversations are usually with lawyers. The objection will, however, alert you to the possibility that such versions exist, and you can request them in discovery or pretrial discussions about exhibits. If the deponent has seen such specially prepared exhibits or helped prepare them, the privilege objection is unlikely to succeed. Non-text exhibits may also show up on videotapes, computer displays, visualizer presentations, slides, and other methods of presentation. See Chapter 9. Ask each deponent if he or she knows anything about such preparations.

Most non-text documents are not within the hearsay definition, and therefore no hearsay exception need be established. Any writing is subject to Rule 1002, however, which requires, when the exhibit is offered to prove its content, that the original be produced unless the rules allow use of a duplicate or copy. You will usually use duplicates rather than originals as deposition exhibits. As a part of the deposition record, you should ask for, or record the prior agreement to, a stipulation as to the status of duplicates.

Example

(After questioning of the deponent about Exhibit 82 has been completed)

Q. *(To opposing counsel)* Can we stipulate that the table that is Exhibit 82 is a duplicate of the original as to which there is no objection under Rule 1003?

Opposing Counsel: I don't think so.

Q. *(To the deponent)* So far as you know, is Exhibit 82 an accurate reproduction of the original document?

A. So far as I know it is. I don't see anything to the contrary.

Q. So far as you know, is there any question as to the authenticity of the original of Exhibit 82?

A. I don't know of any.

Q. *(To opposing counsel)* Can you state for the record any reason why Exhibit 82 is not an accurate reproduction of an authentic original so that I have a fair opportunity to examine while this witness is available?

Opposing Counsel: I am not prepared to state any at this time.

If opposing counsel fails to state a ground for objecting to the document under Rule 1002 at a time when the necessary information could be obtained from the witness, the court likely will not allow the same objection to be made at trial. See Section 2.6.4.

If the deposition exhibit has any writings, stamps, or markings that were not on the original, you need either to lay a foundation for the additions (by having the witness identify and explain them) or go to Rule 1004 and establish one of the grounds for using a non-duplicate copy: the original is lost or damaged, not obtainable, or in the hands of your opponent. See Section 2.2.3.

Plan the foundation for non-document exhibits

Consider whether you need to cover with the witness any known physical objects (see Chapter 5); photographs, x-rays, videotapes, or sound recordings (see Chapter 6); models, demonstrations, or reconstructions (see Chapter 7); or computer drawings, simulations, or animations (see Chapter 8). If so, list the foundation requirements for each such exhibit and determine what you can obtain from this witness. Each type of non-document exhibit will require some special foundation facts. Even if you know of no exhibits in these categories and the existence of any is unlikely, ask open-ended questions to find out what the witness knows about possible exhibits of these types.

10.1.3 Depositions of Experts

Techniques for dealing with expert witnesses primarily relate to matters beyond the scope of this book. This section sets out some basic guidelines for the exhibits that are used with experts.

Direct examination

If you are deposing an expert such as a medical doctor or foreign scientist whose testimony you need but whom you do not expect to produce at trial, you need to give careful thought to the foundation for each exhibit to be qualified by the expert and possible objections that might be raised.

The first decision is whether to use as exhibits the sources of the data relied on by the expert in forming an opinion. You need not qualify documents relied on by an expert, if the opinion alone is sufficient, because, under Rule 703, the facts or data upon which the opinion is based need not be admissible in evidence. If you want the underlying materials in evidence for some reason, perhaps for use with another witness, then you must qualify each exhibit with an adequate foundation and the necessary bases to meet hearsay and original document objections.

Exhibits that illustrate, incorporate, or constitute the expert opinion should be qualified as evidence. These typically are the materials covered in Chapters 3 through 8. The examples set forth there give guidance as to the foundation requirements and the ways to meet objections. You will need to use in the direct examination of the expert at deposition the exact same exhibit presented at trial.

Cross-examination

If you are deposing an expert whose testimony you expect to be presented by your opponent at trial, you need to ensure that you are not surprised at trial by any exhibit presented by that expert.

One way to proceed is to make a list of each category of potential exhibits and to ask of the expert early in the deposition whether he or she used any such materials, had such materials made available by your opponent that were not used, or considered or attempted to use any such materials. You may want to start with objects, substances, and site views (Chapter 5); then go to maps, diagrams, drawings, and sketches (Chapter 4); next ask about photos, x-rays, videotapes, and sound recordings (Chapter 6). Most experts can waste a fair amount of your deposition time discussing documents, so it may be most efficient to cover text documents (Chapter 2) after you have finished with more interesting and productive categories.

Some categories of exhibits can be either input to an expert opinion or an illustration or expression of that opinion. These include charts, graphs, time lines, tables, and computer printouts (Chapter 3); models, demonstrations, and reconstructions (Chapter 7); and computer drawings, simulations, and animations (Chapter 8). Make sure you know whether the expert has any such exhibits. Find out how the expert classifies the potential exhibit (as input or output) at the outset of your examination about it.

When deposed, experts will often present black-and-white copies of the exhibits they intend to sponsor and then turn up at trial with brilliantly colored versions, making it more difficult to cross-examine effectively from the deposition testimony. Pin down any plans in that regard. Make sure what you are seeing at the deposition is the same thing you will be seeing at trial. Ask about enlargements, transparencies, slides, videotapes, computer displays, and other presentation options explained in Chapter 9.

10.1.4 Depositions of Third Parties

The depositions of third parties range from the very friendly depositions of those who support your client, to the neutral third parties, to the very hostile and difficult depositions of those who support your opponent. Because some of these witnesses will quite likely be unavailable to testify, the transcript of the deposition may be the only way to provide a foundation for some classes of exhibits necessary to the case.

As with the depositions of a party opponent, it is useful to focus first on potential hearsay problems and deal with those under the available exceptions. Separate the text documents (which are subject to hearsay objections) from the non-text documents and other potential exhibits. Code the text documents for the exceptions that should be established in depositions.

Business records exception

The focus of the depositions of third parties with respect to text documents is generally on the business records exception to the hearsay rule. The rule has a very broad scope and supports the admissibility of a wide range of text and non-text documents.

There are four requirements under Rule 803(6) and the foundation must include each:

(1) Type of exhibit: "A memorandum, report, record, or data compilation, in any form, of acts, events, conditions, opinions or diagnoses . . . if it was the regular practice of [the] business activity to make the memorandum, report,

record, or data compilation . . . ." This covers most paper records and computer data storage media. It also covers routine videotapes with sound recordings, such as those made by surveillance cameras. Photographs, physical objects and substances, models and computer animations are not "statements" and therefore require no exception to the hearsay rule unless attached to and made a part of a report or record.

(2) When created: "[A]t or near the time" of the "acts, events, conditions, opinions or diagnoses" that are recorded or reported. This requirement attempts to screen out documents that were created after the fact to improve a litigating or negotiating position.

(3) By whom created: "[B]y, or with information transmitted by, a person with knowledge. . . ." The knowledge required under the business records exception is not the "personal knowledge" required by Rule 602 to qualify as a competent witness. The broader scope of Rule 803(6) is intended to cover normal business situations in which persons record and report information about which they have no first hand knowledge but about which they have sufficient knowledge and experience to serve the business purposes at hand.

(4) Where kept: The record must be "kept in the course of a regularly conducted business activity." The rule specifically provides that: "The term 'business' as used in this paragraph includes business, institution, association, profession, occupation, and calling of every kind, whether or not conducted for profit."

You may not get "yes" answers to the standard leading questions that paraphrase the rule (see example of the questions in Section 2.1.2) in a deposition of a hostile, well-prepared witness. If this happens, you should break the questions down and make sure that you cover every aspect.

Example

Q. I am handing you what has been marked by the reporter as Exhibit 99. That is a memorandum from Mr. Stampel, the Vice President, to all employees, isn't it?

A. Yes.

Q. And in the memorandum, Mr. Stampel reports the latest sales figures, doesn't he?

A. Well, not exactly.

Q. What is Mr. Stampel reporting in this memo?

A. He is giving the trends.

Q. The information about sales is one way to keep up with the conditions in your business, isn't it?

A. Yes.

Q. And it is a regular part of the business activity of your company to report sales trends, isn't it?

A. I don't know what you mean by that.

Q. You've seen these reports of sales trends before, haven't you?

A. Yes. But they don't come out every week like clockwork, if that's what you mean.

Q. When there are trends observed by management and they think those trends should be reported, it is a regular part of their management activity to report them, isn't it?

A. Yes.

Q. And, in fact, there were six of those reports of sales trends in the last year alone, weren't there?

A. I don't know exactly how many, but there were several.

Q. This memorandum about sales was created at or near the time the data became available, wasn't it?

A. I don't know when the data became available.

Q. The memorandum contains the most recent information about sales, doesn't it?

A. Yes.

Q. Mr. Stampel is the person whose responsibility it is to know the sales figures, isn't he?

A. Lots of people in the company work with sales figures.

Q. Mr. Stampel is one of those, isn't he?

A. Yes.

Q. This memorandum was put in the company's files, after it was circulated to the employees, wasn't it?

A. I put my copy in the files in my office. I don't know what other people did with theirs.

Q. You kept this memo in your regular files at the office?

A. Yes.

Q. So that it would be there if you needed to refer to it in your work?

A. I don't usually refer to these things after they are put out, but I might need to find it some time.

The questioner is permitted to use leading questions because this is a matter of establishing foundation. You must keep after a hostile witness until you establish all the elements. Once you have worked through this formulation a few times, the witness may grow weary of the game and give more responsive answers.

Medical records exception

The medical records exception in Rule 803(4) is intended to do for medical records what the business records exception does for business records. All medical records qualify so long as they were made for a proper purpose and have proper content.

> (1) Purpose: "Statements made for purposes of medical diagnosis or treatment" qualify for the exception. These statements can be made by doctors, nurses, technicians, or any other medical personnel.
>
> (2) Content: Statements describing (a) medical history, (b) past or present symptoms, (c) pain, or sensations, or (d) the cause of the history, symptoms, pain, or sensations "insofar as reasonably pertinent to diagnosis or treatment."

Unlike the business records rule, there is no temporal requirement here. Statements qualified for the exception are not limited to those made at or near the time of the information being acquired by the person who made the record. Also unlike the business records rule, this exception does not require trustworthiness of the source; that is, the information need not come from a person with knowledge or from information transmitted by a person with knowledge. The statements in a medical report need only be sufficiently worthy to be pertinent to diagnosis or treatment.

Other exceptions

Some of the other hearsay exceptions may assist you with third party documents. The most useful are:

- Recorded recollections (such as date books, calendars, and personal memos) are covered by the exception under Rule 803(5).

- Public records held by the third party should qualify for an exception under Rule 803(8).

- Documents that are 20 years old or more are covered by Rule 803(16).

- Stock market reports and commercial tabulations, lists, or directories held by the party opponent are covered by Rule 803(17).

Occasionally a potential exhibit will qualify for more than one exception. If the exhibit is important, either get a stipulation from your opponent that the testimony you have elicited qualifies for one particular exception or use the deposition to establish all possible bases for admissibility.

10.1.5 Creating Exhibits at Depositions

Witnesses often explain things at depositions that could be clarified with the assistance of markings by the witness on an exhibit or by a sketch or drawing by the witness. You should not hesitate to ask the witness for this kind of testimony. The witness (or her counsel) may not cooperate, and judges' practices differ as to orders compelling a witness to mark on an exhibit or make a sketch. But regardless of whether the witness cooperates, you have gained useful information for which you may be able to find a tactical use at trial.

Here are some examples of requests that trial lawyers make of witnesses in depositions after laying a foundation that the witness has the requisite knowledge:

Text documents: Mark the portions of the document that you (the witness) wrote; mark the portions that someone else wrote; underline the statements that are wrong.

Charts and graphs: Circle the data points that are particularly significant to you; mark the data points that you used in your analysis; mark the data points that you think should not have been used by (the expert witness).

Maps: Mark the place on the map where you started; mark the route that you followed; mark the place where you ended up.

Diagrams: Mark the lines of authority on this organization chart that you believe are not correct and put in the correct ones.

Photographs: Mark where you were standing at the time (of the events at issue); mark where (other witnesses)

were standing; mark anything in the photograph that
you believe was not there at the time you witnessed (the
events at issue).

If the witness refuses to mark an exhibit for you, be sure to ask whether
he or she is able to do what you ask and is refusing to do it. Either way,
you have almost certainly prevented the witness from doing this for
your opponent at trial.

If the witness has described a physical location of which you do not
have a map or photograph, you can ask her to draw a sketch of the
location and mark the significant objects on the sketch. If you have a
SoftBoard (see Section 9.6.7) and you are taking the deposition in your
office, you may want to invite the witness to draw on the board. This
has the feel of working with a blackboard and many witnesses are more
open to drawing on a blackboard or whiteboard than they are to making
a sketch on a piece of paper. The SoftBoard is the equivalent of writing
on a piece of paper, however, because the board automatically creates a
computer file that can be stored and printed. You can then mark the
printout as an exhibit.

10.1.6 Defending Depositions as to Exhibits

When defending a deposition at which you expect your opponent to
use or try to lay the foundation for exhibits, you should make a request
well before the deposition for copies of the exhibits that your opponent
intends to use with the deponent. Your opponent is not required to turn
these over, but you may be able to persuade a judge to order this
production if there are difficulties in completing depositions in the case
without undue wrangling and waste of time.

When you review potential exhibits, decide whether you will
stipulate as to the genuineness of signatures and original document
requirements as to duplicates or copies. The lawyer taking the
deposition is entitled to ask for such stipulations, and you should give
them unless there is a real question in your mind about the exhibit.
When giving stipulations on exhibits used at a deposition, it is useful
to add a condition that your stipulation is based on the present state of
discovery, and later acquired facts may invalidate the stipulation.

Explain to the deponent, or ask the deponent's own counsel (if
separately represented) to explain, what foundation questions may be
asked about a document and why they are important to the
admissibility in evidence. Explore the fair limits of the deponent's
personal knowledge as to each potential exhibit so that questions can
be answered accurately. When the questioner gets beyond the witness's

personal knowledge, object on the grounds of lack of personal knowledge, speculation, or conjecture.

Be sure you know the rules with respect to privilege in your jurisdiction and object to the use of any documents that should be privileged. Objections should be made with respect to exhibits that relate to insurance, subsequent remedial measures, settlement offers, improper character evidence, and improper lay opinion where an instruction not to answer is proper.[2]

10.2 OPENING STATEMENTS

The lawyer's function in the opening statement is to explain what the case is all about. If the case is tried to a jury, you will be addressing a group of people you have met only very briefly. You will know relatively little about their collective or individual interest, attention span, or capacity to learn. Using tangible evidence permits you to put your arguments forward on several levels. The graphics or other visual aids present the material on the simplest level to help along jurors who are slow in adjusting to an unfamiliar role, while the oral presentation gives a richer detail for those who are ready to absorb it. Tangible evidence will also help judges, who have many cases, motions, and other matters on their dockets, to focus on the case at hand.

An opening statement is an opportunity to tell the fact-finder what the facts are going to be and to develop your theory of the case.[3] Visual materials should be simple and geared to help you present the opening statement without notes.

You can use three kinds of tangible evidence in opening statements: key exhibits that will be used in the case; presentation aids such as prepared charts or lists that are not exhibits but assist in making the statement; and notes, sketches, or other marks made on a sketch pad, whiteboard, or blackboard during the opening statement.

10.2.1 Exhibits That Are Evidence

Any text document, table, diagram, or other type of tangible evidence that you reasonably intend to offer as an exhibit is a candidate for use during the opening statement. The reverse is also true. Photographs, maps, and other types of tangible evidence that would require an evidentiary foundation and are not intended to be offered as exhibits are not appropriately presented by the lawyer in an opening statement.

Unless the judge has made pretrial rulings, exhibits will not be in evidence yet, so it is important to find out from your opponent whether he or she will object to the admissibility of any substantive exhibit you plan to use in the opening statement. If they have an objection that you do not work out in advance, that objection can be made in the midst of your opening statement, possibly detracting from its effectiveness. Moreover, even if your opponent does not object during the opening statement, you should not describe something as evidence in an opening statement that later is excluded during trial because of objections. The usual procedure is to submit the proposed exhibits to be used in the opening statement (perhaps together with other exhibits) to opposing counsel with a proposed stipulation as to admissibility. If they do not object and it is probable that the exhibit will be admitted in the proceeding, most courts will allow you to use the exhibit during the opening statement.

Example

Counsel: This case is about a letter. Here it is *(holding up the exhibit)*. This letter has already been marked as Exhibit 109. You will hear it referred to by its number because that is a convenient way of keeping track of things during a trial. It is a rather long letter, as you can see. It has 8 pages. But the idea expressed in this letter is straightforward. The XYZ Company, whose Vice President, Mr. Brown, is sitting at that table over there, offered to sell to the Bilt-Rite Machinery Company, whose General Manager, Ed Wells, is sitting here at this table with me, an Assembot II robot that was fully tested, proven, and ready to go. In fact, the Assembot II robot was not fully tested, it was not proven, and it was not ready to go. We will prove that the statements made in this letter *(holding up the exhibit)* are not true, and the XYZ Company knew these statements were not true when they made them.

In this case, if the letter is the contract at issue in the case, you know it will be admitted in evidence (or it already has been admitted in pretrial proceedings) so there is no risk of a successful objection when it is used during opening statement.

If you do not use items of tangible evidence during the opening statement itself, do not outline or refer to exhibits that you will present. Preserve the element of surprise and wait until the exhibit is introduced.

In the case of videotapes, you may want to use excerpts of key videos or depositions to support the opening statement. Your opponent may object to the editing even if the videotape itself is admissible, so it is usually helpful to resolve these questions in advance. Alternatively, if your opponent refuses to stipulate and the exhibit is important to the opening statement, ask the court at a pretrial conference for a ruling on the use of the exhibit during the opening statement.

If you are in a court where there is any question about the appropriateness of using exhibits with an opening statement, always try to get a ruling in advance. Judges have considerable discretion in such matters and may exercise it differently from jurisdiction to jurisdiction.

10.2.2 Presentation Aids

Specially designed charts or presentation aids that illustrate or summarize points to be made during the opening statement are very useful, particularly where the opening may be more than 15 minutes long. The ground rules are unclear, however, with respect to something prepared specially for an opening statement (and not intended to be offered as an exhibit). One rule of thumb is that you can put anything on a visual aid that you could say. Words, graphs, and charts are appropriate so long as they contain information that would be appropriate in the lawyer's statement itself. The traditional limitations on what you can say during an opening statement are:

- no irrelevant material—the statement must stick to the issues in the case;
- no reference to any matter not reasonably believed to be supported by admissible evidence;
- no personal views, opinions, or assertions of personal knowledge; and
- no argument—arguments are reserved for closings and are improper in an opening statement.

The most effective visual aids for an opening statement are those that illustrate the relationship among the parties or key witnesses; assist in the explanation of a key statute, contract provision, or other written material; or describe damages.

No foundation is required for any visual aid used in an opening statement. Simply introduce the chart or board at the appropriate moment:

Example

Counsel: We have prepared an enlargement showing this contract section in order to provide a clearer explanation on this point. *(Puts board up on easel)* Now with respect to the first point . . . *(Continues statement)*.

Nothing requires you to show the visual aid to your opponent before the opening statement or, once you have unveiled it, to give your opponent an opportunity to examine it before you continue your statement. Local practice varies, however. Some courts require all visual aids used in opening statements to be disclosed in the final pretrial conference and examined for possible objection.

You will want to make sure, in the opening statement, that the jury understands who the main players are. A simple diagram is usually effective for this purpose.

Example

Counsel: There will be testimony in this case about the people who were responsible for the statements made in the letter sent by the XYZ Company that is Exhibit 109. I am putting up here on the easel a diagram that shows you who these people are. *(Puts 30 x 40" enlarged organization diagram on the easel facing the jury.)* I have marked this as Exhibit 55 so we can keep track of it. The person at the top is Sharon McGelvey. *(Points to top box on the diagram.)* She's the President of the XYZ Company. The person next in line here is Mr. Brown, who is sitting over there at counsel table. He is the Vice-President for Sales. *(Points to box on next level of the diagram.)* There are also Vice Presidents for Engineering and for Manufacturing. You see them here. *(Points to other boxes on diagram.)* You will hear testimony that these people, the Vice Presidents for Engineering and Manufacturing, didn't know that statements were being made about the Assembot II robot being fully tested, proven, and ready to go . . . .

A simple diagram that helps explain who the players are should not draw an objection because any such objection will be overruled. So long as this diagram does not contain irrelevant material, inadmissible facts, personal opinions of the lawyer, or arguments about the facts, it falls within the general rule of material that could be explained orally and therefore can also be explained using a visual aid.

One caution: there is probably nothing worse than having opposing counsel find some flaw in your visual aid and harp on it during his or her opening statement. If you use a visual aid with your presentation, you must be sure it is absolutely accurate; or that its possible inaccuracies can be defended and are defended in advance.

Icons are a different form of presentation aid for opening statements. Icons are representational figures or pictures that encapsulate ideas necessary to presenting the theory of the case. See Fig. 57. They are drawn from the general idea in a computer's interface with its human operator. In that context, small figures or cartoons appear on the screen to express a command or direction: an arrow pointing backward means "please undo the last thing that I did and take me back to what I had before that"; or a drawing of a pair of scissors means "please cut out this whole section I've marked because I've decided to do something else with it."

In the context of an opening statement, icons help you speak in a way that jurors can understand. Cases often involve disputes about matters with which jurors have no personal familiarity. During the opening statement, you may have to explain several new concepts and then go on to link the concepts together before pointing the way to a conclusion. When you identify each concept with an icon, it helps the jurors recognize each concept without getting confused.

Example

Counsel: *[After initial explanations about the parties and the time frame]* I have put up an exhibit frame over here so that I can show you how the evidence in this case will fit together. The first transaction that happened here was the joint venture between the XYZ Company and the Svensk Technology Company. So I'll put this "handshake" figure up here *[places first icon on the exhibit frame]* with the XYZ Company on one side of the handshake and the Swedish company on the other side. Here is how this joint venture came about. *[Explains evidence as to the joint venture . . .]*

Now, the next transaction that happened here was a contract between the Swedish company and the Belchfire Boiler Company. That contract provided the Swedish company would transfer know-how about coal burning industrial boilers. So I'll put this figure with a piece of paper and a light bulb up here *[places second icon on the exhibit frame]* to represent this second transaction—the contract to transfer know-how. *[Explains evidence as to technology transfer contract . . .]*

The third transaction that happened was the sale of a coal burning boiler by Belchfire Boiler Company to the New Age Power Company right here in this state. I'll put this figure with a piece of paper and a boiler up here *[places third icon on the exhibit frame]*. New Age Power Company was a customer of the XYZ Company. Nevertheless, XYZ Company lost this sale, and many others, because the Swedish company revealed XYZ's technology that they promised, over here in the joint venture *[points to the first icon]*, that they would not do.

Using these icons allows the lawyer to identify the transactions easily, by pointing, rather than with a lot of words that could lead to confusion. Once the icons are on the exhibit frame (see discussion of exhibit frames in Section 9.3.1), other explanatory information can be added, such as dates or key phrases, to help crystallize an overview of what happened. A piece of foamboard covered with Velcro, a computer display, a visualizer, or a magnetized board can be used to the same effect. See discussion in Chapter 9.

10.2.3 In-Court Lists, Notes, and Sketches

You can write or draw as the opening statement proceeds. Write key dates to emphasize the chronology being developed. Spell out the full names of key witnesses so that the fact-finder gets them straight from the start. Draw basic diagrams to illustrate the verbal description of what the evidence will show.

The same rules apply to in-court lists, notes, and sketches made by the lawyer during the opening statement as apply to prepared visual aids discussed in Section 10.2.2. Basically, anything that is proper as an oral presentation can also be written down or drawn during the opening statement.

You can use a large sketch pad mounted on an easel or a whiteboard. Blackboards are also available in most courtrooms, although this is a less desirable medium. See Section 9.3.1.

No in-court list, note, or sketch should be attempted without either prior experience or plenty of pretrial practice. Even a simple list needs to be written in letters that are large enough for the jury to see easily, that do not slant downhill, and that fit on the page. One practical suggestion in this regard: do not write as you talk. Talk first, then write, then talk. Talking while you are writing is distracting both to you and to your audience.

10.3 CLOSING ARGUMENTS

A closing argument brings together the key evidence in a persuasive summary that explains why the requested verdict is necessary and just. If exhibits have been an important part of the evidence, then they will be an equally important part of the closing argument.

By the time you get to the closing argument, the exhibits are already admitted in evidence and can be used, without any permission from the court, in summing up the case. You can display the entirety or any part of any document exhibit, and you can play excerpts from videotapes and segments of computer animations admitted in evidence.

You can also use new presentation aids, made specially for closing argument, that outline or illustrate the points you are making orally. Even in areas where no exhibits were used with the testimony at trial, it may increase the effectiveness of the closing to use a list of points, a diagram of relationships, or some other graphic display to help hammer home the logic of the argument.

The rules governing the use of exhibits with a closing argument are not codified anywhere unless some provision in this regard is included in local rules. Rule 611(a) is sometimes cited in deciding disputes about closing arguments. It provides that: "The court shall exercise reasonable control over the mode and order of . . . presenting evidence so as to (1) make the . . . presentation effective for the ascertainment of the truth [and] (2) avoid needless consumption of time . . . ." The lawyer's use of exhibits, like the oral description of the evidence, must be fair and within the boundaries of evidence admitted at trial.

Exhibits have only a supporting role in the closing argument. You must cull them vigorously to get down to the critical items about which the jury must be persuaded in order to arrive at a verdict in your favor. Using too many exhibits in the closing argument will dissipate its effect.

10.3.1 Entire Admitted Exhibits

You may use an admitted exhibit in its entirety in the closing argument so long as it is properly identified by exhibit number or otherwise and the oral description of the facts with respect to the exhibit is fair and accurate.

If you do not describe the exhibit by its number or a ready shorthand description, your opponent does not have a fair opportunity to determine if your use of the exhibit during your closing is proper, and he or she may object on that ground, interrupting your flow.

Example

(A closing argument involving Exhibit 43 described in Section 2.1.2)

Counsel: We have proved that the Fifer Company represented its Assembot II robot was available immediately for installation in the Jackson plant. This letter *(holding up an exhibit)* came from their own agent right before the . . . .

Opposing Counsel: Objection, the exhibit to which counsel is referring has not been identified and thus we are deprived of the opportunity to object, if necessary, to the description of it.

Counsel: The letter is Exhibit 43.

Opposing Counsel: Objection. There is no proof that Fifer Company represented the Assembot II was available immediately, and the letter doesn't say that.

Court: Objection sustained, please rephrase your description.

Counsel: This letter, Exhibit 43, came from their own agent right before the order form was signed by the plant manager at the Jackson plant, and it says, and I quote: "The Assembot II is available to be installed in your plant in California within 30 days after an order was received. The Assembot II has been fully tested and is ready to go." The plant manager, Mr. Ordway, testified that he would never have considered the Assembot II if it had not been ready to be installed right away. . . .

The objection may be readily overcome, but the failure to describe the document adequately may be interpreted by some jurors as an effort by counsel to slip something by them. If you make sure each exhibit is described by its number when you first refer to it, this kind of objection can be avoided. After the first reference, the exhibit can be described as "this letter" or "the agent's letter" and no further objection will be sustained.

10.3.2 Parts of Admitted Exhibits

You may use any part, paragraph, sentence, or phrase from an admitted exhibit, so long as you properly identify the exhibit and acknowledge that you are using only an excerpt of the exhibit. You may also take parts of an exhibit out of order or use parts of one exhibit with parts of another exhibit so long as the oral description of the facts portrayed is fair and accurate.

Example

(A closing argument involving Exhibit 7 described in Section 1.1.4 and Exhibit 91A described in Section 9.2.1)

Counsel: We have proved that the method used to guard against injuries is reasonable.

First, we have Exhibit 7. *(Holds up exhibit.)* This is a publication issued by the Occupational Health and Safety Administration in January just last year. This is the agency of the United States Government that has the responsibility for deciding what safety measures should be required in workplaces. *(Puts Exhibit 7 on the visualizer.)* Here on page 129, in the third paragraph, OSHA says, and I am putting this up on the screen so you can read along with me, quote: Two hand stops and two foot stops on a cutting machine is sufficient protection for the operator, unquote. That's what OSHA says is sufficient.

> Second, we have Exhibit 91A. *(Holds up videotape cassette.)*
> This is the tape of Mr. Kling's demonstration of the cutting
> machine in the fabricating department of the Riverside plant.
> I am going to play one excerpt from Mr. Kling's
> demonstration. *(Puts hand held scanner over bar code to play
> just one segment of the videotape which is controlled by the
> visualizer.)* Here you see two hand stops; and here you see two
> foot stops. Just what OSHA said was sufficient.

Here, counsel used one sentence in a report containing hundreds of
pages and a 30-second portion of a 10-minute videotape. The entirety
of the report and the videotape have been admitted in evidence, so any
portion, no matter how small, may be used in the closing argument.

10.3.3 Testimony Aids

Testimony aids that have been used with witnesses may also be used
in whole or in part in closing argument. Testimony aids are exhibits
that have been marked but have not been offered or admitted in
evidence. They have, however, been accepted by the court because they
assist the witness in presenting his or her testimony or assist the judge
or jury in understanding the testimony being represented. See
discussion in Section 1.2 and Section 1.3.7.

Example

*(A closing argument involving Exhibit 24A described in Section
1.2.1)*

Counsel: We have proved when the delays occurred and what
    caused them. This is Exhibit 24A *(puts exhibit on easel in
    front of jury)*, which Mr. Jackson, the project inspector, used
    to tell you about his work. He testified that there were no
    delays in Phase 1, from December through mid-March, which
    involved this work on the site *(points at a section of Exhibit
    24A relating to Phase 1)*. Everything was on schedule until
    then . . . .

Some lawyers recommend that testimony aids not be used in closing
argument because the court generally does not give them to the jury
during the deliberation. But post-verdict interviews often confirm that
familiar testimony aids used during trial are helpful to jurors in putting
testimony into context. Using the testimony aids that relate to key facts
helps jurors recall the testimony itself and understand why it was
important.

10.3.4 Lawyer-Generated Summaries

Like testimony aids, lawyer-generated summaries created during direct and cross-examination can be very useful during closing argument. Anything that appeared before the jury during trial can be brought back during closing argument.

Example

(A closing argument involving Exhibit 32 described in Section 1.2.2)

Counsel: The facts about what was supposed to happen under this contract are simple. This is Exhibit 32 which I wrote down as Mr. Morgan testified. *(Turns the pages of the sketch pad over to show the page marked as Exhibit 32.)* The order was placed on January 15 *(points to first line written on the pad)*. The robot was supposed to arrive between February 15 and March 1 *(points to second line written on pad)*. Installation would take about 10 days *(points to third line written on pad)*. And the production line would be in full operation by March 15 *(points to fourth line written on pad)*. 60 days total time from the order on January 15 to full production on March 15. That's what Mr. Morgan testified, and there is no contrary evidence about what was expected. Now, let's look at what actually happened . . . .

The lawyer-generated summary made during trial is brought back to illustrate the same point again during closing argument.

10.3.5 New Presentation Aids

You are not limited during closing argument to existing exhibits, testimony aids, and lawyer-generated summaries. You may also create new materials for closing argument. The basic rule is that anything you could say during your closing argument you can also write down and display before the jury as you talk. You may make a list of dates, phrases, or points as you talk or the new material may be prepared ahead of time by graphic arts specialists and used during the final argument. These new materials are not limited to words; they may include illustrations, icons, or other graphic materials so long as they are within the bounds of the oral presentation allowed in closing argument.

Example

Counsel: We are required to prove five things in order to recover for a misrepresentation. They are listed here *(puts a large exhibit listing five items on the easel in front of the jury)*. The court will instruct you that we are required to prove that a statement was made *(points to first item on the list)* by the

> defendant, Albert Zeigler. We did that. Here it is. Exhibit 110 is the letter signed by Albert Zeigler in which he said, and I quote, the scientific testing of the new drug to cure Alzheimer's disease has been completed and FDA approval will be forthcoming, end quote *(makes check mark against first item with black marker)*. Next, the court will instruct you that we are required to prove this statement was false *(points to second item on the list)*. We did that . . . .

Using a new exhibit to summarize proof is permitted in closing argument so long as everything on the exhibit is something that you are permitted to present orally in closing argument. Complicated jury instructions often require explanation from counsel as to how the evidence presented at trial meets the requirements of the instructions. An exhibit made specially for closing argument is useful in this regard. Inferences from complicated facts are also explained more readily with visual assistance.

A time line that summarizes the evidence in the case month-by-month or year-by-year is often effective in drawing the fact-finder's attention to the overall picture while the lawyer's closing argument explains how each piece fits the pattern. With a complicated case, when the courtroom configuration permits, you can do this dramatically using a 10' or 15' long roll-out chart.

When two or more witnesses who saw the same events have testified dramatically differently about those events, sometimes you can use an enlargement of a list that summarizes opportunity to observe and the other elements of credibility to demonstrate that one witness is more trustworthy than another. If a particular bit of trial testimony is crucial, you can have the reporter produce a certified transcript and use a blowup of the transcript. Damages charts are also important in discussing why your client is entitled to the amounts claimed.

10.3.6 Advance Planning

The visual aids used in any presentation by a lawyer need to be a part of the natural flow of the explanation. They must appear and disappear gracefully and not cause any disruption in the attention of the fact-finder to the argument that is being made. Visual aids are only supporting props; they are not the argument.

As the trial proceeds, you will want to have a separate section of your trial notebook where you put thoughts about the additions to the closing argument. When your opponent makes a particularly effective point with an exhibit, put down your thoughts about how to handle that visually in your final argument. If the presentation of some of your exhibits gets ensnared in evidentiary objections and the evidence comes in piecemeal or with cautionary instructions, consider straightening this out in the jury's mind with an explanation during closing argument.

The technology you choose for trial will affect closing argument. You have to be ready to respond quickly and flexibly. A paper graphics system where hard copy exhibits are displayed on an easel or a projector screen system requires you to give graphic artists two or three days' advance notice to prepare new materials for closing. An electronic system, where hard copy exhibits are presented on a video monitor through a visualizer or videotape player usually requires less time to get ready. A digital system, where all exhibits have been digitized and are controlled through a computer system, is the most flexible and provides the greatest range of support for a closing argument.

Experienced trial lawyers often draft the closing argument well in advance of the opening of the trial while exhibits are being assembled and testimony is being prepared. When designing exhibits to be used with various witnesses, you will want to give some thought to how those exhibits might be used in a series at closing argument. You can effectively tie in the theory of the case together at the end if, in the closing argument, the evidentiary exhibits or testimony aids used with some of the key witnesses come together in a series that makes a persuasive argument.

Color is one simple device that ties exhibits together visually for use in the final argument. For example, if witnesses A, B, and C testify about a number of subjects and it is particularly important to tie together their testimony about one subject, perhaps construction costs, you can use the same color band for the heading or outline of each witness's exhibit on this subject. Thus, when your engineering witnesses testify about construction costs, the relevant exhibit may be a chart or a table with a distinctive green band. When your accounting witnesses testify about construction costs, their relevant chart or table also has a green band. And when your safety expert testifies about that same subject, her exhibit is similarly identified. When you do your final argument, you bring out the green color coded exhibits from each witness, put them side by side, and argue how this testimony all meshes together to support the overall proposition. The visual color coding of the green bands will help make the point. You can accomplish the same sort of color coding with exhibits that cover more than one subject. Assign each important subject its own color code, so that at the end you can show the judge and jury how the pieces fit together. It is a simple, but effective device.

If you are using a computer system or an electronic system to present exhibits during trial, you will want to integrate these display capabilities into your closing argument. If there are many bits and pieces of evidence to be drawn together, this equipment can help create a smooth, flowing presentation that maximizes impact within the time available. For example, excerpts from the trial transcripts, videotapes of depositions played at trial, and documentary exhibits can be put together in a computer display prepared specially for the closing arguments. With all the materials in one place, the lawyer need only press a button to display the next piece of evidence as the closing argument is made.

ENDNOTES

1. *See The Effective Deposition* (giving a detailed and practical discussion of how to prepare for and conduct a successful deposition).

2. *See Model Rules of Professional Conduct* Rule 3.4(e) (1995) (codifying these limitations to some extent).

3. *See generally Steven Lubet, Modern Trial Advocacy, ch.1* (NITA 1993).

APPENDIX A

FEDERAL RULES OF EVIDENCE

for United States Courts
and Magistrates
Effective July 1, 1975
as amended to July 9, 1995

ARTICLE I
General Provisions

Rule 101 – Scope

These rules govern proceedings in the courts of the United States and before United States bankruptcy judges and United States magistrate judges, to the extent and with the exceptions stated in Rule 1101.

Rule 102 – Purpose and Construction

These rules shall be construed to secure fairness in administration, elimination of unjustifiable expense and delay, and promotion of growth and development of the law of evidence to the end that the truth may be ascertained and proceedings justly determined.

Rule 103 – Rulings on Evidence

(a) Effect of erroneous ruling. Error may not be predicated upon a ruling which admits or excludes evidence unless a substantial right of the party is affected, and

(1) Objection. In case the ruling is one admitting evidence, a timely objection or motion to strike appears of record, stating the specific ground of objection, if the specific ground was not apparent from the context; or

(2) Offer of proof. In case the ruling is one excluding evidence, the substance of the evidence was made known to the court by offer or was apparent from the context within which questions were asked.

(b) Record of offer and ruling. The court may add any other or further statement which shows the character of the evidence, the form in which it was offered, the objection made, and the ruling thereon. It may direct the making of an offer in question and answer form.

(c) Hearing of jury. In jury cases, proceedings shall be conducted, to the extent practicable, so as to prevent inadmissible evidence from being suggested to the jury by any means, such as making statements or offers of proof or asking questions in the hearing of the jury.

(d) Plain error. Nothing in this rule precludes taking notice of plain errors affecting substantial rights although they were not brought to the attention of the court.

Rule 104 – Preliminary Questions

(a) Questions of admissibility generally. Preliminary questions concerning the qualification of a person to be a witness, the existence of a privilege, or the admissibility of evidence shall be determined by the court, subject to the provisions of subdivision (b). In making its determination it is not bound by the rules of evidence except those with respect to privileges.

(b) Relevancy conditioned on fact. When the relevancy of evidence depends upon the fulfillment of a condition of fact, the court shall admit it upon, or subject to, the introduction of evidence sufficient to support a finding of the fulfillment of the condition.

(c) Hearing of jury. Hearings on the admissibility of confessions shall in all cases be conducted out of the hearing of the jury. Hearings on other preliminary matters shall be so conducted when the interests of justice require, or when an accused is a witness and so requests.

(d) Testimony by accused. The accused does not, by testifying upon a preliminary matter, become subject to cross-examination as to other issues in the case.

(e) Weight and credibility. This rule does not limit the right of a party to introduce before the jury evidence relevant to weight or credibility.

Rule 105 – Limited Admissibility

When evidence which is admissible as to one party or for one purpose but not admissible as to another party or for another purpose is admitted, the court, upon request, shall restrict the evidence to its proper scope and instruct the jury accordingly.

Rule 106 – Remainder of or Related Writings or Recorded Statements

When a writing or recorded statement or part thereof is introduced by a party, an adverse party may require the introduction at that time of any other part or any other writing or recorded statement which ought in fairness to be considered contemporaneously with it.

ARTICLE II
Judicial Notice

Rule 201 – Judicial Notice of Adjudicative Facts

(a) Scope of rule. This rule governs only judicial notice of adjudicative facts.

(b) Kinds of facts. A judicially noticed fact must be one not subject to reasonable dispute in that it is either (1) generally known within the territorial jurisdiction of the trial court or (2) capable of accurate and ready determination by resort to sources whose accuracy cannot reasonably be questioned.

(c) When discretionary. A court may take judicial notice, whether requested or not.

(d) When mandatory. A court shall take judicial notice if requested by a party and supplied with the necessary information.

(e) Opportunity to be heard. A party is entitled upon timely request to an opportunity to be heard as to the propriety of taking judicial notice and the tenor of the matter noticed. In the absence of prior notification, the request may be made after judicial notice has been taken.

(f) Time of taking notice. Judicial notice may be taken at any stage of the proceeding.

(g) Instructing jury. In a civil action or proceeding, the court shall instruct the jury to accept as conclusive any fact judicially noticed. In a criminal case, the court shall instruct the jury that it may, but is not required to, accept as conclusive any fact judicially noticed.

ARTICLE III
Presumptions in Civil Actions and Proceedings

Rule 301 – Presumptions in General in Civil Actions and Proceedings

In all civil actions and proceedings not otherwise provided for by Act of Congress or by these rules, a presumption imposes on the party against whom it is directed the burden of going forward with evidence to rebut or meet the presumption, but does not shift to such party the burden of proof in the sense of the risk of non-persuasion, which remains throughout the trial upon the party on whom it was originally cast.

Rule 302 – Applicability of State Law in Civil Actions and Proceedings

In civil actions and proceedings, the effect of a presumption respecting a fact which is an element of a claim or defense as to which State law supplies the rule of decision is determined in accordance with State law.

ARTICLE IV
Relevancy and Its Limits

Rule 401 – Definition of "Relevant Evidence"

"Relevant evidence" means evidence having any tendency to make the existence of any fact that is of consequence to the determination of the action more probable or less probable than it would be without the evidence.

Rule 402 – Relevant Evidence Generally Admissible; Irrelevant Evidence Inadmissible

All relevant evidence is admissible, except as otherwise provided by the Constitution of the United States, by Act of Congress, by these rules, or by other rules prescribed by the Supreme Court pursuant to statutory authority. Evidence which is not relevant is not admissible.

Rule 403 – Exclusion of Relevant Evidence on Grounds of Prejudice, Confusion, or Waste of Time

Although relevant, evidence may be excluded if its probative value is substantially outweighed by the danger of unfair prejudice, confusion of the issues, or misleading the jury, or by considerations of undue delay, waste of time, or needless presentation of cumulative evidence.

Rule 404 – Character Evidence Not Admissible to Prove Conduct; Exceptions; Other Crimes

(a) Character evidence generally. Evidence of a person's character or a trait of character is not admissible for the purpose of proving action in conformity therewith on a particular occasion, except:

(1) Character of accused. Evidence of a pertinent trait of character offered by an accused, or by the prosecution to rebut the same;

(2) Character of victim. Evidence of a pertinent trait of character of the victim of the crime offered by an accused, or by the prosecution to rebut the same, or evidence of a character trait of peacefulness of the victim offered by the prosecution in a homicide case to rebut evidence that the victim was the first aggressor;

(3) Character of witness. Evidence of the character of a witness, as provided in rules 607, 608, and 609.

(b) Other crimes, wrongs, or acts. Evidence of other crimes, wrongs, or acts is not admissible to prove the character of a person in order to show action in conformity therewith. It may, however, be admissible for other purposes, such as proof of motive, opportunity, intent, preparation, plan, knowledge, identity, or absence of mistake or accident, provided that upon request by the accused, the prosecution in a criminal case shall provide reasonable notice in advance of trial, or during trial if the court excuses pretrial notice on good cause shown, of the general nature of any such evidence it intends to introduce at trial.

APPENDIX A — FEDERAL RULES OF EVIDENCE

Rule 405 – Methods of Proving Character

(a) Reputation or opinion. In all cases in which evidence of character or a trait of character of a person is admissible, proof may be made by testimony as to reputation or by testimony in the form of an opinion. On cross-examination, inquiry is allowable into relevant specific instances of conduct.

(b) Specific instances of conduct. In cases in which character or a trait of character of a person is an essential element of a charge, claim, or defense, proof may also be made of specific instances of that person's conduct.

Rule 406 – Habit; Routine Practice

Evidence of the habit of a person or of the routine practice of an organization, whether corroborated or not and regardless of the presence of eyewitnesses, is relevant to prove that the conduct of the person or organization on a particular occasion was in conformity with the habit or routine practice.

Rule 407 – Subsequent Remedial Measures

When, after an event, measures are taken which, if taken previously, would have made the event less likely to occur, evidence of the subsequent measures is not admissible to prove negligence or culpable conduct in connection with the event. This rule does not require the exclusion of evidence of subsequent measures when offered for another purpose, such as proving ownership, control, or feasibility of precautionary measures, if controverted, or impeachment.

Rule 408 – Compromise and Offers to Compromise

Evidence of (1) furnishing or offering or promising to furnish, or (2) accepting or offering or promising to accept, a valuable consideration in compromising or attempting to compromise a claim which was disputed as to either validity or amount, is not admissible to prove liability for or invalidity of the claim or its amount. Evidence of conduct or statements made in compromise negotiations is likewise not admissible. This rule does not require the exclusion of any evidence otherwise discoverable merely because it is presented in the course of compromise negotiations. This rule also does not require exclusion when the evidence is offered for another purpose, such as proving bias or prejudice of a witness, negativing a contention of undue delay, or proving an effort to obstruct a criminal investigation or prosecution.

Rule 409 – Payment of Medical and Similar Expenses

Evidence of furnishing or offering or promising to pay medical, hospital, or similar expenses occasioned by an injury is not admissible to prove liability for the injury.

Rule 410 – Inadmissibility of Pleas, Plea Discussions, and Related Statements

Except as otherwise provided in this rule, evidence of the following is not, in any civil or criminal proceeding, admissible against the defendant who made the plea or was a participant in the plea discussions:

501

(1) a plea of guilty which was later withdrawn;

(2) a plea of nolo contendere;

(3) any statement made in the course of any proceedings under Rule 11 of the Federal Rules of Criminal Procedure or comparable state procedure regarding either of the foregoing pleas; or

(4) any statement made in the course of plea discussions with an attorney for the prosecuting authority which do not result in a plea of guilty or which result in a plea of guilty later withdrawn. However, such a statement is admissible (i) in any proceeding wherein another statement made in the course of the same plea or plea discussions has been introduced and the statement ought in fairness be considered contemporaneously with it, or (ii) in a criminal proceeding for perjury or false statement if the statement was made by the defendant under oath, on the record and in the presence of counsel.

Rule 411 – Liability Insurance

Evidence that a person was or was not insured against liability is not admissible upon the issue whether the person acted negligently or otherwise wrongfully. This rule does not require the exclusion of evidence of insurance against liability when offered for another purpose, such as proof of agency, ownership, or control, or bias or prejudice of a witness.

Rule 412 – Sex Offense Cases; Relevance of Victim's Past Sexual Behavior or Alleged Sexual Predisposition

(a) Evidence Generally Inadmissible. The following evidence is not admissible in any civil or criminal proceeding involving alleged sexual misconduct except as provided in subdivisions (b) and (c):

(1) Evidence offered to prove that any alleged victim engaged in other sexual behavior.

(2) Evidence offered to prove any alleged victim's sexual predisposition.

(b) Exceptions.

(1) In a criminal case, the following evidence is admissible, if otherwise admissible under these rules:

(A) evidence of specific instances of sexual behavior by the alleged victim offered to prove that a person other than the accused was the source of semen, injury or other physical evidence;

(B) evidence of specific instances of sexual behavior by the alleged victim with respect to the person accused of the sexual misconduct offered by the accused to prove consent or by the prosecution; and

(C) evidence the exclusion of which would violate the constitutional rights of the defendant.

(2) In a civil case, evidence offered to prove the sexual behavior or sexual predisposition of any alleged victim is admissible if it is otherwise admissible under these rules and its probative value substantially outweighs the danger of harm to any victim and of unfair prejudice to any party. Evidence of an alleged victim's reputation is

admissible only if it has been placed in controversy by the alleged victim.

(c) Procedure to determine admissibility.

(1) A party intending to offer evidence under subdivision (b) must

(A) file a written motion at least 14 days before trial specifically describing the evidence and stating the purpose for which it is offered unless the court, for good cause requires a different time for filing or permits filing during trial; and

(B) serve the motion on all parties and notify the alleged victim or, when appropriate, the alleged victim's guardian or representative.

(2) Before admitting evidence under this rule the court must conduct a hearing in camera and afford the victim and parties a right to attend and be heard. The motion, related papers, and the record of the hearing must be sealed and remain under seal unless the court orders otherwise.

Rule 413 – Evidence of Similar Crimes in Sexual Assault Cases

(a) In a criminal case in which the defendant is accused of an offense of sexual assault, evidence of the defendant's commission of another offense or offenses of sexual assault is admissible, and may be considered for its bearing on any matter to which it is relevant.

(b) In a case in which the Government intends to offer evidence under this rule, the attorney for the Government shall disclose the evidence to the defendant, including statements of witnesses or a summary of the substance of any testimony that is expected to be offered, at least fifteen days before the scheduled date of trial or at such later time as the court may allow for good cause.

(c) This rule shall not be construed to limit the admission or consideration of evidence under any other rule.

(d) For purposes of this rule and Rule 415, "offense of sexual assault" means a crime under Federal law or the law of a State (as defined in section 513 of title 18, United States Code) that involved—

(1) any conduct proscribed by chapter 109A of title 18, United States Code;

(2) contact, without consent, between any part of the defendant's body or an object and the genitals or anus of another person:

(3) contact, without consent, between the genitals or anus of the defendant and any part of another person's body;

(4) deriving sexual pleasure or gratification from the infliction of death, bodily injury, or physical pain on another person; or

(5) an attempt or conspiracy to engage in conduct described in paragraph (1)-(4).

Rule 414 – Evidence of Similar Crimes in Child Molestation Cases

(a) In a criminal case in which the defendant is accused of an offense of child molestation, evidence of the defendant's commission of another offense or offenses of child molestation is admissible, and may be considered for its bearing on any matter to which it is relevant.

(b) In a case in which the Government intends to offer evidence under this rule, the attorney for the Government shall disclose the evidence to the defendant, including statements of witnesses or a summary of the substance of any testimony that is expected to be offered, at least fifteen days before the scheduled date of trial or at such later time as the court may allow for good cause.

(c) This rule shall not be construed to limit the admission or consideration of evidence under any other rule.

(d) For purposes of this rule and Rule 415, "child" means a person below the age of fourteen, and "offense of child molestation" means a crime under Federal law or the law of a State (as defined in section 513 of title 18, United States Code) that involved—

(1) any conduct proscribed by chapter 109A of title 18, United States Code, that was committed in relation to a child;

(2) any conduct proscribed by chapter 110 of title 18, United States Code;

(3) contact between any part of the defendant's body or an object and the genitals or anus of a child;

(4) contact between the genitals or anus of the defendant and any part of the body of a child;

(5) deriving sexual pleasure or gratification from the infliction of death, bodily injury, or physical pain on a child; or

(6) an attempt or conspiracy to engage in conduct described in paragraphs (1)-(5).

Rule 415 – Evidence of Similar Acts in Civil Cases Concerning Sexual Assault or Child Molestation

(a) In a civil case in which a claim for damages or other relief is predicated on a party's alleged commission of conduct constituting an offense of sexual assault or child molestation, evidence of that party's commission of another offense or offenses of sexual assault or child molestation is admissible and may be considered as provided in Rule 413 and Rule 414 of these rules.

(b) A party who intends to offer evidence under this Rule shall disclose the evidence to the party against whom it will be offered, including statements of witnesses or a summary of the substance of any testimony that is expected to be offered, at least fifteen days before the scheduled date of trial or at such later time as the court may allow for good cause.

(c) This rule shall not be construed to limit the admission or consideration of evidence under any other rule.

ARTICLE V
Privileges

Rule 501 – General Rule

Except as otherwise required by the Constitution of the United States or provided by Act of Congress or in rules prescribed by the Supreme Court pursuant to statutory authority, the privilege of a witness, person, government, State, or political subdivision thereof shall be governed by the principles of the common law as they may be interpreted by the courts of the United States in the light of reason and experience. However, in civil actions and proceedings, with respect to an element of a claim or defense as to which State law supplies the rule of decision, the privilege of a witness, person, government, State, or political subdivision thereof shall be determined in accordance with State law.

ARTICLE VI
Witnesses

Rule 601 – General Rule of Competency

Every person is competent to be a witness except as otherwise provided in these rules. However, in civil actions and proceedings, with respect to an element of a claim or defense as to which State law supplies the rule of decision, the competency of a witness shall be determined in accordance with State law.

Rule 602 – Lack of Personal Knowledge

A witness may not testify to a matter unless evidence is introduced sufficient to support a finding that the witness has personal knowledge of the matter. Evidence to prove personal knowledge may, but need not, consist of the witness' own testimony. This rule is subject to the provisions of Rule 703, relating to opinion testimony by expert witnesses.

Rule 603 – Oath or Affirmation

Before testifying, every witness shall be required to declare that the witness will testify truthfully, by oath or affirmation administered in a form calculated to awaken the witness' conscience and impress the witness' mind with the duty to do so.

Rule 604 – Interpreters

An interpreter is subject to the provisions of these rules relating to qualification as an expert and the administration of an oath or affirmation to make a true translation.

Rule 605 – Competency of Judge as Witness

The judge presiding at the trial may not testify in that trial as a witness. No objection need be made in order to preserve the point.

Rule 606 – Competency of Juror as Witness

(a) At the trial. A member of the jury may not testify as a witness before that jury in the trial of the case in which the juror is sitting. If the juror is called so to testify, the opposing party shall be afforded an opportunity to object out of the presence of the jury.

(b) Inquiry into validity of verdict or indictment. Upon an inquiry into the validity of a verdict or indictment, a juror may not testify as to any matter or statement occurring during the course of the jury's deliberations or to the effect of anything upon that or any other juror's mind or emotions as influencing the juror to assent to or dissent from the verdict or indictment or concerning the juror's mental processes in connection therewith, except that a juror may testify on the question whether extraneous prejudicial information was improperly brought to the jury's attention or whether any outside influence was improperly brought to bear upon any juror. Nor may a juror's affidavit or evidence of any statement by the juror concerning a matter about which the juror would be precluded from testifying be received for these purposes.

Rule 607 – Who May Impeach

The credibility of a witness may be attacked by any party, including the party calling the witness.

Rule 608 – Evidence of Character and Conduct of Witness

(a) Opinion and reputation evidence of character. The credibility of a witness may be attacked or supported by evidence in the form of opinion or reputation, but subject to these limitations: (1) the evidence may refer only to character for truthfulness or untruthfulness, and (2) evidence of truthful character is admissible only after the character of the witness for truthfulness has been attacked by opinion or reputation evidence or otherwise.

(b) Specific instances of conduct. Specific instances of the conduct of a witness, for the purpose of attacking or supporting the witness' credibility, other than conviction of crime as provided in Rule 609, may not be proved by extrinsic evidence. They may, however, in the discretion of the court, if probative of truthfulness or untruthfulness, be inquired into on cross-examination of the witness (1) concerning the witness' character for truthfulness or untruthfulness, or (2) concerning the character for truthfulness or untruthfulness of another witness as to which character the witness being cross-examined has testified.

The giving of testimony, whether by an accused or by any other witness, does not operate as a waiver of the accused's or the witness' privilege against self-incrimination when examined with respect to matters which relate only to credibility.

Rule 609 – Impeachment by Evidence of Conviction of Crime

(a) General rule. For the purpose of attacking the credibility of a witness, (1) evidence that a witness other than an accused has been convicted of a crime shall be admitted subject to Rule 403, if the crime was punishable by death or imprisonment in excess of one year under the law under which the witness was convicted, and evidence that an accused has been convicted of such a crime shall be admitted if the court determines that the probative value of admitting this evidence outweighs its prejudicial effect to the accused; or (2) evidence that any witness has been convicted of a crime shall be admitted if it involved dishonesty or false statement, regardless of the punishment.

(b) Time limit. Evidence of a conviction under this rule is not admissible if a period of more than ten years has elapsed since the date of the conviction or of the release of the witness from the confinement imposed for that conviction, whichever is the later date, unless the court determines, in the interests of justice, that the probative value of the conviction supported by specific facts and circumstances substantially outweighs its prejudicial effect. However, evidence of a conviction more than 10 years old as calculated herein, is not admissible unless the proponent gives to the adverse party sufficient advance written notice of intent to use such evidence to provide the adverse party with a fair opportunity to contest the use of such evidence.

(c) Effect of pardon, annulment, or certificate of rehabilitation. Evidence of a conviction is not admissible under this rule if (1) the conviction has been the subject of a pardon, annulment, certificate of rehabilitation, or other equivalent procedure based on a finding of the rehabilitation of the person convicted, and that person has not been convicted of a subsequent crime which was punishable by death or imprisonment in excess of one year, or (2) the conviction has been the subject of a pardon, annulment, or other equivalent procedure based on a finding of innocence.

(d) Juvenile adjudications. Evidence of juvenile adjudications is generally not admissible under this rule. The court may, however, in a criminal case allow evidence of a juvenile adjudication of a witness other than the accused if conviction of the offense would be admissible to attack the credibility of an adult and the court is satisfied that admission in evidence is necessary for a fair determination of the issue of guilt or innocence.

(e) Pendency of appeal. The pendency of an appeal therefrom does not render evidence of a conviction inadmissible. Evidence of the pendency of an appeal is admissible.

Rule 610 – Religious Beliefs or Opinions

Evidence of the beliefs or opinions of a witness on matters of religion is not admissible for the purpose of showing that by reason of their nature the witness' credibility is impaired or enhanced.

Rule 611 – Mode and Order of Interrogation and Presentation

(a) Control by court. The court shall exercise reasonable control over the mode and order of interrogating witnesses and presenting evidence so as to (1) make the interrogation and presentation effective for the ascertainment of the truth, (2) avoid needless consumption of time, and (3) protect witnesses from harassment or undue embarrassment.

(b) Scope of cross-examination. Cross-examination should be limited to the subject matter of the direct examination and matters affecting the credibility of the witness. The court may, in the exercise of discretion, permit inquiry into additional matters as if on direct examination.

(c) Leading questions. Leading questions should not be used on the direct examination of a witness except as may be necessary to develop the witness' testimony. Ordinarily leading questions should be permitted on cross-examination. When a party calls a hostile witness, an adverse party, or a witness identified with an adverse party, interrogation may be by leading questions.

Rule 612 – Writing Used to Refresh Memory

Except as otherwise provided in criminal proceedings by section 3500 of title 18, United States Code, if a witness uses a writing to refresh memory for the purpose of testifying, either

(1) while testifying, or

(2) before testifying, if the court in its discretion determines it is necessary in the interests of justice, an adverse party is entitled to have the writing produced at the hearing, to inspect it, to cross-examine the witness thereon, and to introduce in evidence those portions which relate to the testimony of the witness. If it is claimed that the writing contains matters not related to the subject matter of the testimony the court shall examine the writing in camera, excise any portions not so related, and order delivery of the remainder to the party entitled thereto. Any portion withheld over objections shall be preserved and made available to the appellate court in the event of an appeal. If a writing is not produced or delivered pursuant to order under this rule, the court shall make any order justice requires, except that in criminal cases when the prosecution elects not to comply, the order shall be one striking the testimony or, if the court in its discretion determines that the interests of justice so require, declaring a mistrial.

Rule 613 – Prior Statements of Witnesses

(a) Examining witness concerning prior statement. In examining a witness concerning a prior statement made by the witness, whether written or not, the statement need not be shown nor its contents disclosed to the witness at that time, but on request the same shall be shown or disclosed to opposing counsel.

(b) Extrinsic evidence of prior inconsistent statement of witness. Extrinsic evidence of a prior inconsistent statement by a witness is not admissible unless the witness is afforded an opportunity to explain or deny the same and the opposite party is afforded an opportunity to interrogate the witness thereon, or the interests of justice otherwise require. This provision does not apply to admissions of a party-opponent as defined in rule 801(d)(2).

Rule 614 – Calling and Interrogation of Witnesses by Court

(a) Calling by court. The court may, on its own motion or at the suggestion of a party, call witnesses, and all parties are entitled to cross-examine witnesses thus called.

(b) Interrogation by court. The court may interrogate witnesses, whether called by itself or by a party.

(c) Objections. Objections to the calling of witnesses by the court or to interrogation by it may be made at the time or at the next available opportunity when the jury is not present.

Rule 615 – Exclusion of Witnesses

At the request of a party the court shall order witnesses excluded so that they cannot hear the testimony of other witnesses, and it may make the order of its own motion. This rule does not authorize exclusion of (1) a party who is a natural person, or (2) an officer or employee of a party which is not a natural person designated as its representative by its attorney, or (3) a person whose presence is shown by a party to be essential to the presentation of the party's cause.

ARTICLE VII
Opinions and Expert Testimony

Rule 701 – Opinion Testimony by Lay Witnesses

If the witness is not testifying as an expert, the witness' testimony in the form of opinions or inferences is limited to those opinions or inferences which are (a) rationally based on the perception of the witness and (b) helpful to a clear understanding of the witness' testimony or the determination of a fact in issue.

Rule 702 – Testimony by Experts

If scientific, technical, or other specialized knowledge will assist the trier of fact to understand the evidence or to determine a fact in issue, a witness qualified as an expert by knowledge, skill, experience, training, or education, may testify thereto in the form of an opinion or otherwise.

Rule 703 – Bases of Opinion Testimony by Experts

The facts or data in the particular case upon which an expert bases an opinion or inference may be those perceived by or made known to the expert at or before the hearing. If of a type reasonably relied upon by experts in the particular field in forming opinions or inferences upon the subject, the facts or data need not be admissible in evidence.

Rule 704 – Opinion on Ultimate Issue

(a) Except as provided in subdivision (b), testimony in the form of an opinion or inference otherwise admissible is not objectionable because it embraces an ultimate issue to be decided by the trier of fact.

(b) No expert witness testifying with respect to the mental state or condition of a defendant in a criminal case may state an opinion or inference as to whether the defendant did or did not have the mental state or condition constituting an element of the crime charged or of a defense thereto. Such ultimate issues are matters for the trier of fact alone.

Rule 705 – Disclosure of Facts or Data Underlying Expert Opinion

The expert may testify in terms of opinion or inference and give reasons therefor without first testifying to the underlying facts or data, unless the court requires otherwise. The expert may in any event be required to disclose the underlying facts or data on cross-examination.

Rule 706 – Court Appointed Experts

(a) Appointment. The court may on its own motion or on the motion of any party enter an order to show cause why expert witnesses should not be appointed, and may request the parties to submit nominations. The court may appoint any expert witnesses agreed upon by the parties, and may appoint expert witnesses of its own selection. An expert witness shall not be appointed by the court unless the witness consents to act. A witness so appointed shall be informed of the witness' duties by the court in writing, a copy of which shall be filed with the clerk, or at a conference in which the parties shall have opportunity to participate. A witness so appointed shall advise the parties of the witness' findings, if any; the witness' deposition may be taken by any party; and the witness may be called to testify by the court or any party. The witness shall be subject to cross-examination by each party, including a party calling the witness.

(b) Compensation. Expert witnesses so appointed are entitled to reasonable compensation in whatever sum the court may allow. The compensation thus fixed is payable from funds which may be provided by law in criminal cases and civil actions and proceedings involving just compensation under the fifth amendment. In other civil actions and proceedings the compensation shall be paid by the parties in such proportion and at such time as the court directs, and thereafter charged in like manner as other costs.

(c) Disclosure of appointment. In the exercise of its discretion, the court may authorize disclosure to the jury of the fact that the court appointed the expert witness.

(d) Parties' experts of own selection. Nothing in this rule limits the parties in calling expert witnesses of their own selection.

ARTICLE VIII
Hearsay

Rule 801 – Definitions

The following definitions apply under this article:

(a) Statement. A statement is (1) an oral or written assertion or (2) nonverbal conduct of a person, if it is intended by the person as an assertion.

(b) Declarant. A declarant is a person who makes a statement.

(c) Hearsay. Hearsay is a statement, other than one made by the declarant while testifying at the trial or hearing, offered in evidence to prove the truth of the matter asserted.

(d) Statements which are not hearsay. A statement is not hearsay if –

(1) Prior statement by witness. The declarant testifies at the trial or hearing and is subject to cross-examination concerning the statement, and the statement is (A) inconsistent with the declarant's testimony, and was given under oath subject to the penalty of perjury at a trial, hearing, or other proceeding, or in a deposition, or (B) consistent with the declarant's testimony and is offered to rebut an express or implied charge against the declarant of recent fabrication or improper influence or motive, or (C) one of identification of a person made after perceiving the person; or

(2) Admission by party-opponent. The statement is offered against a party and is (A) the party's own statement in either an individual or a representative capacity or (B) a statement of which the party has manifested an adoption or belief in its truth, or (C) a statement by a person authorized by the party to make a statement concerning the subject, or (D) a statement by the party's agent or servant concerning a matter within the scope of the agency or employment, made during the existence of the relationship, or (E) a statement by a coconspirator of a party during the course and in furtherance of the conspiracy.

Rule 802 – Hearsay Rule

Hearsay is not admissible except as provided by these rules or by other rules prescribed by the Supreme Court pursuant to statutory authority or by Act of Congress.

Rule 803 – Hearsay Exceptions; Availability of Declarant Immaterial

The following are not excluded by the hearsay rule, even though the declarant is available as a witness:

(1) Present sense impression. A statement describing or explaining an event or condition made while the declarant was perceiving the event or condition, or immediately thereafter.

(2) Excited utterance. A statement relating to a startling event or condition made while the declarant was under the stress of excitement caused by the event or condition.

(3) Then existing mental, emotional, or physical condition. A statement of the declarant's then existing state of mind, emotion, sensation, or physical condition (such as intent, plan, motive, design, mental feeling, pain, and bodily health), but not including a statement of memory or belief to prove the fact remembered or believed unless it relates to the execution, revocation, identification, or terms of declarant's will.

(4) Statements for purposes of medical diagnosis or treatment. Statements made for purposes of medical diagnosis or treatment and describing medical history, or past or present symptoms, pain, or sensations, or the inception or general character of the cause or

external source thereof insofar as reasonably pertinent to diagnosis or treatment.

(5) Recorded recollection. A memorandum or record concerning a matter about which a witness once had knowledge but now has insufficient recollection to enable the witness to testify fully and accurately, shown to have been made or adopted by the witness when the matter was fresh in the witness' memory and to reflect that knowledge correctly. If admitted, the memorandum or record may be read into evidence but may not itself be received as an exhibit unless offered by an adverse party.

(6) Records of regularly conducted activity. A memorandum, report, record, or data compilation, in any form, of acts, events, conditions, opinions, or diagnoses, made at or near the time by, or from information transmitted by, a person with knowledge, if kept in the course of a regularly conducted business activity, and if it was the regular practice of that business activity to make the memorandum, report, record, or data compilation, all as shown by the testimony of the custodian or other qualified witness, unless the source of information or the method or circumstances of preparation indicate lack of trustworthiness. The term business as used in this paragraph includes business, institution, association, profession, occupation, and calling of every kind, whether or not conducted for profit.

(7) Absence of entry in records kept in accordance with the provisions of paragraph (6). Evidence that a matter is not included in the memoranda reports, records, or data compilations, in any form, kept in accordance with the provisions of paragraph (6), to prove the nonoccurrence or nonexistence of the matter, if the matter was of a kind of which a memorandum, report, record, or data compilation was regularly made and preserved, unless the sources of information or other circumstances indicate lack of trustworthiness.

(8) Public records and reports. Records, reports, statements, or data compilations, in any form, of public offices or agencies, setting forth (A) the activities of the office or agency, or (B) matters observed pursuant to duty imposed by law as to which matters there was a duty to report, excluding, however, in criminal cases matters observed by police officers and other law enforcement personnel, or (C) in civil actions and proceedings and against the Government in criminal cases, factual findings resulting from an investigation made pursuant to authority granted by law, unless the sources of information or other circumstances indicate lack of trustworthiness.

(9) Records of vital statistics. Records or data compilations, in any form, of births, fetal deaths, deaths, or marriages, if the report thereof was made to a public office pursuant to requirements of law.

(10) Absence of public record or entry. To prove the absence of a record, report, statement, or data compilation, in any form, or the nonoccurrence or nonexistence of a matter of which a record, report, statement, or data compilation, in any form, was regularly made and preserved by a public office or agency, evidence in the form of a certification in accordance with Rule 902, or testimony, that diligent

search failed to disclose the record, report, statement, or data compilation, or entry.

(11) Records of religious organizations. Statements of births, marriages, divorces, deaths, legitimacy, ancestry, relationship by blood or marriage, or other similar facts of personal or family history, contained in a regularly kept record of a religious organization.

(12) Marriage, baptismal, and similar certificates. Statements of fact contained in a certificate that the maker performed a marriage or other ceremony or administered a sacrament, made by a clergyman, public official, or other person authorized by the rules or practices of a religious organization or by law to perform the act certified, and purporting to have been issued at the time of the act or within a reasonable time thereafter.

(13) Family records. Statements of fact concerning personal or family history contained in family Bibles, genealogies, charts, engravings on rings, inscriptions on family portraits, engravings on urns, crypts, or tombstones, or the like.

(14) Records of documents affecting an interest in property. The record of a document purporting to establish or affect an interest in property, as proof of the content of the original recorded document and its execution and delivery by each person by whom it purports to have been executed, if the record is a record of a public office and an applicable statute authorizes the recording of documents of that kind in that office.

(15) Statements in documents affecting an interest in property. A statement contained in a document purporting to establish or affect an interest in property if the matter stated was relevant to the purpose of the document, unless dealings with the property since the document was made have been inconsistent with the truth of the statement or the purport of the document.

(16) Statements in ancient documents. Statements in a document in existence twenty years or more the authenticity of which is established.

(17) Market reports, commercial publications. Market quotations, tabulations, lists, directories, or other published compilations, generally used and relied upon by the public or by persons in particular occupations.

(18) Learned treatises. To the extent called to the attention of an expert witness upon cross-examination or relied upon by the expert witness in direct examination, statements contained in published treatises, periodicals, or pamphlets on a subject of history, medicine, or other science or art, established as a reliable authority by the testimony or admission of the witness or by other expert testimony or by judicial notice. If admitted, the statements may be read into evidence but may not be received as exhibits.

(19) Reputation concerning personal or family history. Reputation among members of a person's family by blood, adoption, or marriage, or among a person's associates, or in the community, concerning a person's birth, adoption, marriage, divorce, death, legitimacy,

relationship by blood, adoption, or marriage, ancestry, or other similar fact of personal or family history.

(20) Reputation concerning boundaries or general history. Reputation in a community, arising before the controversy, as to boundaries of or customs affecting lands in the community, and reputation as to events of general history important to the community or State or nation in which located.

(21) Reputation as to character. Reputation of a person's character among associates or in the community.

(22) Judgment of previous conviction. Evidence of a final judgment, entered after a trial or upon a plea of guilty (but not upon a plea of nolo contendere), adjudging a person guilty of a crime punishable by death or imprisonment in excess of one year, to prove any fact essential to sustain the judgment, but not including, when offered by the Government in a criminal prosecution for purposes other than impeachment, judgments against persons other than the accused. The pendency of an appeal may be shown but does not affect admissibility.

(23) Judgment as to personal, family or general history, or boundaries. Judgments as proof of matters of personal, family or general history, or boundaries, essential to the judgment, if the same would be provable by evidence of reputation.

(24) Other exceptions. A statement not specifically covered by any of the foregoing exceptions but having equivalent circumstantial guarantees of trustworthiness, if the court determines that (A) the statement is offered as evidence of a material fact; (B) the statement is more probative on the point for which it is offered than any other evidence which the proponent can procure through reasonable efforts; and (C) the general purposes of these rules and the interests of justice will best be served by admission of the statement into evidence. However, a statement may not be admitted under this exception unless the proponent of it makes known to the adverse party sufficiently in advance of the trial or hearing to provide the adverse party with a fair opportunity to prepare to meet it, the proponent's intention to offer the statement and the particulars of it, including the name and address of the declarant.

Rule 804 – Hearsay Exceptions; Declarant Unavailable

(a) Definition of unavailability. "Unavailability as a witness" includes situations in which the declarant–

(1) is exempted by ruling of the court on the ground of privilege from testifying concerning the subject matter of the declarant's statement; or

(2) persists in refusing to testify concerning the subject matter of the declarant's statement despite an order of the court to do so; or

(3) testifies to a lack of memory of the subject matter of the declarant's statement; or

(4) is unable to be present or to testify at the hearing because of death or then existing physical or mental illness or infirmity; or

(5) is absent from the hearing and the proponent of a statement has been unable to procure the declarant's attendance (or in the case of a hearsay exception under subdivisions (b)(2), (3), or (4), the declarant's attendance or testimony) by process or other reasonable means.

A declarant is not unavailable as a witness if exemption, refusal, claim of lack of memory, inability, or absence is due to the procurement or wrongdoing of the proponent of a statement for the purpose of preventing the witness from attending or testifying.

(b) Hearsay exceptions. The following are not excluded by the hearsay rule if the declarant is unavailable as a witness:

(1) Former testimony. Testimony given as a witness at another hearing of the same or a different proceeding, or in a deposition taken in compliance with law in the course of the same or another proceeding, if the party against whom the testimony is now offered, or, in a civil action or proceeding, a predecessor in interest, had an opportunity and similar motive to develop the testimony by direct, cross, or redirect examination.

(2) Statement under belief of impending death. In a prosecution for homicide or in a civil action or proceeding, a statement made by a declarant while believing that the declarant's death was imminent, concerning the cause or circumstances of what the declarant believed to be impending death.

(3) Statement against interest. A statement which was at the time of its making so far contrary to the declarant's pecuniary or proprietary interest, or so far tended to subject the declarant to civil or criminal liability, or to render invalid a claim by the declarant against another, that a reasonable person in the declarant's position would not have made the statement unless believing it to be true. A statement tending to expose the declarant to criminal liability and offered to exculpate the accused is not admissible unless corroborating circumstances clearly indicate the trustworthiness of the statement.

(4) Statement of personal or family history. (A) A statement concerning the declarant's own birth, adoption, marriage, divorce, legitimacy, relationship by blood, adoption, or marriage, ancestry, or other similar fact of personal or family history, even though declarant had no means of acquiring personal knowledge of the matter stated; or (B) a statement concerning the foregoing matters, and death also, of another person, if the declarant was related to the other by blood, adoption, or marriage or was so intimately associated with the other's family as to be likely to have accurate information concerning the matter declared.

(5) Other exceptions. A statement not specifically covered by any of the foregoing exceptions but having equivalent circumstantial guarantees of trustworthiness, if the court determines that (A) the statement is offered as evidence of a material fact; (B) the statement is more probative on the point for which it is offered than any other evidence which the proponent can procure through reasonable efforts; and (C) the general purposes of these rules and the interests of justice will best be served by admission of the statement into evidence. However, a statement may not be admitted under this exception unless the

proponent of it makes known to the adverse party sufficiently in advance of the trial or hearing to provide the adverse party with a fair opportunity to prepare to meet it, the proponent's intention to offer the statement and the particulars of it, including the name and address of the declarant.

Rule 805 – Hearsay Within Hearsay

Hearsay included within hearsay is not excluded under the hearsay rule if each part of the combined statements conforms with an exception to the hearsay rule provided in these rules.

Rule 806 – Attacking and Supporting Credibility of Declarant

When a hearsay statement, or a statement defined in Rule 801(d)(2), (C), (D), or (E), has been admitted in evidence, the credibility of the declarant may be attacked, and if attacked may be supported, by any evidence which would be admissible for those purposes if declarant had testified as a witness. Evidence of a statement or conduct by the declarant at any time, inconsistent with the declarant's hearsay statement, is not subject to any requirement that the declarant may have been afforded an opportunity to deny or explain. If the party against whom a hearsay statement has been admitted calls the declarant as a witness, the party is entitled to examine the declarant on the statement as if under cross-examination.

ARTICLE IX
Authentication and Identification

Rule 901 – Requirement of Authentication or Identification

(a) General provision. The requirement of authentication or identification as a condition precedent to admissibility is satisfied by evidence sufficient to support a finding that the matter in question is what its proponent claims.

(b) Illustrations. By way of illustration only, and not by way of limitation, the following are examples of authentication or identification conforming with the requirements of this rule:

(1) Testimony of witness with knowledge. Testimony that a matter is what it is claimed to be.

(2) Nonexpert opinion on handwriting. Nonexpert opinion as to the genuineness of handwriting, based upon familiarity not acquired for purposes of litigation.

(3) Comparison by trier or expert witness. Comparison by the trier of fact or by expert witnesses with specimens which have been authenticated.

(4) Distinctive characteristics and the like. Appearance, contents, substance, internal patterns, or other distinctive characteristics, taken in conjunction with circumstances.

(5) Voice identification. Identification of a voice, whether heard firsthand or through mechanical or electronic transmission or recording, by opinion based upon hearing the voice at any time under circumstances connecting it with the alleged speaker.

(6) Telephone conversations. Telephone conversations, by evidence that a call was made to the number assigned at the time by the telephone company to a particular person or business, if (A) in the case of a person, circumstances, including self-identification, show the person answering to be the one called, or (B) in the case of a business, the call was made to a place of business and the conversation related to business reasonably transacted over the telephone.

(7) Public records or reports. Evidence that a writing authorized by law to be recorded or filed and in fact recorded or filed in a public office, or a purported public record, report, statement, or data compilation, in any form, is from the public office where items of this nature are kept.

(8) Ancient documents or data compilation. Evidence that a document or data compilation, in any form, (A) is in such condition as to create no suspicion concerning its authenticity, (B) was in a place where it, if authentic, would likely be, and (C) has been in existence 20 years or more at the time it is offered.

(9) Process or system. Evidence describing a process or system used to produce a result and showing that the process or system produces an accurate result.

(10) Methods provided by statute or rule. Any method of authentication or identification provided by Act of Congress or by other rules prescribed by the Supreme Court pursuant to statutory authority.

Rule 902 – Self-Authentication

Extrinsic evidence of authenticity as a condition precedent to admissibility is not required with respect to the following:

(1) Domestic public documents under seal. A document bearing a seal purporting to be that of the United States, or of any State, district, Commonwealth, territory, or insular possession thereof, or the Panama Canal Zone, or the Trust Territory of the Pacific Islands, or of a political subdivision, department, officer, or agency thereof, and a signature purporting to be an attestation or execution.

(2) Domestic public documents not under seal. A document purporting to bear the signature in the official capacity of an officer or employee of any entity included in paragraph (1) hereof, having no seal, if a public officer having a seal and having official duties in the district or political subdivision of the officer or employee certifies under seal that the signer has the official capacity and that the signature is genuine.

(3) Foreign public documents. A document purporting to be executed or attested in an official capacity by a person authorized by the laws of a foreign country to make the execution or attestation, and accompanied by a final certification as to the genuineness of the signature and official position (A) of the executing or attesting person, or (B) of any foreign official whose certificate of genuineness of

signature and official position relates to the execution or attestation or is in a chain of certificates of genuineness of signature and official position relating to the execution or attestation. A final certification may be made by a secretary of embassy or legation, consul general, consul, vice consul, or consular agent of the United States, or a diplomatic or consular official of the foreign country assigned or accredited to the United States. If reasonable opportunity has been given to all parties to investigate the authenticity and accuracy of official documents, the court may, for good cause shown, order that they be treated as presumptively authentic without final certification or permit them to be evidenced by an attested summary with or without final certification.

(4) Certified copies of public records. A copy of an official record or report or entry therein, or of a document authorized by law to be recorded or filed and actually recorded or filed in a public office, including data compilations in any form, certified as correct by the custodian or other person authorized to make the certification, by certificate complying with paragraph (1), (2), or (3) of this rule or complying with any Act of Congress or rule prescribed by the Supreme Court pursuant to statutory authority.

(5) Official publications. Books, pamphlets, or other publications purporting to be issued by public authority.

(6) Newspapers and periodicals. Printed materials purporting to be newspapers or periodicals.

(7) Trade inscriptions and the like. Inscriptions, signs, tags, or labels purporting to have been affixed in the course of business and indicating ownership, control, or origin.

(8) Acknowledged documents. Documents accompanied by a certificate of acknowledgment executed in the manner provided by law by a notary public or other officer authorized by law to take acknowledgments.

(9) Commercial paper and related documents. Commercial paper, signatures thereon, and documents relating thereto to the extent provided by general commercial law.

(10) Presumptions under Acts of Congress. Any signature, document or other matter declared by Act of Congress to be presumptively or prima facie genuine or authentic.

Rule 903 – Subscribing Witness' Testimony Unnecessary

The testimony of a subscribing witness is not necessary to authenticate a writing unless required by the laws of the jurisdiction whose laws govern the validity of the writing.

ARTICLE X
Contents of Writings, Recordings, and Photographs

Rule 1001 – Definitions

For purposes of this article the following definitions are applicable:

(1) Writings and recordings. Writings and recordings consist of letters, words, or numbers, or their equivalent, set down by handwriting, typewriting, printing, photostating, photographing, magnetic impulse, mechanical or electronic recording, or other form of data compilation.

(2) Photographs. Photographs include still photographs, X-ray films, videotapes, and motion pictures.

(3) Original. An original of a writing or recording is the writing or recording itself or any counterpart intended to have the same effect by a person executing or issuing it. An original of a photograph includes the negative or any print therefrom. If data are stored in a computer or similar device, any printout or other output readable by sight, shown to reflect the data accurately, is an original.

(4) Duplicate. A duplicate is a counterpart produced by the same impression as the original, or from the same matrix, or by means of photography, including enlargements and miniatures, or by mechanical or electronic re-recording, or by chemical reproduction, or by other equivalent techniques which accurately reproduces the original.

Rule 1002 – Requirement of Original

To prove the content of a writing, recording, or photograph, the original writing, recording, or photograph is required, except as otherwise provided in these rules or by Act of Congress.

Rule 1003 – Admissibility of Duplicates

A duplicate is admissible to the same extent as an original unless (1) a genuine question is raised as to the authenticity of the original or (2) in the circumstances it would be unfair to admit the duplicate in lieu of the original.

Rule 1004 – Admissibility of Other Evidence of Contents

The original is not required, and other evidence of the contents of a writing, recording, or photograph is admissible if –

(1) Originals lost or destroyed. All originals are lost or have been destroyed, unless the proponent lost or destroyed them in bad faith; or

(2) Original not obtainable. No original can be obtained by any available judicial process or procedure; or

(3) Original in possession of opponent. At a time when an original was under the control of the party against whom offered, that party was put on notice, by the pleadings or otherwise, that the contents would be a subject of proof at the hearing, and that party does not produce the original at the hearing; or

(4) Collateral matters. The writing, recording, or photograph is not closely related to a controlling issue.

Rule 1005 – Public Records

The contents of an official record, or of a document authorized to be recorded or filed and actually recorded or filed, including data compilations in any form, if otherwise admissible, may be proved by copy, certified as correct in accordance with rule 902 or testified to be correct by a witness who has compared it with the original. If a copy which complies with the foregoing cannot be obtained by the exercise of reasonable diligence, then other evidence of the contents may be given.

Rule 1006 – Summaries

The contents of voluminous writings, recordings, or photographs which cannot conveniently be examined in court may be presented in the form of a chart, summary, or calculation. The originals, or duplicates, shall be made available for examination or copying, or both, by other parties at reasonable time and place. The court may order that they be produced in court.

Rule 1007 – Testimony or Written Admission of Party

Contents of writings, recordings, or photographs may be proved by the testimony or deposition of the party against whom offered or by that party's written admission, without accounting for the nonproduction of the original.

Rule 1008 – Functions of Court and Jury

When the admissibility of other evidence of contents of writings, recordings, or photographs under these rules depends upon the fulfillment of a condition of fact, the question whether the condition has been fulfilled is ordinarily for the court to determine in accordance with the provisions of rule 104. However, when an issue is raised (a) whether the asserted writing ever existed, or (b) whether another writing, recording, or photograph produced at the trial is the original, or (c) whether other evidence of contents correctly reflects the contents, the issue is for the trier of fact to determine as in the case of other issues of fact.

ARTICLE XI
Miscellaneous Rules

Rule 1101 – Applicability of Rules

(a) Courts and judges. These Rules apply to the United States district courts, the District Court of Guam, the District Court of the Virgin Islands, the District Court for the Northern Mariana Islands, the United States Courts of Appeals, the United States Claims Court, and to United States bankruptcy judges and United States magistrate judges, in the actions, cases, and proceedings and to the extent hereinafter set forth. The terms "judge" and "court" in these rules include United States bankruptcy judges and United States magistrate judges.

(b) Proceedings generally. These rules apply generally to civil actions and proceedings, including admiralty and maritime cases, to criminal cases and proceedings, to contempt proceedings except those in which the court may act summarily, and to proceedings and cases under title 11, United States Code.

(c) Rule of privilege. The rule with respect to privileges applies at all stages of all actions, cases, and proceedings.

(d) Rules inapplicable. The rules (other than with respect to privileges) do not apply in the following situations:

(1) Preliminary questions of fact. The determination of questions of fact preliminary to admissibility of evidence when the issue is to be determined by the court under rule 104.

(2) Grand jury. Proceedings before grand juries.

(3) Miscellaneous proceedings. Proceedings for extradition or rendition; preliminary examinations in criminal cases; sentencing, or granting or revoking probation; issuance of warrants for arrest, criminal summonses, and search warrants; and proceedings with respect to release on bail or otherwise.

(e) Rules applicable in part. In the following proceedings these rules apply to the extent that matters of evidence are not provided for in the statutes which govern procedure therein or in other rules prescribed by the Supreme Court pursuant to statutory authority: the trial of misdemeanors and other petty offenses by United States magistrate judges; review of agency actions when the facts are subject to trial de novo under section 706(2)(F) of title 5, United States Code; review of orders of the Secretary of Agriculture under section 2 of the Act entitled An Act to authorize association of producers of agricultural products approved February 18, 1922 (7 U.S.C. 292), and under sections 6 and 7(c) of the Perishable Agricultural Commodities Act, 1930 (7 U.S.C. 499f, 499g(c)); naturalization and revocation of naturalization under sections 310-318 of the Immigration and Nationality Act (8 U.S.C. 1421-1429); prize proceedings in admiralty under sections 7651-7681 of title 10, United States Code; review of orders of the Secretary of the Interior under section 2 of the Act entitled An Act authorizing associations of producers of aquatic products approved June 25, 1934 (15 U.S.C. 522); review of orders of petroleum control boards under section 5 of the Act entitled An Act to regulate interstate and foreign commerce in petroleum and its products by prohibiting the shipment in such commerce of petroleum and its products produced in violation of State law, and for other purposes, approved February 22, 1935 (15 U.S.C. 715d); actions for fines, penalties, or forfeitures under part V of title IV of the Tariff Act of 1930 (19 U.S.C. 1581-1624), or under the Anti-Smuggling Act (19 U.S.C. 1701-1711); criminal libel for condemnation, exclusion of imports, or other proceedings under the Federal Food, Drug, and Cosmetic Act (21 U.S.C. 301-392); disputes between seamen under sections 4079, 4080, and 4081 of the Revised Statutes (22 U.S.C. 256-258); habeas corpus under sections 2241-2254 of title 28, United States Code; motions to vacate, set aside or correct sentence under section 2255 of title 28, United States

Code; actions for penalties for refusal to transport destitute seamen under section 4578 of the Revised Statutes (46 U.S.C. 679); actions against the United States under the Act entitled An Act authorizing suits against the United States in admiralty for damage caused by and salvage service rendered to public vessels belonging to the United States, and for other purposes, approved March 3, 1925 (46 U.S.C. 781-790), as implemented by section 7730 of title 10, United States Code.

Rule 1102 – Amendments

Amendments to the Federal Rules of Evidence may be made as provided in section 2072 of title 28 of the United States Code.

Rule 1103 – Title

These rules may be known and cited as the Federal Rules of Evidence.

APPENDIX B

SUPPLIERS FOR EQUIPMENT AND TECHNICAL ASSISTANCE

This Appendix provides information about manufacturers, systems providers, production firms, and graphic arts specialists so that the lawyer considering a new type of exhibit or display will have a starting point in the search for a supplier. Part I covers equipment for displaying exhibits as described in Section 9.1. Part II covers specialized exhibits such as computer animations and videotape exhibits. Part III covers general graphic arts suppliers who can provide assistance with text documents, charts, graphs, time lines, tables, maps, diagrams, drawings, and other explanatory materials. Part IV lists jury research firms who can help with the focus groups described in Section 9.8.

As explained in Section 9.7, the process of selecting a firm or firms to assist with trial exhibits is like selecting an expert. Individual lawyers have particular preferences, and clients have litigation budget limitations. These critical considerations cannot be assessed here. This Appendix is intended only as a helpful starting point, generally in alphabetical order.

PART I: EQUIPMENT FOR DISPLAYING EXHIBITS

Digital systems
(Section 9.6)

DOAR Communications Inc.
Sam Solomon, President
Bonnie Seidler, Executive VP
743 West Merrick Road
Valley Stream, NY 11580-4826
(516) 285-1100
Fax: (516) 285-1145
http://www.doar.com
e-mail: sam@doar.com

DOAR supplies complete
courtroom display systems
(computer, monitors, switcher,
cabling, backup) and in-court
services for the installation and
operation of the equipment.

Visualizer/Visual Presenter/Document Camera
(Section 9.5.3)

DOAR Communications Inc.
743 West Merrick Road
Valley Stream, NY 11580-4826
(516) 285-1100
Fax: (516) 285-1145

Current model: DVP-2000. Doar
provides a Visual Presenter which
has been specially optimized for
courtroom use.

Toshiba America Consumer
 Products
Video Communications and
Information Systems Division
Multimedia Group
1010 Johnson Drive
Buffalo Grove, IL 60089-6900
(800) 344-8446
http://www.toshiba.com

Current model: Toshiba
MediaStar. This is a combined
document camera and LCD
projector.

Overhead projector
(Section 9.4.1)

3M Product Information Center
3M Center Building 515-3N-06
St. Paul, MN 55144
(800) 952-4059
http://www.mmm.com/office
e-mail: presentations@mmm.com

Current model: 3M 9850

Apollo Presentation Products
60 Trade Zone Court
Ronkonkoma, NY 11779
(800) 777-3750
http://apollo.pb.net
e-mail: sales@apollo.a-v.com

Current model: Co-Star 575

Boxlight Corporation
17771 Fjord Drive NE
Poulsbo, WA 98370
(800) 762-5757
http://www.boxlight.com

Current model: 4810

DOAR Communications Inc.
743 West Merrick Road
Valley Stream, NY 11580-4826
(516) 285-1100
Fax: (516) 285-1145
http://www.doar.com
e-mail: sam@doar.com

Current model: Special adaptation
for courtroom use

InFocus Systems, Inc.
27700B SW Parkway Ave.
Wilsonville, OR 97070-9215
(800) 294-6400
http://www.infs.com

Current model: 410P

Minnesota Western
921 Parker Street
Berkeley, CA 94710-2572
(800) 444-9350
http://www.minnwest.com

Current model: 4320

Sharp Electronics Corporation
Sharp Plaza Box G
Mahwah, NJ 07430
(800) 237-4277
http://www.sharpmeg.com

Current model: XGE100U

LCD panel projector
(Section 9.6.6)

An LCD (liquid crystal display) panel is designed to fit on top of the projection surface of an overhead projector. The panel is square or rectangular, 8 to 10 inches in size, and weighs about 7 lbs. The LCD panel is connected to the video port of a computer. The panel provides the display and the overhead projector provides the light source and projecting optics. The crispness of the image projected by the panel depends on the resolution of the panel and the lumens of the overhead projector. LCD panels may have a resolution of 640 x 480 up to 1024 x 768. To project images from an LCD panel successfully, the overhead projector needs to produce at least 3,000 lumens (a standard measure of light intensity). The projection size (image on the screen) is about 10 feet. LCD panels may be active or passive matrix. Active matrix costs more, but produces sharper, clearer, steadier images and better color reproduction.

3M Product Information Center
3M Center Building 515-3N-06
St. Paul, MN 55144
(800) 952-4059
http://www.mmm.com/office
e-mail: presentations@mmm.com

Current model: 3M 6750; fits on top of the 3M 9850 overhead projector.

Apollo Presentation Products
60 Trade Zone Court
Ronkonkoma, NY 11779
(800) 777-3750
http://apollo.pb.net
e-mail: sales@apollo.a-v.com

Current model: Vison Q4

Boxlight Corporation
17771 Fjord Drive NE
Poulsbo, WA 98370
(800) 762-5757
http://www.boxlight.com

Current model: Boxlight 1820

Epson America
20770 Madrona Ave.
Torrance, CA 90503
(800) GO-EPSON
Fax (310) 782-5220
http://www.epson.com

Current model: ELP-3300

Hitachi Multimedia Systems Division
3890 Steve Reynolds Blvd.
Norcross, GA 30093
(770) 279-5600
http://www.hitachi.com

Current model: CPL540

InFocus Systems, Inc.
27700B SW Parkway Ave.
Wilsonville, OR 97070-9215
(800) 294-6400
Fax (503) 685-8887
http://www.infs.com

Current model: Lite Pro 760

Panasonic
One Panasonic Way
Secaucus, NJ 07094
(800) 742-8086
http://www.panasonic.com

Current model: PT-L104

Philips
One Philips Drive
Knoxville, TN 37914
(800) 223-4432
http://www.philips.com

Current model: LC1200

LCD digital projector
(Section 9.6.6)

An LCD (liquid crystal display) digital projector is a self-contained portable unit that combines the LCD display, the light source, and the projecting optics. The unit weighs more than a panel projector. The projector connects to the video port of a computer and projects the images from the computer onto a screen. The LCD matrix inside the projector has the same characteristics as the LCD panel for projection with an overhead projector. Because the light source is built in, it can be varied to accommodate the type of display and the ambient conditions. LCD digital projectors usually produce higher quality images than LCD panel projectors. The image size is also larger than that produced by panels. The capability of various models differs considerably with respect to use in particular courtrooms.

3M Product Information Center
3M Center Building 515-3N-06
St. Paul, MN 55144
(800) 952-4059
http://www.mmm.com/office
e-mail: presentations@mmm.com

Current model: 3M MP8030; 500 ANSI lumens of brightness; compressed SBGA (800 x 600) resolution; compact, 24 lbs.; four input channels; built-in video; VirtualMouse remote with power zoom, power focus, and built-in timer and blank presentation tools; built-in speaker; audio output for external speakers.

CTX Opto, Inc.
1257 Tasman Drive, Suite B
Sunnyvale, CA 94089
(888) 289-6786

Current model: EzPro 500 Personal Multimedia LCD Projector; weighs 9.25 lbs.; works in lighted room; accepts input from computer and video sources; has remote, built-in audio, and carry case.

Hitachi Multimedia Systems Division
3890 Steve Reynolds Boulevard
Norcross, GA 30093
(770) 279-5600
http://www.hitachi.com

Current model: CP-L540; accepts input from laserdisc player, computer, camcorder, or VCR; uses metal halide lamp; has hand-held remote control unit; power zoom; and built-in audio system.

APPENDIX B — SUPPLIERS FOR EQUIPMENT AND TECHNICAL ASSISTANCE

NEC Technologies, Inc.
1414 Massachusetts Ave.
Boxborough, MA 01719
(800) 338-9549
http://www.nec.com
e-mail: tech-support@nectech.com

Current model: MultiSynch
MT600; weighs less than 16 lbs.;
true-640 x 480 resolution and
compressed 800 x 600 resolution;
bright 400 ANSI lumen image;
power zoom focus lens.

InFocus Systems, Inc.
27700B SW Parkway Ave.
Wilsonville, OR 97070-9215
(800) 294-6400
Fax (503) 685-8887
http://www.infs.com

Current model: LitePro 210;
weighs 16 lbs; has built-in JBL
speakers; auto-sensing software
adjusts the picture; remote control;
active matrix LCD panel and
metal halide lamp. CableWizard
feature reduces cables to one cord;
modular upgrades.

Panasonic
One Panasonic Way
Secaucus, NJ 07094
(800) 742-8086
http://www.panasonic.com

Current model: PT-L390U

Philips
One Philips Drive
Knoxville, TN 37914
(800) 223-4432
http://www.philips.com

Current model: Philips ProScreen;
takes input from computer, CD-I
unit, VCR, or live TV feed.

Sharp Electronics Corporation
Sharp Plaza Box G
Mahwah, NJ 07430
(800) 237-4277
http://www.sharpmeg.com

Current model: XGE650 Mk1; uses
metal halide lamp technology.

DLP projectors
(Section 9.6.6)

DLP (digital light processing)
projectors use a DMD (digital
micromirror device) which is a
RAM (random access memory) chip
painted with microscopic
aluminum mirrors that can be
switched on and off individually to
reflect light. Each individual
mirror corresponds to one pixel.
The light is generated by a
high-intensity source such as a
metal halide bulb located in close
proximity to the mirrors. This
technology, developed and licensed
by Texas Instruments, improves
the quality of images over the LCD
technology.

nView
860 Omni Blvd.
Newport News, VA 23606
(800) 736-8439
http://www.nview.com

Current model: Diamond D-400
projector; 23 lbs; accepts both
computer and video input.

InFocus Systems, Inc.
27700B SW Parkway Ave.
Wilsonville, OR 97070-9215
(800) 294-6400
http://www.infs.com

Current model: 410P

Proxima Corporation
9440 Carroll Park Drive
San Diego, CA 92121-2298
(800) 447-7692
http://www.prxm.com

Current model: DP2750B

Electrohome
890 Wellington Street North
Kitchener, Ontario,
Canada N26 4J6
(800) 266-2171
Fax: (519) 749-3136
http://www.electro.com

Current model: Vista

Sony Electronics, Inc.
10833 Valley View Street
Cypress, CA 90630
(714) 220-9100
http://www.sel.sony.com

Current model: VPH1001

CRT projection units
(Section 9.6.6)

CRT (cathode ray tube) projectors
are high end products that are less
portable and more expensive than
LCD projectors. They weigh 50 to
75 lbs. and produce the largest,
brightest, highest resolution
images. Most CRT projectors have
three separate phosphor-coated
tubes (red, green, and blue) each
with its own video amplifier and
lens system. When these three
separate images are projected onto
the screen, they merge to form the
final image. Alignment of the final
image is dependent on the distance
from the projector to the screen, so
in-court adjustments are necessary.

Panasonic
One Panasonic Way
Secaucus, NJ 07094
(800) 742-8086
http://www.panasonic.com

Current model: PT-M1085U
Graphic Projector

Sony Electronics, Inc.
10833 Valley View Street
Cypress, CA 90630
(714) 220-9100
http://www.sel.sony.com

Current model: VP-1001Q

Presentation video monitors
(Section 9.6.4)

Presentation video monitors are
larger versions of the desktop
monitors used with ordinary
computer systems. Monitors for
courtroom use come in sizes up to
40". The monitor should have a
variable scan display so that it can
synchronize itself to signals from a
variety of sources. The remote
control for the monitor may be
either tethered or wireless;
monitors may have built-in
speakers; and the video controls
may be on the front or back. Each
of these features affects how the
monitor is used in the courtroom.
The crispness of the display is
determined by the resolution,
which may range from 640 x 480
on the lower end to 1280 x 1024 or
more on the higher end.

JVC
41 Slater Drive
Elmwood Park, NJ 07407
(800) 582-5825
http://www.jvc.com

Current model: TM270SU

APPENDIX B — SUPPLIERS FOR EQUIPMENT AND TECHNICAL ASSISTANCE

Mitsubishi America
5665 Plaza Drive
Cypress, CA 90630
(714) 220-2500
http://www.mitsubishi.com

Current model: XC2930C

NEC Technologies, Inc.
1414 Massachusetts Ave.
Boxborough, MA 01719
(800) 366-0476
http://www.nec.com

Current model: MT600

Panasonic
One Panasonic Way
Secaucus, NJ 07094
(800) 742-8086
http://www.panasonic.com

Current model: DT2730MS

Philips
One Philips Drive
Knoxville, TN 37914
(800) 223-4432
http://www.philips.com

Current model: 21A

Sony Electronics, Inc.
10833 Valley View Street
Cypress, CA 90630
(714) 220-9100
http://www.sel.sony.com

Current model: RVP4010

SoftBoard
(Section 9.6.7)

Microfield Graphics, Inc.
9825 SW Sunshine Court
Beaverton, OR 97005
(800) 334-4922
Fax: (503) 641-9333
e-mail: sb_info@mfg.com

Current model: Model 203 is a full-sized board integrated with a rolling stand.

SMART Technologies Inc.
Suite 600
1177 Eleventh Ave. SW
Calgary, Alberta,
Canada T2R 1K9
(403) 245-0333
Fax: (403) 245-0366
e-mail: sales@smarttech.com
http://www.smarttech.com

Current model: SMART Board

Poster generator

DOAR Communications Inc.
743 West Merrick Road
Valley Stream, NY 11580-4826
(516) 285-1100
Fax: (516) 285-1145
http://www.doar.com
e-mail: sam@doar.com

Exhibit frame
(Section 9.3)

MF Graphics
12700 S.E. Crain Highway
Brandywine, MD 20613
(301) 372-1245

Exhibit Resource Center, Inc.
8229 Tory Road
Springfield, VA 22152
(703) 569-2725
Fax: (703) 569-8018

Note: The author acknowledges reference material for Part I with respect to projectors and monitors from Knowledge Industry Publications, Inc., 701 Westchester Ave., White Plains, NY.

PART II: SPECIALIZED EXHIBITS

Computer animations
(Section 8.3)

Z-Axis Corporation
Raymond C. Hauschel, Vice
    President
116 Inverness Drive East
Suite 110
Englewood, CO 80112
(303) 792-2400
Fax: (303) 792-2416

Z-Axis constructs computer
animations and provides the
courtroom display equipment
including electronic systems
(laserdisc player and television
monitor) and digital systems
(computer system and video
monitor) plus in-court services to
install and operate the equipment.

Digital trial consultants

DOAR Communications Inc.
743 West Merrick Road
Valley Stream, NY 11580-4826
(516) 285-1100
Fax: (516) 285-1145
http://www.doar.com
e-mail: sam@doar.com

Videotape exhibits
(Section 9.5)

Legal Video Services, Inc.
Avi Stachenfeld, President
1431 Center Street
Oakland, CA 94607
(510) 918-6011
Fax: (510) 836-1420

Seacoast Video Productions
Leslie Sanguinetti
3446 Hancock St., Suite A
San Diego, CA 92110
(619) 297-6113

PART III: GENERAL GRAPHIC ARTS SPECIALISTS

This is a list of firms that are
members of the Demonstrative
Evidence Specialists Association
available as of publication date.
For the current list, contact
Demonstrative Evidence
Specialists Association, Attn:
Brian Hendrix, Browning &
Company, 815 Walker Suite 1553,
Houston, TX 77002, (713) 223-1226.

ALPS—Evidence and Photo
George Pearl
2139 Liddell Drive, N.E.
Atlanta, GA 30324
(404) 872-2577

Applied Litigation Research
Dorie Buckley
Five Civic Plaza
Newport Beach, CA 92660
(714) 760-8100

Artistic Evidence
Debra Schechter
19 Winterbranch
Irvine, CA 92714
(714) 559-4748

Berenson Associates
Lanny Berenson
P.O. Box 1645
Glen Ellen, CA 96442
(415) 485-1025

Bioforce
Willma Wagner
2619 Sailboat Drive
Houston, TX 74508
(409) 766-1355

APPENDIX B — SUPPLIERS FOR EQUIPMENT AND TECHNICAL ASSISTANCE

Browning & Company
Brian Hendrix
815 Walker Street, Suite 1553
Houston, TX 77002
(713) 223-1226

Courtroom Graphics
Holly Hobbs-Bussey
4330 Dumaine, Suite A
New Orleans, LA 70119
(504) 482-8400

Creative Imagery, Inc.
Roy W. Walston
Yvonne Wylie Walston
1048 County Line Road
Tijeras, NM 87059
(505) 281-9847

Drawing Attention
Sharon Cavanaugh
90 High Street
South Windsor, CT 06074
(203) 644-5157

Engineering Animation, Inc.
Matthew Rizai
Jeff Trom
2625 N. Loop Dr, Suite 300
Ames, IA 55010
(515) 296-9908

Exhibit A
Gregory De Santis
7010 Brookfield Plaza, Suite 547
Springfield, VA 22152
(703) 451-9204

Exhibit A America
Penelope Johnston
3 Neck Road
Old Lyme, CT 06371
(203) 434-3941

Goffe Photographic Associates
Jerry Goffe
3108 Monte Vista Blvd., N.E.
Albuquerque, NM 87106-2118

Hans Duus and Associates
Hans Duus
15108 Kercheval Avenue
Grosse Pointe, MI 48230
(313) 822-7703

IFT Technical Services, Inc.
David Frey
2322 Sixth Street, Suite 107
Berkeley, CA 94710
(510) 548-3451

Innovative Media, Inc.
Scott Groves
506 SW Sixth Ave., Suite 401
Portland, OR 97204
(503) 796-0774

Judicial Graphics
Steve Mayhall
38 Wood Lane
Groton, MA 01450
(508) 448-5529

Jurix Graphix Consulting, Inc.
Gail Jaquish
21311 Hawthorne Blvd., Suite 106
Torrence, CA 90503
(310) 792-0506

Just in Case
Nancy Samovar
3001 Motor Avenue
Los Angeles, CA 90064
(213) 558-0726

Legal Arts, Inc.
James Gripp
Jim Jacobsen
401 B Street, Suite 306
San Diego, CA 92101
(619) 231-1551

Legal Graphics
Sam Anderson
228 Robert S. Kerr, #310
Oklahoma City, OK 73102
(405) 232-5242

Legal Graphics
Gale D. Heilman
16835 Algonquin, No. 265
Huntington Beach, CA 92649
(714) 840-4114

Legal Graphics, Inc.
Jan Krafsur
208 South LaSalle Street #1318
Chicago, IL 60604
(312) 332-1212

Legal Model & Display
Mike Russo
P.O. Box 306
N. Scituate, RI 02857
(401) 647-7769

Legal Visuals
Jill Goff
18730 Wimbledon Circle
Lutz, FL 33549
(813) 949-0190

LitCom
Bruce Turkel
2871 Oak Avenue
Miami, FL 33133
(305) 446-8877

Litigation Communication
Theodore D. Ciccone
1009 Duke Street
Alexandria, VA 22314
(703) 739-0400

Litigation Communications, Inc.
Ted Mussenden
1209 Prince Street
Alexandria, VA 22314
(703) 739-0400

Litigation Graphics
Marsha Drebelbis
8150 Brookriver Dr., Suite 606
Dallas, TX 75247
(214) 951-0032

Litigation Graphics
Susan Whaley
1022 East 28th Avenue
Spokane, WA 99203
(509) 838-9898

Litigraphix
John Phelps
438 Main, Suite 207
Rochester, MI 48307
(810) 650-8118

Lou Glist Art
Lou Glist
13615 Pinerock Lane
Houston, TX 77079
(713) 468-6622

Madison Reprographics
William Young
P.O. Box 55193
Madison, WI 5370-5
(608) 836-8890

Med Art & Legal Graphics Co.
Shelly Coy
2108 Braewick Circle
Akron, OH 44313
(216) 869-5330

Medi-Lex Courtroom Visuals
Mark Pearson
4303 Ostrom
Lakewood, CA 90713
(213) 425-0699

MediVisuals
Tom Sims
1221 River Bend Drive, Ste. 240
Dallas, TX 75247
(214) 634-3996

Medical Graphics
Lynne Waltman
P.O. Box 470889
Fort Worth, TX 76147
(817) 560-7856

APPENDIX B — SUPPLIERS FOR EQUIPMENT AND TECHNICAL ASSISTANCE

Medical Visual Communications
Kathleen Harris
P.O. Box 17112
Milwaukee, WI 53217
(414) 352-5515

Nimmer Legal Graphics
Laurence Nimmer
5296 El Carro Lane
Carpenteria, CA 93013
(805) 566-0163

Perry Ballard/Adv. Inc.
Mary Schroder
P.O. Box 240, 526 Upton Dr., East
St. Joseph, MI 49085
(616) 983-0611

Seacoast Video Productions
Leslie Sanguinetti
3024 Hancock Street
San Diego, CA 92110
(619) 297-6113

Southeast Consulting Group
Carole Garlin
450 N. Park Road, Suite 605
Hollywood, FL 33021
(305) 983-6159

Standard Testing Labs
Glenn D. Follen
Lee Spencer
1845 Harsh Ave. SE
Massilon, OH 44648
(216) 833-8548

The Reporter Company
Ken Walter
181 Delaware Street
Walton, NY 13856
(607) 865-4131

Trial Art
Mark E. Vander Hart
1801 Eastern Avenue, S.E.
Grand Rapids, MI 49507
(616) 245-1944

Trial Arts
1801 North Lamar, Suite 110
Dallas, TX 75202
(214) 720-0040

Trial Arts
Cherie Virden
P.O. Box 1560
Santa Ynez, CA 93460
(805) 688-4296

Triodyne
Anthony Provensano
5950 West Touhy Avenue
Niles, IL 60648
(708) 647-8866

Visual Evidence
Dan Copfer
812 Huron Road, S.E., Suite 201
Cleveland, OH 44115
(216) 241-3443

Visually Speaking
Susie Y. Anderson
3746 Pukalani Place
Honolulu, HI 96816
(808) 732-3144

Wilson Management Associates
Ed Josiah
80 Glenhead Road
Glenhead, NY 11545
(516) 759-2300

PART IV: FOCUS GROUP RESEARCH FIRMS

Marjorie Fargo
Litigation Communications
1209 Prince Street
Alexandria, VA 22314
703/739-0400

Dr. Allan H. Colman
DecisionQuest
2050 West 190th Street
Suite 205
Torrance, CA 90504
310/618-9600
http://www.decisionquest.com

Arline Lowenthal
4016 Gresham Street, D-3
San Diego, CA 92109
(619) 272-1662

APPENDIX C

SELECTED SOURCES ON TANGIBLE EVIDENCE

This appendix lists some of the sources published after the second edition that are available for additional research or information on points covered in this book. Some treatises, books, and articles are more useful than others where the task is to get a particular exhibit admitted in evidence. The list set out below is not exhaustive, and many helpful pieces may exist that are not included. Earlier publications are listed in the appendices to the first edition (1978-1982) and the second edition (1983-1989).

TREATISES

Moore, James W., et al. *Moore's Federal Practice*. 2d ed. Matthew Bender & Co., Inc., 1988.

Strong, John W., et al., eds. *McCormick on Evidence*. 4th ed. West Publishing Co., 1992.

Wigmore, John. *Evidence in Trials at Common Law*. 3d ed. Little, Brown and Company, 1983.

BOOKS

Bocchino, Anthony J., and David A. Sonenshein. *A Practical Guide to Federal Evidence*. 3d ed, rev. NITA, 1996.

Broun, K. S., and W. J. Blakey. *Evidence*. West Publishing Co., 1994.

Cotchett, J. W., and Arnold B. Elkind. *Federal Courtroom Evidence*. With Contributions by Charles E. Wagner. Butterworth Legal Publishers, 1993.

Elwork, Amiram, Bruce D. Sales, and James J. Alfini. *Making Jury Instructions Understandable*. Michie Co., 1982.

Jeans, James W. *Trial Advocacy*. West Publishing Co., 1975.

Lubet, Steven. *Modern Trial Advocacy: Analysis and Practice*. Chap. 6. NITA, 1993.

MacGregor, A. *Graphics Simplified: How to Plan and Prepare Effective Charts, Graphs, Illustrations, and Other Visual Aids.* University of Toronto Press, 1979.

Malone, David M., and Peter T. Hoffman. *The Effective Deposition, Techniques and Strategies That Work.* 2d ed. NITA, 1996.

Monmonier, Mark. *How to Lie with Maps.* 2d ed. University of Chicago Press, 1996.

Philo, Harry M., and Harry M. Philo, Jr. *Lawyers Desk Reference.* 8th ed. Clark Boardman Callaghan, 1993.

ARTICLES

Bailey, William S. "Videotape Evidence: Show Me, Don't Tell Me (Proving Damages: The Mechanics of a Case)." *Trial* (March 1991): 52.

Bailey, William S. "Making the Most of Day-in-the-Life Films." *Trial* (April 1994): 28–30.

Bailey, William S. "Storyboards: Inexpensive and Effective." *Trial* (Sept. 1994): 64.

Bailey, William S. "The Artful Lawyer: More Show, Less Tell in Opening Statement." *Trial* (Oct. 1993): 28–30.

Barr, Stephen. "Legal Video Takes the Stand." *Corporate Video Decisions* (Jan. 1990): 33–39, 62–63.

Betts, Mitch. "Multimedia Takes Stand at Simpson Trial." *Computerworld* (9 Jan. 1995): 28.

Borelli, Mario. "The Computer as Advocate: An Approach to Computer-Generated Displays in the Courtroom." *Indiana Law Journal* (Spring 1996): 439–56.

Brain, Robert D., and Daniel J. Broderick. "The Derivative Relevance of Demonstrative Evidence: Charting Its Proper Evidentiary Status." *University of California Davis Law Review* 25, no. 4 (Summer 1992): 957–1027.

Brain, Robert D., and Daniel J. Broderick. "Demonstrative Evidence: Clarifying Its Role at Trial." *Trial* (Sept. 1994): 73–74.

Branson, Debbie Dudley, Frank L. Branson, William H. Carpenter, Windle Turley, J. Kendall Few, John C. Few, Joseph M. Matthews, John W. Norman, and Charles F. Moser. "Saying It Well Without Language." *Trial* (Sept. 1995): 40.

Cerniglia, Timothy W. "Computer-Generated Exhibits—Demonstrative, Substantive or Pedagogical—Their Place in Evidence." *American Journal of Trial Advocacy* (Summer 1994): 1–35.

Chatterjee, I. Neel. "Admitting Computer Animations: More Caution and New Approach Are Needed." *Defense Counsel Journal* (Jan. 1995): 36–46.

Christy, Gary. "A Storybook Approach." *Trial* (Sept. 1994): 70–71.

Clancy, James T., Jr. "Computer Generated Accident Reenactments: The Case for Their Admissibility and Use." *Review of Litigation* (Winter 1996): 203–28.

APPENDIX C — SELECTED SOURCES
ON TANGIBLE EVIDENCE

Curriden, Mark. "At the Creation: With the Generative Power of a Computer, Lawyers Can Shape an Adam or Eve to Demonstrate All Sorts of Medical Conditions. And What They See Is Good." *ABA Journal* (Aug. 1994): 76.

Dedman, James M., III. "What You Are About to See . . . ." *Prosecutor, Journal of the National District Attorneys Association* (July–Aug. 1993): 5.

Dilworth, Donald C. "Virtual Reality: Coming Soon to a Courtroom Near You?" *Trial* (July 1993): 13.

Douglas, Preston. "'A Day-in-the-Life' Videos." *Trial Lawyers Quarterly* (Fall–Winter 1995): 13–17.

Fadely, Kathlynn G. "Use of Computer-Generated Visual Evidence in Aviation Litigation: Interactive Video Comes to Court." 55 *Journal of Air Law and Commerce* 839 (1990).

Feller, H. J. "Photographic Evidence: More Than Meets the Eye." *Maine Bar Journal* (Nov. 1993): 372–74.

Garcia, R. "Garbage In, Gospel Out: Criminal Discovery, Computer Reliability, and the Constitution." *UCLA Law Review* (June 1991): 1043–1145.

Gass, J. Ric. "Trying Cases Visually." *Trial Lawyers Guide* (Winter 1994): 553–600.

Gass, J. Ric, and Samuel H. Solomon, "Trying Cases Visually: Understanding the Effective Use of Visual Communications in Your Legal Practice," in *Coping with Psychiatric and Psychological Testimony*, ed. J. Ziskin (Law Psychology Press 1995), 299-337.

Ghazi, Juliane Kay. "Courtroom Animation: The Cutting Edge of Demonstrative Evidence." *Law Office Computing* (Oct.–Nov. 1992): 30.

Giannelli, P. C. "Forensic Science: Dental and Bite Mark Evidence." *Criminal Law Bulletin* (May/June 1992): 276–84.

Hansen, Mark. "Unfettered Filming; Court Bars Defense Lawyers From Set of Day-in-the-Life Video." *ABA Journal* (Feb. 1992): 32.

Heninger, Stephen D. "Cost-Effective Demonstrative Evidence." *Trial* (Sept. 1994): 65–66.

Henke, M. J. "Admissibility of Computer-Generated Animated Reconstructions and Simulations." *Trial Lawyers Guide* (Winter 1992): 434–47.

Howarth, Don, Suzelle M. Smith, and Mary La Cesa. "Rules Governing Demonstrative Evidence at Trial: A Practitioner's Guide." *Western State University Law Review* (Fall 1992): 157–70.

Jessen, J. E. "Electronic Data as Evidence: A Litigation Tool." *Washington State Bar News* (Oct. 1992): 40–41.

Joseph, Gregory P. "Computer Evidence." *Litigation* 22, no. 1 (Fall 1995): 13–16.

Kalinski, Jane A. "Jurors at the Movies: Day-in-the-Life Videos as Effective Evidentiary Tool or Unfairly Prejudicial Device?" *Suffolk University Law Review* (Fall 1993): 789–823.

Kelner, Joseph, and Robert S. Kelner. "Demonstrative Evidence—Exhibiting Injuries." *New York Law Journal* 214, no. 16 (25 July 1995): 3.

Kelly, Mary C., and Jack N. Bernstein. "Virtual Reality: The Reality of Getting It Admitted." *The John Marshall Journal of Computer & Information Law* (Oct. 1994): 145–73.

Kennedy, W. K. "Demonstrative Evidence in Vehicle Accidents." *Practical Litigator* (Nov. 1993): 37–45.

Krieger, Roy W. "Now Showing at a Courtroom Near You . . . Sophisticated Computer Graphics Come of Age—And Evidence Will Never Be the Same." *ABA Journal* (Dec. 1992): 92–96.

Krieger, Roy W. "Photorealistic Computer Graphics: New Horizon for Evidence." *Trial* (Feb. 1993): 46.

Lederer, Fredic I. "Revolution in Courtroom Technology Presents Opportunity and Risk." *Trial* (Nov. 1994): 86–90.

Leighton, Richard J. "The Use and Effectiveness of Demonstrative Evidence in Federal Agency Proceedings." *Administrative Law Review* 42, no. 1 (Winter 1990): 35–63.

Lucas, J. R. "Props: An Overview of Demonstrative Evidence." *American Journal of Trial Advocacy* (Spring 1990): 1097–1139.

Lynch, Hon. Daniel J., and Ian Brenson. "Computer Generated Evidence: The Impact of Computer Technology on the Traditional Rules of Evidence." 20 *Loyola University of Chicago Law Journal* (Summer 1989): 919-936.

Marcotte, Paul. "Animated Evidence: Delta 191 Crash Re-Created Through Computer Simulations at Trial." *ABA Journal* (Dec. 1989): 52–56.

Martin, E. X., III. "Demonstrative Evidence: Using Computer-Generated Demonstrative Evidence." *Trial* (Sept. 1994): 84–88.

McElhaney, James W. "Seeing the Facts: Tapping the Power of Seeing as Well as Hearing." *ABA Journal* (Dec. 1992): 102–3.

Mulroy, Thomas R., Jr., and Ronald J. Rychlak. "Use of Real and Demonstrative Evidence at Trial." *Trial Lawyer's Guide* (Winter 1990): 550–63.

Oade, K. Preston, and Leslie C. Annand. "Winning with Visual Evidence." *Colorado Lawyer* (Jan. 1996): 35.

Powell, Carole E. "Computer Generated Visual Evidence: Does Daubert Make a Difference?" *Georgia State University Law Review* (Jan. 1996): 577–99.

Reuben, Richard C. "Stuntpersons Add Drama to Cases; Accidents are Re-Created to Support Litigants' Version of Events." *ABA Journal* (Nov. 1995): 14.

Rosen, William W. "Altered Photographs? New Evidentiary Considerations." *Trial* (Sept. 1994): 67–70.

Ryan, J. W., Jr. "Techniques for Success in Preparing and Using Demonstrative Evidence." *Defense Counsel Journal* (April 1991): 188–97.

Ryan, J. W., Jr. "Videotaped Reenactments in Civil Trials: Protecting Probative Evidence from the Trial Judge's Unbridled Discretion." *John Marshall Law Review* (Winter 1991): 433–62.

Rychlak, R. J., and S. Dulaney. "To Tell the Truth: Accuracy in Demonstrative Evidence." *Practical Litigator* (March 1994): 47–62; (May 1994): 41–48.

APPENDIX C — SELECTED SOURCES
ON TANGIBLE EVIDENCE

Sargeant, Georgia. "Defense Lawyers Banned From Scene of Day-in-the-Life Videos." *Trial* (Dec. 1991): 80.

Sargeant, Georgia. "Day-in-the-Life Videos: Candid Camera or Special Effects?" *Trial* (July 1991): 92.

Saraceno, David A., and Paul Bernstein. "A.D.A.M.: An Evolutionary New Tool for Demonstrative Evidence." *Law Office Computing* (Dec.–Jan. 1993): 94.

Savage, E. Scott. "Demonstrative Evidence: Seeing May Not Be Believing But It Beats Not Seeing at All." *Utah Bar Journal* (Nov. 1995): 17–19.

Schlueter, David A. "Gruesome Photos." *Texas Bar Journal* (May 1991): 453.

Seiden, M. D. "Physical Evidence in Criminal Cases." *Trial* (August 1992): 106–110.

Selbak, John. "Digital Litigation: The Prejudicial Effects of Computer-Generated Animation in the Courtroom." *High Technology Law Journal* (Fall 1994): 337–67.

Seltzer, Robert. "The Keys to Admissibility (Special Section: Demonstrative Evidence)." *California Lawyer* (Feb. 1990): 78.

Setterberg, Fred. "Roger Rabbit Goes to Court; Computer Graphics Specialists are Producing Dazzling Demonstrative Evidence Using PC Software and Lots of Imagination." *California Lawyer* (Feb. 1990): 70.

Simmons, Robert, and J. Daniel Lounsbery. "Demonstrative Evidence: Admissibility of Computer-Animated Reenactments in Federal Courts." *Trial* (Sept. 1994): 78–83.

Thapedi, Andre M. "A.D.A.M.—The Computer Generated Cadaver: A New Development in Medical Malpractice and Personal Injury Litigation." *The John Marshall Journal of Computer & Information Law* (Winter 1995): 313–41.

Turbak, Nancy I., William S. Bailey, Stephen D. Heninger, William W. Rosen, and Gary Christy. "If a Picture's Worth a Thousand Words . . . ." *Trial* (Sept. 1994): 62.

Turley, Windle. "Effective Use of Demonstrative Evidence: Capturing Attention and Clarifying Issues." *Trial* (Sept. 1989): 62–68.

Twiggs, Howard F. "Do-It-Yourself Focus Groups: Big Benefits, Modest Cost." *Trial* (Sept. 1994): 42–45, 117.

Wagner, M. J. "Choosing and Using Demonstrative Evidence." *Practical Litigator* (Sept. 1993): 39–49.

Weinberg, David. "Animation in the Court: Scientific Evidence or Mickey Mouse? A Proponent of Reconstructed Evidence Walks Judges Through This Evidentiary Quagmire." *Judges Journal* (Spring 1995): 11.

White, T. S. "The Time Line: Culpability Writ Large." *Trial* (Nov. 1991): 55–58.

Wilson, Thomas W. "Image Processing by Computer Analysis—Potential Use and Application in Civil and Criminal Litigation." *Legal Medicine* (1990): 87–103.

Zimmerman, M. "Educating the Judge and Jury: The Technology Tutorial." *Computer Lawyer* (May 1990): 1–8.

Note, "Computer Simulation May Be Considered Real Evidence." *Prosecutor, Journal of the National District Attorneys Association* (Nov.–Dec. 1995): 17.

Note, "Demonstration and Discussion of Technological Advances in the Courtroom." *Indiana Law Journal* (Fall 1993): 1081–91.

Note, "Demonstrative Evidence Directory." (Special Section: Demonstrative Evidence) (directory), *California Lawyer* (Feb. 1990): 79.

FORMS FOR USING EXHIBITS AT DEPOSITION AND TRIAL

Four basic forms provide the organization you need at trial. The exhibit foundation checklist shows the four elements of foundation for each of the exhibits to be presented in your case and indicates how potential objections will be overcome. The exhibit objection checklist shows any objections to be made by you to your opponent's exhibits. The two exhibit tracking lists—one for your exhibits and one for your opponent's exhibits—tell you which exhibits have been numbered, offered, admitted, and subjected to special instructions.

This Appendix includes an example of each of these forms. Each form should be dated so that you know you are looking at the right version. Each form should carry the name of the case to avoid accidental mixups and should have a standard title. Typically the completed checklists are each printed on a distinctive color paper—pink, green, or blue—so that you can turn to the right one quickly. You may want to shade some of the columns to help guide your eye to the right columns quickly.

Exhibit foundation checklist

The exhibit foundation checklist serves two purposes: it ensures that you have thought through how you will present each required element of the foundation, and it provides you with a handy reference when your opponent challenges the foundation for or objects to one of your exhibits. In a case involving a large number of exhibits, you probably cannot keep in mind the details with respect to each exhibit. The exhibit foundation checklist collects these details and serves as a ready reference.

The structure for the checklist is simple so that it is easy to use under the stress of an active trial. The first two columns deal with the identification of the exhibit—its number and a short description. The next four columns cover the four elements of foundation for exhibits—competence, relevance, identification, and trustworthiness. The last four columns explain how to deal with potential objections.

The exhibit foundation checklist serves an important function during the preparation of the case. It makes you get down to specifics about how you are going to get each particular exhibit into evidence. If there are flaws in the current planning with respect to exhibits, the checklist should flush them out. If objections to exhibits are dealt with at a pretrial conference in your jurisdiction, you will use your exhibit foundation checklist at that time and then add a column for the court's tentative rulings.

Exhibit number and description

As you collect potential exhibits for your case, add them to your exhibit foundation checklist by entering the exhibit number and a short description. Some lawyers dispense with the description and rely solely on the number identifier. It is easier, however, to have a short description to help you focus on each exhibit quickly. The practice varies with respect to how much description to put into the checklist. Some lawyers make do with "letter" or "memo" or a similar short description indicating what kind of exhibit this is. Others want the date and author of a letter or the subject of a memorandum, for example, in order to feel comfortable with the checklist.

Competence

This column identifies the witness who will sponsor the exhibit and provides a brief indication of the competence of the witness to identify and explain the exhibit. A lay witness must have personal knowledge about the exhibit. An expert witness must have knowledge about the exhibit arising out of knowledge, skill, experience, training, or education sufficient to assist the trier of fact to understand the exhibit. Indicate in this column the source of the sponsoring witness's knowledge about the exhibit. Be sure it meets the criteria in Rule 602 and Rule 702. If you are relying on a deposition transcript to provide foundation, indicate the pages where the evidence of the competence of the witness to testify about the particular exhibit is located.

Relevance

This column identifies the fact at issue in the case to which the exhibit relates. Under Rule 401, the fact must be one that is of consequence to the determination of the action. Make sure you can state this concisely so that, when you look at your list after a relevance objection has been made, you can start your defense of the exhibit by explaining to the court the fact to be established. Once the fact at issue is identified, the test for relevance is whether the exhibit has any tendency to make the existence of that fact more probable or less probable than it would be without the exhibit. The broad sweep of this language makes this part of the argument relatively easy.

Identification

This column states the way that you have complied with Rule 901(a) by eliciting testimony identifying the exhibit or the way that the exhibit is distinguished from all other things.

Trustworthiness

This column indicates whether any additional proof of trustworthiness is required. If so, it indicates which subsection of Rule 902 on self-authentication or Rule 901 on methods of authentication applies. When filling in this column, you should examine carefully whether any of the common law requirements apply such as testimony that the condition of the exhibit at the present time is substantially the same as it was at the time at issue or testimony about the basis for identifying nonunique items.

Hearsay objections

There are two basic ways to deal with hearsay objections: either the exhibit is not hearsay and therefore the rule against hearsay does not apply; or the exhibit is hearsay but it fits under one of the exceptions to the hearsay rule. There are two columns with respect to hearsay objections so that you can see very quickly whether your position is that the exhibit is not hearsay or that the exhibit is hearsay and you are relying on an exception. If the exhibit is not hearsay, there will be something in the first of the two columns. If the exhibit is hearsay, there will be something in the second of the two columns. The "not hearsay" entries usually will be one of the three possibilities: (1) the exhibit is not a statement and thus not covered by the definition in Rule 801(a); (2) the exhibit is not offered to prove the truth of its contents and thus is not covered by the definition in Rule 801(c); or (3) the exhibit is a statement of the opposing party and thus is not hearsay under Rule 801(d)(2). The "exception" entries should state the subsection of Rule 803 or Rule 804 on which you are relying and should include a short entry to remind you what the cited subsection covers.

Original document objections

Original document objections are made less often and therefore have a place farther to the right on the checklist. Put in this column the citation to Rule 1001 through Rule 1007 on which you will rely, and note whether you will claim that the exhibit is an original, a duplicate, a non-duplicate copy, or an item to which the original document rule is not applicable.

Policy, completeness, and surprise objections

Anticipate objections on grounds of policy, completeness, or surprise. Under Rule 403, you must consider whether your opponent has any policy objection based on a claim of unfair prejudice, confusion of the issues or misleading the jury, waste of time, or needless presentation of cumulative evidence. Under Rule 106, you need to think about what will happen if you are offering only a part of a documentary exhibit, and how you will respond if your opponent wants to require you to introduce more of it. Anything not turned over in discovery or at a pretrial conference will be subject to an objection based on "surprise" and, as to any such exhibits, you need to indicate in this column how you plan to explain the non-disclosure.

The exhibit foundation checklist set out as an example has been filled in with entries about the exhibits numbered 1 through 10 from the examples in this book. This sample checklist treats these exhibits as if they were from one case (which they are not) in order to show how the checklist might look for exhibits for which there is some context. Exhibit 1 is in Section 1.4; Exhibit 2 is in Section 5.1.1; Exhibit 3 is in Section 1.1.4; Exhibit 4 is in Section 2.1.1; Exhibit 5 and Exhibit 6 are in Section 4.1.1; Exhibit 7 is in Section 1.1.4; Exhibit 8 is in Section 2.3.3; Exhibit 9 is in Section 2.6.2; and Exhibit 10 is in Section 1.1.4 and also in Section 1.7.2.

ELLEFF v. XYZ CO.

EXHIBIT FOUNDATION CHECKLIST

[Date]

Ex. No.	Description	Competence	Relevance	ID	Trustworthy	Not Hearsay	Exception	Original Document	Other (Policy, Completeness, Surprise)
1	Letter	Wilson: wrote it	Sets schedule	Signature	No extra proof		803(6) Business record	1001(4) Duplicate	None
2	Sprocket	Gordon: inspected it	Part that broke	Initials	In same condition now	Not a statement		1002 Not applicable	None
3	Sales report	Ellis: uses it	Loss of sales	Recognizes it	901(b)(9) Process		803(6) Business record	1001(3) Original	None
4	Contract	Sanders: expert qualif.	Contract at issue	Analyzed signature	No extra proof	Not offered for truth		Original	None
5	Plat	Martin: did appraisal	Shows location	Got it from gov't	902(5) Official publ.		803(14) Property record	1001(4) Duplicate	None

ELLEFF v. XYZ CO.

EXHIBIT FOUNDATION CHECKLIST

[Date]

#	Item	Witness		Prepared it	Standard published source	Not a statement			Notes
6	Map	Gerardi: v-isited locations	Shows locations					Original	Possible surprise; not produced
7	OSHA report	Thomas: job covers it	States proper methods	Recognizes it	902(5) Official publ.		803(8) Public record	1001(3) Original	Possible completeness objection; using short excerpt
8	Analysis of competition	Mell: worked on it	Shows competition	Recognizes it	No extra proof		803(6) Business record	1001(3) Original	Possible completeness objection; sound files not offered
9	Depo videotape	Siegfried: expert qualif.	Shows damages	Reporter certificate	No extra proof		FRCP 32 (a)(3)(E); 803(24)	Original	Possible completeness objection; using excerpts
10	Note	Sutton: wrote it	Company knew	Signature	No extra proof		803(3) State of mind	Original	Note: May be a problem because paper is ripped

APPENDIX D — FORMS FOR USING EXHIBITS AT DEPOSITION AND AT TRIAL

Exhibit objection checklist

Deciding when and about what to object is a key part of trial strategy. The Exhibit Objection Checklist is a place to collect your thoughts about potential objections and to assess the likelihood of success. The exhibits used in this sample form are the same as those used in the sample Exhibit Foundation Checklist form in order to illustrate how both plaintiff and defendant would look at the same exhibits.

Exhibit number and description

The first step is to list all of your opponent's exhibits by number and by short description. Those are the first and third columns in the sample form set out below. Then make a tentative decision about how important each exhibit is to your case.

Ranking or rating

Your strategy on objections is dictated, in part, by whether the exhibit makes any difference to the case. A simple four-letter system is sufficient, as shown in the second column of the form below. An opponent's exhibit designated as "A" is very harmful to your case and needs to be kept out of evidence if at all possible. An opponent's exhibit designated as "B" does quite a bit of harm, and serious consideration should be given to any available objection. The "C" category is used for exhibits that are harmful but can be overcome by exhibits or testimony from your witnesses. These exhibits are not very dangerous and only very good objections would be made. The "D" category is reserved for exhibits that are not harmful, and only objections with an almost certain chance of prevailing would be made.

Foundation objections

Once you have categorized your opponent's exhibits by how harmful they are to your case, examine whether there is a likely challenge to foundation, from what you now know about your opponent's witness who is likely to sponsor each exhibit. Speculate about how your opponent may go about laying the foundation, and elements that may be lacking or overlooked. These thoughts about ways to challenge the foundation go in the fourth column.

Hearsay objections

Next, consider whether the hearsay rule applies and, if so, whether any exception is available to your opponent. If you know that there is a response to the potential objection that should succeed, you may still elect to object if you think your opponent may not be able to defend against the objection. This decision should be made cautiously, however, as the court will not appreciate an abundance of objections to which there is an adequate response. Possible challenges under the hearsay rule, and the likely responses of your opponent, go in the fifth column.

Original document objections

Give some thought to the original document rule and how it applies to the exhibits your opponent is offering. Objections on this ground are not often successful because Rules 1001 through 1007 favor admissibility. Occasionally, however, your opponent will be stuck with a non-duplicate copy that was not authenticated properly during depositions and for which no adequate excuse exists for not having the original.

Policy objections

Policy objections are usually made more successfully if thought out and prepared in advance. If your opponent has a number of exhibits on the same point, consider a policy objection as to needless cumulative evidence. If an exhibit is unfairly prejudicial, you may want to make a motion in limine before trial to exclude it. Look carefully at labels and titles on charts, graphs, maps, drawings, and similar exhibits to see if they are possibly misleading or confusing.

Completeness objections

Any multi-page document is a candidate for an objection under Rule 106 as to completeness if your opponent does not offer all of it in evidence. Look for portions that you might want to add to the exhibit, perhaps to blunt the effect of the excerpt that your opponent has chosen.

Surprise objections

Any evidentiary exhibit not produced in discovery well before trial is a candidate for an objection based on "surprise." One of the sanctions for discovery abuse is rejection of exhibits offered in evidence. Any testimony aid not produced for inspection sufficiently before being used with a witness to allow meaningful scrutiny for accuracy may also be objected to on the basis of "surprise."

[Date]

ELLEFF V. XYZ CO.

EXHIBIT OBJECTION CHECKLIST

Ex. No.	Rank	Description	Foundation objection	Hearsay objection	Original document objection	Policy objection	Completeness objection	Surprise objection
1	C	Letter		Yes, but 803(6) available	Yes, but 1001(4) available			
2	A	Sprocket	May not be in same condition as time at issue					
3	B	Sales report	May be no basis for computer accuracy	Yes, but 803(6) available	Yes, but 1001(3) available	Perhaps needless cumulative		
4	A	Contract						
5	D	Plat		Yes, but 803(14) available	Yes, but 1001(4) available			
6	D	Map						
7	A	OSHA report		Yes, but 803(8) available	Yes, but 1001(3) available	Unfair prejudice; not describe machine at issue	Yes, only excerpt used. Add pp. 17-95	

ELLEFF V. XYZ CO.

EXHIBIT OBJECTION CHECKLIST

[Date]

8	B	Analysis of competition	May be trustworthiness problem due to different authors	Yes, but 803(6) available	Yes, but 1001(3) available	Yes, if all multimedia parts not offered
9	B	Depo videotape	32(a)(3)(E) No exceptional circumstances as basis for not using live witness	Yes, but 803(24) available if 32(a)(3)(E) is available		Yes, if whole deposition not offered; add pp. 25-78; 152-67
10	A	Note	May not be in same condition now as time at issue	Yes, but 803(3) may be available unless not an expression of witness's own frame of mind		

APPENDIX D — FORMS FOR USING EXHIBITS AT DEPOSITION AND AT TRIAL

Exhibit tracking list

The Exhibit Tracking List tells you the current status of each exhibit. Most lawyers use one tracking list for their own exhibits and a separate tracking list for their opponent's exhibits. The format of the two tracking lists is, however, the same. The exhibits used in this sample are taken from examples in the book. The sample tracking list assumes that all of these exhibits are from a single case (which they are not) in order to provide some context. Exhibit 11 and Exhibit 12 are in Section 2.1.1. Exhibit 13 is in Section 2.3.5. Exhibit 14 is in Section 2.3.4. Exhibit 15 is in Section 1.1.2, Section 1.1.3, Section 1.1.4, Section 1.1.5, and Section 1.7.2. Exhibit 16 is in Section 4.1.1. Exhibit 17 is in Section 3.2.2. Exhibit 18 is in Section 3.2.1. Exhibit 19 and Exhibit 20 are in Section 2.3.2.

Number, date, and description

For tracking purposes, you need the number, date, and a short description of the exhibit. This will allow you to deal with a judge who runs rapidly through rulings or tentative rulings on exhibits.

Deposition cross-references

You may need to know that the exhibit you are offering as Exhibit 8 at trial, for example, was Exhibit 21 at the Mell deposition. It was also Exhibit 10 at the Patterson deposition; Exhibit 27 at the Wilson deposition, and so on. Deposition testimony is sometimes important in providing foundation or bases for overcoming objections. Adding the page numbers of the deposition transcripts in this column ensures that you have the necessary information if a question arises at trial.

Trial witness

The name of the witness (or witnesses) whose testimony laid the foundation for the exhibit is often useful in reminding the court when the exhibit was presented.

Date offered and transcript page citations

The date on which the exhibit was offered in evidence may be important if you need to locate the testimony supporting the exhibit. The page citation to the transcript gets you to the court's ruling on the record. At the end of the trial, the court or clerk may read off a list of exhibits that have been admitted. If disputes arise about whether a particular exhibit was admitted and whether a limiting instruction was called for, the court will not want to wait while you research the transcript to find the quote on which you are relying. You will need to have all the information immediately at hand if you are to prevail.

Ruling and citation to record

This column will tell you whether the exhibit was admitted, an objection was sustained, or the court reserved ruling.

Notes and instructions

If the exhibit was offered for a limited purpose, you should make sure a limiting instruction is given to the jury at the time the exhibit is admitted and is repeated during the final instructions.

ELLEFF V. XYZ CO.

PLAINTIFF'S EXHIBIT TRACKING LIST

[Date]

Ex. No.	Ex. Date	Description	Depo cross-reference	Trial witness	Date/page offered	Ruling	Notes and instructions
11		Price list	Edwards depo, Ex. 22, pp.75-77; Jackson depo, Ex. 2, pp. 31-33	Edwards	10/14 p. 253	Admitted	
12		Letter	Andrews depo, Ex. 43, pp. 105-07; Pepper depo, Ex. 4, pp. 23-25	Andrews	10/14 p. 270	Admitted	
13		E-mail	Toeffler depo, Ex. 22, p. 111; Bailey depo. Ex. 45, p. 220	Toeffler	10/15 p. 75	Admitted	Signature at issue; instruction on consideration of evidence
14		Research paper	None	Berrie	10/14 p. 47	Admitted	
15		Gear	Jones depo, Ex. 1, pp. 14-47; Mason depo, Ex. 1, pp. 17-37	Jones	10/16 p. 115	Reserved	Subject to testimony of person who kept Exhibit 15

ELLEFF V. XYZ CO.

PLAINTIFF'S EXHIBIT TRACKING LIST

[Date]

16	Map	Jensen depo, Ex. 5, pp. 33-51	Jensen	10/16 p. 176	Admitted	
17	Performance testing data	Akbar depo, Ex. 12, pp. 41-67; Beardwood depo, Ex. 23, pp. 141-49	Akbar	10/14 p. 47	Reserved	Pending memo on legal points from defendant
18	Time line	None	Evans Moriarty Werner Adson	10/17 p. 55	Admitted	
19	E-mail	Jones depo, Ex. 13, pp. 118-31; Mason depo, Ex. 13, pp. 38-45	Jones	10/16 p. 134	Admitted	
20	Fax	Jones depo, Ex. 14, pp. 135-147	Jones	10/16 p. 157	Admitted	

INDEX

INDEX

P

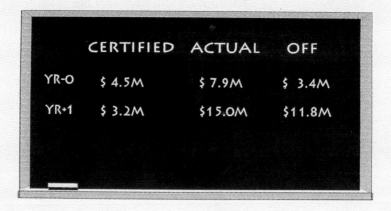

Figure 1. Lawyer-sponsored visual aid. Facts elicited during the cross-examination are written on a blackboard as an aid to understanding testimony.

Figure 2. Carrying case. This standard artist's carrying case holds up to ten 30 x 40" foamboard exhibits. It is easy to carry to and from the courthouse or to check as luggage on an airplane.

Figure 3. Text document. Enlarged and highlighted text points out what is significant about a document.—TrialGraphix (by permission of Scientific-Atlanta)

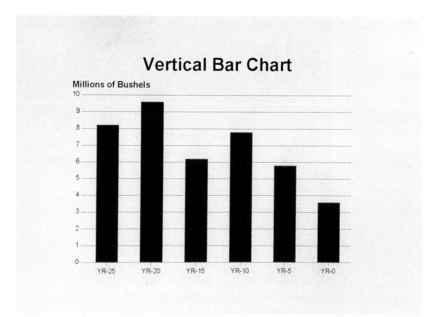

Figure 4. Vertical bar chart. Bar chart columns are separated by white space to make them distinct when viewed from a distance. Columns should be of equal width.

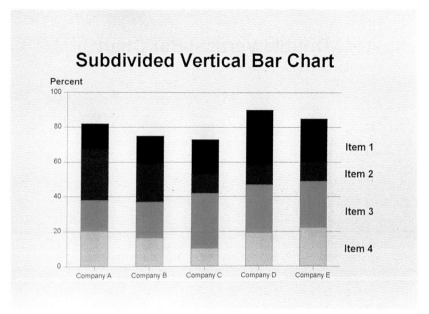

Figure 5. Vertical bar chart, subdivided bars. This chart compares individual quantities and totals over a period of time. Because the upper subdivisions of the columns on this kind of chart lack a common baseline, they can be hard to compare visually.

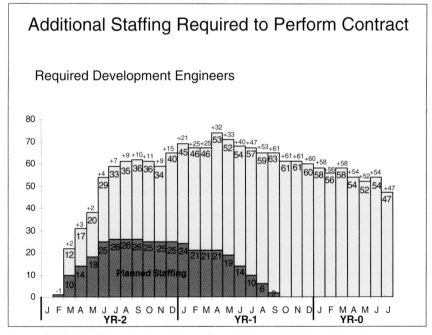

Figure 6. Vertical bar chart, with overlays. This vertical bar chart shows levels of staffing planned at the contract's outset and has an overlay of a comparable vertical bar chart that shows the staffing levels ultimately required under the contract. The overlay demonstrates the level of additional work.—LITIGATION COMMUNICATIONS

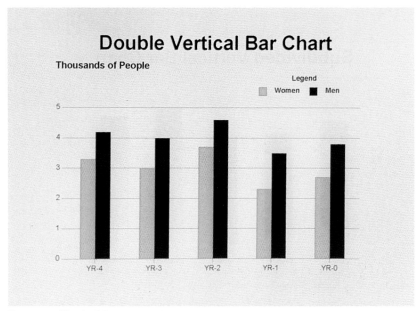

Figure 7. Vertical bar chart, double bars. This type chart compares two independent sets of data over time. The columns are done in different colors. A shorter space between columns in a pair than between pairs makes the chart easier to read.

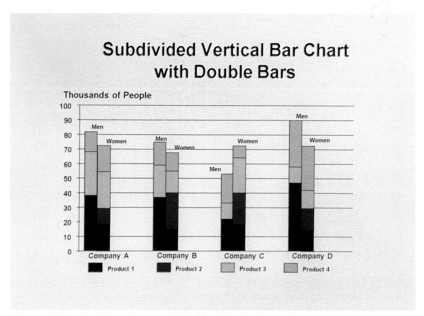

Figure 8. Vertical bar chart, subdivided double bars. Use this type chart only if you can keep it relatively simple.

FIGURES

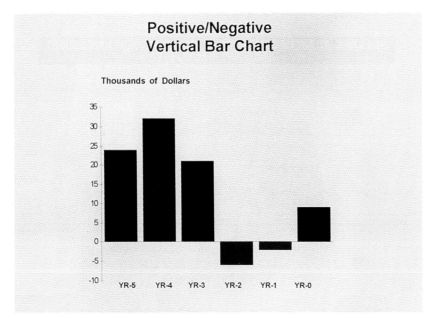

Figure 9. Positive/negative vertical bar chart. In this type of chart, the zero point is set above the baseline, and both positive and negative values are shown on the vertical axis, preferably in different colors.

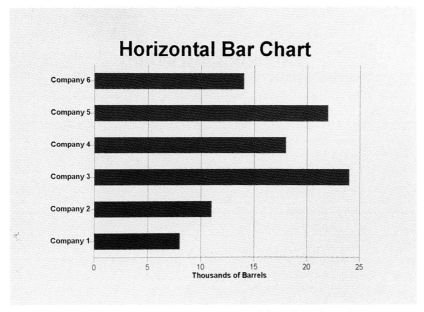

Figure 10. Horizontal bar chart. The horizontal bar chart has white space between the bars to improve visual impact. All bars should be of equal width.

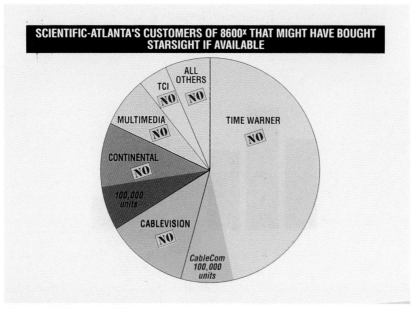

Figure 11. Pie chart. This chart uses percentage segments of the circumference of a circle to show the relation of parts to the whole. Arrange segments clockwise in decreasing order of size.—TrialGraphix (by permission of Scientific-Atlanta)

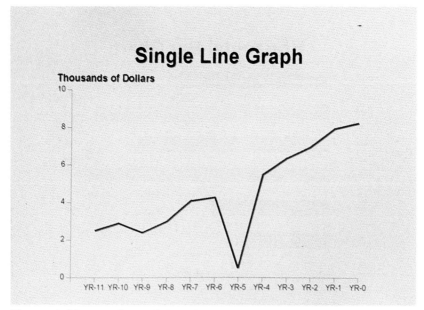

Figure 12. Line graph, single line. Line graphs show trends. Time is generally plotted on the horizontal axis and changing events on the vertical. The plotted line should be heavier than the axis lines.

FIGURES

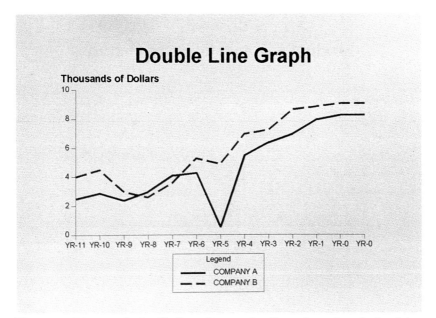

Figure 13. Line graph, double line. Contrasting lines show the relationship between two or more items over time.

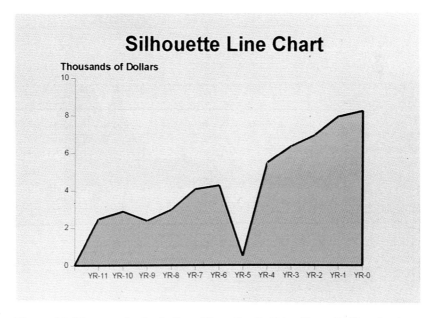

Figure 14. Line graph, single line silhouette. In this silhouette line chart, the curve is filled in to emphasize the trend. Here time is plotted on the horizontal axis and dollars spent on the vertical.

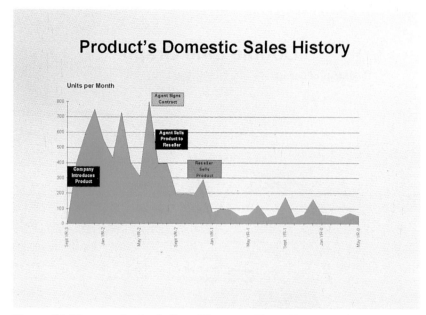

Figure 15. Line graph, single line silhouette. This silhouette line chart shows sales of a product over a period of time, with key events added with color overlays.—LITIGATION COMMUNICATIONS

Shortfall of Funds - YR-7 to Present

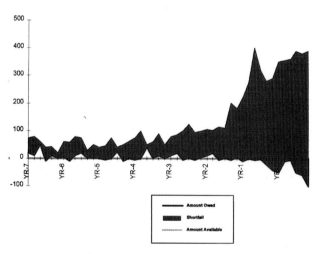

Figure 16. Line graph, double line silhouette. The silhouette provides a shaded area between the two lines to emphasize the difference. The bottom line shows money collected and the top line shows money owed. The shaded area emphasizes the increasing amount of debt over the time period.—LITIGATION COMMUNICATIONS

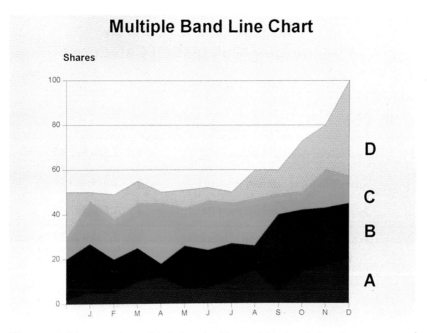

Figure 17. Line graph, multiple bands. The width of each band represents a value and the top line the total of all values. The graph should show the least active band at the baseline and the most active band at the top.

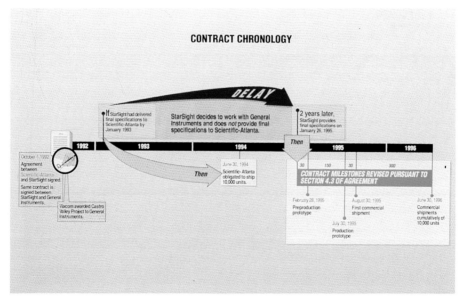

Figure 18. Time line. This time line shows major chronological events in a contract agreement.—TrialGraphix (by permission of Scientific-Atlanta)

Damage Claim Totals by Accounting/Calculation Categories

Category	Claim Amount
Percent of Contract Value	$ 7,576,592.45
From Cost Accounting Records	$ 2,876,904.19
Percent of Cost Accounting Records	$ 1,566,987.46
From Contemporaneous Records	$ 2,664,436.52
From Identifiable Activities	$ 6,759,736.75
Other	$ 836,137.35
	$ 22.280.794.72

Figure 19. Table. This table summarizes a damages claim. It sets out the type and amount of damages, in a simple format.—LITIGATION COMMUNICATIONS

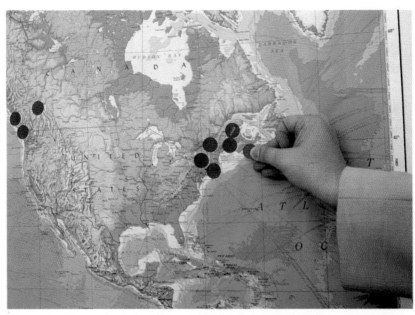

Figure 20. Map, color keys. This exhibit uses a commercially available map of North America as a backdrop for information about particular locations referenced in a case. It uses color labels to identify the locations.

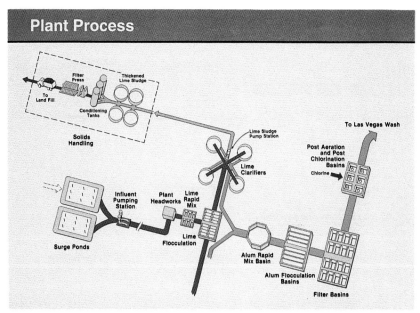

Figure 21. Diagram, technical process. This diagram outlines the processing facilities at a waste water treatment plant, using color for easy reference to particular features. Company and expert witnesses used it to explain how the plant works.—LITIGATION COMMUNICATIONS

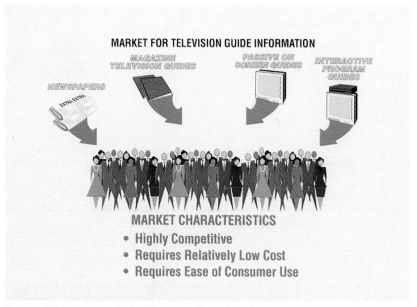

Figure 22. Diagram. This diagram of market characteristics uses symbols, colors and labels in clear, simple type so jurors can comprehend it at a distance.—TrialGraphix (by permission of Scientific-Atlanta)

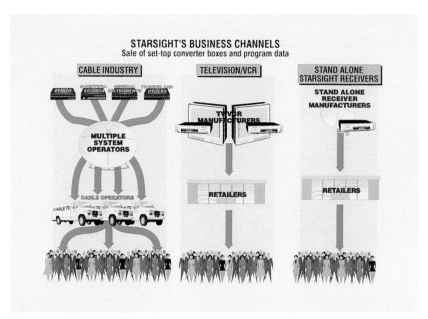

Figure 23. Diagram. This diagram helps jurors quickly comprehend a company's distribution channels.—TrialGraphix (by permission of Scientific-Atlanta)

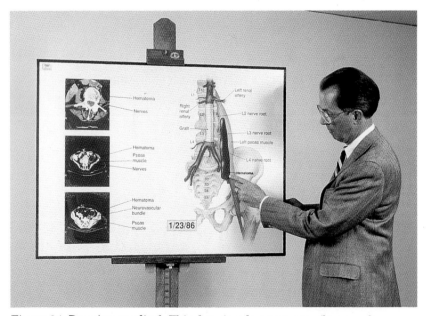

Figure 24. Drawing, medical. This drawing demonstrates (by use of a transparency overlay) the size and location of a hematoma that developed following graft surgery. The blow-ups of the CT study on the left side of this diagram were used to locate the anatomy and the hematoma.—LONG & JAUDON

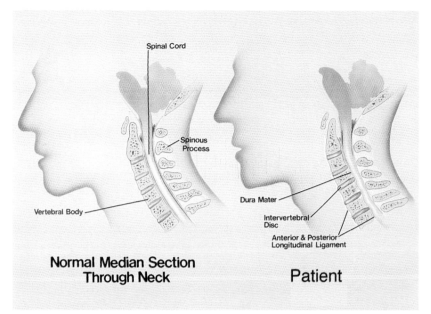

Figure 25. Drawing, medical. This anatomical drawing of the cervical spine shows a normal segment of spine on the left and a plaintiff's spinal segment on the right. The data came from CT and MRI studies. The drawing assisted in teaching general anatomy to the jury and showing the differences between a normal spine and the plaintiff's spine.—LONG & JAUDON

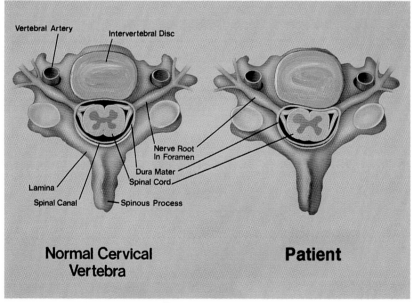

Figure 26. Drawing, medical. This drawing was used to show the normal anatomy of cervical vertebra with surrounding structures as compared to the anatomy of the plaintiff's cervical vertebra. The information for these drawings came from CT and MRI studies of the patient.—LONG & JAUDON

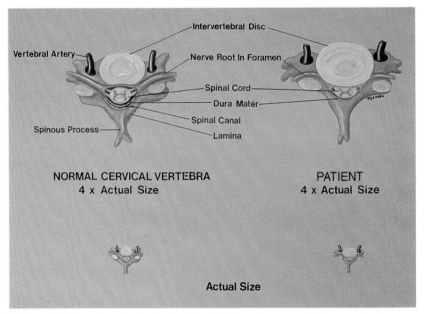

Figure 27. Drawing, medical. Anatomical drawings made in a cervical degenerative arthritis case showing a cervical disk impinging on the patient's nerve, causing severe pain, numbness and tingling in the upper extremities. The anatomical drawings, based on CT scans, compare normal anatomy with the plaintiff's anatomy.—LONG & JAUDON

Figure 28. Plastic mounting. This mounting of a small piranha fish was designed to be handled by jurors so they could examine the teeth and understand its size.—LAW GRAPHICS

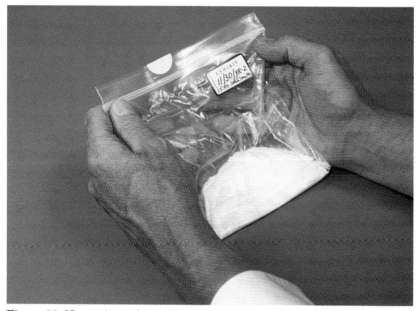

Figure 29. Non-unique object. This sample of a substance that cannot be differentiated by sight alone has been placed in a plastic container, sealed and labeled.—LAW GRAPHICS

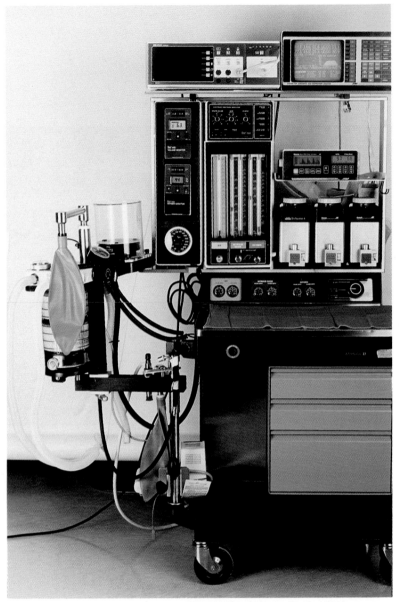

Figure 30. Photo, medical device. This life-size photo shows the actual anesthesia machine used during the surgery at issue in the case. The readings on the gauges and monitors were constructed comparable to those on the monitors at the time in question. Actual monitors were fastened to the exhibit by Velcro so they could be removed and used by witnesses during testimony, and by the jurors after the exhibit was admitted into evidence.—LONG & JAUDON

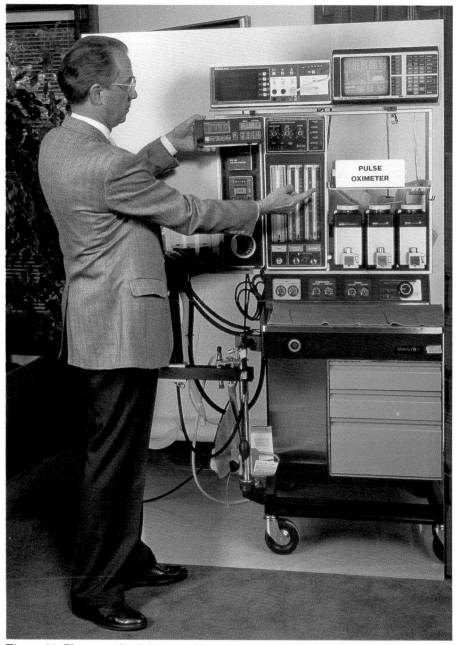

Figure 31. Photo, medical device, add-on pieces. Life-size photo of anesthesia machine with monitor removed from main exhibit.—LONG & JAUDON

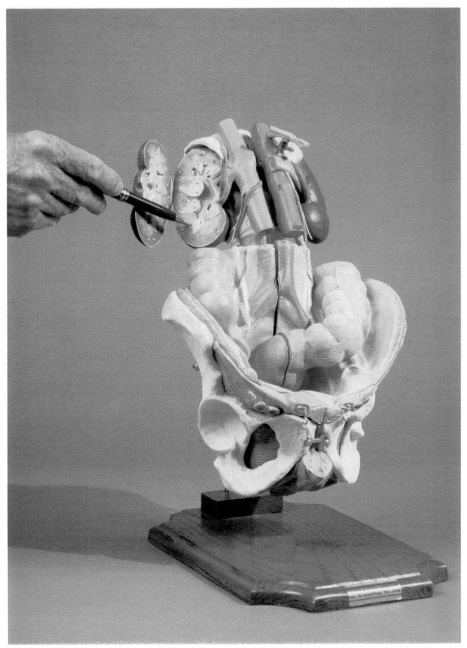

Figure 32. Life-size model. This anatomical model shows the female reproductive organs and allows jurors to visualize the injury at issue better than they could with photographs or drawings.—Thomas H. Singer, Esq.

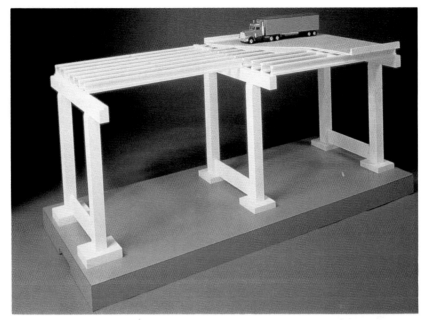

Figure 33. Scale model, bridge. This scale model of a bridge, built from engineering documents, was used to show how the bridge was assembled and where the problems developed that led to litigation.—LITIGATION COMMUNICATIONS

Figure 34. Scale model, bridge. This scale model of a bridge construction is built to a scale that shows one of the critical components.—LITIGATION COMMUNICATIONS

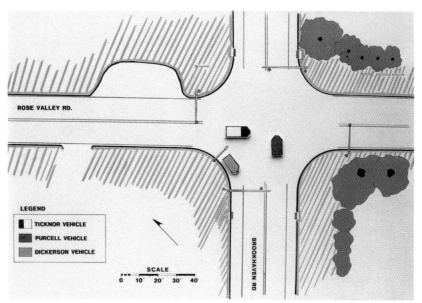

Figure 35. Magnetized map. This intersection map is mounted on a magnetized sheet on which models of the vehicles can be moved to illustrate how the collision happened.—LEGAL GRAPHICS

COST CATEGORY	8/76** ($M)	8/77** ($M)	8/78† ($M)	1/79† ($M)	8/79† ($M)	5/80† ($M)	7/80† ($M)	11/80† ($M)
Labor	$2.59	$2.60	$2.62	$			~~72	$6.42
Maintenance	3.02	2.95	2.89				73	9.47
Supplies	.57	.30					42	.42
Fuel Oil	.03	.01			$4.50		42	.42
Electricity	3.62	4.20	5.14		4.50		12	6.06
Insurance	.13	.15	.22		.30		54	.54
Administrative					.30		47	.60
Rental Equipment			.39		5.70			
Chemicals								
Water								
Pest Control								
Trucks							.10	
Uniforms							.03	
Consultants							.21	
Interest on Working Capital			.44					
			.35				3.33	$28.11
Contingency					.15			
		$9.96	$10.21	$12.05				
TOTAL					1.58			
					.90			

...in Contingency ("other")
...of Base Estimate to 1981
Estimate

Figure 36. Add-on board. Add-on exhibits use Velcro strips pasted unobtrusively on a foamboard exhibit. As the testimony progresses, small sections can be added to make a particular point.

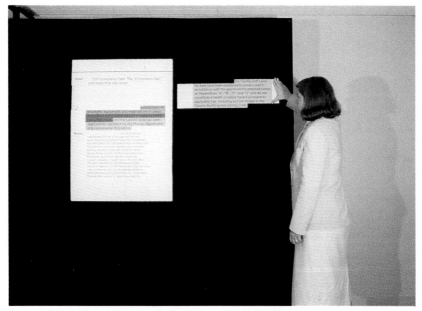

Figure 37. Take-apart board. Take-apart boards show the entire exhibit at the outset and then are disassembled to make a point.

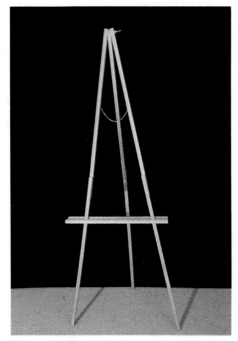

Figure 38. Easel. A standard artist's easel holds most 30 x 40" exhibits adequately. Adjust the easel up or down to set exhibits at desired heights, and fold it up into an easy-to-carry package.

Figure 39. Exhibit frame and carry case. This tubular aluminum frame comes out of its compact case in one piece.

Figures 40-41. Exhibit frame. The tubular frame expands into place and Velcro mats are fastened to the frame.

FIGURES

Figure 41.

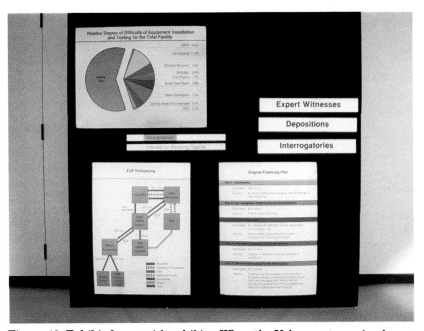

Figure 42. Exhibit frame with exhibits. When the Velcro mats are in place, the exhibit frame provides enough room for the display of a number of related exhibits. You can place and remove exhibits from the exhibit frame by pressing or separating the two Velcro surfaces, one on the exhibit's back and the other on the frame's mat.

Figure 43. Poster generator. A poster generator uses a built-in scanner to create inexpensive enlargements of document and photographic exhibits. They are especially useful when an unexpected document becomes important and you need an enlargement to use with a witness.—DOAR COMMUNICATIONS

Figure 44. Mylar overlays for exhibit. Clear mylar sheets as overlays for exhibits display cumulative information. This offers a substantial advantage when you want to build a picture that has a number of sequentially related elements.

FIGURES

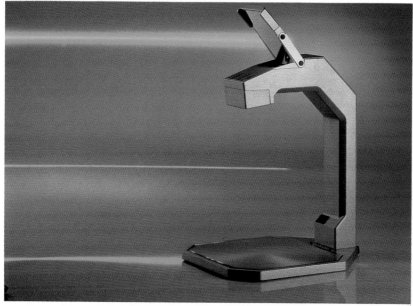

Figure 45. Overhead projector. A small, portable overhead projector displays images photocopied on transparencies.—APOLLO PRESENTATION PRODUCTS

Figure 46. Rear-screen slide projector. Slides are projected onto the rear of the screen producing a television-like image on the front. This unit is useful when you need a high degree of clarity or when a room's natural light cannot be blocked out during the slide presentation.—LAW GRAPHICS

Figure 47. Opaque projector. This unit projects whatever is put on its surface, such as pages of open books, documents, photographs, and objects.—DOAR COMMUNICATIONS

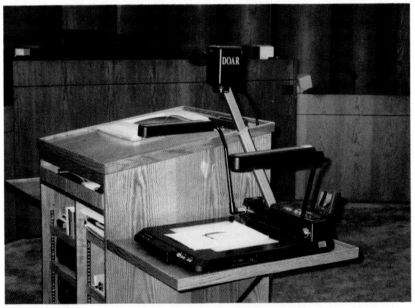

Figure 48. Visual presenter. The presenter features a miniature television camera mounted over a surface with a sufficient light source to get good images from the camera. An exhibit placed on the display surface appears immediately on the television monitor.—DOAR COMMUNICATIONS

Figure 49. Visual presenter with exhibit. A visual presenter displays text documents, charts, graphs, computer data printouts, maps, drawings, diagrams, objects, photographs and x-rays. —DOAR COMMUNICATIONS

Figure 50. Visual presenter with light pen. A light pen is used with a visual presenter for drawing or pointing capability on the television screen.—DOAR COMMUNICATIONS

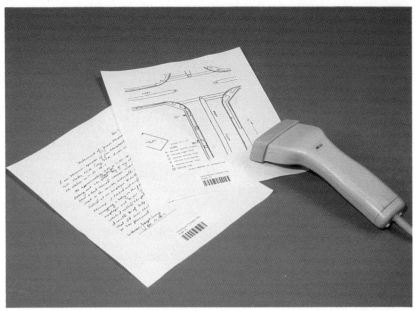

Figure 51. Bar code stickers. Bar codes can be produced on small stickers or labels that are easily attached to the lawyer's notes or the witness outline. The lawyer uses a hand-held bar code reader to transmit the necessary information to the computer system that controls the litigation display.—LAW GRAPHICS

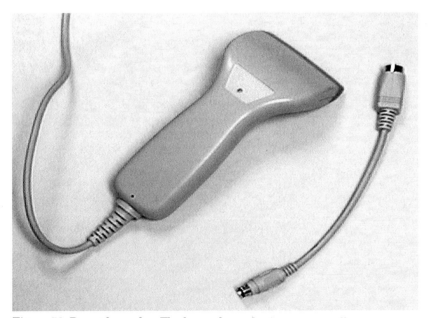

Figure 52. Bar code reader. The bar code reader is a very small scanner which transmits the information from the bar codes to the computer and, with one click of the control button, displays the image on the video monitor.—DOAR COMMUNICATIONS

Figure 53. Touch screen. A touch screen controls a computer system used for litigation displays. When you touch the screen at a point indicated by a button labeled for a specific exhibit, information to retrieve and play the exhibit is transmitted to the computer and the exhibit is displayed nearly instantaneously on the video monitor.—Z-AXIS CORPORATION

Figure 54. LCD panel. This projection aid is placed on top of a standard overhead projector and cabled to a computer to display an enlargement of the computer output.—APOLLO PRESENTATION PRODUCTS

Figure 55. Digital projector. This unit takes output directly from the computer and projects a high color resolution image onto a 10-foot screen.—INFOCUS SYSTEMS, INC.

Figure 56. SoftBoard. This unit acts as a computerized version of a blackboard. The large drawing surface is connected to a computer. Anything drawn on it with special markers becomes a digital image which you can store, save and print out from the computer.—MICROFIELD GRAPHICS INC.

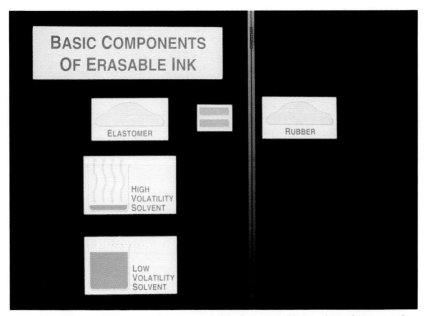

Figure 57. Icons. When used on an exhibit frame or Velcro board mounted on an easel, icons are a versatile means for showing how things (or concepts) relate to one another. These icons were used to show that a variety of substances could be substituted for each other as basic ingredients of erasable ink.—Robert P. Taylor, Esq., HOWRY & SIMON